Firuz Kazemzadeh is Emeritus Professor of History at Yale University. He has taught at Harvard and Yale universities and was subsequently appointed Commissioner to the United States Commission on International Religious Freedom by President Clinton. Professor Kazemzadeh is also the author of *The Struggle for Transcaucasia*.

'Professor Kazemzadeh's book is to be welcomed as a major contribution to the field ... a formidable and monumental work that far surpasses any other book on modern Iranian international relations.... . The author has done an outstanding job of research in Russian, Britain and Persian sources ... and has presented a far fuller view of his subject than has hitherto been available. ... Both students and scholars should put it on their must reading lists.'
Nikki I. Keddie, *Iranian Studies*

'A first class piece of scholarship.'
A.P. Thornton, *American Historical Review*

'A valuable study of Anglo-Russian relations in Persia.'
Ann K.S. Lambton

RUSSIA AND BRITAIN IN PERSIA

Imperial Ambitions in Qajar Iran

FIRUZ KAZEMZADEH

I.B. TAURIS
LONDON • NEW YORK • OXFORD • NEW DELHI • SYDNEY

I.B. TAURIS
Bloomsbury Publishing Plc
50 Bedford Square, London, WC1B 3DP, UK
1385 Broadway, New York, NY 10018, USA
29 Earlsfort Terrace, Dublin 2, Ireland

BLOOMSBURY, I.B. TAURIS and the I.B. Tauris logo
are trademarks of Bloomsbury Publishing Plc

First published by Yale University Press 1968
This edition published by I.B. Tauris 2013
Paperback edition published 2021

Copyright © Firuz Kazemzadeh 1968, 2013

Firuz Kazemzadeh has asserted his right under the Copyright,
Designs and Patents Act, 1988, to be identified as Author of this work.

All rights reserved. No part of this publication may be reproduced or
transmitted in any form or by any means, electronic or mechanical,
including photocopying, recording, or any information storage or retrieval
system, without prior permission in writing from the publishers.

Bloomsbury Publishing Plc does not have any control over, or responsibility for,
any third-party websites referred to or in this book. All internet addresses given
in this book were correct at the time of going to press. The author and publisher
regret any inconvenience caused if addresses have changed or sites have
ceased to exist, but can accept no responsibility for any such changes.

A catalogue record for this book is available from the British Library.

A catalog record for this book is available from the Library of Congress.

ISBN: PB: 978-0-7556-4447-6
ePDF: 978-0-8577-2173-0
eBook: 978-0-7556-1291-8

To find out more about our authors and books visit
www.bloomsbury.com and sign up for our newsletters.

Contents

Preface		vii
Note		xi
Introduction		xiii
1.	Anglo-Russian Conflict in Central Asia: Genesis and Evolution	3
2.	Reuter and Falkenhagen: Two Failures and a Beginning	100
3.	"Pénétration Pacifique": Rivers, Railways, Trade and Foreign Advisers	148
4.	The Tobacco Régie: Britain's Retreat and Russia's Offensive	241
5.	Loans, Concessions and Political Power		302
6.	Seistān and the Persian Gulf: Gates to India		386
7.	War, Revolution and the Reconciliation of the Antagonists	448
8.	The Uneasy Alliance		510
9.	"The Strangling of Persia"		581
Bibliography		681
Index		699

TO CATERINA

Non perch'io creda sua laude finire

Preface

This book is a history of Anglo-Russian relations in Persia during the half century preceding World War I. The interests of the two great powers clashed at many points from Turkey to China, but only in Persia and Central Asia did the imperialist giants meet face to face. It was my purpose to describe the confrontation.

The literature on the subject was surprisingly inadequate, only a few episodes such as the Agreement of 1907 having received more or less detailed treatment. I had to construct *de novo* a continuous narrative, working from a mass of unpublished and published documents. Sifting through them, interpreting, evaluating, and putting the pieces together was a task that occupied me for several years.

The book would have been twice as long had I not rigorously limited myself to the re-creation of Russian and British activities in Persia. Only when these could not be properly understood without a larger context did I touch upon events elsewhere.

Diplomatic history is somewhat unfashionable these days. Yet in Persia diplomacy was the main instrument of policy, and diplomats exercised great influence on the course of events. Though military power always loomed in the background, it was seldom used. Economic competition was largely a by-product of political conflict and never played a decisive role.

The nature of the subject inevitably turned this work into a case study of imperialism. I have nowhere defined the term and have refused to generalize about its nature. Whatever the nature of imperialism may be, its significance is plain. Believing that objectivity is not synonymous with indifference and that historians must feel in order to know, I have not concealed my own reactions to persons and events described in this book.

I am grateful to many scholars and institutions for their kind assistance. The study was begun under the auspices of the Russian Research Center and the Center for Middle Eastern Studies at Harvard University. Professor William L. Langer, then director of both centers, encouraged my early efforts. Professor Richard N. Frye of Harvard University was always ready to listen to my stories of shahs, ministers, generals, and adventurers of all sorts. Dr. Khodadad Farmanfarmaian, now deputy director of the Central Bank of Iran, patiently explained to me some of the intricacies of international high finance.

Yale University granted me two leaves, one to conduct research in England, another to complete the writing. Professors George W. Pierson and Arthur F. Wright invariably showed interest in my work. Miss Loueva F. Pflueger, executive secretary of the Department of History, arranged for the typing and retyping of the manuscript.

Professor Nikki Keddie of the University of California at Los Angeles read the manuscript and offered a number of valuable suggestions. My old friends Professors Amin Banani of the University of California at Los Angeles and Mario Rodriguez of George Washington University know what is in the book without having read it. Professor Howard Garey of Yale University, my next-door neighbor at Trumbull College, found himself reading a manuscript that dealt with matters far from his own field. I am grateful for the many suggestions he made.

Mrs. Marian N. Ash, managing editor of the Yale University Press, and Miss Casey Miller made a significant contribution invisible to the reader but known to the author and valued by him.

I wish to record my gratitude to the staff of the Commonwealth Relations Office Library and its director, Mr. Joseph Sutton, and to the staff of the Public Record Office in London for their unfailing help. I also feel compelled regretfully to record that the gentlemen at Reuter's news agency in Fleet Street refused me access to the archives of their organization. I am at a loss to explain their reluctance to expose secrets which are more than ninety years old, as well as the brusk, not to say rude, manner of their refusal.

Most of all I am indebted to my father, Kazem Kazemzadeh, whose diplomatic experience in Iran and Russia made him an invaluable critic and who obtained for me a number of documents from the archives of the Iranian Ministry of Foreign Affairs.

F. K.

New Haven, Conn.
April 1967

Note

Some twenty years ago the Persian government addressed a note to the governments with which it maintained diplomatic relations, requesting that in all official transactions the native name, Iran, be substituted for Persia. This has given rise to all sorts of mistaken notions. Though the matter has been dealt with many times before, one feels compelled to say once more that as far as the Persians were concerned they had not changed the name of the country, which to them has always been Iran. It was the ancient Greeks who first called all of Iran by the name of one of its parts, Persia, the modern Fārs; just as the Iranians referred, and still refer, to all of Hellas as Ionia. The tradition established by the Greeks prevailed in the West. There over the centuries the name Persia acquired rich connotations which Iran lacks. Yet to an Iranian Persia is only a province. In this book the two names are used interchangeably throughout, as one would use interchangeably America and the United States.

Introduction

This book was published almost half a century ago and has become a standard work on the diplomatic history of Anglo-Russian rivalry in Iran from the middle of the nineteenth century to the First World War. It pleases me that after many decades out of print, it has been resurrected in its original English version while an excellent Persian translation and a pirated Russian edition have made it accessible to readers of those two languages.

While writing *Russia and Britain in Persia,* I was painfully conscious that the inaccessibility of Russian archives could make my work one-sided. Published government sources could not be relied upon, as I knew from a simple comparison of some of the documents in a collection produced by the Russian Ministry of Foreign Affairs in 1911 and the same documents reissued by the Soviet government after the Revolution of 1917. Would the inaccessibility of original documents vitiate my narrative and my conclusions? Yet a relative paucity of original documentation should not stop a historian from attempting to reconstruct the past to the best of his ability.

Unanticipated radical change in the life of the Soviet Union made it possible for me in 1990 to work in the archives of the Russian Ministry of Foreign Affairs. An examination of relevant materials relieved my anxiety and persuaded me that the basics of my narrative needed no modification and neither did my conclusions. Although a large number of works on Iran has appeared in the last forty years, few have dealt with the topics covered in *Russia and Britain.* I felt that I needed to make no change in the original text.

The book ends with the onset of the First World War, but the rivalry of the two great powers continued. The Russian government had not been satisfied with the gains made under the agreement of 1907 and, in 1915, concluded another agreement with Britain that amounted to a virtual annexation to Russia of her sphere of influence in Persia at the small price of ceding to Britain the insignificant neutral zone. Exigencies of war muted the old conflict.

The collapse of the Russian Empire and the establishment of the Soviet regime created an entirely new situation. Russia withdrew from the War and concluded a humiliating peace with Germany, creating a grave threat to the Allies on the Western Front. Russian troops withdrew from Persia and left behind a vacuum that Britain hastened to fill, out of fear that Persia would descend into anarchy and open the door to an ideology that called for an armed struggle against European imperialism and the overthrow of the old colonial order. Appealing to all peoples of colonial and semi-colonial countries, the Soviet government repudiated various treaties that had given Russia rights and privileges in countries such as Persia and China. This would, of course, undermine Britain's position throughout the colonial world. Thus the old rivalry was resuming under new names and new flags.

In 1919, hoping to consolidate Britain's position and assure the defense of India, Lord Curzon bribed a number of leading Persian officials to sign an agreement which, had it come into force, would have turned their country into a British protectorate. Persia's parliament, the *Majles*, refused to ratify the agreement. Curzon's policy was in shreds. Tribes were in rebellion, the central government under the ineffective Ahmad Shah was paralyzed, and an anti-colonialist movement established itself in the province of Gilan, attracting the support of communist-leaning radicals and welcoming a contingent of Soviet Russian troops. A Soviet Republic of Gilan was proclaimed, hailed by Moscow, and ready to advance on Tehran. The only force that could stop the advance was the Cossack Brigade created by Russia half a century before but now commanded by

Persian officers headed by Rezā Khan, an energetic and ambitious young officer.

Britain, exhausted by a long war, evacuated its troops from northern Persia. At the urging of its minister in Tehran, and in spite of Curzon's misgivings, the British government decided to back Rezā Khan and the Cossack Brigade as the only force capable of preventing Tehran, and perhaps all of Persia, from falling to the Soviets. Rezā Khan marched on Tehran, staged a *coup d'état*, and succeeded in stopping the troops of the Gilan Republic. Internal conditions compelled Soviet Russia to abandon the Gilan Soviet, whose leaders fled to Russia, there to form a nucleus of Persian Communist opposition. Soon the Persian government, now entirely dominated by Rezā Khan, concluded a treaty that recognized Soviet Russia, established regular diplomatic relations between the two countries, and helped to stabilize the domestic situation in Persia, permitting Rezā Khan to consolidate his authority, overthrow the Qajar dynasty and have a constituent assembly proclaim him Rezā Shah Pahlavi.

Russia's threat to British interests in Persia was averted, although Rezā Shah proved not to be Britain's obedient tool. Even before ascending the throne, he created a national army which he successfully used to centralize the country by destroying the autonomy of southern tribal leaders such as the Bakhtiāri khans and the Sheykh of Muhammarah, who had long been Britain's clients. After 1925, a balance of Russian and British influence was achieved that lasted up to the Second World War and a joint occupation of Iran reminiscent of what had occurred in the First World War.

In their sphere of occupation, as elsewhere in Iran, the Soviets proceeded to encourage the growth of Communist parties, while in Azerbaijan and Kurdistan they promoted separatist movements that would, at the War's end, create a serious crisis, but this time Russia's principal antagonist would be the new super-power, the United States.

Before the Second World War, America had no significant interests in Persia. Regular diplomatic relations between the two were not established until 1882. A few Protestant missionaries had been active in Persia since the mid-nineteenth century but Muslims could not be converted and the missionaries worked mostly among Armenian and Assyrian Christians. They were allowed to open a number of schools that educated non-Christian Iranians, including members of prominent families. An American, Morgan Shuster, briefly Iran's Treasurer General, was forced to leave when Russia demanded his dismissal in an ultimatum and sent troops to occupy northern Persia. The US government neither sponsored nor supported the Shuster mission.

The Second World War and the Cold War changed the situation. Fear of the Soviet Union became America's main concern in the conduct of her foreign policy. Britain might have compromised on the issue of oil and acquiesced in the acquisition of rights to the exploitation of northern Iran's fields by the Soviets, but the United States took a strong position. The Soviets, not yet in possession of an atom bomb, abandoned their demands for an oil concession and left their *protégées* in Azerbaijan to their fate.

When an upsurge of national sentiment led to the nationalization of the Anglo-Iranian Oil Company, Britain had to persuade the US government, apprehensive of a Communist takeover in Iran, to participate in the overthrow of Mosaddeq and the return of the Shah from his brief exile. Russia chose not to support Mosaddeq, concentrating instead on cultivating a network of agents within Iran, a network that was soon smashed by the Shah with the support of the United States.

The establishment of the Islamic Republic once again dramatically changed relationships among Iran, Russia, Britain and the United States. For the first time in two hundred years Iran was free to determine its own domestic and foreign policies. Rivalries among great powers had lost much of their relevance, although the history of those rivalries determined, and is determining, many of the actions of the current regime. In novel conditions, under very different circumstances, the past continues to exercise its influence.

In the Preface to this book when it was first published, I gratefully acknowledged the assistance of several individuals and institutions.

I now take this occasion to add my thanks to Professor Rudi Matthee of the University of Delaware for suggesting to I.B.Tauris that they reissue this book.

Firuz Kazemzadeh
2013

Russia and Britain in Persia, 1864–1914

A Study in Imperialism

1

Anglo-Russian Conflict in Central Asia:
Genesis and Evolution

> Turkestan, Afghanistan, Transcaspia, Persia—to many these words breathe only a sense of utter remoteness or a memory of strange vicissitudes and of moribund romance. To me, I confess, they are the pieces on a chessboard upon which is being played out a game for the domination of the world. George Curzon

Russia's advance into Central Asia, the spectacular conquests she carried out in the second half of the nineteenth century, and the consequent expansion of her Empire, startled Europe. The deserts and oases of Central Asia, the unexplored mountains of Afghanistan, the legendary cities of Khorāsān, suddenly invaded the front pages of the leading newspapers and became a lively topic of conversation in Berlin, Paris, and London.

As their troops won easy victories over the hordes of Kazakhs, Uzbeks, and Turkomans, the gap that separated the Russians from the British, slowly making their way toward Baluchestān and Afghanistan, narrowed, and conflict threatened the peace precariously maintained between the major powers. When viewed from London, Russia's penetration of Central Asia seemed disturbing, if not frightening. From St. Petersburg it appeared natural, being only the climax of a long series of efforts that had begun three centuries earlier in the reigns of Ivan the Terrible, Feodor Ivanovich, and Boris Godunov. While the British, themselves strangers in Asia, were shocked to discover the Cossack on the banks of the Oxus, the Russians felt at home among the Turkic peoples who for hundreds of years had been by turns their neighbors, masters, and subjects.

The conquest of Kazan opened the way for Russia's approach

to the Caspian, while the acquisition of Astrakhan inevitably involved her in the affairs of Tarki and Kabarda, which in turn led to contacts with Georgia, Turkey, and Iran.[1] In 1560 Russia was already sending troops to fight against the Mountaineers of Daghestan. The marriage of Ivan the Terrible to the daughter of the chieftain Temriuk resulted in the stationing of Russian troops in Kabarda.[2]

Russia's attempts to subdue Daghestan failed when Prince Ivan Andreevich Khvorostinin was defeated in 1594 and forced to retreat, after losing three thousand men.[3] Her first "Caucasian war" inaugurated a struggle that was to continue until the capitulation of the intrepid Sheykh Shamil at Gunib in 1859. Boris Godunov made another attempt to establish Russian rule over the Mountaineers, but Turkey and Iran aided the tribes of Daghestan in resisting the Streltsy and the Cossacks. By 1605 Russia was too absorbed in domestic troubles to embark upon new conquests. No further moves were made in the Caucasus until the reign of Peter the Great.

Under him, the Empire expanded in every direction. While fighting for a foothold on the Baltic, the Tsar nursed dreams of Asiatic campaigns. "For all the concentration of his main energies upon Europe," writes B. H. Sumner, "he had from his earliest years taken a lively interest in Asia. The enthusiasm of the explorer was allied with the gold-dazzled phantasy of the prospector and the merchant."[4] Khiva, Bukhara, Persia, and beyond these fabulous India, excited Peter's imagination. He sent a force of thirty-five hundred men under Prince Bekovich-Cherkasskii to conquer Khiva and find the road to India. The force fell into a trap and was exterminated.

About the same time Peter ordered one of his younger officers, Artemii Volynskii, to travel to Persia to gather political, economic, and military intelligence. Volynskii was instructed to find

---

1. For a history of Russia's first contacts with Daghestan and Kabarda, see Boris Nolde, *La formation de l'Empire Russe*, 2 (Paris, 1953).

2. Ibid., p. 307.

3. Ibid., p. 318.

4. B. H. Sumner, *Peter the Great and the Emergence of Russia* (London, 1956), p. 171.

out, among other things, whether there were in Persia any navigable rivers that flowed from India into the Caspian Sea. Upon his return, Volynskii strongly urged the Tsar to conquer Persia, which was in a state of anarchy and disorder. Once the Northern War was over, Peter launched an attack on Iran. He met practically no resistance, for the country had been invaded by the Afghans, the Shah was a captive, and the government nonexistent. The Russians occupied Baku, Gilān, Māzandarān, and Astarābād. However, Peter's Persian conquests proved ephemeral. His immediate successors, faced with the resurgent power of Iran led by Nāder Shah, and having no interest in the East, gave up every bit of the territory Peter the Great had acquired at great cost in men and treasure.[5]

During the closing decades of the eighteenth century Russia resumed her activity in the Caucasus. In 1801 Georgia was annexed. Persia, refusing to acquiesce in the loss of a land it had ruled for centuries, went to war and was badly defeated.[6] By the Treaty of Golestān she lost most of her Caucasian possessions, including Baku, Darband, Ganjeh, and Georgia, gave up her right to maintain a navy on the Caspian, which thereby became a Russian lake, and accepted an unfavorable arrangement in regard to tariffs. Perhaps the most damaging provision of all was contained in Article 5 of the treaty by which Russia recognized Prince Abbās Mirzā as the rightful heir to the throne and promised him assistance in case succession was disputed, thus obtaining a useful instrument for direct interference in Iran's internal affairs.

Persian desire for revenge and Russian encroachment along the newly established frontier led to another war and another Russian victory. Russian troops captured Erivan and Tabriz, and threatened Tehran. In 1828 at the village of Torkamanchāy a peace treaty was signed. It was destined to regulate Russo-Persian rela-

5. On Peter's Persian war and his relations with the Turks, the Georgians, and the Armenians, see V. P. Lystsov, *Persidskii pokhod Petra I, 1722–1723* (Moscow, 1951), and D. M. Lang, *The Last Years of the Georgian Monarchy, 1658–1832* (New York, 1957), pp. 111–17.

6. The best account of the complicated situation that led to the annexation of Georgia is in D. M. Lang, *The Last Years of the Georgian Monarchy*, Chaps. 9, 11–13. *Akty sobrannye kavkazskoiu arkheograficheskoiu kommissieiu* (12 vols. Tiflis, 1868–1904), are a rich source for this period.

tions until 1917. In addition to further territorial losses, Persia had to pay an indemnity of 20 million rubles. A commercial treaty concluded at the same time set the maximum duty on Russian goods imported into Persia at 5 percent *ad valorem*, established a regime of capitulations for Russian subjects, and extended to Russian merchants many privileges never before enjoyed by foreigners in the domains of the Shah. Thus in one generation Russia had vaulted the Caucasus, absorbed Georgia, northern Āzarbāyjān, and a part of Armenia, acquired extensive commercial rights and strong political influence in Persia, and established herself in the vicinity of British India. The stage was now set for a long duel between Russia and Britain, a duel that was the determining factor in Central Asiatic and Middle Eastern affairs until British power waned after the Second World War.[7]

The complexities of the Eastern question, the savage resistance of the Mountaineers under Shamil, and the fear of provoking a major conflict with Great Britain restrained Russia from undertaking any further encroachment on Persian territory west of the Caspian. The frontier drawn up at Torkamanchāy has remained substantially unchanged to this day. East of the Caspian no definite frontiers existed between Persia and her nomadic neighbors, between the various Central Asiatic khanates, or between the khanates and Russia. Political instability and economic stagnation were the lot of the various ephemeral states that periodically sprang up in Turkestan. A vast power vacuum, stretching all the way from the Caspian Sea to the borders of China, from Afghanistan to the edge of the Siberian plain, could not fail to exercise an irresistible attraction upon the Russians.

The European powers, jealously watching every move Russia made in the direction of Constantinople, seemed almost entirely unaware of her steady advance in Central Asia. Neither the disaster that overtook General V. A. Perovskii in his attempt to capture Khiva in 1839, nor the victories that gave Russia Aq-Masjid (Ak Mechet) in 1853, elicited a reaction from the Euro-

7. The Persian view of the two Russo-Persian wars is presented in Jamil Qozānlu, *Jange dah-sāle yā jange avvale Irān bā Rus* (Tehran, 1937); and his *Jange Irān-Rus, 1825–1828* (Tehran, 1938). For the Soviet interpretation, see M. S. Ivanov, *Ocherk istorii Irana* (Moscow, 1952). For the British view, see Sir Percy M. Sykes, A History of Persia (London, 1915), 2, Chap. 76.

pean states.⁸ The Crimean War interrupted Russia's activity in Central Asia; but, after a brief period of recuperation, the forward movement was resumed.

Its initiator and inspirer was one of the most remarkable figures of nineteenth-century Russia, though his stature has not yet been sufficiently recognized. General Dimitrii Alekseevich Miliutin was a soldier, a teacher, a statesman, a reformer, and a close collaborator of Alexander II throughout the latter's reign. It was Miliutin who played the principal part in reforming the antiquated serf army of Nicholas I and restoring Russia's military power. It was he who championed every advance, every conquest in Central Asia, often against the wishes of the more cautious and European-minded Chancellor, Prince A. M. Gorchakov. It was Miliutin who was responsible for the appointment of K. P. von Kaufmann to the post of Governor-General of Turkestan in 1867, and who was intimately connected with the pacification, administration, and exploitation of Russian Central Asia.⁹

While Miliutin urged the Tsar forward, Gorchakov counseled caution. Too rapid an advance in the direction of India would alarm the English to whom even the vastest deserts, highest mountains, and deepest seas did not seem sufficient to protect their dearest possession. Ever since Napoleon had toyed with the utterly impractical scheme of invading India with the help of Tsar Paul and Fath Ali Shah, the British had been obsessed with fear and suspicion, which Gorchakov would have preferred not to increase. On one occasion, when the Foreign Ministry argued this point, Miliutin angrily wrote: "it is not necessary to apologize to the English Minister for our advance. They do not stand on ceremonies with us, conquering whole Kingdoms, occupying alien cities and islands; and we do not ask them why they do it." For the next twenty years Gorchakov, and after him his successor, N. K. Giers, attempted to restrain the military, while providing them with brilliant tactical support abroad. The very tension between Miliutin and Gorchakov, the generals and the diplomats,

---

8. The most recent American contribution to the study of Central Asia is Richard A. Pierce's *Russian Central Asia, 1867–1917* (Berkeley, 1960). See also M. A. Terent'ev, *Istoriia zavoevaniia Srednei Azii* (St. Petersburg, 1906).

9. See A. M. Zaionchkovskii, "D. A. Miliutin: Biograficheskii ocherk," in *Dnevnik Miliutina* (Moscow, 1947), 1, 35.

made Russian policies unusually flexible and vigorous. Since there was no disagreement about ends, and since no one questioned the final authority of the Tsar to determine policy, there was little danger from this interdepartmental rivalry.

In 1864 several special ministerial conferences were held in St. Petersburg on orders of the Tsar to discuss the Central Asiatic question. Extensive military preparations were made for new advances. When the armies began to march, the diplomats were ready with justifications. In December, Gorchakov sent to Russian representatives abroad a circular dispatch, requesting them to use its arguments as a guide "in any explanations you may give to the Government to which you are accredited, in case questions are asked, or you may see credence given to erroneous ideas as to our action in these distant parts." The dispatch of November 21/December 3, 1864, became a landmark in the history of Russian diplomacy. Gorchakov wrote:

> The position of Russia in Central Asia is that of all civilized States which are brought into contact with half savage, nomad populations, possessing no fixed social organization.
>
> In such cases it always happens that the more civilized State is forced, in the interests of the security of its frontier and its commercial relations, to exercize a certain ascendency over those whom their turbulent and unsettled character make most undesirable neighbours.
>
> First there are raids and acts of pillage to put down. To put a stop to them, the tribes on the frontier have to be reduced to a state of more or less perfect submission.

Once pacified, these tribes have a right to protection against their neighbors; but "the moral force of reason" will not accomplish this, since "It is a peculiarity of Asiatics to respect nothing but visible and palpable force." Thus the civilized state is placed in a dilemma: it must either abandon all attempts at civilization, or "lunge deeper and deeper into barbarous countries."

Such has been the fate of every country which has found itself in a similar position. The United States in America,

France in Algeria, Holland in her Colonies, England in India —all have been irresistibly forced, less by ambition than by imperious necessity, into this onward movement where the greatest difficulty is to know where to stop.

Faced with the dilemma common to all civilized states with "savage" neighbors, Russia decided to rectify her Central Asiatic frontier, drawing it in such a way that it should run through a fertile area, to insure both supply and regular colonization, "which alone can prepare a future of stability and prosperity for the occupied country." It was urgent to lay down this line definitively, so as to escape the danger of being carried away, as is almost inevitable, by a series of repressive measures and reprisals, into an unlimited extension of territory.[10]

Russia wanted to absorb the nomads but not the sedentary agricultural and commercial populations "who are good neighbors." The new line

> puts us in the immediate neighbourhood of the agricultural and commercial populations of Khokand. We find ourselves in the presence of a more solid and compact, less unsettled and better organized social state, fixing for us with geographical precision the limit up to which we are bound to advance and at which we must halt.[11]

No sooner had the British government been informed of the Gorchakov circular by the Russian ambassador, Baron E. Brunnow, than events in Central Asia cast doubt on the sincerity of the document. An attack was launched against Tashkent, a town inhabited by a sedentary people engaged in agriculture and commerce. On June 10, 1865, Gorchakov told the British ambassador in St. Petersburg, Sir Andrew Buchanan, "that the Russian Government would not retain the city, but would act up to their declarations 'in regard to that country.'"

Tashkent was taken by storm (June 15–17, 1865). When the

---

10. Correspondence, from 1864 to 1881, respecting the movements of Russia in Central Asia and her relations with Afghanistan; F. O. 65/1202. Hereafter cited as Correspondence.

11. Id.

victory was publicly announced, a St. Petersburg newspaper, *Russkii invalid*, wrote:

> Our troops can only occupy the town for a short time, until its independence of Kokand is no longer menaced. After having given independence to Tashkend . . . Russia, who has no desire to annex the place, will only have to watch over the tranquility and security of her commercial relations with Central Asia.[12]

The British were not reassured. Lord John Russell, Secretary of State for Foreign Affairs, wanted a formal exchange of notes in which the two powers would "declare that they had no intention of extending their territories in such a manner that their frontiers would approach each other more than they then did." If one of the powers felt compelled to expand, it would inform the other of the causes that compelled it to do so "and the extent of the contemplated increase of territory." Both parties would respect the "present state of possessions" in Central Asia and "both Powers would respect the independence of the Persian monarchy; would be careful not to encroach on the territory of Persia; and would act in concert to support and strengthen the authority of the Shah." [13]

The India Office approved of the spirit of such an understanding, though it opposed a formal convention. Russell agreed and approached Gorchakov, who was handed excerpts from Russell's dispatch of July 31 expressing the wish of Her Majesty's Government "to remove every cause of danger which might threaten the future good understanding between England and Russia." The two powers would engage not to disturb the status quo in Central Asia. "Her Majesty's Government will also respect the independence of the Persian Monarchy, will be careful not to encroach upon the territory of Persia, and will act in such a manner as may best support and strengthen the sovereignty of the Shah." [14]

12. Correspondence, ibid.
13. Id.
14. Id.

Gorchakov pretended not to understand Russell's point. Had not Russia already proclaimed her pacific intention in regard to Central Asia? As for Persia,

> His Excellency said that he could not understand the connection between Central Asia and the Persian monarchy which had induced this declaration.
> The declaration itself was of very satisfactory nature, and one which was quite in accord with the views of the Imperial Government, but, while receiving it with pleasure, he must say that he had never suspected Her Majesty's Government of any intention of encroaching upon the territory of the Shah.[15]

One wonders whether Russell sensed Gorchakov's irony. By affirming with an air of naïve innocence his faith in England's good intentions, he evaded the issue and kept Russia uncommitted. When, on September 3, Sir Andrew Buchanan intimated that the terms of Gorchakov's circular of 1864 were not sufficiently explicit to reassure the British government in regard to Persia, which had not even been mentioned in it, Gorchakov replied that "he could not believe that an unfavourable interpretation would be given to that omission, as it was impossible for any one acquainted with the policy of the Imperial Government to suspect it of designs against the independence of the Persian monarchy." Gorchakov added that he was prepared to instruct his ambassador in London to give Russell confidential assurances that Russia had no intention to violate the independence and integrity of Persia, but that the Turkomans were not the subjects of the Shah, and that Russia found it necessary to punish them for depredations against her commerce. The significance of this remark was not understood by the British for many years.[16]

The reference to the Turkomans was not fortuitous. Late in 1864 a Special Conference composed of representatives of the Foreign Ministry, the Army, the Navy, and several other depart-

15. Id.
16. Id.

ments, met on orders of the Tsar to discuss the question of establishing Russian power in Turkoman lands on the eastern coast of the Caspian. It was decided to occupy the village of Qizil-Su (Red Water, Krasnovodsk). The Tsar approved the decision on February 22, 1865.[17] The proposed outpost would enable Russia to control the sea as well as a strip of land stretching the entire length of the Caspian and, perhaps, to remove her naval station from the island of Āshurādeh. The station had been established on Persian territory without Persia's consent. Its purpose had been to stop Turkoman piracy and to prevent Persia from evading the provisions of Article 8 of the treaty of Torkamanchāy which prohibited her from maintaining armed vessels on the Caspian. Because the naval station was located on Persian territory, it was a constant irritant which stimulated the Shah's suspicions of Russian intentions. A base at Krasnovodsk would provide the same, or even greater, advantages as Āshurādeh, without the disadvantages of the latter.[18] Complications on the borders of Bukhara and Kokand prevented the immediate implementation of the decision, but Gorchakov was carefully preparing the diplomatic basis for military action in Transcaspia.

Contrary to its promises of 1865, the Russian government did not evacuate Tashkent. In May 1866, relations with Bukhara having broken down, General D. I. Romanovskii led his troops against the Bukharans and routed them at Irjar. In June Khojent was occupied. On the twenty-seventh, Lord Clarendon, now Foreign Secretary in Lord John Russell's cabinet, instructed Sir Andrew Buchanan at St. Petersburg to let the Russian government know that, while Britain recognized Russia's right to use force to procure the release of her ambassador imprisoned in Bukhara,

> the changes which were being made in Russia's borders are scarcely consistent with the professed intention of the Russian Government to respect the independence of the States of Central Asia. Russia seems to have made a steady advance

17. Minister of Foreign Affairs, A. M. Gorchakov, to the Director of the Ministry of the Navy, October 15/27, 1869; A. Il'iasov, ed., *Prisoedinenie Turkmenii k Rossii* (Ashkhabad, 1960), No. 1, pp. 19–23. Hereafter cited as *Prisoedinenie*.
18. Id.

in this direction, taking permanent possession of territory not required solely for making a good frontier.[19]

To Buchanan's question about the limits of Russian conquests, Gorchakov replied that only the military were competent to decide such issues, and added that it was absurd to suppose that Russia's moves could threaten British India.[20]

The pattern was now established. Year after year Russian troops would penetrate deeper into the heart of Asia. A flurry of alarm would run from Calcutta, or Simla, to Whitehall. The British ambassador in St. Petersburg would call on Russia's Minister of Foreign Affairs, ask for an explanation, receive assurances of the Tsar's determination not to annex an inch of land anywhere, send a dispatch to that effect to Her Majesty's Principal Secretary for Foreign Affairs, and leave the matter there until Russia's next move reopened the whole issue.

The Government of India was divided in its opinions in regard to the Russian threat. While a number of lesser officials advocated strong measures, even to the occupation of Afghanistan, the Viceroy, Sir John Lawrence, preached the doctrine of masterly inactivity. "He belonged to the generation which had drawn natural but mistaken conclusions from the lamentable war of 1839. He held strongly that Britain had no interests beyond the line which the Sikhs had formerly held, and that the defence of India should be based on the Indus." [21]

In a minute dated October 3, 1867, Lawrence, opposing a British advance, argued that the further Russia penetrated into Central Asia, the longer her supply line would become, while the length of the British supply line would remain the same. A British advance into Afghanistan might be interpreted by Russia as a challenge. Moreover Russia might actually prove a good neighbor.

> I am not myself at all certain that Russia might not prove a safer ally, a better neighbour, than the Mahomedan races of

19. Correspondence; F. O. 65/1202.
20. Id.
21. John Allan, *The Cambridge Shorter History of India* (London, 1934), pp. 804–05.

Central Asia and Kabul. She would introduce civilization, she would abate the fanaticism and ferocity of Mahomedanism, which still exercises so powerful an influence in India.[22]

W. R. Mansfield, Commander in Chief in India, shared the Viceroy's optimism on military grounds:

the alarm testified with regard to Russia, as affecting British interests in India, is more unreasonable than it is possible to describe. As a military and vast political Power, we have literally nothing to fear from Russia, whether she stop at her present limits, or spread her power even to our own borders. A great mischief is done by those who, from whatever cause, occupy themselves in preaching the falsehood of our weakness in India.

We are simply invincible in that country against all the powers in the world, provided only we are true to ourselves. If we choose to commit ourselves to a policy of aggression, we can go and establish ourselves wherever we like.[23]

In London the Cabinet was reluctant to take any but diplomatic steps. The change from a Conservative to a Liberal government in 1868 did not result in a change of policy. The new Secretary of State for Foreign Affairs, Lord Clarendon, made an attempt to reach an agreement with Russia by creating a neutral zone between India and Russian possessions. On March 27, 1869, Brunnow transmitted to Clarendon a letter from Gorchakov giving assurances in regard to the neutrality of Afghanistan. Six weeks later Russian troops entered Samarkand, and the British ambassador in St. Petersburg once again "tried to ascertain how far the conquests of Russia were likely to extend." [24]

Clarendon made another attempt to obtain from Gorchakov a commitment that Russia would not absorb the independent

---

22. Correspondence; F. O. 65/1202.
23. Minute by Commander-in-Chief in India, suggested by Sir H. Rawlinson's Memorandum on the questions connected with Central Asia, December 24, 1868, No. 11, Foreign Department, Political. Confidential, No. 1, January 4, 1869; *Letters from India*, 4, 1869. Hereafter cited as *L.I.*
24. Correspondence; F. O. 65/1202.

khanates of Central Asia. The two statesmen met in Heidelberg on September 3, 1869. The conversation began with Gorchakov's expressing satisfaction that England and Russia had no conflicting interests anywhere in the world. When Clarendon pointed out that Central Asia was such an area, Gorchakov said that the Emperor had no intention of advancing further south. Clarendon replied that the events of the last five years made it impossible to doubt that Russian armies were "impelled forward either by direct orders from St. Petersburg, or by ambitions of Generals in disregard of the pacific intentions of the Emperor." Gorchakov promptly agreed and blamed the military "who had all exceeded their instructions in the hope of gaining distinction." [25] Thus Clarendon and Gorchakov jointly created the legend of insubordination having been the principal cause of the conquest of Central Asia. This notion, which had an inexplicable appeal to British statesmen up to and including Sir Edward Grey, was extremely useful to the Russians. With the passage of time it assumed the status of a venerable tradition and was enshrined by statesmen and historians in various articles and books.

The Clarendon-Gorchakov pourparlers neither did nor could lead to an understanding. St. Petersburg was aware of the indecision in London. If anything, Britain's conciliatory attitude and the acceptance of Gorchakov's version of the causes of Russian conquests in Central Asia encouraged further moves southward and eastward. Negotiations, exchanges of notes, reminders concerning old pledges, and expressions of dissatisfaction on the part of the British had not the slightest effect upon Russian planning and execution of conquests. Now that Tashkent and Khojent had been annexed, it was Khiva's turn to fall before the armies of the Āq-Khān (the White Tsar). Beyond the deserts and the oases of Ākhāl and Marv lay Khorāsān and Herāt. Neither Persia nor Afghanistan could escape involvement in the Great Game.

The Persian government was much disturbed by the rapid Russian movement toward Khorāsān. Already in 1868 a number of Tekke Turkomans appeared in Tehran to warn of the Russian threat. They told Charles Alison, the British minister, that they

25. Id.

would not submit to the Russians but would like to serve Britain in return for British protection. Alison assured the Turkomans that Russia would not dare to go beyond the Oxus, advised them to form a union of tribes, but said nothing about British aid.[26] The Persian government could not be put off as easily as the Tekke.

At an audience granted to Alison shortly before his scheduled departure for England, the Shah, Nāser ed-Din, said that it was more important than ever "that the closest intimacy should exist between the two States now that Russia is making such advances in Central Asia." The sentiments of Fath Ali Shah, he went on, continued to exist. It was Persia's "foremost thought . . . to be guided and supported by England." However, the Shah complained, in his repeated attempts to ascertain clearly the policy of Her Majesty's Government, he met "with some reserve on their side." He hoped that during his visit in England Alison would "explain fully his anxieties and elicit from the Queen's Government such a frank declaration of their views as would enable him satisfactorily to understand his true position and the best course to pursue." [27]

The Minister of Foreign Affairs, Mirzā Said Khān Mo'tamen ol-Molk, echoed his master's words. The Shah, he told Alison, was anxious to place his relations with England "on the same cordial footing as they were in the time of Fath Ali Shah." Nāser ed-Din hoped that Britain would send him military instructors and was even prepared to pay them, though he knew that once the English decided on a course of action, money was not a consideration.[28]

Alison's visit to London did not result in closer Anglo-Persian cooperation. The Government of India had been for some time quite sceptical about the idea of British officers serving in the Iranian army. "Persia," wrote Colonel R. Taylor in a memorandum prepared for the use of the government, "appears to me to

---

26. Mr. Charles Alison to the Earl of Clarendon, No. 2, Tehran, January 11, 1869; F. O. 60/318. See also M. A. Terent'ev, 2, 61.

27. Alison to Clarendon, No. 49, Tehran, May 5, 1869; F. O. 60/318.

28. Alison to Clarendon, No. 50, Tehran, May 6, 1869; ibid.

be so weak . . . that she is practically under the control of Russia, and utterly unable to resist the influence of that power." [29]

The British government itself was not disposed to send a military mission to Iran, and perhaps provoke a violent Russian reaction.

Ever since armed force had been used in 1857 to prevent Persia from retaining Herāt, Britain preferred to employ strictly diplomatic means in the Middle East. The hope of reaching a formal agreement with Russia, guaranteeing the independence and integrity of Persia, lived in the hearts even of such "imperialistic" Englishmen as Sir Henry Rawlinson, who, in 1860, felt that Russia could not refuse to guarantee the integrity of Persia. To refuse would mean to show her hand. The French minister in Tehran, although he knew how keenly the Shah desired international assurances of Iran's territorial integrity, realized that Russia had no reason to tie her hands in the Middle East by giving such guarantees. The true guarantee of Persia, he told Mirzā Saīd Khān, reposed less in treaties than in the jealous rivalry of the two great powers. Acting wisely, balancing one against the other, Persia could preserve her independence and integrity.[30]

British statesmen felt that their policy in Persia was "very friendly and very plain." It consisted of supporting the independence of Persia. To do this it was necessary constantly to remonstrate with the Russian government at St. Petersburg, thus endangering Anglo-Russian relations and, incidentally, exposing the Shah to ever greater pressure from the north.

> I agree with the Shah [Russell wrote in 1860] that the use of our good offices at St. Petersburg must be employed with great discretion and seldom. There is nothing which the Russian Government would resent so much.
>
> But on the other hand we could not look upon their aggressions in silence, and on a sudden make them the ground of hostilities.

29. Memorandum by Col. R. Taylor, November 23, 1868, Foreign Department, Political, Confidential, No. 1, January 4, 1869; L. I., 4, 1869.
30. M. le Baron Pichon a M. Thouvenel, Direction politique, 1602, Tehéran, 13 fevrier 1860; Archive des Affaires Entrangères, Perse, tome 31.

It is fit that Russia should perceive that her conduct is not unobserved and that the relations of Great Britain and Persia are of the most friendly character. Russia may draw her own inferences. In the mean time we can make no engagements; nor can we from selfishness or jealousy obstruct the advances of Russian Commerce in Central Asia, so long as trade is the main object of such advances.[31]

It is this kind of "very friendly and very plain" statement that the Shah and his ministers had difficulty understanding. How could they comprehend the meaning of British friendship when the only action the British minister, Mr. Charles Alison, had been allowed to promise since his arrival in Tehran in 1860 was intercession before Russia at St. Petersburg? What could they think of the value of British support when year after year the advice they received from Alison was to take "a cautious, accommodating attitude toward Russia"?[32] What was the Shah to expect from the British now that Russian troops had crushed Kokand and Bukhara, were preparing to crush Khiva and subjugate the Turkomans of Transcaspia?

On November 10, 1869, a Russian ship anchored opposite the Turkoman village of Qizil-Su. A small force landed on the shore, occupying the village. For several days thereafter ships brought more troops. Persian merchants at Astarābād, having learned of their presence up the coast, asked Russian authorities for permission to trade with them but were turned down lest the Persian government be informed too soon of what was taking place at Qizil-Su (Krasnovodsk).[33]

The precaution was superfluous since the Persian government already knew of the landings and was sufficiently disturbed to remind the Russian minister that the Persian frontier lay north of Qizil-Su (Krasnovodsk), the point at which the troops had landed, and that their action constituted a violation of the sovereign rights of the Shah. The Russian minister, Aleksandr Fedorovich Beger, denied that Iran's frontier extended beyond

31. Russell to Rawlinson, No. 24, March 8, 1860; F. O. 248/185.
32. Russell to Alison [Instruction], No. 3, April 24, 1860; ibid.
33. Report of the Commanding Officer of the Astarābād Naval Station to the Russian Minister in Iran, November 17/29, 1869; *Prisoedinenie*, No. 3, pp. 26–27.

the Atrak River. Moreover, Beger maintained, Persia had never exercised authority over the Turkomans "who professed to be, and in reality were, an independent population." Mirzā Said Khān retorted that temporary failure to exercise authority over a nomadic tribe did not imply abandonment of sovereign rights. "Russia would not, he supposed, be prepared to admit such arguments if applied to the Kirghize and other refractory tribes in Central Asia." [34]

The British minister at Tehran, Charles Alison, agreed with his Russian colleague that Persia exercised no influence north of the Atrak. He informed Clarendon that "he was not aware upon what grounds they [the Persians] could claim Kyzyle Su [Krasnovodsk] as part of their territory." [35] Lacking British support, the Persian government could not press its claims very far. Rather it tried to obtain from A. F. Beger written assurances that Russia would not interfere with the nomads living along the Gorgān and Atrak rivers, would not build fortifications, and would admit Persian sovereignty there. On December 25, 1869, Beger informed Mirzā Said Khān "that the Imperial Government recognizes Persian dominion up to the Atrak and therefore does not intend to build any fortifications in that area." [36] In St. Petersburg the Tsar referred to the occupation of Krasnovodsk in a conversation with Sir Andrew Buchanan, the British ambassador. He implied that no conquest had been made since the territory "had been almost without a sovereign," and informed Buchanan that most positive assurances had been given to Persia that her Atrak frontier would be respected.[37]

The Krasnovodsk issue was closed. The Shah himself admitted this in a Decree (Farmān) to the Governor of Astarābād, stating that Russian presence at Krasnovodsk was not injurious to Persia and that the Russians were free to build what they pleased on the right bank of the Atrak.[38]

34. Mr. Thomson, November 14, 1869, Central Asia, No. 2 (1873), Correspondence; F. O. 65/1202.
35. Correspondence; ibid.
36. The Russian Minister in Iran to the Iranian Minister of Foreign Affairs, December 13/25, 1869; *Prisoedinenie*, Document No. 6, pp. 31–32.
37. Correspondence; F. O. 65/1202.
38. Id.

Whatever Russian diplomats might say about the motives that brought the Tsar's troops to Krasnovodsk, Tehran and Calcutta felt that Khiva would be the next victim of Russian expansion. In St. Petersburg itself no one but high government officials pretended that this was not the case. Even before Krasnovodsk had been occupied, St. Petersburg newspapers wrote that the conquest of Khiva was inevitable. Gorchakov "denied positively the existence of any such intention," but Sir Andrew Buchanan obtained evidence from other sources that a campaign was indeed being prepared. The Government of India, far less complacent under Lord Mayo than it had been under Lawrence, admitted that to secure her commerce Russia might have to punish the Khan of Khiva, but would not need to annex the country. However, it was the possible effect of the conquest of Khiva on Persia that worried the Government of India most. This was clearly expressed in a secret dispatch (No. 28, dated May 26, 1871) to the India Office: "It is unnecessary to point out . . . that occupation or annexation of Khiva by Russia would be a fatal blow to Persian independence. Should such an event occur, she must either submit to the absolute influence of Russia, or seek for protection from British or Turkish power." [39]

No one seemed certain what course of action to take. The confused and contradictory advice of Lord John Russell, the self-assured pronouncements of Sir John Lawrence, and the general optimism of British political outlook made it difficult to admit that the policies pursued by Britain in Persia since the conclusion of the treaty of Paris in 1857 had been inadequate. Characteristically enough, the man who dared to question and condemn these policies was a neurotic, though capable, junior diplomat, Edward B. Eastwick. Unlike many of his colleagues, he mastered the language and acquired a fairly solid knowledge of the history of Persia. Generally speaking, British diplomats who served in Tehran fell into two distinct categories: those who liked or appreciated at least some features of Persian life and culture, and those who did not. Eastwick belonged to the first category. Even after he left Persia as a result of a sordid clash with his superior,

39. Id.

Charles Alison, Eastwick kept up his interest in Persian affairs. His concern led him to compose a memorandum which, in the spring of 1871, he submitted to the Foreign Secretary, Lord Granville.

Eastwick noted that up to the conclusion of the treaty of Torkamanchāy, British influence in Persia had been paramount. After 1828 Britain set herself "to limit Persia to her *de facto* possessions, inhibiting her from advancing in the direction of Afghanistan, Seistan, Mekran, and Arabia, and discouraging every other effort on her part to acquire or regain territory."

> In 1835 Haji Mirza Aghassi, by birth a Russian subject, became the Prime Minister of Muhammad Shah, and when that Shah in November 1837 laid siege to Herat the change of policy on the part of the two Great European Powers toward Persia had reached its culminating point, and a strange spectacle was witnessed of Russian officers and a Russian battalion serving with the Persian army, and a Russian Minister, Count Simonich, urging on the operations of that army, while an English officer was leading the sorties against it, and the English Minister, Mr. MacNeil, threatened the Shah with war.[40]

A few months later all British officers had been dismissed from Persian service, but relations between the two countries remained correct until 1855. A year later they were at war, which was terminated by the treaty of Paris signed in March 1857.

> but, except during the short interval that Sir H. Rawlinson was Minister, and the very brief period in 1862/63 when the writer of this Memorandum was chargé d'affaires there has been no return to cordiality in our relations with Persia. At the present moment . . . nothing but the sense of his own inability to cope with us prevents the Shah from coming to an open rupture with our Government . . . it is certain that matters are in such a state that the Shah might easily be induced to connive at, or, perhaps, even openly assist a Rus-

40. The Policy of Great Britain towards Persia [a memorandum by E. B. Eastwick], London, June 16, 1871; F. O. 60/340.

sian occupation of Herat and advance towards the frontier of Sindh.[41]

Anticipating the objections of those who defended this policy on the grounds that it had prevented war with Russia, and that Persia would make an extremely unreliable ally, Eastwick argued that Persia could be made into a "safe outer defence of India, impenetrable to Russia and to every other power." The Persians, Eastwick wrote, were far from degenerate mentally or physically. Sickly children die early and only the hardy survive. "Hence, notwithstanding their vices, they are a fine athletic race, with an amount of nerve, which Europeans might envy." Eastwick urged a change in Britain's approach to Iran. Herāt could not be given back to Persia as yet, but it could be detached from Kābul. The Shah could be encouraged to reestablish Persian dominion over Marv. "Above all, English officers should be sent at once to discipline the Shah's troops." [42]

The paper was circulated in various departments of the government at home and in India. Sir Henry Rawlinson, scholar, colonial administrator, and diplomat, wrote a memorandum of his own, expressing general agreement with Eastwick's views. Placed on the flank of "Debatable Land" between the Caspian and the Indus, Persia would largely determine "when a contact may take place between Russia and British India." A strong and friendly Persia might be able to postpone such contact indefinitely, a weak Persia would make it inevitable. "It should then be to our interest to conciliate her friendship and at the same time to give her strength and confidence in her own resources, any expense to which we may be put on this account being regarded as a sort of premium on the Insurance of India." [43]

However, Rawlinson did not endorse all of Eastwick's proposals for specific measures through which Persian friendship might be won. He did not doubt that approval "of her encroachments" in Seistān and Mekrān, encouragement to occupy Marv,

41. Id.
42. Id.
43. Memorandum on the policy of Great Britain towards Persia [by Eastwick], Comments by Sir H. Rawlinson; July 4, 1871; ibid.

concessions in the Persian Gulf and the promise of Herāt would make British influence paramount at Tehran; but Rawlinson did not believe Persia was strong enough to digest such acquisitions. The result would be rebellion and intervention by both the Russians and the Turks.

Rawlinson shared Eastwick's opinion that Britain should furnish officers to train the Persian army. He added a suggestion of his own: strengthen the legation at Tehran. To Rawlinson, who had been long associated with the Government of India, the latter was the proper locus of control over Britain's Persian policy. He therefore advocated the transfer of the Tehran legation from the jurisdiction of the Foreign Office to that of the Government of India.[44]

Eastwick's memorandum was studied with care at Fort William, where there had developed a feeling of frustration over the indecisive British attitude toward Russia. Unlike his predecessor, Lord Mayo did not want to defend India on the Indus. To him it was a cardinal point of Anglo-Indian policy that friendly relations be maintained with Kelāt, Afghanistan, Yār-Kand, Nepal, and Burma, and that their freedom from domination by another European power be preserved by supporting them with money, arms, "and even, in certain eventualities, with men."[45] His sentiments were shared by many of his subordinates, one of whom wrote:

> We either pretend not to know, or care not to know this [the need for proper defense of India's frontiers] ourselves, because we are in the hands of irresolute party politicians, who will not realize what is perfectly well known by Powers like Russia, whose interests are opposed to our own in every part of the world, and whose boldness is only the result of our timidity . . . But the one Power I fear is Russia, which seems fated to be the disturber of peace through Eastern Europe and the Eastern world.[46]

44. Id.
45. Cited in O. T. Burne, *Memories* (London, 1907), p. 107.
46. Ibid., pp. 118–19.

However, the determination to defend the approaches to India did not extend to the defense of Persia. The Government of India was just as determined not to provoke Russia, not to seek a confrontation in the Middle East, as was the Cabinet in London. Commenting on Eastwick's memorandum, and Rawlinson's thoughts on it, the Government of India stated that it attached the greatest importance to the maintenance of Persia's independence, but refused to encourage the Shah to collide with Russia.

> We cannot too strongly express our concurrence with Sir Henry Rawlinson upon this point and declare our opinion that it should be almost a crime upon our part, for the mere purpose of obtaining a temporary ascendency in Persian politics, to urge her to so perilous a course as any attempt to extend her dominions either in a north-easterly direction, or by encroachments upon Afghanistan or its feudatory tribes.[47]

On the issue of British officers for the Persian army, the Government of India differed from both Eastwick and Rawlinson. It felt that British officers should not serve Asiatic countries:

> The ways of Oriental Governments are not our ways, and in peace as well as in war, Officers placed in such a position must be cognisant of deeds, and participators to some extent in actions which no man of honour can approve. If British Officers cannot be in supreme command they should not enter on such service.[48]

This bit of Victorian cant was followed by the real reason for not wanting to interfere with the Persian army.

> In our present relations with Russia, we should view with great suspicion the admission of a number of the Officers of the Russian army to the command of Persian troops. A similar proceeding on our part would probably call forth a strong remonstrance from the Cabinet of St. Petersburg.[49]

47. The Government of India to the Duke of Argyll, Secretary of State for India, No. 4 of 1872, Secret, Fort William, January 19, 1872; L.I., 11, 1872.
48. Id.
49. Id.

It is noteworthy that neither Rawlinson nor the Government of India in their comments on the Eastwick memorandum made any serious suggestions for dealing with the Russian menace in Central Asia and maintaining Britain's position in Persia. The insistence of both papers upon the need for "an able and energetic Anglo-Indian statesman" to take the post of minister in Tehran, gaining the confidence of the Shah and restoring the balance of influence in the Persian government, was only an expression of an unfounded faith in a panacea which, like all panaceas, did not exist. The discussions and correspondence about Persia bore no fruit.

As far as the Russian government was concerned, the next important task was the conquest of Khiva. The occupation of Krasnovodsk had been carried out in preparation for a Khivan campaign, as had been the careful surveying of the deserts that protected the khanate better than its ragtag army. Once again Miliutin, assisted by Kaufmann, was the chief advocate of conquest. Gorchakov was to play his by now familiar role of laying a smoke screen of assurances and promises. The final decision to annex Khiva was made at a meeting "under the presidency of the Emperor," late in 1872. It was then that Alexander II uttered his famous sentence to Kaufmann: "Konstantin Petrovich, take Khiva for me."[50] At the beginning of January 18, 1873, Adjutant General Count Petr Andreevich Shuvalov, Chief of the Gendarmes and of the Third Section of His Majesty's Chancery (the secret police), was sent to London, where he told Lord Granville that the Emperor not only had no intention of conquering Khiva but had given special orders that this should not happen. Granville wrote the British ambassador in St. Petersburg, Lord Augustus Loftus: "Count Schouvaloff repeated the surprise which the Emperor, entertaining such sentiments, felt at the uneasiness which it was said existed in England on the subject, and he gave me most decided assurance that I might give positive assurances to Parliament on this matter."[51] Indeed Granville failed to understand Russia's actions. In a letter to the Duke of Argyll he stated: "I like to see my way when dealing with such sharp practi-

50. N. N. Knorring, *General Mikhail Dmitrievich Skobelev* (Paris, 1939), p. 26.
51. Granville to Loftus. January 8, 1873, Correspondence; F. O. 65/1202.

tioners as our friends at St. Petersburg. I can conceive the Russians pining for Constantinople; but why they should push on the extreme East, I cannot understand." [52]

In a tone of contempt which the Russian military habitually assumed when speaking or writing of civilians, General M. A. Terent'ev tells of Gorchakov's promise to the English not to annex Khiva:

> Negotiations were conducted by Shuvalov. Our diplomats apparently trusted in our fighting generals who will always be able to prove that military circumstances prevent the exact fulfilment of that which was promised. When the English finally settled down to celebrate their would-be victory, our troops were already on their way to Khiva.[53]

By the spring of 1873, General von Kaufmann had concentrated under his command an army of thirteen thousand men with sixty-two guns. Among the officers who waited impatiently for the excitement of an expedition against the "savages" were such illustrious personages as the Grand Duke Nikolai Konstantinovich and the Duke Eugene of Leuchtenberg, who had traveled to Central Asia for the purpose of enjoying the campaign.[54] Khiva fell in May. Count Petr Shuvalov, who had to explain it all to the British, invented far-fetched alibis and put the blame on that old black sheep of Russian diplomacy—insubordinate generals.[55] This time it was Kaufmann who was the culprit in London.

The conquest of Khiva was such a clear case of violation on the part of Russia of all her recent pledges that even the moderately Russophile and immoderately optimistic Lord Augustus Loftus,

---

52. Granville to Argyll, January 6, December 2 [sic], 1872; cited in E. Fitzmaurice, *The Life of Granville George Leveson Gower, Second Earl of Granville, K. G., 1815–1891* (London, 1905), 2, 410.

53. Terent'ev, *Istoriia zavoevaniia Srednei Azii*, 2, 83.

54. Various aspects of the conquest of Khiva are described in Terent'ev, 2. See also Eugene Schuyler, *Turkistan* (New York, 1877), 2, 334; A. Lobanov-Rostovsky, *Russia and Asia* (Ann Arbor, 1951), p. 158; R. A. Pierce, *Russian Central Asia*, p. 31.

55. Augustus Loftus, *The Diplomatic Reminiscences of Lord Augustus Loftus, 1862–1879*, 2nd Series (London, 1894), 2, 105.

British ambassador at St. Petersburg, felt compelled to sound the alarm. He warned his government that Russia had now acquired a foothold in the Turkoman steppes from which she could

> menace the independence of Persia and Afghanistan and thereby become a standing danger to our Indian Empire . . . if events are allowed to pass unobserved and without comment, if no preventive measures are adopted, or precautionary warnings given, England may, at a later period, reproach herself with having tacitly witnessed the encroachment of Russia to the detriment of her own prestige and power.[56]

In Tehran the British repeatedly pointed out to the Persian government that the Russians would soon begin operations against the Turkomans of the Atrak and further east in the direction of Sarakhs and Marv.[57] Only Granville stubbornly clung to the opinion that the Tsar had been "perfectly sincere" when he sent assurances through Shuvalov that Khiva would not be annexed. It was out of weakness that Alexander had bowed to the demands of the military. Replying to a letter of the Duke of Cambridge, who called for some kind of action, Granville admitted that Britain had the right to resent Russia's breach of promise; "but your Royal Highness does not suggest how we are to resent it. Is it to be by biting or merely by barking?" Indulging in wishful thinking, Granville continued:

> In the meantime the Russians are opening a sore in their own body; they have excited the bitterest hatred in the inhabitants of Central Asia; they are embarrassing their finances; and if it is to come to a struggle, the nearer that struggle takes place to Afghanistan, the stronger we are, and the weaker they must be.[58]

As if to increase British fears, General N. P. Lomakin, the new military commander in Transcaspia, addressed a letter to the khans of several Turkoman tribes, announcing his appointment

56. Lord A. Loftus. No. 304. August 28, 1874, Correspondence; F. O. 65/1202.
57. Correspondence; ibid.
58. Granville to the Duke of Cambridge, December 20, 1873, cited in Fitzmaurice, 2, 410–11.

and demanding that delegates from the tribes come to him to negotiate as to how "the August will" of the Āq-Pādeshāh (White Tsar) in regard to the establishment of peace and order could be carried out.[59]

The Russian government fully anticipated British and Persian protests against Lomakin's activities. Khiva had been conquered so recently that the process of consolidation in the khanate was not yet sufficiently advanced. A respite was needed before a new move could be made, a move which would carry the Russian flag to the Ākhāl oasis and beyond, perhaps to Marv and even Herāt. The problem was discussed at a Special Conference chaired by Grand Duke Konstantin Nikolaevich, Admiral-General of the Navy, and attended by the Grand Duke Mikhail Nikolaevich, Viceroy and Commander in Chief of the Caucasus; General Miliutin, Minister of War; Vladimir Westmann, Acting Minister of Foreign Affairs; and representatives of other departments. It was decided to proceed with caution, avoiding the use of force against the Turkomans, especially those who regularly migrated from Iranian to Russian territory and back.[60]

The British government was also trying to formulate a policy in regard to Central Asia and Persia. The starting point was a dispatch from the British minister in Tehran, W. Taylour Thomson (No. 136 of June 25, 1874) in which he revived Eastwick's proposal of 1871 that aid be given Persia in order to prevent Russia from taking over the Turkoman lands, including Marv. Thomson, like Eastwick, felt that British officers should be sent to Tehran to train and discipline the Iranian army, and that they should be paid by the British government. Eventually it might even become necessary to subsidize Persia "for the purpose of securing that country as a barrier for British India against Russia." [61]

---

59. Address of the Chief of the Transcaspian Section [Lomakin] to the Khans and Elders of the Tekke. April 2/14, 1873; *Prisoedinenie*, No. 61, pp. 155–56.

60. Journal of a Conference of the Special Committee on questions of strengthening political and commercial ties with the Turkomans, July 27/August 8, 1874; *Prisoedinenie*, No. 67, pp. 167–73.

61. Minute on Persia by Lord Northbrook, May 30, 1875, Government of India, Foreign Department, No. 123 of 1875; L. I., 4, 1875.

Complying with a request of the India Office for the opinion of the Government of India on Thomson's proposals, the Viceroy, Lord Northbrook, wrote that Persia was unreliable. The Shah and the Grand Vizier spoke of their friendships for Britain, yet granted a railway concession to a Russian.[62] Some Persian politicians look for an English alliance, but there are others, who represent a strong anti-English party. But even the professed friends of England cannot be trusted. "From all accounts," Northbrook wrote, "there are few Persian statesmen whose incorruptibility is beyond question, and the elements of an honest and reliable Government appear to be almost wholly wanting."[63]

Britain, Northbrook pointed out, was under no treaty obligation to protect Persia by force of arms, nor should she encourage her to take any action that might give umbrage to Afghanistan, a country whose interests were identical with those of India. Even if Britain desired to do so, she could not protect northern Persia from a Russian attack. The distance from the Gulf was too great, the Caucasus was too near, and

> Persia is so unable to defend herself, even for a time, that England, unless by general result of a war in which the principal scene of operations would be in Europe, would be unable, in my opinion, to ensure the integrity of those provinces. It is unlikely that any of the great Powers of Europe would consider an attack upon Persia by Russia as a *casus belli*, and in a war in Europe between Great Britain and Russia, singlehanded, neither power is in a position to inflict any serious injury upon the other. Our position therefore does not appear to be such as to authorize us to encourage Persia to suppose that she can depend upon receiving material assistance from us.[64]

Northbrook admitted the existence of the Russian threat:

---

62. A reference to the Falkenhagen Concession. See below, Chapter 2.
63. Minute on Persia by Lord Northbrook, May 20, 1875; Government of India, Foreign Department, No. 123 of 1875; L. I., 4, 1875.
64. Id.

in the event—which, to judge from the recent information which we have received, I cannot regard as improbable of a substantial annexation of Persian territory by Russia, I am far from saying that a just cause of war between England and Russia might not arise. The interests of England are intimately involved in the maintenance of free communication between England and India, and an attempt to extend Russian territory, or a Russian protectorate, to the shores of the Persian Gulf would be so direct a menace to India that it would, in my opinion, justify a resort to arms for the purpose of securing our present supremacy in the Persian Gulf. But the action of Her Majesty's Government under such circumstances should be left free and unfettered by any previous engagements.[65]

Having admitted this much, Northbrook failed to suggest any effective program for the prevention of that very situation which, in his opinion, would justify war. The best he could do was to propose the assignment to Tehran of a military attaché from the Indian Service, and vaguely to wish for the opening of communications "between the Persian Gulf and the interior of Persia."

The Commander in Chief in India, Napier of Magdala, strongly disagreed with the Viceroy. "I confess," he wrote, "I think there is a great danger in this shrinking policy, which increases as it grows old, and would lead us to be inactive, perhaps fruitlessly protesting and being disregarded, until Russian bases of action shall have been formed on the salient points around India." Britain should do everything to keep Russia at arm's length from Afghanistan and Persia, "and to this end I would give Persia the friendship she needs." [66]

Turning to Northbrook's moralizing about Persian fickleness, Napier pointed out that "it does not become us to condemn her for her fickleness, as our own policy has not been free from reproach on that ground." He questioned the usefulness of retaining the shores of the Persian Gulf if the northern part of Persia were occupied by Russia, and concluded with a call to action:

65. Id.
66. Minute by the Commander-in-Chief, Napier of Magdala; Government of India, Foreign Department, No. 123 of 1875; 4, L. I., 1875.

We should immediately oppose any further encroachment on Persian territory. By increasing our diplomatic influence in Persia, we shall best be able to prevent that country from giving Russia cause for aggression, but should we be driven to war, the people of Persia, supported by a British contingent and aided by British arms, supplies, and officers, would render the task of conquering the country as difficult and exhaustive as the conquest of the Spanish Peninsula was to France.[67]

A majority of the members of Viceroy's Council ranged themselves against the views expressed by Northbrook. E. C. Bailey put the issue in the simplest possible terms: "As far as Persia is concerned, the question at present really raised is plainly whether we are prepared to support or to abandon her."[68] He conceded that the upper classes of Persia were, "as individuals, almost without exception, corrupt, selfish, debased, and shamelessly unprincipled to a degree which it is scarcely possible to conceive," but felt that "even they as a class would doubtless see that their interests lay with us." He supported the proposal to send English officers to Persia, and noted the success which such missions had achieved in the past.

In conclusion Bailey stated that, in preparing his argument, he had assumed that Russia would act loyally toward British possessions in the East. If one made no such assumption, the urgency of the danger would appear much greater. "And I for one having all my life had opportunities of knowing Russian feelings believe in no such loyalty at all, either on the part of the Russian Government, on the part of its officials, or even of the nation generally."[69]

The disagreement among the members of the Viceroy's Council was such that the Government of India was unable to present a set of concrete proposals and a coherent policy to the Cabinet in London. At the India Office Lord Salisbury inclined toward stronger action, but the Foreign Office under Lord Derby dis-

---

67. Id.
68. Minute by E. C. Bailey, Government of India, Foreign Department, No. 123 for 1875; L. I., 4, 1875.
69. Id.

approved. As a result nothing was accomplished at all. Britain continued to bombard Russia with memoranda, notes, inquiries, questions, etc., etc. never to any effect, while Persia was left to deal with her formidable neighbor to the north as best she could.

The Persian government tried to maintain its claims to the Turkoman lands and tribes. During his European trip in the summer of 1873, the Shah told the Viceroy of the Caucasus, Grand Duke Mikhail Nikolaevich, that action against the Tekke Turkomans should be undertaken jointly by Russia and Persia. Early in 1874 Mirzā Hoseyn Khān returned to the issue with A. F. Beger. The latter understood Hoseyn Khān's motives: to strengthen Persia's position among the Turkomans and also to "declare to us [the Russians] their pretentions to the Tekke tribe which never submitted to Persia but was always a threat to her Khorāsān frontier." [70]

Persia was not in a position to press the issue. If effective representations were to be made, Britain's backing was indispensable. For a short time it seemed to the Persian government that Britain intended to champion its cause. On November 17, 1874, Lord Augustus Loftus called on V. Westmann, Acting Minister of Foreign Affairs, and showed him dispatches from London and Calcutta requesting explanations of Lomakin's actions. Westmann claimed that the incident with Lomakin's proclamation had been a *mal entendu* resulting from a faulty translation, and that the Persian government had been perfectly satisfied with the explanation it received from Russia. Westmann then expressed his surprise

> that an explanation should have been asked by Her Majesty's Government of an incident of so little importance in itself, and which solely concerned Russia and Persia. It was not customary, His Excellency observed, to interfere in the international relations between two independent States, and he could not comprehend in what way the incident referred to could affect Great Britain.[71]

70. Report of the Russian Minister in Iran to the Viceroy of the Caucasus, January 23/February 4, 1874; *Prisoedinenie*, No. 54, pp. 129–30.
71. Loftus to Derby, November 17, 1874, Correspondence; F. O. 65/1202.

Loftus replied that in Asia Britain had an Empire of two hundred million people over whose interests she watched. The conversation grew tenser as the usually mild and friendly Loftus continued: "the advance of Russia in Central Asia of late years was a subject of watchful interest, although it was not one of either jealousy or fear to the Government of India." As for interference with Russo-Persian relations, he cited the exchanges between Palmerston and Nesselrode in 1835 and 1838 in which both countries agreed to maintain the integrity of Persia. "I did not, therefore," Loftus concluded, "comprehend the surprise expressed by His Excellency on the Communication I had made." [72]

Encouraged by the interest Britain showed in the Lomakin incident, the Persian government hoped for additional support when it received information early in December 1874 that Lomakin had appeared with six hundred men intending to occupy Qara Qal'e, a village on the Atrak River. Mirzā Hoseyn Khān turned to W. T. Thomson, British minister in Tehran, for moral support. Lord Derby, who had succeeded Granville at the head of the Foreign Office, wrote that Britain regretted Russian inroads into the Tekke territory as likely to lead to disputes which might ensue in a misunderstanding between England and Russia, but doubted that protests in this case would be justified. Once again Britain refused to intervene.[73]

The never-ending barrage of protests and complaints emanating from London did not stop Russia's forward movement in Central Asia. However, it did annoy the Tsar, the military, and even the master diplomat, Gorchakov. On April 17 the latter wrote a long memorandum to Count Shuvalov to be shown to Lord Derby. This document may be styled the Second Gorchakov Memorandum and deserves to be quoted at some length.

> The Cabinet in London [Gorchakov began] appears to derive, from the fact of our having on several occasions spontaneously and amicably communicated to them our views with respect to Central Asia, and particularly our firm resolve not to pursue a policy of conquest or annexation, a conviction

72. Id.
73. Derby to Thomson, January 8, 1875, Correspondence; ibid.

that we have contracted definite engagements toward them in regard to this matter.

Owing to the fact that events have forced us against our will, to depart, to a certain extent, from our programme, they seem to conclude that the Imperial Cabinet have failed to observe their formal promises.

Lastly, in view of the successive steps which we have been forced to take in these countries, they infer that it is the right and duty of England to take on her side measures to restrain our action, paralyze our influence, and to secure herself against eventual aggression.

These conclusions, Gorchakov stated, were not in agreement either with facts or the spirit and letter of the conventions established between the two governments.

It has always been understood, he continued, that either party retained complete liberty of action. Russia had made clear since 1864 that she would not expand beyond the limits of necessity. The British, with their experience in India, knew full well what such necessities might be. It had been expressly recognized by the two powers that it was impossible "to consider the Russian and English frontiers in Asia as incapable of alterations," and that therefore "an international agreement on that point would be ineffectual."

To Gorchakov the "understanding" existing between Britain and Russia meant that for this purpose it was desirable to have an intermediate zone between them and that Afghanistan should constitute such a zone if its independence were secured on either side.[74]

Lest the British be too much provoked by the firm tone of the memorandum, the old diplomat, who did not wish for a full-scale confrontation with Britain, appended a note which reaffirmed that

His Imperial Majesty has no intention of extending the frontiers of Russia such as they exist at present in Central Asia, either on the side of Bokhara, or on the side of Krasnovodsk

74. Gorchakov's Memorandum of April 5/17, 1875, Correspondence; ibid.

and the Attrek. We have no inducement to do so. On the contrary, the Emperor deems any extension of our frontiers in those parts as being opposed to our interests . . . The orders of the Emperor are formal in this respect. They have been notified by His Imperial Majesty to the military authorities, who are charged with their execution.[75]

It took the British government several months to digest Gorchakov's April memorandum. In a paper prepared for the use of the Cabinet, the Foreign Office noted that Russia had reserved to herself full freedom of action everywhere north of Afghanistan. The Foreign Office pretended not to doubt the sincerity of Russia's promises not to expand further, but did not omit to mention that on previous occasions declarations fully as sincere as the present one were followed by actions of quite different sort. Lord Salisbury, Secretary of State for India, expressed the opinion that Britain could not accept the inactive role Russia wished to impose upon her in Central Asia. He suggested that Britain inform Russia that her interpretation of past agreements was unacceptable to the British.[76] The Government of India listed the various pledges Gorchakov, Shuvalov, and Alexander II himself had made, and concluded that, if these were ignored, the agreements regarding Afghanistan would also lose their value, "and the British Government would be at liberty to adopt whatever policy beyond the limits of Afghanistan the circumstances of each case, as it arises, may be deemed to require." [77]

Before the British had time to reply to Gorchakov's April memorandum, Russian troops struck again. In July a rebellion had erupted against the unpopular Khan of Kokand, Khodāyār. He fled to the Russians and the wrath of the rebels turned on the infidels who protected him. On September 3 General von Kaufmann defeated the main rebel force of some thirty to fifty thousand men at Mahram. "The natives left 90 dead in the fortress, but Cossacks led by Colonel M. D. Skobelev pursued the

75. Id.
76. F. O. Memorandum, June 22, 1875, Correspondence; ibid.
77. The Government of India to the India Office, Secret, No. 37, August 23, 1875, Correspondence; ibid.

fugitives along the bank of the Syr-Daria for several miles and killed over 1,000 more. The Russians lost only six killed and eight wounded in the entire action." [78]

Five months later the following Imperial Proclamation was issued:

> We, Alexander, II, etc., yielding to the wishes of the Khokandi people to become Russian subjects, and likewise recognizing the absolute impossibility of restoring the Khanate to peace and tranquility by any other means, command that the Khanate of Khokand be immediately incorporated with our dominions and that it shall henceforth form the "Fergana province" of our Empire.[79]

It must be noted that the annexation of Kokand had been strongly urged by the military. On January 27, 1876, generals Miliutin and Kaufmann were received by the Tsar. They brought with them a plan for a final incorporation of Kokand in the Russian Empire and for the strengthening of the army in Turkestan. The Tsar, whose diplomats had so very recently assured the British that no further conquests were contemplated, hesitated but finally had to accept the inevitable. Gorchakov had not even been consulted. The Tsar left it to Miliutin and Kaufmann to inform the Chancellor of the Empire that he had been overruled in absentia. Miliutin was satisfied. Gorchakov's defeat pleased him for it was the Chancellor "who has always opposed any extension of our possessions in Asia." [80]

The annexation of Kokand did not satiate the expansionists but only whetted their appetite and made them cry out for more. Russian society was entering a period of prolonged crisis. The promise of the early years of Alexander's reign had not been fulfilled. His reforms had not sufficed to reverse the process of social and spiritual disintegration. The irresponsible upper class composed of landowning nobles had not lost its political power in spite of the insecurity of the economic foundations on which that

78. Pierce, p. 35.
79. Correspondence; F. O. 65/1205.
80. *Dnevnik Miliutina*, 2, 11.

power rested. The growing bourgeoisie, deprived by the nobility of a share in determining the policies of the state, occupied itself almost exclusively with a narrow and selfish pursuit of wealth. The intelligentsia, alienated and angry, abandoned its former liberalism for a radical dogmatism and an intolerance as vicious as that of the government. From its ranks emerged the first revolutionaries, who declared war on the old order and initiated a campaign of terror that culminated in the assassination of the Tsar in 1881. In such an atmosphere foreign adventures, colonial wars, and conquests were irresistibly attractive to the upper strata of Russian society. They distracted attention from the frightening domestic situation, created the illusion of national unity and community of effort, and provided a romantic escape from the unpalatable reality of a decaying social order. An end to expansion would have forced the ruling class to cope with problems with which they were incapable of coping.

No sooner had Kokand been taken over than a suggestion for the occupation of Turkoman lands in Transcaspia was made to D. A. Miliutin by Grand Duke Mikhail Nikolaevich, Viceroy and Commander in Chief of the Army of the Caucasus. Grand Duke Mikhail wanted to send an expedition in the direction of the Turkoman village of Ashkhabad (Russian corruption of the Turkoman Ashqabat, which in turn is a corruption of the Persian Eshqābād), a point located some four hundred miles from Krasnovodsk and two hundred miles from Marv.[81] Miliutin replied, "This point lies at a distance of only 360 versts from Merv, that sore spot of the most recent Central Asiatic policy of Great Britain." A clash with the Turkomans and their possible flight to Afghanistan could create complications which, considering present relations between Russia and England, should be avoided.[82]

The Russian government could well imagine British fears for Marv and Herāt. These half-ruined, dusty cities, once centers of a flourishing civilization, were considered keys to India. The

81. The Commander in Chief of the Army of the Caucasus to the Minister of War, January 24/February 5, 1876; *Prisoedinenie*, No. 85, pp. 204–08.

82. The Minister of War to the Commander in Chief of the Army of the Caucasus, February 19/March 8, 1876; ibid., No. 87, pp. 209–11.

Persians had done their best to draw the attention of the British government to Marv. Already in 1874 the Persian minister in London, Malkam Khān, had warned Lord Derby that Russia could establish her rule there "almost without Europe being aware of it," though it was a strategically important intersection of the lines of communications between Mashhad, Bukhara, Khiva, and Herāt.

> On the day when the Russian flag restores order and security in Merv [Malkam Khān wrote], that destined capital will be re-established; and nature itself, aided by Russian administration, will inevitably render it the most active centre of new enterprises and certain success; for we may be sure, when Merv is once in the hands of Russia, all barriers will be broken down, and all neighbouring states blotted out.[83]

If in fact the British government was less concerned about Marv than the Persians hoped and the Russians feared, it was not known in St. Petersburg.

Gorchakov, cautious as usual but more than usually disturbed about the possible consequences of a rash move in the direction of Marv, begged Miliutin to exercise his considerable influence with the Tsar so as to prevent an expedition into the heart of Turkoman lands. Count Shuvalov, who had returned to St. Petersburg for a brief stay, joined the Chancellor in pleading for restraint. "The cautious and reserved Lord Derby," Shuvalov reported, "said in a conversation . . . that our advance toward Merv is a casus belli." [84]

Unlike many of his military colleagues, Miliutin was a soldier-statesman. He would not rush the Tsar when the goals of expansion could be reached just as certainly but at a smaller risk by waiting a few years. On April 8, 1876, he wrote the Viceroy that the Tsar persisted in his decision and "ordered me to inform your Highness that the troops of the Transcaspian region are not to be permitted under any pretext to make moves in the direction of

83. Malkam Khān to Derby, 1874; as cited in Government of India, Foreign Department, Secret, No. 21 of 1877, Simla, July 2, 1877; L. I., 17, 1877.
84. *Dnevnik Miliutina*, 2, 31.

the upper Atrak and to the lands of the Ākhāl-Tekke in the direction of Askhabad." [85]

The Grand Duke obeyed but did not change his mind, and neither did Miliutin's closest collaborator, K. P. von Kaufmann, Governor-General of Turkestan. A younger officer, M. D. Skobelev, veteran of several Central Asiatic campaigns in which he displayed both great military talents and equally great brutality, wrote about the relative positions of Russia and Britain in Asia. As a Pan-Slavist, Skobelev was uninterested in Turkestan except as a means for the solution of the Eastern question. "Otherwise the hide is not worth the tanning, and all the money sunk in Turkestan is lost." [86] From Turkestan Russia must exercise pressure on the British, whose position in India seemed weak to Skobelev. An invasion of India, he admitted, would be a difficult and risky enterprise, but the stakes were high and the gamble worthwhile.

> Competent English authorities [Skobelev wrote] admit that an overthrow of the frontiers of India might even produce a social revolution in England, because for the last 20 years England has been tied closer than ever to her Indian possessions by reasons and phenomena (including incapacity for war) identical with those of France. The downfall of the British supremacy in India would be the beginning of the downfall in England.[87]

The decision of the Russian government to abstain temporarily from the conquest of the Turkoman lands seemed to offer Persia the last opportunity to establish authority over her nominal subjects, the Tekke Turkomans of the Ākhāl oasis. The task of persuading them to accept Persian sovereignty fell to Abd ol-Hasan Khān, son of Shojā od-Dowleh, Ilkhāni (hereditary ruler) of Quchān. Abd ol-Hasan was a most unreliable servant of the Shah. He had for years maintained close relations with the

85. Ibid., p. 263, note 2.
86. H. Sutherland Edwards, *Russian Projects Against India from the Czar Paul to General Skobeleff* (London, 1885), p. 285.
87. Ibid., pp. 277–78; a more detailed examination of Skobelev's position is given in N. N. Knorring, *General Mikhail Dimitrievich Skobelev*.

Turkomans, often helping them to raid Persian territory and carry off his compatriots to Central Asiatic slavery. So closely had Abd ol-Hasan allied himself with the Tekke that he even married a Turkoman woman. The nearness of the Russians, or perhaps the fear that the Shah would not permit him to succeed his father at Quchān, made Abd ol-Hasan try to mend his ways. He persuaded a large number of Tekke (forty thousand families according to a report, undoubtedly exaggerated, by the Russian chargé d'affaires in Tehran), to submit to the Shah and send a delegation to Tehran to beg His Majesty's favor.[88]

The arrival of Turkoman elders in Tehran did not escape the attention of the Russian legation, which immediately inquired about it at the Ministry of Foreign Affairs. The Persians were evasive, saying only that the Turkomans had come to assure the Shah of their desire to live in peace.[89]

To prevent Persia from carrying out her designs, the Russian government, in October 1876, ordered Major General N. P. Lomakin to march from the sea shore to the Turkoman village of Qizil Ārvāt and occupy it, to show to the Tekke tribesmen and the Persians that Russia did not recognize Persia's claims to the area and would not allow an extension of Persian authority there. Lomakin was admonished not to use force without pressing need and to hold Qizil Ārvāt for a short time only. On May 19, 1877, the Russians occupied the village without opposition, but five days later the Turkomans attacked. Lomakin's force was small, the outbreak of war with Turkey having made it impossible to get reenforcements, food was short, and sickness began to spread among the troops. Though the battle of May 24 was won by the Russians and the Tekke suffered heavy losses, Lomakin was forced to retreat. However, he had accomplished his mission. The Persians dropped their plans to bring the Tekke under their sway.[90]

Lomakin urged his superiors to fight on. Never before had so

88. Chargé d'Affaires in Iran to the State Chancellor, September 20/October 2, 1876; *Prisoedinenie*, No. 118, pp. 253–55.

89. Id.

90. Report of General N. P. Lomakin to the Chief of the Caucasian Mountain Administration, July 5/27, 1879; ibid., No. 213, pp. 413–26.

Anglo-Russian Conflict

many Turkomans banded together. Never before had popular fanaticism, fanned by Turkish agitators and the pro-Persian party, manifested itself with such force. Exemplary punishment must be meeted out to the nomads; "it is necessary once for all to beat out of them all desire to worry not only our troops but our military-commercial route and our Yomuts as well." Lomakin asked permission to march through the Ākhāl oasis, sending out raiding parties

> to devastate and destroy Tekke villages, through which actions the Tekke, on the one hand, will suffer due retribution and will not be likely quickly to regain their wits and to recover so as to be able to resume their old looting and raiding, and on the other hand we would thus demonstrate in fact our ownership of this territory.[91]

Lomakin's plea coincided with a turn toward greater belligerence on the part of the Russian government. Mr. Ronald F. Thomson, British chargé d'affaires at Tehran, and brother of W. Taylour Thomson, obtained a copy of a paper which Russia's War Minister, General Miliutin, was reported to have presented to the Council of State on June 2. The document began with an attack on Britain: "The peace of Europe cannot possibly be secured until the greed and rapacity of the Despot of the Seas have been restrained. An inordinate desire for gain has extinguished in the hearts of the English all honourable feeling in connection with other nations." [92] Britain's only objective was to destroy the commerce of the nations competing with her. Russia had long acted in a friendly and sincere manner, but Britain was not after friendship. She wanted to exclude Russia from commerce and influence in Asia.

> England advances boldly against those who retreat before her. But it is indispensable now that Russia should abandon

---

91. The Commander of the Transcaspian Military Sector to the Chief of the Caucasian Mountains Administration, June 9/21, 1877; ibid., No. 169, pp. 323–25.

92. R. F. Thomson to Salisbury, No. 16, Tehran, April 26, 1878; Copy to the Viceroy of India; L. I., 18, 1878.

this policy of inaction, that, instead of halting, we should advance towards the enemy; that we should show the English that the patience of Russia is exhausted, and that she is ready to retaliate and to stretch out her hand towards India.[93]

When Russian troops begin to march, the people of India would rise against the British. The Afghans would take the opportunity to avenge themselves. Once India was lost, Britain's economy would collapse and she would no longer be a threat.

Since Russian archives are not generally open to non-Soviet investigators, the authenticity of the above document cannot be proved. Considering the fact that it was transmitted to the British minister by someone who stole or bought it from the Russian legation in Tehran, or may even have forged it for profit, its contents must remain suspect. However, its tone is authentic, and the views it expresses can be found scattered through Miliutin's writings and the writings of many other Russian officers and government officials.

The British had every reason to expect a further Russian advance, this time to the Ākhāl oasis and thence to Marv. The usual steps were taken in St. Petersburg, where Ambassador Loftus, on Derby's instructions, again warned the Russian government that "so close an approximation of the outposts of the two Empires" in Central Asia was in itself undesirable, and expressed the hope that the Emperor would issue the strictest orders to his officers not to advance in the neighborhood of Marv.[94] This demarche had no more effect than all the others in the past dozen years. However, in India the temper of the government had changed.

Lord E. Lytton, who had succeeded Northbrook as Viceroy in April 1876, was a proponent of the "forward policy." The conclusion of a new treaty with the Khan of Kalāt and the occupation of Quetta, opening the road to Qandahār, were signs of a new and a more aggressive attitude on the part of the Government of India. In a dispatch to the India Office, dated July 2, 1877, Lytton

93. Id.
94. Correspondence; F. O. 65/1202.

revived the issue of British policy in Persia and Central Asia, and imparted to it an urgency it had never had before.

A review of the history of Russian expansion in Central Asia led Lytton to believe that the occupation of Qizil Ārvāt had not been a random act of aggression but an "important step in a long meditated and well prepared movement." From reports of Captain Napier, who, to the consternation of the Russians [95] traveled among the Turkomans, Lytton learned that Russia's troops were within 150 miles of Marv and Herāt, and that she had established contacts with the Turkomans whom she was about to subdue.

> For these reasons, Captain Napier regards the occupation of Kizil Arvat . . . as the most significant, and, in fact, the most formidable, indication yet given by the Russian authorities of definite design, and fixity of purpose, in the notoriously aggressive character of their Central Asian policy.[96]

Turning to the importance and the consequences of a Russian occupation of Marv, Lytton declared that

> unless the course of history were suddenly reversed, or the conditions of the situation materially altered by the active interference of the British Government, the occupation of Herat by the Russians would, within no very distant period, follow as certainly on the occupation of Merv as that of Tashkend on the occupation of Chemkend . . . The occupation of Herat would mean the establishment of Russian sovereignty or influence throughout Afganistan, and its expansion to the present frontiers of British India, carrying with it the command of the passes into Northwestern India.

Lytton wanted the government to decide "at what point in Russia's progress action is to be taken by us, and what the nature of the action must be." When must Britain intervene? Will Russia

---

95. The Commander of the Transcaspian Military Section to the Chief of the Caucasus Mountains Administration, March 2/14, 1877; *Prisoedinenie*, No. 145, pp. 294–96.

96. Lytton to Salisbury, Government of India, Foreign Department, Secret, No. 21 of 1877, Simla, July 2, 1877; L. I., 17, 1877.

"be allowed by Her Majesty's Government to occupy Merv unopposed?"

He proposed that Russia be warned clearly that her next advance in Asia would be regarded by England as casus belli. An understanding should be reached with Persia "if still practicable." She should receive British support in opposing further Russian encroachments, provided she permitted the stationing of British agents with military escort at Mashhad or Sarakhs and gave Britain free access to Marv. In the meantime, Lytton suggested, British arms and officers should be sent to the Turkomans to stiffen their resistance and prevent Marv from falling to a Russian coup de main.[97]

Independently of the Viceroy, W. T. Thomson, British minister in Tehran, urged similar action. He did not doubt that Russia would occupy the Ākhāl and Marv. She would connect these by rail with the Caspian and Turkestan, enabling her to concentrate her forces and threaten the peace of India. Britain would then be forced to maintain such large forces on the Northwest Frontier that her resources would be crippled. Thomson hoped that Marv could be annexed to Afghanistan or, as a last resort, to Persia to prevent its annexation by Russia.[98]

In London, Lytton's and Thomson's warnings made little impression. Even the India Office failed to share the Viceroy's fears. Salisbury expressed his doubts as to whether Russia would attempt a coup de main against Marv. As Dr. R. L. Greaves points out in her detailed study of Salisbury's policy, "The India Office reply to the Viceroy has some traces of a cavalier tone." [99] Salisbury lectured Lytton on the reasons why Marv was of no use to Russia, and claimed that its occupation "would be a needless and wanton waste both of money and military force." Salisbury's own analysis of the situation led him to believe that there was no immediate cause for worry.

97. Id. Cf. Correspondence; F. O. 65/1202.
98. W. T. Thomson to Derby, No. 114, Tehran, July 26, 1877; L. I., 16, 1877.
99. R. L. Greaves, *Persia and the Defence of India, 1884–1892* (London, 1959), p. 30.

Many years must elapse before the Russian frontier can be pushed forward by safe and gradual advances as far as Merv. When the course shall have been entered upon of which the conquest of Merv is to be the end, the time will have arrived for declaring how far and soon the adoption of corresponding military measures may be expedient.

In the meantime any aid given the Turkomans would only expose them to Russia's vengeance and "would be inconsistent with the proclaimed policy of Her Majesty's Government," that is neutrality in the Russo-Turkish war.[100]

That Russia's Central Asiatic policy was not a purely local or isolated phenomenon had been amply demonstrated in the spring of 1877. On April 24, Russia had declared war on Turkey. Britain's attitude toward Russia was hostile, and the possibility of active British intervention in favor of the Ottoman Empire could not be excluded. In May the British government warned Russia against any attempt to blockade the Suez Canal or occupy Egypt. In July the British Cabinet decided to go to war if Russia should occupy Constantinople. Indian troops arrived in Malta, and the Mediterranean fleet was reenforced. When Turkish resistance collapsed and Russian soldiers reached the outskirts of Tsargrad, the British fleet moved into the Golden Horn, bringing the two great powers to the brink of war.

The Russian government had foreseen the possibility of British intervention. Several weeks before declaring war on Turkey, the Tsar had called, and presided over, a Special Conference to consider measures that would be taken against Britain in case of a break with her. The one area where Russia could effectively threaten Britain was Central Asia, Miliutin pointed out. The conference was asked to suggest actions that would accomplish the purpose of intimidating the British, thus keeping them from entering the war on the side of the Turks.

The Privy Counselor, Baron Tornau, suggested that an alliance be concluded with Persia, giving her, at Turkey's expense, the dis-

---

100. Salisbury to Lytton, Secret, No. 68, October 18, 1877, Correspondence; F. O. 65/1202.

tricts of Najaf and Karbalā, sacred to Shiites, in exchange for the Astarābād province. The latter could be used as a staging area for a march across Khorāsān to Herāt. General K. P. von Kaufmann, Governor-General of Turkestan, felt that it was enough to send troops to Shirābād on the Oxus and to Marv, and to reach an agreement with the Amir, Shir Ali, the anti-British ruler of Kābul. The Governor-General of Orenburg, General N. A. Kryzhanovskii, shared Tornau's view that only a threat to Herāt from Khorāsān would suffice to compel Britain to change her behavior. For this a large force, at least a hundred and fifty thousand men, would be needed. Assistant Minister of Foreign Affairs, N. K. Giers, who directed Russian diplomacy during the last years of Gorchakov's tenure of office, the Chancellor having grown too old and feeble to carry the burden, pointed out that an alliance with Persia would bring about quick retaliation on the part of the British, "which would complicate matters and deprive us of the advantages which Persia's neutrality could afford us." [101]

Special conferences had a strictly consultative nature. The final decisions were made by the Tsar together with one or two officials closest to him. As was so often the case, it was Miliutin whose recommendations the Tsar adopted. Miliutin felt that under the existing political and military circumstances a large-scale military operation for the purpose of shaking British dominion over India was undesirable. A demonstration in Central Asia would create enough fear in England to paralyze her forces in India. Persia, exposed to British sea power through the Persian Gulf, should not be involved, Afghanistan should be approached through trusted individuals, or even an official mission, and assured "that the forward movement of our detachments is by no means hostile to Afghanistan but, on the contrary, may be even of advantage to her in support of her independence against the English, and under certain circumstances, even as help against them." [102] Miliutin's other proposals included the reenforcement of the

---

101. Report of the War Minister to the Tsar, April 8/20, 1878; *Prisoedinenie*, No. 177, pp. 332–36.
102. Id.

Turkestan Military District, the dispatch of a number of troops to the shores of the Oxus, a move from Transcaspia toward Marv in order to protect the area and to gain the goodwill of the native populations of the regions where Russian troops might have to operate. The Tsar approved all of Miliutin's proposals and ordered their implementation.[103]

Major General N. G. Stoletov, who had commanded the Russian troops that occupied Krasnovodsk in 1869, was appointed to head a mission to Kābul. On June 7, 1878, General K. P. von Kaufmann provided him with his Instruction (No. 4407) which defined the goals of the mission: "your Excellency's mission to the Afghan Amir has for its main purpose the maintenance in the Amir of distrust of the actions of the English and the encouragement of his further resistance to their attempts to establish themselves in Afghanistan." [104] Stoletov was to explain to the Afghans that Russia, unlike Britain, did not "buy either the rulers themselves or their chief advisers," did not "attempt to enslave neighboring countries" either politically or economically, but, on the contrary, supported the lawful rule of the khans. If the Amir of Afghanistan took advantage of the conflict between England and Russia, he could become the head of a mighty Moslem state, assuming the position and role lost by the Turkish Sultan because the British bribed his officials and advisers. That the Russians considered it below their dignity to offer bribes did not mean that they "would not or could not help an ally with financial means as well, should he really need help." [105] Finally Stoletov was to obtain permission for the passage of Russian troops through Afghanistan; and, in case of need, not only to advise the Amir but even "to assume command of that portion of the country's resources and forces which, in your [Stoletov's] opinion, in agreement with the Amir, would seem the most important defensively or offensively against England." [106]

To British inquiries concerning Stoletov's mission, N. K. Giers

103. Id.
104. Cited in Terent'ev, *Istoriia zavoevaniia Srednei Azii*, 2, 428.
105. Ibid., p. 429.
106. Ibid., p. 430.

replied that no such mission had been or would be sent either by the government or by General Kaufmann.[107] On July 22 the general arrived in Kābul. He was received with great honor by Amir Shir Ali who made him and his companions a gift of 11,000 rupees (equivalent to 10,000 rubles). Instead of sharing the gift, which he had no right to accept in view of Kaufmann's strong prohibition of taking money from Asiatic rulers, Stoletov quickly changed the Indian money into gold and kept it for himself. Naturally, he did not report this to Kaufmann.[108]

In the negotiations with the Amir, Stoletov far exceeded the authority granted him by his superiors. On August 21, 1878, he signed a formal treaty in which Russia promised to give Afghanistan military help in case it were attacked by "a foreign power" (Article 5); regular diplomatic relations were to be established between the signatories; and Russia was to provide technical assistance (to use modern terminology) and military instructors (Article 9).[109] When taking leave of the Amir two days later, Stoletov promised to return with an army of thirty thousand men.[110]

Stoletov left Kābul on August 23, arriving in Tashkent on September 17 after a strenuous and difficult journey. He had already given Kaufmann by messenger highly inaccurate accounts of what took place in Kābul, creating the impression that Shir Ali wanted his country to become a Russian protectorate. This notion greatly pleased Kaufmann, who urged Miliutin that two infantry divisions and four cossack regiments be sent to Turkestan.

107. William Habberton, *Anglo-Russian Relations Concerning Afghanistan, 1837–1907* (Urbana, 1937), p. 44.

108. Terent'ev, 2, 449. For fascinating details of Stoletov's activities in Kābul and the fate of the mission after his departure, see I. L. Iavorskii, *Puteshestvie russkogo posol'stva po Avganistanu i Bukharskomu khanstvu v 1878–1879 gg.* (St. Petersburg, 1882). The author was the mission's doctor and kept a full record of everything he saw or heard. E. L. Steinberg [Shtcinberg], *Istoriia britanskoi aggressii na Srednem Vostoke* (Moscow, 1951), pp. 120–22, gives a highly colored interpretation of Stoletov's mission from the Soviet point of view.

109. The text of the treaty is reproduced in Terent'ev, 2, 451–54.

110. Ibid., p. 450.

to evade this protectorate means to give up Afganistan not only to British influence but perhaps to complete subjugation as well. One must confess that such a turn of events would harm our position in the East . . . All this will demonstrate to the population of Afganistan and India England's power and might and our relative weakness.[111]

The Viceroy of India, Lord Lytton, was a proponent of strong measures. In order to counteract the effect of Stoletov's mission, of whose doings he was well informed, he sent one of his own; but Shir Ali on Stoletov's advice refused to receive the English or even to admit them to Kābul. The situation grew tense. In Tashkent, Kaufmann saw that war might break out at any moment. He had gathered twenty thousand men under his command—the largest Russian force ever to operate in Central Asia. However, Kaufmann did not dare to assume the responsibility for unleashing a war. He sent Stoletov to Livadia, a Crimean resort, to report to the Tsar personally and to receive his orders.[112]

The Anglophobe Miliutin rejoiced in Britain's discomfiture in Afghanistan. On September 22, 1878, he entered in his diary:

In London they cannot digest it that Shir Ali received very cordially the Russian embassy of Stoletov, while refusing to admit the British embassy. But what an outcry will be raised when it is learned that the ruler of Afganistan himself has sent his embassy to Tashkent with the request to take Afganistan under Russia's protection and the declaration that he will not receive the English in Kabul without General Kaufmann's "permission." [113]

That summer the European situation had changed as a result of the Congress of Berlin (June 13–July 13, 1878). The need for a diversion against British India had disappeared. The unfinished task of conquering the rest of Central Asia could be jeopardized by a clash with Britain over Afghanistan. Moreover, an indepen-

111. Kaufmann to Miliutin, September 9/21, 1878; cited in ibid., p. 459.
112. *Dnevnik Miliutina*, 2, 93–94.
113. Id.

dent Afghanistan was preferable to an Afghanistan controlled by Britain. Miliutin saw the disadvantages that would accrue to Russia from further provoking the British and decided not to offer the latter a pretext for an invasion of Afghanistan. On October 4 a telegram was sent from Livadia to Kaufmann "to disabuse the Amir, if the latter is counting upon our material aid." [114]

Kaufmann had been too long absorbed in the immediate affairs of Turkestan to perceive the correctness of Miliutin's judgment. "This protectorate," he pleaded with his chief, "is very tempting. With it we could do everything . . . we could dominate England and oblige her to execute the will of the Sovereign." Furthermore, Kaufmann warned, to abandon Shir Ali would mean risking the "charm" Russia had acquired in Asia.[115] However, Miliutin held Kaufmann to the Instruction the latter had received from St. Petersburg, informing him that a Special Conference had decided that Russia must under no circumstances "go straight to war with England over her present collision with Afghanistan." Even secret help to Shir Ali was not permitted, and Kaufmann was told that the only course of action was to make every effort to bring about a peaceful solution of the Anglo-Afghan conflict "and then to put the English in their previous solitary position." [116]

It was too late to save the peace in Afghanistan. Urged on by Razgonov, Stoletov's successor at the head of the Russian mission, Shir Ali was no less determined to resist than Lytton to break his resistance. On November 2 the Government of India issued an ultimatum, demanding apologies for past insults and the admission of a permanent British mission to Kābul. The Russians in Kābul knew that Shir Ali would get no assistance from them, yet Razgonov continued to press for resistance.[117] From Tashkent Kaufmann entreated Miliutin not to let Afghanistan fall to the British. He admitted to his limited knowledge of European affairs, but thought "that all the existing and potential

114. Ibid., 3, 96.
115. Kaufmann to Miliutin, letter dispatched on October 21/November 2, 1878; cited in Terent'ev, 2, 460.
116. Terent'ev, 2, 461.
117. Ibid., p. 483.

new difficulties in our affairs in Europe derive from England," and that their solution lies in Central Asia. Had Russia been strong there, she could have achieved all she wanted in the Balkans and Asia Minor. If the British settle their affairs in India and secure themselves from external eventualities, they would never yield to Russia on anything.[118]

Shir Ali rejected the British ultimatum and saw his country invaded. Russia did not make a move. In a kind but firm letter, Miliutin spelled out for Kaufmann the reasons for inaction. He had read Kaufmann's dispatch to the Tsar. Neither His Majesty nor the Chancellor, the ancient Gorchakov, denied the validity of Kaufmann's views concerning the connection between the general tenor of British policy and Central Asiatic affairs. Undoubtedly England's success in Asia would make her even more intractable in Europe. But the Tsar had not changed his decision to maintain peace.

> Our collision with that power [Britain] would be a signal for a general and stubborn war under circumstances and in a situation extremely unfavorable to us. The support of the Afgan Amir would be fitting only if a break with England became inevitable. This is what we had in mind at the beginning of the current year when we were preparing for war. Now there can be no question of any active measures on our part.[119]

In 1877, while war blazed in the Balkans, Persia was seemingly quiet. The government watched with mixed feelings the defeat of one hereditary foe by another, more formidable one. Russian prestige increased from day to day, correspondingly lowering the influence of the British, who could not fail to notice the change. The firm tone assumed by Britain when Russian troops approached Constantinople, the appearance of the British fleet in the Golden Horn, and the prominent part played by Disraeli and Salisbury at the Berlin Congress, which deprived Russia of some of the prizes won by her fighting men, helped improve her posi-

---

118. Kaufmann to Miliutin, November 19/December 1, 1878; ibid., p. 464.
119. Miliutin to Kaufmann, December 6/18, 1878; ibid. p. 466.

tion in Tehran, but, in the eyes of English diplomats it was still unsatisfactory.

Ronald Thomson, British chargé d'affaires in Tehran, complained that certain Persian functionaries had the idea that the British government for various reasons could not use force against Persia. He foresaw a further deterioration of England's standing "unless some check is put on the conduct of the officials." Thomson suspected that Persia had made secret promises to cede territory to Russia in Transcaspia, finding here an answer to the question why Turkey had, by the treaty of San Stefano, been compelled to give over to Persia the district of Kotur. Should this be the case, Thomson wrote, Britain should occupy the island of Kharg and threaten Persia with the occupation of Mohammareh (now Khorramshahr). Such an occupation, if carried out, would provide Britain with a number of strategic advantages and "The Russians would hesitate either to force or allow Persia of her own will to place herself in a position which would lead to such results." [120]

On July 7, 1878, Ronald Thomson telegraphed the Viceroy of India that his Astarābād agent reported the landing of a Russian force at Chikishlar. Two weeks later he informed the Government of India that an invasion of the Ākhāl was imminent and that he proposed to go there himself, as well as urge the Persians to send a commission to prevent fighting. Thomson spared no effort to persuade the Persian government to protest against Russian military preparations, to claim sovereignty over the Ākhāl, and even resort to "direct action in relation to the tribes." The Persian government, having learned its lessons, refused to move, and intimated "that the Shah would, in fact, prefer the Russians to the Ākhāl Turkomans as neighbours." A few days later the Viceroy received an even more disconcerting bit of news. Captain Napier, still traveling among the Turkomans, gathering intelligence, and, undoubtedly, attempting to organize resistance, reported that Persian officials in Bojnurd, Quchān, and all along

---

120. R. Thomson to Salisbury, No. 84, Secret, Tehran, July 6, 1878; L. I., 20, 1878.

the border, were secretly preparing to supply Russian troops in Transcaspia.[121]

Thomson's and Napier's apprehensions were fully justified. Late in July Stoletov was in Afghanistan. A small force of Russians joined by a cloud of valiant Afghan cavalry could do immense damage in an area the loyalty of whose population was doubtful. Troops had gathered in Turkestan; still other troops had crossed the Caspian from the Caucasian Military District and were preparing to start a long march toward Marv and Herāt. The immense country east of the Caspian was quiet under the piercing rays of the summer sun, but for how long? The successful conclusion of the Berlin Congress seemed to suggest that the danger was over. However, Russian preparations for the campaign continued for another two weeks before the Viceroy of the Caucasus and the Governor-General of Turkestan received word that the Tsar had canceled the planned demonstration against India and ordered that no moves, except of local nature, be made.[122]

Thomson did not learn of the withdrawal of Russian troops until the first week of September. In the interval he continued to cajole and threaten the Persians into protesting against Russian preparations for an invasion of the Ākhāl. He complained to Mirzā Hoseyn Khān, the Minister of Foreign Affairs, that Russia, unlike Britain, possessed great influence in Iran. Hoseyn Khān replied truthfully that

> he had for years endeavoured earnestly to bring Persia under the influence and protection of Her Majesty's Government, and that, if he had not succeeded, and the Shah's sympathies were with Russia to a great extent, it was because we [the British] had refused to take Persia by the hand, and had thrown her aside.[123]

121. Various telegrams from Ronald Thomson to the Viceroy of India in L.I., 19, 1878.

122. The War Minister to the Commander in Chief of the Caucasian Army, Telegram, July 18/30, 1878; *Prisoedinenie*, No. 180, p. 338.

123. R. Thomson to Salisbury, No. 123, Confidential, Tehran, August 14, 1878; L.I., 20, 1878.

Personal appeals to the Shah were equally unsuccessful. On August 14, Nāser ed-Din frankly told Thomson that he could do nothing to stop Russia from penetrating the Ākhāl. By giving up her claims to the territory north of the Atrak, Persia hoped to save her Turkoman lands south of the river. "The time for action, and for England to have concerted measures with Persia to induce the Russians to withdraw altogether from the Turkoman coast, was, His Majesty said, when Persia found herself forced to make that arrangement; but that now it was too late." [124]

The tone of Ronald Thomson's dispatches turned bitter. He felt frustrated and failed to recognize the justice of Mirzā Hoseyn Khān's reproaches. The only success he achieved that summer was ephemeral. Hoseyn Khān promised to send one more note to I. A. Zinov'ev, Russian minister in Tehran, concerning Qara Qal'e, the Ākhāl, and Marv.[125] The Shah, who personally edited the note, struck out Ākhāl and Marv, leaving only a mild request that the Russians not occupy Qara Qal'e, an insignificant village misnamed a fort. Angry and disappointed, Thomson wrote Salisbury:

> It must be obvious now, that the Persian Government will not only make no objection to the acquisition of the whole of the Akhal territory by Russia, but that she is willing to further her views on that country; and that, when the moment arrives for the Russian occupation of Merv, she will further that design also, either by withdrawing, or failing to put forward her claim to that territory . . . or by ceding her rights to whatever extent they should have been meanwhile realized. It matters nothing whether this is done by formal agreement and understanding with Russia, or not. If the views of Persia harmonise so completely with the designs of Russia that she is ready to play into her hands . . . the result, as far as our own interests are concerned, is the same as if a definite agreement had been come to between the two Governments.[126]

124. Id.
125. R. Thomson to Salisbury, No. 131, Tehran, August 17, 1878; ibid.
126. R. F. Thomson to Salisbury, No. 152, Confidential, Tehran, September 8, 1878; ibid.

Thomson's disappointment was natural, but one cannot help wondering what he expected defenseless Persia to do, when mighty Britain herself had been unwilling or unable to stop Russia's advance in Asia. There was an element of the absurd in Thomson's insistence that Persia should expose herself to grave danger to protect the approaches to India, while Britain refused to extend any but "moral" support.

The Persian note on Qara Qal'e was mild and polite. The fortress, it stated, belonged to Persia, having been captured by the Governor of Khorāsān, Prince Heshmat od-Dowleh.

> Although the Foreign Department feels perfectly assured that the Russian Government have always been the upholders and protectors of the rights of Persia, and that the sacred rights of Persia will never be injured or impaired by them, still it is not considered superfluous to request, with the utmost respect, His Excellency the Russian Minister to be so good as to give such informations in the proper quarter as will prevent the Commander of the Russian expedition from interfering either through misapprehension or inadvertence, with the territory or in the affairs of Karee Kala [Qara Qal'e].[127]

Zinov'ev, who knew that Persian representations were the result of British pressure, assumed a conciliatory tone. He expressed appreciation of the confidence Persia had in Russian intentions. As for operations along her frontiers; he wrote,

> La Perse ne s'aurait d'ailleur que profiter de ces efforts dont le succès ne manquera pas de contribuer à l'affermissement de la sécurité le long de ces frontièrs et à mettre le Gouvernement de S. M. le Schah à l'abri de la necessité d'entreprendre des expéditions lointaines et coûteuse.[128]

---

127. Mirzā Hoseyn Khān to Zinov'ev, September 5, 1878 (6 Ramazan 1295), Translation, Enclosure in R. Thomson to Salisbury, No. 166, Confidential, Tehran, September 26, 1878; *L.I.*, 21, 1879.

128. I. A. Zinov'ev to Mirzā Hoseyn Khān, Unsigned and undated, Enclosure in Thomson to Salisbury, No. 166, Confidential, Tehran, September 26, 1878; ibid.

While refusing to admit Persian claims to Qara Qal'e, Zinov'ev promised to transmit Hoseyn Khān's words to Russia.[129] Four days later, he received a reply from the Chief of Staff of the Caucasian Military District that Lomakin had not been ordered to occupy Qara Qal'e and that "Until spring next year he has the right to send toward the Ākhāl only reconnoitering parties." Zinov'ev conveyed this information to Hoseyn Khān. Available records do not show whether he mentioned the words "until next spring," but it can be confidently assumed that he did not.[130]

On September 6 Ronald Thomson, now minister in Tehran, learned that Lomakin was withdrawing. He attributed this to his remonstrances with the Persian Foreign Minister, who was only too happy to maintain the illusion which flattered Thomson and was advantageous to the Persian government. According to Thomson's cheerful account telegraphed to the Viceroy of India, Lomakin had counted on provisions promised by the Governor of Khorāsān. Their delivery was prevented by Thomson, and Lomakin had to retreat. In fact, provisions had been collected in Khorāsān, and their delivery had been prohibited by the Persian government, but Lomakin's withdrawal began even before the prohibition. The Russian minister was annoyed and protested. Mirzā Hoseyn Khān apparently saw an opportunity to make Thomson happy, and so exaggerated the importance of the incident. He told Thomson that Zinov'ev had threatened him, saying that the failure of Lomakin's expedition was due to Hoseyn Khān's "intrigue" and that "no Government had so long a memory for good or for evil as that of Russia." This further convinced Thomson that he had achieved a major diplomatic victory.[131] The Viceroy of India accepted his version and telegraphed his "special acknowledgements."[132]

129. Zinov'ev's telegram of August 24/September 6, 1878; *Prisoedinenie*, No. 184, p. 344.

130. Chief of Staff of the Caucasian Military District [Popov] to the Minister in Iran [Zinov'ev], August 27/September 9, 1878; Russian Minister in Iran to the Chief of Staff of the Caucasian Military District, August 28/September 10, 1878; *Prisoedinenie*, Nos. 185, 186, p. 345.

131. [R.] Thomson to the Viceroy, Telegrams, September 6, October 9, 1878; L.I., 21, 1879.

132. The Viceroy to R. Thomson, Simla, No. 2236P, October 10, 1878; ibid.

Though Lomakin's retreat had not been caused by Thomson's diplomacy, its consequences were harmful to the Russians. The rumor spread among the Turkomans that the *urus* had suffered a reverse. Masses of Tekke cavalry appeared in front of the Russian fort at Chikishlar, and Colonel N. I. Grodekov, the future historian of Turkmenistan's conquest, who had made a courageous journey from Tashkent to Astarābād via Herāt, reported that the Turkomans on the Khorāsān frontier had become insolent to the point of capturing some Russian soldiers in the vicinity of a new Russian fort at Chat.[133] English successes in Afghanistan produced a strong impression in Persia and Central Asia, raising British and lowering Russian prestige.

St. Petersburg was in an ugly mood. The reforms of the sixties had not met the aspirations of the progressive elements of Russian society. The radicals launched a campaign of terror, which would culminate in March 1881 in the assassination of the Tsar. The gentry and the army, twin pillars of the Tsarist regime, were bitter over the results of the Congress of Berlin at which Austria and Britain had robbed Russia, or so they felt, of the fruits of her victory over the Turks. The ruling class called upon the Tsar to embark upon new conquests, to compensate in Asia for failure in Europe. The military saw England as Russia's principal enemy and believed she could be dealt a serious blow only through India.

Count Shuvalov, the Tsar's ambassador in London, who had achieved among the military the reputation of "England's friend," was among the first to call for a decisive advance toward Afghanistan. "Morally we shall not remain dispassionate witnesses of the conquest of Afghanistan," he wrote. "We shall trade England blow for blow . . . If up to now we have refrained from an expedition against Merv, it was only out of respect for England, in order to avoid a break with her." Shuvalov called for action, for the occupation of Marv which would be necessary sooner or later. However, he proposed to take this step only if the British occupied Kābul.[134]

133. *Dnevnik Miliutina*, 3, 108.
134. Shuvalov [presumably to Gorchakov], No. 149, November 27/December 9, 1878, as cited in Terent'ev, 2, 525–26.

Ivan Alekseevich Zinov'ev, Russia's minister in Tehran, emphasized that brief, indecisive expeditions of the 1877 and 1878 type were not only useless but harmful. They did not stop Turkoman depredations, and produced an unfavorable impression in Persia, where British agents interpreted them as failures. British successes in Afghanistan must be answered with an occupation of the Ākhāl if Russian influence in Persia was to be preserved.[135] Zinov'ev was strongly supported by Grand Duke Mikhail Nikolaevich, Viceroy of the Caucasus and Commander in Chief of the Caucasian Army.

The Viceroy's views were reflected in a memorandum produced by his assistant, Prince D. I. Sviatopolk-Mirskii, who argued that diplomacy could not change "the law of gravitation of political bodies": Russia and Britain must unavoidably meet in Asia. No negative measures in Central Asia would bring results. To obtain them one must move with the current, not against it. The way to avoid a clash in Asia was not to agree as to what England and Russia would not occupy, but what they would. Shuvalov was right in advocating action in reply to British entry in Afghanistan. Russia must move on to Herāt across the Ākhāl.[136] From across the Caspian General Lomakin, who had led the expeditions of 1877 and 1878, clamored for action. The Tekke were hostile. They attacked Russian transports and camps. They shot at Russian soldiers. "Only one thing remains—to exterminate this nest of bandits, this shame and stain upon our age." [137]

One of Lomakin's subordinates, Colonel Petrusevich, listed the main reasons for decisive action against Ākhāl. The Ākhāl lay across Russian lines of communication from the Caspian to Turkestan. Russia needed it to open a convenient route to Herāt. The retreat of Russia's armies to Krasnovodsk damaged her

135. Paraphrased in Commander in Chief of the Caucasian Army to the Minister of War, January 22/February 3, 1879; *Prisoedinenie*, No. 197. pp. 377–78.

136. Report of the Assistant Commander in Chief to the Commander in Chief of the Caucasian Army, February 7/19, 1879; *Prisoedinenie*, No. 202, pp. 390–94. Cf. M. N. Tikhomirov, *Prisoedinenie Merva k Rossii* (Moscow, 1960), p. 40.

137. Report of the Commander of the Transcaspian Section to the Chief of Staff of the Caucasian Military District, January 2/14, 1879; *Prisoedinenie*, No. 193, pp. 359–63.

Anglo-Russian Conflict

prestige, which must be restored. Until now she destroyed barbarian forces with one blow, but prolonged and indecisive fighting with Turkomans was making them less fearful of Russians. They were even taking Russians prisoner, equating them with the Persians, and inflicting on them barbarous torture. They must be punished. "Even one pogrom would be enough, because such a pogrom would demonstrate the impossibility of resistance; but, without a trial of strength in battle, Ākhāl will not surrender." [138]

It is probable that the octogenarian Chancellor, Prince Gorchakov, would have opposed the Ākhāl venture; but his health was failing, and he no longer had the strength to influence the course of affairs. Early in 1879 he left on a prolonged leave, thus ending his political career. His assistant, now Acting Minister of Foreign Affairs, N. K. Giers, a gray, cautious, uninspired but professionally competent diplomat, was not an originator of policies. He fully accepted D. A. Miliutin's guidance and followed the War Minister's lead. Thus for the next two years Miliutin in fact directed Russia's foreign policy as well as her armed forces.[139] The Tsar continued to trust him and to follow his advice. No one's opinion had more weight with the sovereign.

On February 2, 1879, a Special Conference was held in St. Petersburg under the chairmanship of the Grand Duke Mikhail Nikolaevich, with Miliutin, Giers, the Chief of General Staff, the Minister of Finance, and several others, including Colonel A. N. Kuropatkin, the future governor of Transcaspia, war minister and supreme commander in the war against Japan, in attendance. Having heard Major General Glukhovskii of the General Staff, and Colonel Kuropatkin, the conference unanimously decided to send an expedition to the Ākhāl in the spring. The main object would be Geok-Teppe, a Turkoman village which had become a rallying center for Tekke tribes. Two days later Miliutin, having noted with satisfaction that even the cautious Giers made no objections, received the Tsar's confirmation of the decision made

---

138. Memorandum by Colonel Petrusevich concerning Khorāsān, the position of Ākhāl in Russia's policy in the Middle East, and the necessity of its immediate occupation, 1879; *Prisoedinenie*, No. 195, pp. 262–74.

139. P. Zaionchkovskii, "D. A. Miliutin: Biograficheskii ocherk," *Dneynik Miliutina*, 1, 51.

by the conference. Miliutin, with his accustomed care, also obtained the Tsar's prohibition of any move to Marv or of crossing into Persian territory. Even operations along the right bank of the Atrak and over the Kopet-Dāgh range could not be undertaken without Zinov'ev's agreement. Only with his cooperation were the Russian commanders allowed to buy food and camels in Persia. The minister in Tehran was made an informal political director of the campaign.[140]

Russian preparations for a new campaign in Transcaspia could not be kept secret. Ronald Thomson knew that it would begin some time in 1879 and made every effort to induce Persia to serve as a shield for India, without Britain's committing herself to anything but nebulous friendship and moral support. Believing that it was his pressure on the Persian government that had caused Lomakin's retreat the previous year, he would use the same tactics again.

Thomson complained to the Foreign Minister that Britain's friendly overtures to Persia were ignored by the latter, and that Persia did nothing to maintain her rights to the Ākhāl.[141] On March 2 and 3 the two held conversations which epitomized the positions of their respective countries in regard to Russian actions in Turkmenistan.

Mirzā Hoseyn Khān told Thomson that he had urged the Shah to "look to the friendship of England as the only power that could protect this country [Persia] against Russia." The Shah admitted this but feared that Persian objections to the Russian advance in the Ākhāl would give umbrage to Russia. "Would England therefore in such a case be prepared to protect Persia against Russian aggression?" If England were prepared to conclude an alliance, to undertake to defend her against a Russian attack, Persia "would object to the Russian occupation of the Ākhāl, would refuse supplies to the Russian troops, would decline to employ Russian officers [who had been invited by the Shah to organize a Persian Cossack brigade], agree to consult England in all important matters, and would substitute English for Russian influence in the country." Thomson replied that Hoseyn Khān

---

140. Terent'ev, 3, 6–7. *Dnevnik Miliutina*, 3, 113.
141. R. Thomson to Salisbury, No. 47, Tehran, March 1, 1879; L.I., 22, 1879.

was mixing together matters that had nothing in common. Britain had the right to expect that Persia, as a friendly power, not allow her territory to be used for the passage of Russian troops or provide the latter with assistance and supplies.[142]

The threat implicit in Thomson's words about Britain's right to expect that Persia prevent Russia from using her territory placed the Shah in a dilemma. To protest to the Russians, to make a gesture of resistance by sending some of his troops into the Ākhāl, would bring upon him the wrath of the Tsar whom the Shah, as his father before him, had learned to fear. Moreover, the practical consequences of playing an anti-Russian game would certainly be disastrous. No protest, and certainly no ragtag Persian regiments, would stop the movement of Russian troops. To oppose them would be to risk the loss of Astarābād, perhaps of Khorāsān itself. But to ignore Britain was also dangerous. She might not want to tangle with the Russians, but nothing could prevent her from taking over Persian islands in the Gulf, pushing into Seistān, landing her troops at Bushehr, and extending her protection to the Sheykh of Mohammareh, as she had already done in Bahreyn. Either way Persia would lose. The only question the Shah and his ministers had to answer was: which course was less dangerous; which was the lesser evil?

The conversation which started on March 2 was resumed the next day. Thomson claimed that Hoseyn Khān's idea of an Anglo-Persian alliance was vague. The Foreign Minister quickly showed that it was not.

> England, he said, was desirous that Persia should protest against the advance of Russian troops, and that she should not employ Russian Military Officers in her service. The Persian Government was convinced that, if they followed the course thus suggested, Russia would take offence to the extent of proceeding to measures of coercion and aggression, and Persia could not expose herself to such resentment unless England would engage to defend her against its consequences.[143]

---

142. R. Thomson to Salisbury, No. 48, Tehran, March 2, 1879; ibid.

143. R. Thomson to Salisbury, No. 51, Secret, Tehran, March 6, 1879; L.I., ibid.

Again Thomson insisted that an alliance, or its absence, had nothing to do with Persia's obligation to maintain her claims to the Ākhāl and not to supply Russian troops in Transcaspia. Thomson stubbornly refused to concede Persia's inability to stand up to Russia. He demanded that she sacrifice herself. Hoseyn Khān, whose sympathies had always been with England, would not promise resistance. Thomson turned to threats:

> I stated to His Highness that if Persia not only allowed, without a word of objection, a Russian force to advance towards Merv and Herat through territory claimed by her, but also afforded material aid to that force by placing her resources at its disposal, it would be considered as an act hostile to England.[144]

Thomson's language was, in nineteenth-century diplomatic usage, almost equivalent to an ultimatum.

In reply Hoseyn Khān once again pleaded for friendship. If only Britain promised to protect Persia, she would consult Britain and "act in accordance with her advice in all future political, and commercial relations with Russia"; she would "act in conjunction with England, and in accordance with her wishes in any action, military or diplomatic, which Her Majesty's Government might consider necessary to check Russian advance in the direction of Afghanistan or India"; she would give every facility to British trade, open the Kārun River to British ships, and grant other such privileges.[145]

Thomson made no promise. Without any consideration for Persia's delicate position, he continued to hammer at Mirzā Hoseyn Khān. On March 13 he demanded to be informed at once what Persia's position was in regard to the anticipated Russian advance in the Ākhāl.[146] Mirzā Hoseyn Khān's answer was embarrassingly relevant and pathetic. Persia, he wrote, did not like disturbances on her borders. Russia's advance toward the Ākhāl placed her in a difficult position.

144. Id.
145. Id.
146. R. Thomson to Mirzā Hoseyn Khān, March 13, 1879, Enclosure in R. Thomson to Salisbury, No. 75, Tehran, March 22, 1879; ibid.

As regards your statement that these proceedings of Russia are taken with a hostile intention against British interests in Asia, it is a matter of surprise that the British Government is silent, and does not even make representations to the Russian Government with a view to preventing her [expedition to Marv]. Although the greatest friendship and cordiality exists between the two Governments, she nevertheless asks from, and insists upon, the Persian Government's giving a promise and so making her position difficult. Moreover, such proposal made by you, and any steps taken by the Persian Government depend on the main question [Anglo-Persian alliance] of which these are only minor details. You do not at all notice the main question, but rather have passed it over in silence and taken no notice of any representations made by us, but you press and insist upon the performance of minor details. The fact of the matter is this, that until the main question between the two Governments is placed on a firm basis, the Persian Government cannot, and does not, perceive it advisable that for the carrying out of a branch subject it should plunge itself into trouble and danger.[147]

Since the "main question," that of a formal Anglo-Persian alliance, remained unanswered, partly because of indecision in London and partly because of misgivings at Simla,[148] the Persian government chose a policy of prevarication and evasion, the only policy left open by the intransigence of her great neighbors.

Once Mirzā Hoseyn Khān was convinced that Britain would not protect Persia's territorial integrity, he did his best to assure Russia of Persia's goodwill. His own position was precarious. For twenty years he had tried to establish firm ties with Britain. Admittedly, in championing the cause of Julius de Reuter, the British businessman who had obtained in 1872 perhaps the largest concession ever granted by any state to a foreigner, he had been

147. Translation of a memorandum from the Sepeh Salar [sic] to Ronald Thomson, Esq.,—dated 17th March, 1879, Enclosure in R. Thomson to Salisbury, No. 75, March 22, 1879; ibid.

148. The Government of India to the Secretary of State for India, Secret, No. 107, Simla, May 1, 1879; ibid.

motivated by a strong desire for personal gain, yet his British sympathies had also played a part. Through the years, as Grand Vizier and later as Minister of Foreign Affairs, he had demonstrated his pro-British tendencies, while succeeding in establishing good relations with the Russian legation. Mirzā Hoseyn Khān hoped that Britain would show the same concern for Persia as she did for Turkey. In view of the events of 1878, when British troops had been sent to Malta and warships to Constantinople, he may well have thought that an Anglo-Persian alliance was possible. Now that the hope was lost, he may have foreseen his own downfall. Other men, less tainted with British sympathies and more friendly to the Russian legation, would be called upon by the Shah to administer the nation's foreign affairs.

In an attempt to propitiate Russia, Mirzā Hoseyn Khān told Zinov'ev that the Shah was willing to cooperate in the planned Ākhāl expedition. As long as Russia did not draft the Turkomans, who were Persian subjects, into her service, the Shah would provide Russian forces in Transcaspia with food and means of transportation. Zinov'ev avoided discussing Persia's Turkomans, knowing that General I. D. Lazarev, who had replaced the luckless Lomakin in command of Transcaspian troops, had already recruited a thousand Ja'farbāy and Ātābāy horsemen, a fact which Zinov'ev denied.[149]

It has often been noted that there existed no secrets in Tehran. One can imagine Thomson's anger upon learning of the Shah's offer to assist the Russians in their move toward the Ākhāl, a move that would undoubtedly constitute only a step on the road to Marv and Herāt. Once again he demanded explanations and assurances. Hoseyn Khān produced an undated autograph letter from the Shah in which His Majesty stated: "as regards this expedition of the Russians against Akhal and the Turkomans, I now state categorically, and in the form of an oath, that in no matter whatsoever has the Persian Government had any communication respecting a share in the matter." [150]

149. Report of the Minister in Iran to the Minister of Foreign Affairs, April 17/29, 1879; *Prisoedinenie*, No. 207, pp. 403–04.

150. Nāser ed-Din Shāh to Mirzā Hoseyn Khān Moshir od-Dowleh, the Sepahsālār, undated, received May 5, 1879, Translation, Enclosure in R. Thomson to Salisbury, No. 122, Tehran, May 17, 1879, L.I., 23, 1879.

The Shah was no less exasperated than Thomson. He felt not merely abandoned but betrayed by the British whose insistence on Persia's opposition to Russia might lead to disaster. He could no longer contain his feelings, which burst forth in bitter taunts: "as the British consider the matter of so much importance and so injurious to themselves, why with all the adequate power which they possess by land and sea, do they not take steps to prevent the Russians from undertaking this expedition against the Turkomans." If the British attach such importance to the expedition, why don't they stop it? And if it is not all that important, why threaten the Persians and accuse them of hostility? Moreover, if Britain deems the situation serious, "and yet she does not consider herself sufficiently strong to prevent Russia from carrying out her design, how could Persia"? And in conclusion: "As I have already said, it would be better that the British Government, instead of discussing and pressing these minor and useless details, should, if they can, put a stop to the military movement of the Russians in this direction so as to free themselves of these schemes."

Having read the letter, Thomson lost his temper and wrote to Hoseyn Khān that "England will judge for herself what steps shall be taken in direct action with Russia, and it may be safely assumed that she will look after her own interests," but she will also expect Persia to do nothing against such interests. If Persia, Thomson continued, should fail to protest the interference of Russia with Qara Qal'e; make no objection to the expedition in the Ākhāl; not protest in writing against the employment of her subjects to assist the campaign; and supply the expedition, "undertaken with and avowedly unfriendly motive" toward Great Britain, with material aid, "and that notwithstanding the assurances to the contrary given, and conveyed, by her to England, these will constitute facts from which Her Majesty's Government will have no difficulty in drawing their own conclusions, and which are not susceptible of disguise." [151]

Faced with what amounted to an ultimatum, Persia pretended to comply. What followed was a farce with sinister overtones.

151. Memorandum by Ronald F. Thomson, Esq. [for Mirzā Hoseyn Khān], dated Tehran, May, 1879, Enclosure in Thomson to Salisbury, No. 122, Tehran, May 17, 1879; ibid.

Mirzā Hoseyn Khān proposed that Thomson himself draft the note which he wanted the Persian government to hand to the Russian legation. This seemed like complete surrender to British pressure, while in fact it was not. By drafting the note Thomson deprived himself of the right to complain that Persian protests were insufficient. Moreover, the moral responsibility for the consequences of the protest was laid on Thomson's shoulders. He must have felt it, for the note he drafted was fully as mild as those composed by the Persians themselves. Qara Qal'e and Ākhāl were mentioned, but not Marv. The tone was friendly and inoffensive.[152] By making Thomson do the work of foreign minister, Mirzā Hoseyn Khān not only disarmed him but also created an effective alibi for the Persian government before the Russians. There can be no doubt that the Russian legation learned of the authorship of Persia's protest. Mirzā Hoseyn Khān could easily show the Russians that he was not a free agent, that the note did not represent the views of the Persian government, and that it could not be held responsible for acts committed under political duress.

While the British minister in Tehran cast thunderbolts, his counterpart in St. Petersburg, Lord Dufferin, made polite inquiries at the Foreign Ministry concerning Russian intentions in Transcaspia. On May 16, 1879, Count Shuvalov gave Salisbury the traditional assurances about Marv and heard from the Secretary of State for Foreign Affairs that "'Her Majesty's Government would take grave exception to any operations by which Merv was menaced,' and would, 'object to any encroachments upon Persian territory.'" On July 9 Giers repeated the same bland assurances to Dufferin. However, a new and disturbing note was sounded by A. G. Jomini, Senior Counselor of the Ministry of Foreign Affairs, who said to Dufferin:

> although we do not intend to do anything which may be interpreted as a menace to England, you must not deceive yourselves, for the result of our present proceedings will be

---

152. R. Thomson to Salisbury, No. 122, Tehran, May 17, 1879, and Enclosure (Translation of a Memorandum sent by the Persian Minister of Foreign Affairs to the Russian Legation, dated 12th May, 1879); ibid.

to furnish us with a base of operations against England hereafter, should the British Government by the occupation of Herat threaten our position in Central Asia.[153]

The warning was ominous and clear. Dufferin reported to his chief that "the language held by Baron Jomini leaves little doubt as to the nature of the position which the Russians are seeking to prepare for themselves eastward of the Caspian."[154] Another assurance, this one given to Dufferin on August 12 by the Tsar himself, was eagerly grasped by the British government.[155] The very next day Mr. Stanhope, Undersecretary of State for India, rose in Parliament to say that Russia had given solemn promises not to march on Marv. On August 25 Giers told Dufferin that Stanhope had gone too far. Russia did not intend to march on Marv now, but it was impossible to say that she would not do so in different circumstances. Russia had not given a pledge of never going to Marv.[156]

The Ākhāl expedition began in an atmosphere of diplomatic tension and uncertainty. Its appointed commander, General Lazarev, died on the eve of the campaign, leaving Lomakin to lead the troops. On September 8 the first skirmishes with the Turkomans took place. Intelligence was obtained that the Tekke had massed near the village of Geok Teppe. Lomakin marched his force of eighteen hundred men over dry sand in merciless summer heat and, on September 10, threw them into battle against a Turkoman horde many times as numerous. Both sides fought bravely, but for the first time in the history of Russia's Central Asiatic expansion, her troops failed to route the enemy. Russian losses were heavy: 6 officers and 170 men, almost a tenth of the force, killed; 20 officers and 248 men wounded; 8 men missing. The troops could not fight another battle. The transportation system had disintegrated. Half of the four thousand

---

153. Dufferin to Salisbury, No. 321, St. Petersburg, July 15, 1879, as cited in Correspondence; F. O. 65/1202

154. Same to same, No. 362, St. Petersburg, July 30, 1879, as cited in Correspondence; ibid.

155. Correspondence; ibid.

156. Id.

camels in the supply train had died. There was nothing Lomakin could do but retreat.[157] The War Minister, General D. A. Miliutin, commented in his diary:

> Thus fate has decreed for Lomakin for the second time to show his weakness and inability before the half-savage Turkomans. Instead of correcting last year's mistakes, he repeated this year the same shameful retreat before that scum and thereby definitely stained the honor and decreased the charm of Russian arms in Central Asia.[158]

Exactly a week before Lomakin's defeat at the hands of the Tekke, Sir Louis Cavagnari, head of the British mission established at Kābul by the terms of the peace treaty which had ended, or so it seemed, the Second Afghan War, was murdered together with his two secretaries, a doctor, and most of his escort of eighty-two men. British troops had to return to Afghan soil. On October 12, 1879, General Sir Frederick Roberts occupied Kābul. Yaqub Khān, Shir Ali's wayward son and successor, abdicated and was deported to India. Afghanistan was in chaos. Under these circumstances the British government had to work out as rapidly as possible a policy to be followed in regard to Herāt, the last stage on the road from the Caspian Sea to the gates of India. Unnerved by the relentless approach of the Russians, grasping at straws, the British conceived the idea of reversing their attitude toward Persia, making her "instead of Afghanistan the main bulwark in Indian defence," and the keeper of Herāt.[159]

---

157. Acting Commander of the Transcaspian Section [Lomakin] to the Commander in Chief of the Caucasian Army, September 15/27, 1879; Report of the Commander of the Transcaspian Military Section [Lieutenant General Tergukasov who relieved Lomakin] to the Commander in Chief of the Caucasian Army, September 24/October 6, 1879; Telegram of the Commander in Chief to Alexander II, September 28/October 10, 1879; *Prisoedinenie*, Nos. 231, 232, 235, pp. 442–57.

158. *Dnevnik Miliutina*, 3, 168. The term charm, *obaianie*, was widely used by the officials of the Tsarist regime when referring to fear and dread, which Russia inspired. One wonders whether they remembered the Russian saying about the dog's love for the stick.

159. Greaves, *Persia and the Defence of India*, p. 50.

Anglo-Russian Conflict

Lord Salisbury asked for Ronald Thomson's views. On October 28 Thomson wrote that giving Herāt to Persia might be expedient, but there were also advantages to keeping it as an "independent" principality under a "dependent" ruler. To such a ruler, Thomson wrote, "we could dictate our own terms." He liked the prospect of gaining the goodwill of Persia too, though with reservations.

> To cede Herat . . . to Persia, permanently and absolutely, would, in my opinion, be a hazardous measure. Persia, having obtained all that we could give would feel no gratitude and we should have lost our hold upon her. She would then be more open to Russian advances, in a better position to serve Russia and her services would be worth a higher price. Russia would moreover be entitled under the Treaty [of Torkamanchāy] to place agents at Herat, if transferred permanently to Persia, which would in itself make it a hot-bed of Russian intrigue.[160]

To prevent such a situation from arising, Thomson advised that Herāt be turned over to Persia on condition that she faithfully fulfill all her obligations. The latter were enumerated by Thomson for the Persian Minister of Foreign Affairs:

1. Herāt would be provisionally transferred to Persia, "her occupation to continue only so long as she had the confidence of Her Majesty's Government."
2. Britain would retain the right of military occupation of Herāt "should there be danger of its falling into wrong hands."
3. England would determine the size of the garrison to be maintained there.
4. Her officers would train the garrison and supervise the defense.
5. "Persia would not allow any Foreign agents or travellers, excepting English, to reside at, or visit Herat."
6. Persia, with Britain's moral support, would take steps to prevent the occupation of Marv by Russia.

160. R. Thomson to Salisbury, No. 255, Secret, Tehran, October 28, 1879; F. O. 60/422.

7. Persia would "do all she possibly can to check the advance of Russia in the Turkoman country," would "object strenuously to the passage of Russian troops through any territory belonging to or claimed by her," and would give "no assistance of any kind to any military expedition advancing Eastwards from the Caspian."

8. Persia would conclude a commercial treaty favorable to Britain.[161]

In addition, Thomson told Mirzā Hoseyn Khān that Persia should give England "a preponderating influence, and be guided by our [British] advice in important political questions." She should also allow the construction of a wagon road from Bushehr to Tehran and Esfahān to Shushtar, and open the Kārun River to free steam navigation. In the event of the above conditions not being fulfilled or "of its being found that the continued occupation of Herat by Persia was incompatible with the security of our Indian frontier, or of its being requisite, in consequence of the possible occupation of Merv by Russia, that the arrangement should cease, it should be set aside, and Persia would then revert to her stipulations with England under the Treaty of 1857."[162] The conditions attached by England make it quite clear why the Shah hesitated to accept the offer.

To recover Herāt, the center of a Persian-speaking province tied to the rest of Iran by many bonds, was a dream of every Persian ruler since the years of anarchy which followed the death of Nāder in 1747. Āqā Mohammad Khān, the first Qājār on the Persian throne, was too busy elsewhere to attend to Herāt. Under his successor, Fath Ali Shah, Abbās Mirzā led a campaign against the Sādozāi ruler of the city but died without achieving success. Mohammad Shah laid siege to the city, but was forced to give it up when Britain threatened war.[163] His son, Nāser ed-Din, captured Herāt in 1856. Britain struck in the Gulf. Persia was quickly defeated and promised never again to interfere with Afghanistan. But the dream lived on. Would

161. Id.
162. Id.
163. See W. K. Fraser-Tytler, *Afghanistan* (London, 1950), pp. 82–105.

Herāt be returned to Persia by the power which had kept it out of her reach? The temptation to accept Britain's conditions was intolerably great.

Russian silence gave Nāser ed-Din Shah courage to proceed with the negotiations. In late November the Minister of Foreign Affairs satisfied one of the eight conditions made by Thomson when he informed the latter that the Shah "considered Merv as his territory and that he therefore now declared that if Russia made any movement upon that place, Persia would not only protest, but would do all in her power to prevent it." [164] A month later Thomson informed the Shah that Her Majesty's Government agreed to the provisional transfer of Herāt to Persia. The Shah expressed his pleasure.

> His Majesty further observed that by thus allowing Persia to occupy Herat, England would place him under an obligation which he should not forget, that Persia would be a sure barrier to check any intrigues which might be directed . . . against . . . India, and that he could undertake to do all that was in his power to protect British interests and to further the views and policy of Her Majesty's Government.[165]

The next stage in negotiations about Herāt must inevitably involve Russia. No major change in Central Asia was possible without her. In January 1880, Mirzā Hoseyn Khān told Zinov'ev of Thomson's proposals. The Russian minister telegraphed Giers who, in turn, communicated them to Miliutin. The latter commented that British conditions would make of Persia a vassal of England and force her to assume an anti-Russian position.[166] A test of strength was in the offing. That it did not develop was due entirely to British domestic politics. On November 26, 1879, William Gladstone opened his campaign with a speech at the Edinburgh Music Hall. For the next several months he and his party attacked almost every policy, domestic and foreign, of Beaconsfield's government. On March 31 a general election

164. R. Thomson to Salisbury, No. 248, Secret, Tehran, November 26, 1879; F. O. 60/422.
165. R. Thomson to Salisbury, No. 4, Secret, Tehran, January 3, 1880; ibid.
166. *Dnevnik Miliutina*, 3, 202.

began, and by April 3 the Liberals had a majority in the new Parliament. "The political horizon is clearing up," the jubilant Miliutin wrote in his diary.[167] Lord Salisbury, who together with Lord Lytton was a chief advocate of the transfer of Herāt to Persia, was gone. The Viceroy, too closely identified with the Conservative party to remain in office under a Liberal cabinet, resigned his post. The Liberals did not intend to follow a forward policy in Afghanistan. They craved for a return to the old "masterly inactivity" of John Lawrence. One of the first actions of Lord Granville, once again Secretary of State for Foreign Affairs, was to break off negotiations with Persia concerning Herāt.

Whereas Britain under Gladstone momentarily veered away from imperialism and expansion, or at least tried to, Russia's imperial policies remained unchanged. No sooner had the news of Lomakin's defeat been digested than new plans began to be drawn in St. Petersburg, Tiflis, and Tashkent. Colonel Pozharov, Chief of Staff of the Twenty-first Infantry Division of the Caucasian Army, argued in a memorandum that the occupation of the Ākhāl by Russia was of the first importance for her struggle against Britain, a struggle that was determined by the latter's political aspirations. The Ākhāl and Marv would allow Russia to strike at Britain's most sensitive spot. Should Russia succeed in reaching the Indian frontier with sufficient military forces, two hundred million natives of India would inevitably manifest their desire for independence and would probably join the struggle against England.[168] Memoranda advocating the conquest of the Ākhāl and of Marv were produced by several other officers, among them General A. A. Tergukasov and Colonel Malama of the General Staff.[169]

Not everyone among Russia's military and government leaders favored a new advance in Central Asia. The Chief of the General Staff, Count Fedor Logginovich Heiden [Geiden], felt that money should be invested in "the construction of a railway from

---

167. Ibid., p. 248.

168. From a memorandum of the Chief of Staff of the 21st Infantry Division to the Chief of Staff of the Caucasian Military District, December 21/January 2, 1880; *Prisoedinenie*, No. 240, pp. 463–64.

169. *Prisoedinenie*, No. 240, p. 463, n. 1.

Orenburg to the Turkestan Military District rather than spent on expeditions in waterless deserts."[170] The Minister of Finance, Adjutant General Samuil Alekseevich Greig, insisted that during the contest with the terrorist underground Russia needed "quiet and tranquility." The conquest of Turkmenistan would bring no positive results and lead only to new political, military, and financial difficulties.[171]

At a special meeting held on March 9 under the chairmanship of the Tsar and attended by the heir to the throne, Grand Duke Aleksandr Aleksandrovich; the Viceroy of the Caucasus, Grand Duke Mikhail Nikolaevich; Miliutin, Giers, Jomini, Greig, and generals Heiden, Skobelev, and Obruchev, the Transcaspian question was discussed at length. N. N. Obruchev and M. D. Skobelev argued in favor of an active policy. Skobelev in particular emphasized that an advance was necessary because "of the aggressive policy of the English." Heiden spoke against an advance. When Greig, another opponent of the "forward policy," a term even more descriptive of Russian activities in Central Asia than of British activities in India, suggested that Russia was provoking England, inviting her to fight, the Tsar rather severely interrupted him. "We parted dissatisfied with one another," Miliutin wrote in his diary that day.[172]

Miliutin's own opinion was, as usual, decisive. The Turkoman lands must be occupied in order to link the Caucasus with Turkestan. This must be done without delay, for the British were already intriguing among the Turkomans. "The occupation by the English of Quetta and Qandahār, their rapid construction of a railway to that point from the Indus, and their endeavour rapidly to ensconce themselves in Herat, clearly indicate that shortest road on which an Anglo-Russian collision, or reconciliation, must occur."[173]

170. Memorandum of February 7/19, 1880, as cited in *Dnevnik Miliutina*, 3, 297, n. 93.
171. Memorandum of February 28/March 12, 1880, as cited in *Dnevnik Miliutina*, 3, 293, n. 95.
172. *Dnevnik Miliutina*, 3, p. 224.
173. Central State Military-Historical Archive, f. V.U.A., d. 6863, 11. 42–43, as cited in E. L. Steinberg, "Angliiskaia versiia o 'russkoi ugroze' Indii v XIX–XX v.v.," *Istoricheskie zapiski*, 33, 1950, p. 59.

Miliutin's memorandum to the Tsar asked for the conquest of the Turkoman lands, as a preventive measure.

> To judge on the basis of facts, England is still very far from making peaceful pronouncements. On the contrary, she still pursues against us a policy of advance, a policy which becomes more widespread every year. Having subjugated Asiatic Turkey, having destroyed Afghanistan, having established close ties with the Turkomans, and trying to win Persia to her side as well, she is beginning deliberately to threaten the Caspian region.[174]

Miliutin knew that Britain had not subjugated Asiatic Turkey, that her allegedly close ties with Turkomans consisted of a number of visits by British agents, and that she certainly was not beginning to threaten Transcaspia. The vehemence and the inaccuracy of his argument may be explained not only by his increased dislike, or rather hatred, for Britain, but also by the opposition to his plans for Transcaspian conquests on the part of such important personages as the Chief of the General Staff and the Minister of Finance. The Tsar accepted Miliutin's views. On March 18 the Chief of Staff of the Caucasian Military District was informed by telegram that the Tsar had permitted the resumption of military operations in Transcaspia, that for the years 1880 and 1881 10,000,000 rubles had been appropriated for this purpose, and that General M. D. Skobelev, a hero of the recent war with Turkey and an old *turkestanets*, had been appointed to lead the expedition.[175]

The political direction of Skobelev's expedition was entrusted to I. A. Zinov'ev, the Russian minister in Tehran and perhaps the ablest representative Russia had ever had in Iran. A graduate of Moscow's Lazarev Institute, Zinov'ev knew Persian, as well as some Turkish and Arabic, and was intimately familiar with the

---

174. Miliutin's memorandum of February 29/March 12, 1880, as cited in Zaionchkovskii, "D. A. Miliutin: Biograficheskii ocherk," *Dnevnik Miliutina*, 1, 54.

175. General Gurchin to the Chief of Staff of the Caucasian Military District, March 6/18, 1880; *Prisoedinenie*, No. 246, pp. 471–72.

country where he had made his diplomatic career. His devotion to Russian imperialist ideals was as great as his mistrust and dislike of Great Britain. Zinov'ev had worked diligently to prepare the ground for Skobelev's campaign. He not only succeeded in keeping the Persian government quiet but managed to obtain its support in the vital matter of supply and transportation.[176] Russian officers in mufti arrived in Khorāsān to buy large quantities of wheat and many camels. Where Persian officials showed signs of hostility, a token of Russian esteem would invariably lead to a change of mind. During a conversation with the chief of the purchasing mission, Colonel N. I. Grodekov, the Governor of Khorāsān, Rokn od-Dowleh, a brother of the Shah, hinted that he would appreciate the gift of a landau. When delivery was delayed, the prince-governor happily settled for the cash value of the carriage—2,000 rubles, the sum coming from the funds of the Russian military command in Transcaspia.[177]

Close cooperation between Zinov'ev and Skobelev was one of the important factors in assuring the success of the expedition. Unlike Lomakin, Skobelev prepared his campaign with utmost care. Supply bases were established in Persian territory with provisions sufficient to feed an army of over ten thousand men. Though in command of a force several times the size of Lomakin's, Skobelev never became overconfident. He sought help and cooperation wherever they were to be found. He even suggested that Zinov'ev enlist the services of Khorāsān Kurds who would devastate the land between Geok-Teppe and Ashkhabad. "It is vital to burn the Tekke's stores and property and to take their cattle," he wrote.[178] On Zinov'ev's advice this idea was abandoned as likely to cause political difficulties in Tehran. Upon the successful termination of the campaign, Skobelev generously

---

176. For a detailed account of the conquest of Ākhāl, the problem of logistics, and Zinov'ev's role in solving it, see N. I. Grodekov, Voina v Turkmenii, 4 (St. Petersburg, 1884).

177. Otchet v raskhode ekstraordinarnoi summy, assignovannoi na Akhaltekinskuiu ekspeditsiiu 1880–1881 gg., Grodekov, 4, Appendix 106, p. 112 of supplementary matter. (Accounts of the expenditures of the Akhāl expedition of 1880–81).

178. Skobelev to Zinov'ev, June 20/July 2, 1880; Prisoedinenie, No. 251, p. 478.

acknowledged Zinov'ev's part. "To his advice and cooperation we owe to a significant degree the success of the expedition." [179]

Skobelev's campaign began in November and centered on Geok-Teppe, defended by over twenty thousand Turkomans, only eight thousand of whom had firearms. During the several weeks' siege, thousands died inside the mud village as a result of the heavy Russian bombardment. On January 24 the Russians stormed the fortress. A mine, which was exploded under the walls, opened a breach into which Colonel A. N. Kuropatkin led his column. Resistance collapsed. Thousands of Turkomans, men, women, and children, fled into the desert pursued by Cossack cavalry. In addition to sixty-five hundred bodies found in the fortress, eight thousand fugitives "of both sexes" were caught and hacked to death by a furious soldiery. Only fifty-nine Russians were killed.[180] Thus was civilization introduced to the Turkomans. Their former nominal sovereign, Nāser ed-Din Shah, received the news of the Russian victory from a special messenger sent by I. A. Zinov'ev. He expressed great pleasure and the conviction that the victory would increase the security of the frontiers and of the population of Khorāsān.[181]

A brief debate flared up among Russian officials concerning the future of the Ākhāl. Colonel Grodekov had recommended massacre and devastation. The Tekke survivors would be forced to surrender their horses, thus ensuring peace in the Ākhāl. "Furthermore approval was expressed of Kaufmann's order for the extermination of the Yomuds as the most humanitarian decree ever published." [182] Should such a policy be adopted, the annexation of the Ākhāl would be unnecessary.

The Ministry of Foreign Affairs requested Zinov'ev's opinion on whether it was necessary to annex the Ākhāl or possible to

179. General Skobelev to the Minister of Foreign Affairs, N. K. Giers, No. 87, St. Petersburg, December 9/21, 1881; Grodekov, 4.

180. Journal of the Military Operations of the Ākhāl expedition for January 1881 [Signed: Major General Grodekov] May 2/14, 1881; Prisoedinenie, No. 263, pp. 497–529.

181. Nāser ed-Din Shah to Zinov'ev, 25 Safar 1298 [January 14/26, 1881] as reported in Zinov'ev to Skobelev, No. 32, January 16/28, 1881; Grodekov, 4, 52.

182. Terent'ev, 3, 227.

bring the Tekke to submission and establish peaceful relations with them without permanently occupying their territory. Zinov'ev replied that there could be "no question of any peaceful understanding with the Tekke" unless it rested on Russian "military might in the oasis," a might that would constantly serve as a reminder to the Turkomans that Russia had the ability severely to punish any recalcitrance on their part. The Tekke did not constitute a state, and the independence of each individual precluded the possibility of a stable agreement. Moreover, Zinov'ev went on, one should not lose sight of the other independent center of Tekke population, the Marv oasis, whose inhabitants were hostile to Russia.

The evacuation of the Ākhāl, Zinov'ev argued, should lead logically to the evacuation of Krasnovodsk, since the latter "could serve only as a military base for expeditions into the steppes, but would lose all significance as soon as we [Russians] renounce the spread of our dominion to the east of the Caspian." It should not be forgotten that one of the causes that had impelled Russia to move eastward from the Caspian was the need to impress England and to prevent her from carrying out her anti-Russian designs in Central Asia. The turmoil in Afghanistan might lead to a British annexation of that country.

> If Gladstone's Cabinet rebels against such a turn of events, the English Conservatives, in case of their return to power, would probably not hesitate to find in the impossibility of pacifying Afghanistan sufficient pretexts to begin carrying out their political program which tends toward the spreading of England's influence in Central Asia to extreme limits to the detriment of the importance of Russia.
>
> Our advanced post on the northwestern edge of Khorāsān, connected with a base on the Caspian Sea by dependable means of transportation would undoubtedly compel the English to be more restrained in their ambitious designs, since all the routes to the east and south-east would be open to us.[183]

183. Zinov'ev as cited in Grodekov, 4, 101–05. Grodekov gives neither the number nor the date of the dispatch. In the margin of the copy of Grodekov's

Zinov'ev's dispatch, together with Skobelev's proposals on Ākhāl's borders, formed the basis of the government's decision. On May 18, 1881, at Gatchina, one of the Imperial residences near St. Petersburg, the Tsar issued an ukase proclaiming the annexation of the lands of the Tekke Turkomans and the formation of the Transcaspian *oblast* of the Russian Empire.

The extension of Russian power to the Ākhāl necessitated a delineation of the Russo-Persian frontier in that area. Secret negotiations were conducted in Tehran by Zinov'ev and Mirzā Said Khān Mo'tamen ol-Molk, a politician of marked pro-Russian sentiments who had replaced Mirzā Hoseyn Khān as Minister of Foreign Affairs. The British continued to receive fairly complete information from their sources in the Persian bureaucracy and were aware that Persia would give up her old claims to the various Turkoman lands. The near approach of Russia to Afghanistan and the extent of Russia's territorial encroachment on northeastern Persia were matters of considerable interest to the Government of India. The Secretary of State for India, Lord Hartington, stated as much in Parliament on August 1, 1881. Later the same month the India Office communicated to the Foreign Office Hartington's views in regard to the Persian problem.

Hartington knew that there had never been a formal Anglo-Russian treaty guaranteeing Persia's integrity, "yet the understanding reached on this subject in 1834–38 has, up to the present time, been considered on both sides to subsist in full force." It was apparent, the India Office wrote, that a modification of the Persian frontier was likely and that as a result the Shah's domain might be seriously reduced.

> The bearing of any such measure upon British Indian interest is obvious; and it was with a view to avert complications that Lord Hartington lately suggested to the Secretary of State for Foreign Affairs that a British officer should be associated

---

work at the Sterling Library at Yale University there is a notation in a well-formed nineteenth-century hand "dispatch of January 26 [February 7], 1881, No. 7." The date and the number fit the case.

with any Boundary Commission that might be appointed by the Russian and Persian Governments.[184]

Ronald Thomson felt that the Shah probably would not object to the inclusion of a British officer on the commission for border demarcation, but that the slightest hint of Russian displeasure would make His Majesty exclude the British from participation. On September 4, 1881, Thomson wrote that there was one danger the British should guard against: "a direct and secret understanding between the Russian Minister here and the Shah, negotiated without reference to the Persian Ministers." In such a case the British legation would not be informed until it was too late, just as it had happened with the agreement on the Atrak frontier in 1869. To forestall any secret agreements between Zinov'ev and the Shah, Thomson told the latter on October 24 that Britain would regard them with disfavor.[185]

The Russian government did object to British participation in negotiations of the Russo-Persian frontier issue. Though not entirely secret, the negotiations were conducted without the British, Thomson being able to do no more than urge Mirzā Said Khān to press Persia's claims to the Akhāl and Marv. The Persians paid no attention.

Mirzā Hoseyn Khān, who had been appointed governor of Khorāsān upon the failure of negotiations regarding Herāt, had addressed a letter to the elders of Marv inviting them to submit to Persia for the sake of peace and tranquility. The letter included the usual threats to those who did not obey the commands of the Shah.[186] However, the Marv Turkomans had no fear of Iran. If they submitted, it would be only to avoid Russian domination. Nāser ed-Din Shah, whose armies had suffered a terrible and humiliating defeat at the hands of the Marvis twenty years earlier, had no power to compel submission, as he was fully aware.

184. India Office to Foreign Office, August 26, 1881, as cited in Correspondence; F. O. 65/1202.
185. Correspondence, ibid.
186. Mirzā Hoseyn Khān Moshir od-Dowleh to the elders of Marv, July 1881; *Prisoedinenie*, No. 284, p. 551.

The former governor of Khorāsān, Rokn od-Dowleh, the one who had been bribed by Grodekov, told Thomson that the only way Persia could establish her claim to the Turkomans was by force of arms, "and this the Persian Government would not attempt." The Shah had issued orders that for the time being there should be no further interference with the affairs of Marv. When Thomson asked Mirzā Said Khān whether Persia had informed Russia of the Shah's decision, the latter replied

> that he had received . . . an unsigned Memorandum from the Russian Minister, stating that, as Persia had failed to establish her authority over the Tekkeh tribe at Merv, Russia could not now recognize her claim to that territory, and that he had replied in the same informal manner that Persia's territorial rights could not be invalidated on the ground stated, but that she had no present intention of interfering with those tribes, and would take no action with respect to her claim to their allegiance without previous communication with the Russian Government.[187]

On December 21, 1881, Ivan Alekseevich Zinov'ev, Russian minister in Tehran, and Mirzā Said Khān, Persian Minister of Foreign Affairs, signed a treaty delineating the border between the two countries from the Caspian Sea (Bay of Hasan Qoli) to the vicinity of the village of Bābā Dormez. Further east in the area of Sarakhs some one hundred miles of the frontier remained undelineated.[188] Nine months later the Persian government secretly promised Russia not to interfere in the affairs of the Turkomans of Tejen.[189]

The short distance between Bābā Dormez and the point where the borders of Iran and Afghanistan meet made it certain that soon the latter would have Russia for a neighbor. The *Novoe*

---

187. Paraphrase of Thomson's telegram of January 4, 1882, Correspondence; F. O. 65/1202.

188. Convention between Iran and Russia delineating the border to the East of the Caspian; *Prisoedinenie*, No. 327, pp. 602–05.

189. Minister of Foreign Affairs to the Chargé d'Affaires at Tehran, October 25/November 6, 1882; *Prisoedinenie*, No. 264, pp. 653–55.

Vremia had already reported that P. M. Lessar, an engineer active in politics, was surveying the country between Ashkhabad and Herāt. A knowledgeable English observer commented that "This could have but one meaning, that Russia had in view the possibility of a further advance, which, of course, was only to be expected." [190] The British government felt that it was more than ever necessary to press both Russia and the Shah for a definitive settlement of the entire frontier question. Thomson was instructed to raise the issue in Tehran once more. He did so and reported to Granville that Mirzā Said Khān would be happy to have the entire frontier demarcated, but that Persia "would not move openly in the matter, least she should cause umbrage to Russia." Mirzā Said Khān wanted Britain to reach an agreement with Russia before involving Persia in difficult and dangerous disputes. Thomson inferred that Persia was sure of a Russian advance to Marv and was not willing to oppose it. Persian ministers, he wrote, would not risk the displeasure of Russia "without being assured of something more than moral support from England." [191]

The Government of India pressed London for a settlement of the Russo-Persian frontier issue. It also felt that the time to negotiate a treaty, securing Afghanistan from Russian interference, was before Russia absorbed the last remaining territories next to Afghanistan. Should Marv and Sarakhs fall to the Tsar, there would remain no basis for bargaining, nothing to give Russia in return for a commitment to keep her hands off Afghanistan.[192]

Lord Granville talked to the Russian ambassador in London (Prince Alexei Borisovich Lobanov-Rostovskii, who had succeeded Count Shuvalov) about the still undefined portion of the Russo-Persian frontier between Bābā Dormez and the Hari-rud. He handed Lobanov an undated, unsigned memorandum propos-

---

190. J. F. Baddeley, *Russia in the 'Eighties: Sport and Politics* (London, 1921), p. 121.

191. Granville to Thomson, No. 21, January 7, 1882; Thomson to Granville, No. 31, January 12, 1882; Correspondence; F. O. 65/1202.

192. Government of India to Lord Hartington, No. 6 of 1882, Secret, Fort William, January 16, 1882; L.I., 31, 1882.

ing demarcation in order "To promote the stability and integrity of the Persian Empire," which was "a matter of equal interest to England and Russia"; to obtain a settled frontier; to avoid "actual territorial contact between the two powers in Central Asia, or any collision between the Asiatic states within the circle of their influence." The memorandum further stated that Britain had demonstrated that she did not want to extend her territory "but it is by no means certain that it will be possible for H. M.'s Government to maintain this attitude, unless Russia will consent, on her part, to adopt and follow a similar policy." Granville proposed that the two powers agree "to aid the Shah in effectively establishing his authority over Sarakhs, and the Atak and Tejend lands." In conclusion Granville warned that in the absence of an agreement concerning the tracts between Russia and Afghanistan, "a state of things might occur which would not be of advantage to the continuance of good relations now existing between this country and Russia." [193]

Lobanov took the position that the delineation of Persia's northern frontier was a matter of exclusive Persian and Russian concern. Lord Hartington, Secretary of State for India, rejected this view and stressed the danger that would arise should Russia reach Afghan borders. Hartington wanted the Russians to conclude a formal agreement with Persia and Britain, recognizing the Shah's sovereignty over Marv and thus "interposing a comparatively civilized State between the territories of the Czar and our own uncivilized allies and dependents on the North West frontier of India." [194]

The India Office was so involved in the Persian frontier question that Lord Hartington sat in on conversations between Granville and Lobanov in March 1882. Hartington proposed to Lobanov that the "undoubted right" of the Shah to the territory between Bābā Dormez and Sarakhs be recognized by Britain and Russia, and that Persia be encouraged to establish her authority over the Tekke in that area. Lobanov replied that Persia had not been able to control the Tekke, and that she would not be

193. Pro Memoria [no date, number, or signature]; F. O. 65/1202.
194. India Office to Foreign Office, Secret and Immediate, February 21, 1882; ibid.

Anglo-Russian Conflict

able to control them at Marv either. Russia had never interfered with arrangements between Britain and Afghanistan. On her part she expected to be left free "to take any measures with regard to the States within the sphere of her influence which might be required for purposes of security." Granville said that from Lobanov's words one might infer that Russia felt free to advance to Sarakhs. Lobanov did not offer any further explanation. The conversations achieved nothing.[195]

Through the rest of 1882 and most of 1883 an uneasy truce prevailed in Central Asia. Persia had definitely given up hope of reasserting her sovereignty over Marv; Mirzā Said Khān told Ronald Thomson that too large a force was needed to subjugate and garrison Tekke lands.[196] The Persians were not prepared to make an effort which, considering Russia's designs on the area, was doomed to failure. Even diplomatic talk was growing softer. The rival players in the great game seemed tired.

The apparent calm was deceptive. Russian authorities, carrying out their long-range plans, succeeded in promoting a pro-Russian party among the elders of Marv, who received gifts and medals for their services. Russian agents displayed unusual tact in handling the Marvis. "The endeavor to attract the Turkoman leadership compelled the Tsarist command to show tolerance even toward the enemies of Russia." [197] The pro- and anti-Russian groups engaged in bitter squabbles, but no one had the heart for another round of fighting which could end only in defeat and, most likely, in another massacre.[198] Rather than face the Russians, the Turkomans staged looting raids on Persian villages in Khorāsān. Tehran officials believed that the raids had been instigated by Makhdum Qoli Khān and other Russian partisans at Marv to show the Persians that they could not control the Turkomans and should relinquish their claims even to such clearly Iranian areas as Sarakhs. However, the British agent at Mashhad and his cor-

195. Granville to Sir E. Thornton [Ambassador at St. Petersburg], Draft, No. 99, March 22, 1882; ibid.

196. R. Thomson to Granville, No. 23, Tehran, February 13, 1882; ibid.

197. M. N. Tikhomirov, *Prisoedinenie Merva k Rossii*, pp. 61–62.

198. Report of Lieutenant Colonel Nazarov, February 1884; *Prisoedinenie*, No. 406, pp. 715–16.

respondent at Marv saw no reason to suppose that this was the case.[199]

On January 13, 1884, the pro-Russian elders, who had prevailed at Marv with the help of Russian agents, addressed to the Tsar a petition for admission to the Empire.[200] It was a foregone conclusion that the petition would be accepted at St. Petersburg. Though Alexander II had been assassinated in March 1881, and his faithful War Minister, D. A. Miliutin, the main architect of Russian expansion, had been dismissed by the new Tsar, the basic policy of the government in regard to Central Asia had not changed. The new War Minister, General Petr Semenovich Vannovskii, had troops ready to occupy Marv. Giers, uncertain that the pro-Russian party would be able to prevent resistance by anti-Russian elements, advised caution. Bloodshed must be avoided. If resistance developed, troop movements must be postponed and "moral pressure" used first.[201]

On February 14 it was officially announced in St. Petersburg that General A. Komarov, Chief of the Transcaspian Region, had informed the Tsar of the formal submission of Marv. Twenty-four deputies representing four Turkoman tribes had taken the oath of allegiance at Ashkhabad. "The Khans and representatives state," Komarov reported, "that the Mervees have decided on this step, because conscious of their inability to govern themselves, and convinced that your Majesty's powerful Government alone is capable of establishing and consolidating order and prosperity in Merv." [202]

The next day Giers casually informed the British ambassador,

199. R. Thomson to Granville, No. 167, Tehran, December 5, 1883; Correspondence respecting the occupation of Merv by Russia and her proceedings on the Khorasan frontier of Persia, India, Political and Secret Department, August 15, 1884; F. O. 65/1209; hereafter cited as Correspondence respecting Merv.

200. Vsepoddanneishee proshenie mervskikh turkmen k Aleksandru III ob ikh priniatii v russkoe poddanstvo, January 1/13, 1884 [Petition of Mary Turkomans to Alexander III to become Russian subjects]; *Prisoedinenie*, No. 380, pp. 688–89.

201. Giers to Vannovskii, January 28/February 9, 1884, *Prisoedinenie*, No. 395, pp. 700–01

202. Extract from the *Official Gazette* of St. Petersburg in Correspondence respecting Merv, F. O. 65/1209.

Sir Edward Thornton, that the Emperor had decided to accept the allegiance proffered him by the Turkomans of Marv.

The moment for the annexation of Marv was well chosen. In Britain the Liberals were in power, and the Russians relied on Gladstone and his colleagues not to go beyond the usual weak remonstrances when confronted with a fait accompli. Russia's international position was strong, whereas Britain was isolated. The rapprochement which had occurred between St. Petersburg and Berlin, and which would result in the renewal of the Alliance of the Three Emperors in March 1884, secured Russia's position in the West.[203] Moreover, Britain was in deep trouble in the Sudan. In November 1883 an Egyptian force commanded by General Hicks was cut to pieces by the rebellious forces of the self-styled Mahdi, Muhammad Ahmad. Other British-led Egyptian detachments were defeated in the months that followed. Soon Khartum was besieged. It was clear that the Egyptians would not be able to put down the Mahdi; but if Britain must reconquer the Sudan, she would not be able simultaneously to offer strong resistance to Russia in Central Asia.

The British were well aware that the Egyptian-Sudanese trouble was "an encouragement to the Russians as it is to every enemy of this country." [204] However, they could only complain:

> Her Majesty's Government [Granville wrote to Thornton] are not aware that any new circumstances have occurred which can be held to create a pressing necessity for the course that had been decided upon; but even if such were the case, it seems entirely inconsistent with the whole tenour of the mutual explanations between the two Governments that one of them should take a step which appears to be in contradiction with the assurances which have on so many occasions been received both from the Emperor and his Government, without any previous communication of their change of views.[205]

203. Cf. W. L. Langer, *European Alliances and Alignments, 1871–1890* (New York, 1931), p. 342.

204. Currie to Kimberley, private, January 12, 1884; loose papers, Pte Kimberley Papers; as cited in R. L. Greaves, *Persia and the Defence of India*, p. 64.

205. Granville to Thornton, Draft, No. 42c, February 29, 1884; F. O. 65/1203.

In reply to Thornton's note of March 12, embodying Granville's complaints, Giers stated that Russia had not assumed any restrictive obligations in Central Asia but had preserved for herself entire liberty of action except in respect of the northeastern frontiers of Afghanistan. Russian occupation of Marv had for its purpose the pacification of the steppe "dans son intérêt et dans celui de la Perse." Giers was not prepared to discuss the probable future actions of Russia in Asia. British interpretations of past Russian assurances made it necessary for her "to be very circumspect" in this regard.[206]

Though Giers did not refer to the Sudan, the thought that Russian action was expertly timed to coincide with Britain's discomfiture there was present in many minds. In an attempt to clear his country of any suspicion of perfidy, Baron Artur Pavlovich Mohrenheim, Lobanov's successor at the Russian embassy in London, claimed that the reproach made by Granville that Britain had been treated discourteously in being faced with an accomplished fact, was undeserved. The Russians would have informed the British in advance had they foreseen the submission of the Marvis. "They would, at all events, have endeavoured, had the matter depended upon them, to prevent the decision from being taken at a moment when Her Majesty's Government were embarrassed by the affairs of the Sudan." [207]

In the Parliament the opposition decried the lack of policy and decision on the part of the government. Lord Lytton "sarcastically observed that if the Liberals would create two new departments of the Foreign and War Offices 'devoted to the careful preparation of measures to be taken only when too late' they would be the busiest in Downing street." [208] Baron Mohrenheim tried to win the Liberals by making it appear that the explanations he had given the government about the annexation of Marv were a favor to their party. In a memorandum to Granville he declared "that, if any other Government but that of Mr. Glad-

206. Giers to Thornton, St. Petersburg, March 17/29, 1884, Enclosure No. 1 in Thornton to Granville, No. 84, St. Petersburg, March 31, 1884; F. O. 65/1204.
207. Correspondence respecting Merv, F. O. 65/1209.
208. R. L. Greaves, p. 66.

stone had been in office, the Russian Government would have formally declined to discuss the matter at all." [209]

Having renounced their claims to Marv, the Persians had held aloof from the entire issue. They were unpleasantly surprised when they saw Russian troops advancing toward the right bank of the Tejen River and the village of Old Sarakhs. There the Persians, freed of the scourge of Turkoman raids, had planted crops and established their authority over small groups of Tekke and Salors. The thought of losing these newly reclaimed lands to Russia pained Nāser ed-Din Shah.

Early in May 1884 the rumor spread in Russia that Persia had ceded Sarakhs. It had probably originated in a visit which the Chief of the Transcaspian Region, General A. V. Komarov, paid to Old Sarakhs on the right bank of the Tejen. As was customary, the British ambassador in St. Petersburg immediately inquired at the Ministry of Foreign Affairs into Russia's intentions and was assured that "Sarakhs on the West Side of the Tejend which has a garrison of Persian troops and to which the Persian Government lately sent a battalion, has not been and will not be ceded by Persia to Russia." [210] As for the Sarakhs on the eastern side of the Tejen, that was nothing but a few mud huts inhabited by Turkomans. "M. de Giers added that it was to this latter place that General Komaroff recently went in order to settle disputes which had arisen about the water supply." [211]

Poor communications made it impossible for the Shah to ascertain what was happening in the extreme northeast of his empire. For all he knew Russia might be preparing to annex all of Khorāsān. Fear drove him to seek once more that same British support of which he had on so many previous occasions despaired. The Shah privately acquainted Ronald Thomson with the situation to the extent to which it was known to him, adding that Persia's

209. Granville to Thornton, No. 81B, April 9, 1884; F. O. 65/1205.

210. Thornton to Granville, Telegram, No. 10, St. Petersburg, May 12, 1884; ibid.

211. Thornton to Granville, St. Petersburg, No. 145, May 12, 1884; Correspondence respecting Merv; F. O. 65/1209.

right to the entire Sarakhs district was clear, and that "he would do all in his power" to maintain it.[212]

When the new Russian minister, Aleksandr Aleksandrovich Melnikov, learned of Persia's attempts to secure the Sarakhs district, he appealed to St. Petersburg to order the Transcaspian authorities immediately to settle there a number of Turkomans owing allegiance to Russia.[213] Two hundred families of Salor Turkomans accompanied by two Cossack squadrons under Colonel Alikhanov, one of the principal figures in the events which had led to the annexation of Marv, were sent to Old Sarakhs.[214] The Persians were driven out without a fight, and Prince Aleksandr Mikhailovich Dondukov-Korsakov, Commander of the Caucasian Military District, wrote Melnikov that the troops had arrived to establish Russian rule in the area.[215]

The Shah was not prepared to acquiesce silently in the loss of a territory that had been long acknowledged as his. The British minister in Tehran summed up the situation in the following words:

> Persian remonstrances, even if followed by a protest which I understand the Shah is at present not disinclined to make, are not likely to have much weight with the Russian Government in determining their action with regard to Sarakhs, but it is possible that the feeling of dissatisfaction which has been produced here by these proceedings may leave an unfavorable impression on the Shah's mind which will not readily be effaced.[216]

For a Persian protest to be at all effective, it had to have the back-

---

212. R. Thomson to Granville, No. 78, Tehran, May 23, 1884; Correspondence respecting Merv; ibid.

213. Telegram of the Russian Minister in Iran to the Chief of the Transcaspian Region, May 13/25, 1884; *Prisoedinenie*, No. 420, p. 734.

214. Commander of the Caucasian Military District [Prince A. M. Dondukov-Korsakov] to the Russian Minister in Iran, May 14/26, 1884; ibid., No. 421, pp. 734–35.

215. Dondukov-Korsakov to Melnikov, June 9/21, 1884; ibid., No. 425, p. 744.

216. R. Thomson to Granville, No. 94, June 16, 1884; Correspondence respecting Merv, F. O. 65/1209.

ing of the British. The Shah was therefore "anxious to know whether Persian remonstrances, and formal protest, if made, would be supported by Her Majesty's Government at St. Petersburg." [217]

The Government of India felt that Persia should be supported.

> Retention of old Sarakhs district by Persia [Lord Ripon telegraphed] would interrupt direct communications between Akhal and Herat territory and conjointly with Afghan occupation of Panjdeh it would prevent Russia occupying any part of Heri Rud valley.
>
> It is certain that more than fifty years ago Persia drove Salors out of Old Sarakhs, and since then the Turkomans who occupy lands have done so by Persian permission. New Sarakhs depends on old Sarakhs district and is useless by itself.[218]

Upon consulting Lord Kimberley, the Secretary of State for India, Granville authorized Ronald Thomson confidentially to inform the Persian government that it would be better for the latter "to exhaust every means of arriving at an understanding with Russia before appealing to Her Majesty's Government for support." However, if in spite of the Shah's protests Russia should "insist upon appropriating territory which can be shown to have been under Persian rule at a recent date, Her Majesty's Government will be ready to consider any application which Shah may make for their good offices at St. Petersburg." [219]

In Tehran the new Minister of Foreign Affairs, Nāser ol-Molk, complained that Persia was not in a position to defend herself and warned Thomson that "if English interests were not concerned to an extent which would require the interference of Her Majesty's Government . . . the only course which the Shah could safely pursue would be to cease expostulation and allow his claim to be

217. Same to same, June 21, 1884; ibid.
218. Telegram from the Viceroy [to Thomson] June 24, 1884; F. O. 65/1208.
219. Granville to Thomson, July 3, 1884; Correspondence respecting Merv; F. O. 65/1209.

set aside." [220] No understanding could be reached with Russia, whose minister answered every representation with the statement "that Persia had undertaken not to interfere with the Turkomans residing on the right bank of the Tejjen," from which promise the Russians inferred that Persia had given up her claims to the territories now or recently occupied by the tribes.[221]

Thomson noticed the discontent and anxiety of the Persians over the treatment they had received at Sarakhs.

> The knowledge of this state of popular feeling [he reported], and the offensive and humiliating manner in which the seizure of the place was effected, no previous notice having been given to the Persian Government in order that they might withdraw their guards instead of leaving them to be expelled from the district by the Cossacks who were sent to take possession, have probably caused more annoyance to the Shah than the actual loss of territory which was involved.[222]

But he was equally well aware of their reluctance to provoke Russia's displeasure without first obtaining definite and specific promises of British support.

The British were not anxious to commit themselves in a situation fraught with unknown dangers. Where did the limits of the Persian Empire in the northeast actually lie? Which territories had the Persians given up by secret agreements that they had, according to rumors, concluded with the Russians in the previous year? When Thomson asked these questions, Nāser ol-Molk pleaded ignorance.[223] He requested that Lord Granville give new assurances of British interest in Persia's territorial integrity, pointing out that if England allowed Russia to absorb Sarakhs,

> the Shah could no longer feel any certainty that further encroachments by Russia on Persian territory would not be

---

220. R. Thomson to Granville, Confidential, No. 106, Tehran, July 8, 1884; F. O. 65/1208.

221. Id.

222. Id.

223. R. Thomson to Granville, Confidential, No. 118, Tehran, July 21, 1884; ibid.

regarded with indifference by Her Majesty's Government. The Caspian Provinces, or Boojnoord, or Kuchan might next be appropriated by that Power, and if England did not interfere, Persia was powerless to protect herself, and she might eventually be thrown entirely under Russian domination.[224]

The Persian minister in London, Mirzā Malkam Khān, wrote Granville that the Shah wanted to know what measures Britain would take if Russia committed new acts of aggression, and whether the assurances in regard to Persian territorial integrity which he had received during his visit to London in 1873 were still in effect.[225] Granville replied that the old promises held good, except for the territories that Persia herself had given up since then. The British were prepared to make representations in behalf of Persia, but—the tone of the memorandum suddenly changed—they could not conceal from Persia that British support largely depended "upon the amount of sympathy which is felt by the British nation toward that country." Then came what amounted to a series of conditions for extending the support that had in the past often been offered unconditionally when unasked for.

This feeling [of sympathy for Persia] is undoubtedly checked by the almost entire absence of Commercial intercourse between England and Persia and especially by the obstacles which exist to trade with the southern provinces of Persia, which if these obstacles were removed would be easily accessible to English and Indian commerce.

The repeated efforts of H. M.'s Minister at Tehran, to obtain the opening of the Karoon river to trade and navigation, have hitherto been unsuccessful, and the want of good and safe roads from the interior to the Persian Gulf a serious drawback to enterprise.

Now the British government wanted the Shah to open the Per-

224. Id.
225. Malkam Khān to Granville, Confidential, London, August 11, 1884; F. O. 65/1209.

sian Gulf area to British commerce, thus assuring its speedy development.[226]

The price set by Granville on British support of Persian claims to Sarakhs was too high. The Shah did not feel that the strip of land along the Tejen was worth the sacrifices demanded by the English. He decided to make one more attempt at direct negotiations with the Russians, and sent to St. Petersburg as a special envoy Yahyā Khān, the younger brother of Mirzā Hoseyn Khān. Though much indebted to the latter for his career, Yahyā Khān managed to retain the Shah's favor at the time of his brother's exile to Mashhad in 1881. When Hoseyn Khān suddenly died in mysterious circumstances, his old title, Moshir od-Dowleh, was bestowed upon Yahyā Khān. Yahyā's skill in palace intrigue and "adjustment" was such that he won the confidence of his late brother's old rival, the Russophile Mirzā Said Khān.

At St. Petersburg Yahyā Khān requested in the name of the Shah that Russia withdraw her troops from Old Sarakhs, leaving the entire district to Persia. Giers firmly refused to comply and pointed out that only Russia's conquest of the Turkomans made it possible for the Persians to cultivate the banks of the Tejen.[227] Giers had a point. Ever since 1861, when a Persian army was cut to pieces by the Marvis, the northern border of Khorāsān had been in perpetual turmoil. Turkoman raids never ceased, thousands of Persians were abducted and sold into slavery in Khiva, Bukhara, Marv, and other Central Asiatic cities. Russian armies had imposed order on chaos, liberated Persian slaves, and made it possible to resume peaceful cultivation in the oases along the Kopet-Dāgh and in the river valleys. Yahyā Khān capitulated, winning for himself the goodwill of the Russians.[228]

226. Granville to Malkam Khān, Draft, August 16, 1884; ibid. The first draft of the document mentioned the opening of the Gulf to "the trade of this and other countries." In the margin Granville wrote: "Is there any necessity to mention other countries? What the Shah wants is our support, and though of course we should not ask for any exclusive commercial privileges our position in the Persian Gulf is very peculiar and we have always endeavoured to keep out of the Gulf the influence of other European nations."

227. The Minister of Foreign Affairs [Giers] to Russia's Minister in Iran [Melnikov], September 15/27, 1884; *Prisoedinenie*, No. 436, pp. 765–67.

228. Id.

No sooner had Persia renounced her claims to Old Sarakhs, and settled the issue of her Khorāsān frontier, than a conflict of first magnitude erupted further to the east. With Persia out of the picture, Afghanistan became the principal target of the continuing Russian advance. Every bit of news telling of British difficulties in the Sudan made the Russian military grow bolder. The political temperament in St. Petersburg rose sharply with the approach of winter in 1884.

Miliutin, considered too liberal by Alexander III, was in retirement. Gorchakov was dead. The new War Minister, General Petr Semenovich Vannovskii, was strongly influenced by Pan-Slavist extremists and led the opposition to the cautious Giers.

> Monsieur de Giers [Sir Edward Thornton wrote] has undoubtedly a good many bitter enemies and very few true friends. His excellency enjoys no social position except that allowed him by the Office he holds, and has no fortune. Count Ignatieff [the leading exponent of aggressive Pan-Slavism] is one of his bitterest and most unscrupulous enemies, partly because he attributes it to Monsieur de Giers' influence that the Emperor called upon him to resign his post of Minister of the Interior, and partly because he is extremely desirous of himself occupying the Office of Minister of Foreign Affairs. The strongest opposition is also made to Monsieur de Giers by the Minister of War and all military men, whose ambitious views are thwarted by His Excellency's peaceful policy.[229]

Giers lacked not only wealth and social position but character as well. "Timidity and indecision were perhaps his principal qualities." He was mortally afraid of Alexander III. "When Giers went to report to the Tsar, his assistant, Lamsdorff, would go to church to pray for a successful issue of the audience." [230] His aristocratic though far less able successor, Prince Lobanov-Ro-

---

229. Thornton to Granville, No. 4, Confidential, St. Petersburg, January 10, 1885; F. O. 65/1216.

230. V. M. Khvostov, "Avstro-germanskii soiuz i vozobnovlenie dogovora trekh imperatorov," V. P. Potemkin, ed., *Istoriia diplomatii* (Moscow, 1945), 2, 56.

stovskii, is reported to have quipped: "Que voulez-vous. Il n'a été que consul général toute sa vie." [231]

On January 26, 1885, Khartum fell to the dervishes of the Mahdi. The news of the massacre of General Gordon and the British garrison was received with unconcealed jubilation in the military circles of St. Petersburg. The Pan-Slavist press called for immediate action to take advantage of Britain's embarrassment in the Sudan and to defy her in Central Asia. On February 13, *Vedomosti* wrote:

> Europe would calmly receive the intelligence that Heratees, discontented with the rule of the Emir, were desirous of following the example of the Mervees and requesting the protection of Russia at a time when all barbarous and semi-barbarous nationalities are either seeking or being taken under the protection of a Great Power.[232]

The British military attaché at St. Petersburg, Colonel F. Trench, reported that among the Russian military there was no desire for the settlement of the Afghan border issue. They understood well that such a settlement would be to Britain's advantage.

> At St. Petersburg, however, no secret is made of the fact that they do not wish to hamper their future movements, and they do not mean whatever assurances to the contrary they may make, to be bound to a definite frontier for the very reason that they fully intend to take the first opportunity of seizing Herat.[233]

Trench warned that "a month or two hence, as soon as a large portion of our forces are locked up in Egypt and the Sudan," the Russians would, under some pretext, occupy Herāt.[234]

The locus of the approaching clash was the Panjdeh oasis near

---

231. K. Skalkovskii, *Vneshniaia politika Rossii i polozhenie inostrannykh derzhav* (St. Petersburg, 1901), p. 20.

232. Enclosure in Thornton to Granville, No. 27, St. Petersburg, January 14, 1885; F. O. 65/1236.

233. Colonel F. Trench, February 17, 1885; ibid.

234. Id.

Anglo-Russian Conflict

Kushk. Amir Abd or-Rahmān of Afghanistan had occupied the area in the summer of 1884, in spite of Russian objections that he was trying to establish his authority in anticipation of the work of the boundary commission.[235] Sir Edward Thornton defended the Amir, claiming that Panjdeh had always belonged to Afghanistan.[236] While the diplomats talked, the military deployed their forces. From St. Petersburg, Colonel Trench urged the dispatch of British troops to Herāt. Their presence in the city would be so distasteful to the Russians that they would be prepared to sign a border agreement on British terms.[237].

While the Russian force under General Komarov took up positions in front of Panjdeh, the British continued to drag their feet. On March 28 in an unpleasant conversation with Thornton, Giers accused Britain of preparing for war. A force was being assembled in northern India under Sir Frederick Roberts, with the Duke of Connaught in command of the reserve. Sir Henry Drummond Wolff, an influential politician, had asked in Parliament whether a fleet would be sent to the Baltic at the opening of navigation. The Russian military and naval authorities, Giers continued, were asking him what all of this meant and whether the army and the naval base at Kronstadt should be prepared to withstand an enemy attack. Did Britain really intend to go to war?

Thornton replied that England could do nothing in secret, and that any movements of her troops would be immediately known to all. The last thing Britain wanted was war, but she had "engagements with the Ameer of Afghanistan" which she was bound to maintain and "could not allow him to be deprived of territory which His Highness claimed, and which Her Majesty's Government believed to belong to Afghanistan, without an impartial investigation" of his rights. "I added," Thornton wrote home, "that any attempt on the part of the Russian troops to approach or occupy Herat, would be equivalent to a declaration of war and would be accepted as such by Her Majesty's Government." Giers

235. Undated and unsigned memorandum from the Russian Ministry of Foreign Affairs to the British Embassy in St. Petersburg, Enclosure in Thornton to Granville, No. 194, St. Petersburg, June 23, 1884; F. O. 65/1207.
236. Thornton to Granville, No. 201, St. Petersburg, June 24, 1884; ibid.
237. Colonel Trench, February 17, 1885; F. O. 65/1236.

disclaimed any intention on the part of Russia of attacking Herāt.[238] He put these assurances in writing in a memorandum delivered to Thornton on March 30, 1885.[239]

That same day General Komarov's troops lashed out at the Afghans within sight of General Lumsden, the members of his commission, and their military escort of several hundred men. The Afghans fought bravely, suffered heavy losses estimated at over five hundred dead and several hundred wounded, but were no match for the disciplined, well-equipped, and well-trained Russians, who lost only nine men and had forty-seven wounded. It was all over in a few hours on the banks of the Kushk River.[240]

For the next several weeks war seemed inevitable. Sir Edward Thornton told John F. Baddeley, correspondent for the *Standard:* "Yes, I have just seen de Giers. There had been a battle at Penjdeh—the Afghans were defeated and five hundred of them killed. Some of our officers were present . . . There is nothing to do but to pack up; war is inevitable; I shall be told to demand my passports tomorrow." [241]

The Foreign Office printed documents announcing a state of war between Britain and Russia. The Viceroy of India was informed that the Admiralty had ordered all Russian ships to be watched. He prepared to send twenty-five thousand men to Quetta, and was promised reinforcements from home. In the Far East Vice Admiral Sir William Dowell, Commander in Chief of the China Station, occupied Port Hamilton, which could be used as a base of operations against Vladivostok.[242]

Queen Victoria, who had personally appealed to her "cher frère," Alexander III, to avoid bloodshed, was now in a belligerent mood. Even Gladstone, who had been consistently conciliatory toward Russia, found it imperative to act. He denounced

238. Thornton to Granville, No. 77, Confidential, St. Petersburg, March 29, 1885; F. O. 65/1238.

239. M. de Giers, Memorandum, St. Petersburg, March 18/30, 1885, Enclosure in Thornton to Granville, No. 80, St. Petersburg, March 30, 1885; ibid.

240. Report of the Chief of the Transcaspian region [Lieutenant General Komarov] to the Commander of the Caucasian Military District, March 30/April 11, 1885; *Prisoedinenie,* No. 445, pp. 776–88.

241. Baddeley, *Russia in the 'Eighties: Sport and Politics,* p. 217.

242. R. L. Greaves, *Russia and the Defence of India,* pp. 72–73.

Russian aggression in Parliament and asked for £11,000,000, a large sum for that day, "of which six million and a half were to meet the case for preparations rendered necessary by the incident of Penjdeh." [243]

The forward movement of Russia in Central Asia during the winter and spring of 1885, culminating in the battle of Panjdeh, kept the Shah and his ministers in a state of unrelieved fear. Though continuing to pose as a friend of Russia, Nāser ed-Din sought some guarantee from Britain that she would protect his territories from Russian encroachment. In February he advised Britain to occupy Herāt, convinced "that if England did not now take possession of Herat, Russia would certainly do so, and in that case he considered that Khorasan would no longer be safe." Nāser ol-Molk urged Ronald Thomson to communicate the Shah's ideas to Her Majesty's Government.[244]

In May Thomson asked what course of action Persia would pursue in case war broke out between the two great powers. Nāser ol-Molk told Thomson, now Sir Ronald, that the Shah had decided to maintain the strictest neutrality and would resist all pressure to involve him in hostilities.[245] Persia's position was clear and simple, whereas Britain had not informed the Shah of her own. Early in June Nāser ed-Din asked Sir Ronald for "a more precise and definite statement of the policy which England would pursue in event of an unprovoked aggression being made by Russia upon Persian territory." The Shah said frankly that if the people of Persia, meaning himself, did not feel that British friendship could be relied upon, they would realize their helplessness before Russia and would not even attempt to resist her any longer. Reporting the conversation to Granville, Thomson advised that the Shah be reassured.[246]

243. W. Habberton, *Anglo-Russian Relations Concerning Afghanistan*, pp. 53–54.
244. R. Thomson to Granville, No. 26, Secret, Tehran, February 27, 1885; F. O. 65/1236.
245. Sir Ronald Thomson to Granville, No. 52, Tehran, May 4, 1885; F. O. 65/1242.
246. Thomson to Granville, No. 65, Secret, Tehran, June 9, 1885; F. O. 65/1244.

By this time the danger of war had somewhat receded. Lord Dufferin, the Viceroy of India, did not relish the thought of a Central Asiatic campaign. Amir Abd or-Rahmān of Afghanistan had had a sufficient demonstration of Russian power and was prepared to forget the humiliation of Panjdeh. The resignation of Gladstone and the formation of a Conservative cabinet on June 23 did not stop the cooling off process, for Lord Salisbury, who had become Prime Minister and Secretary of State for Foreign Affairs, was a cautious, rather slow-moving statesman not given to unreasoned action. No less than his predecessor, he realized the weakness of Britain's position, especially in view of the stand taken by Bismarck, who, loyal to his Russian alliance, made strong representations to the Porte demanding the closing of the Dardanelles to the British navy. "Turkey was compelled to comply, and the British plan of action in the Black Sea against Odessa and Batumi was disrupted." [247] On the other hand, the verbal violence of the initial British reaction, coupled with concrete and visible preparations for resistance, convinced Russia that she could advance no further without provoking a major war. Alexander III would not repeat his grandfather's blunder. Faced with the threat of a tangible force, Russia's forward movement, which had not been checked for over twenty years, ground to a halt.

When Mirzā Malkam Khān, the Persian minister, raised the issue of Anglo-Persian relations with Lord Salisbury in August 1885, there was no sense of pressure that would compel the latter to promise anything. Malkam Khān complained of the lack of sympathy shown by England toward Persia. He begged for "advice." Whether intentionally or not, Salisbury misunderstood Malkam Khān's meaning. What the latter wanted was a guarantee of Persia's territorial integrity and British advisers in the Persian government, the advisers serving essentially as a symbol of British commitment to Iran. Salisbury said that it was not for him to offer advice; but, as an example of what could be done to help Persia, he suggested that the capital be moved from Tehran,

247. F. A. Rothstein (Rotshtein), *Mezhdunarodnye otnosheniia v kontse XIX veka* (Moscow, 1960), pp. 123–24. Also V. M. Khvostov, "Kolonial'naia ekspansiia velikikh derzhav," Potemkin, ed., *Istoriia diplomatii*, 2, 74.

"where it is constantly in danger of a Russian blow," to Esfahān, which is closer to "the friendly shores" of the Persian Gulf, and that corruption in the government, especially in the administration of justice, "be somewhat remedied." Salisbury was very much disturbed when he learned that his offhand remarks had been communicated to Tehran as if they were the official advice volunteered by the British government.[248]

In view of the progress of Anglo-Russian negotiations concerning the Afghan border and the rapid diminution of tension between the two powers, the Persian problem no longer appeared pressing. In September the Russian ambassador, Baron Georgii Staal, and Lord Salisbury signed a protocol defining the frontier between Russia and Afghanistan. The Russians kept every bit of ground their armies had conquered, but Afghanistan at least had a border.[249] Diplomacy solved other issues that periodically cropped up between the two great powers in Asia. With the disappearance of the power vacuum, the limits of Russian expansion north of Persia and Afghanistan were set.

248. Salisbury to Sir R. Thomson, No. 75A, August 6, 1885; F. O. 65/1248.
249. For the text see E. A. Adamov, ed., *Sbornik dogovorov Rossii s drugimi gosudarstvami. 1856–1917* (Moscow, 1952), No. 37, pp. 264–66.

2

Reuter and Falkenhagen:

Two Failures and a Beginning

The development of an industrial capitalist society in nineteenth-century Europe made it impossible for non-European nations to persist in their old isolation. The dynamic, rich, technologically and militarily superior West could not even be resisted by those who sought to keep it out. The paradox of opening the doors, or windows, to the West in order to preserve one's political and spiritual independence was experienced at different times by Russia, Turkey, Japan, Iran, and many other societies.

Persia's isolation had begun to crumble in the days of Napoleon. His officers were the first of a long line of military advisers to the Persian army. Russia, whose own transformation into a modern society was far from complete, played the role of a Western nation on the Persian scene. The crushing defeats she inflicted on Persia in two wars proved the superiority of European arms and organization. Abbās Mirzā, the able heir of a dull monarch, fully realized this but had the misfortune to die before his father. In 1834 the throne went to Abbās Mirzā's son, the untalented, narrow, and superstitious Mohammad Shah who was utterly incapable of dealing with problems of state, which he entrusted to Hāji Mirzā Āghāsi, a vicious and ignorant opportunist. For another generation Persia remained relatively unexposed to the West.

However, the West continued to exercise its attraction. In the 1850s, Count Gobineau reports, a Persian attended the French military college at Saint Cyr. Later he made the first Persian translation of Descartes. But it was not Descartes that fascinated and attracted Nāser ed-Din Shah and the tiny group around him who ruled and owned Persia. Even a useful invention such as the telegraph did not appeal to the rather limited imagination of the Shah. The one thing he understood well was money, of which he never had enough yet, which seemed to flow in abundance in Europe.

England, France, Germany, were gripped by the moneymaking fever. The stock exchange, no less than Henry Adams' dynamo, was a central symbol of a new age. Banks, countinghouses, factories, railways, spread their influence throughout the world, carrying misery to millions and unimagined riches to a few. The exquisite Crown jewels of Persia's King of Kings, sparkling reminders of the loot of India, brought no income, but stories of a new India, an India of stocks and bonds, of coupons and interest, of concessions and loans, excited his cupidity. Persia could not long remain unaffected by the moneymaking passion of the age, nor did her rulers want to stay outside the magic circle of cascading gold.

Diplomacy was enlisted in the service of the Shah's purse. In Paris and London Persia's representatives approached a number of entrepreneurs, painted attractive pictures of easily gained wealth, and encouraged investment in Iran.

As early as 1864 a certain Monsieur Savalan appeared in Tehran with a project for the construction of a railway and the exploitation of mines. Though he failed to win a concession,

> in consideration of a money payment to the Persian Ministers, he obtained an engagement from the Shah's Government, that for a period ending in 1873 . . . no concession for railways or mines should be given by them without his having received formal notice thereof, in order that he might have the option of accepting any proposals made on the same conditions.[1]

Two years later Mohsen Khān Moin ol-Molk, Persian minister in London, persuaded Dr. Strousberg, a Prussian businessman involved in railway promotion in Rumania "as well as numerous other vast undertakings," to take up a concession for a line from Tehran to the shrine of Shāhzādeh Abd ol-Azim. On arriving in

1. Mr. R. F. Thomson to the Earl of Granville, No. 8, Commercial; Tehran, September 12, 1872; F. O. 60/405.

Tehran, Strousberg's engineers, "although provided with full powers and backed by the strong recommendations of the Persian Envoy," found the authorities uncooperative. Negotiations and bribes removed some of the obstacles, but Strousberg soon decided that the risk was too great. He preferred to pay Mohsen Khān 4,000 pounds sterling as a quitclaim and be rid of a concession that promised nothing but unlimited loss.[2] It seems that the money was pocketed by Mohsen Khān who, upon the failure of Strousberg's concession, claimed that the Prussian had wanted to cheat the public and "proposed gifts," a euphemism for bribes. "In spite of extreme need, I swear by your dear life that I did not accept them," he wrote to Mirzā Hoseyn Khān Moshir od-Dowleh, the Grand Vizier.[3]

Next Mohsen Khān offered the same concession to several other capitalists, among them C. W. Siemens of the firm of Siemens Brothers, but "these practical men of business, without hesitation, firmly declined entertaining the matter or having anything whatever to do with the project."[4] The Persian government was already beginning to acquire a reputation for bad faith in financial matters.

The £4,000 received from Strousberg had whetted Mohsen Khān's appetite. Undaunted by Siemens' lack of interest, he offered the concession to Sir E. Watkins, a director of Britain's South Eastern Railway. Watkins consulted the Foreign Office, stating that he proposed to "further the scheme, if Her Majesty's Government would give support." The government refused to encourage him,

> as it was not believed that Persia seriously desired any such development as was foreshadowed in this Concession, but

2. Mr. Shee to the Earl of Granville; London, July 14, 1873; F. O. 371/1185.

3. Mohsen Khān Moin ol-Molk to Mirzā Hoseyn Khān Moshir od-Dowleh; London, 22 Rabi os-Sāni 1287; The Ghani Collection, Sterling Memorial Library, Yale University, New Haven.

Already in 1871 the British minister in Tehran, Mr. Charles Alison, had warned that the Persians had from time to time entertained projects for railways, "principally as a means of profit to the Persian Ministers and the agents employed by them." Alison's opinion was that such transactions with Persian agents abroad "ought not . . . to be concluded without good advice." C. Alison, Esq. to the Earl of Granville, No. 90, Gulahek, July 17, 1871; L.I., 1, 1871.

4. Shee to Granville; London, July 14, 1873; F. O. 371/1185.

that the real object of the Shah's Ministers was the making of those profits which are incidental to the negotiation of great contracts, and the acquisition by the Persian Government of a short railway from Tehran to Shah Abdul Azim [the shrine] at the cost of the Concessionaire.[5]

Without official backing Watkins lost interest in Mohsen Khān's schemes.

The Persian minister redoubled his efforts, claiming that his repeated failures had been caused by the jealousy and greed of his colleagues in Tehran and that the construction of a railway in Persia had become a matter of principle which he would accomplish in spite of all obstacles. He realized that his government's reputation had been lowered in European financial circles: "Only the London market had remained unpolluted with our filth, and that one did not stay clean," he wrote to Mirzā Hoseyn Khān.[6]

Since reputable firms hesitated to invest in Iran, Mohsen Khān turned his attention to capitalists of a more adventurous type, and discovered Baron Julius de Reuter. Born in Germany, where he achieved considerable success operating a commercial news service, Reuter moved his business to London, the financial heart of the world. He became a British subject in 1857, prospered greatly, and in 1871 bought the title of Baron from the Duke of Coburg Gotha. His interests multiplied, and with wealth came power, until "by a Royal Warrant dated Nov. 6, 1891 he was recognized in this country [England] as Baron von Reuter."[7] However, official recognition did not bring full social acceptance, and it has been suggested that Anthony Trollope was inspired by the dazzling career of Baron Julius de Reuter to create the character of Augustus Melmott in *The Way We Live Now*.

It was to Reuter that Mohsen Khān Moin ol-Molk now took his scheme. The former was quick to see its inherent possibilities. Having obtained the backing of the rich and influential firm of

---

5. "Railways in Persia," Memorandum by R. C. Dickie, February 17, 1911; Persia No. 6824, February 23, 1911; ibid.

6. Mohsen Khān to Mirzā Hoseyn Khān; London, 22 Rabi os-Sāni 1287; The Ghani Collection.

7. "Railways in Persia," Memorandum; F. O. 371/1185. A brief, laudatory account of Julius Reuter is found in Graham Storey, *Reuter's Century* (London, 1951).

Matthiessen and Jardine, he needed no further financial support and was "bent on carrying the affair through, so to speak, single-handed." [8] To make sure of Mohsen Khān's continued support, Reuter offered him and his brother, Mohammad Āqā, then serving as secretary of the Persian legation in London, an interest in the future company.[9] It has been claimed that Mohsen Khān was bribed to the sum of 20,000 pounds sterling.[10]

Early in 1872 a certain Mr. Edouard Cotte, employed as agent by Reuter, arrived in Tehran where he laid his proposals before the Grand Vizier (Prime Minister), Mirzā Hoseyn Khān Moshir od-Dowleh, who had served for several years as ambassador at Constantinople where he acquired a taste for innovation, especially the kind that promised to add to his fortune. The Shah, anticipating large profits for himself, was as eager as his Prime Minister to bring the affair to a successful issue. He feared that opposition to the proposed concession might develop, and urged Mirzā Hoseyn Khān to keep the plans secret. "Beware of Cotte being frightened and scared away," the Shah cautioned him, and added, "Curses upon the fathers of traitors." [11]

The Shah had reason to fear opposition, for Reuter's scheme envisaged the creation of a monopoly that would exploit all the mineral resources, build and run all the railways, tramways, irrigation dams and canals, manage forests, operate banks, etc. Mr. Cotte was also aware of the need for secrecy. He was careful not to inform the British legation in Tehran of the exact nature of Reuter's proposals. Only two weeks before the concession was granted did Mr. Ronald Thomson, chargé d'affaires at Tehran, convey to Earl Granville, the Foreign Secretary, a brief outline of the proposed concession, and even then his information was incomplete. Not until July 16, 1872, nine days before the signing, did Thomson find out that Cotte had proposed "to farm all Customs throughout the Persian Territory, at a somewhat higher

8. Shee to Granville; London, July 14, 1873; F. O. 371/1185.

9. Mr. W. T. Thomson to Granville, No. 28, Confidential, Tehran, February 6, 1874; F. O. 60/406.

10. Ebrāhim Teymuri, Asre bikhabari yā tārikhe emtiāzāt dar Irān (Tehran, 1332), p. 107. Hereafter cited as Teymuri, Asre bikhabari.

11. Ibid., p. 104.

rate than is now paid to the Shah's Treasury," and that he wanted the Persian government to agree, "in the event of a bank being established in this country, that any concession to be given for such a purchase shall, in the first instance, be offered to him." [12]

Before signing the contract, Nāser ed-Din Shah ordered a number of his highest officials to give him their opinion concerning this vital manner. Their deliberations did not take long. Aware of their master's wishes and liberally paid by Mr. Cotte, the ministers wrote the Shah that the concession was in Persia's best interests. She would reap enormous benefits without giving in return anything but some empty lands which had never been, and were not likely to be, of any use in the future. "Should you sign your blessed August name to this concession, one stroke of your pen will bestow upon the land and the people more good and truer existence than have been given them by all the Kings of Iran over thousands of years." [13]

The concession was signed in Tehran on July 25, 1872. Article 1 authorized Baron Julius de Reuter to form in London "one or more societies with the object of undertaking and executing throughout the whole extent of the Empire, the works of public utility which form the subject of this Concession." For a period of seventy years Reuter was granted the "exclusive and definitive right" of constructing and operating a railway line from the Caspian Sea to the Persian Gulf with "such branch lines as he shall think fit." His company was permitted to institute tramways at its discretion.

Article 4 promised the Company "all lands being Crown property which may be necessary for the construction and working of the line of double rails, sidings, stations, employes' houses, workshops, yards, and sheds." Privately owned lands which the company might need would be obtained for it by the government at current prices, by compulsory expropriation if necessary.

---

12. R. F. Thomson to Granville, No. 2, Commercial; Tehran, July 9, 1872, and postscript of July 16; F. O. 60/405.

13. Cited in Teymuri, *Asre bikhabari*, pp. 106–07. The letter was signed by Dust Ali Khān Moayyer ol-Mamālek, Minister of Finance; Mirzā Said Khān, Minister of Foreign Affairs; Amin ol-Molk, Minister of Justice; Mohammed Hoseyn Khān Dabir ol-Molk, Minister of the Interior, and several others.

Article 5 permitted the company to take gratis, on Crown property, building and maintenance materials such as stone and gravel. Utensils, provisions, and beasts of burden would be supplied at current prices.

Article 6 exempted from duties all materials the company would import for the construction of the railway.

> The same privilege of exemption shall apply to all the undertakings and works of the Company; their employes shall be exempt from all taxes in the interior, all their lands shall be free of all taxes and duty, and the produce of their industry of every kind shall be allowed free circulation of every kind throughout the Empire and free export, with exemption from all duty.

Article 7 stipulated that the schedule for the completion of the line would be the subject of a separate agreement.

Article 8, which later proved of major importance, read:

> Caution money, to the amount of 40,000 £ sterling, shall be deposited in the Bank of England in the name of the Persian Government and of the "concessionaires" on the day on which the contract is signed. It shall be confiscated in the event of the works not having been commenced within fifteen months of the date of the present contract, except in case of compulsion or of obstacles over which the Company has no control, such as war, shipwreck, or suspension of communications with foreign countries. The caution money will be returned to the Company in exchange for a receipt from the Governor of Resht, reporting the arrival at Enzellee of the quantity of rails necessary for the construction of the line from Resht to Tehran.

In Article 9 the company engaged to pay the Persian government yearly "2- per cent. on the net returns of the working of the line." At the expiration of seventy years, Article 10 stated, if no new arrangements were made, all the assets of the company in Iran would be turned over to the government without reimbursement or indemnity.

In Article 11 the government granted

the said "concessionaires," as long as their Concession lasts, the exclusive and definitive privilege to work, all over the Empire, the mines of coal, iron, copper, lead, petroleum, etc., and every other mine at their pleasure, with the exception of mines actually being worked by private individuals . . . The Government reserves the mines of gold, silver, and precious stones, in respect of which it may come to special arrangements with the Company.

The Persian government was to receive 15 percent of the net profit of every mine worked by the company (Article 12), to provide the land gratis, and to provide other privileges in the manner identical to that stipulated for the railway in Article 10.

Further, the company was given the exclusive right

to execute throughout the Empire the necessary works for changing the course of rivers or water courses, for making bars, Artesian wells, canals, reservoirs, taking and bringing to every point they may judge fit water over which the Government shall as yet have granted no right . . .

The Company shall have the right to cultivate and to dispose at its will of all barren lands, reclaimed by the water it has brought to the spot. The Company must come to an amicable arrangement with the Government as to the price of the water it sells. The Government shall receive 15% annually of the new profits. [Article 14]

The management and profits of state forests throughout the country were also turned over to the company (Article 15), and the government guaranteed it an annual interest of 5 percent on its investment "with an additional annual 2 per cent as a sinking fund" which would eliminate all risk of loss to the investors (Article 17).

In Article 19 the government engaged

to grant the "concessionaires" the "regie" of the Customs for a term of 20 years from the 1st March, 1874. The "concessionaires" shall pay the Government the sum now paid by the contractors for the Customs, and in addition a yearly premium of 500,000 fr[ancs]. (20,000 £ sterling).

These are to be the conditions for the first 5 years. From the beginning of the sixth year the premium of 500,000 fr. shall be exchanged for a premium of 60 per cent. of the net profits over and above the contract price.

Should the government decide to form a bank, the Company would be "assured preference over any other party" (Article 20). Moreover,

> The "concessionaire" shall have a prior claim over any other parties as regards such enterprises as gas, the paving and decorations of the capital, roads, postal and telegraphic arrangements, mills, manufacturies, and factories for which privileges might be hereafter requested. [Article 21]

The company was free at any time to transfer its privileges to other persons (Article 22).[14]

Thus without any pressure having been exercised by foreign powers, without the slightest interference from the British legation, the King of Kings, the Shadow of God, gave away practically the entire resources of his impoverished and misgoverned nation to a greedy business manipulator of dubious reputation. For paltry sums which would not suffice even to maintain the Imperial Court, Nāser ed-Din Shah did not hesitate to sell the future of generations of his subjects. The pretty phrases about benefiting the country by bringing the fruits of European progress to Iran and the pretense at concern for the well-being of the people made the actions of the corrupt ruler and his equally corrupt ministers still more offensive by adding hypocrisy to treasonable greed.

The enormity of the deed perpetrated by the Shah and Mirzā Hoseyn Khān aroused immediate opposition in various quarters. The Russian legation had been suspicious for some time. The negotiations between Cotte and the Grand Vizier had been enveloped in secrecy. Since very few people participated in them, and all had a personal interest in their successful conclusion, no reliable information could be obtained. Shortly after the contract

---

14. Concession of H.I.M. the Shah to Baron Julius de Reuter (Translation), Enclosure in W. T. Thomson to Granville, No. 36; Tehran, May 20, 1873; F. O. 60/405.

had been signed, Mirzā Hoseyn Khān reported to the Shah that the Russians were displeased. "Though they do not yet know the articles and conditions of the agreement, they are enumerating its shortcomings and dangers." [15] In the margin of the Vizier's report the Shah scribbled:

> I have well understood the advantages of this [the concession]. Let the Russian Legation be as unhappy as it pleases. What right do they have? Of course, the power of this Company from the Caspian Sea to the Persian Gulf is no good for Russia, but, God willing, it is good for Iran.[16]

Reuter had foreseen Russian objections to his concession and understood the need for official British support, which he requested in September 1872. In a letter to Lord Granville he claimed that

> In undertaking this gigantic task it is not only my earnest desire both to improve the social condition of the Persians, and to open up the great natural resources of their country for the benefit of the world at large, but also to render my concession of the highest value to Great Britain.

Having pointed out that a Select Committee of the House of Commons had recommended the construction of a railway to the east via the Euphrates valley, Reuter said:

> Your Lordship is doubtless aware that the Russians are making great progress with their railways toward the Caspian Sea, having already partly completed three lines, each leading in that direction . . .
>
> Under these circumstances, I need not point out to your Lordship the importance of my Concession I have [sic] obtained from the Shah, which as before mentioned is of an exclusive character and secured to me for a period of 70 years.
>
> I desire to serve this my adopted country, by introducing my enterprise under English auspices alone; and I shall have

15. Mirzā Hoseyn Khān to Nāser ed-Din Shah, n.d. [1872]. Cited in Teymuri, *Asre bikhabari*, p. 114.
16. Id.

pleasure in so doing without soliciting a subsidy or other material support from Her Majesty's Government. I nevertheless desire to feel assured that, in the event of differences arising between the Persian Government and myself, Her Majesty's Government will recognize the validity of my scheme, and protect my rights as a British subject, so far as may be in their power.[17]

The Foreign Office did not like the terms of the concession and was not impressed with Reuter's patriotic effusion. "This gentleman," as the Foreign Office minutes sometimes designate him, was not trusted. It was felt that "if wholly repulsed," he "might renounce his acquired British nationality and place himself under Russian protection, a course which it appears he had not obscurely hinted at."[18] Nevertheless, after a month's delay, the Foreign Office sent its cold, official answer:

In reply to the letter of September 12 I am to acquaint you that, whilst Her Majesty's Government would view with satisfaction the efforts of the Shah's Government to increase by means of railways and roads, the resources of Persia, they cannot bind themselves officially to protect your interests while carrying out your engagements with that Government.[19]

Reuter's apprehension in regard to his concession's future was fully justified. Mr. Cotte, his agent in Tehran, was certainly aware of the opposition it aroused among the Persians. Not only the reactionaries, who would fight any innovation whether harmful or beneficial, but also those who welcomed progress and had looked forward to the introduction of railways and industries to Iran, were dismayed and voiced their dissatisfaction.[20] The Russian legation encouraged the opposition and championed the half-

17. Mr. de Reuter to Earl Granville; 18 Kensington Palace Gardens, London, September 12, 1872; F. O. 60/405.

18. "Railways in Persia," Memorandum; F. O. 371/1185.

19. Viscount Enfield to M. Julius de Reuter, Foreign Office, October 15, 1872; F. O. 60/405.

20. W. T. Thomson to Granville, Telegram, Tehran, April 7, 1873; ibid.

forgotten cause of Monsieur Savalan, whose option to build railways would not expire until the end of the year 1872. Russian intervention in behalf of Savalan was a serious matter. To remove all legal pretexts for it, the Persian government did not hand over to Cotte, Reuter's agent, the signed text of the concession when he was about to leave Tehran in September 1872, but promised to deliver the documents later in London.[21]

Early in 1873 Reuter and the Shah seemed to have surmounted all obstacles. Though the British minister at Tehran, W. Taylour Thomson, expressed the opinion that "The completion of a railroad between the Caspian Sea and Tehran, under existing political circumstances," would involve "the question of Persia ceasing to be an independent Power," by giving Russia military and economic preponderance in the country, Britain remained officially silent.[22] Nor was there any serious pressure on the Persian government from the Russian legation. Mirzā Hoseyn Khān Moshir od-Dowleh, the chief proponent of the concession, was in a slightly nervous yet optimistic mood when he wrote his brother Yahyā Khān, in London, that Reuter's engineers had surveyed the land and were about to start the construction of the railway from the Caspian shore to the capital. There shall be no opposition, Hoseyn Khān predicted, as "The advantages and profits have been explained to the entire people." Moreover, he would not allow anyone to obstruct the railway agreement, since such obstruction would be equivalent to treason. Hoseyn Khān urged Yahyā Khān to exert all his efforts for a speedy arrival on Persian soil of construction materials, and concluded by boasting that the Shah left all the affairs of state up to him.[23]

Urged by his Westernizing Vizier, supplied with ample funds by Baron de Reuter, Nāser ed-Din Shah decided to tour Europe. Mohsen Khān Moin ol-Molk having been promoted to the embassy in Constantinople, the new minister of the Shah in

21. R. F. Thomson to Granville, No. 8, Commercial, Tehran, September 12, 1872; ibid.
22. W. T. Thomson to Granville (Telegraphic), Tehran, April 7, 1873; and same to same, No. 10, Confidential, Tehran, April 17, 1873; ibid.
23. Mirzā Hoseyn Khān to Yahyā Khān; Tehran, 29 Zi Hajjeh 1289 A.H.; The Ghani Collection, Yale University.

London, Mirzā Malkam Khān, called on Lord Granville on March 30, 1873, to tell him that both the Shah and his Prime Minister were determined to cultivate England's friendship and to attract British capital. To further this purpose and "to judge for himself the advanced state of civilization" in Britain, the Shah proposed to visit that country. Granville replied that the Shah would meet with a hearty welcome and "that it was a matter of satisfaction to hear of the encouragement which the Shah was prepared to give to the introduction of English Capital for the development of such a naturally rich country as Persia." [24]

The Shah was undoubtedly interested in attracting British capital to Persia, anticipating great profits to himself. He was also childishly curious about Europe, which had replaced India in the Persian mind as the land of wonders and wealth. Last but not least, he hoped to secure from Britain a guarantee of Iran's territorial integrity which was threatened by the recent Russian involvement in Transcaspia; or, as Hoseyn Khān put it to W. Taylour Thomson in February 1873, Persia hoped to obtain from Russia, through the intervention of England, a formal assurance "that Persian territory would not be encroached upon." [25]

In May 1873 the Shah, accompanied by Mirzā Hoseyn Khān, the Grand Vizier; a vast number of officials and retainers; his favorite wife, Anis od-Dowleh, with several female servants; and Dr. Joseph Dickson, his British physician, left for Russia. At Anzali, the Shah was met by Prince Menshikov, acting as the representative of the Tsar.

During a brief stopover in Moscow, the Shah had to deal with trouble in his traveling harem.

> Some said that the Persian women wanted to amuse themselves, to go to the theatres, and to go about unveiled. Others said that an embarrassment arose as to the reception of the Shah's wife at foreign Courts. The Grand Vizier was called in, and induced the Shah to send them all back to Tehran, in charge of a high priest and three or four other fanatics,

24. Granville to W. Taylour Thomson, Draft, No. 8, F. O. April 17, 1873; F. O. 60/358.
25. F. O. to Mr. [W. T.] Thomson, No. 16, April 24, 1873; F. O. 60/348.

who would eat nothing but what they had brought with them.[26]

Anis od-Dowleh would never forgive Mirzā Hoseyn Khān for this. She turned into one of his bitterest and most persistent enemies. Her home became a center of political intrigue and propaganda directed against the Grand Vizier and all his measures.

At St. Petersburg the Shah was met by Tsar Alexander II who conducted him to the Winter Palace where he was lodged. The Tsar decorated his guest with the order of St. Andrew. Thanking Alexander for the honor, Nāser ed-Din

> expressed . . . his warm friendship for the Emperor, and his anxious wish for the continuance of cordial relations between the two countries. The Emperor, after accepting the friendly assurances of the Shah, turned to M. Jamasoff, the Russian interpreter, and expressed through him his regret that there were some persons who were not too friendly disposed to Russia, and that his sentiments toward the Shah had been misinterpreted to His Majesty. This speech was very embarrassing to the Shah, and still more so to the Grand Vizier, who felt that the allusion of the Emperor more particularly referred to himself.[27]

The Shah's stay in St. Petersburg consisted of two parts: one was magnificently staged, enjoyable and public, the other extremely unpleasant but more or less private. Russian society, while turning out for receptions and dinners in honor of the Shah, sneered at him. After attending a dinner given by Prince Oldenburg, the War Minister, D. A. Miliutin, commenting on Nāser ed-Din's table manners, wrote in his diary: "It appears that the ruler of Persia is a complete stranger to European manners; we have to begin his education and even teach him how to sit at a European table." [28]

26. Augustus Loftus, *The Diplomatic Reminiscences of Lord Augustus Loftus,* 2, 72.
27. Ibid., pp. 70–71.
28. D. A. Miliutin, *Dnevnik D. A. Miliutina,* 1, 84.

Behind the scenes serious conversations were held between the Shah, Mirzā Hoseyn Khān, and Prince A. M. Gorchakov, Russia's Chancellor. The British ambassador, Lord Augustus Loftus, learned that strong recommendations had been made to the Shah against the Reuter concession, but believed that they had failed, which was not the case.[29] When Gorchakov complained against the concession, saying that it violated Persian sovereignty and independence, the Shah replied:

> In any case now the signed Concession is in his [Reuter's] hands. If he should carry out his promises and obligations we would be able to do nothing . . . However, if he should show the least negligence, in the future we will under no circumstances give him aid and support and will annul this agreement.[30]

The Shah went further, telling Gorchakov that his country could not remain without railroads, the building of which would necessitate agreements with other companies. "It is up to you to aid us in such a case." [31] Gorchakov assured the Shah that he would try to find a company to suit his purposes. The opportunity that had suddenly opened before Russia was not missed by the veteran diplomat. The Ministry of Foreign Affairs immediately produced an entrepreneur willing to invest in Iran: a retired Russian general, Baron von Falkenhagen (Falkengagen), who came supplied with the best references. He was invited to go to Tehran to negotiate a contract.[32] Thus with a few words the Shah committed himself to break Reuter's contract and to transfer at least a part of the latter's concession to a Russian subject. Gorchakov had won an easy but impressive victory.

Traveling through Germany and Belgium, Nāser ed-Din Shah reached London on June 18. The British government,

29. A. Loftus, 2, 110.

30. Mirzā Hoseyn Khān to Sāed ol-Molk, Persian minister at St. Petersburg, 22 Jamādi os-Sāni 1291, as cited in Teymuri, Asre bikhabari, p. 120.

31. Id.

32. Correspondence between General Falkenhagen and the Persian Minister of Foreign Affairs, Translated by J. Ibrahim, Enclosure in W. T. Thomson to the Earl of Derby, No. 211, Gulahek, October 8, 1874; F. O. 60/406.

mindful of the Russian threat in Central Asia, hoped to establish closer relations with Iran. The Shah was therefore received with great pomp, the Prince of Wales, the future King Edward VII, being his principal host.[33]

There were troop reviews, receptions, parties in country houses, and a visit to Windsor where Queen Victoria, "nervous and agitated at the great event of the day," [34] greeted the Shah "at the foot of the grand staircase." [35] Wearing dazzling rubies and diamonds, the Shah looked impressive as he was led into the state reception room to be invested with the Order of the Garter and, in turn, to invest the Queen with the Order of the Lion and the Sun.[36] There were no untoward incidents or breeches of manners at table, the Queen noting in her diary only that "the Shah ate fruit all through luncheon . . . and drank quantities of ice water." [37]

While the Shah acted the tourist, Mirzā Hoseyn Khān, who had been unnerved by the bluntness of Russian displeasure with him, sought to strengthen his and his country's position by obtaining some form of British guarantee of the territorial integrity of Persia. He inquired "as to the nature of agreements which subsisted between Great Britain and Russia as to the integrity of Persian territory" and was told by Granville that there were none save the understanding of 1834,

> that that understanding was based on the sincere desire of the two Govts. to maintain not only the internal tranquility, but also the independence and integrity of Persia; that in the year 1838 Count Nesselrode adverted to the agreement entered into by the two Govts. as still subsisting in full force . . . and that H. M's Govt., as they recognized for themselves the principles which guided the general policy of Great Britain and Russia in favour of this integrity and

33. Sidney Lee, *King Edward VII* (London, 1925), 1, 278.
34. Extract from the Queen's Journal, Windsor Castle, 20th June, 1873; G. Buckle, *The Letters of Queen Victoria*, 2nd series (London, 1926); 2, 258.
35. O. T. Burne, *Memories*, p. 155.
36. Buckle, 2, 259–60.
37. Ibid., p. 260.

independence of Persia in the year 1834, had reason to believe from information which they had received from Lord A. Loftus, H. M.'s Amb. at St. Petersburg, that the Russian Govt. referred with satisfaction to the mutual assurances that were made on this subject in 1834, and in 1838, and that H. M's Govt. considered that the best mode of confirming both Powers in those sentiments was that Persia, while steadily maintaining her rights as an independent Power, should studiously fulfil in all respects her treaty engagements with each, and so ensure the continuance of the friendship which both Powers even for their own interests should desire to maintain with her.[38]

If Mirzā Hoseyn Khān, or the Russian ambassador in London, Baron Brunnow, to whom Granville later repeated the conversation, understood the sense of this wordy statement, they realized that in fact no agreement concerning the integrity of Persia existed, and that Granville's advice to Persia was to be good and hope for the best. Neither the Shah nor his Prime Minister succeeded in turning the many expressions of friendly sentiment they heard in London into a straightforward promise of support. Britain's obvious interest in Iran seemed to conflict with the unwillingness of her government to take a stand. The Persians must have left England utterly confused. Would Britain defend Reuter's rights against Russian pressure? Would Britain stand by Persia and extend to the Shah her protection against Russia's wrath?

Of the latter there could be no doubt. The Shah was on his way home when reports of what had transpired between him and the Russian government began to reach London in increasing volume. On July 10, 1873, Granville had a conversation with the Russian ambassador, Baron F. I. Brunnow, in which he mentioned the fact that the Reuter concession "had been made a matter of state importance" in St. Petersburg. Granville must have suspected that the Russians saw in that concession a British plot to disturb the balance of power in Persia. He assured Brunnow that it was a strictly private venture, that many British capitalists engaged in

---

38. Granville to Loftus, No. 116, July 10, 1873; F. O. 60/405.

business throughout the world, "and that it was not the policy of our Govt. to mix themselves up in their affairs." The British government, Granville said, made this clear to both Baron de Reuter and the Persian minister in London, Mirzā Malkam Khān.[39] Granville may have hoped to impress upon the Russian government his country's disinterestedness in the Reuter concession and thus to allay Russia's fears. He achieved his purpose but in a manner that could not have been pleasing to him. Russia had been preparing for a contest with mighty Britain. Now she was facing only Reuter, Nāser ed-Din Shah, and his Prime Minister, Mirzā Hoseyn Khān. The first must be driven out of Persia, the second taught a lesson, the third overthrown.

On his homeward journey the Shah had to pass over Russian territory once more. His party traveled from Poti to Tiflis, and thence to Baku, accompanied by high Russian officials. Everyone noted "that the Grand Vizier was received with marked coolness by the Grand Duke Mikhail, the Viceroy of the Caucasus."[40] Only a few knew that a determined effort was being made in Tehran to remove Mirzā Hoseyn Khān and cancel the concession, though the Russians made no effort to hide their belief that Mirzā Hoseyn Khān would not remain in office much longer. The Shah's British physician, Sir Joseph Dickson, who had accompanied him on his European trip, reported: "While in Russia I was told by Russian officials and others in conversation that the Sadrazam [Prime Minister] would last only until the Shah's return at Enzellee."[41]

At the center of the conspiracy stood the Shah's favorite wife, Anis od-Dowleh, who had not the slightest concern for concessions, patriotism, or politics, but was merely trying to repay Mirzā Hoseyn Khān for the affront and disappointment he caused her by sending her home from Moscow. Anis od-Dowleh, being an inhabitant of the Imperial harem, had not the freedom of movement, the experience, and the knowledge required for the

39. Id.
40. W. G. Abbot, H. M.'s Consul at Resht to H. E. W.Taylour Thomson, H. M's Minister at Tehran, No. 27; Resht, September 10, 1873; F. O. 60/351.
41. Sir Joseph Dickson to Mr. W. Taylour Thomson, Resht, September 10, 1873, Enclosure No. 2 in W. T. Thomson, No. 115, Confidential, 1873; ibid.

conduct of a serious political intrigue. However, she had the services of Mirzā Said Khān, the Minister of Foreign Affairs and a notorious Russophile. Several princes, important officials, and high mullas participated, as did the Persian consul at Tiflis, where the conspiracy may have, in fact, originated.[42] The harem, the Minister of Foreign Affairs, the princes, the clerics, and, in the background, the Russian legation, made a powerful combination when advocating opposition to a concession that was inherently vicious. It was easy to persuade the public "that it [the concession] is a scheme of the Sadr Azem's [the Prime Minister's] to place Persia virtually in the hands of the English." [43]

Early in September eighty "highly placed persons," including Farhād Mirzā Mo'tamed od-Dowleh, President of the Council of State (who in the Shah's absence had performed the duties of regent), signed a petition for the dismissal of Mirzā Hoseyn Khān. The British minister, aware of the position of Mirzā Said Khān, the Foreign Minister, made an attempt to persuade him of the untimeliness of such a move since "the downfall of the Grand Vizier . . . cannot fail to make the most unfavourable impression through Europe, being at the very moment of His Majesty's return to his own Dominions on the conclusion of a tour of Europe." [44] Thomson's advice was disregarded, and the petition was telegraphed to Anzali where the Shah received it as he disembarked.

The telegram which the Shah received on September 7, 1873, from Farhād Mirzā Mo'tamed od-Dowleh, told of a large number of princes, clergy, and other dignitaries, taking *bast* (sanctuary) in the house of Anis od-Dowleh. Next day at Rasht the Shah learned that several more princes took *bast* in the royal stables, refusing to leave unless the Grand Vizier were dismissed. Nāser ed-Din Shah, unable to estimate the seriousness of the situation in the capital, was frightened. Attached though he was

42. W. T. Thomson to Granville, No. 107; Gulahek, September 7, 1873; ibid.

43. "Memorandum of a confidential conversation which took place this afternoon (Tuesday, October 7th) between H. E. Moetemed el Mulk [Yahyā Khān] and Sir Joseph Dickson, Tehran, October 17, 1873," Enclosure No. 13 in H. M.'s Minister at Tehran to the Secretary of State for Foreign Affairs, No. 128, Secret and Confidential, Tehran, October 8, 1873; L.I., 16, 1873, 362–63.

44. W. T. Thomson to Granville, No. 107, Gulahek, September 7, 1873; F. O. 60/351.

to his Grand Vizier, he did not want to provoke a conflict with a large section of the ruling class. Mirzā Hoseyn Khān obligingly tendered his resignation, which was accepted at once.[45] Two days later the Shah changed his mind. In a brief outburst of courage he reinstated Mirzā Hoseyn Khān and scolded the princes.

> They all got frightened, admitted their fault, begged for pardon and swore that they were ready to obey implicitly H. M.'s commands. The Shah then desired them to go and make it up with the Sadr Azam [Prime Minister], which they did. H. H. asked them all to dinner and swore that he would retain no rancour against them.[46]

The Grand Vizier realized that the quick capitulation of the princes who were in attendance upon the Shah meant very little. The chief members of the opposition, including Anis od-Dowleh and the Foreign Minister, Mirzā Said Khān, were in Tehran, in close touch with the Russian legation. He therefore asked the Shah's physician, Sir Joseph Dickson, to request the British minister "to let him know by return courier the real state of affairs in the capital," and to point out to Mirzā Said Khān the dangers of opposing the will of the King of Kings.[47]

Having learned of Mirzā Hoseyn Khān's dismissal but not of his subsequent reinstatement, the British minister immediately wrote the Shah:

> I venture to trust . . . that as a tried well wisher of this State Your Majesty will permit me to express the sincere regret with which I learned that the late Grand Vizier had deemed it necessary to tender his resignation at the very moment when Your Majesty had completed a tour of such unexampled brilliance throughout the greater part of Europe that it is destined, please God, to form one of the bright spots in the history of the civilized world.[48]

45. W. G. Abbott to W. T. Thomson, No. 27, Resht, September 10, 1873; ibid.
46. J. Dickson to W. T. Thomson, Rustemabad, September 11, 1873, Enclosure No. 3 in W. T. Thomson No. 115, Confidential, 1873; ibid.
47. Id.
48. W. T. Thomson to Nāser ed-Din Shah [no date], Enclosure in Thomson to Granville, No. 113, Gulahek, September 14, 1873; ibid.

Thomson's intervention was in vain. On September 13, the day before the letter was written, the Shah, who was slowly making his way to Tehran, had received alarming messages from the leading mojtaheds and commanding officers of the army in Tehran, repeating their demands that Mirzā Hoseyn Khān be removed from the government. Again the Shah lost his courage, dismissed Mirzā Hoseyn Khān, and ordered him not to enter Tehran.[49]

Mirzā Hoseyn Khān quickly understood the precariousness of his position. Every victory of the opposition added to its strength. Every humiliation inflicted upon the King of Kings increased the Imperial need for a scapegoat, a role which a fallen minister traditionally filled. He may well have recalled the day in March 1861 when, in the midst of a famine, a hungry mob had gathered in front of the palace, pleading with their ruler for bread.

> His Majesty is said to have been in some trepidation upon the appearance of the tumultuous assembly before the Ark [citadel]; immediately summoned the Lord Mayor of Teheran to his presence, and after a few words of Royal censure committed him to the work of the Executioner. The Chief Magistrate was thus put to death on the spot, and his body denuded and dragged through the streets [and] amidst the execrations of the multitude was hung up by the heels at one of the city gates.[50]

Private favors shown him by the Shah even after his dismissal did not sufficiently reassure Mirzā Hoseyn Khān. When Sir Joseph Dickson spoke with him on September 15 at the Royal Camp at Āqā Bābā, near Qazvin,

> The fallen Minister seemed quite disheartened, and with tears in his eyes said that he did not feel sure of his life. He has full confidence in his sovereign, who is most gracious and kind to him, but he fears the enmity of the clergy . . .
> He particularly requested me to send a courier to inform

---

49. Dickson to [W. T.] Thomson, Menjil, September 13, 1873, Enclosure No. 4 in Thomson No. 115, Confidential, 1873; ibid.

50. Charles Alison, Esq. to Lord John Russell, No. 27, Tehran, March 3, 1861; F. O. 248/194.

you of his forlorn position. "Tell the British Minister," he continued, "with my kindest regards, that I have been all along a friend of England, and remind His Excellency that I have been invested by Her Majesty the Queen with the Grand Order of the Star of India and that therefore my person should be protected against any violence or undue humiliation. Say that I implore His Excellency to address, together with his colleagues, a collective note to His Majesty the Shah, soliciting an assurance that my life is safe and my person respected." [51]

That same day Dickson interceded for the fallen minister with the Shah. Without a trace of humor he compared the attack launched against Mirzā Hoseyn Khān to the opposition of the nobles, the clergy, and the ladies of the court to Bismarck. But the good Emperor, Dickson said, remained firm and as a result Prussia was now blessed with a good government, a constitution, a parliament, and one of the finest armies in the world. "How I should wish Your Majesty," Dickson appealed to the Shah, "to follow the example of the Great Emperor and how the whole of Europe would praise the conduct of Your Majesty." The Shah then confided to Dickson that he had no intention to deprive himself permanently of the services of his Bismarck and would return him to power as soon as he put down "the movement that has been organized against him." [52]

Upon his return to Tehran the Shah abolished the post of Grand Vizier and published a new list of ministers in which Mirzā Hoseyn Khān's name was not included.[53] The latter's discharge and the retention of the Russophile Mirzā Said Khān as Minister of Foreign Affairs were designed to placate the Russians and disarm the opposition. A few days later Mirzā Hoseyn Khān was summoned to Tehran, graciously received by the Shah

51. Dickson to [W. T.] Thomson, Royal Camp, Aga Baba near Cazveen, 15th September 1873; Enclosure No. 5. in Thomson, No. 115, 1873; F. O. 60/351.

52. Dickson to W. T. Thomson, Aga Baba, September 15, Enclosure No. 6 in Thomson, No. 115, 1873; ibid.

53. "Persian Official Gazette," October 3, 1873, Enclosure No. 12, H. M.'s Minister at Tehran to the Secretary of State for Foreign Affairs, No. 126, Tehran, October 7, 1873; L.I., 16, 1873.

but, for the time being, not given any official position. However, this was enough to alarm the Russian minister, A. F. Beger, who called on the British minister in an attempt to discover why the former Prime Minister had come to Tehran. Beger disparaged Mirzā Hoseyn Khān and spoke favorably of the opposition. W. Taylour Thomson strongly disagreed. In his opinion

> the action taken by them was not simply against the Sadr [Premier] but against the prerogatives of the sovereign . . . and that it appeared to me those who had brought about the present state of affairs had laid the germ of clerical pretentions and popular excitements which, if not speedily quashed, might eventually lead to the establishment of a form of Government by no means to be desired and for which Persia was altogether unprepared.[54]

These were, indeed, prophetic words. To break an outrageous concession Russia had encouraged a reactionary camarilla made up of princes, mullas, and Imperial wives. Their motives were private and low, but their rallying cry was independence of foreign control and the protection of religion. They dared to thwart the will of the autocrat and won a brief victory. The lesson was not lost on the Russians, the British, and the Persians. A pattern was established here which would recur with ever-increasing violence until the Qājār dynasty's final downfall.

Such thoughts were far from Taylour Thomson's mind when, on October 15, he told the Shah in person and by means of a memorandum that the attack on Mirzā Hoseyn Khān was a conspiracy against the prerogatives of His Majesty's Crown "full of evil consequences for the future." [55] He was fighting an old-fashioned political duel with his Russian colleague, supporting a friendly, pliant Persian, doing his best to maintain British influence and to prevent Russia from scoring a point. He was least of all concerned with Baron de Reuter and a few of his engineers

---

54. H. M.'s Minister at Tehran to H. M.'s Secretary of State for Foreign Affairs, No. 134, Secret and Confidential, Tehran, October 13, 1873; ibid.

55. W. T. Thomson to Granville, No. 137, Secret and Confidential, Tehran, October 15, 1873; F. O. 60/351.

who were at that very time going through the motions of tracing a railway from Rasht to Tehran.

Mirzā Hoseyn Khān was still in fear of his life and begged Taylour Thomson for protection. The British minister tried to allay his fears and also pointed out the fatal results of foreign intervention in the case of Nāser ed-Din's first Prime Minister, Mirzā Taqi Khān Amir Nezām, who was put to death after the Shah had learned that he had obtained the protection of the Russian government through the efforts of Prince D. I. Dolgorukov, its minister in Tehran.[56] However, Mirzā Hoseyn Khān's fears were greatly exaggerated. The Shah remained loyal to his favorite. In another two weeks he was again a regular visitor at the palace and charged with the conduct of the delicate negotiations aimed at the cancellation of Reuter's concession.

On November 8, Mirzā Hoseyn Khān asked Taylour Thomson to call on him in connection with some very important business entrusted to him by the Shah. When they met the same day, Mirzā Hoseyn Khān, who was still without an official position, said that the Shah was in a difficult situation. His European trip had confirmed him in his desire to bestow upon Persia the benefits of progress and civilization, but upon his return

> he found himself unable to carry out the course he had laid down for himself in consequence of the events which had been brought about by the action of traitors left in high posts during his absence. He [Hoseyn Khān] said His Majesty found himself in so delicate a position towards his own subjects, whose cry was that he had delivered his country and religion into the hands of the Europeans, and that the opposition of the clergy in particular was so formidable that contrary to his wishes he believed it was necessary that the concession should be cancelled.[57]

Both the Shah and Mirzā Hoseyn Khān believed that they could void the concession on the basis of articles 8 and 23, which

---

56. W. T. Thomson to Granville, No. 133, Secret and Confidential, Tehran, October 13, 1873; ibid.

57. W. T. Thomson to Granville, No. 158, Tehran, November 8, 1873; F. O. 60/405.

provided for the commencement of work on the railway line within fifteen months of the signing of the contract. Mirzā Hoseyn Khān asked for Thomson's opinion on this, but the latter, realizing that the Persians had already decided the case and were only looking for loopholes in the text of the contract, advised him to consult some British law firm in London. Thomson stressed the fact that "from the time of his [Hoseyn Khān's] departure, when he gave me a certified copy of the concession, until now, I had held myself aloof from the question, speaking neither in favour nor against it." [58] Reporting to the Shah on his conversation with Thomson, Mirzā Hoseyn Khān quoted him as saying:

> From the day the negotiations with Reuter began, the British Government has remained entirely neutral, i.e., it has not negotiated with the Persian Government on this subject until today. It has given neither support and encouragement nor has it objected and placed obstacles. Officially I must follow the policy of my Government and remain neutral and silent.[59]

Mirzā Hoseyn Khān correctly interpreted Thomson's attitude as one of disinterestedness in the fate of the Reuter concession. On November 10 the *Tehran Gazette* announced its cancellation. The Russian minister, A. F. Beger, immediately inquired into the matter and was advised to seek further information from Mirzā Hoseyn Khān, who had been appointed by the Shah to deal with Henry M. Collins, now Reuter's agent in Tehran. Mirzā Hoseyn Khān was in turn instructed by the Shah to meet Beger and give him the desired information. No longer afraid of banishment or death, Mirzā Hoseyn Khān complained that Beger was the only foreign representative who had failed to call on him since his return to Tehran. He wrote Beger, requesting the latter to call. In reply Beger claimed to be too ill to leave the legation, but invited Mirzā Hoseyn Khān to visit him there. The latter obliged, and

58. Id.
59. Mirzā Hoseyn Khān Moshir od-Dowleh to Nāser ed-Din Shah, n.d.; cited in Teymuri, *Asre bikhabari*, p. 137.

two days later Beger, completely recovered from his diplomatic illness, returned the visit.⁶⁰

The conversation between Beger and Mirzā Hoseyn Khān was not unpleasant. The Russian minister was delighted with the turn of events. Hoseyn Khān communicated to him the text of a statement by the Shah reminding Gorchakov that he had lived up to his promise of canceling the Reuter concession and hoped: "You [Gorchakov] will not forget the promises of increased friendship between Iran and Russia which you made in the name of the Emperor." ⁶¹ The same point was stressed by Hoseyn Khān.⁶²

The new friendliness between the former Vizier and the Russian minister did not escape the observant Mr. W. T. Thomson. Evidently the Shah desired to establish good relations between his favorite and the Russian legation,

> but as yet I am unable to form a clear opinion as to the motive for doing so, whether it be with the view of engaging His Highness to adopt a Russian instead of an English policy, or merely for the temporary purpose of overcoming the formidable political crisis in which he is involved, and later to carry out the program of reforms meditated by the ex-Grand Vizier.⁶³

Whatever suspicions Thomson may have harbored in regard to Hoseyn Khān's loyalty to Britain were dispelled almost immediately by the former Grand Vizier's assurances of continued friendship. Hoseyn Khān went so far as to consult Thomson as to whether or not he should accept the post of Minister of Foreign Affairs when it was offered to him by the Shah early in December. He emphasized that his refusal would mean the retention in that office of Mirzā Said Khān, the notorious Russophile.

60. W. T. Thomson to Granville, No. 172, Confidential, Tehran, December 4, 1873; F. O. 60/405.

61. Nāser ed-Din Shah to Mirzā Hoseyn Khān Moshir od-Dowleh, n.d.; cited in Teymuri, p. 122.

62. Mirzā Hoseyn Khān Moshir od-Dowleh to Nāser ed-Din Shah [December 3, 1873]; cited in ibid., pp. 140–41.

63. W. T. Thomson to Granville, No. 172, Confidential, Tehran, December 4, 1873; F. O. 60/405.

Thomson did not hesitate: "I at once counselled its acceptance and offered him my congratulations on the spot." [64]

One of the first acts of the new Foreign Minister was the dispatch of a lengthy memorandum to Persian representatives abroad, explaining in great detail the Reuter concession and giving the official reasons for its cancellation. Though composed to justify the Shah's actions, the memorandum threw some light on the more obscure episodes of the Reuter case.

The memorandum began its review of events with the spring of 1872 when Reuter made his first proposal to build a railway across Iran, and sent a representative to Tehran to negotiate the project. The Persian government was willing, since His Majesty the Shah

> is and always has been anxious to promote civilization in his Kingdom, and was well aware of the great advantages which arise from a railway and of the wealth which would be derived by the public from this source, which would also improve the country and be the cause of increasing friendly intercourse with Foreign Crowns.

The contract was quickly negotiated and signed. Reuter received "certain concessions such as mines, waters, and forests," as a guarantee for the sums he had to spend for the construction of a railway from Rasht to Bushehr. Work had to begin within fifteen months of the signing of the contract on the penalty of forfeiture of £40,000 which Reuter had deposited as security in the Bank of England. In Article 23 of the concession, Reuter engaged to begin building the railway and working the mines and the forests simultaneously. The Persian government thought it strange that such vast tasks should be undertaken all at once,

> and yet Mr. Cotte, his Agent, made such statements as to the wealth, position and riches of Baron Reuter and his associates, that we entertained no further doubts that this gentleman would exert himself heartily in carrying out his engagement faithfully, and that he would not allow any delays to take place in the work, thus rendering it useless.

64. W. T. Thomson to Granville, No. 186, Confidential, Tehran, December 15, 1873; F. O. 60/352.

When he visited Europe with the Shah, Mirzā Hoseyn Khān continued, he learned that Reuter

> had no associates or partners and that he positively would not be able to perform the thousandth part of what he had engaged to do, and that his object in obtaining this concession was nothing but a mere speculation of purchase and sale with gain to himself, and that no trust or confidence could be placed on his promises and engagements.

To illustrate Reuter's bad faith, Mirzā Hoseyn Khān revealed that Reuter, anticipating his own financial needs in Iran, had offered to advance £200,000, payable in various European capitals, to the Shah during his trip. Within six months of each payment, its equivalent would be turned over to Reuter's account in Tehran. After the initial payment of £20,000, Mirzā Hoseyn Khān claimed, Reuter had refused to carry out the agreement, "thus putting us to great trouble."

The Persian Government was now convinced of Reuter's bad faith but

> out of respect for its signature and the promise it had made, it remained silent, awaiting the expiration of the time fixed by the contract, and imagining that perhaps he would be enabled to make his arrangements.

The fact that Reuter's engineers had leveled the road for a distance of about one mile did not change the government's opinion, as they were convinced that this was intended "merely to confuse matters." Moreover, no work had been started on mines, waters, and forests, not "even with the object of confusing matters." Under the circumstances, the Persian government "officially intimated to Baron Reuter, and to Mr. Collins, his Agent at Tehran, that the contract and its concessions were null and void." [65]

Hoseyn Khān's memorandum was, of course, less than completely honest. It failed to mention the eagerness with which the

---

65. His Highness the Minister of Foreign Affairs to the Persian representatives Abroad, undated [translated at the British Legation in Tehran], Enclosure in W. T. Thomson to Granville, No. 9, Tehran, January 21, 1874; F. O. 60/361.

Shah and his ministers welcomed anyone who would sign a contract, no matter what the contract contained. It failed to mention the enormous bribes received by Mirzā Hoseyn Khān himself, Mohsen Khān Moin ol-Molk, Malkam Khān, and others. Very understandably, it failed to mention Russian intervention and domestic difficulties, which were the only causes of the cancellation of the government's agreement with Baron Reuter. Whatever the legal strength of Persia's case may have been, the last point of the memorandum was well taken. Reuter had not begun construction, the one mile of leveled roadway to the contrary notwithstanding. Had Mirzā Hoseyn Khān had access to the files of the British Foreign Office, he could have cited a dispatch of his friend Taylour Thomson to Granville, telling of Reuter's engineers clearing the way through the forest near Rasht: "But this," the British minister had written, "was probably with the view to their being able to show the Shah on his return from Europe something which would cause His Majesty to believe that the Railway to connect the Port with the capital was really begun." [66]

Henry M. Collins, Reuter's agent in Tehran, had been notified of the cancellation of the concession on November 5. Several weeks passed before Reuter received the pertinent documents and could compose a reply. He termed the conclusions reached by the Persian government erroneous and claimed to have fulfilled all his obligations. Work on the railway had begun on September 11, 1873, in the presence of British and Russian consuls, and Reuter was in possession of a letter from the Minister of Public Works, thanking him for it officially in the name of the Shah.[67] In another statement, Reuter himself, who was now fighting not only for the dream of future profits, or the recovery of a considerable investment already made in bribes, surveys, and travel expenses for his agents, but also for the £40,000 of caution money deposited in the Bank of England and claimed by the Persian gov-

66. W. T. Thomson to Granville, No. 91, Confidential, Gulahek, August 2, 1873; F. O. 60/405.

67. Julius Reuter to Mirzā Hoseyn Khān Moshir od-Dowleh, Received January 7, 1874, Enclosure in W. T. Thomson to Granville, No. 8, Tehran, January 19, 1874; F. O. 60/406.

ernment, wrote a longer rebuttal which repeated the above points and made additional ones. The new document stressed the fact that the Persians had indulged in every form of procrastination from the day the concession was signed in July 1872. The text of the agreement, Reuter rightfully claimed, was not delivered to him for a very long time. His engineers could not leave England until January 1873, and it was spring before they were able to start surveying. Malkam Khān, appointed to discuss details with Reuter, dragged things out for months. In spite of lack of cooperation from Persian officials, dense forests, climate, and other difficulties, work had begun on September 1, as was witnessed on September 11 by the British and the Russian consuls at Rasht. Rails had been ordered and contracts placed to have them delivered at Anzali by October 20. Thus before October 2, the date by which work must begin, "not only had one kilometre of earthwork been completed, but ballast and sleepers had been laid throughout a great part of that length. Everything was indeed in readiness to place and fix the rails on the line as soon as they might arrive."[68] Reuter's apologia convinced no one, while his attempt to use the British and Russian consuls as witnesses to the fulfilment of his obligations to the Persian government provoked the British minister in Tehran to state in a dispatch to Lord Granville:

> I would observe that although the Consuls were present at the occasion . . . Mr. Abbot was not there in his Consular capacity, nor was he in a position to know whether the works of the Railway were opened in conformity with the Articles of the Concession granted by the Persian Government, and I am inclined to believe that this observation is equally applicable to the Russian as well as to the British Consul.[69]

The British government, which had been sceptical about Reuter's concession from the first, tacitly approved its cancellation. Lord Derby, Foreign Secretary in the government formed by

68. Summary by Mr. Collins, Enclosure in W. T. Thomson to Granville, No. 68, Tehran, March 23, 1874; ibid.
69. W. T. Thomson to Granville, No. 8, Tehran, January 19, 1874; ibid.

Disraeli as a result of a Conservative electoral victory in February, thus expressed its position:

> it appears to H. M.'s Govt. exceedingly doubtful whether the Persian Govt. could ever have carried out the Contract, as its effect would have been to place the administrative resources of the State at the disposal of a single individual who might have in turn alienated them to others or even to a Foreign Govt. And although Baron Reuter may have suffered disappointment and possibly even injustice, from the failure to secure the Contract, H. M.'s Govt. are not prepared to say that the Persian Govt. were [here the word "probably" had been originally written, then crossed out to strengthen the sentence] otherwise than well advised in cancelling it, when they came to appreciate its true bearing, at the earliest opportunity wh. [which] presented itself.[70]

In Tehran Henry Collins, Reuter's representative, in the name of his employer asked the British legation for assistance. W. T. Thomson informed him that he was already in receipt of definite instructions from Lord Derby, that his Lordship "looked upon Baron Reuter's undertaking entirely as a private one in which Her Majesty's Government cannot interfere," and that the British minister "was not authorized or instructed to use diplomatic influence or good offices on his behalf" except in obtaining for Reuter the hearing before the Persian government to which every British subject doing business in Persia was entitled.[71] Collins, who was considerably more patriotic than his employer, readily admitted that "the construction of the Railway from Resht was not of the general advantage which was to be desired, as it was Russia alone which in a commercial point of view would profit by it." [72]

On April 23, 1874, Collins informed the Persian government that Reuter had submitted his case to Her Majesty's Advocate General, whose opinion it was that there had been no just cause

70. Derby to Mr. [W. T.] Thomson, Draft, No. 34, Confidential, March 27, 1874; ibid.
71. W. T. Thomson to Derby, No. 84, Tehran, April 7, 1874; ibid.
72. Id.

Reuter and Falkenhagen

for the cancellation of the concession. Reuter had addressed himself to the Foreign Office and received a reply "of a favourable nature." Mirzā Hoseyn Khān frankly inquired of W. T. Thomson whether such instructions, "favourable to the pretensions of Baron Reuter in the matter of his Concession," had been received. The British minister's reply relieved the Persian government of any apprehensions they may have felt after talking with Collins. In guarded but clear language, Thomson repudiated Reuter:

> I said that it was the case that I had received an instruction . . . in that matter; that the term "favourable" was a very indefinite one and usually meant more than was applicable in this case; but that I was instructed to obtain for the representations of Baron Reuter's Agent to the Persian Government the same hearing to which the representations of other British Subjects who had entered into contracts with the Persian Government would be entitled.[73]

In London Reuter was conducting a campaign for the recovery of his "rights." He had written several letters to Lord Derby, protesting the actions of the Persian government and demanding redress. On March 27 he received a reply:

> this Government [the Foreign Office told him] could not bind themselves officially to protect your interests while carrying out your engagements with the Persian Government. Lord Derby looks upon the undertaking as an entirely private one in which HM's Govt. cannot interfere.[74]

On the same day Derby wrote Taylour Thomson concerning Reuter:

> I have informed this gentleman that although prepared to instruct you to obtain for his representative to the Persian Govt. the same hearing to which the representatives of any other British subject who had entered into a contract with that Government would be entitled, I cannot authorize you

---

73. W. T. Thomson to Derby, No. 99, Tehran, April 28, 1874; F. O. 60/406.
74. F. O. to Baron Reuter, Draft, March 27, 1874; ibid.

to use any diplomatic influence or good offices on his behalf except in this respect. You will accordingly strictly confine your proceedings in the matter within these limits.[75]

Lord Derby was prepared to concede that "although the Persian Govt. had no doubt done wisely in cancelling the contract, he could not but feel that the step involved considerable hardship upon Baron Reuter." Thomson was even instructed to let the Persian government know that although the British government would not support the Baron's contract, it "would be glad if he were allowed to benefit by any part of it which the Persian Govt. might think free of objection." [76] The Shah and Mirzā Hoseyn Khān considered the Reuter case closed and paid no attention to the mild, almost reluctant, representation of the British legation.

Having failed to obtain assistance by pleading, Julius Reuter resorted to blackmail. In a private and confidential letter to Derby, he declared that a Russian company had offered him certain terms for the transfer of his concession but that if

"high political reason" made it seem advisable to Lord Derby that he should surrender the concession to the Persian Govt. in consideration of an indemnity for his expenses and his labours, and if Lord Derby could bring about an amicable arrangement between the Persian Government and himself he should not be disposed to raise objections.[77]

The threat implied in Reuter's letter had to be taken seriously. The gentleman had never been trusted by the British, partly because of religious and social prejudice, Reuter being a Jew, partly because he was a foreigner, and, last but not least, because of his own often questionable conduct. Already in the summer of 1873, after Lord Granville's statement of British position in regard to his concession, rumors circulated in Tehran that Reuter "had proposed to the Russian Government to place himself under its protection." [78] In October 1873, W. T. Thomson telegraphed

75. Derby to T. Thomson, Draft, No. 33, March 27, 1874; ibid.
76. Foreign Office Memorandum, Baron Reuter's Concession, August 10, 1878; F. O. 60/416.
77. Id.
78. W. T. Thomson to Granville, No. 91, Confidential, Gulahek, August 2, 1873; F. O. 60/405.

the Foreign Office that Reuter had obtained the support of a number of great European powers and was determined to place his concession under international protection.[79]

In the summer of 1874, Reuter traveled to several European capitals, including St. Petersburg. With typical lack of precision, the Persian minister in St. Petersburg, Mirzā Abd or-Rahim Khān Sāed ol-Molk, reported that Reuter stayed in Russia "for two or three weeks."

> His main purpose [Sāed ol-Molk wrote] was to sell his rights to the Russian Government if possible; and if this did not work, to take some wealthy people into partnership. He even succeeded in softening up several people at the English Club which he visited every day. As soon as the authorities learned of this, they suggested to these people to keep away from him.[80]

Almost simultaneously W. T. Thomson reported his suspicions from Tehran. "I am inclined to believe," he wrote, "that an understanding has been come to directly or indirectly between Baron Reuter and the Russian Government on the subject."[81]

In his reply to Reuter's threat to sell his rights to the Russians, Lord Derby stated that, since the concession had been canceled, Reuter had nothing to sell. Yet the uneasiness felt at the Foreign Office showed through in Derby's suggestion that if Reuter abandoned all his claims, the British government would be prepared to instruct its minister in Tehran to seek compensation for "his actual expenses and labours, it being clearly understood that no claim could be pressed diplomatically."[82] Had the Foreign

---

79. W. T. Thomson to Granville, No. 136, Secret and Confidential, Tehran, October 15, 1873; ibid.

80. Mirzā Abd or-Rahim Khān Sāed ol-Molk to Mirzā Hoseyn Khān Moshir od-Dowleh, St. Petersburg, 4 Zel Qa'deh 1290 A.H. Cited in Teymuri, Asre bikhabari, p. 142.

81. W. T. Thomson to Derby, No. 149, Confidential, July 22, 1874; F. O. 60/406.

82. Foreign Office Memorandum, Baron Reuter's Concession, August 10, 1878; F. O. 60/416. Derby's letter dated July 6, 1874. Reuter eventually claimed £1,000,000 in compensation. Taylour Thomson had telegraphed home on September 17, 1874, that Reuter had actually incurred expenses to the sum of £200,000 and had promised £180,000 as bribes. "The balance therefore would

Office been certain that the Russian government would not buy Reuter's rights, he would not have been offered even this limited hope of assistance. Reuter, who had utterly failed to gain the backing of any government in Europe, and whose concession the Russians would under no circumstances wish to keep alive, replied that he did not consider his concession void "but expressed his willingness to relinquish it and accepted the assistance proffered." [83] The Reuter case, which for almost two years had agitated three capitals, seemed to be coming to an end. Nothing short of a major change in the political situation at Tehran could revive it. The sudden appearance of a new concession hunter accomplished such a change and breathed new life into the dying body of the Reuter concession.

The Shah's unguarded remark to Gorchakov that it was up to Russia to help Iran build railways was not forgotten in St. Petersburg. Once the threat to Russian interests from Reuter's monopoly of the Persian economy had been removed, the time was ripe for a countermove. In Russian eyes the indifference displayed by the British to the fate of a concession that could have given them complete control of the Shah's vast domain was in itself most encouraging. With Gorchakov's warm support, several projects were prepared in the latter part of 1873.[84] Baron von Falkenhagen, a retired general who had built railways in Transcaucasia, was put forward by the government and placed under the direction of the Ministry of Foreign Affairs.[85] Falkenhagen was instructed by the government to seek a concession for the construction of a railway from the Russian border at Jolfā on the Araxes to Tabriz, the second largest city of Persia and provincial capital of Iranian Āzarbāyjān. In addition he was to secure for the future railway company the right to exploit coal mines in a fifty-mile zone along the Jolfā-Tabriz track, should deposits of coal be discovered there.[86]

---

represent his personal labours." Evidently the Baron could not resist the temptation to cheat.

83. Reuter's reply was dated July 14, 1874; F. O. 60/416.

84. A. Popov, "Stranitsa iz istorii russkogo imperializma v Persii," *Mezhdunarodnaia zhizn*, Nos. 4–5 (1924), p. 134.

85. Cf. G. N. Curzon, *Persia and the Persian Question* (London, 1892), 1, 615–16. A. Popov, p. 135.

86. P. A. Rittikh, *Zheleznodorozhnyi put cherez Persiiu* (St. Petersburg, 1900), p. 12.

Though the Russian legation in Tehran was instructed not to take part "openly" in Falkenhagen's dealings with the Persian government, it was the legation that carried the main burden of negotiations.[87]

Falkenhagen arrived in Tehran in June 1874. An attempt was made to keep his mission secret, which served only to increase the curiosity of the British legation. In his first report on Falkenhagen, W. T. Thomson noted that "Unlike other Russian officers visiting this country he has held himself aloof from the European Society of the place." [88] Since no secret was ever kept in Tehran for more than a few days, Thomson quickly found out that Falkenhagen's object was to obtain a concession to build a railway from Jolfā to Tabriz.[89] In another few days Thomson discovered that Falkenhagen had "a letter of recommendation from the Russian Department for Foreign Affairs to the Russian Minister here," and that he had asked the Persian government to guarantee a 6½ percent return on the capital he would invest in the railway. From one of his numerous sources, Thomson learned also that Hāji Mirzā Javād, "the influential High Priest of Tabreez, ... has warmly recommended to the Shah the concession of this line and promised to use all his influence in Azerbaijan so that the requisite land be obtained free of charge from the several proprietors." [90]

Shortly after his arrival in Tehran and a friendly meeting with the Foreign Minister, Mirzā Hoseyn Khān, Falkenhagen submitted to the Persian government the draft of a concession for a railway. He engaged to build and operate one at his own expense between Jolfā and Tabriz. Article 1 stated:

> In order that he may connect this line with those of Europe, the Govt. of H. M. the Shah promises to induce the Govt. of H. M. the Emperor of Russia to construct a Railway from Tiflis to the Persian frontier at Julfa, or at some other point on the Aras near Julfa.

87. The Chancellor [Gorchakov] to the Minister in Tehran, Secret, February 12/24, 1874; as cited in A. Popov, p. 135.
88. W. T. Thomson to Derby, No. 135, Gulahek, June 25, 1874; F. O. 60/406.
89. Id.
90. W. T. Thomson to Derby, No. 144, Confidential, Gulahek, July 7, 1874; ibid.

The concession could not be transferred to any party except a company which Falkenhagen himself would form and which would conform "to the laws of Russia respecting Railway companies" (Article 2).

The construction of the Jolfā-Tabriz line would begin no later than six months after the commencement of construction of the Tiflis-Jolfā line. A sum to be specified later would be deposited by Falkenhagen in a Russian bank as security for the fulfillment of this obligation (Article 3).

The concession would run for a period specified in Article 3 and for forty-four years from the opening of the line, during which period the railway would be in the company's possession (Article 6).

Article 8 of Falkenhagen's draft read:

> The Govt. of H. M. the Shah guarantees to the Company, from the day of the completion and the commencement of the working of the Railway until the expiration of the term of this Concession, a yearly net profit of 6½ per cent. upon the capital of the Company—that is, 223,600 Russian Ducats [rubles] a year—representing the profit upon the nominal Capital of the Company and a sinking fund during a period of 44 years.
>
> If the working of the Tabreez Railway should not produce a net income of 223,600 Russian Ducats, in that case the Govt. of H. M. the Shah engages to make good the deficit, whatever it may be, by paying in cash to the Company every year half the amount due for the first six months on the 1-st of January and the next half on the 1-st of July, according to the European calendar; and to pay this money to the Company punctually during the whole term of the Concession from the day of the commencement of the working of the line.

The Company would in turn engage to pay the Persian Government 50 percent of its net profits, whenever such profits are made, until it got back all the money it may have paid out as guarantee and 5 percent interest (Article 9). However, to ensure that the annual profit of 6½ percent upon the whole nominal capital of the Company—which is the minimum profit guaranteed by Persia—may be received by the Company at the periods stipulated in Art. VIII, the Persian Govt. makes over to the Company for the entire period of the Concession the Customs of Tabreez, which shall be transferred to an international Board of Customs at the village of Julfa, or at some other part of the frontier, which will be fixed in a separate convention between the Govt. of H. M. the Shah, and that of Russia. The Govt. of H. M. the Shah promises to make at once an arrangement with that of Russia for the conclusion of a convention for the purpose of establishing on the River Aras a united Russian and Persian Custom House under an International administration similar to those which exist on the Great Railways between some of the European States. [Article 10]

In addition to the guaranteed 6½ percent return on its investment, Falkenhagen's company would take 10 percent of net profits for a reserve fund to be used for repairs, building, etc. Should any money remain in the fund at the time the concession expired, it would be distributed to the shareholders (Article 11).

At the expiration of the concession, the Persian government would take possession of the railway with all its rolling stock, except for engines and carriages,

> which it may have added to those which existed when the line commenced to work . . . All buildings, and movable or immovable property, which the Company may have purchased or erected with its own money, independently of that assigned for the construction of the Railway, shall remain and be considered as the property of the Company. [Article 12]

The company would be entitled to fix passenger and other rates (Article 13), build a telegraph line along the track (Article 14), and be allowed to mine coal, if any were found, within a fifty-mile zone along the entire length of the railway (Article 17). The company would be exempted from customs dues and taxes on materials and tools needed for building and running the line (Article 19), as well as from taxes on transactions, land, or income (Article 20).

The company would appoint a board of directors: "This agency and all those in the service of the Company shall be under the protection of the Russian Legation and consulates in accordance with sacred treaties" (Article 21). All disputes involving the company would be adjudicated by a mixed commission, two of whose members would be appointed by the company and two by the Persian government, with the Russian consul general presiding. Decisions, which would be binding, would be reached by a majority vote, the president being allowed to break a tie vote (Article 22). Such were the major provisions of Falkenhagen's draft.[91]

Though Falkenhagen's proposed concession was much smaller in scope than the one granted to Reuter, in every other respect its terms were more onerous. What purported to be a private enterprise was actually an attempt to impose Russian government control upon a part of Persia and do it at Persia's expense. Under Article 8 the Persian government would be obliged to subsidize the railroad, but since the Shah's financial resources were at best uncertain, as Article 9 frankly acknowledged, the customs of Tabriz would be mortgaged. Indeed, this was the first attempt to make the Shah hypothecate the customs.

The risk to the investor has been the classical justification of profit on capital. Falkenhagen, or rather the Russian government, was not prepared to take any risks. He would get his 6½ percent free of all taxes, even if his company never made a single *shāhi*. The Persian government could not even look forward to the acquisition of a railway and rolling stock forty-four years from the date on which operations began. Article 12 provided that Persia would take over only those engines or cars which had been in service for forty-four years, by which time nothing would have been left of them.

The Persian government was not given any control over the

---

91. Draft of Concession for a Railway from the Town of Tabreez to the village of Julfa, Enclosure in W. T. Thomson to Derby, No. 169, Confidential, Gulahek, August 13, 1874; ibid.

railway, and the commission for settling disputes was so organized, in Article 22, that every dispute must inevitably be won by Russia. In fact the Russians would sit in judgment on themselves. Perhaps the most frightening aspect of the proposed concession was its official character, the need to deal with the Russian government, the obligation to abide by Russian laws regulating the activities of Russian railways, the joint operation of Āzarbāyjān customs, the authority of the Russian consul general in settling disputes.

Both the Shah and his Foreign Minister understood the implications of Falkenhagen's proposals; neither was patriotic enough to turn them down outright. The only thing that bothered the two was the possible loss of money through the obligation to guarantee Falkenhagen a 6½ percent return on capital invested and giving up of control over Tabriz customs. The Shah and his minister were not prepared to protect the country, but they would jealously guard the royal purse. Mirzā Hoseyn Khān freely admitted this to W. T. Thomson, whom he told that, as long as Falkenhagen insisted upon the articles on customs and guarantees, Persia would refuse to grant the concession, but might agree to it should these be withdrawn.[92]

Procrastination seemed the best method of dealing with Falkenhagen. He was allowed to wait in Tehran but received no answer to his proposals. Had he been representing a private firm, as Cotte and Collins had, the method would have succeeded. However, behind Falkenhagen stood A. F. Beger, the Russian minister. Repeatedly and insistently he urged the Shah to sign the contract. On July 30, 1874, at a private audience with the Shah, with Mirzā Hoseyn Khān present, the Russian minister accused the latter of being hostile to Russia and insisted that the Shah accept Falkenhagen's proposals. The scene was immediately reported by Mirzā Hoseyn Khān to W. T. Thomson.[93]

A few days later Beger called upon several Persian ministers and finally upon Mirzā Hoseyn Khān. He complained about the

92. W. T. Thomson to Derby, No. 168, Confidential, Gulahek, August 13, 1874; ibid.

93. W. T. Thomson to Derby, No. 162, Most Secret, Gulahek, August 4, 1874; ibid.

suspension of the negotiations, noted that his British colleague, W. T. Thomson, "had made frequent visits of late to His Highness," and asked whether the suspension of negotiations was brought about on Thomson's advice or was the work of Hoseyn Khān alone. Mirzā Hoseyn Khān admitted that Thomson was kept informed of the negotiations but claimed that he himself, since Beger's attack on him in the presence of the Shah, had withdrawn from them.[94]

The pressure applied by the Russian legation had grown so intense that the Shah, on Hoseyn Khān's advice, sent a pathetic telegram to the Persian minister at St. Petersburg, begging to be relieved:

> Say to Gortchakoff that the Russian Minister and General Falkenhagen insist upon having an immediate answer regarding Railway concession; that an affair of this nature cannot be terminated in a few days, and is not a subject for official negotiation; that full time should be allowed to study the question; that the Russian Legation interferes as if this matter were an official one; that in the matter of the Reuter Concession from the Commencement until now neither the British Government nor its Legation have interfered either verbally or in writing.[95]

As was his custom in times of stress and crisis, Nāser ed-Din Shah left the harrowing task of confronting Beger to his ministers and departed the capital to indulge in the pleasures of the chase.

The Shah's plea had no effect in St. Petersburg. In Tehran, Falkenhagen demanded a reply to his proposals so that he "may, if it be possible meet those [Persian] views, or else return without further loss of time to my country."[96] On September 17, 1874,

---

94. W. T. Thomson to Derby, No. 168, Confidential, Gulahek, August 13, 1874; ibid.

95. W. T. Thomson to Derby, No. 166, Most Secret, Gulahek, August 11, 1874; ibid.

96. Correspondence between General Falkenhagen and the Persian Minister of Foreign Affairs, Enclosure in W. T. Thomson to Derby, No. 211, Gulahek, October 8, 1874; ibid.

Mirzā Hoseyn Khān informed Falkenhagen that the Shah refused to accept the articles dealing with the guarantee and the customs. "Whenever these two conditions are removed from the Convention the Persian Ministers will be ready to negotiate with you, and will be most happy to enter into the necessary discussion respecting the other articles." [97]

Falkenhagen sensed evasion in Hoseyn Khān's letter. Pressing the issue, he wrote back that he was unable to give an answer concerning the guarantee and the customs without consulting his "partners" but would like to have the definitive views of the Persian government on the other articles before leaving for Russia and consultations with his "associates."

> The best plan is for the Persian Ministers to take into consideration the whole of the terms of my concession with full care and justice, whichever is favorable let them accept and show the difficulties existing in the others, so that I may place the whole case before my partners at the same time when the business will be settled at once.

In concluding, Falkenhagen sounded a threatening note:,

> I am quite certain that the Persian Ministers will not, in consideration of the endeavours made by the Russian Govt. in carrying out this desire of H. M. the Shah, make any such exorbitant proposals to me as will be impossible for a company of any nation or country to accept, and the exertions of the Russian Govt. in this affair will not remain fruitless.[98]

At this stage all pretense was dropped, and the dealings of the supposedly private entrepreneur with Mirzā Hoseyn Khān were revealed as an encounter between hapless Persia and her mighty northern neighbor.

On September 21 Beger renewed his assault on Mirzā Hoseyn Khān's already frayed nerves, informing the latter of a telegram just received from St. Petersburg and reporting that the Russian ambassador in London had written,

97. Id.
98. Letter dated September 20, 1874; ibid.

that a foreign influence had been exerted over the Shah to spoil (gâter) the affair Falkenhagen and that this foreign influence had been instigated (provoquée) by him [the Persian Minister of Foreign Affairs] . . . [Beger further stated] . . . that all this had been made known to the Emperor and that the Emperor was indignant at his conduct (et que l'Empereur était indigné de votre conduite).[99]

Mirzā Hoseyn Khān was coming to the end of his diplomatic resources. The only way to stop Russia from forcing Falkenhagen's concession on Persia was to appeal for British support. He had prudently kept Taylour Thomson au courant, finding in him a sympathetic, though by no means disinterested, listener. At the Foreign Office Lord Tenderden proposed to use Reuter's claims to prevent Russia from obtaining that which a British subject had lost. The Foreign Secretary, Lord Derby, hesitated. From Tehran came W. T. Thomson's reports, which indicated that General Falkenhagen, who was now negotiating with the Minister of Public Works, Hasan Ali Khān, might, for political reasons, sign the concession without the guarantee clauses.[100] Lord Derby hesitated still. A few days later the Persian minister in London, Mirzā Malkam Khān, saw Lord Tenderden at the Foreign Office and "pressed him to use every effort" to prevent the realization of Falkenhagen's concession: ". . . 'would the English tamely look on while such a Concession as that of Baron Reuter was wrested from her [Britain's] influence at the dictation of Russia and transferred to the Russian Govt.?' "[101]

While Lord Derby hesitated, W. T. Thomson made some preliminary moves for the revival of Reuter's claims as a weapon against Russian demands. On October 8 he mentioned to Mirzā Hoseyn Khān, in words intended for A. F. Beger at the Russian legation, that

> as improper pressure had been exerted by the Russian Government in furthering General Falkenhagen's contract, if it

99. W. T. Thomson to Derby, No. 215, Very Confidential, Tehran, October 12, 1874; ibid.
100. W. T. Thomson to Derby, No. 211, Gulahek, October 8, 1874; ibid.
101. Minute by Lord Tenderden, October 30, 1874; "Railways in Persia," Memorandum by R. C. Dickie; Persia No. 6824, February 23, 1911; F. O. 371/1185.

should be conceded to him Her Majesty's Government would be entitled to change the employment of their good offices in the matter of the Reuter Concession, to which they had hitherto limited themselves, into official intervention on their part.[102]

The conversation was followed by a brief note, again intended for Russian eyes:

> Sachant qu'une concession pour la construction d'un chemin de fer entre Djoulfa et Tabriz, à la suite de l'intervention de la Légation de Russie, est en voie de négotiation . . . permettez-moi de vous observer que comme toute concession de cette nature serait nuisible aux intérêts du Baron Reuter dont la concession, quoique déclarée nulle et vide par le Gouvt. Persan, reste encore une question ouverte, il est de mon devoir de vous prévenir par ce moyen que je réserve à mon Gouvt. le droit de prendre les mesures qu'il jugerait convenables dans les circonstances ci-dessus mentionnées.[103]

Reuter did not need much encouragement to renew his claims. Henry Collins sent Mirzā Hoseyn Khān a protest couched in legal language, stating:

> Now these Presents witness that it having come to the knowledge of the said Baron Julius de Reuter that the Persian Ministers have granted, or are about to grant to a Russian individual, party, Company, or Association a concession for the construction of a line of Railway from the Russo-Persian frontier at Julfa to Tabreez, I, the undersigned duly appointed Agent to Baron Julius de Reuter at Tehran, declare such concession to be an infringement and violation of the right absolutely and exclusively conferred on the said Baron Julius de Reuter . . . and in his name and on his behalf I hereby formally and solemnly protest against such a proceed-

---

102. W. T. Thomson to Derby, No. 211, Gulahek, October 8, 1874; F. O. 60/406.

103. W. T. Thomson to Moshir od-Dowleh [Mirzā Hoseyn Khān], October 17, 1874; Enclosure in W. T. Thomson to Derby, No. 220, Tehran, October 17, 1874; ibid.

ing holding as I here do the said Persian Government solely responsible for all losses and damages which Baron Julius de Reuter may thereby directly or indirectly sustain.[104]

Mirzā Hoseyn Khān replied that the Persian government had repeatedly explained the grounds on which the concession had been annulled, and that in view of its cancellation the Persian government had complete freedom of action, while Reuter's "so called protest" was illegal.[105]

The British minister, who finally received Derby's instructions to intervene officially in Reuter's behalf, supported Collins' protest with a blunt note, again intended not so much for the Persian government as for the Russian legation. Thomson recalled that the British government would not support Reuter's contract "as it stood," but now

> Her Majesty's Government feel that Baron Reuter has a good cause to complain that if the Persian Govt. desire or consent to have a Railway constructed to Tabreez the Concession should be granted to any one else, and I am therefore instructed to urge upon the Persian Govt. the propriety of suspending any action in regard to the Concession to the Russian Company until Baron Reuter's claims have been duly considered and a settlement arrived at with him.[106]

The Russian legation was fully aware that it had a new opponent in Tehran. It would be almost impossible to intimidate the Persian government into signing Falkenhagen's contract now that it had British support. If a Russian railway were to be built to Tabriz, a quick compromise with the Shah was necessary. Unfortunately, no Russian documents dealing with this affair have been published, nor are Persian sources sufficient to determine exactly

---

104. Henry M. Collins, Agent, Baron Julius de Reuter to Mirzā Hoseyn Khān Moshir od-Dowleh, Minister of Foreign Affairs, Undated, Enclosure in W. T. Thomson to Derby, No. 250, Tehran, November 30, 1874; ibid.

105. Mirzā Hoseyn Khān to Henry M. Collins, Tehran, November 15, 1874, Enclosure in W. T. Thomson to Derby, No. 250, Tehran, November 30, 1874; ibid.

106. W. T. Thomson to Mirzā Hoseyn Khān Moshir od-Dowleh, November 14, 1874, Enclosure in W. T. Thomson to Derby, No. 250, November 30, 1874; ibid.

what transpired in late November and early December 1874. Circumstantial evidence suggests that Falkenhagen, without consulting Gorchakov, signed a contract with the Persian government on the basis of the original Draft Concession but without the guarantee clauses. It is reported that, to induce the Shah to sign the contract, Falkenhagen gave Mirzā Hoseyn Khān

> as a douceur, a promissory note for Fifty thousand (50,000) Russian Imperials to be cashed when the Concession was made effective, and that this document was immediately transferred by the Minister to the Shah, who deposited it in the private coffer which His Majesty reserves for the safe keeping of documents having reference to matters personal to himself.[107]

The Russian government was disappointed. It had planned to acquire an important concession at no cost to itself. The contract had been signed, but its implementation involved two extremely distasteful things—the investment of a fairly large sum without any guarantee of profit or even a prospect of a return, and the exacerbation of relations with Britain. Russia's finances were in the state of perpetual crisis. Her domestic railways were being built with foreign, largely French, capital. The Ministry of Finance must have been strongly opposed to a scheme that promised nothing but loss of money. The old Chancellor, Prince Gorchakov, must have felt that the gain to accrue to Russia as a result of controlling a railway to Tabriz would not be commensurate with the price she would have to pay in antagonizing Britain. There were other and more important issues on which the two great empires might clash. Falkenhagen was instructed to write Mirzā Hoseyn Khān that his "Company" declined the railway concession which had been signed by him and the Persian government but would be prepared to undertake it if the Persian government would insert into the text the old clauses about the guarantee and the customs.[108] In Tehran the dragoman of the Russian legation told Mirzā Hoseyn Khān that the Tsar was

107. W. T. Thomson to Derby, No. 19, Confidential, Tehran, February 13, 1875; F. O. 60/407.
108. W. T. Thomson to Derby, No. 2, Tehran, January 4, 1875; ibid.

greatly vexed by "the unacceptable terms on which the Falkenhagen Concession had been concluded." [109]

The Persian government, fearful of the consequences which might follow the collapse of Falkenhagen's concession, made friendly overtures to Russia, even proposing new and more favorable terms to the general. In a letter to the latter dated January 19, 1875, Mirzā Hoseyn Khān wrote that the Shah, "being desirous for certain reasons that this important transaction should not be set aside," was willing to guarantee the Company a yearly income of 102,000 tumāns by making up the difference between that sum and the amount gained from the operation of the Jolfā-Tabriz railway. As for the question of customs, Hoseyn Khān was willing to assign their revenues to the company. "But the Persian Govt. will itself recover the revenue of the place in question and pay the amount to your Company." [110] The guarantee now being offered to Falkenhagen amounted to 3 percent on the Russian investment. Had fear of financial risk been the dominant factor in Russia's considerations in regard to the concession, she could have accepted the offer. However, it had already been decided to abandon the entire project. On May 5, 1875, Falkenhagen telegraphed Mirzā Hoseyn Khān, requesting that the "Railway Concession granted to him be considered null and void." [111]

As far as the two rival powers were concerned the concession issue was closed. Only Reuter failed to understand that once again he was the loser. He persisted in his attempt to regain at least a part of his original concession, or be compensated in cash. Day after day Henry Collins bombarded Mirzā Hoseyn Khān with complaints, claims, and proposals; but the British minister, who had lost all interest in Reuter's affairs as soon as Falkenhagen withdrew from the scene, failed to provide him with diplomatic support. On October 2, Collins left Tehran. A year later the French Minister in Tehran noted in a letter:

109. W. T. Thomson to Derby, No. 5, Tehran, January 5, 1875; ibid.
110. Mirzā Hoseyn Khān Moshir od-Dowleh to General Falkenhagen, Tehran, January 19, 1875, Translation, Enclosure in W. T. Thomson to Derby, No. 16, Tehran, January 28, 1875; ibid.
111. W. T. Thomson to Derby, No. 64, Tehran, May 6, 1875; ibid.

En y réfléchissant, en effet, la concession Reuter a été dans les dernières années, très utile à la Légation d'Angleterre pour combattre toutes les tentatives du meme genre qui ont été faites en Perse. C'est sur les droits du Baron Reuter que M. Thomson s'est appuyé pour protester contre le chemin de fer Falkenhagen . . . L'Angleterre ayant toujours cherché à dominer en Perse à l'exclusion des autres nations et luttants constamment dans ce but avec la Russie, je ne serais pas étonné que le Cabinet de St. James ait fait comprendre au Baron Reuter que le maintien de son agence était nécessaire aux intérêts britanniques à Téhéran.[112]

112. De Balloy à M. le Duc Decazes, Ministre des Affaires Etrangères, Direction Politique, 16° 13; Téhéran 13/27 Octobre 1876; Archive des Affaires Etrangères, Perse, tome 37.

3

"Pénétration Pacifique": Rivers, Railways, Trade, and Foreign Advisers

Unkind fate placed Persia between the Russian hammer and the British anvil. The struggles of the two giant empires, whether for Constantinople, Central Asia, or the Far East, were instantly reflected and echoed at Tehran. Through the two decades of Russia's uninterrupted advance in Turkestan and Transcaspia, Persia felt the pressure from both St. Petersburg and London. Though truly isolationist in spirit, her government was constantly threatened, or seduced, into involvement in issues that were not of her making and could result in nothing but harm.

Neither Russia nor Britain could leave Iran alone. Her richest, most populous provinces were easily accessible to Russian armies from the Caucasus, while the Gulf shore lay at the mercy of the British navy. Both great powers had had diplomatic relations with Persia for several centuries and, since the time of Napoleon, maintained permanent missions in Tehran. Trade between Persia and her two neighbors was conducted on a rather small scale, but the potential value of her market was recognized, keeping alive hopes for a great commercial future.

Though driven by different motives, Russia and Britain pursued somewhat similar policies. Each endeavored to impose her own hegemony upon Persia, through a combination of means, the more important of which were: influence over the persons of the Shah and his chief ministers; commerce; concessions; intimidation. To use any of these, Britain and Russia each needed to provide herself with access to as much of Persian territory as possible, while denying it to others. This explains the crucial importance attained by the problem of transportation in the last quarter of the nineteenth century.

"Pénétration Pacifique" 149

Every major city of Persia was sufficiently distant either from the Caspian Sea or from the Persian Gulf to make the transportation of goods and persons difficult. On the way from Anzali to Tehran, the Alborz range must be crossed. Traveling from Baghdad to Kermānshāh and Hamadān one has to negotiate the Zagros. It is no easier to climb to the central plateau from the Persian Gulf coast. In the absence of roads and railways, neither goods nor armed forces could easily make their way into the interior. The river Kārun provided the only water route of some length into the southwestern corner of Iran.

As early as 1871, Gray, Paul and Company, an established commercial firm at Bushehr, felt capable of organizing a steamer service on the Kārun between Mohammareh (now Khorramshahr) and Shushtar. The Company believed that while it took thirty to thirty-five days for goods to reach Esfahān from Bushehr by caravan, the Kārun would make it possible for the same goods to reach Esfahān from Mohammareh in ten days. The company asked the British political resident in the Persian Gulf to request the British minister in Tehran to negotiate a navigation concession with the Persian government.[1] The resident, Lewis Pelly, forwarded the request to Mr. Charles Alison with a covering letter supporting Gray, Paul and Company. Having first visited the Kārun with Sir James Outram (presumably during the Anglo-Persian war in 1857), Pelly wrote, he had "long been impressed with the physical advantages of the line." Obviously goods shipped into the interior of Persia via the Kārun would have a competitive advantage over those shipped by land.[2]

The Government of India, when informed of Gray, Paul and Company's request, expressed its interest and asked Alison to inform it of the results of his negotiations with the Persian government.[3] The latter refused to discuss the issue. A few years

---

1. Gray, Paul and Co. to Lieutenant-Colonel Lewis Pelly, H.B.M.'s Political Resident in the Persian Gulf, Bushire, July 22, 1871; F.O. 60/336.
2. Lieutenant-Colonel Lewis Pelly to His Excellency Charles Alison, No. $\frac{817}{38}$, Bushire, July 31, 1871; ibid.
3. C. Aitchison, Secretary of the Government of India, to C. Alison, No. 2232, Foreign Department, Political, Simla, October 17, 1871; ibid.

earlier the Persian government, having partly recovered from the disruption and demoralization inflicted upon the country by the savage suppression of the Bābi movement, and having somewhat restored its army after it had been shattered by the British in 1857 and the Turkomans in 1861, made an attempt to reimpose its authority on various border regions where local rulers had become practically independent. The Shah pressed for the return to Persian sovereignty of Bandar-Abbās, which had been occupied by the Imam of Masqat (Muscat), and, simultaneously moved against the various khans of Seistān, Kelāt, and Mekrān.

The Persian government felt that its relations with the khans were a purely domestic matter and tried to keep the British out of negotiations with them.[4] However, when in March 1869 the Persians advanced on Kelāt, the Viceroy of India and the Governor of Bombay asked Charles Alison to intervene. Mirzā Said Khān, the Foreign Minister, explained in a memorandum that the territories in question had always been recognized as Persian, and that the government was only trying to reestablish order.[5] The Government of India refused to accept this reasoning. In 1842 it had concluded an agreement with the Khan of Kelāt, promising him assistance against "foreign powers," and in 1854 obtained from him the pledge to "enter into no negotiations with other States" without British consent. Now the Government of India urged London to deal firmly with the Shah and settle the question once for all, otherwise the British position and authority in Baluchestān would suffer.[6]

Simultaneously Persia became involved with Britain in a dispute, unsettled to this day, over the island of Bahreyn, where the various members of the ruling Khalifeh family engaged in fratricide and practiced piracy as a source of income supplementary to that derived from pearl fishing. During one of the recurrent periods of anarchy the British had interfered, and had placed the

---

4. R. Thomson to the Viceroy of India [Lord Mayo], August 29, 1869; L.I., 5, 1869.

5. W. J. Dickson to Alison, Tehran, March 16, 1869; Enclosure in Alison to the Earl of Mayo, Tehran, March 23, 1869; L.I., 4, 1869.

6. The Government of India to the Duke of Argyll, Secretary of State for India, Foreign Department, No. 22, Fort Williams, November 13, 1869; L.I., 5, 1869.

son of the recently murdered Sheykh Mohammad in power, getting rid of the murderer, who happened to be the late Sheykh's brother. Lieutenant Colonel Lewis Pelly, British resident in the Persian Gulf stationed at Bushehr, had conducted the operation and later prevented Persian authorities from reestablishing their nominal authority over the island.[7]

Realizing that the pirate sheykhs of the Gulf could not be controlled without sea power, and interpreting an ambiguous statement made by Clarendon on April 29, 1869, to mean that Britain would restore Bahreyn to Persia if the latter were able to exercise naval control, the Persian government applied to France for advice and assistance in acquiring a warship.[8] In a dispatch to the Viceroy of India, Charles Alison explained that the Shah considered that the possession of a few ships in the Gulf would enable him to assert his authority and protect his interests with greater efficacy against "the designs proceeding from Muscat," and might be useful against Bahreyn.[9] Mr. Alison felt that Britain should not create obstacles to the legitimate attempts of Persia to defend her shores and islands.

The Government of India took a less generous view. It expressed the opinion that it was "neither necessary nor expedient that the Shah should maintain in the Persian Gulf any number of armed craft." The British navy was sufficient to keep the peace in the Gulf. Persia needed ships for the sole purpose of asserting her "unreasonable claims" to suzerainty over Bahreyn. Under such circumstances the Government of India felt that it had a duty "to remonstrate against the organization of such an armed force as might endanger a State, the independence of which we are bound to maintain."[10] London followed India's advice. Pressure was

---

7. *Letters from India*, volume 6 for 1869, contains the correspondence between Alison and Clarendon, W. T. Thomson and Clarendon, Pelly and W. T. Thomson, and various other relevant materials. For a study of the Bahreyn question from the Persian point of view, see F. Adamiyat, *Bahrein Islands* (New York, 1955). For the controversial Clarendon note of April 29, 1869, see J. C. Hurewitz, *Diplomacy in the Near and Middle East* (Princeton, 1956), 1, 172–73.

8. Thomson to Clarendon, No. 71, Tehran, October 19, 1869; L.I., 7, 1870.

9. Alison to the Viceroy, Tehran, May 29, 1870; ibid.

10. Government of India to the Duke of Argyll Secret, Simla, July 22, 1870; ibid.

brought to bear on the Shah and he was compelled to drop the plan of creating a navy.

Incidents such as these did not endear the British to the Persian government. Only the greater fear of Russia, who had occupied Qizil-Su (Krasnovodsk), an area the Shah considered his own, prevented him from joining Russia against Britain. The Shah certainly would not open to British steamships the only navigable river of his Empire, or at least would resist the opening as long as he possibly could.

The Kārun issue was revived in the latter part of 1875. By that time Russia had conquered Khiva, connected the Black Sea port of Poti with Tiflis by a railway which was soon to reach the Caspian at Baku, and established regular steamship service between the mouth of the Volga and Persian ports. Russian goods appeared in the bazars at Esfahān and even further south.[11] The firms of Gray, Paul and Company and Gray, Dawes Company urged again that measures be taken for the opening of the Kārun, while the Government of India declared its willingness to subsidize the navigation of that river.[12]

The Persian government was in trouble. It had provoked Russian hostility by granting a monopolistic concession on most of the country's resources to Reuter, then cancelled the concession and turned a part of it over to a Russian subject, General Falkenhagen. This alarmed the British. The Falkenhagen concession fell through, but it, and Reuter's monopoly, left a residue of anger and suspicion. Persia was unwilling to antagonize the British further, especially when her territory in the northeast was threatened by Russia. In view of all this, the Shah appointed a council of twenty-one ministers, princes, and high officials to study the Kārun problem. After a month's deliberation the council endorsed the idea of free navigation.

11. Major B. V. Champain, Memorandum on the proposal to establish communication between Central Persia and the Sea by way of the Karoon River, Bushire, March 30, 1876, Enclosure No. 2 in Government of India, Foreign Department, No. 21, Secret; L.I., 8, 1876.

12. Memorandum by L. Pelly on *Messrs. Gray, Dawes'* scheme for developing the line of trade via Karoon between Mohammerah and Ispahan, Enclosure No. 1 in Government of India, Foreign Department, No. 21, Secret; ibid.

The British, who had assumed that the matter had been settled to their satisfaction, were very much disappointed when Mirzā Said Khān, Minister of Foreign Affairs, informed a Mr. Mackenzie of the Gray, Dawes Company that Persia would claim navigation and port dues customary in Europe. To Mackenzie's protestations that such dues were collected only for the maintenance of port facilities, docks, and lighthouses, none of which existed on the Kārun, Mirzā Said Kāhn replied that his government would build a lighthouse. Commenting on this unexpected development, an English officer wrote:

> No one acquainted with the Persian character can be otherwise than certain that this arrangement is simply a subterfuge and a pretext for the indefinite postponement of the whole question. Until the interview mentioned above nothing whatever had been said on the subject of dues, and it is more than probable, if not abundantly clear, that the idea was suggested by the Russian Legation, who are of course perfectly alive to the effect which the encouragement of southern trade would ere long have on Russian commerce and political influence in the Persian Empire.[13]

The Government of India was convinced that Russia was behind Persia's refusal to allow free navigation. It brought to the attention of the Cabinet in London an article from the *Sankt-Peterburgskie Vedomosti* of March 18/30, 1876, which dwelt "with scarcely concealed satisfaction on the alleged definitive rejection of the Project by the Shah's Government."[14] The British minister in Tehran, W. Taylour Thomson, felt that the case had been badly handled. Acting for Gray, Dawes Company, Mackenzie had appointed a Persian, Mokhber od-Dowleh, head of the Telegraph Department, as his agent. This lead to intrigues among the Persians, and difficulties arose. Though Thomson never states it in so many words, one suspects that Mokhber od-Dowleh was bribed to use his influence and to corrupt others to

13. Major B. V. Champain's Memorandum, Bushire, March 30, 1876, Enclosure No. 2 in Government of India, Foreign Department, No. 21, Secret; ibid.

14. The Government of India to Lord Salisbury, Secretary of State for India, Foreign Department, No. 21, Secret, Simla, May 11, 1876; ibid.

take a favorable stand on the Kārun question. Thomson was "determined to await a favorable moment before pressing this matter further upon the Persian Government," but refused to guess when the favorable moment might arrive.[15]

The energetic and impatient Viceroy of India, Lord Lytton, was angered by Thomson's slow tactics. In a dispatch whose tone was unusually severe, the Government of India told Thomson that it regarded the opening of the Kārun of importance to the interests of India. "And the Governor-General [Lytton] in Council cannot refrain from expressing his regret that Your Excellency should not see your way to arriving at an early understanding with the Persian Government on this subject." [16] Lytton also complained to Salisbury in London. If Britain were to wait for a favorable opportunity, such an opportunity might never arise. Thomson should be instructed to create the opportunity.[17] Salisbury transmitted Lytton's message to Lord Derby at the Foreign Office, and Thomson was told that he had not done enough for the opening of the Kārun. Defending his record, he protested that he had done his best, but that the Persian government was not always willing to do what was asked of it, especially if Russia was opposed. "It is only to be expected that in all matters favorable to our political and commercial interest in this country and opposed to their own, the influence of the Russian Mission here would be adversely exerted." However, the British had also had victories. Thomson noted the Falkenhagen concession among "the schemes which have been proposed for the benefit of their trade in the north of Persia," and which "have been not unsuccessfully opposed by us." [18]

In obedience to his instructions, Thomson handed the Persian Foreign Minister, now Mirzā Hoseyn Khān Moshir od-Dowleh, a note in which he reiterated the argument in favor of the open-

15. W. T. Thomson to the Viceroy, Tehran, July 1, 1876, Enclosure No. 1 in Government of India, Foreign Department, No. 43, Secret; L.I., 9, 1876.

16. T. H. Thornton, Secretary to the Government of India, to W. T. Thomson, No. 2186P, Simla, September 25, 1876; Government of India, Foreign Department, No. 42, Secret; ibid.

17. Government of India to Salisbury, No. 42, Simla, September 28, 1876; ibid.

18. W. T. Thomson to Derby, Commercial, No. 9, Tehran, October 30, 1876; L.I., 12, 1877.

ing of the Kārun to all flags. The English and Indian governments were anxious, in the interests of commerce, that navigation be allowed without delay. "They express also their surprise and regret that the Persian Government should have deferred so long the adjustment of a matter gravely affecting the welfare of this country, and the interest of friendly powers holding commercial relations with Persia."[19] Thomson did not go beyond such representations. The Persian government continued to evade the issue, and the matter was dropped.

Though Russia concentrated her main efforts on the conquest of Central Asia, she did not relinquish Persia to Britain. The problem of access to Persia's interior was as important to her as it was to her rival. In 1870 the Russian minister, A. F. Beger, obtained from the Shah the long-coveted permission for Russian ships to enter the lagoon at Anzali.[20] In 1873–74 he fought successfully against Reuter and unsuccessfully for Falkenhagen. The failure of the latter's concession did not put an end to Russian interest in Asiatic railways. Various schemes were advanced by capitalists, engineers, and the military, Russian and foreign. Ferdinand de Lesseps, builder of the Suez Canal, proposed to General N. P. Ignat'ev, Russian ambassador at Constantinople, to construct a line from Orenburg to Samarkand and thence to India.[21] Ignat'ev was favorably disposed, but it was more than a year before the Russian government seriously looked at the plan.[22]

Lesseps' project of a great Indo-European railway was discussed in a conference of high officials on January 15, 1875. Prince Gorchakov, General Miliutin, as well as the ministers of communications and finance agreed that the idea was not realistic and would bring Russia more harm than good. Only the Governor-General of Turkestan, K. P. von Kaufmann, defended the scheme.[23] During the rest of the winter and spring a number of

19. W. T. Thomson to Mirzā Hoseyn Khān, Tehran, November 10, 1876; ibid.
20. Ronald Thomson, Chargé d'Affaires, to the Earl of Clarendon, No. 16, Tehran, February 15, 1870; F.O. 60/325.
21. Lesseps to Ignat'ev, May 1, 1873, Archive des Affaires Etrangères, Correspondence Politique, Perse, tome 36, folio 358–59.
22. Ignat'ev to Lesseps, Pera, April 23/May 5, 1873, France, Archive des Affaires Etrangères, Correspondence Politique, Perse, tome 36, folio 352–53.
23. Dnevnik Miliutina, 1, 181.

other projects were looked into. On April 15, 1875, a conference was held at the home of Prince Gorchakov with the Crown Prince Alexander; Grand Duke Konstantin Nikolaevich; the ministers of War, Communications, and Finance; Count Petr Shuvalov, Ambassador to England; and a number of lesser figures in attendance. It was agreed that a railway to the Persian frontier in the Caucasus should be built, though different opinions were voiced as to the exact routing of the line.[24] No proposals were made at the time to extend the projected line into Persian territory.

The parade of concession seekers which had been opened by Monsieur Savalan in 1864, and in which Reuter was by far the most conspicuous, continued in spite of repeated disappointments suffered by European adventurers. Neither Britain nor Russia was anxious to see enterprises belonging to subjects of other European nations established in Iran. Britain effectively blocked the Tholozan concession, while jointly Britain and Russia prevented Alléon from realizing his.

Dr. Tholozan, the Shah's French physician, used his position to persuade the Shah to grant him, and a number of Paris entrepreneurs, a concession for mines, irrigation, public works, and railways. Having learned of Tholozan's proposed concession, W. Taylour Thomson telegraphed London that Baron Reuter, who had refused to accept the cancellation of his concession and was still pressing his claims, be told to include among them the exclusive right to irrigation works.[25] Tholozan's concession, if granted, would have resembled the one won and lost by Julius Reuter. The draft proposal included such wide-ranging statements as the following: "le Gouvernement Persan accorde à la Compagnie le privilège d'établir en Perse des usines, etc." As W. T. Thomson pointed out in a dispatch to Lord Derby, the clause included a great deal, "and to make the clause even more comprehensive, the general term et cetera, so unusual and inappropriate in documents of this nature, is inserted." Thomson continued:

> Bearing in mind the importance of preventing if possible the establishment of a French, or other Foreign, colony in

24. Ibid., pp. 184–85.
25. W. T. Thomson to the Foreign Office, Telegram in cypher, Tehran, December 30, 1875; F.O. 60/407.

the Province of Khuzistan, which might prejudice British interests there and at Mohammerah . . . I have thought it advisable to endeavour to impede the acceptance of Dr. Tholozan's scheme until Baron Reuter's new proposals have been received and considered by the Persian Government.[26]

For well over a year nothing further was heard about Dr. Tholozan's scheme. It came to light again during Nāser ed-din Shah's stay in Paris in the spring of 1878, when he was presented with a new and revised draft concession. Upon returning to Tehran, Tholozan and several Persian officials interested in the project, and probably heavily bribed by the good doctor, persuaded the Shah to grant the concession over the objection of the British chargé d'affaires, Ronald F. Thomson.[27] The latter was told that Tholozan's concession would profit the country. As far as Reuter's claims were concerned, the Persian government felt that "the sense of justice entertained by Her Majesty's Government" would lead them to agree that Reuter had failed to carry out the provisions of his contract and was "entitled to no concession or privilege whatever." The Persian government, Mirzā Hoseyn Khān wrote, considered themselves "excused from entering into a discussion of the matter." [28]

Mr. Thomson disagreed. The Persian government claimed that Reuter had forfeited his rights by failing to carry out the articles of his contract. "This, however, has not up to the present time been established, certainly not to the satisfaction of Her Majesty's Government." [29] He was obviously using the defunct Reuter concession to block Tholozan's project, therefore no Persian argument showing the justice of the Persian case had any chance

26. W. T. Thomson to Derby, No. 1, January 1, 1876; F.O. 60/379.

27. R. F. Thomson to Salisbury, No. 161, Tehran, September 20, 1878; L.I., 22, 1879. Thomson to the Viceroy of India, Tehran, October 26, 1878; ibid. Thomson to Salisbury, No. 205, Tehran, November 6, 1878; ibid. Ronald Thomson was Taylour Thomson's younger brother.

28. Memorandum of the Persian Minister of Foreign Affairs, Tehran, November 12, 1878, Enclosure in [R. F.] Thomson to Salisbury, No. 225, Tehran, December 5, 1878; L.I., 22, 1879.

29. R. Thomson to Mirzā Hoseyn Khān, November 12, 1878, Enclosure in R. F. Thomson to Salisbury, No. 225, Tehran, December 5, 1878; ibid.

of being accepted by Her Majesty's Government or its representative in Tehran.

British discomfort over the proposed Tholozan concession was understandable. The concession would turn over to a French company that very Kārun river that was the only available route from the Persian Gulf into the interior. Article 8 of the agreement provided for the building and running of tramways, railways, and roads along the Kārun as well as for navigation. Article 10 granted the company the right to cultivate all land, from Ahvāz, where the company would build a dam, to the Persian Gulf. Thus the British were facing the prospect of a French colony being established at the head of the Persian Gulf.

The Persian government was not deeply committed to the Tholozan project. Those who had received bribes had already made their profit. British pressure was increasing, while Russia had no reason to apply counterpressure in favor of a French company. On December 15 Mirzā Hoseyn Khān told Thomson that the government had resolved to cancel the Tholozan concession. "His Highness requested me to state to Lord Salisbury that this decision was in consequence of the memoranda communicated by me to the Persian Government, which had opened their eyes to the objectionable nature of the scheme." [30]

The Tholozan concession was not the only one the Shah granted during his European trip of 1878. A certain Monsieur Alléon, representing a Paris firm, obtained the right to build a railway from Anzali to Tehran. The terms of his concession followed the pattern which had become standard by that time. Its duration would be ninety years. Crown as well as private lands would be turned over to Alléon for the purposes of railway construction. The Persian government would guarantee 6½ percent on the capital invested, pledging customs receipts for that purpose. Of the profits in excess of 6½ percent on the invested capital, Persia would get 50 percent. Alléon's company would be entirely tax exempt.[31]

30. R. Thomson to the Viceroy of India, Tehran, December 16, 1878; ibid.
31. Text of the Concession signed at Paris on June 29, 1878, Enclosure in R. Thomson to Salisbury, No. 161, Tehran, September 20, 1878; ibid.

In his classic work *Persia and the Persian Question*, Lord Curzon stated that "The project came to grief because of the refusal of the Persian Government to give a guarantee for the 7% interest promised on the capital to be raised."[32] Actually the reasons for Alléon's failure were quite different.

The railway Alléon proposed to build would pay for itself only if it carried European goods which would have to traverse Russia and cross the Caspian Sea. A high Russian tariff on transit would make the whole enterprise unprofitable. To make sure that the railway would not be paralyzed, Mirzā Hoseyn Khān asked the Russian minister at Tehran, I. A. Zinov'ev, to give the Persian government a guarantee that "in the event of their granting the concession . . . no restrictive conditions would be imposed by the Russian Custom House authorities upon the transit trade by that line to and from Persia." Zinov'ev refused to give such a guarantee. Moreover, he told Hoseyn Khān that in Russia's opinion it was inadvisable to build a line to the Caspian. Russia, he said, was about to connect the Tiflis-Poti line with Jolfā by a railway running through Aleksandropol. A branch from the Tiflis-Poti line would be built to Batum. Persia should take advantage of this and build a railway from Tabriz to Jolfā. Russia would do her best to find a concessionaire to undertake such a project.[33]

For once the Russians and the British were united. Ronald Thomson also opposed the Alléon concession, though he strongly objected to Zinov'ev's plan for a Tabriz-Jolfā line as well.[34] Thomson saw a serious threat to British commerce in the Alléon scheme, or in any other railway running from northern to central Persia. Russia already had a geographic advantage over Britain in being much closer to the Persian market. In spite of this, British merchants competed successfully at least as far north as Esfahān and even Tehran. They would surely lose out if Alléon built his railway. In such a case the British government would have to take "counteracting measures." "It would, in fact, be imperative on

---

32. Curzon, *Persia and the Persian Question*, 1, 616.

33. R. Thomson to Salisbury, No. 193, Confidential, Tehran, October 20, 1878; L.I., 22, 1879.

34. R. Thomson to the Viceroy of India, Tehran, November 4, 1878; ibid.

Her Majesty's Government to insist upon the opening of the Karoon to steam navigation or else to give way to Russian trade." [35] Alléon's scheme stood no chance against the combined opposition of the two legations. In March 1880, Mirzā Hoseyn Khān informed Thomson that the concession would be canceled. The latter had the pleasure of going over the text of the agreement and suggesting to the Persian Foreign Minister the best way of terminating the contract. Thomson was quite unoriginal, borrowing the excuses which Mirzā Hoseyn Khān had used in Reuter's case. Alléon was to be informed that his concession was being revoked because he had failed to complete all plans, surveys, etc. within a year of the signing of the contract. A telegram to that effect was sent to Paris on March 17.[36]

Tholozan's attempt to obtain a concession on the Kārun demonstrated to the British the uncertainty of their own position in that area. In the fall of 1878, Thomson was instructed to raise once again the issue of freedom of navigation on the river. In a memorandum addressed to Mirzā Hoseyn Khān on September 21, 1878, he repeated arguments that had already been used without success by the British legation at Tehran.[37] It seemed for a moment that the Persians would give in. Mirzā Hoseyn Khān was favorably inclined and expressed his confidence that the Shah would agree to the opening of the river. Suddenly the mood of the Persian government changed. Thomson felt that the Shah had misgivings that once the British obtained a foothold at Mohammareh, they would "take advantage of an opportunity to secure its possession." [38]

Thomson continued to press Mirzā Hoseyn Khān, and the tone of the negotiations grew less friendly. When the Foreign Minister, trying to gain time, informed Thomson that no navigation rights could be granted until after the trip which the Shah

35. R. Thomson to Salisbury, No. 3, Commercial, Tehran, July 30, 1879; L.I., 32, 1883.
36. R. Thomson to Salisbury, No. 69, Tehran, March 21, 1880; F.O. 60/428.
37. Memorandum from R. F. Thomson to the Sepeh Salar [sic] Mirzā Hoseyn Khān, September 21, 1878, Enclosure in R. Thomson to Salisbury, No. 216, Confidential, Tehran, November 20, 1878; L.I., 22, 1879.
38. R. Thomson to Salisbury, No. 216, Confidential, Tehran, November 20, 1878; ibid.

"Pénétration Pacifique"

was planning to make to Khuzestān, Thomson answered: "I cannot conceal from Your Highness my regret and disappointment at having received so unsatisfactory a reply from the Persian Government, amounting, as it does, to a virtual refusal to accede to the reasonable and urgent request of a friendly Power." Moreover, Thomson complained, the Shah had granted a concession to a French subject "giving him a virtual monopoly of the trade of the Karun." There followed more complaints and some thinly veiled threats.

> The present decision . . . cannot fail to be regarded by Her Majesty's Government in any other light than that of an unfriendly action towards England, the more so that Persia is actually doing herself an injury in order to give effect to that unfriendly act.
>
> Whilst offering facilities for trade with Russia, by making and improving roads and adopting other measures in the north of Persia, the Persian Government has done nothing for improving roads or for affording similar facilities for the trade of England in the south.[39]

Thomson's importunity offended Nāser ed-Din Shah, and made him lose his temper. He complied with the British request to give reasons for his refusal to open the Kārun. In a letter addressed to Mirzā Hoseyn Khān but intended for Thomson, he wrote:

> For fifty years you [the English] have carried on trade with Persia, and there has never been a word; what has happened now that you want the Karoon river? Moreover, such rivers as these, are like the door of one's house; and why should you desire to enter by force and without consent? Wait until we have looked around us and visited those places and understood the outlet and ingress of the river; then if we see that it is for the interest and welfare of our country, permission will be granted.

39. R. Thomson to H. H. Hajji Mirza Hussein Khan, G.C.S.I., etc., etc., Tehran, January 10, 1879, Enclosure in Thomson to Salisbury, No. 20, Tehran, January 27, 1879; ibid.

Without any kind of preamble all at once you insist and precipitate matters. [The following sentence was delected in the copy given to Thomson but seen by him in the original.] If my consent is asked for, I decline to give it. Entering by force is a different thing; but for the present it is better to have patience.[40]

Undaunted, Thomson kept up his campaign. He had succeeded in eliminating the threat posed by Dr. Tholozan and his associates. Working along parallel lines with Zinov'ev, he had prevented Alléon from carrying out his railway project. But the swift and muddy Kārun, so temptingly accessible, eluded all his efforts to make it a British highway. Desultory talks continued for months without any effect, except on Thomson's nervous system. He began to dispatch hortatory messages not only to Mirzā Hoseyn Khān, who, in this case, was impervious, but to Lord Salisbury as well. In July 1879 he wrote the latter:

We have suppressed piracy and maintained full security along the Persian coast. Persia could not have done this for herself. She has had all the advantages of our protection, and we have a right, therefore, to expect that she will not capriciously exclude us from a natural highway existing for trade into the interior of her territory.[41]

Thomson's bitterness may have been increased by Persia's compliance with Russian demands. It was no secret that Khorāsān was used as a supply base by Russian troops operating in Transcaspia. Without stores and camels procured in Persia with the connivance of Persian authorities, Skobelev would not have been able to stage his Ākhāl campaign (1880–81). It was galling for Thomson to witness the uninterrupted diplomatic successes of his Russian colleague, the shrewd, well-informed I. A. Zinov'ev. The very fact that both had served in Persia for over twenty years, and were well acquainted, must have added a touch of personal jealousy and deepened the resentment Ronald Thomson felt at his utter lack of success.

40. Translation of a letter from H. M. the Shah to the Sepeh Salar (n.d.), Enclosure in R. Thomson to Salisbury, No. 20, Confidential, January 27, 1879; ibid.
41. R. Thomson to Salisbury, No. 3, Commercial, July 30, 1879; L.I., 32, 1882.

"Pénétration Pacifique" 163

In March 1881 Mirzā Said Khān, Hoseyn Khān's predecessor and successor as Minister of Foreign Affairs, requested Britain's support in a border dispute with Turkey involving some Kurds. Foolishly he dangled before Thomson "as an inducement to such action a promise that Persia would shape her policy henceforward in conformity with the views of Her Majesty's Government, and would concede the free navigation of the Karun river." The Englishman retorted angrily that

> it is the duty of the Persian Government to carry them [measures for the advancement of trade, i.e. the opening of the Kārun] out independently of any question of the Kurds. Any delay on their part in the execution of their engagements or attempt to make a bargain for their performance can only therefore be regarded by Her Majesty's Government as an unfriendly act, which is a very unsatisfactory return for the efforts which they have already made . . . in favor of Persia as regards the question of the Kurdish insurrection.[42]

Mirzā Said Khān was friendly and conciliatory. He even showed Thomson some minutes he had written in favor of the opening of the Kārun. He also had suggested to the Shah that the entire issue be placed in the hands of Zell es-Soltān.[43]

Mas'ud Mirzā Zell es-Soltān was the Shah's eldest son. Since his mother was a commoner, Zell es-Soltān was excluded from the succession, which would go to his younger half-brother, Mozaffar ed-Din Mirzā, the Vali Ahd (Crown Prince). The Shah, who disliked his heir, heaped honors on Zell es-Soltān, adding province after province to the domain over which the ambitious and cruel prince ruled from Esfahān. By 1882, Zell es-Soltān controlled about one third of Persia. He had raised and trained several regiments, which he armed with 6,000 Martini-Henry rifles, thus creating a force that was reputed to be the best in the country. The British, with their special interest in the south, were very much aware of Zell es-Soltān's growing power.[44]

42. R. Thomson's Memorandum to Mirzā Said Khān, Tehran, July 6, 1881; ibid.
43. R. Thomson to Granville, No. 156, Tehran, October 29, 1881; ibid.
44. R. Thomson to Granville, No. 32, Tehran, February 25, 1882; ibid.

They would undoubtedly have looked for means of winning his goodwill. Zell es-Soltān made the search easy.

On January 6, 1882, the man who was then British political resident in the Persian Gulf and consul general for Fārs, Lieutenant Colonel E. C. Ross, telegraphed the Viceroy of India that he had received a private message from Zell es-Soltān to the effect that the latter had been given by the Shah full power to deal with the Kārun question, and "that he is disposed to meet the wishes of British Government and hopes in return to receive a decoration. It is probable that if decoration is promised point would be carried."[45] The Viceroy inquired from Thomson whether he advised giving Zell es-Soltān the Star of India and whether it was true that he had the power to open the Kārun.[46] Thomson thought it might be expedient to initimate to Zell es-Soltān that he would receive a present from the Government of India, should he succeed in opening the Kārun. However, Thomson was not certain that the Prince should be decorated. He telegraphed the Viceroy: "fear grant of Star of India to him would be extremely distasteful to heir-apparent, who regards present position of his brother with great jealousy." The Viceroy preferred to bestow decorations rather than make expensive presents. In reply to Thomson he said that he understood a decoration would be the only effective inducement to Zell es-Soltān. "Moreover present given must be very costly. I should prefer recommending decoration if you could arrange matter to be given only on condition of success."[47]

Zell es-Soltān wanted the Grand Cross of the Star of India. The Governor of Bushehr, who served as an intermediary between the Prince and E. C. Ross, showed him a letter he had received from Zell. It deserves to be quoted at some length:

> It is necessary for them to give the decoration and receive this [grant of the] opening [of the Kārun]; either let the decoration be given or a promise of the decoration be sent me

---

45. The Resident, Bushire, to Foreign Department, Calcutta, Telegram, January 6, 1882; L.I., 31, 1882.

46. Viceroy, Calcutta, to Minister, Tehran; Telegram No. 57 E.P., January 11, 1882; ibid.

47. Thomson, Tehran, to Viceroy, Calcutta, Telegram, January 11, 1882; Viceroy, Calcutta, to R. Thomson, Telegram, No. 143 E.P., January 21, 1882; ibid.

officially and this [grant of the] opening will be received in exchange . . .

Now you must conduct your negotiations with the resident to a conclusion. If he be anxious for this opening [up of the Kārun] let the decoration very quickly reach me and the arrangement about it be completed by you. In proportion as the business of the decoration is delayed, the "opening" is also delayed.[48]

One suspects that Thomson was not very happy about relations between Zell es-Soltān and E. C. Ross. His experience must have told him that in the last analysis it was only the Shah who would decide whether the Kārun were to be opened. Decorating Zell would not change the Shah's mind but would alienate Mozaffar ed-Din Mirzā, the heir apparent. Moreover, Thomson may have felt a pang of disappointment that E. C. Ross should succeed where he had failed. If Thomson entertained such sentiments, he did not allow them to interfere with his duties. In April he gave Zell es-Soltān to understand that the decoration would be granted if the Kārun were opened. Simultaneously he suggested to the Viceroy that the award "be deferred pending the fulfilment by him of above engagement."[49] Once again the Shah was adamant. Neither Thomson nor Zell es-Soltān could make him change his mind. The evidence now at hand does not fully explain the Shah's stubborn refusal to open the Kārun. What were the roles of I. A. Zinov'ev and his successor, A. A. Melnikov? The full answer will not be known until Russian archives are made available, but it is probable that the Shah's natural fear of British encroachment was stimulated and sustained by the Russian legation.

In their preoccupation with the Kārun and, after 1879, with Transcaspia, the British paid little attention to an event of major importance for the future—the formation of the Persian Cossack Brigade.[50]

---

48. Instructions of H. H. Zil-es-Sultan to Governor of Bushire, communicated by the latter, March 8, 1882, Enclosure in E. C. Ross to C. Grant, Secretary of the Government of India, No. 65, Bushire, March 10, 1882; L.I., 32, 1882.

49. Thomson, Tehran, to Viceroy, Simla, Telegram, April 8, 1882; ibid.

50. The following account incorporates portions of my article on "The Origin

Early in the nineteenth century, Persia still possessed considerable military strength. Her armies, though ultimately defeated by Russia, put up serious resistance and even won a number of hard-fought battles in the Caucasus. In 1821–23 Mohammad Ali Mirzā and Abbās Mirzā, the Shah's sons, defeated the Turks. The general decline of the country in the reign of Mohammad Shah, however, brought about a catastrophic deterioration of the armed forces. They were able to cope with Afghan tribesmen, but were routed by greatly inferior numbers of the English in 1856–57. After the disastrous campaign against the Turkomans of Marv in 1861, the Persian army virtually ceased to exist.

In theory Nāser ed-Din Shah favored an army reform. During his first European trip he had been much impressed with the orderly maneuvers and beautiful uniforms of various armies, particularly the Austrian. However, he had neither the ability nor the strength of character to act the part of a Peter the Great. Childishly fickle and lazy, he never carried any undertaking to a successful conclusion. On his second European trip, the idea of an army reform returned to his inconstant mind. The Shah traveled through Transcaucasia, which teemed with Russian troops after the recently concluded Turkish war. He was everywhere escorted by a detachment of Cossacks whose smart appearance, bright uniforms, and fine horsemanship appealed to Nāser ed-Din so much that he told the Viceroy of the Caucasus, Grand Duke Mikhail Nikolaevich, that he intended to organize a similar cavalry unit in his own country.[51]

The Grand Duke suggested to the Tsar that a number of instructors be sent to Persia for that purpose. Alexander II gave his permission, and the Chief of Staff of the Tiflis Military District, General Pavlov, selected Lieutenant Colonel of the General Staff Aleksei Ivanovich Domantovich to head a small military mission to Iran. Pavlov gave Domantovich extremely vague instructions. It seems that no one, the Shah, the Grand Duke, or

---

and Early Development of the Persian Cossack Brigade," *The American Slavic and East European Review*, 15 (October 1956), 351–63.

51. A. Domantovich, "Vospominaniia o prebyvanii pervoi russkoi voennoi missii v Persii," *Russkaia starina*, February 1908, pp. 332–33.

Pavlov himself, knew what the exact nature of Domantovich's assignment was.⁵²

Domantovich arrived in Tehran in January 1879. The Russian Minister, I. A. Zinov'ev, assigned the dragoman of the legation, a Russianized Arab, Grigorovich, to act as his guide. Grigorovich, who had spent many years in Tehran, knew everyone in the official circles. Mixing his metaphors, Domantovich, whose sword must have been a great deal mightier than his pen, wrote of Grigorovich:

> It seems that for him there were no secret springs with which the Persians tried to hide their diplomatic secrets. At difficult moments he would go to the Persian Ministry of Foreign Affairs where he would find a way of getting at secrets which were covered mostly with the English chain of gold.⁵³

The British legation disapproved of the employment of Russian officers by the Shah. Ronald Thomson complained to Mirzā Hoseyn Khān, but did not press the issue too far, not wishing to endanger the outcome of negotiations he was then conducting on the subject of the Kārun navigation. The Shah refused to open the Kārun and brushed off Thomson's objections to the hiring of Domantovich in the same letter addressed to Mirzā Hoseyn Khān. He wrote:

> We have officers and *employes* of every nation and sect in our service. We also wished to have one single Russian to drill and instruct a few hundred of our horse as Cossacks. This is the officer who has come.
>
> Persia is not Afghanistan that they should entertain such suspicions. She is an independent Power, and always considers it her interest to be on friendly and cordial footing with all Powers, especially with those of England and Russia.⁵⁴

52. Id.
53. Domantovich, *Russkaia starina*, March 1908, pp. 578–79.
54. Translations of a letter from H. M. the Shah to the Sepeh Salar (sic, n.d.), R. Thomson to Salisbury, No. 20, Confidential, Tehran, January 27, 1879, L.I., 22, 1879.

In spite of British objections and the intrigues of some Persian officers jealous of his position, Domantovich, with Zinov'ev's backing, organized a force and trained it so rapidly that at the end of the summer of 1879, he was able to present it to the Shah. The Brigade immediately won Nāser ed-Din's admiration, and Domantovich became a leading member of the governing circle. I. A. Zinov'ev began to feel that he was losing control over the Russian officer. A personal quarrel between the minister's wife and Madame Domantovich spoiled the relations between the colonel and the legation to such an extent that the former accused the latter of attempting to undermine him and his work.[55] In 1881 Domantovich's contract expired and was immediately renewed by the Shah. Having been granted a leave of four months, Domantovich went to Russia, never to return. Zinov'ev was a strong man with excellent connections among the military. The Caucasian Army Command refused to send Domantovich back to Persia in spite of the insistence of the Shah that he be permitted to serve out the term of his second contract.[56]

Under its next four Russian commanders the Cossack Brigade deteriorated, but even then the French chargé d'affaires could report that it was the only experiment with foreign military instructors that showed any signs of success.[57] The incompetence of its commanders, the puny and irregular appropriations it received, and the lack of interest on the part of the Russian legation may have convinced the British that the Brigade was not worth bothering about. When in 1894 it was put under an exceptionally capable officer, V. A. Kosogovskii, who speedily turned it into a disciplined and effective force and an instrument of Russian pressure, it was too late to protest. The Cossack Brigade had become an accepted part of the Persian scene.

British concentration on the Kārun issue to the exclusion of almost all other problems save that of Central Asia was officially

55. V. A. Kosogovskii, "Ocherk istorii razvitiia persidskoi kazach'ei brigady," *Novyi Vostok*, No. 4 (Moscow, 1923), p. 392.

56. Ibid., pp. 392–93.

57. M. Souhart a M. Duclere [Minister of Foreign Affairs], No. 16, 8 Decembre 1882, Teheran, Direction politique; Archive des Affaires Etrangères, tome 39, folio 80–81.

justified by the requirements of commercial competition. Russia, whose proximity to the Persian market was supposed to bestow special advantages upon her, must not be allowed to drive British trade out of Iran. In reality British trade was in no danger from Russian commercial firms. When competition increased in the closing years of the nineteenth century, and when early in the twentieth, British goods began to be forced out of most of Persia by Russian goods, the contest was waged not between Russian and British private business but between the Russian government on one side and a few British commercial houses on the other.

Not only in the south, where Britain held a virtual monopoly on foreign trade, but in the north as well, Russian business found it difficult to strike roots in spite of the favorable provisions of the treaty of Torkamanchāy. In the 1850s a Russian merchant, Kokarev, formed a commercial company that soon closed down in the face of European competition. N. N. Konshin, a man of great wealth, imported 660,000 rubles worth of goods into Persia between 1884 and 1889, and lost 100,000 rubles in the process.[58] F. A. Bakulin, a Russian official well acquainted with Persian markets, wrote that in 1870–71 the main item of Persian import was cotton goods, most of which came from England. Russia was not in competition, Bakulin wrote, because British cottons were cheaper and better satisfied the taste of the consumers. He complained that while Russia was endeavoring to increase the sale of her manufactured goods in Central Asia, she neglected the familiar Persia, which was open to exploitation by foreign firms.[59]

Of the five Russian firms operating in Tabriz, every one dealt directly with Britain, France, Austria, and Turkey. What Russian goods made their way into Persia were imported by petty Armenian merchants, Bakulin complained.[60] More than thirty years later an official of the Russian Discount and Loan Bank in Tehran wrote to the Minister of Commerce and Industry that up to 1901 the import of Russian goods into Persia was not large. Trade was

---

58. M. L. Tomara, *Ekonomicheskoe polozhenie Persii* (St. Petersburg, Ministry of Finance, 1895), pp. 102–03.

59. F. A. Bakulin, "Ocherk vneshnei torgovli Azerbaidzhana za 1870–1871 g.g.," *Vostochnyi Sbornik* (St. Petersburg, 1877), pp. 205–08.

60. Ibid., p. 208.

mostly concentrated at Nizhnii-Novgorod, where Persian merchants sold their raw materials and stocked up on Russian goods in relatively modest quantities. Goods of Russian origin spread mostly in provinces adjacent to Russia—in Māzandarān, Gilān, Āzarbāyjān, Khorāsān—but even then in limited amounts.[61]

Clearly in the 1870s and 1880s Russian trade was not endangering Britain's commercial position in Persia. Yet the alleged need to equalize Britain's competitive position with that of Russia was frequently mentioned as a principal motive in raising the Kārun issue. Her Majesty's minister in Tehran, Ronald Thomson, worried that the acquisition of Batum would allow Russia to lure to the Caucasus the European transit trade. In July 1879 he wrote Salisbury:

> The Russians are at this moment in a very favourable position as regards Persia for the successful prosecution of their trade. In recent years steam navigation has been greatly developed on the Volga and the Caspian, and Russia can now land her goods along the northern coast of Persia at extremely low rates, at Enzeli within 100 miles of Kasveen and 200 of Tehran.[62]

Transcaucasian railways did not improve Russia's competitive position in Persia. On the contrary, they made possible a veritable invasion of northern Persia by German and Austrian goods carried over the Black Sea to Batum and thence through the Caucasus to Tabriz. The transit trade brought Russia 800,000 to 900,000 rubles yearly, even before the annexation of Batum and the construction of a railway from Tiflis to the Black Sea.[63] But although the income from this source was increasing rapidly, the Russian legation in Tehran was unhappy at the sight of Russian railways serving to facilitate and increase the volume of European trade in

61. Memorandum of I. S. Rosenblum to the Minister of Commerce and Industry, October 7/20, 1910, as cited in A. A. Zonnenshtral-Piskorskii, *Mezhdunarodnye torgovye dogovory Persii* (Moscow, 1931), pp. 151–52.

62. R. Thomson to Salisbury, No. 3, Commercial, Tehran, July 30, 1879; L.I., 32, 1882.

63. P. M. Romanov, *Zheleznodorozhnyi vopros v Persii i mery k razvitiiu russko-persidskoi torgovli* (St. Petersburg, 1891), pp. 3–4.

"Pénétration Pacifique"

Persia. In 1883 I. A. Zinov'ev, then Director of the Asiatic Department of the Ministry of Foreign Affairs, submitted to his superiors a report on the commercial situation, urging that restrictions be imposed on European goods in transit to Persia as a measure designed to win the north for Russian commerce.[64] Alexander III accepted Zinov'ev's proposal, and a heavy tariff was imposed. That the Tsar and his diplomats were politically motivated there can be no doubt. The conquest of the north Persian market was seen from St. Petersburg as a part of the larger task of establishing Russian hegemony in the Middle East.

> This act [wrote a contemporary observer], dictated by the rivalry in Persia of England and Russia, the latter wishing to establish its political supremacy there based on economic domination, dealt the entire foreign trade in Northern Persia a powerful blow and immediately gave a great advantage to Russian commerce, which from then on began quickly to develop and strengthen.[65]

The primacy of political motives in Russia's activities in Iran, and indeed in all Russian imperialism, has baffled Soviet writers who must, by virtue of adherence to Lenin's views, profess a theory that does not always correspond to the facts of history. If imperialism is the highest stage of capitalism, "*parasitic* or *decaying* capitalism," "the last stage of capitalism the main feature of which is the substitution of monopoly for free competition," then Russia's conquest of the Caucasus and Central Asia, her actions in Persia, her rule over Poland, Finland, and other subjugated nations, was not imperialism at all,[66] at least not until the very end of the nineteenth century when her economy began to assume a capitalist character.

The incongruity between the wide scope of Russian political

64. M. P. Pavlovich, *Imperializm i borba za velikie zheleznodorozhnye i morskie puti budushchego* (Moscow, 1918–19), 2, 27.
65. L. A. Sobotsinskii, *Persiia* (no place of publication given, 1913), p. 159.
66. For a number of definitions of the term "imperialism" in a Soviet textbook, see *Politicheskaia ekonomiia*, a collective work published by the Institute of Economics of the Academy of Sciences of the U.S.S.R. (Moscow, 1954), pp. 224, 236, 254, 257.

activity and the narrow scope of her economic involvement in Iran was admitted by some Soviet writers. One of them went so far as to state that the Russian government's "commercial policy in Persia was subordinated more to the general foreign policy than to its immediate economic interests in Persia." [67] In his posthumous work on *International Relations at the End of the 19th Century*, the veteran Bolshevik diplomat and scholar, F. A. Rothstein [Rotshtein], states that commercial capital did not dictate the conquest of new colonies by Russia. The conquests were motivated by the desire to grab that which could be grabbed.

> History had placed that Empire [Russia] in circumstances which permitted her to expand with impunity to the east, where she met no geographic obstacles and did not come up against serious resistance. Meanwhile the military-feudal nature of the tsarist autocracy itself demanded conquests, territorial acquisitions, the widening of the sphere of landowners', fiscal, and bureaucratic exploitation and, not the least, the widening of the sphere of "activity" of military officers, members of the gentry, the pillar of the Tsar's authority. The desires of the merchants or manufacturers then played a secondary role in this decisive context.[68]

Every age has its own language, its own set of slogans, its own notions of what is and what is not legitimate. Identical phenomena, identical motives, find a different expression depending on the ideological climate of the time and the place. The primordial human desire to conquer, to dominate, may be justified in one period by the requirements of honor and glory, in others by the need to convert the heathen, to reach natural frontiers, to reclaim a lost patrimony, to secure markets, to fulfill one's destiny, or to take up the "white man's burden." Nineteenth-century Europe, awestruck before the power of its own economy, deified the economic process. The new god was then called upon either to condemn or to justify any condition, action,

---

67. Zonnenshtral-Piskorskii, p. 80.
68. F. A. Rotstein, *Mezhdunarodnye otnosheniia v konstse XIX veka* (Moscow, 1960), pp. 161–62.

"Pénétration Pacifique"

or policy, depending upon the needs of the particular believer who was making the invocation. When Ronald Thomson insisted upon the opening of the Kārun or the construction of roads into the interior of Persia, he justified his proposals in terms of a generally accepted economic ethos. His counterpart, Ivan Alekseevich Zinov'ev, who was not at all concerned for the welfare of a few dozen Armenian merchants in northern Persia, used almost identical language.

The partial settlement of the Afghan border dispute following the Panjdeh incident in 1885 led to a temporary relaxation of tension in Tehran. By that year both I. A. Zinov'ev and Ronald Thomson had left Persia. For two and a half years the British legation was headed by a chargé d'affaires, Arthur Nicolson, a man who knew little of Persia and cared less. In the summer and fall of 1885, London made overtures to Berlin, hoping to involve Germany in the "development" of Persia, or in plain language to gain Bismarck's support for British attempts to keep Russia out.[69]

The Shah was making attempts in the same direction. In the spring of 1885, Germany opened a legation in Tehran. In the fall, Mohsen Khān Moin ol-Molk was sent to Berlin to beg Bismarck for military instructors and an administrative adviser, that is to try to involve Germany in Persia. All Mohsen Khān accomplished was to hire two retired German generals. Sir Edward Malet, British ambassador in Berlin, was no more successful. He forwarded to Bismarck a new proposal by Reuter for an international company for railway-building in Persia, noting that the Chancellor might favor the scheme. Bismarck refused the bait. His marginal comment was clear and brief: "Nein." [70]

Anglo-German negotiations concerning Persia encouraged Reuter to resume his efforts to obtain compensation for his concession. On the basis of the latter, several plans for railway construction were presented by Britain to Persia in 1886 and 1887.[71]

69. See R. L. Greaves, *Persia and the Defence of India, 1884–1892*, Chap. XI, pp. 85–100.

70. B. G. Martin, *German-Persian Diplomatic Relations, 1873–1912* ('S-Gravenhage, 1959), pp. 33–34.

71. See, for instance, Draft concession for the Formation of a Railway from

Sporadic attempts were also made by the Shah to find a neutral builder for Persian railways. In the spring of 1886 Yahyā Khān Moshir od-Dowleh negotiated with an American, a Mr. Winston. Both Melnikov and Nicolson were kept informed. The former told Yahyā Khān that

> the establishment in Persia of American capitalists and enterprizes cannot be for us as politically inconvenient as the establishment in Persia of British capital and enterprizes but that Mr. Winston's proposal has for us serious commercial disadvantages since, by connecting Tehran with the Persian Gulf by a railroad, it would open the way for European goods to Persian markets and would push Russian goods out of them.[72]

The Winston project was killed by Arthur Nicolson, who told the Shah that the granting of a concession to the American would produce the most unfavorable impression in London and that Reuter would demand the restitution of his rights. The Shah "frightened by such representations of the English chargé d'affaires hurried to annul Winston's concession." [73]

In the summer of 1886, the Persian minister in London, Mirzā Malkam Khān, returned to Tehran for consultations with his government on the same railway question. The Russian ambassador, E. Staal, reported from London that Malkam Khān had told him the Shah was determined to build railways but was not sure of the direction they should take. Those linking the capital with the south would necessarily benefit British trade, while those going north would benefit the Russians. Malkam Khān, the good friend of the English, did not hesitate to assure Staal that he would do his best to have railways built from Tehran northward.[74]

Ahwaz to Tehran, via Dizful, Khoramabad, Burrojird, Sultanabad, and Kum, January 11, 1887; F.O. 60/485.

72. Melnikov to the Minister of Foreign Affairs, Giers, May 17/29, 1886, as cited in A. Popov, "Stranitsa iz istorii russkogo imperializma v Persii," pp. 136–37.

73. Melnikov to Giers, Zargandeh, July 5/15, 1886; as cited in A. Popov, p. 137.

74. Staal to Giers, July 11/23, 1886; A. Meyendorff, *Correspondance diplomatique du Baron de Staal* (1884–1900) (Paris, 1929), 1 (1886), No. 26, 303.

St. Petersburg watched with interest the attempts of the various entrepreneurs to construct railway lines in Iran. Prince Nikolai Sergeevich Dolgorukov, the new Russian minister in Tehran, felt that such lines should be built. He "understands all the grandeur of this idea," the court minister, Count I. I. Vorontsov-Dashkov wrote to K. P. Pobedonostsev, "and is completely convinced that it could be built without encountering difficulties on the part of Persia." Dolgorukov was concerned only about having the railways built by Russia.[75]

Moscow merchants who, since the introduction of the restrictive transit tariff of 1883 had built up a certain interest in the Persian market, feared the introduction of railways in Persia. A certain V. P. Osipov wrote to Pobedonostev about his discovery of a group of Jews in Berlin who had formed a company for that purpose. Osipov expressed apprehension lest the success of the "Jewish scheme" lead Persia into debt and turn her into another Egypt. The company in question would seek Russian cooperation, but unless the Government preserved the right to control the rates, Russian trade would suffer. The interests of the shareholders must not be allowed to predominate over the interests of Russian commerce. "As to the question how well our commercial interests would be represented by a company of Jews in Russian dress, one hardly needs to expatiate on it." [76]

The Moscow merchants had nothing to fear. Shortly after his arrival in Tehran, Prince Dolgorukov obtained from the Shah a precedent-setting document. His Majesty wrote to the Russian minister in September 1887 that out of friendship and affection for the Emperor of Russia, who had always shown his friendship and affection for the Shah, the latter decided

> not to give orders or permission to construct railways or waterways to companies of foreign nations before consulting with His Majesty the Emperor; and this advice and consultation will meet with our consideration, in as much as, should

---

75. K. P. Pobedonostsev, *Pobedonostsev i ego korrespondenty* (Moscow, 1923), 1, 697.

76. V. Osipov to K. P. Pobedonostev, Moscow, October 5/17, 1887; ibid., No. 673, pp. 696–97.

those concessions contain an article or clause detrimental to Persian interests we can utilize the Emperor's consultation and advice in order to avoid it, and protect ourselves against detriment.[77]

Thus Russia now held what amounted to a right of veto over Persian railway construction.

Arthur Nicolson was unable, or perhaps unwilling, to pursue a vigorous policy. He ingratiated himself with the Shah, encouraging him to hope for a British guarantee of his country's independence, a guarantee no one in London was prepared to give. The chargé d'affaires felt that Britain should not waste her "energies in endeavouring to counter-act Russian influence on the Central Government at Tehran." He was perhaps the first British diplomat to despair of the possibility of contesting Russia's position.

> This part of the world [he wrote to Lord Dufferin, the Viceroy of India] is lost to us and we should devote the modicum of attention which we seem disposed to give to Persia to the south alone. If we could persuade some other power, say Germany, to join us in some definite assurances . . . well and good. But failing this, we could not single-handed undertake so serious a responsibility as any definite commitment.[78]

Such a policy must inevitably lead to the partition of Persia. Concentrating on the south alone, attempting to win the friendship of Mas'ud Mirzā Zell es-Soltān, "the Satrap at Ispahan," would be to invite Russia to divide the country. Nicolson did not advocate such a course, not yet. Twenty years later, with cold determination, he would help cut Persia in three parts and give the largest to Russia. His son and biographer writes:

> When asked, in later years, why he was so convinced in the necessity of an Anglo-Russian Convention, he replied unhesitatingly, "From what I saw in Persia in 1886." And already in February of that year he had written tentatively to

---

77. The Shah to Prince N. S. Dolgorukov, Month of Zi Hajjeh 1304 A.H. (August 21–September 18, 1887), Memorandum on Persian Railways, Secret, India Office, June 20, 1911; F.O. 471/1186.

78. H. Nicolson, *Portrait of a Diplomatist* (Boston, 1930), p. 49.

"*Pénétration Pacifique*"

Sir Philip Currie: "Of course if we could come to a mutual understanding with Russia on the integrity question—that would be the best solution of all." [79]

The Cabinet in London and the Government of India were unsure what policy to adopt. Though he gave in to Russia on almost every issue, the Shah never ceased begging Britain for guarantees, for an alliance which would offer Iran a firm assurance of support against Russian encroachments. As a matter of fact, the Shah pleaded for help against Russia with anyone who came along. Thus in 1883, when the United States opened a legation in Tehran, the Persian Minister of Foreign Affairs told Mr. Samuel G. W. Benjamin, United States minister and consul general, that Persia was threatened by Russia. He went on to suggest that a political treaty be concluded between the two nations, demonstrating thereby his total lack of knowledge of the position then occupied by the United States in the world.[80] Five years later the first Persian minister in Washington, Hāj Hoseyn Qoli Khān, presented to President Grover Cleveland "what must be one of the most colorful documents in American diplomatic history."

> The Persia knows herself capable for any kind of progress, and she is always desirous for opening every branches of modern civilization and advancement of mankind . . .
>
> And She never refuses any of those advantagious intercources for Her country and the people, But we have two great neighbours which instead of assisting us in those holy thoughts, they are always internally endeavouring to prevent us, the truth and clear is that they are entirely repulsing us from our progress. And want to do every important and needful of our affairs according to their own interest not for both sides, And because they are our neighbours, in any of those affairs they want to enter with us in an agreement which is not suitable for us and we cannot carry their proposes, because if the Government accepts what they say, it seems as She wants to hand her country to them. And if a

---

79. Ibid., p. 50.
80. A. Yeselson, *United States–Persian Diplomatic Relations, 1883–1921* (New Brunswick, 1956), p. 27.

company of any impartial nation wants to do with us an agreement which is convenient for us, they try to hinder and stop it.[81]

Malkam Khān continued to agitate in favor of closer ties between Britain and Persia. As a result of a conversation with the persuasive Persian minister, Lord Cross, Secretary of State for India, agreed that "it would be expedient to take measures to strengthen British influence in Persia." Since Colonel Murdock Smith, head of the Persian section of the Indo-European telegraph, was about to leave London for his post, the government entrusted him with a special mission to the Shah. He was to impress upon His Majesty the advantages of a railway connecting Tehran with Ahvāz and of opening the Kārun to steam navigation. He was also to obtain permission to station an agent at Esfahān, the headquarters of Zell es-Soltān.[82]

The Viceroy of India, Lord Dufferin, agreed with Cross that it was "expedient and important to strengthen British influence" in Persia, but the years he had spent as ambassador at St. Petersburg made him pessimistic about the chances of British success.

> We do not conceal from ourselves [he wrote] that the geographical situation of Russia, her energetic policy, and the rapid development of her military resources in the east, have given her great power at Tehran; and it seems improbable that any exertions on our part would now regain for us the position which we once held at the Court of the Shah.[83]

In this short passage Dufferin revealed the loss of nerve which would gradually affect large numbers of English statesmen when they confronted Russia. The twenty years of empty protests over Russia's advance in Central Asia must have undermined their confidence in their own power. The inability of Britain to stand up to any great continental power, unless in an alliance with

---

81. State Department Documents, Persia, Notes, 1, October 1888; as cited in Yeselson, pp. 39–40.

82. The Viceroy to Viscount Cross, Government of India, Foreign Department, No. 100A, Secret, External, Simla, June 24, 1887; L.I., 50, 1887.

83. Id.

"Pénétration Pacifique" 179

another continental nation, must have created a sense of insecurity in the hearts of even the loudest of imperialists. Did Gladstone, Salisbury, and the rest sense more than a quarter century before the First World War that Britain was not a first-rate military power? Russia's rulers answered this question in the affirmative.

While giving up hope for a full restoration of England's old position at Tehran, Dufferin believed "that something may yet be done to prevent, or at least retard, the complete subjection of Persia to Russian domination." Like Arthur Nicolson, and perhaps under his influence, for the latter repeatedly expressed such views in his letters to the Viceroy, Dufferin advocated concentrating on the southern and western provinces "where Russia has at present made little way." It was advisable to win over Zell es-Soltān by bestowing on him the decoration which he had coveted for years. As for the proposed Ahvāz-Tehran railway, Dufferin was for it, but felt that a guarantee to investors whose money would build it "would not be a legitimate application of Indian revenues, and would meet with hostile criticism from the Indian tax-payer." [84] Again Dufferin revealed a fundamental British weakness, the profit and loss approach to foreign and imperial policy, an approach that made Britain militarily weak and politically timid by comparison with Russia whose industrial, commercial, and fiscal resources were greatly inferior to her own. Of the members of the Viceroy's Council, only the Commander in Chief and a certain Mr. Scoble felt it advisable for political reasons to pledge public money as a guarantee on capital to be invested in the railway from Ahvāz to Tehran.[85]

In Tiflis and St. Petersburg, unlike Simla and London, statesmen were dreaming of new advances, not of saving some vestiges of a shattered influence. The confidence in the future, the dynamic and aggressive character of Russian planning, is evident from a report of Adjutant General Prince Aleksandr Mikhailovich Dondukov-Korsakov, Commander in Chief and principal administrative officer of the Caucasus, dated January 14/26, 1887. He

84. Id.
85. Id.

dealt with the role of Transcaspia as "an advanced post from which Russia can act successfully against the hostile designs of England," and with such problems as

> the gradual extension of our influence over the adjoining countries, the possible extention of material prosperity throughout the newly acquired territory, with the object of drawing therefrom the greatest advantage to ourselves, and of securing the subjugation of the population, not only by an exhibition of our strength, but by the introduction of new conditions of life.

Turning to Persia, the Prince stated that the frontier settlement of 1881 east of the Caspian was unsatisfactory. The headwaters of the streams that irrigated the fertile valleys along the border were on the Persian side, and the Transcaspian railway ran too close to the Persian frontier. Therefore the frontier should be moved further south. There was also the question of succession to the Persian throne. At the death of the reigning Shah, disturbances would break out everywhere and especially in Khorāsān, where the authority of the central government was weak. The local ilkhāns (tribal rulers) would attempt to reestablish their independence,

> and in order to secure the success of their designs, would seek our assistance and protection, or, what is even more probable, the inhabitants themselves of the parts of Khorasan adjoining the Russian frontier, being drawn more strongly toward the north than toward Persia, would turn to the administration of Trans-Caspia with a prayer to be received as subjects of Russia.

Insisting on the importance of Khorāsān, Dondukov-Korsakov pleaded for control over that province since without it the Herāt valley could not be incorporated into the Empire. The death of the Shah would certainly result in disorders in Persia, and Russia,

> by the force of circumstances, will be driven to active interference in the affairs of that country. The present Shah may

"Pénétration Pacifique"

. . . rule another ten years, or may die any day. The second son of the Shah, residing at Tabriz, is acknowledged by Russia as the legitimate heir to the Persian throne, but it is well known that his elder brother, Zil-i-Sultan, who rules at Ispahan, and administers about one half of Persia, is an honorable and determined man, who would not willingly submit himself to the rule of his younger and weak-minded brother.

A third son of the Shah, Kāmrān Mirzā Nāyeb os-Saltaneh, Minister of War and Governor of Tehran, might take advantage of his position in the capital and attempt to ascend the throne.

Hence spring the questions: Should we support absolutely the son whom we have recognized as the legitimate heir to the Persian Throne, and give him active assistance in troops and other means, if he should turn to Russia for them? Or should we remain inactive spectators of civil war in Persia, only taking measures for the protection of our interests, and eventually acknowledge as Shah that one of the brothers who shall have overcome the others? Or lastly, taking advantage of these quarrels, should we not, under pretext of preserving tranquility in Trans-Caspia, occupy certain important points in Khorasan, and then offer our protection to that one of the pretenders to the throne who would consent to conclude a Treaty with Russia for the delimitation of a new frontier for the Trans-Caspian Province, in accordance with the lines I have already laid down? [86]

Though Dondukov-Korsakov's report was not followed in its entirety, much of its analysis and many of its suggestions were accepted by the Russian government. The problem of succession did not arise until 1896 when Nāser ed-Din Shah was shot dead by a follower of Jamāl ed-Din Asadābādi (Afghāni). The

86. Report of Adjutant-General Prince Dondukov-Korsakov, St. Petersburg, January 14/26, 1887, Enclosure No. 2, Memorandum on the Condition of the Trans-Caspian Province, Secret (Translation); Mr. Dering to the Marquis of Salisbury, No. 294, Received August 27, 1888. (Note: This report was obtained and translated by Lieutenant-Colonel Herbert); F. O. 65/1460.

disorders predicted by Dondukov-Korsakov did not occur. Over the previous decade the central government had acquired sufficient control over Khorāsān to prevent serious outbreaks. No struggle for the throne developed among Nāser ed-Din's sons. On both these counts Dondukov-Korsakov proved an indifferent prophet. However, his recommendations in regard to Khorāsān and the extension of Russian influence within Iran were acted upon. A number of Moslem religious leaders were recruited and became Russian agents, conducting especially effective propaganda at Mashhad, the location of the shrine of Imam Rezā, Persia's greatest saint.[87] Simultaneously anti-Shiite propaganda was conducted by other Russian agents among Turkoman, Baluch, and other Sunnite tribes of Khorāsān and Seistān in the hope of securing their adherence to Russia in case civil strife broke out in Iran. Lord Curzon, a perceptive and well-informed observer, wrote, after visiting the area:

> along the entire circumference of Khorasan, from north-west to south-east, occur a succession of points at which Russian interference, influence, or intrigue is being actively pushed forward; and so the Muscovite toils are steadily and surely being wound round the body of the intended victim.[88]

Dondukov-Korsakov's speculations and proposals were symptomatic of a growing Russian interest in and concern for Iran's internal affairs. So was the appointment in November 1886 of Prince Nikolai Sergeevich Dolgorukov, scion of one of Russia's most distinguished aristocratic families and personal friend of the Tsar, to the post of minister in Tehran. Driven by insatiable

---

87. A British intelligence agent reported from Mashhad: "The Russian Consul General has given a present of a hundred tumans to a leading preacher at Meshed, who spoke in favour of the Russian Government in the course of one of his sermons. The other Ulemas of the Shrine reported the matter to the Governor-General, who has called upon the preacher to explain why he is in communication with the Russian Consul General, and what right he had to speak of the Russian Government in the pulpit." Memorandum of information regarding the course of affairs beyond the North-Western Frontier, received during the month of June 1890, Enclosure in Letter to H. M.'s Secretary of State for India, No. 81, July 7, 1890, Simla, Foreign Department, Secret, Frontier; *L.I.*, 60, 1890.

88. G. N. Curzon, *Persia and the Persian Question*, 1, 201.

ambition, a sense of his own and his country's superiority, and a strong dislike for the bureaucrats of the Giers-Zinov'ev type, Dolgorukov "was convinced that the torch of Russia's historic mission in the East had been handed to him personally that he might encompass some great deed by its light." [89] A master of court intrigue, polished and charming when necessary though boorish and arrogant by nature, Dolgorukov, upon arriving in Tehran, assumed with the Shah and his ministers the tone of ruler of a conquered province.

The Shah was offended and frightened by the high-handed behavior of the new envoy. He turned for help to the British chargé d'affaires, Arthur Nicolson.

> If England would protect him from the consequences and if she would give him strength to resist the demands of Russia, which he was convinced would be impossible and exacting . . . he would do all that Her Majesty's Government desired. He would be guided absolutely and entirely by us [the British] and place himself with confidence in our hands. But without such support, alone and unaided, he could not face the consequences.[90]

Thus once again Nāser ed-Din was pleading for an alliance or a guarantee, and once again the British gave an evasive answer.

Nicolson explained that his government could not run ahead of public opinion which "did not as yet understand the importance to British interests of the integrity and independence of Persia." The British public, he continued, thought in terms of trade and progress, and only if the Shah "opened the southern trade routes and introduced democratic reforms" would there be enough support for the government to assume responsibilities for the protection of Persia.[91] The Shah was certainly able to translate Nicolson's phrases about trade and democratic reforms into the language of real power relations. Their meaning was plain: Britain

---

89. A. P. Thornton, "British Policy in Persia, 1858–1890," *The English Historical Review*, 69, No. 273 (October 1945), 579.
90. Nicolson to Salisbury, July 5, 1887, as cited in H. Nicolson, pp. 50–51.
91. H. Nicolson, p. 51.

might support Persia if the latter opened her gates to British capital, but no definite promises would be given.

The Shah may have also been alarmed by Nicolson's wooing of Zell es-Soltān, who, Nicolson hoped, might be able to obtain for Britain the right to build a railway north from the Persian Gulf. Once before the British had tried to circumvent the Shah. Ronald Thomson and E. C. Ross had failed when they attempted to use Zell es-Soltān to open navigation on the Kārun. In his desire to obtain a railway concession, Nicolson made the same mistake. Zell es-Soltān still wanted the Grand Cross of the Star of India, and Nicolson took it upon himself to champion his cause, partly out of fear that the prince, disappointed in the British, might turn to Russia.[92]

In September 1887 the India Office at last decided to decorate Zell es-Soltān. A few months later he was called to Tehran and dismissed from all his posts save the governorship of Esfahān. The supposed strong man, around whom Nicolson would build the British policy for Persia, proved that he was at least clever enough to realize his own weakness and made no attempt whatsoever to disobey his father. His position was ruined but his life was safe. Zell es-Soltān survived even Nicolson's requests to the Shah that he be reinstated in all his former governorships.[93]

If Arthur Nicolson was not a complete failure as chargé d'affaires at Tehran, he was not a success either. It was felt in London that a stronger personality was needed at the court of the Shah, and that whoever was appointed to that post must enjoy some standing at home. The Foreign Office found such a person in Sir Henry Drummond Wolff.

Henry Drummond Wolff, son of the courageous traveler who was among the first Europeans to penetrate Bukhara, was a remarkable and colorful individual. Well educated, clever, outwardly cynical, overflowing with energy, he poured forth an unending stream of commercial and diplomatic ideas, projects, and schemes. Sir Henry had ties to both the City and Westminster.

92. Various Foreign Office and India Office documents (including a private letter of Nicolson to Rawlinson, April 26, 1887) cited in R. L. Greaves, *Persia and the Defence of India*, pp. 150–52.

93. Greaves, pp. 153–54.

"Pénétration Pacifique"

He had made a career as a diplomat, sat in the House of Commons, was a founder of the Primrose League, and numbered among his friends the Rothschilds, the Sassoons, Julius de Reuter, and Lord Randolph Churchill. Indeed he was, or at least seemed to be, a perfect embodiment of the spirit of Imperialism as defined by Lenin. Though it is unlikely that he either knew or read Marx, Sir Henry firmly believed in the primacy of economics. Government and diplomacy were only means for the achievement of economic ends. Yet, contrary to the Leninist view of what an imperialist should be like, Sir Henry was simultaneously a vocal exponent of finance capital and an upholder of international peace. Long association with Lord Randolph Churchill made him also believe in the need for an Anglo-Russian entente.

Churchill introduced Wolff to the Prince of Wales, who enjoyed "the cynical frankness of Wolff's conversation and his lively epistolary style." [94] In 1885 Wolff left Parliament and returned to the diplomatic service. At this time the future Edward VII was exposed to a number of influences in favor of better relations with Russia. Unlike his predecessors, Shuvalov, Lobanov, and Mohrenheim, the new Russian ambassador, Staal, found favor with the Prince of Wales. His "attractive manner made him a popular figure in English society, and intimacy with the Prince developed steadily during the Ambassador's nineteen years' tenure of office." Sir Robert Morier, a protégé of the prince, to whom he owed his appointment as ambassador at St. Petersburg, was also inclined toward an understanding with Russia. However, the most vigorous proponent of an Anglo-Russian agreement was the flamboyant Lord Randolph Churchill. Toward the end of 1887 he and his American wife visited Russia, where he "proclaimed in all Russian quarters—official and social—a complete identity of interests between England and Russia." This was too much even for Sir Robert Morier, who declared that Churchill was "a dangerous man." The Queen herself urged her son to prevent his friend from expressing in public "such dangerous doctrines." [95]

94. S. Lee, *King Edward VII* (London, 1925), 1, 685.
95. Ibid., p. 681.

When in October 1887 Salisbury appointed Wolff minister to Iran, he must have been aware of the latter's Russian sympathies. Yet, as Dr. R. L. Greaves points out in her study of Salisbury's Persian policy, "the object of the Wolff mission, as the Foreign Office envisaged it, was the revitalization of the buffer policy." [96] Thus Wolff would inevitably have to work against the interests of Russia. Salisbury explained that the principal questions which would concern the minister were: "the integrity of Persia, the development of its resources, and the maintenance of a strong, independent and friendly Government." [97] Before Wolff left for his post he was given explicit instructions as to the talks he was expected to pursue.

The main goals of British policy were thus summarized:

It is to the interest of this country that the integrity of Persia should be maintained, that its resources should be developed, and that its Government should be strong, independent, and friendly. It is to the promotion of these objects that your attention should be directed, and so long, at least, as there is any reasonable hope of their being realized, the efforts of Her Majesty's Government would be to frustrate any policy incompatible with them.[98]

Wolff was told to watch the developments on Persia's northeastern border, and to encourage the Persians "to do their utmost in strengthening the administration and police of the frontier districts." He was also to continue urging the Shah to develop communications between the capital and the Persian Gulf. This would involve the opening of the Kārun to navigation up to Ahvāz, from which point a railway could be constructed no further than the plateau north and northwest of Dezful. The Persian government should be persuaded to guarantee a fair return on capital invested by pledging the revenue of its customs, which should be placed under European supervision. There was not a word about endeavoring to reach an understanding with Russia.

96. Greaves, p. 157.
97. H. D. Wolff, *Rambling Recollections* (London, 1908), 2, 337.
98. Salisbury to Wolff, No. 14, Very Confidential, February 29, 1888; F. O. 60/491. This document has been published in Greaves, Appendix IV, pp. 256–71.

Salisbury had raised the Persian question with the Russian ambassador, Staal, suggesting that the two great powers renew the assurance that they would respect Persia's integrity, that their rivalry over the development of Persian commerce was inexpedient and an agreement on railways desirable, and that it was also desirable to settle the question of the Russo-Persian frontier east of the Caspian. At Staal's request, Wolff called upon him on March 3, 1888, to be told that Giers agreed with the first suggestion. The question of railways, he felt, should be treated with the Shah. "As to the delineation of the Russo-Persian border, Giers considered this a problem to be dealt with by Russia and Persia alone." A diplomat more experienced in dealing with the Russians would have understood at once that St. Petersburg was not interested in a rapprochement. A person of finer grain would have sensed Russian reluctance to pursue the subject. Wolff's statement to Staal that he was instructed to keep on most friendly terms with Prince Dolgorukov and, "as far as possible, to act in cooperation with him" must have sounded alarming to the Russians for whom any departure of the British from their customary passive policy was a potential threat.[99] Indeed the Russians saw a challenge in the very appointment of Sir Henry Drummond Wolff, as did the representatives of other nations at Tehran. Monsieur de Balloy, the French minister, believed that Sir Henry had come to Tehran with the express idea of combating Russian influence and reestablishing England's old hegemony. In his dispatches Balloy repeatedly attributed to Wolff the desire to gain for England an "exclusive" influence in Persia. He wanted to open Persia to British commerce, to create industries, to construct railways, in order to build up British economic interests to the point where the Parliament would find it impossible not to support a strong Persian policy. Thus in the opinion of the French legation, the Foreign Office was promoting commercial interests in Persia so as to compel the Parliament to support the Cabinet's political position there.[100]

Marie René Davy de Chavigné de Balloy may have slightly

99. Wolff, 2, 338–39.
100. Balloy to Ribot, Direction politique, No. 38 [n.d.; stamp of the *Cabinet du Ministre*, January 27, 1891]; Archive des Affaires Etrangères, Correspondance Politique, Perse, tome 42, folio 242.

overstated the case, yet he was entirely right in attributing political motives to British attempts to develop their Persian commerce. Economically there was not, nor could there be at the time, much advantage in investing money in Iran when South Africa, Latin America, Canada, and even the United States were ready to absorb vast amounts of capital at a fraction of the risk involved in Persian investments. Sir Henry Drummond Wolff, friend of the Sassoons and of Reuter, would certainly try his best to promote their business, but the British government, and Salisbury first of all, looked upon the development of British economic interests in Persia in the spirit noted by Balloy.

The promotion of economic enterprise in Persia was a thankless if not an impossible task. The country lacked many of the essential prerequisites of economic development, including the will to develop. During most of Nāser ed-Din's reign, conditions in Persia were deteriorating. The savage suppression of the Babis in 1848–52 and the systematic persecution of the Baha'is in later years sapped the strength and prevented the growth of a progressive urban middle class. The close cooperation between the mullas and the government in opposing the Babi-Baha'i movement was almost entirely to the advantage of the clergy, which increased its hold on the Shah and the bureaucracy, and stigmatized as a Babi any Persian who dared to open his mind to Western influence.

The government was incredibly lawless and corrupt. Even critical foreign observers either did not see the extent of demoralization that prevailed in Iran, or could not bring themselves to tell the whole story. Curzon softened the colors when he described the government of Persia in his classic work. It is in secret diplomatic dispatches, diaries, and private correspondence that the depth of the country's degradation is fully revealed. The commander of the Persian Cossack Brigade, Colonel V. A. Kosogovskii, who served in Tehran in the mid eighteen-nineties, left a small gallery of frightening sketches of Persia's rulers. Either monarchic sentiments or a certain delicacy of feeling prevented him from saying too much about the new Shah, Mozaffar ed-Din (the diary entries were made in 1896–97), but of the Crown Prince, Mohammad Ali Mirzā, Kosogovskii says: "The Valiahd's mind is not well developed. He is dull, greedy, and takes the most shameful bribes. Indulging in unnatural vices, he has, according to his own brothers, been infected with syphilis." [101]

The new Shah's third son, Sālār od-Dowleh, engaged in a feud with his father's brother-in-law, favorite and War Minister, Farmānfarmā, and without a trace of embarrassment shouted for the whole palace to hear, "this *pedar-sukhteh* [son of a burnt father], this dog Farmānfarmā, has grabbed everything from my stupid daddy, including the War Ministry. I, Sālār od-Dowleh, and not that rogue, that stinking cur Farmānfarmā, should be Minister of War." [102] Prince Farmānfarmā, the victim of such tirades, was characterized by Kosogovskii as "a jesuit." When the Shah had suddenly fallen into an anticorruption mood, Farmānfarmā, famous for looting whole provinces, pretended to honesty, "while never letting go of an opportunity to grab wherever possible ... And the Shah himself ... quietly sold batallions from one commander to another for two or three thousand tumāns." [103]

Kāmrān Mirzā Nāyeb os-Saltaneh, Kosogovskii wrote, "has neither conscience, heart, nor sense of gratitude, and, like a true Qājār, and Oriental despot, is cowardly and fawning in adversity and, conversely, heartless and perfidious when in power." [104] His elder brother, Mas'ud Mirzā Zell es-Soltān, G.C.S.I., was a vicious, unscrupulous tyrant. Ronald Thomson, who had courted him in the line of duty, described how the prince, anticipating an increase in the price of grain, bought, or rather took at nominal prices, a large quantity. When the famine on which he had hoped to make a killing failed to occur, His Imperial Highness "endeavored to dispose of this grain at forced high prices." Disturbances broke out and were only quelled with the help of two army regiments.[105]

From the capital, the rot spread to the provinces. Life and

---

101. V. A. Kosogovskii, *Iz tegeranskogo dnevnika polkovnika V. A. Kosogovskogo* (Moscow, 1960), p. 133.
102. Ibid., p. 110.
103. Ibid., p. 105.
104. Id.
105. R. Thomson to Salisbury, No. 130, June 5, 1879; F.O. 60/421.

property were nowhere safe. The clergy were as lawless as government officials. The Emām Jom'e of Esfahān ordered the assassination of two prominent Baha'i merchants to avoid repaying a debt he owed them. The chief mulla of Ardebil terrorized the town to such an extent that the inhabitants begged the British consul general at Rasht to save them from the scourge. The list of swindles, torture, crime, and perversion could be continued indefinitely.[106]

Under such conditions it was plainly impossible to promote the economic development of the country. Immediately upon his arrival in Tehran in April 1888, Sir Henry Drummond Wolff, whose optimism was boundless, devised the means for the reform of the system. "My first efforts," he writes in his memoirs, "were directed towards inducing the shah to issue a proclamation securing the rights and property of his subjects."[107] The Shah, looking forward to advantages that would accrue to himself, and hoping to secure a British guarantee of his country's integrity, published the proclamation suggested by Wolff. It promised to the peoples of the Empire freedom and independence in matters of property. The Shah's subjects now had the right to form companies and engage in the promotion of "any branch of the branches of civilization and wealth." The sovereign himself proclaimed it his duty to protect this right, and stated that "no one shall have the right or power to lay hands upon, or take possession of, or interfere with, the life or property, or punish or chastise the subjects of the Persian Government, except it be in execution of the religious and civil laws."[108]

As far as the Persian people were concerned, the proclamation might just as well not have existed. A vast majority of city dwellers, let alone the peasantry, never heard of it, and those who did could have interpreted it to mean only that such was the Shah's momentary whim. Lord Curzon noted that the proclamation made very little difference in the provinces. Actually, outside

---

106. Id.
107. Wolff, 2, 343.
108. Proclamation securing the property rights of the Persians, May, 1888; as cited in Wolff, 2, 341.

"Pénétration Pacifique" 191

the small European colonies in the larger cities, it made no difference at all.[109]

Sir Henry Drummond Wolff felt that the Shah's property rights' proclamation had been his triumph. The next step in his private program for Persia, as distinguished from the policy set by Salisbury and the Foreign Office, was to arrive at an amicable understanding with Russia, whose minister, Prince Nikolai Dolgorukov, Wolff approached. Dolgorukov showed no interest in informal conversations. If Britain was serious, let Wolff state his proposals in writing so that they might serve as a basis for negotiations. After exchanging a number of telegrams with Salisbury, Wolff wrote Dolgorukov a confidential letter. "It was," he reports, "absolutely personal on my part, and could in no respect compromise Her Majesty's Government." [110]

Wolff suggested to Dolgorukov the abandonment of the old Anglo-Russian rivalry and a new approach to the Persian problem. The object of the settlement he had in mind was not egotistic, nor was it designed "for the exclusive advantage of our two Governments." Wolff's aim was rather to "civilize" Persia.

> It seems to me [he wrote] that by establishing the prosperity of this country, and by assisting in the development of her resources, her two neighbours will interpose between their frontiers a neutral territory, which, while profiting by their support and legitimate influence, would remove the friction which is the inevitable result of a state of uncertainty.[111]

Dolgorukov would have been blind not to see what Wolff's strategy was. In the long duel between Britain and Russia in the Middle East, the former was proposing to try new weapons. That Britain was a world champion in industry, commerce, and banking, while Russia tottered on the brink of insolvency, could not have been overlooked by Wolff when he put forth a policy that would surely lead to Russia's being pushed out of Iran. Dolgorukov read the letter, thanked Sir Henry, and remarked "that the

109. See Curzon, *Persia and the Persian Question*, 1, 466.
110. Wolff, 2, 346.
111. Ibid., p. 347.

principal difficulty in the way of an arrangement was the fact that where British commerce flourished, Russian trade failed." [112]

Exchanges of letters and conversations with Dolgorukov did not stop Wolff from pursuing his more concrete tasks, among which the opening of the Kārun River was the most pressing. More than any of his predecessors in Tehran, Sir Henry was conscious of the potential wealth of Khuzestān, of which the Kārun was the forbidden highway. He waxed poetic describing the abundance of the province.

> Tobacco, rice, dates, grain—especially barley—cotton, indigo, and opium could all be grown there. Sugar had, at one time, been very abundant. Tentcloths and coarse woollens were extensively manufactured. White naphtha and bitumen were also produced, and there are signs of old irrigation works. Khuzistan, with little care, could be made a second Egypt.[113]

Sir Henry found a strong supporter in the Shah's new favorite, Mirzā Ali Asghar Khān Amin os-Soltān. He was a grandson of a Georgian who had been captured by the Persians during Āqā Mohammad Khān's campaign of 1795. The Georgian prisoner was presented to a certain Qāsem Khān Qājār in whose household he remained as a servant to the end of his life. Having embraced Islam, Zāl Khān (the name by which the Georgian was known in Persia), married an Esfahāni woman and raised a family. When Qāsem Khān died, the family stayed on with their late master's daughter. The young lady married Mohammad Shah, and Zāl Khān found himself in the service of the Empress of Iran. When her son, the boy Nāser ed-Din Mirzā, was appointed Governor of Āzarbāyjān, Zāl Khān's four sons were sent along to run his household. The third of these, Ebrāhim, was especially liked by the young Prince. In 1848 Nāser ed-Din ascended the throne. Ebrāhim moved to Tehran and married a second wife, an Esfahāni girl who bore him six sons and two daughters. The eldest of these children was Ali Asghar, the future favorite and Prime Minister of Nāser ed-Din Shah.

112. Ibid., p. 346.
113. Ibid., pp. 343–44.

Ebrāhim spared no pains or expense in educating his eldest son. By the time he was sixteen, the bright and good-looking Ali Asghar was an accomplished Persian and Arabic scholar. It was said that he was very much attracted to the life of a dervish, to Sufi poetry, and to learning, but that his father, now an important Court official bearing the title of Amin os-Soltān (the Trusted One of the King), prevailed upon him to enter the service of the Shah. When Āqā Ebrāhim died in 1883, Nāser ed-Din Shah bestowed the father's title on Mirzā Ali Asghar Khān. Thereafter his rise was swift.

In 1884 he was employed in secret negotiations with the British legation, where he was considered a friend. He was close to Arthur Nicolson and worked with him against the Russian minister, A. A. Melnikov. By the time Wolff arrived in Tehran, Mirzā Ali Asghar Khān Amin os-Soltān was, next to the Shah, the most important man in Persia.[114] Clever, sensitive, well-mannered, ambitious, unscrupulous, and financially corrupt, Amin os-Soltān remained the Shah's favorite until the latter's assassination in 1896. Yahyā Khān Moshir od-Dowleh, Qavām od-Dowleh, Amin od-Dowleh, and two of the Shah's sons—Zell es-Soltān and Nāyeb os-Saltaneh—were among the favorite's enemies. None was able to undermine his position, and the decline of Zell es-Soltān's fortunes in 1888 was often attributed to his influence.

It was Wolff's good fortune to have such a person for a friend and collaborator in the Kārun matter. Sir Henry appreciated Ali Asghar Khān's qualities. He wrote that he was a cool-headed, able, and judicious man, who inevitably inspired regard in all who knew him.

> He was accused of being in favor of Russia; but once he said to me, "It is absolutely necessary for me to hold the balance between England and Russia. Russia has a frontier of twelve hundred miles on the country, and without declaring war she

114. Note by Nawab Hasan Ali Khan on the Descent, Biography, and Character of Ali Asghar Khan, Sadre Azam, dated September 22, 1895, Appendix 2 in Memorandum by Sir M. Durand on the Situation in Persia, prepared for the use of the Foreign Office, December 1895, Confidential (6704); F.O. 60/581.

can at any time do great injury to Persia by raising against her some of the numerous Yamoot Turcoman frontier tribes." [115]

Wolff's trust and confidence in Amin os-Soltān were fully justified. The Shah and his Prime Minister were seeking British support against ever-increasing Russian pressure. Prince Dolgorukov's behavior in Tehran was offensive, but the cold intransigence of I. A. Zinov'ev, Director of the Asiatic Department of the Ministry of Foreign Affairs, formerly minister in Tehran, was even more frightening. The Persian minister in Vienna once told Prince A. B. Lobanov-Rostovskii that his government's English orientation was due entirely to the behavior of the Russians themselves. The people were beginning to suspect that Russia intentionally tried to keep Persia low and "to obstruct the growth of her trade and her development out of egotistic considerations of domination." Commenting on the Persian diplomat's complaint, Vladimir Nikolaevich Lamsdorff, assistant to Giers at the Foreign Ministry, jotted down in his diary: "These considerations do not lack justice, and the Minister [Giers] talked about it more than once, calling Zinov'ev's attention to the dangerous side of the system of intimidation and constant refusals of Persian requests adopted by him." [116]

For the Persian government, Russian displeasure could be costly. Thus Amin os-Soltān's words about Russia's raising Turkoman tribes referred to a rebellion that was either still in progress or had just been put down. It had been provoked, no doubt, by traditional Persian misgovernment. To suppress it the government fielded an army of 13,000 men. The governors of Khorāsān and Astarābād and the khans of Quchān and Bojnurd mismanaged the campaign, stole their soldiers' pay, and generally demoralized the men to the point where regiments of one thousand or two thousand men would run from a few hundred Yomuts. The rebellion was finally quelled by diplomacy, or treachery, when the government succeeded in sowing discord

---

115. Wolff, 2, 328–29.
116. V. N. Lamsdorff, *Dnevnik V. N. Lamzdorfa* (1886–1890) (Moscow, 1926), p. 90.

"*Pénétration Pacifique*"

among the tribes, and the leading rebel, Hāji Nazar Khān of the Ātābāi tribe, was lured into a trap and murdered. The Russians did not make a move. However, the Persian government did not miss the significance of the fact that the Yomuts were armed with Russian rifles and cartridges.[117]

For the sake of a British guarantee, Nāser ed-Din Shah was now willing to open the Kārun and make other concessions. Various details which had, in previous negotiations, turned into insurmountable obstacles were swept away. Amin os-Soltān asked only for a written document, an insurance policy against Russian encroachment. On October 24, 1888, Wolff, with the approval of his government, gave Amin os-Soltān a written statement to the effect that

> In the event of any power making an attack without just cause or provocation on Persia, or attempting to take possession of Persian territory against the will of the Persian Government, Her Majesty's Government engage to make earnest representations against such proceedings, and to take such steps as may in their judgement be best calculated to prevent any infringement of the integrity of Persia.[118]

On October 30 the Shah published a firman opening the Kārun to "commercial steamers of all nations, without exception." [119]

St. Petersburg, which received the news of the opening of the Kārun before the decree had been published, was both angered and discouraged. It seemed for a moment that all past efforts to hold the Shah firmly in hand had collapsed. In the margin of a telegram in which the Russian chargé d'affaires in Tehran, Poggio, suggested means of influencing Nāser ed-Din, Alexander III wrote: "Unfortunately, we know well how the Shah has put himself in the hands of the English and does nothing without

---

117. Curzon, 1, 190–91.

118. H. D. Wolff to Salisbury, No. 233, Tehran, October 28, 1888, as cited in Memorandum on Persian Railways, Secret, India Office, June 20, 1911; F. O. 371/1186.

119. Wolff published the text of the firman of October 30, 1888 (24 Safar 1303) in his *Rambling Recollections*, 2, 344.

their advice."[120] The high society and the press were in an uproar. "British intrigues once again became a favorite theme of the Russian literature devoted to the Persian question."[121] Prince Dolgorukov, who happened to be in St. Petersburg when the event occurred, was hurt in his pride. A year later Giers admitted to Sir Robert Morier that the storm raised in Russia over the Kārun was partly the result of the fact that

> it was a diplomatic struggle between Prince Dolgorouki and Sir Henry Wolff, in which the former, *tout fin qu'il est*, got the worst of it. I [Morier] said that in that case it was entirely the Prince's fault, who, instead of accepting the candid and straight forward cooperation of Her Majesty's Minister, had suspected tricks, and looked for a *midi a quatorze heures*.[122]

The violent reaction of the Russian press elicited no reply from Tehran, but in Constantinople, a city with a relatively large colony of Persian merchants, the Persian language newspaper *Akhtar* bitterly accused Russia of trying to prevent Persia from achieving prosperity and progress. In 1873, *Akhtar* wrote in its issue of December 5, 1888, Russia had prevented an English company from constructing a railway between Rasht, Tehran, and Bushehr. Her "real object" was to avoid Persia having intercourse with the nations of Europe and that she might not be awakened from her slumber to improve her condition." It was for this same reason that Russia prohibited the transit of European goods through the Caucasus, thus preventing Persia's progress and, simultaneously pursuing her own unjust policy through a Dolgorukov, a military man ignorant of diplomacy.

> Prince Dolgorouki is rough, proud and ambitious . . . Recently it was published in one of the French papers (very probably at the instigation of the Prince himself) that Prince

---

120. Marginal note by the Tsar, Alexander III, on Poggio's secret telegram of October 14/26, 1888, Ministry of Foreign Affairs file "O plavanii inostrannykh sudov po reke Karunu i vdol beregov persidskogo zaliva," No. 589, 1889–92; cited in A. Popov, "Stranitsa . . . ," p. 138.

121. A. Popov, p. 138.

122. Morier to Salisbury, No. 341, Secret and Confidential, St. Petersburg, November 6, 1889; F. O. 65/1379.

"*Pénétration Pacifique*" 197

Dolgorouki's influence in Persia has attained such a high degree that Persia has assumed the character of one of the provinces of Russia and all the internal affairs of Persia are transacted in the cabinet of the Prince and with his knowledge.

The *Akhtar* expressed its belief in the peaceful intentions of both the Tsar and his Foreign Minister, Giers. But there were others who could do things against the Emperor's wishes. Alexander II had not wanted to fight a war against Turkey but was forced into it by General Ignat'ev. The Russians complained that Persia changed her formerly friendly policy toward Russia.

If the envoy and agents of Russia would restrain themselves from their autocratic bearing in Persia it is evident that there would be no change in the policy of Persia toward Russia, and that Persia would strive more than ever to maintain the old friendship so long existing between them but what a pity that this is improbable in as much as the Russian envoy and agents will not abstain from that misplaced arrogance which is beyond their duty and role . . . Russian statesmen should know that Persia's soil is a den of braves and lions and that the inhabitants of that noble land are not to be compared with barbarous desert haunting Turkomans devoid of any spirit of patriotism.[123]

The article is significant, for it touches upon themes and expresses sentiments that will recur year after year. The phraseology itself, a mixture of whine and Hāji Bābā bombast, will become standard in Persian periodicals abroad. What is unusual about *Akhtar's* article is the insight into the situation and the largely correct information it conveyed. One is tempted to speculate on its sources, for it is not impossible that the article was inspired by the Persian or even the British embassy at Constantinople.

The opening of the Kārun was seen everywhere as a great victory for Great Britain. The Shah was "alarmed at what he had

---

123. Translation, From the gazette Akhter [sic], No. 102, December 5, 1888, Enclosure No. 1 in Wolff to Salisbury, No. 25, Tehran, January 22, 1889; F. O. 60/549.

done" and "nervous of the possible demands of Russia." [124] No one in Tehran doubted that the Russian government would seek compensation for the advantage gained by its rival in the south. The Persians had reasons to anticipate fresh demands for extensive railway concessions.

In the summer of 1888 a Belgian company had built a narrow-gauge railway from Tehran to the shrine of Shāhzādeh Abd ol-Azim. The line, less than six miles long, was opened on June 25 to the great delight of the Shah, who had at last endowed his Empire with this important symbol of progress. The Belgians, who had large capital at their disposal, then proposed to build a line from the Caspian to Tehran and southward to the Persian Gulf. Prince Nikolai Sergeevich Dolgorukov reacted violently, threatening to leave Persia if the government granted such a concession. The British muttered about Reuter's rights. The Belgians scaled down their requests and got busy building a horse tramway in Tehran.[125]

Dolgorukov, who had for some time favored the idea of a Russian-built railway in Persia, became the strongest advocate of Russian entrepreneurs who expressed their willingness to undertake such a venture. Among them was V. P. Osipov, a Moscow merchant who has been mentioned earlier in connection with his complaint to Pobedonostsev about some Berlin Jews who intended to promote a railway in Persia. In January 1888, Osipov submitted to Ivan Alekseevich Vyshnegradskii, the Minister of Finance, a project for the construction of a line from Rasht through Tehran and Esfahān to Bushehr. Osipov and a number of his Moscow associates would obtain from the Shah a concession to build the railway if their capital were guaranteed a 6 percent profit. In a memorandum to Giers, Vyshnegradskii said that in his opinion "the construction of the above named railway would appear important and desirable in the interests of the development of Russian trade in Persia." Moreover, it would furnish "Russian factories work and orders for the manufacture of railway equipment for the above named road." However,

---

124. Wolff to Salisbury, No. 16, Confidential, Tehran, January 20, 1889; ibid.
125. A. Popov, "Stranitsa . . . ," pp. 137–38.

"Pénétration Pacifique" 199

Vyshnegradskii continued, in the interests of Russia the road should be built in sections, beginning at Rasht. Only after the traffic on the Rasht-Tehran section developed sufficiently could the section from Tehran to Esfahān be built.

As for the last section from Esfahān to the Persian Gulf, in my opinion its construction could be started not before Russian industrial and commercial influence in Persia becomes so firm, due to the projected railway, that it would not be endangered by competition from the influence of other states.

The Persian government must guarantee the capital invested in the railway by pledging its customs revenues, and the Russian government should participate in this beneficial scheme by opening credit for the railway company at the Russian State Bank.[126]

Later in the year two other proposals were submitted to the Russian government, one from a wealthy businessman, Lazar Poliakov, the other from the ubiquitous Baron de Reuter. Lazar Solomonovich Poliakov came from a poor Jewish family of Orsha. He displayed his great commercial talents while still a very young man, when he turned railway contractor and became a millionaire. Wealth enabled him to overcome the disabilities the Russian government placed on its Jewish subjects. L. S. Poliakov was one of the very few Jews to have been granted the rank of privy counsellor (*tainyi sovetnik*).

Under the aegis of M. Kh. Reutern (Reitern), Finance Minister from 1862 to 1876 and an advocate of laissez-faire, Russia's economy raced forward. Rapid development led to feverish speculation and the emergence of the first industrial-capitalist fortunes. Lazar Poliakov and his brother Samuil invested their money in a variety of enterprises. Lazar was the founder of the Banking House of Poliakov, founder and director of the Moscow and the Yaroslav-Kostroma Agricultural banks, the Orel Commercial Bank, the South Russian Industrial Bank, the Riazan Commercial Bank. He was the animating force behind the Moscow Lumber Company and the Moscow Housing Construction Society. He in-

---

126. Minister of Finance, I. Vyshnegradskii, to the Minister of Foreign Affairs, N. Giers, January 1888, Secret; Pobedonostsev, *Pobedonostsev i ego korrespondenty*, 1, 844–46.

vested in paper, railways, rubber, and a number of other industries.[127] Poliakov was among the first to rush into the Central Asiatic market once Turkestan had been pacified. He organized the Persian and Central Asiatic Industrial and Commercial Society. The company opened a match factory in Tehran, investing in it 400,000 rubles. Poor location (far from the sources of match wood), low quality, and high price, however, made it impossible for Poliakov's matches to compete with the Austrian import. The Persian venture lost him money.[128]

Considering his wide business interests, his propensity to take risks, and his previous connections with Persia, it was almost inevitable that Poliakov should enter the Persian railway race. He must have gauged the political situation in St. Petersburg, after Persia opened the Kārun to navigation, and decided that the Russian government would surely endeavor to counteract this British coup by promoting railways in northern Persia. In such a case the government might be reluctant to build railways openly, and would perhaps prefer to subsidize private builders. Millions of rubles in government grants would flow to him who knew how to attract fiscal grace. Poliakov began by recruiting such "whales" of the Moscow business community as Rukavishnikov and Morozov. N. N. Konshin, "who is a man of good social position," as an English diplomat characterized him, undertook to represent their nascent company in the official world of St. Petersburg. Konshin had entrée to Prince Dolgorukov and to the various ministries. He guided the latest Poliakov scheme through the bureaucratic labyrinth of St. Petersburg.[129] Poliakov, in a memorandum submitted to the government on December 8, 1888, proposed either to form a purely Russian company for the construction of a railway from Rasht to Tehran, or to enter into partnership with the already functioning Belgian Société Anonyme.[130]

127. P. I. Liashchenko, *Istoriia narodnogo khoziaistva S.S.S.R.* (Leningrad, 1952), 2, 179, 457.

128. M. L. Tomara, *Ekonomicheskoe polozhenie Persii* (St. Petersburg, 1895), pp. 104–05.

129. Memorandum compiled from confidential but official data by John Mitchell, St. Petersburg, February 6, 1889, Enclosure in Morier to Salisbury, No. 41, Confidential, St. Petersburg, February 6, 1889; F. O. 65/1377.

130. A. Popov, "Stranitsa . . . ," p. 139.

Another group to come forward with a Persian railway project was that of N. A. Khomiakov, marshal of the nobility of Smolensk province; Baron P. L. Korff; and S. E. Palashkovskii. From the technical and economic points of view, this was certainly the group best qualified to build a railway. S. E. Palashkovskii was a highly talented engineer who had proved his ability in the construction of the Transcaucasian line, of which he was also one of the principal shareholders. He had owned some oil wells in Baku and was the author of a plan to lay a pipeline across Persia for the conveyance of Baku oil to the Persian Gulf. Cheap Russian oil in the Gulf, he hoped, would drive out American oil from the Middle East and India. (Though nothing came of the project when it was submitted to the government in 1883, almost twenty years later S. Iu. Witte revived the idea.) Having failed to win government backing for his pipeline project, Palashkovskii sold his oil wells to Baron Rothschild and devoted himself to the promotion of Persian railway schemes.

Unlike other promoters, Palashkovskii was technically competent and had elaborate blueprints for several railways.[131] He also had connections in France, where he could get financial backing. Zinov'ev gave Palashkovskii no encouragement, but his partner Khomiakov had friends at Court and succeeded in obtaining the blessings of His Imperial Majesty for the construction of a line from Rasht to Chāhbahār on the Arabian Sea. The partners entered into a preliminary agreement with the Parisian Banque d'Escompte, which undertook to raise 300,000,000 francs. In the fall of 1888 prospects looked bright.[132]

As for Reuter, he was aware that Russia considered the opening of the Kārun a blow to her and a victory for Britain. He entered into communication with the Russian ambassador, Baron Staal.

---

131. Palashkovskii's reputation was such that his plans were coveted by rival promoters. They were stolen in 1885 and sold to a certain von Derviz, a well-known capitalist. Derviz was negotiating with German banks for funds with which to realize the project, when Palashkovskii, having discovered where his plans were, claimed them back. Derviz had no choice but to return the blueprints to their author and owner. Confidential Memorandum on Russian railway schemes in Persia, by J. Mitchell, February 6, 1889, Enclosure in Morier to Salisbury, No. 41, Confidential, February 6, 1889; F. O. 65/1377.

132. P. A. Rittikh, *Zheleznodorozhnyi put cherez Persiiu*, p. 13.

> Supposing that our [Russian] Government would incline to restore the disturbed balance through the acquisition of new and greater commercial advantages in Northern Persia, Baron Reuter proposes to undertake the construction of a railway from the shores of the Caspian Sea, at points which the Russian Government would indicate, to Tehran. Baron Reuter himself would provide all the capital necessary for this work, but would not refuse, if we so desired, to enter into relations with a Russian banking house.[133]

The enterprising baron, whose British patriotism was as recent as his title and much less valued by himself, was perfectly willing to sell out the interests of his adopted country. One can only wonder whether his friend and champion, Sir Henry Drummond Wolff, knew anything about such behavior or even suspected it.

Dolgorukov, who was in St. Petersburg when the Kārun was opened, worked actively in favor of a Russian railway in Persia, but met strong opposition in the Ministry of Foreign Affairs, particularly from the director of the Asiatic Department, the veteran diplomat I. A. Zinov'ev. Rumor had it that Dolgorukov had obtained a million rubles "for miscellaneous projects" which he would promote on his return to Tehran; but it was also said that

> His return is in direct opposition to the wishes of M. de Giers, and Monsieur Zinovieff as well as those of all the military authorities, and is due entirely to the personal influence which he has brought to bear upon the Czar. He has succeeded in inflicting a heavy blow on M. Zinovieff whose opposition to him he has represented as a piece of class enmity as that of a man with ultraradical opinions, in a word "un rouge," caring for national ideas only, and hating him, the "grand seigneur" whose sole idea was loyalty to the Emperor; of M. de Giers he has spoken, if not to His Majesty, at least to His Majesty's immediate *entourage* as a "vieux bonnet de nuit." He has made the Emperor believe that all that required to be done was to wipe [sic] out the stains inflicted

---

133. Russian Ambassador in London, Staal, to the Minister of Foreign Affairs, Giers, 4/16, 1888; cited in A. Popov, p. 139.

"*Pénétration Pacifique*" 203

on His Majesty's honor by the Karun concession. If an "amende honorable" were made, however small, and if only one in appearance, an immense hubbub would be made about it, and Prince Dolgoruky would return to Tehran in triumph.[134]

Dolgorukov's quarrel with Zinov'ev was long and bitter. The "grand seigneur," scion of a princely family which outshone the Romanovs themselves, felt contemptuous of Zinov'ev, part intellectual, part bureaucrat, whose father had been a professor of Oriental languages at the Lazarev Institute, and who had to work for a living. Yet it was whispered in St. Petersburg that Prince Nikolai Sergeevich was not a disinterested party. The British ambassador discovered that Dolgorukov was connected with Konshin, the front man for the Poliakov group, who was trying to obtain a railway concession in Persia.

Prince Dolgorouki [Sir Robert Morier wrote] who would regard the grant of such a concession to Russian merchants as a set off to the opening of the Karun, and therefore as a personal satisfaction to his own *amour propre*, and who would, it is asserted, not be averse to combining a moral victory for Russia with pecuniary profit to himself, is believed to have undertaken to push this project, and use his influence to overrule any objection which may be raised to its details at Tehran, as well as the opposition in principle of the St. Petersburg Foreign Office to the introduction, under present circumstances, of European enterprise in any form into Persia.[135]

The aristocrat stooped to intrigue and intimidation. He not only denounced Zinov'ev as a Red, but attacked Prince Dondukov-Korsakov, against whom he nursed a personal grudge. He told the Emperor that the Commander in Chief of the Caucasus had proposed to Drummond Wolff, when the latter stopped in Tiflis

134. Sir Robert Morier to Salisbury, No. 6, Secret, St. Petersburg, January 9, 1889; F. O. 65/1377.
135. Morier to Salisbury, No. 9, Secret, January 11, 1889; ibid.

on his way to Tehran, that Russia and Britain partition Persia.[136] Dondukov-Korsakov may not have known what Dolgorukov was saying behind his back, but Zinov'ev and his chief, Giers, were informed of every word uttered by the prince. Soon the feud spilled over onto the pages of the St. Petersburg newspapers.

The *Sankt-Peterburgskie Vedomosti* ran an article that reviewed the history of Russo-Persian relations since Torkamanchāy. It claimed that Russian interests had been neglected and Britain had full control until Zinov'ev appeared on the scene. He restored Russian influence, secured the rights of Armenians, signed an agreement on the Khorāsān frontier, and acquired the Atak area. Thanks to him Russian troops were regularly supplied during the Transcaspian campaign. His influence with the Shah was so great that ministers were not appointed without his sanction and approval. Russian military instructors appeared on the scene, and the British star waned over Tehran. The appointment of Dolgorukov changed all this. Since 1886 Russia had suffered a series of diplomatic defeats. Her good friend Yahyā Khān Moshir od-Dowleh was dismissed from the post of Minister of Foreign Affairs. The energetic British minister, Sir H. D. Wolff, pushed various British enterprises and obtained the opening of the Kārun, while Dolgorukov looked on.

On January 10/22 *Novoe Vremia*, a nationalist paper close to Court circles, published a reply by S. Tatishchev. Tatishchev, a diplomat turned official historian, denied that Russian influence had been nil before Zinov'ev's appointment to Tehran. As a matter of fact, Zinov'ev did not carry much weight with the Persians, especially during Skobelev's Turkoman campaign. Tatishchev quoted a private letter written by Skobelev, stating that in spite of Zinov'ev's efforts, Persia either could not or would not give Russia any sincere support. Tatishchev pointed out further that Zinov'ev had been minister in Tehran during the unsuccessful campaigns of Lomakin, Lazarev, and Tergukasov. Moreover, if Russian influence in Tehran had been established by Zinov'ev, "the fabric erected by him could not have been very strong since it rapidly crumbled to pieces with Prince Dolgoruky's

---

136. Same to same, No. 6, St. Petersburg, January 9, 1889; ibid.

arrival, and while furthermore Mr. Zinovieff was the Prince's coadjutor at St. Petersburg, as Director of the Asiatic Department." [137]

Dolgorukov was hated and feared by the Persians as well. Mirzā Mahmud Khān, Persian minister at St. Petersburg, was afraid that the Shah would sign anything the prince demanded, unless the British legation came to the Shah's rescue. He bitterly complained to Sir Robert Morier of the violent revival of the Persian question in the Russian press, and blamed "that scoundrel Dolgorouki" (*"ce coquin de Dolgorouki"*).[138] On one occasion Mahmud Khān confided to Morier this story:

> "Whenever" he said, "I pay a visit to the old Princess [Prince Nikolai Dolgorukov's mother], she threatens me with the anger of the Czar, the Empress, and the Court, if her son meets with difficulties in Tehran. Madam, I answer (leaving it to her to interpret the real meaning of my language) the Shah knows the power of Russia, he understands his position in relation to her; rest assured that he will act in the manner most in harmony with the interests of his country.

It was clear to Morier that Mahmud Khān bitterly hated "ce polichinelle, cet Achille, ce Boulanger" as he called Dolgorukov. He ascribed Dolgorukov's hostility to himself to an article, which the prince attributed to his authorship, outlining quite accurately Russia's aims. Mirzā Mahmud was convinced that Dolgorukov believed him "too well informed and too quick to detect Russia's purpose to serve as a blind devoted tool, which a Persian Minister at the Russian capital was expected by her diplomacy to be." He was certain that Dolgorukov would try to undermine him at Tehran. Morier caught the hint and wrote Salisbury that Mahmud Khān, though timid and "sometimes wanting a clear grasp of probabilities and facts," was an honest and able man. Long residence in Russia, both in St. Petersburg and the Caucasus, provided him with experience and sources of information "which a new Minister could hardly possess, and which even if he did, he

137. Abstract from Russian press by Mitchell, Enclosure in Morier to Salisbury, No. 21, St. Petersburg, January 24, 1889; ibid.
138. Morier to Salisbury, No. 20, Secret, St. Petersburg, January 23, 1889; ibid.

would scarcely place with equal readiness, especially if he owed his appointment to Russia, at the disposal of Her Majesty's Embassy." [139]

Mirzā Mahmud's one hope was that Dolgorukov's ambition and vanity would recoil on himself and ruin his career.

> "There was once a man in Persia" he exclaimed, breaking suddenly into a fable, "who made his livelihood by the washing of dead bodies before burial. This man in his selfish eagerness to make his fortune speedily, without regard for the happiness of others, one day prayed that there might be a plague. God heard his prayer and sent the plague but the first person to die of it was himself. So it will be with Dolgorouki." [140]

Sir Robert Morier was uncertain which of the two policies— "the ambitious personal schemes of Prince Nicholas Dolgorouki, or the prudent if somewhat cynical counsels of Monsieur de Giers and Monsieur Zinovieff"—would prevail with the Emperor. Mirzā Mahmud Khān, much as he hated Dolgorukov, hoped that railways would be built "to rebound in the long run to the advantage of Persia's progress and independence, and thus recoil upon the heads of their promoters." Giers repeatedly told him that the question of Persian railways was still being studied, but the Persian minister was convinced that all the efforts of the Foreign Ministry were directed "towards shelving the whole scheme" in opposition to Dolgorukov and his business collaborators.[141]

Neither Sir Robert nor Mirzā Mahmud Khān saw the instructions the Foreign Ministry issued to Dolgorukov the day before he left for Tehran. Giers, who was reluctant to battle the powerful prince openly, temporized. The instruction read in part:

> Having good reasons to doubt the usefulness of railways for Persia, we cannot, however, lose sight of the fact that our endeavors to incline the Shah toward an indefinite postpone-

---

139. Same to same, No. 13, Secret, January 16, 1889; ibid.
140. Same to same, No. 32, Secret, St. Petersburg, February 4, 1889; ibid.
141. Same to same, No. 9, St. Petersburg, January 11, 1889; ibid.

ment of the solution of this question could arouse in him doubts concerning our sincerity. In view of this we should attempt to eliminate railway projects which are inconvenient for us and give this affair, as far as possible, a direction compatible with our politico-economic interests.

This meant first of all the denial of Reuter's claims and the prevention of the construction of any railway that would begin at the Persian Gulf. The least that Dolgorukov was instructed to do was "to make the Persian Government stop the granting of any railway concessions for a certain period of time." [142]

While Dolgorukov fought his battles with Giers and Zinov'ev, neither Sir Henry Drummond Wolff nor the Russian legation remained idle. With Wolff's arrival in the spring of 1888, political activity at Tehran accelerated and intensified. Dozens of concession seekers, among them George Reuter, the baron's son, poured into the capital. In December 1888 the Foreign Minister, Mirzā Abbās Khān Qavām od-Dowleh, renewed an expiring concession granted originally in 1879 to several Russian subjects to fish the entire length of the Persian Caspian shore from Āstārā in the west to the mouth of the Atrak in the east. The Russian, or rather Russian-Armenian, businessmen had been paying the Shah 50,000 tumāns a year for this profitable privilege. By 1888 only one of the original partners, Stepan Martynovich Lianozov, remained to sign the new ten-year agreement. Few could have foreseen how lucrative Lianozov's business would become in another few years when he would hold what almost amounted to a world monopoly of caviar.[143] The Persian government, or rather the Shah, received 60,000 tumāns, or only a small fraction of Lianozov's yearly profit.

On the eve of Dolgorukov's return, the Russian legation demanded Persian acquiescence in the opening of a Russian consulate general at Mashhad. The Ākhāl-Khorāsān border treaty of 1881 entitled Russia to maintain agents at Persian frontier posts. Under this provision the Russians appointed Petr Mikhail-

---

142. Secret dispatch from the Minister of Foreign Affairs to Prince Dolgorukov, December 31, 1888/January 12, 1889; A. Popov, "Stranitsa . . . ," p. 140.
143. Iran, Archives of the Ministry of Foreign Affairs, Shilāt [Fisheries] File.

ovich Vlasov, formerly consul at Rasht, to Mashhad before the Persian government agreed to receive him there. The Shah, who "was informed that he must ratify the appointment," resisted for a while but finally gave in and accepted the inevitable.[144] To the Russians, Mashhad was a valuable listening post. The city was a great Shiite religious center, attracting tens of thousands of pilgrims yearly, and it was close to Herāt. The British, naturally, wanted to place their own consul at Mashhad. Once the Russians had gotten in, the Shah saw no reason to keep out the English. In fact he invited them to come and balance out the Russian presence.[145]

The British acted with great dispatch. General C. Maclean of the Perso-Afghan frontier commission, who was appointed consul general, reached the city before Vlasov, thus gaining diplomatic precedence over his Russian colleague.[146] However, the Russians regained the initiative through the purchase of a large residence, the flying of the flag over the doorway, the stationing of an imposing guard, and the assignment to the consul of a mounted Cossack escort whenever he moved about town. Lord Curzon, who personally observed the scene, wrote

> that the presence of a capable Russian official and staff, and the impression produced by ample surroundings and an imposing abode must have done much to augment Russian influence in the capital, and, if that influence is sometimes exercised with an abrupt and imperious insistence, the effect, even though it be the reverse of welcome to those on whom it is produced, will not thereby have been lessened in intensity. A vigorous Russian representative in Meshed is a visible symbol of the great power whose movements and intentions form the subject of conversation in every Oriental bazaar, and whose ever-swelling shadow, witnessed with a sort of paralyzed quiescence by the native peoples, looms like a thunder-cloud over the land.[147]

144. Curzon, *Persia and the Persian Question*, 1, 170.
145. Greaves, *Persia and the Defence of India*, p. 171.
146. Curzon, 1, 171.
147. Id.

"Pénétration Pacifique"

Curzon noted that originally the British consulate had lodged in a building that afforded "the scantiest possible evidence of the rank and importance of its inmate. It is little short of discreditable that the British Consul-General should be compelled to reside in such attentuated and miserable surroundings."[148] Soon conditions improved. A better building was obtained, and a private guard, consisting of five Indian and seven Persian soldiers, was posted to the consulate.[149] In Mashhad for the time being the score was even.

Sir Henry Drummond Wolff was hunting bigger game. He was determined that his friend Reuter should salvage at least a part of his concession of 1872. The most suitable part to save seemed to be Article 20, which had given Reuter priority in opening a bank. Amin os-Soltān and Qavām od-Dowleh were willing to cooperate, but some high officials opposed the scheme. E'temād os-Saltaneh, for instance, pointed out in a letter to the Shah that while the opening of the Kārun had given equal rights and privileges to all nations who might wish to navigate the river, a bank concession would be an expression of preference for one side as against the other. Is it advisable, E'temād os-Saltaneh asked, to give up a safe and healthy impartiality and to abandon neutrality between the two powers?[150]

Whether E'temād os-Saltaneh knew it or not, the Shah had already made up his mind. Not even the fury of Poggio, Russia's chargé d'affaires, could stop him this time. Poggio demanded that the Persian government give no concession to Julius de Reuter. As for his son, George, the Persians should "either send him away or strike him in the mouth if he again ventured to open it concerning his concession."[151] Poggio's feelings can be readily understood when one considers the scope of the banking concession. It was known, for instance, that Reuter and Wolff were pressing not just for an institution that would engage in financial transactions,

---

148. Ibid., pp. 172–73.
149. Ibid., p. 173.
150. E'temād os-Saltaneh to Nāser-ed-Din Shah, 23 Jamādi ol-Avval 1306 A.H., January 26, 1889; cited in Teymuri, *Asre bikhabari*, p. 200.
151. Wolff to Salisbury, No. 253, Secret and Confidential, October 30, 1888; as cited in Greaves, p. 170.

but for one that would hold a monopoly on the exploitation of all minerals save gold, silver, and precious stones. The Russian legation may have been tipped off when on January 15, 1889, Amin os-Soltān wrote to Joseph Rabino, an agent of Reuter, that the Shah approved of the bank's organizing a mining company in Iran.[152]

On January 30, 1889, George Reuter, Mirzā Abbās Khān Qavām od-Dowleh, and Mirzā Ali Asghar Khān Amin os-Soltān signed the agreement granting the bank concession. The concession of 1872 was at last proclaimed void and mutual claims settled. Article 1 gave Reuter the right to establish a state bank in Persia under the title "Imperial Bank of Persia." The concession would run for sixty years. The head office and domicile of the bank would be in Tehran, but branches might be opened in other Persian towns and abroad. The bank,

> outside any operations which appertain to a financial institution, may undertake on its own account or on account of third parties all matters financial, industrial or commercial which it may think advantageous to this end, on the condition, however, that none of these enterprises be contrary to Treaties, Laws, usages, or the religion of the country.

Article 2 authorized the bank to issue shares in London, Paris, Berlin, Tehran, Vienna, and St. Petersburg so that a total of £4,000,000 could be subscribed. The bank could begin its operations as soon as £1,000,000 became available.

Article 3 stated:

> The Imperial Bank shall, as State Bank, have the exclusive right of issuing notes to bearer payable at sight . . . These notes shall be accepted by all the agents and employee's of the Imperial Government, and they shall be legal tender for all transactions in Persia. But as soon as the Bank be unable to pay the value of one of its notes, the circulation of bank-

---

152. Mirzā Ali Asghar Khān Amin os-Soltān to Mr. Joseph Rabino, January 15, 1889; Iran, Archives of the Ministry of Foreign Affairs, File 44/Folder 8, Registry No. 3.

notes shall be prohibited throughout the Empire, and the Bank shall be compelled to pay all its notes.

Furthermore, the Persian government undertook "not to issue any kind of paper money during the term of this Concession, nor to authorize the creation of any other bank or other institution possessing a like privilege."

Article 5 carried the usual stipulation exempting the bank, its offices, branches, shares, notes, receipts, checks, etc., from taxation, while Article 6 appointed it payments' agent for the government.

> Further, the bank, after its formation, shall always hold itself at the disposal of the Imperial Government for all loans and advances of which the Government may be in need. These advances or loans shall be made on security to be agreed upon in each case by the Persian Government and the bank, or else they shall be considered to form part, *pro tanto*, of the reserve fund to be held by the bank as the guarantee for the paper money.

Article 7 assigned to the Persian government 6 percent of the Bank's annual net profit or £4,000, whichever sum was larger. By curious coincidence Article 11 dealt with the same subject as Article 11 of the original Reuter concession, stating in part:

> The Imperial Bank being ready to incur forthwith the sacrifices necessary for developing the resources of the country by exploitation of its natural riches, the Persian Government grants to the said bank for the term of the present Concession, the exclusive right of working through the Empire the iron, copper, lead, mercury, coal, petroleum, manganese borax, and asbestos mines which belong to the State, and which have not already been conceded to others . . . All the mines which the bank has not commenced working within ten years of its formation shall be deemed to have been abandoned by it, and the State may dispose of the same without consulting the Bank.

Article 13 gave Persia 16 percent of the annual net profit from all mines worked by the bank, and in Article 15 Reuter formally relinquished all claims arising out of his former concession.[153] Shortly thereafter the newly formed Imperial Bank of Persia informed the government that a mining company would be formed in London with a capital of £1,000,000. It would have 200,000 shares of stock of which 130,000 would be common and the rest preferred. Common stock would be held by the bank. Preferred stock would be offered to the public at £5½, except for 14,000 shares which would be given to Persians.[154] The language of the letter is so vague that it is impossible to determine whether the 14,000 shares were offered to Persians gratis, as a bribe, or at the same price as on the London exchange.

Considering the strength of Russian opposition to the bank concession, the Persian government was prepared for a veritable explosion both in Tehran and St. Petersburg. Mirzā Mahmud Khān mentioned the agreement to Giers and Zinov'ev, minimizing its importance and representing it as a purely commercial transaction. Both took the news calmly, though Zinov'ev remarked that this was a very important piece of news. The Persian minister attributed the unexpectedly reasonable attitude of the Russian Foreign Ministry to the absence of Dolgorukov, "the chief promoter of agitation and disturbance." Mahmud Khān, Sir Robert Morier reported, "seemed to regard the late irritation of the Russian Government, or rather of the Emperor's *entourage*, whose passions the Foreign Office were compelled to reflect, as due mainly to the unceasing efforts of the Dolgorouki clique." [155]

The weakness of Russian opposition to the bank was indeed surprising. Undoubtedly St. Petersburg was fully aware of the potential power of a bank that had the exclusive right of emission and also held a monopoly on mining. A dozen years later a Russian writer referred to the Imperial Bank concession as "all-encompassing" and emphasized the fact that the bank was a

---

153. Translation of the text of the agreement signed by Baron George de Reuter, in behalf of Baron Julius de Reuter on October 30, 1889, and by Qavām od-Dowleh and Amin os-Soltān on 28 Jamādi ol-Avval 1306 A.H. (the year of the Mouse) corresponding to October 28, 1889 A.D.; F.O. 60/576 and F.O. 65/1378.

154. Iran, Archives of the Foreign Ministry, File 44/Folder 8.

155. Morier to Salisbury, No. 32, Secret, St. Petersburg, February 4, 1889; F. O. 65/1377.

"Pénétration Pacifique"

purely British institution. He singled out Article 11 as the most important one but noted with satisfaction that the English had failed to take advantage of it.[156] The Russian legation in Tehran showed its displeasure. One of its secretaries, son of Russia's Foreign Minister Giers, told the Shah that the Imperial Bank would not be able to raise the required capital. Failure to raise the capital within the specified period of time would give the Shah the right to cancel the concession, and Giers urged that this be done. Nāser ed-Din pretended to accept the advice and promised not to prolong the time in which the capital must be acquired and the bank opened. Amin os-Soltān at once reported the matter to Wolff.[157]

Both the opening of the Kārun and the granting of the bank concession to Reuter occurred while Dolgorukov was absent from Tehran. His return was anticipated with dread by the Persians and with some apprehension by that indomitable promoter of business ventures, Sir Henry Drummond Wolff. The latter had not been certain until the last moment whether Reuter would get the bank concession. The sudden appearance of an infuriated Dolgorukov, armed with the confidence of the Emperor, might ruin Wolff's plans. Moreover, he could foresee the granting of a railway concession to Russia (and Dolgorukov would undoubtedly demand one in "compensation" for the opening of the Kārun). In an attempt to react to an event which had not yet occurred, Wolff telegraphed Salisbury:

> I think it would be well if before his [Dolgorukov's] arrival articles appeared in English papers saying that England had no objection to railways even if made by Russia if projected so as to develop the resources of Persia. This would prevent the semblance of a sudden diplomatic defeat if they are granted.

At the Foreign Office someone wrote on the telegram, over Salisbury's distinctive S: "If we do this *before* the concessions are granted, the Russians will increase their demands, the purpose of

156. S. Lomnitskii, *Persiia i persy* (St. Petersburg, 1902), pp. 192–93.
157. Wolff to Salisbury, No. 122, Most Secret and Confidential, Tehran, April 12, 1890; F. O. 60/511.

which is not to get railways, but to make an appearance of recovering their position by obtaining some concession to which we are opposed." Then in Salisbury's hand: "No action." [158]

Wolff's fears were entirely justified. No sooner had Dolgorukov arrived than demands began to rain upon the Shah and his ministers. In the same dispatch in which Wolff informed London of Dolgorukov's return, he reported that the latter had already raised the railway issue. The Shah was afraid to refuse and afraid to grant the request. "He proposes to tell Prince Dolgorouki that he cannot give this concession without granting one to England from the south. But against this there is the secret agreement the violation of which would entail hostilities. His Majesty wants immediate advice before seeing Prince Dolgorouki on Sunday." [159] The next day Wolff cabled that a line such as Dolgorukov was said to have in mind (one running from the southeastern corner of the Caspian to Shāhrud and Tehran) "would be strategically dangerous." To meet this danger Wolff advised that Britain build two lines—Shushtar to Tehran and Quetta to Seistān. Given Salisbury's approval, Wolff telegraphed, "I think I could get Reuter's Agent at once to apply for the former." Wolff also needed permission to reassure the Shah, who would be again facing the formidable Dolgorukov. "If we can now inspire the Shah with confidence, I think great good may ensue. But it would be disastrous if he thought that we abandoned him or were lukewarm." [160]

Salisbury's reply was calm and slightly sceptical. "His Majesty ought certainly to represent that he cannot grant this concession to Russia without giving similar ones to England in the South." Should Dolgorukov appeal to the secret agreement, the Shah might insist that he could not turn down the English without giving them an adequate reason, and that he must let them know of the agreement. "We could then argue the question." The tele-

158. Wolff to Salisbury, Decypher, Very Secret, January 24, 1889; F.O. 65/1377.
159. Wolff to Salisbury, No. 36, Telegram, Urgent and very secret, Tehran, February 8, 1889; ibid.
160. Wolff to Salisbury, No. 37, Telegram, Urgent and very private, Tehran, February 9, 1889; ibid.

"Pénétration Pacifique" 215

gram ended on a philosophical note: In the past many schemes had broken down; so might this one.[161]

On February 13, 1889, Wolff and Dolgorukov held a conversation in the course of which the latter admitted that Britain had long ago informed Russia of her intention to seek the opening of the Kārun. However, he said, "Russia was not annoyed only with the action of England but there was altogether a change in the attitude of Persia for which as well as for the opening of the Karun some compensative advantage must be given Russia." The prince placed the blame for the Persian attitude of noncooperation equally upon the policy of Lord Salisbury and Wolff's personal instigation. Sir Henry tried to show that his activities had not been directed against Russia, but were merely attempts to protect British commercial interests. In regard to Reuter, he argued that the bank was a compensation for the original concession and not a new one. Dolgorukov replied that Russian public opinion was inflamed by the whole course of affairs in Persia. Wolff detected "considerable personal annoyance in the language of Prince Dolgorouki which was not entirely hidden by his desire to appear cordial. No doubt much of this feeling is derived from the consciousness that he is not quite so overwhelming as represented by his friends in the Press." [162]

In mid-February Dolgorukov presented his demands. He proclaimed strong attachment to Persia and declared that, though he was a Russian official, he wanted Persia to progress. He complained that during his absence from Tehran the just balance between England and Russia had been destroyed by the grants to Britain of Kārun navigation and the bank. He was instructed, therefore, to make proposals which would help restore the balance. "If they were rejected he had in reserve some other instructions."

Dolgorukov wanted (1) the right to navigate the Anzali Lagoon (Mordāb); (2) the right to navigate all other rivers flowing from Persia into the Caspian; (3) the construction by Persia of a

161. Salisbury to Wolff, Draft, No. 22, Telegram, Very secret, February 9, 1889; ibid.
162. Wolff to Salisbury, No. 35, Confidential, Tehran, February 14, 1889; ibid.

road from Anzali to Tehran and from Ardebil to Āstārā; (4) and an undertaking on the part of the Persian government not to grant concessions for railways for five years, during which Russia would draw up a plan of railway construction, "specifying what lines she will construct herself, Persia being then free to give concessions for the remainder to others." [163]

Amin os-Soltān communicated the demands and a draft of the Persian reply to Wolff, though the negotiations with Dolgorukov were supposed to be secret. Over the next two weeks a final version was worked out and shown to Sir Henry by the Minister of Foreign Affairs, Mirzā Abbās Khān Qavām od-Dowleh. The Persian note granted the Russian demand for the navigation of the Anzali Lagoon, but proposed that the Russians themselves build highways in the north. As for railways, the Shah would allow Russia four years to select one line from the north to Tehran. At the end of that period, or at any time that a concession was granted to Russia, the Shah could grant similar concessions to others as he saw fit. Wolff told Mizrā Abbās Khān that Britain had three demands of her own to make:

1. That as soon as the concession was given to Russia in the North a similar concession was to be given for the South to any Company named by Her Majesty's Government.
2. That no concession to the South should be granted to any Company unless approved by Her Majesty's Government.
3. That the carriage road already promised in connection with the opening of the Kārun from Shuster [sic] to Tehran should be carried out forthwith.[164]

Dolgorukov strongly objected to the four-year term offered by the Persians, instead of the five years he had asked for. Giers was disturbed by his "fatal passion," but the prince had his way.[165] The Persians sent him a new note containing six articles, the last of which said that the Russians might build a railway anywhere

163. Wolff to Salisbury, No. 41, Confidential, Tehran, February 18, 1889; ibid.
164. Wolff to Salisbury, No. 49, Tehran, March 4, 1889; F. O. 65/1378.
165. V. N. Lamsdorff, *Dnevnik V. N. Lamzdorfa*, pp. 151, 154.

they found necessary. Five years were allowed for planning and negotiations. During the five years Persia would give no concession to any other company.[166] Dolgorukov triumphantly telegraphed Giers that complete success had been achieved. Giers' closest collaborator and assistant at the Ministry of Foreign Affairs V. N. Lamsdorff, commented:

> These telegrams . . . created the impression of a brilliant success, but the wonderful Prince forgot to inquire whether the Shah is postponing for five years all decisions in regard to railways in general, or . . . at the end of this period intends simultaneously to give England an exclusive concession for all railways in South Persia . . . Mr. Giers decides to ask our Minister at Tehran about this before replying to the Shah who apparently wanted only to pacify us by a ruse, not to notice which, as Prince Dolgorukii perhaps wished to, would have been uncautious and impractical.[167]

On March 25 Dolgorukov telegraphed Zinov'ev that the Shah had given him an autograph statement confirming the promise not to grant railway concessions to any but Russian companies for five years. Thus the British could not get a concession in the south before 1894.[168]

Having satisfied Dolgorukov, the Persian government must satisfy Wolff as well. Dolgorukov was told that several months prior to its pledge not to grant railway concessions to non-Russian companies, Persia had given Britain priority for such concessions in the south. This meant that Russia would not be allowed to control a line stretching all the way from the Caspian to the Persian Gulf. Since actually no such promise had ever been made, the Shah, Amin os-Soltān, and Sir Henry engaged in a bit of forgery when the Shah wrote a letter to his Foreign Minister ordering him to

> Convey these commands to H. E. the Minister Plenipo. Even give him this very autograph in order that he may keep it and

---

166. Iran, Archive of the Foreign Ministry, File 44/Folder 3, Registry No. 6.
167. Lamsdorff, p. 156.
168. Ibid., p. 177.

be satisfied that our former promises with regard to the priority of the English Govt. over others in the construction of a Southern Railway to Tehran continues to hold good; and certainly, whenever railway Concessions in the North, etc. are given to others, immediately a concession for a railway from Tehran to Shuster, or such a one, will be given to the English Company.[169]

Giers and Zinov'ev had been right in their suspicions. Dolgorukov had failed to achieve his purpose. Should Russia build a railway from Bandare Gaz to Tehran, Britain would respond by building one from Bushehr or Mohammareh to Tehran. Such a situation was a far cry from the monopoly the prince believed he had gained for his country.

The struggle for railways was not over. Sir Henry Drummond Wolff was no less anxious than Dolgorukov to gain easy access by railway to Persia's interior. The prospect of a Russian line running through Khorāsān was especially unpleasant. To counter this potential threat, Wolff proposed that a strategic railway be built from Quetta to Seistān. General Maclean, soon to be appointed consul at Mashhad, believed that the railway would have a commercial purpose, too, carrying Indian goods into Khorāsān. Wolff felt that "the railway through Beluchistan would entirely alter these conditions advantageous to Russia and give to England such a hold on Persia as would neutralize the commanding position achieved by Russia by means of the Transcaspian line for carrying on her designs on Afghanistan and Turkistan." Wolff recognized that it might be difficult for the Government of India to finance this project, but Sir Henry had a solution for that: "I cannot help thinking that Baron Reuter might be induced to build it if he could obtain from the Persian Government some concession in Seistan, and if the Indian Government would undertake to lease the Railway when built or to work it at a fair rate." [170]

169. Wolff to Salisbury, Enclosure in No. 62, Tehran, March 20, 1889; F. O. 65/1377. See also "Railways in Persia," F. O. Memorandum by R. C. Dickie, Persia No. 6824, February 23, 1911; F. O. 371/1185.

170. Wolff to Salisbury, No. 42, Most Confidential, Tehran, February 19, 1899; F. O. 65/1377.

"Pénétration Pacifique" 219

The very thought that Russia might build a railway through Khorāsān sent shudders down the spines of the British military. Almost equally frightening was the idea of a line from the Caspian to the Persian Gulf. A north to south railway and a line through Khorāsān would, the War Office felt, give Russia "control of the whole of the Persian Kingdom, and gain [for her] a position on the Indian Ocean that would necessitate an increase of British naval forces in the Indian waters, and add to our already heavy burdens." [171] General Sir Henry Brackenbury, Director of Military Intelligence, wrote to the Foreign Office:

> Khorasan is not only the base from which serious operations against India will be undertaken, if ever they should be attempted, but its possession is essential to Russia for sustained operations in Western Afghanistan. This is clearly set forth in important Russian secret official papers.
>
> Even if we admit that sooner or later Khorasan must become a Russian province, and that Herat and Northern Afghanistan must fall to Russia, it is desirable to postpone the evil day as long as possible. Nothing would so hasten its arrival as the construction of such railways as are here contemplated, and nothing would so greatly add to Russia's power for still further advances.[172]

The rivalry over railways was interrupted in the early summer of 1889 by the Shah's third European trip. Sir Henry Drummond Wolff was anxious that Nāser ed-Din should gain "a more extensive knowledge" of Britain than he had gained in 1873.[173] By "knowledge of Britain" Wolff undoubtedly meant acquaintance with the business community of the City. The Shah hoped also to visit St. Petersburg, but in spite of hints dropped in Tehran and St. Petersburg, no invitation arrived. The Tsar's anger at Nāser

---

171. Paraphrase of the Memorandum of the Intelligence Department, War Office, March 15, 1889, in Memorandum on Persian Railways, Secret, India Office, June 20, 1911; F. O. 371/1186.

172. Memorandum of the Intelligence Department, War Office, March 7, 1889, as cited in Memorandum on Persian Railways, Secret, India Office, June 20, 1911; ibid.

173. Wolff, 2, 351.

ed-Din stemmed from three telegrams exchanged between Salisbury and Wolff and intercepted by the Russian Intelligence. The telegrams showed that the Shah consulted Wolff on every matter and kept him informed of all negotiations with Dolgorukov. From them, Giers, Lamsdorff, and Zinov'ev understood that "apparently" the Shah had promised Britain a concession for all railways in the south if Russia received one in the north. Alexander III read the telegrams with Giers' explanatory note and returned them with the written comment: "And yet the Shah imagines that we will receive him in St. Petersburg? He will not set foot in Petersburg until he gives in to us on everything we demand." [174]

The Court circles were very angry indeed. Prince Dolgorukov, who belonged to them much more than to the Foreign Ministry, said to Wolff that nothing could be settled with the Persians without the British minister. "In fact discussing matters with the Persian Government is the same as negotiating with the Cabinet of St. James." [175] The Tsar talked of Nāser ed-Din's duplicity, while the Empress claimed that Queen Victoria did not want the Shah to visit London because "he damages the palaces and his visits cost too much." Giers retorted with unwonted courage that even if the Queen personally opposed the Shah's visit, the government found it very desirable. To the Tsar's remark that the Shah should take some other route to Europe, Giers replied that this would hurt Russia's prestige in the East. Alexander gave in, mumbling something which sounded like "We will have to receive him if he continues to insist." [176] Actually the Tsar would have been distressed had the Shah failed to include St. Petersburg in his itinerary. When Dolgorukov telegraphed from Tehran that Sir Henry Wolff ("Sir Wolff" to Dolgorukov) had advised the Shah to travel to Europe via Turkey, the Tsar wrote in the margin: "What an animal and an insolent fellow." [177]

---

174. Lamsdorff, *Dnevnik*, p. 169.
175. Wolff to Salisbury, No. 60, Confidential, Tehran, March 19, 1889; F. O. 65/1378.
176. Lamsdorff, p. 185.
177. Ibid., p. 191.

During the protracted negotiations between Amin os-Soltān and Dolgorukov, the Grand Vizier conveyed to the Russian minister the Shah's wish to spend eight days in St. Petersburg, and his decision to travel with a suite of thirty-four persons. Dolgorukov telegraphed home and was informed that the Tsar was willing to have the Shah for three days and that a suite of twenty was enough. It was the Persian minister in St. Petersburg who, through Zinov'ev's intercession, settled the matter to mutual satisfaction.[178] The Shah's stay in St. Petersburg was memorable chiefly for its unpleasantness. Russian society laughed at Persian manners and mocked Nāser ed-Din Shah's idiosyncratic French. The reception at Court was cold. Rumor had it that Dolgorukov, himself a master of insult, was distressed that the Shah had not been kept in St. Petersburg longer and that Amin as-Soltān had not been bribed. Persia would have signed everything Russia wanted, Reuter's bank concession would have been annulled.

> But they did not want to pay one million, dividing it thus: 500,000 as a gift to the Shah, 300,000 to the Vizier, and 200,000 to other persons. The Shah received a most unimpressive gift—a portrait of the Sovereign set in diamonds. First they wanted to give a vase costing 50,000, but he has received so many from Russian tsars that his people laugh at those vases. . . . Both sides parted dissatisfied.[179]

On July 1, 1889, the Shah arrived in England, where he was much more hospitably received. He was more experienced now than on his first visit in 1873. Under Wolff's influence, he learned to make speeches which delighted the progressive, bourgeois, optimistic English mind of the late nineteenth century. The very fact that a "barbarian" was expressing "English" sentiments was gratifying. Wolff, who accompanied the Shah, was proud of his performance, as a trainer might be proud of the performance of his talking dog.

The language used by the Shah had been very calm and statesmanlike. He had expressed a desire of promoting the

---

178. A. V. Bogdanovich, *Tri poslednikh samoderzhtsa* (Moscow, 1924), p. 99.
179. Ibid., pp. 99–100.

interests of Persia by the introduction of foreign capital and by the development of her great resources. For this purpose he felt he must rely on the friendship of England and Russia. His Majesty said he would be glad if this could be secured by a binding and permanent arrangement.

The Prince of Wales was much struck with the demeanor of the Shah, and by his enlightened way of treating public affairs.[180]

Wolff's short stay in Tehran, where he observed at close quarters the operations of Russian imperialism, served to confirm him in the opinion that an Anglo-Russian understanding in Persia was imperative for the protection of British interests. Looking upon politics through a bank note, it was easy to see Anglo-Russian differences smoothed away to the benefit of the entire world. Wolff tried to persuade himself and others that Russia's objective of gaining access to the Persian Gulf was "legitimate and praiseworthy if carried out in a peaceable manner." He professed not to see "why England should not give her assistance to such a project." [181] Why not come to a friendly agreement along the following lines?

1. The neutralization of Persia;
2. The construction, on certain principles, of a network of railways;
3. An administrative commission of three members, to be respectively appointed by the three contracting Powers;
4. The construction, in the first place, of the line from Enzeli to Mohammerah;
5. The institution of certain transit duties, to be devoted to the service of a loan guaranteed by the three Powers;
6. These duties to be collected at the extremities of the line with the concurrence of the Russian and English Consuls.[182]

Wolff discussed Persian affairs with the Prince of Wales and drew for His Royal Highness enticing pictures of a happy Persia,

180. Wolff, 2, 366–67.
181. Ibid., pp. 372–73.
182. Ibid., p. 375.

"*Pénétration Pacifique*" 223

blessed with the fruits of "civilization" and invisibly divided into Russian and English economic spheres. "The Prince was an attentive listener to Drummond Wolff's scheme of an economic partition of Persia into two spheres of influence, one to be regulated by England, the other by Russia." [183] The two agreed that the Prince of Wales should arrange for a meeting between Sir Henry and Tsar Alexander III, avoiding the necessity of working through such unsympathetic souls as Giers, Zinov'ev, and, perhaps, Salisbury. The latter was not initiated into Wolff's little plan. Early in the fall of 1889, the prince met the Tsar at Fredensborg and obtained Alexander's consent to an interview with Wolff. Salisbury, who had not yet been notified, complained to Queen Victoria. "The Prime Minister resented the direct appeal to the Tsar over his head, but he was not averse to Drummond Wolff's general principles, though he deprecated the precipitate action and judged Wolff's Persian dream unlikely to come true for at least a generation." [184]

Lord Salisbury was not the only one to have misgivings about Wolff's private diplomacy and his notions in regard to Persia. General Brackenbury, Head of the Intelligence Department of the War Office, argued forcefully "that it is in the interests of Great Britain to delay by every possible means the construction of lines in the North of Persia." The general went so far as to declare that "it is little short of treason to every interest of our Empire to connive or assist in any way the promotion of Russian railways in the North of Persia." [185] Sir Robert Morier, British ambassador at St. Petersburg, was convinced that Wolff did not understand the position of the Russian government, or its psychology, and that his initiative in seeking an Anglo-Russian agreement was nothing but meddling.

In the second week of October, Wolff arrived in Berlin for a meeting with Alexander III. He told the Tsar of "the strong necessity which existed for an understanding between England and Russia," and of the great "desire of the commercial community

183. Lee, *King Edward VII*, 1, 686.
184. Ibid., p. 687.
185. Morier to Salisbury, No. 353, Most Secret, St. Petersburg, November 13, 1889; F. O. 65/1379.

everywhere for new markets," the most important of which was in Persia. European governments, Wolff lectured the Emperor, should second the efforts of their merchants. In Persia, where Russia and Britain exercised the preponderant influence, it was in their interests to work harmoniously together instead of engaging in rivalry beyond the ordinary limits of commercial competition.

Alexander was patient and polite. He claimed that "His feelings towards England were of the most friendly nature." If any difficulties arose in Persia, they would rise from the British side. The moves which had already been made in the direction of an understanding, such as Wolff's letter to Dolgorukov, were of a private nature. They would have been looked upon in another light had they come from the British government. Russia, the Tsar went on, did not resent the opening of the Kārun to navigation, "but where the Russian Government felt hurt was at the ease with which Persia had adhered to our [Britain's] wishes while she delayed fulfilling engagements she had undertaken or requests proferred by Russia such as the completion of the Kuchan road, the Meshed Consulate and other pending matters." The Tsar expressed his desire for an understanding with England on the basis of complete reciprocity in the matter of railways, or other industrial and commercial undertakings. "We have no common interests in Europe," he said. "Our common interests lie in Asia." Therefore he wanted to establish an understanding that would enable the two powers to be friends.[186]

Sir Henry was now prepared to go to St. Petersburg personally to negotiate with the Russian government. When Morier informed the Foreign Minister of Wolff's intention, Giers made a terrible grimace (*"épouventable grimace"*) which the British ambassador "faithfully reproduced in writing to Sir Henry," thus effectively dampening Wolff's desire to come. Giers confessed that nothing would have induced him to enter into conversations on the subject of Persian reforms with Sir Robert's "astute colleague." Morier replied that he had feared this would be so.

> This [he said to Giers] is how I explained the matter to Sir Henry: "Having formed a clear idea of what could be done

[186]. Wolff to Salisbury (unnumbered), Secret and Confidential, Vienna, October 14, 1889; F.O. 65/1379; Wolff published this letter in his *Rambling Recollections*, 2, 368–70.

"Pénétration Pacifique"

in the way of raising Persia as a whole, to a higher level of civilization than that which she now enjoys by the cooperation of England in the South and Russia in the North, you believe that such an Utopia would approve itself to the Russian imagination, as it does to yours. But the reverse is the case. Russia is bent on creating an Utopia of her own within the ring fence of her Asiatic annexations by the introduction of the *Pax Romana* within her own dominions, the establishment of order instead of chaos, the advantages of railways and all the other great engines of civilization. She believes that she thus makes herself the cynosure of all neighbouring Asiatic peoples who must sooner or later gravitate towards her. The worse the condition of these neighbours therefore, the more helpless their squalor and decadence, the nearer she is to the attainment of her goal and the less she can look with equanimity at any attempts made to endow them with the blessings of civilization otherwise than as annexes of the Russian Empire; that Persians and other Asiatics similarly situated should go on stewing in their own gravy is the simple *credo* which she opposes to your simple prayers for joint energetic action.[187]

Though these blunt words were part of a conversation "in the form of friendly banter in which His Excellency [Giers] heartily joined," Giers could have had no doubt as to the ultimate seriousness of the accusation thrown in his face by the usually cooperative and Russophile Englishman. Morier's analysis of Russia's motives was extraordinarily perceptive. He had read correctly the minds of Zinov'ev and the other makers of Russia's Persian policy. Of course, Giers denied that Russia held such views. He, like Dolgorukov before him, emphasized the unfairness of the competition which Britain was proposing. For Russia to compete with Britain in Persia on a purely economic level "would be to doom herself to certain defeat," he said.[188]

Several days before the dispatch embodying Morier's observations had reached London, Salisbury, encouraged by the inde-

187. Morier to Salisbury, No. 330, Very confidential, St. Petersburg, October 25, 1889; F.O. 65/1379.
188. Id.

fatigable Sir Henry, wrote to his ambassador in St. Petersburg that since the Shah's last visit, the British commercial community had shown increasing interest in Persian trade. The British government wished "that the material and political progress of Persia should be the cause not of discord but of increased friendliness between England and Russia." Morier was to invite discussions with the view of arriving at a common policy to be pursued by the representatives of the two powers in that country. Salisbury expressed the belief that existing jealousies "could easily be removed by frank explanations and a conciliatory disposition on either side." He proposed that the Russian government instruct its new minister in Tehran, Evgenii Karlovich Bützow (Dolgorukov had just been recalled) to enter into negotiations with Wolff.[189]

Giers was unenthusiastic. He stated, pro forma, that he had no objection in principle to Anglo-Russian cooperation in Persia, but— The construction of railways so dear to Wolff's heart required money. Russia had so many railways to build at home that she was short of capital.

> His Excellency then again reverted to his favorite argument, of the inequality in the conditions of competition between England and Russia in such a race as that proposed in Persia by Sir Henry Wolff. We [the British] had capital, knowledge, resources of every kind specially fitting us for rapidly developing barbarous or semi-civilized countries. Russia's resources were altogether behind ours, and she required them all for the development of her own Empire.[190]

Referring to their recent conversation, during which Morier had accused Giers of preferring that Persia stew in her own gravy until she would wish to be annexed to Russia, Giers said that Morier had "unfairly twitted him." He admitted that such ideas probably "prevailed in certain military heads." He, on the contrary, wished for an improvement of conditions in Persia, but, "having been a long time there as Russian Minister and being

189. Salisbury to Morier, Draft, No. 307, October 28, 1889; ibid.
190. Morier to Salisbury, No. 341, Secret and Confidential, St. Petersburg, November 6, 1880; ibid.

"Pénétration Pacifique"

thoroughly well acquainted with the Government and the people governed, he had little hope of seeing anything done either from within or from without." Morier could not resist the temptation of asking why in such a case Giers had "made such an uproar" about the opening of the Kārun. Giers replied that it was because of the "tremendous explosion of public feeling on the subject and the virulence of the attacks made upon him in connection with this concession."[191] His frankness was commendable, though he should have qualified the term "public feeling." Giers was obviously referring to the imperialist-expansionist segment of Russian society, the one that had gained considerable influence at Court.

Morier did not share Drummond Wolff's enthusiasm for the construction of railways in Persia. His scepticism was largely based on the notion that whatever the Russian military circles wished was bad for England, and the military, whose influence was very strong at the court of Alexander III, advocated railway construction in Persia, Central Asia, and the Far East. When informed by the Foreign Office of the alleged agreement between the Tsar and Wolff, Morier wrote:

> I cannot but fear that, if this is so, the military party, having the Emperor with them, will have an easy victory over Monsieur de Giers and the Russian Foreign Office (for I believe Monsieur Zinovieff is quite as much opposed to the policy of railway construction as his chief) and, though they may find a greater resistance on the part of the Minister of Finance, that resistance, if it should cross the Imperial Will, must be regarded as a minus quantity.

With remarkable clarity of vision, Morier foresaw the pitfalls which Sir Henry's activities opened at the feet of British policy:

> after Sir Henry's great stroke in pushing the Tsar to the foot of the wall and calling upon His M-y in the name of civilization to construct these railways . . . a diplomatic situation will be created, consisting of our using every art to prevent the construction of these railways, whilst using means to con-

191. Id.

struct a trunk line from Mohammerah to Teheran, which will be not only difficult and dangerous but will not conduce to enhance the national reputation for *bona fides*.[192]

Alexander III must have realized, or been shown, that his vague commitment to Wolff had been a tactical error. He had never been a friend of England. Neither his own views nor those of his entourage disposed him to seek cooperation with the British in Asia. On the contrary, he and his intimates saw Britain as Russia's main antagonist. Only a few weeks after his Berlin conversation with Wolff, the Tsar was given a report on the British position in India prepared by the Austrian consul in Bombay and somehow obtained for the Russian government by its ambassador in Vienna. The Austrian consul had written that the British position in India was precarious. The Tsar's reaction was: "Extremely interesting and instructive for us. If, upon checking, all of this proves even half true, we can completely change our tone in our negotiations with England on Asiatic affairs." Lamsdorff commented in his diary that the Tsar, who received Wolff in Berlin, agreed to his every proposal, and expressed his desire to reach an understanding, now suddenly began to talk of "changing our tone." [193]

When Morier made an attempt further to pursue the negotiations which had such a seemingly auspicious beginning in Berlin, Giers expressed complete surprise and said that the Emperor had not told him of any commitment to reach an understanding on Persia. In fact Giers denied outright that the Tsar had made the statements attributed to him by Sir Henry Drummond Wolff. The denial was so positive that Morier accepted it and decided that Wolff must have misunderstood the Tsar, who was not accustomed to discuss politics with foreigners in French.[194] As far as Giers and Morier were concerned, this ended the matter of an agreement on Persia.

In Tehran, however, the irrepressible Sir Henry continued to

---

192. Morier to Salisbury, No. 353, Most Secret, St. Petersburg, November 13, 1889; ibid.

193. Lamsdorff, *Dnevnik*, pp. 212–13.

194. Morier to Salisbury, Secret and Private, St. Petersburg, November 27, 1889; F.O. 65/1379.

battle for an understanding that would allow the construction of a Trans-Persian railway. He was fully convinced of the advantages such a line would bring to England. The problem was to persuade the Russians, who stood to gain a great deal more than the British themselves. In his dispatches to Salisbury, Wolff tried to show that whereas the Suez Canal saved Britain 2,492 miles between London and Bombay, a Trans-Persian railway would save Russia 3,072 miles between Baku and Karachi. The savings on transportation would be enormous. "A thriving trade is generally the earnest of peace," Wolff theorized, "and the sudden stimulus to enterprise that would follow on the adoption of the Persian route would certainly produce great, and it is to be hoped salutary, results, not only commercially but politically." [195] Wolff never explained exactly what it was that Russia would carry to India. The comparison between the imaginary Baku-Karachi trade and the very real London-Bombay trade was ridiculous, but Wolff would use almost any argument to make a point, and the point was that Russia and England should agree that a railway be built by an international company under Persian charter; that the British, the Russian, and the Persian governments be officially represented in such a company; that the railway be declared neutral, "much on the same lines as the neutrality of the Suez Canal"; and that the rates be subject to the approval of the three governments.[196]

Russian businessmen had no intention of cooperating with the City. The Khomiakov and Poliakov groups, originally rivals, drew closer in the face of the obstacles that must be overcome if a railway line were to be built across Persia. Boris Poliakov, a nephew of Lazar, and Lev Rafailovich, Lazar's brother-in-law, appeared in Tehran supposedly as tourists; but the Shah and Amin os-Soltān, who made no secret of their mission, admitted to Wolff that the two gentlemen were seeking a concession and made it clear that the Russian legation was giving them its support.[197]

As soon as he heard of the application made by the Russians for

195. Wolff to Salisbury, No. 49, Most Confidential, Tehran, February 14, 1890; F.O. 60/509.
196. Id.
197. Wolff to Salisbury, No. 70, Most Confidential, Tehran, March 3, 1890; ibid.

a railway concession, Wolff handed Qavām od-Dowleh a note, reminding the Persian government of the Shah's solemn assurances

1. That whenever a railway concession may be given anywhere in Persia, a similar concession shall be granted to an English Company for a line from Tehran to the Persian Gulf.
2. That no concession of any kind will be given for a railway from Tehran to the south except in agreement with this Legation.[198]

Though the note was officially intended as a mere reminder, it contained a clear warning to the Persian government.

Poliakov and his associates knew that they were not likely to obtain a concession without the strong support of their government. Therefore they spent considerably more effort at winning their case in St. Petersburg, where the all-important decisions would be made, than in Tehran. A powerful pressure group had come into being at the Russian capital. In addition to the Poliakov clan with its great wealth and ramified business interests, it included Khomiakov, Tret'iakov, Baron Korff, Palashkovskii, and Konshin. At Court their champion was Prince Dolgorukov, while in the government they found a supporter in the Minister of Roads, Adolf Iakovlevich von Hübbenet (Giubbenet.) Their opponents were few, but among them were some powerful individuals such as P. P. Riabushinskii, a leading Moscow textile manufacturer who claimed that the best defense of Russia's commercial interests in Persia lay in "the elemental monopoly of roadlessness." [199] In the government the opponents of Persian railway schemes had their strongholds in the ministries of finance and foreign affairs.

Having failed to find support in the Ministry of Foreign Affairs, where Zinov'ev ran the Asiatic Department, the Khomiakov-Poliakov group pressed for a special ministerial conference, a kind

---

198. Wolff to Qavām od-Dowleh, in Wolff to Salisbury, No. 35, Tehran, February 5, 1890, as cited in Memorandum on Persian Railways, India Office, June 20, 1911; F.O. 371/1186.

199. L. A. Sobotsinskii, *Persiia*, p. 70.

"Pénétration Pacifique" 231

of general cabinet meeting, in which its friends could rally to the support of the cause of Persian railways. Giers had no alternative and had to agree to a conference, but Zinov'ev did his best to delay it as long as he could. He prepared a detailed memorandum for the Tsar, showing how railways in Persia would harm Russia's interests in that country, but Giers, more experienced in the ways of the Court, talked him out of submitting it to Alexander.[200]

Fed up with Zinov'ev's tactics, the Minister of Roads, Hübbenet, complained to the Tsar about the procrastination and the ill will of the Ministry of Foreign Affairs. Alexander III was furious. "The situation is becoming serious," Lamsdorff entered in his diary, "and could really end badly." [201] The very next day, November 30, 1889, the Tsar upbraided Giers for the slowness of his ministry in the Persian railways' affair, spoke heatedly against Zinov'ev, and on the spot appointed a committee to discuss the entire problem. Zinov'ev, the Tsar said, would not be allowed to participate. The cautious and obedient Giers displayed a high degree of courage when he argued with the autocrat that the chief of the Asiatic Department and former minister to Persia knew the situation and should not be excluded. At last Alexander relented, and Zinov'ev was permitted to participate.[202]

In spite of all the pressure, Giers and Zinov'ev somehow managed to postpone the conference another two months. Zinov'ev preached his doctrine that the Khomiakov project was "incongruous and impossible," and argued that in the interests of Russia it was necessary to oppose all railway construction in Persia. At the expiration of the current moratorium on concessions, it would be possible to obtain its extension, "or, through intimidation, to compel the Persian Government not to build any railways." [203]

The Special Conference on Persia finally convened on February 16, 1890. It was chaired by the former Minister of Finance, now

200. Lamsdorff, Dnevnik, p. 221.
201. Id.
202. Ibid., p. 222.
203. Ibid., p. 240. It may be noted that Lamsdorff felt that in principle such demands on a sovereign state were "unheard of and impossible," though he agreed that from the point of view of practical politics, Zinov'ev's argument had much in its favor.

President of the Department of State Economy of the State Council, Privy Counselor Abaza, and included the ministers of Foreign Affairs, Giers; War, Vannovskii; Finance, Vyshnegradskii; Roads, Hübbenet; the Chief of the General Staff, Adjutant General Obruchev; the Assistant Minister of Foreign Affairs, Vlangali; the Director of the Asiatic Department of the Ministry of Foreign Affairs, Zinov'ev; the newly appointed Minister to the Shah, Bützow; and the former Minister to Persia, Major General of His Majesty's Suite, Prince Dolgorukov.[204]

As Giers had foreseen, the Finance Minister, Ivan Alekseevich Vyshnegradskii, opposed Persian railroad schemes. He pointed out that N. A. Khomiakov and other Russian capitalists did not have the means to build the proposed railway. They were counting on the promises of the Director of the Parisian Banque d'Escomptes, but the bank would provide the funds only if Russia guaranteed the enterprise. Moreover, to make the Persian railway useful, Russia would have to build at government expense a spur line from Vladikavkaz to the railhead of the Persian line, or to allow a foreign company to do so while guaranteeing its investment. Furthermore, the French bank insisted that all orders for railway equipment must be placed with factories designated by the French financial group, showing clearly that the group intended to profit from orders and that there was no hope that any would be placed with Russian factories.[205]

Vyshnegradskii was followed by the War Minister, General Petr Semenovich Vannovskii. The Persian railway issue was not new, he said. It arose in 1873 "after the Shah had been compelled, because of our insistence, to cancel the concession for the construction of a railway which he had given to Baron Reuter without our knowledge." At the time it had been agreed between the ministries of Foreign Affairs and War that in order to counteract the British, it was necessary to build a railway from Tiflis to Tabriz. The strategic importance of such a line would be great, and he was still of the opinion that it should be built, but by the Russian government at its own expense. The War Minister

204. Minutes of the Special Conference of February 4/16, 1890; "Anglo-russkoe sopernichestvo v Persii v 1890–1906 g.g.," *Krasnyi Arkhiv*, 1(56) (1933), 35.
205. Ibid., pp. 36–37.

strongly opposed the idea of a railway touching the shore of the Caspian Sea. "Our policy has always striven to ensure the exclusive character of that sea," he said, "and therefore any enterprise which would assist in attracting foreign interests toward the basin of the Caspian must be recognized as incompatible with our advantages." [206]

The Minister of Roads, Adolf Iakovlevich Hübbenet, spoke in favor of the Khomiakov project, which had been submitted to him in May 1889. He had gotten in touch with the Ministry of Foreign Affairs, hoping to take advantage of the expected arrival of the Shah of Persia, and had been told that it was inconvenient (or embarrassing, "*ne udobno*") to negotiate with the Shah at that moment, but that the latter had been informed of the offers to build railways in Persia and would hear more about it upon his return to Tehran.

At the expiration of the five-year moratorium on railway concessions, Russia must build a Trans-Persian railway so as to gain control of Indo-European transit. Khomiakov and his associates were respectable and trustworthy persons. True, Persian railways would have to be linked with the Russian, but one must not postpone the building of a Persian railway on that account, or one might have to wait ten or more years. The British would take advantage and might deal Russia's position in Persia a heavy blow.[207]

Nikolai Karlovich Giers replied that his ministry watched British intrigues in Asia with care and always opposed them, but the mode of its action varied in accordance with circumstances. In 1873 it had been thought desirable to build a railway to Tabriz. This was not accomplished, yet Russia's position in Persia was not weakened thereby.

During the last two or three years, Giers continued, the English had increased their hostile activities. Sir Henry Drummond Wolff took advantage of the apprehensions aroused in the Shah by the consolidation of Russia's position along the Astarābād and Khorāsān borders to convince him that to secure his safety he must get closer to England. The Shah, with his characteristic

206. Ibid., pp. 37–38.
207. Ibid., pp. 38–39.

timidity, fell for this suggestion, but Russia on her part won from him an obligation not to grant railway concessions for five years, during which she would prepare a project and find a company to carry it out. What Giers wanted the conference to decide was: (1) Should Russia seek a concession for a line to Tabriz, or further south as well? (2) "also—and this may be the main thing —by what means can we prevent the construction of railways in Persia by the British?" [208]

Aleksandr Aggeevich Abaza sided with Vyshnegradskii, Vannovskii, and Giers. In the 1870s a rupture with Britain had been expected over Central Asia. It was partly this expectation that had caused Russia to think of a Tabriz railway as a means of securing her position in Persia. Now that Russian possessions touched Afghanistan and her railway reached Samarkand, her position in Persia was no longer of the same importance as it had been in the seventies. Russia's task must be to prevent the British from extending their influence from south to central Persia. As for northern Persia, nothing could shake Russia's position there, and the Shah could not help but realize this.[209]

The longest and the most carefully thought out presentation was made by Ivan Alekseevich Zinov'ev. His case was stated under four headings:

1. A Trans-Persian railway would hardly become the transit route for the Indo-European traffic, as it would be too long and too slow. It would not be able to compete with shipping through the Suez Canal.

2. The preponderance of India's trade was with Britain. Of the 6,640,832 tons of goods that passed through the Suez Canal in 1888, 5,223,254 tons were carried in British bottoms. It is doubtful that Britain would prefer to ship over a Russian railway which she did not control and which lay on the territory of a power she suspected. Moreover, England could build an Indo-European railway of her own, through Mesopotamia and Asia Minor, such a line being shorter than the one across Russia.

3. Russia could not protect the southern portion of a Trans-Persian railway. The British ruled the Persian Gulf, and Russia would have to establish a naval station there, an extremely com-

208. Ibid., p. 39.
209. Ibid., p. 40.

"*Pénétration Pacifique*"

plicated problem that could have serious consequences and must be given serious and mature consideration.

4. The Tabriz railway was important since the control of Āzarbāyjān could be crucial in another Russo-Turkish war. However, without a link to Russia, such a line would be of no value. Therefore it was better, for the time being, to build a highway from Jolfā to Tabriz and concentrate on preventing the British from building any railways in Persia.[210]

The conference then passed a number of innocuous resolutions, proposing that preliminary research be conducted into the problem of building a railway across Persia, that Caspian shipping be improved, that Persian roads leading to the Caspian be made passable for wheeled vehicles, and that research be undertaken into the building of a railway across the Caucasian chain of mountains and on to Tabriz.[211] Zinov'ev had won a complete victory. His policy of vetoing railway construction in Persia had been approved by the most important government departments. It would be maintained until the downfall of the Imperial regime, and Iran would remain without railroads for more than a generation.

Zinov'ev, of course, was not concerned with the effects of his policy on Persia. Even his colleagues in the Ministry of Foreign Affairs, themselves men of little sentiment or idealism, could not fail to notice his open cynicism. Lamsdorff reports that once in a conversation Zinov'ev thus stated his views:

> "My minor interest should be dearer to me than the major interests of others; in the East principles are inapplicable, there one must be guided by opportunism alone." He [Zinov'ev] is of the opinion that any railway would be advantageous only to foreign commerce and harmful to the Russian. Therefore it only remains to wish Nāser ed-Din Shah a long life and to think how matters could be arranged so that he would be succeeded by the most pliable of the pretenders to the Persian throne.[212]

The decision reached by the Russian government not to allow

210. Ibid., pp. 45–47.
211. Ibid., p. 48.
212. Lamsdorff, *Dnevnik*, p. 347.

any railway construction in Iran was not communicated to the Russian chargé d'affaires in Tehran, A. N. Speyer, for some time. Himself a proponent of railway building, Speyer hoped for a Russian-owned line running from Rasht to Mohammareh. On such a line Russia could establish freight rates favorable to her commerce and unfavorable to Britain's.[213] Speyer spared no effort to obtain a concession for Russian capitalists and worked closely with Boris Poliakov and Lev Rafailovich.

Amin os-Soltān evaded the issue as long as possible. However, in April, Speyer called on him and brought up the railway question. The Russian chargé d'affaires reproached Amin os-Soltān for not granting Poliakov and Rafailovich the concession they sought. Soon the conversation heated up. "Monsieur de Speyer then went on in a very excited manner to declare that it was impossible for England and Russia to exist side by side in Persia. Russia would not allow railways to be made by any but herself and everything should be done to discourage the presence of the English in the country." [214]

Speyer accused Amin os-Soltān of being a partisan of the English, and of having been responsible for the establishment of the Imperial Bank, which would bring ruin to Persia. He urged an immediate grant of a concession to the Russian applicants. Amin os-Soltān replied that he would do so

> on condition that the line should be open to all nationalities without differential rates. Monsieur de Speyer said that this was impossible. Any railway in Persia must give Russia a preference in rates of fifty percent. He went on to say that Russia would not allow England to expend any money on railways in Persia. There must either be no railways at all or they must be Russian. No third countries should make them for they would be bought by England and even if the Shah wished to make them himself the capital must be borrowed in Russia and he would undertake that within a month

213. French Chargé d'Affaires at Tehran, Paulze d'Ivoy de la Poype to the Minister of Foreign Affairs, Telegram, No. 16 [in cipher], Tehran, March 8, 1890; Archive des Affaires Etrangères, Correspondance politique, Perse, tome 42, folio 99.

214. Wolff to Salisbury, No. 122, Most Secret and Confidential, Tehran, April 12, 1890; F.O. 60/511.

"Pénétration Pacifique" 237

the money should be forthcoming. But there must be no British capital.²¹⁵

Amin os-Soltān suggested that the Russian government take up this question directly with the British Foreign Office. The Shah had obligations to Russia in the north and Britain in the south and could not break either. Speyer asked why so much encouragement had been given to the British in Persia, and said "that they should be treated in such a manner as to induce them to leave it." Should Persia throw off all association with Britain, Russia would take the Shah and his dominion under her protection. When Amin os-Soltān protested that Persia needed no protection against the British, Speyer said that the Grand Vizier was well known for his Anglophile tendencies. "If H[is] H[ighness] would entirely change his policy and espouse the interests of Russia, the Russian Government would entirely espouse his cause and take him under its protection." ²¹⁶

Still uninformed of their government's decision, Poliakov and Rafailovich, in close cooperation with Yahyā Khān Moshir od-Dowleh, submitted an application to the Shah. His Majesty was asked for (1) the right to build a railway, (2) a monopoly for the manufacture of paper and cardboard, (3) a *crédit foncier*, (4) a monopoly of opium, (5) the right to refine oil, and (6) the right to open an insurance company. The Shah was offered in return 7,000,000 francs worth of shares in the railway (6,000,000 francs for the railway and 1,000,000 for other concessions). The application was received on April 29. The next day Amin os-Soltān had dinner with Sir Henry Wolff and showed him the letter addressed by Poliakov and Rafailovich to the Shah. The Grand Vizier told Wolff that he intended to advise the Shah against granting the railroad, *crédit fonciér*, and opium concessions, and for the other concessions requested by the Russian businessmen.²¹⁷

Through the spring and summer 1890 the British nervously waited for the outcome of the negotiations between Persia and Russia. Though Amin os-Soltān was on the side of the English,

215. Id.
216. Id.
217. Wolff to Salisbury, No. 156, Confidential, Tehran, April 30, 1890; ibid.

London could not depend on the Shah to withstand great Russian pressure, were such applied. On May 19, 1890, Salisbury instructed Wolff to resist the construction of a railway across Khorāsān, though the Prime Minister himself doubted the efficacy of such resistance. A Russian attempt to build a railway to Tehran was not to be resisted but was to be counteracted by a demand on the Shah to grant the British a concession of equal value.[218] British fears were constantly stimulated by Speyer who talked loudly of Russian railways soon to be built. To the Dutch minister, Knobel, who said that it would be a long time before railways were built, Speyer replied: "Not at all, they will be proceeded with at once. We intend to make a line from the Caspian to Mohammerah or to some port further East." When Knobel observed that this project would probably be opposed by England, Speyer said: "Then it will end by a partition of Persia between England and Russia."[219]

With the arrival in Tehran of the new Russian minister, Evgenii Karlovich Bützow (Biutsov), Russian demands on the Persian government underwent a radical change. Poliakov and other concession hunters were abandoned and the Shah was asked to promise not to build any railways at all. Though a ban on railway construction would deprive Nāser ed-Din of a considerable amount of money, he must have been relieved by the new turn of events. Inaction, after all, was so much simpler, so much less dangerous.

Wolff continued to agitate in favor of a Russo-British agreement, thereby demonstrating his lack of political sensitivity. His position in Tehran deteriorated without his being aware of it.

On November 12, 1890, Bützow and Amin os-Soltān signed an agreement whose first and most important article stated:

> The Persian Government engages, for the space of ten years, beginning from the date of the signature of this agreement, neither itself to construct a railway in Persian terri-

---

218. Salisbury to Wolff, Telegram, May 19, 1890, as cited in Memorandum on Persian Railways, Secret, India Office, June 20, 1911; F.O. 371/1186.

219. Wolff to Salisbury, No. 173, Secret and Confidential, Tehran, May 12, 1890; F.O. 60/511.

"Pénétration Pacifique" 239

tory, nor to permit nor grant a concession for the construction of railways to a company or other persons; and after the expiration of ten years the renewal of the prolongation [sic] shall be immediately discussed between the two parties.[220]

The British went through the motions of protesting against the agreement, which was aptly dubbed "Sterilizing." On November 16 Lamsdorff noted in his diary that the British were displeased. "Thus," he wrote, "even this small, purely negative success of our diplomatic endeavors in Persia excites jealousy." Lamsdorff felt that the British wanted a commitment from Russia to reach an agreement on the issue upon the termination of the ten-year moratorium.[221] Giers was jubilant.

> You will do me the justice to admit [he told Sir Robert Morier] that from the very first I have opposed railway construction in Persia in every form. What this resistance cost me you can have no idea. On all sides and by all parties I have been pestered to grant concessions, and insisting on Persian Government granting concessions. All this is over now, and there will be rest and quiet.[222]

To the continued British complaints, the Russian government firmly replied that it intended to maintain its position.[223]

220. Translation from the Persian of the text of the Russo-Persian Railway Agreement signed at Tehran on November 12, 1890 (1308) by Monsieur de Butzow, and the Amin-es-Sultan, Persian Prime Minister. (From the Persian text in the Persian Foreign Office), Enclosure No. 3 in A. Hardinge, No. 238, Secret, December 1, 1904; F.O. 60/683. The Soviet historian M. S. Ivanov, in his *Ocherk istorii Irana*, p. 189, writes:
> The governments of England and Tsarist Russia signed a convention in which they agreed not to build themselves and generally to oppose the construction of railways in Iran. England was against railway construction in Iran first of all because she endeavored to prevent the approach of other powers to India and to maintain there her monopolistic colonial dominion. Thus, for the sake of the imperialists, Iran was deprived of the right to build railways.

No such convention existed, of course. Needless to say, M. S. Ivanov does not cite the mythical documents alleged to have been signed by the two powers.

221. Lamsdorff, *Dnevnik*, p. 337.
222. Sir Robert Morier to Salisbury [No. 283?], cited in Memorandum on Persian Railways, Secret, India Office, June 20, 1911; F.O. 371/1186.
223. Meyendorff, *Correspondance diplomatique du Baron de Staal (1844–1900)*, 2, No. 48, 120.

Once again, as in the case of Reuter, Falkenhagen, and other concession hunters, the clash of the two powers produced a deadlock. However, the rest and quiet for which Giers longed were not to come to Iran.

4

The Tobacco Régie: Britain's Retreat and Russia's Offensive

Sir Henry Drummond Wolff firmly believed that large-scale investment of British private capital in Persia was the surest means of securing England's position in that country. Though his dream of a Trans-Persian railway never materialized, several of his major endeavors were successful. The Kārun River was opened to commercial traffic, and Reuter was allowed to establish the Imperial Bank. However, navigation, banking, and railways did not exhaust Sir Henry's vivid imagination. Persia was undeveloped and lacked every amenity of modern Western civilization. There was hardly any enterprise that might not be introduced into the country by British capitalists willing to take the risk.

Nāser ed-Din Shah lent a willing ear to the British minister, whose sermons on the virtue of foreign investment provided a patriotic rationalization of the Shah's natural greed. The government and the Court, swept by the moneymaking fever, were anxious to sell to foreign businessmen any concession or privilege they might request. The Shah's entourage, a contemporary Iranian historian writes, "competed in selling the fatherland to foreigners, and from time to time each one of them, for personal gain alone, would show the Shah various paths of treason."[1] The ease and haste with which the Persian government dispensed concessions without regard to consequences proved a source of embarrassment to the British government, particularly when its own subjects were involved. The Reuter concession of 1872 was one such case; another, and even more unsavory one, occurred in 1889-90.

1. Teymuri, *Asre bikhabari*, p. 213.

The principal actor was Mirzā Malkam Khān Nāzem ol-Molk, the Shah's minister to London, a man with a reputation for wit, intelligence, patriotism, and advanced ideas. To this day historians mention him among the precursors of the Persian revolution. (The newspaper, Qānun, which he published in London from 1890 to 1894, has been called "a literary enterprise which undoubtedly was not without its effect in increasing the dissatisfaction at the Shah's extravagances and disregard of the interests of his people which began to prevail in Persia." [2]) Yet this charming, learned, and supposedly patriotic gentleman involved his country in a sordid scandal that helped ruin Persia's reputation in European financial circles.

Soon after his appointment as Minister to Britain, Malkam Khān found his way to London's financial underworld. For over sixteen years he had been closely associated with Julius Reuter, who had paid him £20,000 and promised £30,000 more if Malkam would obtain for Reuter a bank charter. According to Malkam Khān's unreliable testimony, Reuter had refused to honor his pledge and pay the additional sum after the opening of the Imperial Bank. Malkam's appeal to Sir Henry Wolff produced no results.[3]

However, the enterprising diplomat had other friends and associates. The Shah had granted a lottery concession to a certain Buzie de Caerdoel, who was acting in Malkam's behalf and who transferred the concession to the Persian minister. Apparently neither the Shah nor Malkam Khān had any doubts as to the propriety of introducing large-scale gambling into an Islamic country.[4]

With Malkam's encouragement, a number of rather shady dealers formed the Persian Investment Corporation whose board of directors included W. W. Cargill, Director of the New Orien-

---

2. E. G. Browne, *The Persian Revolution of 1905–1909* (Cambridge, 1910), p. 35.

3. Wolff to Salisbury, Secret and Confidential, Berlin, October 12, 1889; F. O. 60/551.

4. Almost simultaneously the Shah granted "to some Europeans" a monopoly on the manufacture and sale of wine and liquor. The concession was later bought by the Société Générale du Commerce et Industrie de la Perse, a Brussels firm. Cf. Curson, *Persia*, 2, 507.

tal Bank Corporation and the Anglo-Asiatic Syndicate, organizations of questionable reputation. Another director of the Persian Investment Corporation was Mikāil Khān, "Councillor of the Persian Embassy," and Malkam's brother. The corporation's prospectus proudly stated that "His Highness Prince Malcom Khan has authorized the constitution of the company" and thus described the objectives of the corporation:

> To acquire any concessions, rights, or privileges for any objects or purposes whatsoever granted or to be granted by his Majesty the Shah of Persia . . .
> To carry on all kinds of financial and banking business, and in particular to negotiate loans and advances, to offer for subscription, place, buy, sell, and deal in shares, bonds, obligations, stocks, bills, notes, and securities of all kinds.
> To carry on all kinds of exploration business.[5]

The prospectus went on to enumerate the types of economic activity in which the company would be engaged: drainage works, road building, markets, lighting of cities, irrigation, construction of residences and stores as well as of public buildings, construction of tramways, amusement, recreation, instruction.

When Sir Henry Wolff picked up rumors that Malkam Khān was connected with the Anglo-Asiatic Syndicate which stood behind the Persian Investment Corporation, he was disturbed and alarmed. The syndicate had issued a number of shares at £100 and saw them appreciate 1,000 percent in a few months "merely on the mysterious hopes held out by anonymous projectors." While Malkam denied any knowledge of the syndicate or its affairs, Wolff found out that one of the men behind it was a certain Mr., or Colonel, Cloete, "recently recommended by Malkham [sic] Khan for the office of Persian Consul General in London." Wolff also discovered "that the real movers in this Association are a Mr. Watson who was mixed up with recent transactions in Hyderabad, and this Colonel Cloete, a man whose antecedents both in England and the Cape of Good Hope are not of the first luster."[6]

5. The Persian Investment Company, *Prospectus*; F. O. 60/551.
6. Wolff to Salisbury, Secret and Confidential, Berlin, October 12, 1889; ibid.

Though not particularly squeamish about the business ethics of his friends, Wolff strongly disapproved of the lottery concession. He expressed his misgivings to Salisbury, who agreed that "It would divert money from profitable trade to gambling and would be a serious injury to the Shah's subjects." [7] The Russian legation was also displeased. Both the Russian chargé d'affaires and the British minister remonstrated with the Shah, who disregarded their representations.[8]

On Wolff's urging, the Foreign Office asked the law officers of the Crown whether any of the objectives of the Persian Investment Corporation were illegal or punishable in English law, and whether persons taking part in the enterprise "were punishable under the Lottery Acts, or whether they were indictable for conspiracy at common law against public morality in fraud of the public." In reply the law officers expressed doubt that criminal proceedings against the members of the corporation would be successful.

> We, however, think [they wrote] that the undertaking is within mischief contemplated by the Laws relating to lotteries and gaming, and that persons receiving money for the purposes of this Company are in fact keeping a lottery within the meaning of these Statutes.
>
> We advise that the Public Prosecutor should be instructed to write to the Secretary of the Company, saying that Her Majesty's Government are advised that the enterprise is unlawful, and that, if continued, the Directors and the Secretary and other persons engaged therein will render themselves liable to proceedings.[9]

While the British government was preparing action against the Anglo-Asiatic Syndicate, the New Oriental Bank Corporation, and the Persian Investment Corporation, the Shah succumbed to combined Russian and British pressure, and canceled the lottery

---

7. Marginal note signed S. Wolff to Salisbury, No. 162, Secret and Confidential, Tehran, November 25, 1889; ibid.

8. Same to same, No. 167, Secret and Confidential, Tehran, November 30, 1889; ibid.

9. The Law Officers of the Crown to the Marquis of Salisbury, Secret, Royal Courts of Justice, December 5, 1889; ibid.

The Tobacco Régie

concession, informing Malkam of this fact on December 5, 1889, by telegram. Keeping the cancellation secret, Malkam sold the concession outright to the Persian Investment Corporation. His brother, Mikāil Khān, received a check for £20,000 which he deposited in Malkam's personal account at the Burlington Gardens Branch of the Bank of England. Since His Highness had already been paid £20,000, his total take from a concession he knew to be invalid was £40,000, a sum roughly equivalent in purchasing power to a million dollars in 1967.[10]

On December 10, 1889, Mirzā Abbās Khān Qavām od-Dowleh officially informed Wolff that, after the concession had been granted to Nāzem ol-Molk (Malkam Khān),

> it appeared that he had put in other games which are contrary to the noble laws of the Mussulman faith and the estabt. of which in Persia might give rise to endless troubles, therefore by obligation the above mentioned concession was annulled and cancelled.[11]

The Persian Government was resorting to lies to save face.

Malkam Khān was not prepared to give up without a fight. He cabled Qavām od-Dowleh that the concession had already been sold and was now the property of thousands of Europeans. The owners would sue the Persian government for damages.[12] The concession was not contrary to religious law, and the company was respectable, having bank directors and members of Parliament on its board. As evidence of his zeal, Malkam Khān had already arranged "that 30,000 tomans on account of future dues be immediately laid at His Majesty's feet." He attributed the cancellation to the intrigues of "foreign sharpers" and asked, "What harm would there be in taking this 30,000 tomans in ready money."[13]

Foreseeing difficulties with his recent associates, whom he had cheated out of a large amount of money, Malkam Khān tried his

10. The Law Officers of the Crown to the Marquis of Salisbury; ibid.
11. Minister of Foreign Affairs [Qavām od-Dowleh] to Wolff, Tehran, December 10, 1889, Enclosure in Wolff to Salisbury, No. 239, Tehran, December 20, 1889; ibid.
12. Malkam Khān to Qavām od-Dowleh, Telegram, London, December 10, 1889, Enclosure in Wolff to Salisbury, No. 239, Tehran, December 20, 1889; ibid.
13. Id.

best to intimidate the Persian government into restoring the concession. Yet he had the temerity to press the syndicate for the rest of the £120,000, the sum it had agreed to pay for the concession. Once the members of the syndicate learned that their concession was nothing but a piece of paper, they protested to the Foreign Office, demanding that Malkam Khān be compelled to return the money he had already received. Again the Foreign Office consulted the law officers of the Crown, who advised it that the British government would not be justified in pressing the claims of the syndicate for loss of prospective earnings.

> It is, however, clear [they wrote] that they [the Syndicate] have parted with the sum of 40,000l. paid by them to General Mikayl Khan, the brother of the Persian Minister in London, and stated to be Councillor to that Legation . . .
>
> We are therefore of the opinion that Her Majesty's Government should press upon the Persian Government the payment to the Memorialist [the syndicate] of this sum of 40,000.[14]

While English law slowly and ponderously made its way through the sordid maze of Malkam's deals, the Shah, embarrassed and angered by his minister's trickery, but unwilling to satisfy the claims of the syndicate or to return the 30,000 tumāns he had received from Malkam, dismissed him from his post, thus depriving him of diplomatic immunity. Faced with a suit in a British court of law, Malkam pleaded with Amin os-Soltān for assistance in his "present precarious position," and simultaneously began publishing a newspaper, Qānun, attacking despotism and calling for a constitutional regime in Persia. British advice that Malkam and the Shah compose their differences "to avoid the scandal which might arise out of legal proceedings" was disregarded by both sides, neither of which would part with the money it had received.[15]

The Persian Investment Corporation brought a suit against Malkam Khān, but the old fox had already transferred his money

14. The Law Officers of the Crown to the Marquis of Salisbury, Royal Courts of Justice, March 12, 1891; F. O. 60/553.
15. R. Kennedy to Salisbury, No. 320, Secret, Gulahek, October 17, 1890; F. O. 60/551.

to the continent. Moreover, the court found that though at the time of the trial Malkam Khān was no longer protected by diplomatic immunity, he had had this protection when the swindle was committed and could not be punished for it. That Malkam was nothing but a charlatan is further evinced by the fact that upon Nāser ed-Din Shah's death he composed his differences with the Persian government and was appointed by Amin od-Dowleh, the new Prime Minister, Persian minister to Rome, a post he occupied till he died a dozen years later. As soon as his salary was resumed, he forgot every principle he had ever advocated in the pages of the *Qānun* and became once again the obedient slave of the blessed threshold of the King of Kings. His subsequent elevation to the pantheon of Persian constitutionalism is a sad joke.[16]

The Malkam swindle weakened Sir Henry Wolff's position in Persia. Circumstances conspired to make the last year of his stay in Tehran disastrous. Since the arrival of Bützow in midsummer 1890, Wolff had lost the initiative. The bitterness the Shah felt toward Malkam was to some extent reflected in his attitude toward the British legation. In September Wolff fell ill. "Left a clear field, de Butzow forgot all about disinterestedness." He pushed Amin os-Soltān and the Shah into the "Sterilyzing" agreement on railways. "Kennedy, the first secretary, found it hard to get an audience of the Shah at all; Gordon, the military *attaché*, made an unguarded remark comparing the position of Persia *vis-a-vis* Russia with that of the Khan of Bokhara, which the Shah deeply resented." [17] The strong position Wolff had built in the first few months of his mission was crumbling before his eyes.

However, Wolff's greatest and costliest mistake was his promo-

---

16. It must be noted in this connection that E. G. Browne's statement that he was ignorant of the identity of the Persian to whom the Shah had granted the lottery concession is utterly incredible. The Malkam swindle and his trial were amply covered in *The Times* and had been public knowledge for many years. Reluctantly one suspects that Browne, whose passions at times betrayed his scholarship, was not entirely candid. Cf. E. G. Browne, *The Persian Revolution*, p. 34. For further materials on the Malkam swindle, see a mass of documents in F. O. 60/551, F. O. 60/553, F. O. 60/557, and Teymuri's *Asre bikhabari*.

17. A. P. Thornton, "British Policy in Persia, 1858–1890," Part III, *The English Historical Review*, 70, No. 274 (January 1955), 68.

tion of a tobacco concession. This seemingly innocent business enterprise opened a new chapter in the history of Anglo-Russian rivalry, a chapter consisting largely of a record of British defeats and Russian victories.

During the summer of the "Year of Evil," as E. G. Browne named 1889, Sir Henry Drummond Wolff introduced to the Shah a friend, Major Gerald F. Talbot, who requested the grant of a monopoly to buy, sell, and manufacture tobacco throughout the Persian Empire for fifty years. Wolff's support and the generous distribution of bribes won Talbot his concession.

The contract, signed on March 8, 1890, promised to pay the Imperial Treasury £15,000 yearly, irrespective of profit or loss, and, in addition, 25 percent of net profit, after the payment of a 5 percent dividend to shareholders (Articles 1 and 3). In return the company was given control over all activities and transactions connected with tobacco. Article 2 read in part:

> Permission for sale etc. of tootoon, tobacco, cigars, cigarettes, snuff, etc. is the absolute right of the concessionaires and no one but the proprietors of this concession shall have the right to issue the above mentioned permits.
>
> The guilds of the sellers of tobacco and tootoon who are engaged in this trade will remain permanent in their local trade and transactions, on condition of possessing permits which will be given to them by the concessionaires.[18]

Article 5 prohibited the "Removal and transfer of tootoon and tobacco in the protected provinces [of Persia] without the permission of the proprietor," except for small quantities travelers might carry with them for their personal daily use. The company would buy the country's entire output of tobacco "at prices agreed upon by buyer and sellers [cultivators]." Disagreements would be solved by compulsory arbitration (Article 6). The contract carried a threat: "Anyone attempting to evade rules of these articles will be severely punished as will be those who are found in possession of tobacco for sale or trade." [19]

18. Text of the tobacco concession given to Major G. F. Talbot on March 8, 1890 (28 Rajab 1307 A.H.), Enclosure in Wolff to Salisbury, No. 104, Tehran, April 3, 1890; F. O. 60/553.

19. Id.

The concession was one of the most vicious ever granted by Nāser ed-Din Shah. Bad as it was, the Reuter contract of 1872, had it been implemented, would not have interfered with the lives of the masses of people. Talbot's concession, on the contrary, hit at every town and village where tobacco was grown, processed, sold, bought, or consumed. Thousands of tobacco merchants and peddlers were virtually sold to a foreign company, and suddenly found their business confiscated in fact if not in law, and themselves turned into salesmen working on commission for an English firm.

Ignorant of the society with which they were dealing, Wolff and his business friends failed to understand the position of the merchants and the power of the bazar in Persia. Unlike the peasantry, city merchants were not defenseless. As a class they enjoyed a much higher status than their counterparts did in Russia or even in Western Europe. Moreover, they had close and vital connections with the clergy, a powerful group none could disregard. Combined and given a modicum of support by outsiders, the merchants and the clergy could throw the country into turmoil.

Much depended on the attitude of Russia. When the tobacco concession was granted and the Régie established, the Russian legation was in the charge of its first secretary, Aleksei Nikolaevich Speyer, Prince Dolgorukov having left and his successor, E. Bützow, having not yet arrived in Tehran. Shortly after the signing of the Talbot contract, Speyer asked Amin os-Soltān whether the rumors of a tobacco monopoly having been granted to an Englishman were true. The Grand Vizier admitted that such was the case. Speyer commented that the Régie would raise the price of tobacco to an exhorbitant extent and would constantly interfere with Persian agriculture. He added that Poliakov and Refailovich protested against the concession since they had first to propose a scheme that included tobacco.[20]

For the next five months the Régie dropped out of sight. Talbot sold his rights, probably making an enormous profit, to a syndicate, which organized the Imperial Tobacco Corporation of

20. Wolff to Salisbury, No. 104, Tehran, April 3, 1890; ibid.

Persia. The Régie had high hopes of success, estimating net annual profits at £371,875, or well over 50 percent on the capital invested. (The corporation was capitalized at £650,000.)[21]

In July 1890, the new Russian minister, Evgenii Karlovich Bützow, arrived in Tehran. Without Dolgorukov's ill-tempered histrionics, Bützow pursued the same policy of fencing off Persia, or at least her northern provinces, from British commerce and influence. The tobacco Régie, which would operate in every town and hamlet of the country, was unpalatable not only to Russian merchants but to the Ministry of Foreign Affairs as well. Unfortunately the Soviet government has not published any documents dealing with the activities of Russia's Ministry of Foreign Affairs and its Tehran legation in the years 1890–92. However, sufficient evidence is available to show that early in September 1890, Bützow lodged his first protest against the Régie, claiming that its monopolistic position violated Article 1 of the Treaty of Commerce appended to the peace treaty of Torkamanchāy and demanding the cancellation of the concession.[22]

A few days later the Russian minister made a formal protest in writing to the Minister of Foreign Affairs against the Régie and asked that the concession be rescinded. "I do not think," Wolff cabled London, "the Persians would give way, but should be glad of instructions." [23]

In his written protest Bützow stated that

> the monopoly, that Concession being so named, is entirely contrary to the stipulations of the treaties, on that account the Impl Govt cannot deem that concession valid and regular. I beg respectfully to draw Y. Es' attention to the aforesaid matters and feel certain that the Persian Govt, who at the time of the granting of that concession, which is entirely contrary of the Treaties, had overlooked the stipulation of the Treaties, will give me an opportunity to inform the Impl

21. E. G. Browne, p. 33.
22. Amin os-Soltān communicated the protest to Sir Henry; Wolff to Salisbury, No. 221, Very Secret, Tehran, September 9, 1890; F. O. 60/553.
23. Wolff, No. 231, Decypher, Telegram, Tehran, September 16, 1890; ibid.

The Tobacco Régie

Govt that the aforesaid Monopoly has been abandoned and stopped.[24]

Ordinarily a strong note from the Russian minister, especially one invoking the "Sacred Treaty" of Torkamanchāy, would have sufficed to intimidate the Persian government. However, this time purely diplomatic means failed. Wolff was not overly optimistic when he stated that in his opinion the Persians would not give way. The main reason for the Shah's and the Grand Vizier's determination to go through with the concession was greed. His Majesty had been promised (and later paid) £15,000. Behind his master's back, Amin os-Soltān had made arrangements to receive an equal sum, but in his case payment depended on performance, thus adding to his zeal in behalf of the Régie.[25] It must be noted that Amin os-Soltān and the Shah were not the only ones to receive money from the Régie. Among the princes and highest officials, Zell es-Soltān, Nāyeb os-Saltaneh, Moshir od-Dowleh, and E'temād os-Saltaneh had been bribed.[26]

Fortified and encouraged by Wolff, the Persian government replied to Bützow's note of September 14 by proclaiming its adherence to the treaty of Torkamanchāy, and continuing:

> but it is not set forth in the Treaty that if the Persian Govt, in its interior, for the benefit of its agriculture, science, treasury or finance should grant a concession to a foreigner it shall not be at liberty to do so, especially if in those Concessions and agreements it should not have prohibited foreign subjects from commerce.[27]

Bützow insisted that the Régie violated the treaty by giving ex-

---

24. Bützow to the Minister of Foreign Affairs [Qavām od-Dowleh], No. 40, 29 Moharram 1308 (September 14, 1890), Enclosure No. 3 in Wolff to Salisbury, No. 286, Very Secret, Gulahek, September 23, 1890; ibid.

25. For a detailed analysis of who bribed whom and how, see Sir Frank Lascelles to the Marquis of Salisbury, No. 18, Secret and Confidential, Tehran, January 29, 1892, and enclosure, including a copy of a letter from Amin os-Soltān to the Shah denying that he received any money in this affair; F. O. 60/554.

26. Id.

27. Persian Government to M. Bützow, 29 Moharram 1308 (14 September 1890), Enclosure in Wolff to Salisbury, No. 286, Very Secret, Gulahek, September 23, 1890; F. O. 60/553.

clusive privileges to a company and preventing Russian subjects from trading freely in Persia.

> Certainly [Bützow wrote] the Persian Govt has the right to make arrangements for the benefit of her agriculture, science, etc. but those arrangements must not in any way whatsoever be contrary to the freedom of commerce stipulated in the Holy Treaty. One of the conditions of free trade is the ability, without anybody anywhere interfering or troubling, to purchase, sell, carry and transport any kind of merchandize of whatever nature there is and if the Persian Govt grants a special privilege to an individual or company in the barter of a commercial commodity and at the same time engages to execute the stipulations of the privilege the rest are prevented from trading in that commodity.[28]

Several days later in a discussion with Mesbāh ol-Molk, a high official of the Ministry of Foreign Affairs, Bützow argued this point orally. When Mesbāh ol-Molk pointed out that tobacco was not a commodity like others, since all governments controlled its production and sale, Bützow retorted that he had nothing to do with other countries, his only concern being that the Russo-Persian treaty should not be violated. "I replied," Mesbāh ol-Molk reports, "that free commerce in Tobacco and Tumbaku was not allowed in Russia even and explained to him how Persian subjects were obliged in Russia to sell their tobacco and tutun to certain individuals only." The two diplomats argued inconclusively over this and other points. At last Mesbāh ol-Molk said that while Russia considered the Régie a violation of the treaty, "The Company and the Legation favouring them will say that it is in accordance with the Treaty. Where will these discussions end!" [29]

The Russian legation had a variety of means of influencing the

---

28. Bützow to the Minister of Foreign Affairs [Qavām od-Dowleh], translation, No. 44, 4 Safar 1308 (September 19, 1890), Enclosure No. 4 in Wolff to Salisbury, No. 286, Very Secret, Gulahek, September 23, 1890; ibid.

29. Translation of a report by Mesbah-ul-Mulk of an interview with M. de Butzow, 7 Safar (September 22, 1890), Enclosure No. 6 in Wolff's No. 286 of September 23, 1890; ibid.

The Tobacco Régie

conduct of the Persian government. Amin os-Soltān, whose testimony is very unreliable but nevertheless indicative of the diplomatic methods current in Tehran, told Navvāb Hasan Ali Khān, native secretary of the British legation, that Bützow, aware of the friendship between the Grand Vizier and the British legation, "suggested to M. Zinovieff that it would, under the circumstances, be advisable to intrigue between the Amin os-Sultan and the British Legation and to cause the latter to suspect the Amin of having come to an understanding with the Russians." Bützow was also reported to have proposed to Zinov'ev that Russia form an "apparent friendship" with Amin os-Soltān, gaining three advantages thereby:

> Firstly this close friendship would rouse the suspicions of the English against the Amin which is the chief point. Secondly it would have the advantage of settling current affairs amicably and easily, and thirdly on account of this close friendship the Amin will be more ready to yield to any important proposals that the Russians may in future make to the Persian Government.[30]

Russian archives being unavailable, it is impossible to determine to what extent Amin os-Soltān's statement to Navvāb Hasan Ali Khān was true. However, he was undoubtedly stating facts when he told Hasan Ali Khān that the Russian minister, his first secretary, Speyer, and the dragoman, Grigorovich, met with Yahyā Khān Moshir od-Dowleh to plot against the Grand Vizier. The British chargé d'affaires, Mr. R. J. Kennedy, reported that "The guarded and significant manner in which the Mushir ed-Dowleh has, on two occasions, spoken to me about the Amin confirms, to a certain extent, the Amin-es-Sultan's information." [31]

The Russian legation was able to recruit to its cause a number of Amin os-Soltān's powerful enemies, among them the Shah's

---

30. Memorandum by Nawab of interview with Amin-es-Sultan, Nov. 29.90. Secret and Confidential, Enclosure in Mr. R. Kennedy to Salisbury, No. 322, Very Secret, Tehran, November 20, 1890; F. O. 60/512.

31. Kennedy to Salisbury, No. 322, Very Secret, Tehran, November 20, 1890; ibid.

favorite son, Kāmrān Mirzā Nāyeb os-Saltaneh, Minister of War and Governor of Tehran, as well as Hāj Mirzā Ali Khān Amin od-Dowleh, a man of great influence and an obvious candidate to take Amin os-Soltān's place at the head of the government.³²

Though Amin od-Dowleh's participation in anti-Régie activities was largely due to his hostility to Amin os-Soltān, it was motivated to some extent by patriotism and sympathy for the plight of tobacco merchants, who begged to be helped. In February 1891 Amin od-Dowleh transmitted to the Shah a petition from tobacco merchants protesting against the Régie. Amin os-Soltān was furious. He attributed the protest to personal enmity. The British legation believed that it had been made "at Russian instigation." ³³ The Grand Vizier was acutely uncomfortable and apprehensive. He may have recalled the events eighteen years before when a combination of princes, mullas, personal enemies, and the Russian legation overthrew his predecessor, Mirzā Hoseyn Khān. History seemed to be repeating itself.

To test the strength of his position, Amin os-Soltān tendered his resignation. The Shah would not hear of it. He would rather part with all his other ministers than with Amin os-Soltān, he said. A council of ministers was convoked to listen to the Shah proclaim his determination that the Régie should stand. It fell to Yahyā Khān Moshir od-Dowleh, Minister of Commerce and one of Bützow's closest collaborators, to explain the situation to the tobacco merchants. A telegram of reassurance was sent to Major Talbot.³⁴

March was deceptively quiet. The Imperial Tobacco Corporation was getting ready to start operations with the full support of Amin os-Soltān, who was now the owner of some five hundred

32. See Note by Nawab Hasan Ali Khan on the Descent, Biography, and Character of Ali Asghar Khan, Sadre Azam, Appendix 2 in Memorandum by Sir M. Durand on the Situation in Persia, December 1895, Confidential (6704); F. O. 60/581.

33. Kennedy to Salisbury, No. 25, Telegram, decypher, No. 25, Tehran, February 23, 1891; F. O. 60/553. The rivalry between Amin os-Soltān and Amin od-Dowleh can be followed in the latter's memoirs, *Khāterāte siāsiye Mirzā Ali Khān Amin od-Dowleh* (Tehran, 1962).

34. Kennedy to Salisbury, No. 25, Tehran, February 23, 1891; F. O. 60/553.

shares of its stock. The Russian legation spun its thick web of intrigue all over Persia and reached to the holy cities of Iraq for clerical support. The British legation at this delicate moment was left in charge of a first secretary who had neither the prestige nor the experience that would have enabled him to extricate his government from an unpleasant situation without suffering a visible defeat.

At the beginning of April, Bützow learned that the Persian government intended to remove Mohammad Taqi Mirzā Rokn od-Dowleh from the governorship of Khorāsān. The prince had served Russian interests faithfully for over a decade, and Bützow was not willing to see a less accommodating official ruling an important province where Russian involvement was growing yearly. Bützow complained to Amin os-Soltān against this "disagreeable surprise." The Russians liked Rokn od-Dowleh, he said, and had even given him a decoration.[35] He did not mention the various expensive gifts the prince-governor had received.

> Monsieur de Butzow went on to warn the Amin us-Sultan against placing too much trust in English support and English friendship. Other nations had done so, and had found to their cost that they were leaning upon a broken reed. Turkey was an instance, and Persia would some day experience similar treatment.[36]

Amin os-Soltān defended his policy of balancing between the two great powers.

> Monsieur de Butzow retorted that his [Amin's] playing off of one Power against the other was contemptible policy, and accused the Amin us-Sultan of having contrived that Russian political and commercial influence which in former years was predominant in Persia should be ousted by the rival power.[37]

The Grand Vizier reported the conversation to the British chargé d'affaires, R. J. Kennedy, the very next day. He made it

35. Kennedy to Salisbury, No. 89, Tehran, April 7, 1891; F. O. 65/1413.
36. Id.
37. Id.

appear that he had bravely stood up to Bützow, telling him that

> Russia had only herself to thank for losing her position and influence in Persia. Her arrogant dictation was submitted to because Persia was a weak Power, but now when a friendly shield had been interposed between her and a drawn sword she was able to maintain her just rights.[38]

Bützow's report of this particular conversation not being available, it is impossible to prove one's suspicions, but the likelihood of Amin os-Soltān's having said anything of the sort is very small. He was probably exaggerating in order to win British favor and to induce London to give him stronger support vis-à-vis Russian pressure. Indeed, the satisfaction of the Foreign Office was expressed in a telegram to Kennedy: "Convey to the Amin es-Sultan my appreciation of the firm and statesmanlike tone of his language to the Russian Minister."[39] Such telegrams and the constant encouragement to stand firm created in the minds of the Shah and the Grand Vizier the impression that they could defy Russia on the issue of the tobacco monopoly.

By late spring the Régie's activities were visible to the population of the larger cities. In Tabriz feelings were particularly bitter. Mr. Robert M. Paton, Acting British consul general, wrote that the most enlightened Persians estimated the annual profits of the Régie at £780,000, of which the Shah would receive only £15,000 plus 20 percent. The monopoly was seen as an injustice and was resented.[40] Yet no one seemed to know much about its proposed methods of operation. Doubt increased fears.

The Armenian tobacco merchants, who were Russian subjects, inquired at the Russian consulate about the effect the Régie would have on their business. The consul told them that their status was determined by the treaty of Torkamanchāy, and that the provisions of the monopoly did not apply to them. They could, he assured them, continue to buy, sell, and import tobacco

38. Id.
39. F. O. to Kennedy, No. 16, Telegram, April 13, 1891; ibid.
40. R. M. Paton to R. Kennedy, Tabriz, May 6, 1891, Enclosure in Kennedy to Salisbury, No. 123, Tehran, May 11, 1891; F. O. 60/553.

as before. The representative of the Régie in Tabriz chose not to tangle with merchants protected by Russia.[41]

In Shirāz, agitators spread the word that the Régie would make hundreds of merchants bankrupt and jobless, that the price of tobacco would rise and the country would be invaded by foreigners. The newly arrived manager of the Régie, Julius Ornstein, telegraphed the manager of the Shirāz branch, a Mr. Binns, to let the public know that "it has never been our intention to deprive the people of their bread but on the contrary to employ and otherwise interest them in our undertaking to the largest possible extent." He argued that the Régie was bringing capital into the country, that for the first time the cultivator would be paid in cash for his crops, that people would buy their tobacco at old prices but fixed in weight and quality, that the company would use the merchants to buy and sell on commission, that hundreds would be employed as clerks and workmen, and that no more than thirty Europeans would be hired. Ornstein instructed Binns to tell the mullas that the British respected Islam everywhere.[42]

Ornstein may have been telling the truth. The cultivator might have benefited from the Régie and the consumer might have been offered a better product, though hardly at the old price. However, the merchants would certainly have lost, and it was they who were the most vocal and, in some ways, the most powerful segment of Persia's urban population. The agitation against the Régie kept growing. The Shirāz mullas refused to enter their mosques until Binns had been expelled from the city. On May 29, Āqā Mirzā Mohammad Ali, a mojtahed, informed the British consular agent that either Mr. Binns or the clergy would have to leave the country.[43]

By midsummer Tabriz was seething. The anti-Régie movement had acquired an organization and was turning to action. At night proclamations appeared in the city. One of them read:

> Woe to those Ulemas who will not cooperate with the nation! Woe to those who will not spend their lives and

41. Paton to Kennedy, Separate and Secret, Tabriz, May 9, 1891, Enclosure in Kennedy to Salisbury, No. 128, Tehran, May 20, 1891; ibid.
42. Ornstein to Binns, Telegram, Tehran, May 29, 1891, Enclosure in Kennedy to Salisbury, No. 138, June 2, 1891; ibid.
43. Kennedy to Salisbury, No. 138, Gulahek, June 2, 1891; ibid.

property! Any one of the Ulemas who will not agree with the people will lose his life. Woe to anyone who may sell one muskal [sic] of Tobacco to the Europeans! Woe to the Europeans who may wish to enforce these customs of the Infidels! We will kill the Europeans first and then plunder their property. Woe to the Armenians who will be killed and will lose their property and their families! Woe to those who will keep quiet![44]

Amin os-Soltān told Kennedy that the Russian consul general at Tabriz had instigated the publication of the proclamation. Bützow had dealt the Régie a blow and given tacit encouragement to resistance when he "informed all Russian subjects that they are at liberty to disregard the existence of the Tobacco Régie and to purchase and sell tobacco without let or hindrance."[45]

That the Russian consul in Tabriz was working actively against the Régie and providing the movement with guidance and inspiration was reported also by R. M. Paton. The mojtaheds preached against the company. During the month of Moharram unusually large crowds of mourners roamed the streets, taking part in the commemorative self-infliction of pain. The sight of blood, the shrieks, the excitement, heightened the tension to the point where a general massacre of Christians was expected. The Mayor of Tabriz was strangely quiet. Paton attributed this to the Russian consul who, it was alleged, had promised to protect the mullas. "In fact," Paton wrote, "it appears to me that this is just the opportunity the Russians have been waiting for." Already Persian employees were resigning from the Régie under pressure.

> I fear [Paton continued] this Tobacco Concession has done much to raise a hostile feeling against the British who till recently were undoubtedly looked upon by very many here as friends of Persia and quite disinterested. Now however they are suspected by the mass of trying to introduce their customs and by and bye [sic] themselves in a surreptitious

---

44. Translation, Kennedy to Salisbury, No. 190, Confidential, Gulahek, July 27, 1891; ibid.
45. Kennedy to Salisbury, ibid.

fashion to them, and their opinion of the British appears to have undergone a complete change and every vile epithet is used towards them.[46]

In spite of warnings received from Shirāz and Tabriz, Kennedy continued to encourage the Shah in his dangerous course. It was believed, quite correctly, that the Tabriz situation had been brought about through skillful planning and could not "have been organized without the secret assistance and knowledge of the Governor of Tabriz," who, both the Shah and Amin os-Soltān admitted, "has been a pliant tool in the hands of the Russians." The Shah wanted to remove him but was "averse from timidity to the adoption of energetic action which may be the cause of disturbances and intervention of Russia in the Province of Azerbaijan." [47]

Tabriz resembled "a forest smeared with petroleum which would be set in a blaze by the smallest spark." The troops were unreliable. It was said that the life of Mozaffar ed-Din Mirzā, heir to the throne and Governor of Āzarbāyjān, was in danger. Amin os-Soltān painted a dark picture for Kennedy when they met on September 1 in the Shah's palace. Kennedy's report read in part:

> The Shah was in an adjoining room and I directed his attention, through the Amin-os-Sultan, to the fact that H. M.'s sovereignty and not the Tobacco Concession was being attacked, and that the other provinces are awaiting the mot d'ordre from Azerbaijan, and that his yielding would be the signal for the rapid spread of the spirit of revolution throughout Persia.
>
> In reply to the offer of the Shah, who was most desirous that the Concession should be cancelled, that he could give some other valuable concession as an equivalent, I stated that

---

46. Paton to Kennedy, Tabriz, August 15, 1891. Same to Same, Tabriz, August 29, 1891; both in F. O. 60/553.

47. Kennedy to Salisbury, No. 177, Paraphrase, September 1, 1891; F. O. 65/1415.

His Majesty would be politically committing suicide; that Persia would be left to decay as no capitalist would again ever enter upon enterprises in Persia, which is the result aimed at by Russia, and that no equivalent could be given.[48]

Pressure from the British legation prevented the Shah from canceling the concession then and there, but Kennedy could not help him to put down the disorders which had broken out in many parts of the country. In desperation the Shah turned for help to those who had the power—the Russians. Bützow insisted that the Régie be abolished before it took root in the country. The Shah argued that this could not be done since he would have to grant other concessions in compensation, and they could turn out to be even more distasteful to Russia. Under pressure Bützow promised to instruct the Russian consul general in Tabriz to exert his influence for the prevention of disorders.[49]

The British government was nowhere near as intransigent as its chargé d'affaires at Tehran. Kennedy's adamant attitude kept the Shah from getting rid of the Régie and pacifying the public. When Kennedy, anxious for approval of his actions, requested guidance, Salisbury replied that it was impossible to judge from London what course of action was most in the Shah's interest. The Foreign Office shrank from the use of force in defense of the Régie.

> Severity should only be employed if he [the Shah] thinks it necessary in the interests of Persia and for the sake of his own authority. We do not wish to assume the invidious position of urging vigorous measures in order that foreigners may make money.[50]

The advice came too late. Nothing but capitulation could now save the Shah from the combined pressure of an aroused people and a determined Russian legation.

In the fall, violence erupted in Tabriz and Shirāz. The leading

---

48. Id.
49. Kennedy to Salisbury, Telegram, No. 181, Gulahek, September 7, 1891; F. O. 60/553.
50. F. O. to Kennedy, Telegram, Confidential, September 6, 1891; ibid.

mojtaheds petitioned the Shah against the Régie, saying that, as the Qur'ān forbade Moslems to be under the influence of infidels, they were "utterly bewildered to see that our Sovereign is selling the whole body of Muslemans [sic], like slaves, to the Kafars." The petition asked the Shah to refrain from innovation.

> and not to allow the Faith to submit to degradation and ruinous changes. His subjects are prepared to sacrifice their lives and property in obedience to his commands but the adherents of the Faith will not consent to his causing the creed to submit to a change. . . . The Moslems prefer death to being mastered over by the Kafars.[51]

This was no idle threat. Through the fall and into the winter riots were an almost daily occurrence in the provinces and even in the capital itself. The mojtahed of Samarra, Hāj Mirzā Hasan Shirāzi, issued a decree forbidding the faithful to smoke. The order was obeyed with remarkable discipline throughout the country.[52]

The Régie's chief manager, Julius Ornstein, realized that the struggle against the combined forces of Russia, the Shiite clergy, and Persian tobacco merchants would be hopeless unless Britain fully committed herself on the company's side. Britain's position was unclear and would not be clarified until the arrival in Tehran of the new British minister, Sir Frank Lascelles. The Régie engineered the formation of a French company, Société du Tombac, with which it entered into an agreement "to undertake the whole of the Tobacco Export trade with Persia." The French ambassador at St. Petersburg was then asked to try to interest the Russian government in this "French company." Ornstein hoped "that by this means an end may perhaps be put to the active Russian opposition against the Persian Tobacco Régie." In a

---

51. Petition submitted to the Shah by the leading mojtaheds [copy secretly transmitted to Kennedy by Amin os-Soltān], Enclosure in Kennedy to Salisbury, No. 225, October 6, 1891; ibid.

52. For detailed accounts of the internal conditions and the resistance to the Régie, see Nāzem ol-Eslām Kermāni, *Tārikhe bidāriye Irāniyān* (Tehran, n.d.); Dr. Feuvrier, *Trois ans à la cour de Perse* (Paris, n.d.); Mehdi Malekzādeh, *Tārikhe enqelābe mashrutiyate Irān* (Tehran, 1331).

memorandum prepared for the Russian government, he argued that very few Russian subjects were involved in the tobacco trade in Persia, and therefore no important Russian interests had been affected by the establishment of the Régie. Leaving the issues of international law to others, Ornstein pointed out that some day Russia might want to establish a tobacco monopoly at home, and would then risk protests by Persia which would cite Russian opposition to the Régie as a convincing precedent. The Régie was willing to be accommodating. If Russia dropped her objections, it would transport Persian tobacco to Europe via the Caspian Sea, providing the Russian government with "permanent and considerable income".[53]

Like many a Western capitalist, Ornstein had implicit faith in the primacy of the economic motive and acted on that faith. However, in trying to conciliate Russia by offering her a share in the profits of the Régie, he demonstrated his lack of understanding of Russian expansionist policy. The same mistake would continue to be made decade after decade by most businessmen and many politicians who, albeit unconsciously, look at international affairs through the prism of economic determinism. In 1891, as in 1873 with Reuter, the Russian government was not interested in making money at the expense of its dominant position in northern Persia. Ornstein's proposals did not even elicit a reply.

In the midst of a mounting wave of demonstrations and riots, a new British minister arrived in Tehran to replace Sir Henry Drummond Wolff, who had returned to England because of illness. Sir Frank Cavendish Lascelles came to Tehran, in November 1891, with much diplomatic experience, having served as an attaché in Madrid and as secretary in Berlin, Paris, Copenhagen, Washington, and Athens. During six years in Bulgaria he had acquired, at least among the Russians, the reputation of a Russophobe. His last post before Tehran was that of minister to Rumania. Thus, unlike Wolff, Lascelles was a professional diplomat well acquainted with Russian policies in the Balkans.[54]

53. Memorandum entitled "La Régie des tabacs de Perse et le commerce russe," by Mr. Ornstein, October 1, 1891, Enclosure in Kennedy to Salisbury No. 226, October 5, 1891; F. O. 60/553.

54. In 1894 Lascelles was appointed ambassador to Russia, a post he occupied for less than a year, being transferred to Berlin, where he stayed until 1908.

Sir Frank's arrival opened a new chapter in the Régie story. R. J. Kennedy's policy of unqualified support was reversed. When in December Amin os-Soltān found further resistance to Russian and clerical pressure impossible, he discovered an unexpected ally in the new British minister. Amin os-Soltān had asked Ornstein to agree to the cancellation of the Régie concession.

The General Manager refused, stating that his instructions were definite and that nothing short of force would induce him to depart from them, and to this attitude he adhered until urgent representations were made to him by Her majesty's representatives in Teheran, that perseverance in it would endanger all other European Institutions in Persia, and even the lives of the Foreign Colony. The General Manager feeling that such representations from such a source would justify him in the eyes of the board [of his Corporation] then yielded.[55]

Salisbury had all along been opposed to the exercise of undue pressure on the Persian government for the purpose of maintaining the Régie. Had the British chargé d'affaires, R. J. Kennedy, been more sensitive he would have abandoned the cause of English investors and saved Britain's prestige. In December it was too late. The proclamation of the cancellation of the Régie on December 28 had no immediate effect on the masses. The clergy did not trust the government and communicated its distrust to the people. The worst outbreak in Tehran occurred a week after the Régie had been canceled.

On January 4, 1892, all shops were closed in the Tehran bazar. Crowds ran toward the Palace. It was said that Amin os-Soltān's house would be sacked. The Shah sent his favorite son, Kāmrān Mirzā Nāyeb os-Saltaneh, Minister of War and governor of the city, to calm the people,

but his appearance had the opposite effect and he was himself threatened and insulted. He beat a hasty and undignified retreat, in the course of which he fell in the mud, and on the

---

55. R. W. Grosvenor (Chairman of the Board of the Imperial Tobacco Corporation of Persia) to the Permanent Under-Secretary for Foreign Affairs, London, February 28, 1892; F. O. 60/555.

whole his conduct was such as to give an unfavourable impression of his personal valour.

Naib's personal guard started shooting into the crowd. Several people (perhaps as many as ten) were killed.[56]

At the first sign of trouble, the Shah had sent for Colonel Schneur, commander of the Cossack Brigade, but the latter,

> instead of giving preliminary orders for the cossacks to assemble and undertake the defense of the Palace, which was then defenseless, and of the Shah himself, did not even go to the Shah . . . [Schneur] himself having gathered the brigade next to the cossack barracks, decided to question them as to who was for the Shah and the Government and who was for the clergy, who was obedient and who was not. Remizov, who was drunk, was shooting his rifle at a target in the yard of the barracks; his friend, Nikolai Zasypkin, a Moscow merchant in cossack uniform, "Muscovite Kabardian" or "Tula Cherkess," rolled out a barrel of red wine for the cossacks, mumbling in a panic: "Brothers, save me, do not ruin an Orthodox soul . . ." the Commander, Colonel Schneur, to whom no one listened any longer, shrugged ["makhnul rukoi," waved his arm as a sign of despair. F. K.] and went to his wife. Megera Medusovna, known to all Persia, who spanked the knight of St. George for leaving her alone at such a critical moment, slammed all the doors locked and did not let her spouse out any more until the end of the mutiny.[57]

The sad state of the Brigade was a result of neglect and poor leadership which had afflicted it since the departure in 1890 of Colonel Kuzmin-Karavaev, the Brigade's third commander who had received strong support from Prince Dolgorukov while the latter was minister in Tehran. However, Schneur's absurd behavior is utterly inexplicable unless one assumes that he had secret orders from Bützow not to use the Brigade in the suppres-

56. Frank Lascelles to Salisbury, No. 2, Tehran, January 14, 1892; F. O. 65/1434.
57. Kosogovskii, *Iz tegeranskogo dnevnika*, pp. 124–25.

The Tobacco Régie

sion of anti-Régie riots. Everything known of the Russian army in 1891 makes the scene, so graphically described by V. A. Kosogovskii, himself an exemplary officer, incredible without such an assumption.

The Imperial Tobacco Corporation of Persia sought compensation for damages and loss of potential profits. The Foreign Office noted that the Persian government appeared "fully to recognize" the corporation's right to compensation and offered its good offices to obtain it.[58] The Persian government was willing to reimburse the corporation's expenses and no more. R. W. Grosvenor, Chairman of the Board, felt that it was "the intention of the Persian Government to cavil at every item with the view of spinning out negotiations to an interminable length." [59]

The corporation's unwillingness to confine its claims to reimbursement for expenses incurred in setting up the machinery of the Régie was understandable. Legitimate expenses had constituted only a fraction of the total invested in Persia, large sums having been paid out in bribes. In a letter to the Foreign Office, R. W. Grosvenor freely admitted that the outstretched palms of influential Persians had to be "crossed." [60] If the bribes were not recovered, the corporation would lose a considerable amount of money. Thus it was necessary for the investors to collect from the Persian government at least a part of the "anticipated profits." Grosvenor proposed arbitration.

The Foreign Office informed him that the Persian government sincerely desired to settle the claims and had offered to pay the corporation £300,000 or £400,000. The country was poor and could afford no more. Sir Frank Lascelles suggested from Tehran that this offer be accepted, "as even if an arbitrator gave a decision more favourable to you, there would be great difficulty in enforcing it." [61]

58. P. W. Currie to R. W. Grosvenor, F. O. January 9, 1892; F. O. 60/555.

59. Memorandum submitted to Lord Salisbury in favour of arbitration as the only means to secure a settlement of the compensation admitted by the Persian Government to be due to the Imperial Tobacco Corporation, February 10, 1892; ibid.

60. R. W. Grosvenor to F. Bertie, Brackley, February 21, 1892; ibid.

61. Francis Bertie to R. W. Grosvenor, F. O., February 27, 1892; ibid.

The Persian government found itself in a difficult and precarious position. The Imperial Tobacco Corporation insisted on compensation. In principle its claims could not be denied, especially since the British government was more inclined to support the defunct Régie than it had been to help Reuter nineteen years earlier. The country was in turmoil, with the clergy and the masses unpacified by the announced cancellation of the concession. Russia was exercising strong pressure on the Shah and Amin os-Soltān, both officially and through her agents among the Persians.

Amin os-Soltān's relations with the Russians had deteriorated to the point of open hostility. Bützow blamed him for the Anglophile attitude of the Shah and for the refusal of the Persian government to cooperate with the Russian legation. During a conversation with the Grand Vizier on January 10, 1892, Bützow said that the Tsar's confidence in the friendship of the Shah had been shaken. "Formerly His Majesty had been willing to listen to the advice of Russia but of late he had apparently become hostile to her and only sought to conciliate England." [62]

Amin os-Soltān retorted that the Shah on his part was losing confidence in Russia, "and this is scarcely surprising when Russian agents had openly declared that Russia meant to annex this country." Bützow denied Russia's having any such intention. "It was however impossible for Russia to remain indifferent, when she saw Persia handed over to the English through the different concessions which had been granted to them." [63]

A month later Bützow returned to the issue and spoke even more bluntly. He told a high Persian official that personally he liked Amin os-Soltān, "but that it was impossible to do business with His Highness who at once repeated everything that was said to him to the British Minister." He had granted British officers permission to visit the Turkoman frontier, refused to satisfy Russia on the Sarakhs water question, and would not cede to her

62. Lascelles to Salisbury, No. 31, Secret and Confidential, February 13, 1892; F. O. 65/1435.
63. Id.

the village of Firuzeh.[64] Amin os-Soltān could not afford Russian hostility. The government was in need of money with which to pay off the Tobacco Corporation. The Shah feared revolution and sought peace above all else. The Prime Minister delicately began to shift his position and to move closer to Russia.

Amin os-Soltān's new attitude could not escape the attention of the English. Lascelles was alarmed that Amin os-Soltān might go too far in the direction of Russia, thus endangering England's position at Tehran. Amin os-Soltān reminded Sir Frank that the latter had on more than one occasion "suggested the advisability of his establishing friendly relations with the Russian Legation" and that he was only following the British minister's advice. Though Amin os-Soltān claimed that his friendship for England had not diminished "in consequence of the better understanding with the Russian Legation," Sir Frank and his subordinates "carried away the impression that the Amin-es-Sultan was keeping something back from us and that he was unwilling to let us know the price he had to pay for Russian friendship." [65]

Through March 1892 the Tobacco Corporation kept pressing for a speedy payment of its claims, calculated at £500,000.[66] The Shah offered £300,000, but Amin os-Soltān "expressed his readiness to again urge upon the Shah to accept the terms of the Company on condition that the £15,000 should be made over to him which he had paid in cash to the Shah for the shares to that amount allotted to H.M." [67] The nation might be the loser, but the Shah and his Grand Vizier would profit nevertheless.

Finally, on April 3, agreement was reached. The Persian government undertook to pay by the end of July £500,000 in cash to the Tobacco Corporation in London against the cancellation of the concession.[68] The problem now was to find the money. The

64. Lascelles to Salisbury, No. 30, Secret and Confidential, Tehran, February 12, 1892; ibid.
65. Lascelles to Salisbury, No. 31, Secret and Confidential, February 13, 1892; ibid.
66. R. W. Grosvenor to P. W. Currie, London, March 8, 1892; F. O. 60/555.
67. T. H. Sanderson to R. W. Grosvenor, F. O., March 11, 1892; ibid.
68. Circular issued to the Shareholders of the Imperial Tobacco Corporation of Persia, Limited, 8 April, 1892; ibid.

Shah approached his French physician, Dr. Tholozan, who suggested that an international company be formed to raise the requisite sum. The doctor hoped to involve both French and British capitalists in this scheme, but neither group showed any interest.[69]

The attempt to secure money from the French having failed, the Persians turned to Sir Frank Lascelles for advice and help. The Finance Minister, Abol Qāsem Khān Nāser ol-Molk, an Oxonian and good friend of the British, was advised to try the Imperial Bank of Persia. When he pointed out to Lascelles that the bank demanded 8 percent interest, Sir Frank retorted that it might well ask more now that Persia had tried and failed to get money elsewhere. In reply to Nāser ol-Molk's pleas for help, Lascelles told him

> that as he had been educated in England he must be fully aware that it would be quite impossible for H. M.'s Government to advance the money themselves. They could not do so without applying to Parliament who would most certainly refuse its consent. It was equally impossible that H. M.'s Government should arrange the terms upon which any bankers should make the loan.[70]

The Shah was growing desperate. He would not dream of using his private funds to help his country and looked to all possible sources save his own treasury. Sensing an opportunity to make a killing, Lazar Poliakov informed the Russian government that if it guaranteed him a 6 percent interest, he would immediately provide Persia with £500,000.[71] Bützow conveyed the offer to Amin os-Soltān, who informed the officials of the Imperial Bank of Persia, and the British legation. Lascelles cabled London that the manager of the bank considered that the acceptance of the Russian offer would be disastrous for the bank and all British enterprise, and "would practically annul all our work during the last four years." Amin os-Soltān was averse to accepting it, and felt that great damage would be done to English interests if the

69. Lascelles to Salisbury, No. 72, Tehran, April 15, 1892; ibid.
70. Lascelles to Salisbury, No. 74, Confidential, Tehran, April 15, 1892; ibid.
71. Id.

The Tobacco Régie

money should be provided by Russia. "I have suggested to His Highness," Lascelles went on, "that he might inform Russian Minister that he must delay definitive reply until he receives answer from Bank, with whom he is negotiating." Amin os-Soltān hoped "for the sake of British interests" that the British government would use its influence to obtain money "on at least equally favourable terms for Persia, and fears that if they fail to do so they will have reason for great regret." [72]

London was annoyed. Undoubtedly the Russians would seek control of the Gulf ports' customs as security for any loan they might issue. "You should state," the Foreign Office instructed Lascelles, "that it will be your duty formally to protest against the validity of any such act." Moreover, Lascelles must point out to the Persians that if at any time in the future the latter should fall in arrears in paying interest on a Russian loan, "they would be inviting a Russian seizure of Khorasan or some other part of the Empire." [73]

Amin os-Soltān instructed the Persian minister in London to tell Salisbury that if the Imperial Bank of Persia refused to advance £500,000, "another [party] is prepared, for the purpose of liberation, to do so at six per cent only and without charging a penny for costs." Sir Frank Lascelles to the contrary notwithstanding, Amin os-Soltān knew that the British government had the means to extricate the Persian government from its plight. He wanted an immediate reply.[74]

On May 2 Amin os-Soltān wrote Lascelles that Bützow strongly urged the Persian government to accept a loan from the Russian bank. Russia would be willing to take forty bills for annual payments to be made from customs revenues. Should the Imperial Bank of Persia offer a loan on identical terms, the Shah would take it, otherwise he would have to deal with the Russians.[75] From St. Petersburg, Sir Robert Morier reported rumors

72. Sir F. Lascelles, Decypher, No. 61, Tehran, April 19, 1892; ibid.

73. F. O. Draft to Sir F. Lascelles, Telegram, Secret, April 22, 1892; ibid.

74. Translation of a Telegram from His Highness the Amin-es-Sultan to the Persian Minister in London (n.d.) F. O. notation—April 23, 1892; ibid.

75. Lascelles to Salisbury, No. 84, Secret and Confidential, Tehran, May 11, 1892; ibid.

of a proposed Russian advance to Persia. There was also talk of Poliakov's seeking road concessions in northern Persia on lines advocated by a military writer, P. M. Romanov, in a recently published work.[76] However, Sir Robert was sceptical. On May 7 he wrote Salisbury:

> My own *a priori* impression is that any serious intention on the part of the Imperial Treasury to pay down into the Treasury of Persia any sum whether quoted in millions or by thousands is absolutely outside the sphere of the probable. That Monsieur Wyshnegradski [Russia's Minister of Finance] should have assented to such a proposal is inconceivable.[77]

The management of the Imperial Bank of Persia did not possess Morier's sangfroid nor did it share his optimism. From the point of view of a British financial institution operating in Persia, a Russian loan would have been a disaster. The bank informed the Foreign Office that it was now prepared to pay the Imperial Tobacco Corporation in bonds, but the corporation saw no reason to give up its agreement with Persia by which it would be fully compensated in cash no later than July 31.[78] Lascelles informed Amin os-Soltān of British objections, "from a political point of view, to a loan being raised in Russia."[79] He did not share the suspicions of some of the Foreign Office staff "as to the genuineness of the Russian offer," nor did he believe that the Persians were "playing with him."[80] Clearly seeing the threat to Britain's position at Tehran, Sir Frank was prepared, if necessary, to disregard the objections of the Tobacco Régie to being paid in bonds instead of cash. Lord Salisbury stated firmly that "H.M.

76. P. M. Romanov, *Zheleznodorozhnyi vopros v Persii i mery k razvitiiu russko-persidskoi torgovli* (St. Petersburg, 1891).

77. Morier to Salisbury, No. 92, St. Petersburg, May 7, 1892; F. O. 65/1420.

78. F. O. to Lascelles, Telegram, April 22, 1892, as cited in Ernest Lehman, Memorandum respecting the Imperial Tobacco Corporation of Persia, Printed for the use of the Cabinet, May 1892, Confidential, F. O., May 9, 1892; F. O. 60/555.

79. Lascelles to Salisbury, No. 84, Tehran, May 11, 1892; ibid.

80. F. O. to Lascelles, Private, Telegram, April 25, 1892; Lascelles to F. O., No. 66, Telegram, April 26, 1892; E. Lehman, Memorandum respecting the Imperial Tobacco Corporation of Persia; ibid.

The Tobacco Régie

Govt had a decided objection to Russian Loan, Corporation have a similar aversion to being paid in bonds. If one or other is inevitable, our influence must support *our* [underlined in the original] objections, not theirs." [81]

Bypassing the Tobacco Corporation, Lascelles worked out an agreement with the Persian government and witnessed its signing by the Shah, Amin os-Soltān, and Joseph Rabino, Manager of the Imperial Bank of Persia.[82] The Imperial Bank undertook to pay the Tobacco Corporation £500,000 (Article 1). The Persian government would repay this sum with 6 percent interest in forty equal annual installments (Articles 2, 3, and 4). Article 5 stated that "The Security for the Payment of the borrowed money will be the receipts of the Customs of the Persian Gulf Ports." [83]

Three weeks later Philip Currie, permanent undersecretary at the Foreign Office, informed the directors of the Tobacco Corporation of the new method of payment. Protesting in behalf of the corporation, R. W. Grosvenor wrote that the government's decision was unjust. It was the British minister in Tehran who had forced Ornstein to disregard the instructions of his board of directors and assent to the cancellation of the concession. The corporation had accepted this and did not even insist on arbitration. On April 3, 1892, an agreement had been reached that represented the limit of the corporation's sacrifices. Now the First Lord of the Treasury was telling Grosvenor that, because Russia was willing to provide Persia with money, creating a situation unsatisfactory for Britain, the corporation should accept the Shah's bonds. The liquidators of the corporation would not accept this.[84] But no one any longer paid much attention to the unhappy investors in the defunct Imperial Tobacco Corporation.

---

81. Salisbury to Lascelles, Draft, Telegram, April 30, 1892 (Copies to Balfour and Goschen); ibid.

82. Lascelles to Salisbury, No. 75, Paraphrase of a Telegram, Tehran, May 15, 1892; ibid.

83. Agreement for the Loan of £500,000 to be made by the Imperial Bank of Persia to the Persian Government, Enclosure in Lascelles to Salisbury, No. 92, Tehran, May 18, 1892; ibid.

84. R. W. Grosvenor to the Permanent Under Secretary of State for Foreign Affairs, June 10, 1892; ibid.

As far as Britain, Russia, and Persia were concerned, the case was closed.

The Tobacco Régie was only the most notorious of the concessions granted by the insatiably greedy Nāser ed-Din Shah to foreign capitalists in the closing years of his long reign. The violent opposition to the Régie had damaged England's position and impelled Amin os-Soltān to seek accommodation with Russia, who had demonstrated her power and her influence on Persia's domestic affairs in a most convincing fashion. While a British enterprise had been attacked and driven out of the country, several Russian businesses had been established.

In his book, *Persia and the Persians*, the Russian writer S. Lomnitskii pointed out that in the Empire of the Shah, "as in all uncivilized countries," the rate of interest was generally very high. "This, and the lack of any institution for small credit, gave birth to wide-spread usury which sprouted deep roots in the life of the population and is blooming in most horrifying forms without finding the smallest obstacle either in the laws or the public opinion of the country." [85] The Poliakov brothers saw an opportunity to make a profit by organizing a loan company which, unlike the Imperial Bank of Persia, would grant small loans secured by jewelry, commercial goods, furniture, and so forth.

In 1890 Iakov S. Poliakov, who had long been involved in Persian trade, put 2,000,000 francs into the venture. Half of this sum was spent "on the concession, i.e. gifts to various Persian officials who helped obtain it." [86] The terms of the concession obtained by Poliakov were generous. Its duration was to be seventy-five years (Article 1). The Iranian Loan Company, as the new business was named, was entitled to lend money on any security except real estate (Article 2). The company was to turn over to the Persian treasury 10 percent of its annual net profits (Article 7), and was to be free of all duties and taxes (Article 8). It was specified that the interest rate would not exceed 18 percent per annum (Article 13). The concession was considered important enough for the Shah himself, as well as his Grand Vizier and the

---

85. S. Lomnitskii, *Persiia i persy*, pp. 196–97.
86. M. L. Tomara, *Ekonomicheskoe polozhenie Persii*, p. 125.

Minister of Foreign Affairs, to sign the contract.[87] In spite of Poliakov's acumen and commercial experience, the Iranian Loan Company did not prosper. It sustained an early blow from a sudden fall in the price of silver. By 1893 it was nothing more than a pawn shop.[88]

To finance their own commercial activities the Poliakovs established in Tehran a branch of the International Commercial Bank of Moscow, an institution they controlled. The Bank's representative, Monsieur François Gunther, was in Tehran in the summer of 1892, talking of the purely commercial and entirely nonpolitical nature of his business. He said that the sole object of the bank was to make money for its shareholders, but that could only be achieved by increasing trade between Persia and Russia, which in turn depended upon the improvement of roads and transportation.[89] Gunther's very protestations indicated that his mission may have been less innocent than he tried to make it out.

Early in 1894, the director of the Iranian Loan Company, one Schaskolsky,[90] traveled to Moscow to report to his employers that the business should be liquidated. The Poliakovs decided to consult the government, and Schaskolsky went to St. Petersburg to discuss the problem with the new Minister of Finance, S. Iu. Witte,[91] a vigorous and ambitious statesman who would turn the Ministry of Finance into a rival of the Ministry of Foreign Affairs.

According to Schaskolsky, Witte told him that the Russian government had decided to buy up all the shares of the Iranian Loan Company (known also as Banque des Prets) and to carry on its business in Tehran. A new director would be appointed, but Schaskolsky could remain, if he wished, at double his old salary. Schaskolsky telegraphed Joseph Rabino, manager of the Imperial Bank of Persia, about the development that had taken place.

87. Iran, Archive of the Ministry of Foreign Affairs, File 44/Folder 21, Registry No. 10 (1326).
88. Tomara, p. 125.
89. Lascelles to Salisbury, No. 132, July 30, 1892, Gulahek; F. O. 65/1439.
90. This is the only spelling in Foreign Office documents. I have never come across the name in any Russian source.
91. Conyngham Greene to the Earl of Kimberley, No. 176, Confidential, Gulahek, August 23, 1894; F. O. 65/1487.

Next day he had another interview with Witte. The Minister of Finance held in his hand the text of Schaskolsky's telegram to Rabino. It had been intercepted on Witte's orders. No information was to be given to the British at the Imperial Bank.[92]

The new director appointed by Witte was not a financier but a political official.

> [Schaskolsky] therefore presumed that banking pure and simple, was not the primary consideration in the future of the New Bank, and that the real reason why the Russian Government had decided to undertake its business was because they feared the loss of their prestige if a Russian institution were to be allowed to collapse in Persia, and further lest the Imperial Bank should take over the business of the Banque des Prets, which, if liquidated, could be acquired for a mere song.[93]

Rabino had been given sufficient information by Schaskolsky to become alarmed at the prospect of competition from a Russian institution with practically unlimited funds. He felt that the move was political and that

> there was a grave danger in the establishment of an enterprise which, though a Bank in name, was in fact purely a Governmental institution, to be used if needful, as a possible political weapon. The very constitution of the Bank under a Director who knows little or nothing of business, and with the avowed object of resuscitating a commercial venture which had been tried and found wanting, was in itself suspicious.

Rabino was afraid that the Russians might buy up in the bazar enough notes of the Imperial Bank to jeopardize its safety by suddenly presenting them for payment.[94]

His fears were not groundless. The infusion of a political

---

92. Id. The information was nevertheless transmitted by Schaskolsky to Rabino personally upon the former's return to Tehran in August. Was Schaskolsky in Rabino's pay?
93. Id.
94. Id.

purpose quickly transformed a failing pawn shop into a powerful bank. Assured of government protection and guaranteed a profit, private money flowed in. According to G. N. Il'inskii, who cites no sources, "Among the shareholders of the Russian Loan and Discount Bank were the Empress Maria Fedorovna and the Minister of Finance, Witte." [95] The bank lent money on the one security which, legally, it was not allowed to accept—land—and came to control vast areas in northern Iran. "Simultaneously it spent enormous sums for bribing the Shah, his courtiers and ministers. In Tehran alone sixteen million rubles were distributed to such 'debtors.'" [96] Ten years after Witte had taken over the bank, a British writer noted that through it the Russian Finance Minister acquired the same influence in the Middle East as he had gained in the Far East through the Russo-Chinese Bank. "Both these institutions are really departments of the Ministry of Finance, and in Persia, as in China, M. de Witte has intended railways and banks to be the Russian weapons of conquest." [97]

The Poliakovs' venture into money lending was but one of the many enterprises they planned and carried out while Persia was in turmoil over the Tobacco Régie. On December 26, 1890, Mark Iakovlevich Mareines, L. S. Poliakov's representative, was granted a monopolistic concession for insurance and transportation. The first article stipulated that the concession would last seventy-five years and that "no one shall have the right within the borders of our Lands to interfere in affairs which concern insurance. And likewise no one shall have the right under any pretext whatsoever, under any title or form to found a transportation company." Poliakov's new company, named "Comptoire d'assurance et de transport" (*Edāreye bime va naqliyāt*), was permitted to insure agriculture, real and personal property, commercial goods, and vehicles (Article 5). The company's central and branch offices, warehouses, employees, and transactions were exempted from all duties and taxes (Article 9). For all these privileges the conces-

---

95. G. N. Il'inskii's chapter on Iran in the late nineteenth and early twentieth centuries in S. N. Rostovskii, I. M. Reisner, G. S. Kara-Murza, B. K. Rubtsov, eds., *Novaia istoriia kolonialnykh i zavisimykh stran* (Moscow, 1940), 1, 527.
96. Id.
97. Geoffrey Drage, *Russian Affairs* (London, 1904), p. 68.

sionaire must pay the incredibly small sum of 300 tumāns per year for the first ten years, 500 tumāns per year for the second ten years, and 1,000 tumāns per year for the remaining fifty years.[98]

A transportation agency would be utterly useless in a country without roads, and Persia in 1891 had none. However, the Poliakovs were prepared to remedy the situation and build the road along which their vehicles, insured by their insurance company, would carry their goods from the Caspian to Tehran. The Russian government, alarmed by the construction of a British-financed road from the Gulf to the capital, was thinking of means to counteract the English move. In October 1891, Vyshnegradskii, then Finance Minister, wrote the Director of the Asiatic Department of the Ministry of Foreign Affairs, the former Minister in Tehran, Zinov'ev, about the desirable direction for a highway that could connect Tehran with the Russian border.[99]

Meanwhile, Lazar Poliakov obtained the right to build a road between Tehran, Tabriz, and Jolfā, on the Russian border, with a branch from Tabriz to Borujerd and Hamadān. He was also allowed to sail two steamships on Lake Urumiyyeh (Article 1). The road was to be completed within four years of the signing of the agreement (Article 2), and the concession was to run for sixty years (Article 10). Persian mails would pay tolls at one half the normal rate (Article 7), the Persian government also receiving 5 percent of the net profits (Article 9).[100] The Russian legation approved of the concession but was not willing to support Poliakov's application for a road from Tehran to Rasht and Anzali on the Caspian. In the absence of Russian archival materials it is impossible to ascertain the reasons why the necessary support was withheld. It may be that the Russian government would have preferred a joint Russo-Persian undertaking. Later in 1892 Bützow told Amin os-Soltān that "engineers would be sent in the spring to study the Resht-Tehran road with a view to the construction of

98. Iran, Archives of the Ministry of Foreign Affairs, Persian text of the concession, File 44/Folder 43, 1326.

99. Vyshnegradskii to Zinov'ev, cited in Popov, "Stranitsa . . . ," p. 143.

100. Undated text. Iran, Archives of the Ministry of Foreign Affairs, File 44/Folder 4.

a chaussée. The scheme should also include the works necessary to make Enzeli accessible to steamers in all weather." However, Bützow insisted that both Russia and Persia contribute capital for the construction. Since no such capital would be forthcoming from the Persian side, a fact Bützow must have known perfectly well, no road would be built on such conditions.[101]

A very different reason was given to Mr. Conyngham Greene, now British chargé d'affaires, by Poliakov's own representative in Tehran, Captain Anatolii Bostelman:

> He [Poliakov] has up till now been hindered by the Russian Government from carrying out the work, partly on account of his being of Jewish extraction, and partly in consequence of the opposition of the Caucasus and Mercury Steam Navigation Company who own practically the whole of the steamships plying with mail and passengers on the Caspian Sea and have up till lately enjoyed a large subvention from the Imperial Government. Some time ago this subvention was reduced to about 10% of the original amount, and the Company in order to recoup themselves offered the Russian Government to undertake the construction of the Resht-Kasvin Road in return for a sum of money which would have practically been equivalent to the loss sustained by them in the matter of the subvention.[102]

If Bostelman is to be trusted, it would appear that two groups of capitalists were fighting for government subsidies. In such a struggle the party with the most contacts in important positions and the most "gifts" to distribute would win.

That Lazar Poliakov won the contest became evident on June 5, 1893, when Bostelman, now director of the Persian Insurance and Transport Company, was given an exclusive right to build a carriage road from Qazvin to the Bay of Anzali. A joint Russo-Iranian company would be formed for this purpose (Article 1). The Persian government would claim no taxes for the duration of

101. Lascelles to Salisbury, No. 193, Tehran, December 20, 1892; F. O. 65/1444.
102. Greene to Kimberley, No. 219, Confidential, Tehran, October 29, 1894; F. O. 65/1488.

the concession, set at ninety-nine years (Article 2). The road must be completed in two years (Article 5). Should the Persian government wish to build a railroad or a highway from Qazvin to Tehran, the Persian Insurance and Transportation Company would have priority in obtaining such a concession (Article 10). Net profits over 12 percent on capital invested would be evenly split between the company and the Persian government (Article 13). The company would have the right to dredge the bay at Anzali on conditions that would be established in a separate agreement.[103]

Shortly thereafter two supplementary contracts were signed. One gave the Insurance and Transportation Company the right to extend the Anzali-Qazvin road to Hamadān, the other to Tehran. Article 4 of the second supplementary contract specified that Amin os-Soltān would receive 750 shares of stock in the Tehran-Azali road.[104]

In St. Petersburg the Ministry of Finance, now under the aggressive leadership of Witte, discussed Poliakov's plea that the government give him financial aid for the construction of the road.[105] In November Bostelman told Sir Frank Lascelles that the road "had now practically been taken over by the Russian Government for whom Mr. Poliakoff was acting as a contractor." The specifications established by the Russian government were such as to make the venture commercially unprofitable, but Poliakov would not sustain a loss because the government would either buy the road at cost plus interest or allow him to collect tolls.[106] A year later the voluble Bostelman told Conyngham Greene that on his last trip to Russia he had discussed Poliakov's project with Witte, who did not want Russia to take over the concession as "there might be practical difficulties with the Shah and diplomatic questions might be raised if the scheme were con-

103. Iran, Archives of the Ministry of Foreign Affairs, File 44/Folder 2.
104. Id. In the margin, in Nāser ed-Din Shah's hand, "The document has been seen. Correct."
105. Report of the Conference in the Ministry of Finance Concerning Trade with Asiatic Peoples, June 9, 16, and 23 (old style), 1893, as cited in A. Popov, "Stranitsa . . . ," p. 143.
106. Lascelles to the Earl of Rosebery, No. 181, Confidential, Tehran, November 11, 1893; F. O. 65/1470.

The Tobacco Régie

ducted under the direct auspices of a foreign Government." [107]

The actual construction of the road over high mountains proved much more difficult and expensive than had been anticipated. The time allotted for its completion was rapidly running out. The Russian military felt that the concession should not be abandoned. The government helped Poliakov by buying all the new shares he issued, and finally bought the entire venture.[108] The Russian chargé d'affaires in Tehran freely admitted to his English colleague that his government "never expected any road of theirs to pay, but that they kept up their roads at a loss in order to maintain the necessary communications and in the hope of thereby benefitting the country." [109] With the Russian government paying the bills and Poliakov acting as its agent, the road was at last completed in October 1899.[110]

Poliakov's various enterprises had demonstrated that a foreign business venture in Persia had but the slimmest chance of success unless vigorously supported either by England or Russia. Reuter's original scheme had not received British backing, and it failed, whereas his bank concession, which was supported, survived. Poliakov lost money and would have been forced to give up all the rights granted him by the Shah. The timely intervention of the Russian Ministry of Finance turned failure into success and gave Russia powerful instruments of influence—the Discount and Loan Bank and the northern highways. General Alfred Lemaire, who had obtained a concession to build a dam on the Kārun at Ahvaz, failed because of British opposition.[111] The so-called

107. Greene to Kimberley, No. 219, Confidential, Tehran, October 29, 1894; F. O. 65/1488.

108. A. Popov, pp. 143–45.

109. Mr. Greene, No. 52, February 19, 1894, as cited in "Roads in Persia" (Russian Concessions), Printed for the use of the Foreign Office, January 14, 1902, Confidential; F. O. 60/661.

110. "Roads in Persia"; *ibid.*

111. Upon learning of Lemaire's concession in April 1892, Salisbury telegraphed Lascelles: "We should strongly object to so comprehensive a concession being granted to a French Company. It would give to France a power and influence on the Karun which it is very undesirable that she should obtain." F. O. to Lascelles, Telegram No. 32, May 9, 1892; F. O. 60/550. Concession du Barrage d'Ahvaz, Enclosure in Lascelles to Salisbury, No. 72, Tehran, April 15, 1892; ibid.

Mining Rights Corporation, a child of the Imperial Bank of Persia,[112] struggled for years and finally decided to recommend to its shareholders to abandon operations in Persia "in consequence of the hostile attitude of the subjects and officials of H.I.M. the Shah, and to make application through Her Majesty's Government for the reimbursement of the Corporation of all that they had hitherto expended on the purchase of the concession and on work which under such circumstances is abandoned." In the absence of the British legation's support, the corporation could not even protect its personnel. When a Mr. Campbell, engineer of the corporation, went to the Governor of Sirjān (Kermān area) to protest against some unlawful exactions,

> in the presence and by the order of the Governor of Sirjan, on some idle pretext, he was seized, stripped, beaten, dragged by his legs to prison and placed in the stocks with native criminals, and chained with an iron collar on his neck, and was only released on the intervention of an influential Syad.[113]

Of the minor entrepreneurs who succeeded with the backing of their government, Cousis and Theophilaktos deserve mention. The two Greek gentlemen, who were Russian subjects and shrewd businessmen, obtained from the Shah for the paltry sum of 1,000 tumāns per annum (Article 8) a monopoly of all olive trees in Gilān for twenty-five years (Article 1). No one else was allowed to buy, sell, or transport olives, or extract olive oil (Article 2). The Persian government, anticipating opposition on the part of growers who were in effect being sold to foreigners, promised to protect the Cousis and Theophilaktos Company against agitation, sedition, and so forth.[114]

At about the same time, Mohammad Vali Khān Nasr os-Saltaneh, Governor of Astarābād and Gorgān, who held an

112. The Persian Mining Rights Corporation was formed by the Imperial Bank of Persia. On April 7, 1890, it signed an agreement with the bank, buying the mining rights granted to the latter by the Persian government in 1889. Text of the agreement in F. O. 60/576.

113. Mining Rights Corporation to Lord Rosebery, October 28, 1893; ibid.

114. Text of concession of June 1890; Iran, Archives of the Ministry of Foreign Affairs, File 44/Folder 22 (1326).

exclusive concession from the Shah to cut down 200,000 boxwood trees in the subtropical forests of the Caspian seashore, turned his rights over to the two Russian Greeks. The original concession lasted four years, with Nasr os-Saltaneh receiving 11,000 tumāns yearly. Undoubtedly Amin os-Soltān and the Shah were cut in on the profit. The contract bears an inscription in Amin os-Soltān's hand to the effect that the Shah had seen it and permitted it to be signed.[115] At the end of the four-year period the concession was renewed. Cousis and Theophilaktos continued for years indiscriminately to devastate the forests of Māzandarān.

The Tobacco Régie fiasco encouraged Russian political and economic activity, while Gladstone's return to power in August 1892 promised the weakening of British opposition. With Amin os-Soltān slowly moving closer to Russia, the Russian government proposed to regularize and improve relations between it and the government of the Shah. Knowing that a rapprochement with Persia would arouse British suspicions, the Russian chargé d'affaires in Tehran, A. N. Speyer, approached Sir Frank Lascelles with the suggestion that it would be desirable for the two powers to come to some sort of an understanding "with regard to their policy in Asia." Speyer professed to believe that "a frank exchange of views between the two Governments might lead to most satisfactory results." As things then stood, Speyer said, the two countries being suspicious of one another, "if by any accident it became necessary for the protection of British interests to send a gun boat to a Persian port, a Russian force would immediately be sent to the borders of Khorassan or Azerbaijan." [116]

Lascelles replied that he was happy to hear of Speyer's interest in a frank exchange of views. He attributed some of the suspicion that existed between the two countries to their agents abroad, "who were apt on the one hand to attribute every want of success they might meet with to the intrigues of their rivals, and on the

115. "In Qarārnāmeh molāheze shod, va az arze khākpāye mobārak gozasht, va ejāzeh farmudand keh emzā' shavad. Lehāzā emzā' shod va sahihast. Amin os-Soltān." Iran, Archives of the Ministry of Foreign Affairs, File 44/Folder 22.

116. Lascelles to Salisbury, No. 149, Confidential, Gulahek, September 30, 1892; F. O. 65/1442. When Lascelles wrote his report, Salisbury was no longer Foreign Secretary, Lord Rosebery having assumed that post in Gladstone's cabinet in mid-August.

other to claim as a diplomatic victory every advantage they gained for their country." He cited Bulgaria as an instance in which the activities of Russian agents had led to the loss of Russian influence.

> I said that I was aware that one of those Agents, General Kaulbars, had done me the honor to attribute his want of success to me personally, and that I had thus obtained the reputation of being an enemy of Russia. Monsieur de Speyer admitted that I had such a reputation and said that the Russian Legation here on hearing of my appointment as British Minister had made preparations to counteract my influence. Monsieur de Butzow, however, after his first conversation with me had seen that I was inclined to be conciliatory and the Russian Legation had not employed the tenth part of the means at their disposal to oppose my action.[117]

Probing further, Speyer said that the existence of buffer states was a mistake, and that Russia and England should have a common frontier in Asia. Lascelles agreed that buffer states tended to become hotbeds of intrigue, but even if such states disappeared, which he doubted, there would still be a point at issue.

> I had always understood from my conversations with Russian diplomatists [he said], and also from the language of the Russian press, that it was the desire of Russia to have an outlet on the Persian Gulf, and I was of opinion that such an idea would be strongly opposed by England. Monsieur de Speyer replied that such an idea was simply madness on the part of Russia. It would place her completely at the mercy of England, as she could never protect such a port against the force which England could at any time bring against it.[118]

Though the conversation was not followed up, Speyer had achieved his purpose. England was interested in establishing a modus vivendi in Persia. She would not raise strong objections to an understanding between Persia and Russia. Lascelles' refusal to

117. Id.
118. Id.

The Tobacco Régie

uphold the Tobacco Régie offered empirical evidence that England was not pursuing a forward policy, at least not at the moment. Russia could, therefore, consolidate her position at Tehran without running major risks.

Early in 1893 she suggested that the treaty of 1881, defining the northern border of Khorāsān, be revised, and Russian occupation of Persian territory at Firuzeh (between Ashkhabad and Quchān) be recognized as permanent in return for territorial concessions in Āzarbāyjān. Russia was also prepared, Bützow told Amin os-Soltān, to meet "the Shah's wishes for the abolition of the clause in the Secret Convention of 1881 which permitted the passage of Russian troops through Khorassan." [119]

The original English reaction to the proposed new treaty was unfavorable. The Persian minister in London reported that Lord Rosebery had confidentially pointed out the importance of Firuzeh and Kheyrābād owing to their proximity to the Russian frontier, their strategic location, and economic potential.[120] However, the warning was mild and easily disregarded. Amin os-Soltān told Sir Frank Lascelles that neither he nor the Shah had ever favored the cession of Firuzeh; and that in response to Russian suggestions for exchange of territory, the Shah had put forward conditions which, he thought, Russia would not accept. Yet Russia accepted them all, and the Shah had no choice but to sign. Lascelles replied that Britain had no objections.[121]

On June 8 the treaty was signed by Evgenii Karlovich Bützow for the Tsar and Mirzā Ali Asghar Khān Amin os-Soltān for the Shah. Persia gave up the village of Firuzeh (Article 1). In exchange she received "a piece of land on the right bank of the river Aras opposite the former fortress of Abbās-Ābād which became a Russian possession on the basis of Article 4 of the treaty made at Torkamanchāy . . . , and (2) the village of Hesār" (Article 2).[122]

Within the next few days Persia received the rest of the pay-

---

119. Lascelles to Rosebery, No. 87, Tehran, May 25, 1893; F. O. 65/1464.

120. The Persian Minister in London to the Sadr Azam, 19 Shaval 1310, Enclosure in Lascelles to Rosebery, No. 74, May 19, 1893; ibid.

121. Lascelles to Rosebery, No. 74, Tehran, May 19, 1893; ibid.

122. Text of the Treaty of May 27/June 8, 1893; F. O. 65/1465.

ment for Firuzeh. At the time of the signing of the treaty, Bützow handed Amin os-Soltān a paper stating that he was authorized by his government to inform the Persians of the nullification of "the whole of the Secret and Separate Articles of the Treaty contracted on the 9th December . . . ," articles that permitted Russian troops to pass over Persian territory in Khorāsān.[123] Furthermore, Bützow formally agreed that Russian subjects living in Persia and employed by various firms operating there might be taxed by the Persian government equally with their Persian co-workers.[124] Finally on June 16 Bützow replied to Amin os-Soltān's request for a written confirmation of a verbal promise to allow Persia to station a consular agent at Ashkhabad.

Bützow's memorandum began with the reaffirmation of Russia's intention not to allow foreign agents in Transcaspia. However, he went on, "After your Highness had conveyed to me H.M. the Shah's wish to appoint a person to watch over the subjects of the Persian Government at Askabad, I transmitted the matter to my Government, who, in consideration of the friendship and amity existing between the two Governments, accepted the appointment of an agent there." [125] Persia was requested to keep in mind the object of the Russian government in not letting foreign agents reside in Transcaspia. The Persians undoubtedly understood the veiled warning that their consul at Ashkhabad should not act as an informant for the British, and should, in any case, watch his step.

Amin os-Soltān's turn toward closer relations with Russia reflected a growing loss of faith among Iran's ruling elite in their own ability to withstand Russian encroachments and in British ability, or desire, to protect the Empire of the Shah. Late in 1892 the Minister of Foreign Affairs, Qavām od-Dowleh, admitted to Lascelles that "the conditions of affairs could not be worse." The

---

123. Text of the Memorandum, Enclosure in Lascelles to Rosebery, No. 102, Secret, Gulahek, June 15, 1893; ibid.

124. Amin os-Soltān to Butzow, May 31/June 12, 1893; Butzow to Amin os-Soltān, June 3/15, 1893, Enclosures in Lascelles to Rosebery, No. 102, Secret, Gulahek, June 15, 1893; ibid.

125. Butzow to Amin os-Soltān, June 4/16, 1893, Enclosure 2 in No. 2, Lascelles to Rosebery, No. 102, Secret, Gulahek, July 21, 1893; ibid.

Minister of Posts said that the Shah himself had no confidence in his country. Other high officials shared these feelings. "They all take a very gloomy view of the situation," Sir Frank reported, "and they all blame the Shah, who seems to have lost much of his energy and to have become even more avaricious than formerly." One of the Shah's brothers, Molk Ārā, compared Persia to "a lump of sugar in a glass of water which was gradually melting away." [126]

Early in 1894 Sir Frank Lascelles was appointed Ambassador to Russia. Immediately rumors spread through Tehran of a secret agreement between the two powers for the partition of Persia. A number of well-informed Persians believed that "the present system could not continue and must necessarily result in such a partition." [127] The rumors were encouraged by, if they did not in fact emanate from, Zell es-Soltān, the Shah's eldest son, who stated repeatedly that upon Nāser ed-Din's death the country would be split, with Mozaffar ed-Din Mirzā, the Crown Prince, taking the north, and Mas'ud Mirzā Zell es-Soltān the south.[128]

On February 10, 1894, after a farewell dinner given in his honor by Amin os-Soltān, Sir Frank asked the Grand Vizier for his views on the situation in Persia. Amin os-Soltān said that he feared the possibility of change in British policy. He had no doubt that, had it not been for England's support, Russia would have long ago occupied northern Iran. "The idea had been gaining ground and had even been entertained by the Shah that Her Majesty's Government would not now oppose the annexation of the northern provinces of Persia by Russia." Persia would not be able to resist, but what of England? "Would it suit her even if she took possession of the south to find herself conterminous with Russia? Was she prepared to abandon Persia altogether? Was she prepared to support a small Persia which might be formed in the south and to leave the north to Russia?" Unable to answer the

126. Lascelles to Salisbury, No. 168, Tehran, November 9, 1892; F. O. 65/1443.
127. Lascelles to Rosebery, No. 18, Confidential, Tehran, January 20, 1894; F. O. 65/1484.
128. Lascelles to Rosebery, No. 22, Confidential, Tehran, January 26, 1894; ibid.

questions, Sir Frank asked how it would be if England tried to obtain from the Russians an assurance that they would not encroach on Persian territory. "His Highness said at once that no assurances that the Russians might give would be of the slightest value." They could always find a pretext for intervention. The only hope for Persia was in strong British support, lacking which the Shah "might be inclined to come to terms with the Russians." [129]

A month later, in the course of a long conversation with the Grand Vizier, Mr. Conyngham Greene, left in charge of the British legation upon the departure of Sir Frank, asked what could be done by England to remedy the situation in Persia. Amin os-Soltān replied that there was only one way: "that was by insisting upon the Shah introducing reforms and, in order to encourage him to do so, by giving him assurance that, if H.M. consented to follow the advice of Her Majesty's Government, they on their side would protect him from attack by Russia or any other power." [130] The Shah, his Prime Minister said, "resisted any attempt to improve the country and refused to take any thought for what might happen after his own death." As long as he had money from the sale of public offices, he wanted only to preserve things as they were. The principal task of the Prime Minister, Amin os-Soltān went on, was to prevent the sovereign from bartering away all of Persia. "I remarked," Greene reported, "that, if that was so, probably H[is] M[ajesty] would have no objection to accept a bid for his Kingdom itself, provided the offer was high enough, and His Highness replied, in all seriousness, that he really believed that the Shah would part with his throne for a suitable consideration." [131] Greene pointed out that the system of selling public posts by auction and the disgraceful condition of the army "were two shameful blots upon the administration of the country." Amin os-Soltān agreed. Speaking of the evil of selling government posts, "His Highness hinted that some-

---

129. Lascelles to Rosebery, No. 42; Confidential, Tehran, February 11, 1894; ibid.

130. Mr. C. Greene to the Earl of Kimberley, No. 67, Secret, Tehran, March 13, 1894; F. O. 65/1485.

131. Id.

The Tobacco Régie

thing could be done in this direction also, provided they were compensated in some other satisfactory pecuniary manner."[132] Thus Iran's Prime Minister stooped to asking the English to pay the Shah to reform his system of government, to bribe him not to take bribes.

England was not prepared to assume additional commitments in Persia. The Liberals' hold on the government was shaky. They were not at all interested in new confrontations with Russia, nor were they willing to spend more money in the pursuit of foreign political goals than was absolutely necessary. When Greene's report of his conversation with Amin os-Soltān made its appointed round of desks at the Foreign Office, an official penned in the margin the routine "approve language," but another official wrote: "I think it would be better to abstain from expressly approving Mr. Greene's language . . . If encouraged, Heaven only knows what he will ask the Sadr Azam next time. Questions of this kind cannot be asked without leaving an impression of indicating a policy. I.W.S." And below: "I agree. Unless we were prepared to interfere actively in Persian affairs, this sort of conversation is misleading. K[imberley] April 9."[133]

"Unless we were prepared to interfere actively in Persian affairs." For over thirty years British policy vacillated between active interference and passive contemplation. During the Liberal administration of 1892–95 neither Rosebery nor Kimberley was able to make up his mind on the course to be pursued in Iran. Gladstone and Rosebery had enough troubles elsewhere. Egypt was in turmoil; so were the rest of Africa and the Far East, where Japan's star was rising unexpectedly and rapidly. The Ottoman Empire once again seemed about to break up. Russia and France, Britain's traditional enemies, moved closer together and, in January 1894, entered into a full-fledged alliance. Rosebery was anxious to improve relations with both. In 1895 he proposed to them joint action in the Armenian question, an undertaking which could possibly lead to the partitioning of the Ottoman Empire.

By early summer Rosebery was out of office and Salisbury re-

132. Id.
133. Id.

turned as both Prime Minister and Secretary for Foreign Affairs. The Russian government did not trust the Tories, whether they were led by a brilliant eccentric such as Disraeli or a solid, old-fashioned statesman such as Salisbury. Giers had died, and the new Foreign Minister, Prince Alexei Borisovich Lobanov-Rostovskii, was much less interested in a rapprochement with Britain, or in joint action in Turkey, with whose Armenian population he did not particularly sympathize. The return of Salisbury to power in June 1895 was a signal for a reevaluation of the Persian situation and of the aims of British policy there. The initiative belonged to Sir Frank Lascelles' successor at Tehran, Sir Mortimer Durand.

Durand was an Anglo-Indian official who had served as political secretary to Sir Frederick Roberts in the second Afghan War, had been undersecretary and then secretary of state in India's Foreign Office. He read and spoke Persian and knew a great deal more about the country than most of his predecessors. On his arrival in Tehran, he had to listen to Amin os-Soltān complain that Russia wanted to turn Persia into a protectorate, and England could not always be depended upon, her friendship being sometimes hot and sometimes cold.[134]

Durand's early impressions of Persia's rulers were unfavorable:

> The Shah is selling appointments and marrying new wives after his wont. Sadr-i-Azam . . . is, I fear, as bad where his own interests are concerned as any other Persian. Fact after fact is coming out which shows him to be deep in all sorts of shady transactions, and my faith in him is becoming seriously weakened.
>
> The country is capable of great development. . . . But all progress and prosperity is made impossible by the universal sale of governorships and other posts to the highest bidder. The governors give the Shah a big bribe and then go off to plunder their respective districts for a year. Pure and patriotic Sadr-i-Azam makes £50,000 a year by farming the customs and some more by flooding the country with copper coin,

134. Sir Mortimer Durand to the Earl of Kimberley, No. 238, Very confidential, Tehran, November 28, 1894; F. O. 65/1488.

The Tobacco Régie

while all the time deploring the villainy of the Mint farmer, with whom I find he is in partnership.

There is no army. The soldiers earn their living as money lenders. . . . I do not believe a shot would be fired if a single Russian brigade were to march on Tehran. The Shah is afraid of the mullas, who do as much as they please, and there is really no government. The only chance of putting things right is by an agreement between us and the Russians, and this I fear is hopeless. The Shah looks to us as the one check on the Russians, and the Russians in many ways seem curiously afraid of us. There is no feeling of inferiority whatever, though as a matter of fact the real strength is with Russia.[135]

Further study confirmed Durand's early impressions of the sad state of the old Empire. In August 1895 the military attaché, Lieutenant Colonel H. Picot, submitted to the minister a series of papers on the ministries of War, Pensions and Charitable Bequests, Justice, Commerce, Posts, Telegraphs, Customs, and Foreign Affairs, as well as the Accounting Department of the army and the Council of State. A harrowing picture of decadence, corruption, and disorganization emerged from the pages of these dry official reports. The entire system of government was run for the financial benefit of a small group of individuals. Graft, bribery, theft reached incredible proportions.[136] Picot felt that British policy in Persia had failed. Nothing short of war could prevent the spread of Russian influence in northern Persia. "The logic of facts proves this to be a hopeless task," he wrote, "and there is little doubt she will acquire predominance in the affairs of the north." [137]

Durand's own views were quite similar. In a long, detailed, and unusually informative memorandum which he submitted to the

---

135. Cited in P. M. Sykes, *The Right Honourable Sir Mortimer Durand* (London, 1926), pp. 231, 232.

136. Memorandum by Lt.-Colonel Picot, Appendix 1 in Memorandum by Sir M. Durand on the Situation in Persia, prepared for the use of the Foreign Office, December 1895, Confidential (6704); F. O. 60/581.

137. Memorandum by Lt.-Colonel Picot on Past and Present Policy in Persia, Appendix 4 in the Memorandum by Sir M. Durand on the Situation in Persia, December 1895, Confidential (6704); ibid.

Foreign Office in December 1895, he poured out his scorn for the Persians and their government.

> The Administration is, and has been for generations, corrupt right through. The first idea of every Persian official is illicit gain. No doubt the proceedings of the Shah and others who ought to set an example tend to increase the prevailing corruption, but they have not created it. Its roots lie deep in the national character. Of all the Asiatics with whom I have had to deal, the Persians appear to me to be the most shameless liars and thieves.* And there is no patriotism upon which one can work. Patriotism is replaced here by national conceit, which makes the Persians look down upon all other countries, but will not make them sacrifice the smallest personal interest for the good of their own.
>
> * The Sadr-i-Azem tells me he has lately found out that the Minister of Posts . . . personally steals from the post office parcels which he believes to be valuable.[138]

Governorships and other high offices were sold by the Shah for short periods. The country was plundered and the administration disorganized. The central government was weak, and was defied not only by the provincial authorities but by the clergy, whose power had become greater than it should have been. The army was a rabble. There were no trustworthy courts of justice, no roads, no stable currency. The Shah's greed was among the principal causes of this state of affairs.

> It is [also] his want of firmness and courage that has led to the regrettable increase in the power of the priesthood, for whom the Persians have little love, and his perpetual demands for money can only be met by starving the public Departments. But the Shah is not the only one in fault. The Heir-Apparent is a man of weak character, and allows his northern Province of Azerbaijan to be dangerously misruled. The Zil-es-Sultan is allowing disorder to spread in the south, if he is not joining with the Mullas to excite it. The Shah's

138. Memorandum by Sir M. Durand on the Situation in Persia, prepared for the use of the Foreign Office, December 1895, Confidential (6704); ibid.

The Tobacco Régie 291

third and favourite son, the Naib-us-Sultaneh, who holds the office of Commander-in-chief, enriches himself at the expense of the troops whom he neglects and robs.

The Grand Vizier, Mirzā Ali Asghar Khān Amin os-Soltān, Durand went on, had concentrated all government authority in his own hands. "Having everything in his own control, he draws from various sources an income generally estimated at something between £70,000 and £100,000 a-year; and the removal of any administrative abuse would almost inevitably deprive him of a portion of this sum." [139]

Backward, misgoverned, defenseless Persia was exposed to constant pressure from the north.

The Shah and his Government seem to be constantly haunted and oppressed by the sense of their proximity to Russia. There can, in fact, be no doubt that in Tehran the influence of Russia is predominant, and I am afraid there can be no doubt that it is antagonistic to our own. I may add that, according to general belief, the influence of Russia is steadily exerted to thwart any measure of reform or progress in Persia —to prevent anything which could tend to strengthen and solidify the country, and arrest its downward course.[140]

However, Durand pointed out with a measure of pride, Russian influence was not exclusive: "England undoubtedly carried great weight." In spite of her unfavorable geographic position, in spite of indifference she had at times shown, Britain had prevented Persia from falling to Russia. "Much as the Russians long for the cool mountain breezes and the fertile plains of Khorassan, they have had to lay their line of advance in Asia through a sandy desert." [141]

Durand was convinced that Russia had no intention of stepping forward in Persia and declaring a protectorate or annexing a province. She had only scattered and small forces in Asia and was just as afraid of England as England was afraid of her. A conversa-

139. Id.
140. Id.
141. Id.

tion with General Kuropatkin had greatly reassured him. A. N. Kuropatkin, Military Commander of Transcaspia since 1890, had made a brilliant career. He took part in a French expedition in the Sahara in 1868; fought under Skobelev at Kokand, Lovcha, and Plevna; directed the Asiatic section of the General Staff; commanded a rifle brigade in Turkestan; and, in 1881, directed the main assault on Geok-Tepe. During a visit to Tehran in February 1895 he told Durand that he had always opposed a forward policy in Asia, and "that in 1885, when selected to command against Afghanistan, he had said in the Council that war with England was a great mistake, that even victory with the conquest of India would weaken Russia, and that defeat would mean the loss of all her provinces in Asia." [142] Durand therefore decided that: "Hereafter, if, for example, a great war should clear the air in Europe and set Russia free, as she was set free by the Crimean War and the Turkish War, to devote herself to the East, and consolidate her recent advances, she may be willing to provoke us in Asia." At present she did not seem to have any wish to do so; and, if this view was correct, there was "no reason to anticipate any serious attempt on her part to disturb the existing situation in this country for some time to come." [143]

If Russia did not intend to encroach on Persia, an agreement with England should be possible. The Persian government, he went on, played off Russia and England against each other with the result that neither could do much, and that Persia remained misruled and undeveloped. "If once England and Russia fairly came together, we might divide Asia between us, and we could do anything we liked in Persia without the smallest difficulty."

However, a fair and honest understanding with Russia was only a dream, and Durand was realistic enough to know it. Russia would probably refuse to cooperate in the regeneration of Persia. If she agreed, she would sooner or later betray England. "Our ways are not her ways, and in the end we would probably be sorry we ever tried to work with her. She might perhaps agree to divide Persia with us, but I do not believe she would seriously help us in trying to regenerate Persia."

142. Sykes, p. 230.
143. Memorandum by Sir M. Durand . . . , F. O. 60/581.

The Tobacco Régie

What policy should Britain adopt? Durand's prescription was not at all as confidently made as his diagnosis. He toyed with, but rejected as impractical and even imprudent, the idea of a vast league of Moslem states under the leadership of England with her sixty million Indian Moslems. He despaired of reforming Persia. Unable to come up with an original plan, he proposed that Britain "should adhere to the line of policy which we have followed with more or less energy for many years past." This would mean, and here Durand sounded exactly like most of his predecessors, that Britain's efforts would be directed toward "preserving the integrity of Persia, gaining the good-will, respect, and confidence of the Persian Government and people, supporting Persia to resist intimidation, watching the proceedings of the Russians, developing our trade with Persia, and taking any opportunities which may occur for advocating measures beneficial to the country." Clearly the minister did not see how meaningless his proposals appeared in the light of his own analysis of the Persian situation.

The only concrete suggestions to emerge from Durand's opus were of minor importance: to issue a warning that in case of a Russian invasion of Persia's northern provinces, England would occupy the south; to establish strong ties with Kurdish, Turkoman, and Bakhtiāri tribes; to appoint additional consuls to provincial towns. He praised the appointment of Mr. Sykes (the future Sir Percy), "a capable, manly young officer," to Kermān. "He has attached firmly to our interests one of the most important men in Persia, the Firman Firma, and has acquired a great reputation for himself." [144]

Durand felt the Persians lacked sufficient respect for the British legation. As a former high official in India, he had undoubtedly been accustomed to being treated as a little god by the "natives." The Persians, though polite and even ceremonious, were too self-assured for his taste. One of his subordinates, Charles Hardinge, felt that Durand's appointment to Tehran had been a mistake because of the Persians' dislike of Anglo-Indian officials. "He was very stiff in his manner toward the Persians, and I found after a short time that they disliked him because of his unbending

144. Id.

manner, his unusual reticence and the bad Persian that he spoke and which they called 'Afghani.' " [145] The polo-playing minister had an easy solution for the problem: "A little wholesome fear, mixed with confidence in our intentions, will tend to make relations between the Persians and ourselves very much more satisfactory than they are at present." [146]

Money being the mainspring of political action in Tehran, Durand believed that the Shah's goodwill could be won by reducing interest on the Régie loan to 3 or 4 percent. "This would save the Persian Government some thousands of pounds a-year; it would look well in Persian eyes; it would apparently cost us nothing, as we could borrow money at a lower rate; and it would put into our hands a very useful lever." [147] Such an arrangement would prevent the Persians from appealing to the Russians, who were ready to lend the money.

Durand's memorandum provoked comments both at the India Office and the Foreign Office. Lord George Hamilton, Secretary of State for India, dismissed Durand's fantasy about an anti-Russian league of Moslem states as "not only chimerical" but also "contrary to the true interests and responsibilities of England in Asia, and dangerous to the peace of the whole continent." Nor did Hamilton agree with the proposal that England should proclaim that she would occupy southern Persia in case of Russian occupation of the north. England should not commit herself prematurely and leave the initiative in Russian hands. It would, moreover, be very difficult to determine ahead of time whether the occupation of points on the Gulf coast would be advantageous. "Such a question must evidently depend upon the particular circumstances of the time and upon the general aspect of the political and military situation." [148]

At the Foreign Office the new Undersecretary, George N. Curzon, then already an expert in the field and author of superb studies of Central Asia and Persia, commented on both the

145. C. Hardinge, *Old Diplomacy* (London, 1947), p. 62.
146. Memorandum by Sir M. Durand . . . , F. O. 60/581.
147. Id.
148. A. Godley [in behalf of Lord George Hamilton] to the Under Secretary of State for Foreign Affairs, India Office, March 2, 1896; ibid.

Durand memorandum and Lord Hamilton's objections. He supported the proposal to warn Russia that aggression in the north would provoke British action in the south:

> There is no necessity to bind ourselves to take the Gulf ports, or to occupy any territory, or indeed to adopt any specific course of action. I cannot see why any such intimation need be so worded (as the India Office seems to fear) as to constitute an obligation upon us to strike, whether the moment is, or is not, opportune. On the other hand, it is surely clear that Russia cannot be suffered to annex Khorassan, or any of the northern provinces of Persia, while we sit still and do nothing. Otherwise, why have a policy and a Minister in Persia at all? [149]

The future Viceroy of India wanted the Russians to know that if, taking advantage of civil strife likely to occur at the death of Nāser ed-Din Shah, they should "slip their troops" into Khorāsān, the British would move in the south. "They [the Russians] want Persia, not merely for the intrinsic value of the northern provinces but in order to get to the Gulf; and they will not rashly take any step that would effectively, and at a blow, prevent the realization of that dream."

Looking into the future, beyond the uncertainties of succession, Curzon wanted to know the long-range policy of the Government of India in Persia. He agreed with Durand that an understanding with Russia was "out of the question." If she tried to reform Persia in agreement with Russia, Britain would "get the kicks and Russia would pocket the halfpence." Where rival interests were frankly divergent, it would be better "for either party to play its own game, instead of affecting a community of interest which does not exist, and which would only be assumed by one party at any rate as a blind."

In Curzon's opinion the only way "of really benefitting Persian administration and at the same time strengthening British influence and popularity in the country," was through a reform of the custom and finances. If Amin os-Soltān, who made a great

---

149. Curzon's Memorandum on the Persian Situation, April 12, 1896, Confidential (6765); ibid.

deal of money on customs, should be afraid of changing the system, it could be shown to him that he stood to make £5,000 a year more than before. "It would seem to be a pity to shelve as impracticable the one real chance of Persian reform simply because the avarice of an individual Minister, and he a Persian, stands in the way." But Curzon had no real faith in the success of Persian reform. He never stopped anticipating the dissolution of the Shah's Empire. Should this occur, what would Britain do about Seistān, the province located on the strategically vulnerable flank of India? "It is certain that when Persia breaks up," he wrote, dropping the subjunctive mood, "we cannot allow it to be quietly absorbed by Russia. If it is so absorbed, she will get to the Gulf. Seistan is a British interest. . . . In proportion to the interest we show in Seistan now will be our opportunity of saving it in the future." [150]

The discussion of Persian policy did not go much further than the exchange of memoranda. No firm lines were established for the guidance of Sir Mortimer Durand, no agreement was reached between Whitehall and the Government of India on the means and methods of protecting Persia against the Russian threat. What emerged clearly from the memoranda was the divergence of opinions and the position of George Curzon, which he would maintain for the next quarter of a century.

Both the English and the Russians had long expected disorders to break out in Persia at the death of Nāser ed-Din Shah, but that inevitable event was always seen in a distant future. Though approaching his fiftieth year as King of Kings, Nāser ed-Din was in excellent health, physically vigorous and youthful when, on May 1, 1896, he was assassinated by a follower of Jamāl ed-Din Afghāni.

The news that the Shah had been shot reached the two legations at two o'clock in the afternoon, but it was only to Colonel V. A. Kosogovskii, commander of the Cossack Brigade, that Amin os-Soltān appealed in this crisis. In a hastily scribbled note, the Grand Vizier charged the colonel "to collect all the cossacks and appoint them in groups to patrol the city to prevent disorders."

150. Id.

The note added that the felicitous being, that is the Shah, was entirely well. To prevent rumors as to the reason for the appearance of the Cossacks in the city, Kosogovskii announced that the Turkish ambassador, Monif Pasha, who was expected in Tehran a few days later, had suddenly arrived and that the Shah had ordered the Brigade to provide a guard of honor. Within minutes the Cossacks were on their way, and soon the entire city was in Kosogovskii's hands.[151]

Having issued the necessary orders, Kosogovskii went to the palace where he found an assemblage of high officials headed by Amin os-Soltān, who seemed firmly in control of the situation. Suddenly, Kāmrān Mirzā Nāyeb os-Saltaneh, the Shah's favorite son and Minister of War, burst into the room. Pale and in despair, his eyes wandering wildly, he exclaimed: "Terrible, straight through the heart . . ." Kosogovskii turned to Amin os-Soltān and said that, from that moment on, he would execute no one's orders but those of the Grand Vizier. Amin os-Soltān was embarrassed in front of Nāyeb os-Saltaneh. He suggested with some hesitation that Kosogovskii should also take orders from the man who, after all, was still Minister of War. Kosogovskii refused to have two masters and demanded an unequivocal instruction as to whose orders he was to obey. Nāyeb os-Saltaneh, who understood the situation, quickly retreated. "Act in accordance with your own understanding and wisdom," he said. "I am so grief stricken that I don't understand anything . . . Better deal with his excellency the Sadre A'zam."[152]

Amin os-Soltān's brief message that the Shah had been shot at, but that there was no cause for alarm, had not satisfied Sir Mortimer Durand. While the Russian legation was being kept informed by the commander of the Cossack Brigade, who was taking an active part in the events of the day, the British minister had to rely on his own resources in gathering information. The legation physician, Dr. Scully, accompanied by the oriental secretary, Navvāb Hasan Ali Khān, drove to Shāhzādeh Abdol Azim. They returned an hour later and reported that the Shah had been

151. V. A. Kosogovskii, "Persiia v kontse XIX veka," *Novyi Vostok*, No. 3 (Moscow, 1923), p. 458.
152. Ibid., pp. 459–60.

killed. Dr. Scully had examined the wound. The bullet, having passed between the fifth and sixth ribs, had entered the heart. Death must have been instantaneous. To prevent panic, Amin os-Soltān put the body in the carriage, propped it up with cushions and took it to the palace as if the Shah were still alive.[153]

At about four o'clock General Maletta, an Italian aide-de-camp of Nāyeb os-Saltaneh, came to ask Durand to visit the prince. Since Nāyeb os-Saltaneh and Zell es-Soltān had long been enemies and rivals of the heir apparent, Durand felt that the chances of a peaceful succession depended upon their conduct. Before meeting Nāyeb os-Saltaneh, he sent word of the invitation to Amin os-Soltān. Durand thus described the interview:

> The Prince was seated on the ground in the middle of the drive. As I approached he got up from the ground and shook hands with me, and we were left alone. He looked shaken and disordered, his face pale and his blue uniform trousers and pointed patent leather boots covered with dust. I offered my sincere condolences, for though a man of no character, he had been his father's favourite son, and it was evident that the Shah's death had been a great shock to him. After a short time however, I found that grief for the loss of his father was not his strongest feeling. He was thoroughly frightened on his own account, and apprehensive of ill treatment at the hands of the Valiahd if the latter came into power. I tried to reassure him, urging him to put himself right with his brother at once. . . . Once he had fully realized the fact that he had no chance of succeeding to the throne, regarding which he had evidently entertained some hopes, he broke down completely, declared that he was in fear of his life, and implored me to protect him . . . Finally he asked whether he could become a British subject. He was talking Persian, but he knows a little French and, to make sure that I understood his exact meaning, the Persian word being rather vague, he said 'Sujet Anglais peut-on devenir Sujet Anglais?' [154]

153. Durand to Salisbury, No. 35, Confidential, Tehran, May 14, 1896; F. O. 65/1528.
154. Id.

A few hours later Colonel Kosogovskii called on the unfortunate prince. He found Nāyeb os-Saltaneh in a "deplorable" condition, talking an incoherent mixture of Persian and French. Kosogovskii's appearance frightened the timid War Minister, but the colonel reassured him and showed him a telegram from the new Shah, who wanted from his younger brother a pledge of loyalty to himself and of obedience to Amin os-Soltān who had been confirmed as Prime Minister. Nāyeb os-Saltaneh swore that he had already sent a telegram to the Shah, then began to whisper into Kosogovskii's ear:

> Now everything is finished for me . . . I don't know what the attitude toward me will be . . . Sadre A'zam, you don't know what an irreconcilable enemy of mine he is . . . My only hope now is Russia . . . Convey to the Chargé d'Affaires [Bützow was on leave] that I seek the protection of Russia; from now on I place myself entirely in the hands of the Russians; let them only assure the life and safety of myself, my family and my property.[155]

Nāyeb os-Saltaneh's last hopes were shattered when the Russian colonel told him that "Not only the Shah, but the Russian and English representatives as well, have recognized the Sadre A'zam [Amin os-Soltān] as the ruler of Persia."[156] *Roma locuta, causa finita.* Like Nāyeb os-Saltaneh, Kosogovskii could imagine resistance to the new Shah, but neither of them could imagine resistance to the representatives of Russia and Britain. Nāyeb os-Saltaneh was beaten. A potential crisis had been averted.

At the palace, Amin os-Soltān had gathered the highest officials of the realm and the representatives of the two great powers whom he wanted to recognize the new Shah, Mozaffar ed-Din, then Governor of Āzarbāyjān. At 7 P.M. G.M.T., the Foreign Office cabled Durand that he could recognize the accession of Mozaffar ed-Din the moment he heard from the Government of India that it was in agreement.[157] The British minister could not wait.

155. Kosogovskii, p. 463.
156. Id.
157. Foreign Office to Durand, May 1, 1896; F. O. 60/578.

Any appearance of hesitation would have done much harm. It would have raised the hopes of others and encouraged them to put forward their claims, thereby endangering the peace of the country, and perhaps making the Valiahd [Mozaffar ed-Din] our enemy for life. It would also have forced the Sadri Azam [Amin os-Soltān] to turn to the Russians, who were known to be in favour of the Valiahd. I should in fact have been playing straight into their hands.[158]

Late at night in the Imperial Palace, standing vigil with Amin os-Soltān and the Russian chargé d'affaires, A. Shcheglov, the British minister was afraid that opposition to Mozaffar ed-Din would bring about Russian intervention. The Russians had already assured the heir apparent of their readiness to "help him in case of need." No pretext whatsoever must be given them for pushing their troops across the frontier. Before midnight Durand sent a telegram to Mr. Wood, British consul in Tabriz, instructing him to recognize the new Shah and to accompany him on his trip to Tehran.[159]

With Russia and England joining in support of Mozaffar ed-Din, no one was foolish enough to contest the succession. Nāyeb os-Saltaneh obtained a promise of Russian protection by signing a paper, renouncing all claims to the throne and humiliating himself before Amin os-Soltān and the Russian legation, assuring them both "that whenever he acted against their interests in the past it was by the direct order of his father, whose autograph letters he offers to produce."[160] The other possible pretender, Mas'ud Mirzā Zell es-Soltān, made no move, though, being the Shah's eldest son, he had long nursed the ambition to wear the crown. As Governor of Esfahān and a declared friend of the British, he thought he had the means of achieving it. He knew that within the Government of India there were those who wished to partition Persia and make him the ruler of a British protected southern half. Several years earlier, when Zell es-Soltān had in-

158. Durand to Salisbury, No. 35, Confidential, Tehran, May 14, 1896; F. O. 65/1528.
159. Id.
160. Id.

The Tobacco Régie

curred the displeasure of his father, it was Sir Mortimer Durand, then India's Foreign Secretary, who helped save him from certain ruin.[161] Now Durand was in Tehran. Might he not call on Zell es-Soltān to contest the succession? The prince waited in silence for the signal that never came. When his hopes died, he sent a message of submission to Mozaffar ed-Din Shah.

Thus for the first time in the history of the Qājār dynasty, a new Shah mounted the throne in peace.

161. H. D. Wolff, *Rambling Recollections*, 2, 333–34.

5

Loans, Concessions, and Political Power

Mozaffar ed-Din Shah was a sickly, weak, good-natured, and entirely uneducated man when, at the age of forty-three, he ascended the throne. Dominated by wives, relatives, astrologers, and chance favorites, he was absorbed in the minutiae of his daily existence and had little time for affairs of state, which bored and baffled him. Throughout his reign he sought the goodwill of Russia, realizing fully that his own fate as monarch depended on it.[1] Yet the initial impression of the British minister at Tehran was that the new Shah did not appear "to be under Russian influence to the extent that was predicted by some who knew him." [2]

For seven months the government continued to function as if Nāser ed-Din were still Shah. Amin os-Soltān's firm espousal of Mozaffar ed-Din's cause on May 1 had won him the gratitude of the new sovereign. However, Mozaffar ed-Din was impressionable and weak, whereas the opposition to the Grand Vizier was strong and efficient. Its leader, Abdol Hoseyn Mirzā Farmānfarmā, "the cousin, son-in-law and brother-in-law" of the Shah, had been denied the war ministry, which he had long coveted. He therefore allied himself with Mohsen Khān Moshir od-Dowleh, Mirzā Ali Khān Amin od-Dowleh, and a group of the Shah's cronies from Tabriz.[3] Together they managed to sway the Shah. On November

---

1. This was acknowledged by Russia's Foreign Minister, Count Lamsdorff, in his "Instruction" to the newly appointed Russian minister in Tehran, A. N. Speyer, in 1904. See *Krasnyi Arkhiv*, 4 (53), (1932), 18–19.

2. Durand to Salisbury, No. 51, Confidential, Gulahek, August 14, 1896; F. O. 60/593.

3. Sykes, *Sir Mortimer Durand*, p. 241.

24, the Shah dismissed the man to whom he largely owed his peaceful accession.[4]

Amin os-Soltān at once sent messengers to Durand and Bützow, requesting the protection of the two legations. That both responded favorably was a high tribute to his political skill. The very next day the two ministers drove in one carriage to the palace, where Bützow addressed to the Shah a plea that the former Grand Vizier be treated honorably.[5] The Shah had no desire to molest the fallen minister. However, Amin os-Soltān had many enemies. The most implacable of them, Farmānfarmā, is reported to have made several attempts to assassinate him. The hired killers failed because of the vigilance of some twenty Cossacks whom Colonel Kosogovskii assigned to guard him day and night.[6]

Bützow was somewhat disturbed by Amin os-Soltān's fall. Durand, on the contrary, welcomed the change. He found the new cabinet "very satisfactorily constituted, especially in view of the prominence achieved by Farmānfarmā, now Minister of War, and Mokhber od-Dowleh, Minister of the Interior. "They," Durand cabled home, "are our best friends in Persia and have both considerable administrative capacity."[7] The newfound influence of Farmānfarmā was especially pleasing to the British.

Almost four years earlier, Captain P. M. Sykes of the Indian army met Farmānfarmā, who had just been appointed Governor of Kermān. The original encounter led to correspondence, fur-

---

4. Colonel Kosogovskii, usually a very well-informed man, reports that the downfall of Amin os-Soltān was partly caused by his brother's indiscretion. The brother, Amin ol-Molk, had frequent parties in his house, with drink, women, and *motrebs* (entertainers). One night the *motrebs* sang a scurrilous song about "ābji" Mozaffar ("sister" Mozaffar). A certain Sheykh Mortezā Amin od-Divān told the Shah. The singers were summoned to the palace and ordered to repeat the performance before His Majesty, who promised them pardon. However, he swore he would show the others what sort of "sister" he was. Kosogovskii claims that this incident decided Amin os-Soltān's fate. V. A. Kosogovskii, *Iz tegeranskogo dnevnika*, p. 93.

5. Durand to Salisbury, Telegram in cypher, No. 81, Tehran, November 25, 1896; F. O. 65/1529. Kosogovskii, *Iz tegeranskogo dnevnika*, p. 85.

6. Kosogovskii, *Iz tegeranskogo dnevnika*, p. 131.

7. Durand to Salisbury, Telegram, cypher, No. 81, November 25, 1896; F. O. 65/1529.

ther meetings, and a friendship that turned out to be exceptionally valuable when, in 1894, Farmānfarmā was reappointed Governor of Kermān where Sykes was now British consul,

> and thenceforward my position as Consul, [he wrote] was most enviable, as I merely had to express my wishes for them to be carried out, while so evident was the friendship of H[is] H[ighness] for H[er] B[ritannic] M[ajesty]'s Government, that all the district officials and local chiefs invariably came to see me, when they visited Kermān, and told me that such were their instructions. Furthermore, the fact that His Highness has invested a considerable sum of money in British securities means that he is bound to our side, as he cannot believe but that H.B.M.'s Government would confiscate his property in England, were he to play us false.[8]

Farmānfarmā had been instrumental in bringing to a successful conclusion the delimitation of the Perso-Baluch frontier, and could give England both support and information. Sykes felt that, "H.H.'s greatest ambition is to receive an English decoration," and recommended that he be given one in view of his services to the British government.[9]

Sykes and Durand were too optimistic about the advantages that would accrue to Britain from the rise of Farmānfarmā. The latter quickly antagonized the Russians. He cut off the funds of the Cossack Brigade, sent 150 mounted Cossacks on plague quarantine duty in Khorāsān, thereby reducing the Brigade's effective strength to two hundred or two hundred and fifty men and winning for himself the undying hatred of its commander, Colonel Kosogovskii.[10] For awhile Russia did not protest, nor did she give open support to the Brigade and its commander, who complained of having been abandoned by his legation,[11] but she undoubtedly worked behind the scenes to bring down the powerful favorite. Within five months her attitude toward the entire

8. Letter of Captain P. M. Sykes, November 20, 1896, Enclosure in Durand to Salisbury, No. 65, Tehran, November 25, 1896; ibid.
9. Id.
10. Kosogovskii, *Iz tegeranskogo dnevnika*, p. 132.
11. Kosogovskii, "Persia . . . ," *Novyi Vostok*, No. 3 (1923), p. 449.

new cabinet, headed by Mirza Ali Khān Amin od-Dowleh, turned openly hostile.

On April 1, 1897, there occurred in Tabriz a minor disturbance. An Armenian employee of the Russian consulate was accused of having "insulted" the wife of a seyyed,[12] who raised an outcry. A crowd collected and demanded the surrender of the alleged offender. The Russian consulate refused to deliver its servant to the bloodthirsty mob, which then went to the Armenian quarter where it sacked three or four houses. Some panic-stricken Armenians sought refuge in the French and Russian consulates, and the Russian consul informed the heir apparent, Mohammad Ali Mirzā, who resided at Tabriz as Governor of Āzarbāyjān, that he had permission to call in Russian troops if the authorities proved powerless to stop the rioting. The British consul, Mr. Wood, was instructed by his legation to urge the authorities to maintain order, "and so to avoid any excuse for armed intervention." [13]

Though order was maintained, the Russian consul informed the authorities that five thousand troops were ready to cross the frontier "to protect the Christians in Tabreez," and demanded a firman from the prince-governor "assuring the safety of all Armenians, compensation to those whose houses had been pillaged, and the public punishment of the ringleaders in the disturbance." [14] In the absence of Sir Mortimer Durand, Mohsen Khān Moshir od-Dowleh consulted Charles Hardinge, the chargé d'affaires, who counseled acceptance of Russian demands. Russia's menacing attitude in such a minor incident baffled Hardinge. "The only explanation that I am able to offer," he wrote Salisbury, "is that it may have been desired to show the preponderating power of Russia in a province adjoining to the frontier or that it may have been inspired by the desire to injure the present Government to whom the Russians are openly hostile." [15]

12. A descendant of the Prophet. Most seyyeds, of course, were impostors.
13. Mr. Charles Hardinge to Lord Salisbury, No. 47, Tehran, April 16, 1897; F. O. 60/584.
14. Id.
15. Id.

Persia's domestic affairs went badly that summer. Disorders broke out here and there, and minor mutinies in the armed forces.[16] The Shah's health was so poor that his death was expected at any time. Rumors spread that Farmānfarmā had tried to have the Shah set aside Mohammad Ali Mirzā as heir apparent and nominate Nāser ed-Din Mirzā, son of Farmānfarmā's own sister, thus assuring himself the post of regent in the probable event of the Shah's death. However, it was said also that the Shah, who was very much attached to Mohammad Ali Mirzā, refused to go along, and Farmānfarmā had to resign. Charles Hardinge wrote to Lord Salisbury five days later:

> Other reasons alleged for the fall of the Firman Firma are non-payment of the troops and the indifference with which he regarded the general robbery of the soldiers by their superior officers, his interference with appointments made by other ministers, and his acceptance of heavy bribes. During the nine months that he has been in office he is said to have received £100,000 in bribes and to have also made another large sum of money by robbing the army of their pay. . . . Nine months have now elapsed since the fall of the Sadr Azam and the accession of the Firman Firma to office and although he at the outset enjoyed a most exceptional position owing to his close relationship with the Shah he succeeded in wrecking his own position and prospects by his want of ability and administrative capacity coupled with unsatiable appetite for intrigue and gain.[17]

Farmānfarmā's resignation was a symptom of a deep crisis. The government, whose expenditures were steadily growing while revenues were decreasing, was on the verge of bankruptcy. Neither the troops nor officials had been paid in months. The authority of the Shah himself was rapidly breaking down. When he tried to get Farmānfarmā out of the capital by appointing

16. A mutiny at Bushehr is graphically described in the Summary of Intelligence for August 1897, Russia in Asia, Persia, Turkey in Asia, Northern China and Korea, Intelligence Branch, Quarter Master General's Department in India; F. O. 65/1549.

17. C. Hardinge to Salisbury, No. 121, Confidential, Gulahek, September 12, 1897; ibid.

him governor of Māzandarān, Farmānfarmā refused the appointment. Neither could the Shah make him leave for Fārs, the governorship he had accepted. "In the meantime, the province of Fars is without a responsible Governor," Hardinge wrote, "and the reports which I have received show that the greatest disorder prevails on the main roads, and that in some places caravans are no longer able to pass." [18]

The government found no other way out than to borrow abroad. Secret negotiations were opened with the firm of Oppenheim of Paris, Cologne, and the Hague. A certain Dr. Ratoul, Polish oculist resident in Persia, was the go-between. The Persian government wanted 40,000,000 francs and was prepared to pledge the customs of Kermānshāh and the Persian Gulf ports as security.[19] The British chargé d'affaires, Charles Hardinge, who did not learn of the negotiations until October 13, notified the Foreign Office. On the fifteenth, Lord Salisbury instructed him to remind the Persians of British views on the control of southern customs as these had been expressed in his dispatch to Sir Frank Lascelles of April 22, 1892. Hardinge at once drew up a memorandum, which he presented to the Shah and the Prime Minister, requesting "an assurance from His Majesty that under no circumstances whatever would the control of the Customs of Southern Persia be ceded to a Foreign Power." [20] Amin od-Dowleh saw no difficulty in giving the requested assurances. On the twenty-third; Hardinge received a letter from Mirzā Mohsen Khān Moshir od-Dowleh, Minister of Foreign Affairs:

> You have written that there was a rumor that the Customs of Southern Persia would be placed under foreign supervision and control as guarantee for a loan. I therefore take this occasion of informing the Legation that this rumour is absolutely without foundation, and that they will never be placed under foreign supervision and control.[21]

18. Same to same, No. 141, Tehran, October 24, 1897; F. O. 60/601.
19. Same to same, No. 140, Tehran, October 23, 1897; F. O. 60/601 and F. O. 65/1549.
20. Id.
21. Id. Also, Hardinge to Salisbury, Telegram, No. 68, Tehran, October 23 1897; F. O. 65/1549.

The Russian chargé d'affaires, A. Shcheglov, who learned of the loan negotiations even later than Hardinge, made no attempt to conceal his annoyance. He reproached the Minister of Foreign Affairs for not having applied to the Russian government, which would have been ready to lend money to Persia.

> He added that as the Russian Government had on previous occasions offered to make a loan to the Persian Government which the late Shah had declined they had a priority of right in the present instance, and he complained bitterly that he and his Legation had been made to appear in the eyes of the Russian Government "comme des imbéciles." [22]

Shcheglov threatened Dr. Ratoul, the go-between, who was a Russian subject. He also persuaded the French chargé d'affaires (it seems that at the moment every legation in Tehran was without its head) to telegraph his government "to prevent the floating of the loan on the French Market." [23] A few weeks later Hardinge cabled Salisbury that loan negotiations had failed, "owing chiefly, as I hear, to the action taken by the French Government to prevent its issue in Paris." [24]

The Persian government made desperate efforts to obtain money elsewhere. It approached the Dutch, but the unusual combination of Russian and British diplomacy frustrated its efforts. The Dutch legation turned unsympathetic, after having been visited by Charles Hardinge.

> In order to avoid any possible misapprehension in the future, I [Hardinge] have thought it best to explain to the Dutch Chargé d'Affaires the views of H.M.'s Government as to the foreign control of the Customs of the south, and have shown to him the text of the assurance received from the Persian Government. He had already strongly urged his Government to discourage the floating of the loan in Holland, and he believes that the negotiations, of which the

22. Hardinge to Salisbury, No. 140; F. O. 60/601.
23. Id.
24. C. Hardinge to Salisbury, Telegram, No. 72, Tehran, November 23, 1897; ibid.

success had hitherto been doubtful, will now probably end in failure.[25]

To add to the government's distress, the clergy began a campaign against the loan and against the cabinet of Amin od-Dowleh, who, Charles Hardinge reported, had "repeatedly resisted their endeavours to extort money from him," and had "shown himself to be indifferent to their aims and influence." [26]

Ever since the agitation leading to the failure of the original Reuter concession, the political power of the mullas had grown and expanded. Whether their zeal had been aroused by devotion to ideals or to Russian gold, they had violently opposed the Tobacco Régie, greatly contributing to its downfall. The death of Nāser ed-Din Shah and the accession of his weak son further increased their arrogance.

In the spring of 1897 the mullas violently attacked Alā od-Dowleh, Governor of Arabestān, for having, they alleged, caused the death of a certain Āqā Sheykh Mohammad Ali, a religious figure in the town of Shushtar. Actually the Sheykh had left town (he later showed up very much alive), but his colleagues were determined to get rid of a governor who intended to assert his authority. The Tehran clergy took the side of their Shushtar brethren, demanding the death of Alā od-Dowleh. To break up the clerical front, the government bribed the chief mojtahed (leading ecclesiastical dignitary) of Tehran, Hāji Mirzā Hasan Āshtiāni. Lieutenant Colonel H. Picot, British military attaché, wrote:

> Seyid Abdullah [Behbehāni], a Mushtahed who stood by this Legation at the time of the Régie, and with whom we are still on excellent terms, took the place of Haji Mirza Ashtiani, and at once sent me messages, to ask the views and wishes of the Legation, adding that he would throw cold water on the whole affair if we were so minded. From another source messages were conveyed to me that if Her Majesty's

25. Same to same, Telegram, No. 69, Tehran, November 3, 1897; ibid.
26. Same to same, No. 152, Tehran, November 17, 1897; F. O. 65/1549.

Legation wished for disorder the Moollahs of Shuster would carry out our instructions to the letter.[27]

Thus the clergy, like the government, was breaking up into two groups: one pro-Russian, the other pro-British.

Alā od-Dowleh had to be recalled, but the cabinet of Amin od-Dowleh survived, partly because of the moderating influence of Seyyed Abdollāh Behbehāni who acted in behalf of the English.

Expecting no advantage from the loan that was being negotiated by Amin od-Dowleh, and sensing an opportunity to overthrow the hated Prime Minister, the clergy unleashed a furious assault on him and his associates. They were described in leaflets and posters as traitors who sold their country to the foreigners and destroyed their religion. According to Charles Hardinge, who observed the situation at close quarters and had excellent sources of information, "In this campaign the Moollahs received the active encouragement and cooperation of the Russian Legation, who, in addition to their hostility to the proposed loan, make no secret of their desire for the fall of the Amin od-Dowleh and for the return to power of the Sadr Azam Amin os-Soltan." [28] Jews were violently denounced in the hope that a pogrom would further discredit the government. Some clerics spoke openly of their intention "to upset the Government and even went so far as to discuss the dethronement of the Shah." [29]

Though the British tacitly agreed with the Russians that Persia should not borrow money in Europe, they did not relish the prospect of clerical domination of the government, nor did they favor the downfall of Amin od-Dowleh. Charles Hardinge sent a message to the Shah through the latter's private physician, Dr. Adcock, that "unless he [the Shah] showed a bold front to the Moollahs at the present moment and supported the Government in power it would mean the extinction of His Majesty's authority and the subservience to the Moollahs of any future Government." Hardinge also urged Amin od-Dowleh to remain firm.

27. Memorandum by Lieutenant Colonel H. Picot, Military Attaché, May 12, 1897; F. O. 65/1547.

28. Charles Hardinge to Salisbury, No. 152, Tehran, November 17, 1897; F. O. 65/1549.

29. Id.

Loans, Concessions, and Power

Being personally acquainted with Syed Abdullah [Hardinge wrote] . . . I sent him a message to the effect that I had heard that he was acting in opposition to the wishes of the Government, and that in the event of his actions getting him into trouble with the Authorities I would be unable to afford him any assistance. This message I am glad to say had an excellent effect as after ascertaining through one of his emissaries that the Government were receiving the support of Her Majesty's Legation and that my message was intended as a serious warning, he withdrew within a few days time from the hostile combination of Moollahs.[30]

The government took courage, arrested a few troublemakers and prevented a massacre of the Jews by dispatching a strong force to the Jewish quarter of the city. But the mullas had not been fully suppressed. The Shah hesitated to push for a showdown. Then, as later, he preferred compromise and conciliation. The crisis had only been postponed.[31]

The identity of Russian and British views on the loan issue did not escape the notice of the Persian government. Throughout the country the belief was growing that Russia and Britain wished to foment disorder as a step preliminary to the division of the country.[32] There were persistent rumors of an impending Anglo-Russian understanding on the problems of the Far East and the Middle East. The rumors were not entirely unfounded. In the fall of 1897 Tsar Nicholas II spent several weeks at Wolfsgarten with his brother-in-law, the Duke of Hesse. One day he spoke to the British chargé d'affaires, George Buchanan, about Asiatic affairs:

---

30. Id.

31. The power and arrogance of the clergy is illustrated by an episode that occurred a few years later. A cholera epidemic struck Kermānshāh in December 1903. Cold weather had stopped its spread in winter, but in the spring it regained its virulence. Under combined Anglo-Russian pressure, the Persian government quarantined the city. However, a great mojtahed from Najaf, Aqā Fāzel Mamaqāni, defied all sanitary precautions. With a band of eight hundred pilgrims, who were joined by four hundred beggars, he set out of Kermānshāh toward Tehran and Mashhad, spreading the disease along the way. The government did not find the courage to stop the great personage and his entourage. Cf. A. Hardinge to Lansdowne, No. 71, Tehran, April 23, 1904; F. O. 60/732.

32. Memorandum by H. Picot, May 12, 1897; F. O. 65/1547.

He did not, he said, believe in buffer States, unless they were strong and independent; and Persia, with its effete and corrupt Government, was too weak to play the role of such a State with advantage. Russia had already quite as much territory as she could manage, and he did not desire to acquire more; but he personally thought that our relations would be more friendly and satisfactory were there no Persia between us.[33]

A few months later, in January 1898, after Russia had occupied Port Arthur, Salisbury indicated at St. Petersburg that he would be prepared to partition China and the Ottoman Empire. Though nothing came of these moves because "Russian diplomacy did not want its hands tied," [34] the Persians must have trembled in fear of the consequences of an Anglo-Russian rapprochement.

Late in November Amin od-Dowleh again complained to Hardinge that the Russian, French, Dutch, and Belgian legations in Tehran had frightened prospective lenders in Europe. A. Shcheglov had offered to obtain money in Russia, but, as the Minister of Foreign Affairs, Moshir od-Dowleh, sarcastically remarked, the Persians were unwilling "to forge new chains for themselves, having already had sufficient proof of Russia's benevolent intentions toward Persia in thwarting every tendency toward the development of the country and in placing every obstacle in the way of progress and reform." [35]

The Persian ministers asked Hardinge whether it would be possible to borrow in London. Moshir od-Dowleh was even prepared to allow the British legation to supervise the expenditure of funds raised in England. Hardinge replied that ever since Malkam Khān's swindle, it had become impossible for Persia to raise money on the London exchange. He pointed out, in monitory tones no doubt, that Her Majesty's Government could not

33. George Buchanan, *My Mission to Russia and Other Diplomatic Memories* (Boston, 1923), 1, 169.

34. V. M. Khvostov, "Nachalo anglo-germanskogo antagonizma," Potemkin, ed., *Istoriia diplomatii* (Moscow, 1945), 2, 127–28.

35. C. Hardinge to Salisbury, No. 157, Tehran, November 24, 1897; F. O. 60/601.

Loans, Concessions, and Power

guarantee a loan "without previous recourse to Parliament and that in England all such ventures were left entirely to private enterprise and initiative." [36] Instead of seeking loans abroad, Hardinge lectured the Persians, the Shah should lend the government £200,000 worth of his own gold, a sum that would not exceed a quarter of the estimated total in his private treasury. Amin od-Dowleh agreed that the proposal was a good one "but that the difficulty consisted in the very strong objections felt by the Shah to opening his Treasury although the gold was lying there absolutely without profit to anybody." [37]

In December the government turned to the Imperial Bank of Persia for a loan of £400,000 at 5 percent interest, offering the customs of Mohammareh and Kermānshāh as security. Charles Hardinge confirmed Amin od-Dowleh's desperate need for funds, and Salisbury agreed that there were no political objections to a loan.[38] However, the bank was not anxious to advance the money, especially since it knew that the Persians continued to make efforts to obtain funds elsewhere. Hardinge, aware of the power of the purse, urged: "I cannot insist too strongly upon the necessity, in their own interests, of the Bank carrying through this loan with the utmost rapidity." [39] The bank was unsure of what it could or should do. The chairman of the board claimed that the public doubted the stability and permanence of Persian investment, a doubt "which is stimulated by the persistent hostility of a small but influential section of the Stock Exchange which considers itself aggrieved by the action of the Persian Government in the matter of a previous concession." The bank was convinced that it was in its own interests, as well as "those of English commerce and influence in Persia" that the loan be granted, but was unable to do so because of the opposition of financial circles of England and Scotland.

36. Id.
37. Id.
38. C. Hardinge to Salisbury, Telegram, No. 85, Secret, Tehran, December 17, 1897, and Salisbury to Hardinge, Telegram, No. 39, December 19, 1897; ibid.
39. C. Hardinge to Salisbury, Telegram, No. 26, Tehran, February 20, 1898; ibid.

Under these circumstances the Imperial Bank of Persia can do no more than urge Her Majesty's Government as strongly as is consistent with propriety, <u>to guarantee a loan of £400,000</u> [underlined in pencil at the Foreign Office] which we believe will be sufficient to meet the needs of the Persian Government and for which the securities offered are amply sufficient.[40]

The chairman pointed out that to turn down Persia's request "would have an extremely *unfortunate and far reaching effect*" (underlined at the Foreign Office). However, the only action open to the bank was to agree to give Persia a small advance if it were guaranteed by the British government. Thus the former lottery syndicate, which had been swindled by Malkam Khān, Amin os-Soltān, and Nāser ed-Din Shah, was settling old scores with the Persian government. The bank notified Persia of the demands of the former lottery syndicate that they be paid off before a Persian loan was floated in London. The Persians refused to pay and turned to the Belgian minister, offering the Belgians control of customs as security on a 40,000,000-franc loan.

The minister immediately consulted Hardinge and was told that the bank was negotiating a similar loan. Hardinge "explained to him the views of H.M.'s Government as to any foreign control of the Customs of the ports, and showed him the guarantee . . . received from the Persian Government." The minister assured Hardinge "that he would tell the Minister for Foreign Affairs that he would take no action whatever so long as negotiations with the Bank were in progress."[41] A word from the British sufficed to keep the representatives of small nations in line. They could not hope to carry out any action in Persia unless backed by one of the two great powers. To Amin od-Dowleh's distress no money was forthcoming from Brussels.

Once again the luckless Grand Vizier approached the Imperial Bank of Persia. Now he was asking for only £250,000, and

---

40. Chairman of the Imperial Bank of Persia to the Marquess of Salisbury, London, March 11, 1898; ibid.

41. C. Hardinge to Salisbury, Telegram, No. 31, Tehran, February 26, 1898; ibid.

Loans, Concessions, and Power 315

offering as guarantee the customs of Mohammareh and Kermānshāh. "The sum asked for is small, and the guarantee could not be better," wrote Hardinge, urging the acceptance of the Persian proposal.[42] The bank wanted the customs placed under the control of Europeans, otherwise the chances of raising money on the Exchange would be slim.[43] On March 7 Amin od-Dowleh wrote a letter to the manager of the Imperial Bank, requesting him to appoint agents to supervise the customs. Again Hardinge urged London: "In view of the very unusual concession made by the Persian Government, for which they have so far nothing in return, I sincerely trust the Directors [of the bank] may be able to meet the wishes of the Persian Government and to profit by the very exceptional advantages offered to them."[44] The concession was indeed extraordinary. For the first time Persia was prepared to turn over to foreigners one of her government departments. The dubious honor of having been the first Persian minister to accept such an arrangement went to Mirzā Ali Khān Amin od-Dowleh.

While waiting for the results of his appeal, Hardinge managed to extract from the Imperial Bank £50,000, thereby saving Amin od-Dowleh from riots which would have broken out on Now-Ruz (New Year) had he been unable to pay at least some of the military and civil officials. The customs of Kermānshāh and Bushehr (the latter was substituted for Mohammareh out of consideration for the feelings of its ruler, Sheykh Khaz'al, a British protégé) were at once placed under the bank's supervision, to the satisfaction of England's chargé d'affaires, who expressed to Salisbury his hope that the rest of the £250,000 would be forthcoming "so that the temporary control which they [the bank] now enjoy at Bushire and Kermanshah may become a permanent institution."[45] Loss of control over two important custom houses and the mortgaging of their revenue was Amin od-Dowleh's Now-Ruz present to his country.

In mid-May the loan question had not yet been settled. The

42. Same to same, Telegram, No. 35, Tehran, March 2, 1898; ibid.
43. Salisbury to Hardinge, Telegram, No. 21, March 5, 1898; ibid.
44. C. Hardinge to Salisbury, Telegram, No. 37, Tehran, March 7, 1898; ibid.
45. Same to same, No. 48, Tehran, March 22, 1898; ibid.

manager of the Imperial Bank of Persia, Joseph Rabino, a man of vast experience and considerable knowledge of the Middle East, strongly favored granting a loan. In a memorandum presented to the British military attaché, Rabino attacked what in his opinion was a series of misconceptions on the loan issue. It was believed in England that the Shah could resolve the country's financial crisis by reaching into his private treasury, that the Persians could not be trusted to pay their debts, and that the establishment of British control over the customs in the south would lead to Russian demands for a similar arrangement in the north.

Rabino argued that the Shah had used his own money to settle government debts but could not be expected to go on doing so. As for Persian dishonesty, he deplored the "astounding ignorance of Persia in England." With the single exception of Curzon's, Rabino declared, he knew of no book which made any attempt to give an impartial view of Persia and her people. In general, he went on, the Persians did pay their debts.

> European honesty and punctuality are proverbial but they are greatly assisted by the existence of many centuries of legislation, of Courts of Justice, or of means of coercion; a sense of honour plus the policeman.
>
> Let us give some credit to the Persian who with none of these stimulants still fulfils his monetary engagements, irregularly and unpunctually if you will, but still fulfils them and that without judicial machinery to make him do so. . . .
>
> On the whole my experience of seventeen years spent in Egypt and Persia is that in overreaching his neighbours the wily Oriental as he is complacently called is very far from being a match for the European business man of unimpeachable morals.[46]

Turning to the possibility of Russia's demanding control over the customs of the north, Rabino claimed that she could not do

---

46. This paragraph was crossed out in pencil at the Foreign Office. In the margin was written the word "omit," indicating that someone felt Rabino's remarks on the business morals of European capitalists unfit for the eyes even of high government officials. J. Rabino to Colonel Picot, confidential, Tehran, May 14, 1898; ibid.

Loans, Concessions, and Power

so without first providing Persia with a loan. He did not entirely agree with the view that blamed Russia for all lack of progress in Persia. Britain brought Persia the benefits of the telegraph, but so had Russia. Economic progress had been supported by Britain, but now the position of the Imperial Bank was in danger.

> Our rivals on the other hand when a small Russian Bank found itself unable to compete with the Imperial Bank not only bought up the undertaking but continued to carry it on at a loss. This may appear an imprudent course, but there now exists an organisation ready to take our place should our discouraged shareholders determine to abandon the business.[47]

Rabino complained that the British government refused to help the bank build a road from the Gulf to Tehran, and it had to be abandoned after £80,000 had been spent. Russia on the other hand had spent a quarter of a million pounds sterling on the Rasht-Tehran road. In conclusion he pointed out that

> whilst we refuse Persia our assistance even upon conditions which imply suspicion on our part, a great financial establishment in St. Petersburg has offered a loan upon easy terms, upon the security of all the customs without any controllers at all, the funds simply to be transmitted to Tehran and this offer is a wise and politic one; little risk and immense advantage to be gained by the operation.
> England has great influence in Persia and the Bank has very considerable power throughout the country but these would be immediately increased by giving our help prudently but unhesitatingly in the critical moment, and would be greatly impaired if not annihilated by our refusal.[48]

The directors of the Imperial Bank of Persia were still discussing matters with their Stock Exchange friends when the Russian legation in Tehran began to move on the loan issue. Seen from the Russian point of view, the picture was quite unlike that painted in Rabino's memorandum. Colonel Kosogovskii, for in-

47. Id.
48. Id.

stance, believed that the English were actually hurrying "to offer their services, using all their efforts not to lose this brilliant opportunity to entangle luckless Persia in their strong nets, as the spider entangles the fly." He marveled at the "equanimity and lack of energy" displayed by Russia. While the loan question was moving ahead rapidly, the Russian legation "condescended to go to picknics in the mountains." To Kosogovskii British proposals were "predatory" while Russian inaction was inexcusable.[49]

Kosogovskii, a dedicated soldier, gave too little credit to the diplomats. He did not know that the legation had already offered Persia 15,000,000 rubles (which equalled 40,000,000 francs or £1,586,250) at 5 percent for sixty-five years. Negotiations, as Rabino pointed out in his memorandum to Picot, were being conducted with the International Commercial Bank of St. Petersburg. Russia was proposing that the revenue of all customs be turned over to the bank, which would pay itself the stipulated interest and part of the principal that came due, and would turn the rest over to the Persian treasury. In case the revenue of any given year was insufficient to meet debt payments, the International Commercial Bank of St. Petersburg would have the right to establish effective control over such revenue. If, in spite of control, payments were still not made properly, the bank "aura le droit de prendre en main la gestion directe de toutes les douanes." [50]

In July Russia received strong support from the former Prime Minister, Amin os-Soltān who, sensing the approaching fall of his hated rival, decided to hasten it in the hope of returning to power. He met Colonel Kosogovskii and asked him to inform the Russian minister, Kimon Manuilovich Argyropoulo, that he was determined to take a desperate step: to sabotage the proposed British loan. On the twenty-first the Russian minister sent word to Amin os-Soltān that Russia had the money ready. "Apparently," Kosogovskii commented, "in St. Petersburg they have understood—though one does not know to what extent—the significance of this loan, since the Minister had received a pro-

49. Kosogovskii, *Iz tegeranskogo dnevnika*, p. 166.
50. Draft Agreement, Enclosure in Durand to Salisbury, No. 71, June 1, 1898; F. O. 60/601.

posal from the Minister of Finance, Witte, to talk with the Persian government about making a loan in Russia." Though the colonel did not know all the terms suggested by Witte, who was using a St. Petersburg bank as a screen, he believed that these included the revenues of all customs, north and south; a single controller of all customs; and "the revenues of all Persia's Caspian Sea fisheries (now predatorily exploited by Lianozov)."[51]

Amin os-Soltān wanted to know what to do if the English applied pressure on the Shah. Kosogovskii said that England would have no right to complain since the money would be provided not by the government but by a private bank. Moreover, Kosogovskii added,

> the Russians propose to issue the shares at eighty-five percent from the start without bargaining; they could issue them higher, up to ninety percent, but do not because they deduct a part for bribes; if you [Amin os-Soltān] should give up the bribes, the Russians would probably agree to issue the loan at ninety percent and perhaps even higher.[52]

The reemergence of Amin os-Soltān's influence led the Persian loan negotiators to change their position. They began to ask the Imperial Bank for £2,000,000 instead of £1,250,000, but offered no additional security. Sir Mortimer Durand, back in Tehran after a prolonged absence, attributed the new difficulties to the machinations of the former Grand Vizier and his followers. He was only partly right.

Russian activity in Persia increased sharply in 1898. Two of her subjects, F. E. Enakiev and A. M. Goriainov, were negotiating a seventy-year concession on mines in the Qarajadāgh area of Āzarbāyjān.[53] The Russian government obtained the right to build a mall and lighthouse at Anzali and to collect tolls from ships using the harbor.[54] In St. Petersburg the Ministry of Finance, animated by Witte, was moving into foreign affairs on a large scale.

51. Kosogovskii, *Iz tegeranskogo dnevnika*, pp. 166–67.
52. Ibid., p. 168.
53. Iran, Archive of the Ministry of Foreign Affairs, File 44/Folder 27, Registry No. 5, 1326.
54. Ibid., File 44/Folder 3.

Simultaneously, the Russian attitude toward Great Britain became daily more negative. The appointment of George Curzon, former undersecretary at the Foreign Office, as Viceroy of India was taken as a challenge and elicited a very hostile reaction in the press. *Novoe Vremia* depicted him

> as a member of "the most extreme Russophobe party, who close their eyes to everything that does not seem to confirm their hardly intelligible hatred towards Russia"; and the writer urged his countrymen "to follow with keen eyes the acts of Mr. Curzon," and warned them that as Viceroy of India he would proceed to give effect to the theories which he had hitherto developed in his books and in the columns of the press.[55]

The year 1898 was an eventful though difficult one for the British Empire. English troops defeated the Dervishes at Omdurman, avenging the memory of General Gordon, but at Fashoda they almost blundered into a war with France. The young and impetuous Kaiser Wilhelm II embarked on a policy of rivalry with Britain and made the Reichstag adopt an ambitious naval construction program to wrest from Britannia control of the seas. Russia occupied Port Arthur, spread her influence over Manchuria, threatened England's position in central China, and increased her activity in Persia. Her government-controlled press spoke of the Anglo-Russian conflict in tones that grew harsher with each passing month. In the spring of 1899, *Novoe Vremia* wrote:

> Two forces alone are struggling for supremacy on the vast expanse of the Continent of Asia—Russia and England. The former founds its claim on the possession of Northern Asia —the second on India. All the other powers may be strong in different parts of the world, but in Asia they are only new comers who are there for the sake of finding fresh markets for their products and to buy raw materials cheap. They are only "guests" as merchants were called in ancient Russia.[56]

55. Ronaldshay, *The Life of Lord Curzon* (London, 1928), 1, 295–96.
56. *Novoe Vremia*, May 9/21, 1899, translated for the F. O.; F. O. 65/1593.

Loans, Concessions, and Power

An understanding with England would be possible only if the two powers had common aims, but

> What common object in the sphere of practical politics can there be in Asia for Russia and England? England whose commercial interests take precedence of ordinary humanity! Can this common object be the construction of railroads over the pathless wastes separating our frontiers and those of England? But, alas, the road which unites India with Central Asia carries English goods from India to the Russian markets and brings us Cholera, and Plague as guests.

Novoe Vremia then spoke of Persia,

> which English politicians have already divided—the South falling under English influence, and the North under Russian. But are all Russia's chances counted in this forecast, and has England sufficient strength to withstand our influence in the south should this influence be supported by three or four hundred versts of railway . . . Our influence in North Persia comes from the definite and inevitable fact of territorial vicinity, while the claim of England to the South is based on an arbitrary usurpation of the Persian Gulf which is recognized by no one. England may look on that Gulf as her own as much as she pleases, and may unofficially call her resident at Bushire the Ruler of the Gulf, but Russia will never recognize this claim . . . War ships, as is well known, possess the quality of floating, and if anything causes them to depart, or if they lose their present exclusive position, the supremacy of British influence in Southern Persia will no longer be a fact. Why do we allow the English to terrify us with this "fact" and thus modify our views with regard to the future.[57]

Russia's first important achievement at Tehran was the deadlock in the negotiations between the Persian government and the Imperial Bank, the second was the return to power of Amīn os-Solṭān, now an acknowledged partisan of Russia. The British legation must have felt how quickly its position deteriorated in

57. Id.

the fall of 1898. General Thomas E. Gordon, a director of the Imperial Bank of Persia, held several conversations with the Grand Vizier in October and November and reported him to be dependent on Russian financial and political support.[58] Amin os-Soltān made it clear that the Shah needed money for a trip to Europe as well as for state needs. He knew that assistance obtained from Russia would mean loss of independence "and perhaps the absorption of the country by that powerful neighbour." He knew, or pretended to believe, that Britain had no such plans. "But the occupation of the Customs posts at Bushire and Kermanshah had alarmed many thoughtful Persians, and raised doubts in their minds as to England's ultimate intentions." [59] Amin os-Soltān himself came to feel that the surrender of control over the customs in the south was a provocation to Russia and voted against the measure in the Shah's Council. Gordon suggested that it might be possible for Britain and Russia jointly to lend Persia money, but Amin os-Soltān showed no enthusiasm for the suggestion.[60]

The British were seriously worried. They began to perceive causal connections between a number of seemingly disparate facts. A run had been organized on the Imperial Bank of Persia and nearly succeeded in wrecking the institution, "not because there was no gold in the Bank, but because it was in gold ingots!" [61] Charles Hardinge was angry with Joseph Rabino, "as the result to British prestige might have been disastrous if the Bank had had to close its doors." [62] The legation also found itself unable to obtain exact information about Russo-Persian loan negotiations and the terms being discussed. When Salisbury asked Alā os-Saltaneh, the Persian minister, whether his country was negotiating a loan with Russia, and was told in reply that such was the case, he instructed Durand to ask the Shah about the terms. Mozaffar ed-Din sent a message to Salisbury:

58. Notes by General Sir Thomas Gordon on his Mission to Tehran in the interests of the Imperial Bank of Persia, Confidential, F. O. 60/630.
59. Id.
60. Id.
61. C. Hardinge, *Old Diplomacy*, p. 65.
62. Id.

You ask to be permitted to see the terms of the loan which I am now making. This is impossible, as the matter is still in course of negotiation. However, I now inform you that I will accept no proposals unless the conditions are more favourable than those proposed by the Imperial Bank of Persia. . . .

Now as regards your statement that you will resist any arrangement tending to place the Customs of Southern Persia in the hands of a Foreign Power, I take this to mean that you have made the statement because the proceeds of the Customs are placed as guarantee to the Régie loan. I now state to you positively that this fact will be taken into consideration.[63]

Amin os-Soltān argued that since the English would not give him the money, he had no choice but seek it elsewhere. "To forbid him," he said, "would be like forbidding a man when dying of thirst to drink water, or when bleeding to death to tie up his wounds. Obedience could not be expected."[64]

In a final attempt to forestall a Russian loan, Durand suggested to Amin os-Soltān that Russia and Britain act jointly in the matter. The Russians had long been opposed to any such arrangement and evaded conversations on this theme.[65] The Shah refused the offer out of hand, regarding it "as almost tantamount to a division of his empire. In this respect, said the Sadr-i-Azam [Amin os-Soltān], His Majesty was not altogether wrong, and his views were shared by the Persians generally."[66] Two days later the Persian Minister of Foreign Affairs frankly told Durand that his government was disappointed in England. Had she wanted to be helpful, she could easily have induced her capitalists to lend £2,000,000 to Persia. Amin os-Soltān, the Foreign Minister said, did not believe Durand's statement "that without guarantees such as would satisfy capitalists" he could not raise the funds.

---

63. Durand to Salisbury, No. 18, paraphrase of cypher telegram, Tehran, March 31, 1899; F. O. 60/630.
64. Id.
65. Kosogovskii, *Iz tegeranskogo dnevnika*, p. 168.
66. Durand to Salisbury, No. 57, Gulahek, August 20, 1899; F. O. 60/630.

Now Persia had to seek friendship elsewhere. Durand noticed the unusual tone assumed by the Foreign Minister, a tone which "appeared to me to be deliberately intended to warn me that the Persian [the word "government" omitted in the original, then penciled in] would no longer regard us as friendly, or behave in a friendly manner toward us, unless we found money for them." [67]

The British minister did not heed the warning. All he could see was that the Grand Vizier hoped "to force our hand by frightening us." Durand's analysis of the situation was simpleminded and faulty. He was convinced that Amin os-Soltān would still be prepared to accept £2,000,000 from Britain even at the risk of Russian annoyance.[68] Actually it was too late for England to stop the Russian loan or to prevent Amin os-Soltān from working in favor of Russia. He owed her too much, depended too heavily upon her continued support, and would never be able to extricate himself from his numerous commitments to her legation.

Through the autumn months of 1899 in Tehran and St. Petersburg, loan negotiations proceeded with speed and dispatch. So thick was the curtain of secrecy behind which Amin os-Soltān, Count Murav'ev, and Witte transacted their business that the usually well-informed British diplomats were left groping in the dark. Neither Russian offers nor Persian counterproposals leaked out, except in the form of totally unreliable rumors.

Russia's final conditions were presented to Persia by the Foreign Minister, Count Mikhail Nikolaevich Murav'ev in a memorandum dated December 14, 1899. Persia was asked to undertake not to borrow money from any other country until the Russian loan had been paid off. Immediately upon receiving money under the new loan, Persia must repay all previous foreign debts. "The Persian Government will renew the previous engagement and undertake that for another ten years excepting the Russian Government no other Government will be given a concession to build railways in Persia." [69] The loan would be guaranteed by the

67. Durand to Salisbury, No. 58, Gulahek, August 21, 1899; ibid.
68. Id.
69. Memorandum by Count Muraviev (translation from the Persian), 10th Shaaban 1371 (December 14, 1899), Enclosure No. 1 in Sir A. Hardinge, No. 238, Secret, December 1, 1904; F. O. 60/683.

revenues of all customs, except those of Fārs and Persian Gulf ports. Should such revenue prove insufficient, all other revenue of the Persian government would serve as a guarantee for the loan. The last provision was the only one rejected by the Shah, who wrote in the lower margin of the memorandum below Murav'ev's signature that it must be canceled.[70]

The agreement was signed in St. Petersburg in January 1900, some of the provisions being made public on January 31. Officially it was a contract between the Persian government, represented by General Mirzā Rezā Khān Arfa' od-Dowleh, Envoy Extraordinary and Minister Plenipotentiary, and the Discount and Loan Bank (the Russian bank in Tehran). Persia borrowed 22,500,000 rubles at 5 percent repayable over seventy-five years (Article 1). The loan was guaranteed by the revenue of all customs except those of Fārs and the ports of the Persian Gulf (Article 4). Should annual payments made by Persia fall below the minimum of 1,156,288 rubles, the bank would have the right to "exercise effective control" over customs' receipts (Article 6). If the Persian government continued to be late in its payments, the bank would have the right to take over the direct administration of all Persian customs, except those of Fārs and the Gulf ports, on the following conditions:

  a. The bank would choose the personnel but they would be Persians, except for twenty-five men, concerning whom the bank would have complete liberty of choice.

  b. The bank must maintain legal tariffs and would have no right to raise them without government consent.

  c. The Persian government would have the right to control the bank's administration of customs.

  d. The expenses of administering customs, and the loan payments having been met, the rest of the revenue would be turned over to the Persian government (Article 7).

From the funds supplied by the bank would be deducted the amount Persia still owed the Imperial Bank on its 1892 and other loans. The bank would pay them off (Article 9). The Persian government could pay off the loan of 1900 at any time after

70. Id.

January 1, 1910, provided six months' notice had been given (Article 13). Until the complete redemption of this loan, Persia would not borrow abroad ("n'émettra pas aucun emprunt extérieur") without prior agreement with the Imperial Government of Russia, nor would it lower tariffs which served as security for the loan (Article 14).[71]

Strange as it may seem, the announcement of the Russian loan surprised the British government and public opinion. Though the danger of Russia's establishing monopolistic control over Persian finances had been present for over two years, it had not been taken seriously. The business mentality of the London Stock Exchange and of the directors of the Imperial Bank of Persia was allowed to prevail over reasons of state that had been clearly expressed in the dispatches of Charles Hardinge from Tehran. Russia, on the contrary, had entirely subordinated economic to political considerations. It was immaterial to Witte or Murav'ev whether Persia could make regular payments. It mattered not whether the loan was profitable or resulted in a heavy loss. The important consideration was to gain exclusive control over Persian finances, which meant exclusive control over the government.

Now that it was too late, the British went through the motions of objecting. At St. Petersburg, Ambassador Sir Charles Scott expressed his government's "profound astonishment" that the loan had been negotiated without an exchange of views with England.[72] Count Murav'ev claimed he had little to do with the loan and suggested that Scott see Witte. The latter assured him that the loan was a private business venture of the Discount and Loan Bank which was under the direction of "Monsieur Poliakoff" and in which neither the State Bank nor the Ministry of Finance had any direct interest. Moreover, Witte went on, Russia had neither sought nor obtained any political advantages, monopoly, or exclusive privileges in connection with this loan. When Scott feebly pointed to the fact that Persia was prohibited from borrowing abroad without the consent of the Russian gov-

71. Loan contract of 1900, Enclosure No. 2 in A. Hardinge to Lansdowne, No. 186, Confidential, Tehran, December 9, 1901; F. O. 60/645.

72. Secretary of State to Viceroy, February 1, 1900, Foreign, Secret, L.I., 70, 1900, No. 335.

ernment, Witte dismissed the objection: Persia could pay off the Russian debt any time and was then free to borrow anywhere. Scott, who must have been aware that Witte's every statement was an out and out lie, chose silence, since altercation would obviously have lead nowhere. Witte was firm.

The loan had been signed and completed and the present wants of Persia had thus been satisfied, there was therefore no occasion for further negotiations in the matter; if there had been any misunderstanding which had led H. M.'s Government to think they had been treated with any want of consideration in not being communicated with again before the negotiations for a loan were completed, he was not responsible for it, and he felt sure that neither Count Lamsdorff nor Count Muraviev had willingly misled me. The matter had been dealt with by him purely on its financial merit and being a private loan not undertaken by the Government, seemed to require no political treatment.[73]

The Russian loan was, Witte to the contrary notwithstanding, a purely political transaction. Poliakov and his partners had not negotiated it, nor would they have risked such a sum. The Discount and Loan Bank had long ago become a branch of the Russian State Bank at the service of S. Iu. Witte, who was the loan's principal architect. Russia had sought and attained several political advantages. She had become Persia's sole source of credit at least until 1910, and probably in perpetuity since Persia was not likely to repay the debt by 1910 but would certainly seek additional funds either before or after that date. This in itself was an enormous political advantage, albeit not the only one.

The promise of money had been dangled before the eyes of the Shah and the Grand Vizier to extract from them an engagement to prolong the "sterilizing" agreement in regard to railway construction. Foreseeing the end of the moratorium, Khomiakov, Tretiakov, and other entrepreneurs dusted off their old plans. Palashkovskii, a talented engineer, submitted a memorandum to the Ministry of Finance advocating the construction of an Indo-

73. Scott to Salisbury, No. 70, Confidential, St. Petersburg, March 10, 1900; F. O. 60/630.

European line through Persia. He frankly admitted that there could be no economic advantage from Persian trade: "What interest do we have in trading with seven or eight millions of lazy ragamuffins . . . ? The task of developing Russo-Persian trade must retreat . . . to the background before the task of monopolizing in the hands of our government the possession of all railway communications." Palashkovskii strongly advocated the construction of a line that would connect either the Caspian Sea or Russian railheads with the shores of the Indian Ocean or the Persian Gulf. Khomiakov and Tretiakov had a similar goal.[74]

What the Russian capitalists wanted was a chance to make money out of railway construction irrespective of the economic, political, or strategic considerations. Technical difficulties of spanning that rugged land would have been enormous, building expenses staggering, and profits to the builders correspondingly high. The capitalists were therefore willing to use any argument to persuade the government to begin the work. However, the Minister of Finance did not agree. Together with a number of most influential Russian statesmen, Witte was fascinated by the Far East, where he hoped for higher returns at lower risk. He wrote: "In the opinion of the Minister of Finance, we should for the time being limit ourselves to the improvement of these roads, for wheeled vehicles or pack animals, which at present connect the economic centers of Persia with the borders of Russia and the Caspian Sea coast."[75] German involvement in the Ottoman Empire and the rising specter of the Baghdad railroad provided the Russian government with additional motives to seek a prolongation of the moratorium on railway building in Persia.

The Ministry of Foreign Affairs urged K. M. Argyropoulo, Russian minister in Tehran, to obtain the Shah's written consent to an extension of the "sterilizing agreement." In his annual report to the Tsar for 1899, the Foreign Minister stated that, "The completion of the Persian loan was conditioned upon the satisfaction of our demands on this issue. The Shah hurried to accept them and to give our Minister a personal promise in the desired

---

74. A. Popov, "Stranitsa . . . ," pp. 145–46.
75. Cited in ibid., p. 146.

Loans, Concessions, and Power

sense."[76] In fact, Russia insisted upon obtaining the Shah's written promise before the completion of the loan negotiation.[77] His compliance with Russian demands elicited an expression of august satisfaction on the part of Nicholas II. This was duly conveyed to Argyropoulo, Amin os-Soltān, and Mozaffar ed-Din Shah.[78]

Sir Mortimer Durand knew he had lost the battle and perhaps the war. "The Russian loan is an accomplished fact," he wrote, "and for a time at least, probably for good, we shall greatly suffer in consequence. Sadr-i-Azam [Amin os-Soltān] had simply sold himself, and I have no doubt he has made various engagements which will militate against us."[79] The Shah's younger son, Shoā' os-Saltaneh, sent a message to the British minister saying that the Grand Vizier had systematically deceived and mislead His Majesty by convincing him of England's unfriendly attitude. "It was only under the impression that Russia was his only hope and that financial aid was absolutely necessary that His Majesty had finally with great reluctance acceded to the loan." Shoā' os-Saltaneh, who would soon become a close friend of the Russians, a Turkish subject, and a source of grave troubles for his country, complained that the government "was in the hands of a man who was more Russian than Persian" and that "no foreign advice could possibly reach the Shah from any but Russian sources if conveyed through the official channel."[80]

If Sir Mortimer blamed himself for having contributed to the Russian victory, he was certainly right. In various memoranda, starting in 1895, he lucidly exposed the dangers that threatened England's position in Persia and proposed many measures that could have improved it. He had received little support from

76. Ibid., p. 147.
77. Draft of a secret telegram to Privy Councillor Argyropoulo. Notation by the Tsar: "I agree. Tsarskoe selo, December 25, 1899/January 7, 1900; *Krasnyi Arkhiv*, 1 (56) (1933), 48.
78. Draft of a secret telegram to Argyropoulo, with the Tsar's notation: "I agree. St. Petersburg January 6/19, 1900"; ibid., p. 49.
79. Cited in Sykes, *Sir Mortimer Durand*, p. 245.
80. Memorandum of conversation [between C. Spring Rice and Shoā' os-Saltaneh], Enclosure No. 1, Durand to Salisbury, No. 13, Secret, Tehran, March 6, 1900; F. O. 60/630.

London and, at least until 1899, from India; yet his own actions had been far from wise.

Curzon wrote Sailsbury, "In view of Russian *mala fides* in respect of Persian loan . . . the moment is favourable for an intimation both to Russian and Persian Governments of our interest in Southern Persia, and our inability to acquiesce in any detriment to it." [81] But the old statesman, tired and in ill health, could only complain in an "injured tone" to General Mirzā Mohammad Khān Alā os-Saltaneh, Persian minister in London, about the Russian loan.

In a dispatch to Alā os-Saltaneh, which he was instructed to show Salisbury, Amin os-Soltān explained his behavior and placed the blame for Persia's acceptance of the Russian loan on the British. "It appears to us that we are more justified to complain than Lord Salisbury," the Grand Vizier wrote.

> In the matter of the loan we are not at all to blame—circumstances, on which we had no control, turned out thus. In fact, the blame rests with their own representatives.
>
> For nearly two years we tried every means of persuasion, and we even addressed entreaties in all directions: through the British Legation, through General (Sir T.) Gordon, who was in Tehran last year, and Mr. Rabino (Director and Manager respectively of the Imperial Bank of Persia) . . . hoping that we may obtain a loan of 60,000,000 fr. which we were in need of. . . .
>
> British representatives treated our words as nonsense, and pretended that everything we said was fiction. They believed that it was impossible for Persia to secure a loan on those conditions in any other quarter.

The British, he went on, now complained that the loan had been obtained without their knowledge, but they had been warned. They had even had conversations about it with the Russians at St. Petersburg.

In conclusion Amin os-Soltān unburdened himself of his old resentment of the studied arrogance affected by Sir Mortimer

---

81. From the Viceroy, Foreign, Secret, February 3, 1900; *L.I.*, 70, 1900, No. 335.

Durand, an arrogance that had been disapproved even by the staff of the British legation, and which the Persians would not forgive. The Shah himself had been repeatedly offended. Amin os-Soltān wrote that the Shah once said to him:

> "You remember a few months ago the British Minister asked me for an audience, and he presented himself before us with a walking-stick in his hand and dressed in a costume such as people wear when they go out for recreation or take a walk in the market place. Is it usual for any Representative to appear at an audience before a Sovereign in such a manner? The fact that we have borne everything in silence is a strong evidence of our great desire to maintain our friendly relations with Her Britannic Majesty's Government." [82]

Even the most optimistic English statesmen saw that the Russian loan to Persia was a severe blow to Britain's position in that country. Russian statesmen had no doubts on this score. The dislike, or even hatred, of England had long been one of the dominant emotions of Russian political life. The Crimean War left painful scars. Even a Turgenev, even an Apukhtin, could write venomous anti-English poems. Pan-Slavist propaganda intensified these feelings by stressing the pro-Turkish and therefore anti-Christian policies of perfidious Albion. Among the extreme nationalists and in certain military circles the idea of a march on India persisted over the decades. The successors of Kaufmann and Skobelev dreamed and made plans. As late as 1898 a Captain V. Lebedev of the Grenadier Guards published a work entitled *To India. A Military, Statistical, and Strategic Sketch. A project of a future campaign.* Lebedev anticipated the occupation of Herāt, Qandahār, and Kābul or perhaps, as a result of future victories over the English, "the creation of a Russo-Indian Empire, or a series of independent principalities, or an alliance of States under Russian suzerainty, or finally, an English retention of supremacy on the condition of a close alliance between Russia and En-

---

82. The Sadr-i-Azam to General Mirza Mohammed Khan, (Translation), undated telegram, communicated to Lord Salisbury February 28, 1900; F. O. 60/630.

gland." Lebedev's own views were relatively moderate. He wanted to establish a protectorate over Afghanistan and the area west of the Indus, leaving England in possession of the rest of India, and, of course, at the mercy of Russia.[83]

Right-wing Russian newspapers promoted hostility and created an atmosphere of tension by conducting a ceaseless campaign against the English, who were represented as murderous, decadent, and utterly contemptible. *Moskovskie Vedomosti* wrote:

> The English are shrieking "the Russians are at the gates of India," but at any rate the cry is premature. When our Ruler orders us we will go to that gate, but why cry out so early? Put your sentries at the gate, but do not venture out and occupy Afghanistan—our Buffer State—or else it will be the beginning of the end and "Finis Britanniae."
>
> Remember that our army is a united one, and as one man believes in God, the Czar, and Fatherland, and that the men are healthy and used to tropical climates, and are different to your siphilitical [sic] English, and the crowd of Natives of every creed and tribe.[84]

Even in works with scholarly pretentions one could read lines such as these:

> They [the English] looted directly, grabbing ships at sea, massacring villages of peaceful Negroes and Polynesians, and they looted indirectly—selling opium, preaching freedom of trade, concluding commercial treaties, promoting the abolition of slavery, unceremoniously establishing their colonies on alien land, sending their emissaries, organizing workers' strikes, finding "English interests" everywhere, etc., etc.[85]

The outbreak of war in South Africa brought anti-English sentiments to the boiling point. The *Sankt-Peterburgskie*

83. Enclosure A141, India Office, September 1, 1899; F. O. 65/1593.

84. *Moscow News* of September 9/21, 1897, Enclosure in Goschen to Salisbury, No. 233, St. Petersburg, September 28, 1897; F. O. 65/1534.

85. K. Skalkovskii, *Vneshniaia politika Rossii i polozhenie inostrannykh derzhav*, p. 116.

Vedomosti ran an article by a military writer who proclaimed that it was time "that we, using the opportune moment, achieve our ancient dreams of reaching the open ocean in the Near East." Bandar Abbās, Qeshm, Hormoz, Lārak, and Hengām must be acquired on the same basis as Port Arthur had been the year before. The Persian government was unlikely to raise obstacles, "it is too much in need of money, and therefore a considerable one-time payment and yearly subsidies will guarantee the success of our cause." However, if Russia failed to act, Britain would occupy the islands of the Persian Gulf as soon as the Transvaal question was settled.[86]

Even moderate papers joined the discussion. *Russakia Mysl* ran an article by "Old Diplomat" who argued that Afghanistan was of no use to Russia:

> What Russia wants is an outlet to the Indian Ocean, but the natural outlet is not through Afghanistan and India, but on the northern shore of the Persian Gulf. . . .
>
> Russia wants no territorial acquisitions in Persia. The uniting of many millions of Mussulmans under the Russian sceptre would only promote Panislamism. We can reach the Persian Gulf without encroaching upon the integrity of Persia.
>
> In view of historical and geographical conditions, Russia has already peacefully conquered the northern, and England the southern, part of Persia. The competition between Russians and English has up to now been a peaceful one, and if both parties strive for peace they can well work hand in hand in the half civilized land. If the Shah, recognizing that Russia wishes to maintain the national existence of Persia, and that a "rapprochement" with that powerful state would be advantageous, were to renew the Treaty concluded ten years ago, by which Russia was given the exclusive right to build railways in Persia [no such right had been given, of course], then all protests on the part of England would be of no avail, and without striking a blow we would acquire some port on

---

86. P. A. Rittikh in *Sankt-Peterburgskie Vedomosti*, No. 287, 1899, reprinted in his *Zheleznodorozhnyi put cherez Persiiu*, Appendix, p. x.

the Persian Gulf suitable for the outlet of a railway running through Persia from north to south.[87]

"Old Diplomat," who sounded more like a railway promoter, felt that the maintenance of buffer states between Russian and English possessions in Asia was a mistake. If England would give Russia an outlet on the Persian Gulf, Russia would not object to British "exploitation" of Afghanistan.

A young American diplomat in St. Petersburg heard a great deal of war talk but felt it was mostly bluff. British reverses in South Africa, he wrote, made many Russians wonder what would happen to England if she were confronted not with a bunch of Dutch peasants but with a great power such as Russia.

> These considerations cause a certain party here a strong feeling for an aggressive move by Russia at the present time against India, Persia and China, and I think it not at all unlikely that such would be made if another Emperor were on the throne. This one, though, hates war, and I think nothing will be done by Russia.[88]

The Russian government gave serious consideration to the possibility of using Britain's embarrassment in South Africa to further its own interest in the East. In January 1900 the Minister of Foreign Affairs, Count Murav'ev, presented to the Tsar a long paper that analyzed the situation and set forth a number of policy recommendations. Murav'ev wrote that over the last half century England had antagonized almost all states of continental Europe through her selfish policy. Taking advantage of their insular position and the might of their navy, "the English sowed discord and trouble among European and Asiatic peoples, always extracting some material advantage for themselves." No wonder the news of English reverses in South Africa "produced everywhere a feeling of moral satisfaction, not to say pleasure." The more deeply Britain got involved, the more clearly public opinion began to preach the necessity of taking advantage of the favorable mo-

87. *Russkaia Mysl* of March 26/April 8, 1900, Enclosure in Scott to Salisbury, No. 103, St. Petersburg, April 14, 1900; F. O. 65/1598.

88. H. Hagerman, *Letters of a Young Diplomat* (Santa Fe, 1937), pp. 131–32.

ment. As usual, the foreign press exaggerated the vague desires of the Russian public and wrote about vast Russian plans for the occupation of Kābul, Herāt, Persian Gulf ports, etc., "certain that Russia who considers England her ancient and most dangerous rival, would take advantage of her difficulties to deal her a sensible blow in Central Asia or the Far East." Such conclusions, Murav'ev stated grandly, had no basis in Russia's traditions. She had gone to war many times "in defense of oppressed peoples of the same faith" but had never been guided by self-interest, nor had she ever looked for gain from the misfortunes of her neighbors. However, since England's difficulties had already led other European states to seek their own gain, Russia should consider the question whether she too should take advantage of favorable circumstances for the solution of certain political issues.

Looking at other great powers, Murav'ev saw the United States definitely and openly refusing to get involved in any alliance. France, where they still remembered Fashoda, reached advantageous agreements with Britain in the old disputes in Shanghai and elsewhere in China. There was reason to suppose that Italy had received promises of British support for her aspirations in North Africa. Austria had no conflict with Britain. The German Emperor, in spite of pro-Boer public opinion in his country, decided to stay neutral. Thus each great power had made her own deals, and Russia could not get allies against England. What goals should she pursue?

The press was mentioning acquisitions in the Mediterranean, the Black Sea, and the Persian Gulf, but Murav'ev felt that Russia should occupy the Bosphorus only if some other power intended to move in. Turning to Persia, he reviewed recent Russian policies there. On the railway question he favored the "sterilizing" agreements since railways would only help British goods to invade northern Persia. In view of British desire to establish themselves firmly on the shores of the Persian Gulf, should not Russia take measures such as (1) the occupation of a port on the Persian Gulf, (2) a formal declaration that Russia would not tolerate any violation of Persia's territorial integrity, or (3) a friendly agreement with Britain on a division of Persia into spheres of influence? Murav'ev rejected the first possibility because a port on the Gulf could not be defended. An open declaration that Russia would not tolerate violations of Persian territorial integrity would "to some extent moderate England's expansionist designs, especially now when all her forces and her attention" were concentrated on the African continent.

> However, our promise at any moment to come to the defense of Persia's territorial rights would place upon us the quite heavy necessity of maintaining upon our border troops in perpetual war readiness, and, in any event, would deprive us of freedom of action in the north of Persia, where we are at present the only and complete masters.[89]

An agreement with Britain to divide Persia would not only be "contrary to the traditions of Russian policy" but would arouse the most harmful discussion in Tehran without bringing Russia any practical gain. In fact, a division of Persia into spheres of influence would give Russia the north and Britain the south,

> but, as has been said above, the north of Persia is in Russia's hands any way and is entirely inaccessible to foreigners; by acknowledging officially England's right to act unilaterally in the south, where her influence is far from being firmly exclusive, we thereby, ahead of time, voluntarily put up a barrier to our further entirely possible movement beyond the limits of Persia's northern provinces.

Murav'ev's prose was turgid and confused, but his intentions were simple and clear. Russia must not in any way erect obstacles to her future southward movement in Persia.

The most effective means of fighting the British on Persian soil was the encouragement of Russian enterprises, the construction of roads leading to Russia, the development of shipping on the Caspian, the improvement of the harbor at Anzali and of postal and telegraphic communications. The recent loan gave Russia a powerful instrument for the strengthening of her economic position and of her "political charm in Persia." [90]

89. Copy of a memorandum of the Minister of Foreign Affairs, "1900. Personnel et très-secret. No. 29," *Krasnyi Arkhiv*, 5 (18) (1926), 4–18.
90. Id.

Murav'ev listed specific proposals:
The Sultan should be stopped from fortifying the Bosphorus and prevented from granting concessions in the provinces on the Black Sea shore. The British government should be informed that Russia would establish direct relations with Afghanistan. Later on, a diplomatic mission should be sent to Kābul. Russia should continue to bring her Turkestan and Transcaspian troops to the state of war readiness.

Such measures always produce an impressive effect upon the British Government, which is aware of the vulnerability of its possessions bordering on Russia and the weakness of its dominion over the freedom loving Indian tribes, whose hostile attitude toward England would, in all probability, increase after her unsuccessful war in the Transvaal.

Russia should speed up railway surveys in Persia and begin the construction of lines in Transcaucasia which would eventually serve as links to a Persian railway system. She should also speed up the construction of the Orenburg-Tashkent line "because of the specially important political, strategic, and commercial significance of this road." She should encourage and cooperate in the development of Russian industrial and commercial enterprises in Persia, promote the construction of highways, which, according to the War Ministry, were of greatest strategic importance, and develop Caspian fishing as well as postal and telegraphic communications.

Russia should continue to strengthen her troops in the Amur Military District and the Kwantung peninsula, and should develop and equip Port Arthur and build a railway over Kwantung. She should not lose sight of the fact that a strong navy was necessary to keep up her might in the Pacific.[91]

Murav'ev's memorandum was circulated to the ministries of the Navy, War, and Finance. Admiral P. P. Tyrtov took a dim view and was sorry that "Russia gains nothing from England's present difficult situation," while all the other powers were making substantial gains. Only Russia would remain vis-à-vis England

91. Id.

in the same position as before, and would be certain to find her in the enemy camp. Any weakening of England was to Russia's advantage, yet Murav'ev had proposed no action except the opening of direct relations with Afghanistan and the attempt to prevent Turkey from fortifying the Bosphorus. Tyrtov agreed with Murav'ev that distant naval bases were useless, meaning bases in the Persian Gulf. His own interests lay in the Far East. He wanted a naval base in Korea.[92]

General Aleksei Nikolaevich Kuropatkin began his comments with a ringing declaration of faith: "I recognize the firm military occupation of the Bosphorus as the most important task of Russia in the present twentieth century. . . . Before this task all other tasks listed in the memorandum have relatively small significance in the nearest historical period." Kuropatkin generally agreed with Murav'ev on Persia but felt that sooner or later Russia would have to reach an agreement with Britain. He deemed it his duty to warn that the military could not give support to negotiations with England in regard to Persia until the completion of a railway connecting European Russia with Central Asia.[93] Like Tyrtov, Kuropatkin was listening to his own thoughts and conducting a monologue in the guise of a critique of Murav'ev's paper.

The Minister of Finance, S. Iu. Witte, pointed out that the measures advocated by Murav'ev would cost a great deal of money. The Siberian railway, a line across Manchuria to Vladivostok, a South Manchurian line, the Orenburg-Tashkent or the Uralsk-Chārjuy line, the occupation of Port Arthur and the defense of occupied territories, all were important but expensive tasks. Excessive strain on the productive capacity of the people, the only source of wealth, would weaken Russia even if particular successes were achieved here and there. The expansion of military forces in Central Asia would make new demands on funds, which were needed elsewhere, and would provoke Britain to increase her own armaments. Thus even if Russia built up a force larger than she had now she would be no stronger relative to other powers.

92. Director of the Ministry of the Navy to the Minister of Foreign Affairs, February 14/27, 1900, No. 341, Very secret; *Krasnyi Arkhiv*, ibid., 18–20.

93. Letter of the War Minister to the Minister of Foreign Affairs, February 16/29, 1900, Very Secret, ibid., pp. 21–22.

In regard to Persia, Witte, who was much more interested in that country than either Kuropatkin or Tyrtov, wrote that his ministry was already considering building highways and assisting in the development of Russian enterprises. In conclusion, Witte flung Murav'ev a challenge to achieve his ends through purely diplomatic means: "Of course, it is hard to create anything without money; but in the political sphere much can be achieved through the art of diplomacy, which is proved by the Ministry entrusted to your excellency." [94]

The Tsar, who was the final arbiter of foreign policy, was undecided. Weak and selfish, Nicholas saw himself at one moment as a great promoter of universal peace, at the next as a world conqueror. In 1898, out of dire necessity, he championed the cause of peace and disarmament; through most of his reign he dreamed of conquest and had no compunctions about going to war. His War Minister, General Kuropatkin, recorded in his diary:

> I told Witte that our sovereign had grandiose plans in his head: to take Manchuria for Russia, to move toward the annexation of Korea to Russia. He dreams of taking under his orb Tibet too. He wants to take Persia, to seize not only the Bosphorus but the Dardanelles as well.[95]

The Tsar, according to Kuropatkin, felt that his ministers were preventing him from realizing his dreams because, unlike him, they failed to understand what would redound to Russia's advantage and glory.

In the end caution prevailed. Murav'ev, though a strong imperialist, was not an adventurer. He sounded out the French as to whether they would join Russia against Britain. Théophile Delcassé professed interest but wanted assurances of safety from Germany. Berlin was willing to participate provided St. Petersburg and Paris joined it in a mutual guarantee of each other's possessions. Russia got nowhere in Europe. In Asia she acted alone. The troops in Turkestan and Transcaspia were reenforced,

94. Letter of the Minister of Finance to the Minister of Foreign Affairs, February 10/23, 1900, No. 28, Very secret; ibid., pp. 22–25.
95. "Dnevnik A. N. Kuropatkina," *Krasnyi Arkhiv*, 2 (1922), 31.

and, in February, Russia informed Britain that needs of commerce and territorial proximity no longer allowed her to abstain from direct political relations with Afghanistan. Russian troops had already been concentrated on the Afghan frontier. Britain, isolated and mired in South Africa, bowed to the inevitable. Peace was preserved.

The intensification of Russian activity in Persia, plainly observable ever since the death of Nāser ed-Din Shah, worried many an English statesman but none more than the Viceroy of India, George N. Curzon. He was exceptionally well informed about Persia, having diligently studied the country and produced a two-volume work which has never been surpassed. He was also a convinced and avowed imperialist.

> "Rightly or wrongly," he told his constituents . . . in 1893, "it appears to me that the continued existence of this country is bound up in the maintenance—aye I will go further and say even in the extension of the British Empire." In glowing sentences he proudly proclaimed himself the convinced and fervent apostle of new Imperialism. When in some distant future Great Britain stood at the bar of history, upon what, he asked, would she be judged? . . . She would be judged, not by her achievements in the domain of domestic legislation, but by the marks she has left on the peoples, the religions, and the morals of the world.[96]

Curzon's appointment to India had been greeted by the Russian press as a challenge to Russia in Central Asia and the Middle East. The press had been right. Less than a year after assuming the post of Viceroy, Curzon dispatched to the Cabinet a long memorandum on Persia, pointing out that there existed in Britain no clear definition of principles upon which a policy toward Persia could be based. Persia was in decay, saved from extinction mostly by the rival ambitions of two great powers who were the real arbiters of her destiny.

> A nation and a government, such as the Persian, may tremble for long upon the verge of certain dissolution, from the

96. Ronaldshay, *The Life of Lord Curzon*, 1, 192–93.

absence of the particular impulse that is required to propel them over the brink. But in the last resort, and often by accident, the impetus is communicated, and the already shattered structure tumbles into irretrievable ruin.[97]

British interests in Persia, Curzon wrote, fell into three categories: commercial, political, and strategic. The latter were of the greatest concern to the Government of India, yet he insisted that he did not contemplate the establishment of a protectorate or the defense of any part of the Shah's realm by force of arms. Not yet, at any rate.

> We can conceive of circumstances that might some day tempt both the Indian and the home Governments from this attitude of reserve, and that would, in a case where the vital interests of the Empire were at stake, force us to consider a burden for which our shoulders are still unprepared. But for the present our ambitions are exclusively limited to making secure the interest which we have already built up, and still more to preventing it from being undermined or taken from us by others, with the result not only of a considerable accretion of strength to them, but a positive detriment to ourselves.[98]

Geography and history gave Russia a dominant position in northern Persia. Britain would do best to concentrate her efforts in the center and south. It was there that she had made the largest investments in trade, shipping, roads, and telegraphs, and it was there that her main strategic interest lay. Curzon gave a detailed account of recent Russian penetration into central and southern Persia and to the shores of the Persian Gulf.

> We desire deliberately to say to Your Lordship, with full consciousness of our responsibility in so saying that difficult as we find it in existing circumstances to meet the financial and military strain imposed upon us by the ever increasing proximity of Russian power upon the northern and north-

97. Curzon's Memorandum of September 21, 1899; F. O. 60/615. Published in full in J. C. Hurewitz, *Diplomacy in the Near and Middle East*, 1, 219–49.
98. Id., 10.

western frontiers of India from the Pamirs to Herat, we could not contemplate without dismay the prospect of Russian neighbourhood in Eastern or Southern Persia, the inevitable consequence of which must be a great increase of our own burdens.[99]

Britain and Russia had repeatedly stated their desire to maintain the integrity and independence of Persia, but

Within the limits of a nominally still existing integrity and independence so many encroachments upon both these attributes are possible, that by almost imperceptible degrees they pass into the realm of constitutional fiction, where they may continue to provide an excercise for the speculations of the jurist, long after they have been contemptuously ignored by statesmen.[100]

In the past the English had often hoped for the regeneration of Persia under the joint auspices of the two great powers. This policy had been discussed and rejected by Sir Mortimer Durand in his memorandum of September 1895.

We concur with Her Majesty's Minister [Curzon wrote] in believing that the reform of Persia by a policy of cooperation between Russia and ourselves is out of the question; and we do so in the main for the reason, which no one familiar with Persia will deny, that Russia is interested not in the reform of Persia, but in its decay; that in the background of her ambition is the vision of a country and a people falling from inherent debility into her grasp; and that any policy which might tend to strengthen the country or to revivify its people, is to be resisted as tending to thwart the fulfillment of those ambitions.[101]

While Russia would not cooperate in regenerating Persia, might she not be induced to divide the country into spheres of interest such as had been recently established by the great powers in

99. Id., 48.
100. Id., 52.
101. Id., 53.

Loans, Concessions, and Power 343

China in regard to railway concessions? Curzon saw the many advantages division would bring, but also the drawbacks. How would one divide the country, and where would the line be drawn? What of Tehran, which was located in the north and would fall into the Russian sphere, making a puppet of the Shah and a proconsulate of northern Persia?

> we do not conceal our anticipation that in the long run such a partition might involve the permanent break up of the Persian Kingdom, and, if it did not ultimately lead to rival Russian and British Protectorates in the north and south, might at any rate result in the selection of another capital, and the rule of more than one native prince in Persia.[102]

Moreover, Russia would still be able to reach the Persian Gulf, either via Mesopotamia or by simply disregarding her promises, as she had done in the past in Central Asia. In spite of all these reservations. Cuzon expressed the opinion that "the experiment of an understanding with Russia as to future spheres of interest . . . is worthy of being made, in the interests both of Persia itself, and still more of harmony between the two great Powers, upon whose relations the peace of Asia may be said to depend." [103]

Curzon then proceeded to make dozens of specific recommendations for British and Indian actions in Persia: the increase of the consular establishment, the furtherance of naval visits to the Persian Gulf ports, the better organization of the telegraph service, and so forth. The all-important question "as to the steps that require forthwith to be taken in order to safeguard British and Indian interests in the so-called British sphere in Persia" he left to the government in London.

Persia had long held an important place in Curzon's mind. In the spring and summer of 1899, when Britain was preoccupied with events in South Africa, he wrote that Kruger was a mere speck of froth on the surface of the ocean.

> If only I could transfer a little of the misplaced anxiety about the Transvaal to Persia and the Persian Gulf, and could get

102. Id., 59.
103. Id., 62.

people at home to see that every month, and still more every year, spent in doing nothing is aggravating a danger that will shortly be at our doors, I should be glad.[104]

In the midst of African troubles few members of the Cabinet were prepared to accept the Viceroy's view, least of all Lord George F. Hamilton, Secretary of State for India.

Upon reading the memorandum, Hamilton wrote Curzon privately that his whole argument was based on the assumption that, "in certain eventualities, we should exercise force to maintain our position in that country" [Persia]. Could Britain possibly resort to force and win in Persia? Hamilton believed not.[105]

Curzon was losing patience. Ever since his arrival in India he had been trying to alert the government. London paid no attention, and he began to sound like a prophet of doom: "One day the crash will come, and then my Despatches will be published and in my grave I shall be justified. Not that I care for that. But I long to see prescience, some width of view, some ability to forecast the evil of tomorrow, instead of bungling over the evil of today." [106]

Months passed, and the India Office maintained a disconcerting silence. The Viceroy watched the Russians grant Persia a monopolistic loan, appoint consuls to new areas, and even invade the quiet waters of the Persian Gulf. On March 16 he telegraphed a reminder to Lord George Hamilton that he had been waiting for six months for a reply to his memorandum. The time had arrived to make "some clear announcement to the Persian Government concerning the nature and extent of the interests of Great Britain and India in Southern Persia." In an obviously sarcastic tone he added: "Presumably it is intended that they should be maintained." [107]

Sir W. Lee Warner, Undersecretary of State at the India Office, wrote a minute suggesting a number of possible actions.

104. Viceroy to the Secretary of State, May 3, 1899, cited in Ronaldshay, 2, 67.
105. Hamilton to Curzon, November 2, 1899, cited in Ronaldshay, 2, 100–01.
106. Curzon to Mrs. Cragie, cited *ibid*.
107. Telegram from Viceroy, March 16, 1900; L.I., 70, 1899.

Loans, Concessions, and Power

The English, he stated, might be content to limit their sphere of influence to the Gulf south of Bushehr.

This would leave Russia and Germany elbow room in the N. of the Gulf. Then, as regards the part of the Gulf in which we mean to claim interest, I would suggest that we inform Persia of our desire to see her independence maintained, and add that if, despite our wishes, it were jeopardized by the intrusion of Russian control on the sea line near to and below Bushire we should be obliged to take precautionary measures. Of course, Persia might say, "Well, if you are interested in my independence join me in an attack on Russia," but we need not lay ourselves open to that challenge. We sincerely desire Persian independence, and will not ourselves begin the game of scramble and take. But if Persia does begin to give way, we shall reserve a veto and an occupation.[108]

The strikingly new element in the above paragraph was the willingness to give up the monopoly of the Gulf and to concede to both Germany and Russia certain rights at least in its northern part, a decisive retreat from the traditional British position. Sir W. Lee Warner was not alone in his views. A sharp difference of opinion developed between the proponents of firmness and the advocates of accommodation, activist imperialists and those who felt that Britain at best could hope to hang on to her possessions but should on no account extend her commitments.

Lord George Hamilton, Secretary of State for India, belonged to the small but increasingly influential group which took the second view. It was inevitable that he should clash with the Viceroy of India, an open and devoted imperialist. Stimulated by Curzon's telegram of March 16 and W. Lee Warner's minute, Hamilton composed a memorandum apparently intended for circulation within the India Office. This remarkable document deserves to be quoted at length.[109]

108. Minute Paper, Register No. 338, Secret Department, Telegram from the Viceroy dated 16th March, 1900, By W. L. W. Subject: Persia, The maintenance of British influence; ibid.

109. As far as I know it has never been published.

In our constant struggle against the growth of Russian influence in Turkey, China, and Persia [Hamilton began], we recently have not sufficiently acknowledged the changed conditions under which the contest proceeds. As Russia annexes territory she contrives with adroitness and determination to so assimilate the territory absorbed that in a short time it becomes a reliable stepping stone for a fresh move. Our base of operations is the sea. We remain where we are: Russia steadily moves on. Our influence stands still: Russia's progresses. We lay down a policy asserting the independence of the country we wish to preserve: Russia gains on land so dominant a position near the capital of the country so guaranteed that the use the sovereign independence is put to is to give to her under cover of concessions and monopolies practical control over a large portion of the country. . . . Our influence in Northern Persia is gone. Do what we like Russia could annex that part of Persia without our being able to effectively resist her. Shall we play the same game in Southern Persia, with the probability of the same result in the future? A nebulous policy supported mainly by bluff must fail when it comes in contact with fixed objects supported by superior material force.

Looking at the past, Hamilton saw England's successes based on her power to concentrate naval forces which no one nation could withstand. Railways had made it possible for others to enjoy on land advantages the British used to enjoy on the sea. But the English had not adapted their policies to new conditions. They constantly asserted their interests over more territories than they could absorb, utilize, or protect. In consequence their assertions, even if acknowledged in theory, were ignored in practice. England enjoyed a monopoly of trade in the Persian Gulf, but could it be maintained? Did England have the right "to say that the civilized world is to be deprived of the benefits of railway access to the Persian Gulf, because it will infringe on the monopoly of sea-borne traffic we there possess?" Could England exclude others from Persia because Persia was next to Baluchestān and Baluchestān next to India? Facts must be faced.

Loans, Concessions, and Power

Britain had interests in the Gulf and in eastern Persia and a prior right to control or annex that territory if Persia broke up. She could not allow Bandar Abbās or any port east of that town to become a coaling station for a foreign navy. England might even claim Bushehr.

> Let us concentrate our attention on that which is essential to us, which we can hold, and let us not interfere with Germany getting her foot in the region. Let us, without in any way encouraging Russia to get a port in the Gulf, avoid basing our whole policy upon the idea that we ought to and can ultimately prevent her from accomplishing this object. By more definitely stating what we want and what Russia is not to have, we may quicken the extension of Russian influence outside the area upon which we have a lien, but we shall avoid the double mortification of knowing that we are pursuing a policy which not only must fail, but which in the process of its failure unites foreign nations against us.[110]

Hamilton's basic assumptions failed to win the day. However, they were largely adopted by men who shaped Britain's foreign policies during the decade immediately preceding the First World War.

It was July 1900 before Curzon received Hamilton's reply to his memorandum of September 1899. Essentially, Hamilton repeated and amplified the views expressed in his intradepartmental memorandum dated April 3, 1900. Russia had already won northern Persia and dominated most of the rest of the country by virtue of her geographical position. As for the Gulf, Hamilton drew the Viceroy's attention to "events . . . which have already modified that theory of 'unchallenged supremacy both naval and commercial'" to which Curzon had referred in his memorandum of September 1899.

> France has recently asserted her right to a joint protectorate over Muscat. . . . Germany is interested in the development of railway enterprise and her agents have lately proceeded

110. Memorandum by G[eorge] H[amilton], No. 338, April 3, 1900; L.I., 70, 1899.

to Kowait. Russian ships have visited Bunder Abbas and adjoining islands, as well as other ports in the Gulf. In these and various other ways the unquestioned position which was formerly asserted and exercised by us, has, even in the Gulf itself, been encroached upon.[111]

Hamilton saw no purpose in opening negotiations with Russia to delimit spheres of interest in Persia. The Russians might inform the Shah, who would take it to mean that Britain was ready to partition his realm. However, the government had taken certain measures to protect British interests in the south. On April 15, 1899, Lord Salisbury informed the Persian government "that it would not be compatible with the interests of the British Empire that any European power should exercise control or jurisdiction over the ports of the Persian Gulf." Moreover, on March 20, 1900, Her Majesty's chargé d'affaires in Tehran was instructed to remind the Persians of their written promise of October 23, 1897, that the southern customs "shall never be placed under foreign supervision or control." In conclusion Hamilton wrote:

> Your Excellency may be assured that all vigilance will be exercised in closely watching the course of affairs in Persia, and that whilst Her Majesty's Government do not propose to adopt for the moment any departure from their past line of action, they readily admit that conditions there may so alter as to necessitate some change in the procedure and measures required for protecting Indian interests in Persia.[112]

The Viceroy and the Government of India had clearly been defeated, but Curzon was not one easily to acknowledge defeat. In an official dispatch of September 6, 1900, he denied that Russia's position in the north allowed her "to dominate and threaten the whole of Persia." In the name of the Government of India he wrote: "We think that the extent to which she is permitted to do so still depends even more upon the action of

111. To H. E. the Right Honourable Governor-General of India in Council, Secret, No. 14, India Office, London, July 6, 1900; ibid.
112. Id.

Her Majesty's Government than it does upon her own."[113] In private letters Curzon was even more emphatic. He was prepared, if Russia struck in the north, to strike back in the south. "I would at once send a force and seize and hold Bunder Abbas, Bushire, or Mohammerah, or all three. That would bring matters to a head." To St. John Brodrick, Secretary of War, Curzon wrote that the whole explanation of Britain's troubles was that "for years no British Minister has consented to look one year ahead." There had been no foresight and no policy. "You have none now for China, Persia, Morocco, Egypt, or any place in the world." Lord Salisbury, Curzon claimed, was adept at handling the present, but the future to him was anathema. Salisbury must have been growing impatient with the learned but passionate Viceroy, of whom he quipped: "He wants me to negotiate with Russia as if I had 500,000 men at my back, and I have not."[114]

His correspondent, St. John Brodrick, tried to moderate Curzon's outbursts.

> You may say that inaction spells future trouble; but, if you were here, I doubt if you would give France, Germany, and Russia a chance of coming together on anything even if that anything were Muscat, Koweit and Bunder Abbas. Don't resent my saying this; I am, as you know, of the forward school and am oppressed by the sometimes needless inertia; but your views, which are well known, rather perturb Arthur [Balfour, First Lord of the Treasury, soon to succeed Salisbury as Prime Minister] and others who are as keen as yourself, because times are difficult.[115]

Both Curzon's desire for a firm policy and Hamilton's discouragement in the face of Russian achievements in Persia could exist side by side in the same mind. Cecil Spring Rice, a secretary of the British legation in Tehran, fully realized in 1899 that Persia was crumbling. "The harvest is in," he wrote, "but the price of

---

113. The Government of India, Foreign Department, Secret, to Lord George F. Hamilton, Secretary of State for India, No. 127, Simla, September 6, 1900; L.I., 76, 1900, No. 1017.
114. Ronaldshay, *The Life of Lord Curzon*, 2, 206.
115. St. John Brodrick to Curzon, August 8, 1901, as cited in ibid., p. 207.

bread keeps up . . . The people are exasperated and talk of looting the Imperial Bank to attract attention of the Government." A new governor cut off the ears of three bakers, which reduced the price of bread for a short time. The Jews were persecuted, but that too proved ineffective. "Between Persia and revolution is the Cossack regiment, officered by Russians, but they are not paid and there is no money to pay them with." [116]

Spring Rice knew that in England they talked about partitioning Persia. Europeans in Tehran, as well as the Persians, laughed at the idea. Russia did not seem to want to annex any part of Persia.

> But if she wants anything she wants the whole. Persia is the route by which she intends to reach the sea, and one end of a road is not much use without the other. Everyone here says "Russia wants the whole and not the part, and you can never come to an agreement with her to stop anywhere." She has been sending agents south and pressing her influence for all it is worth, and wherever there is an enemy of British power or commerce, the agent of Russia is sure to be in communication.

But Russia was not in a hurry. She would not occupy the north for fear of a British occupation of the south, "so that while she opened one door we locked the other." Russia's best policy, Spring Rice felt, was "gradually to prepare the ground, to disintegrate Persia, and prevent Persia improving. To wait an opportunity when England is engaged somewhere and to make a pounce." [117]

Spring Rice had the feeling that Britain would not defend her interests, that she would make declarations while Russia acted. As for Persia, "The Government here is so bad and corrupt and hopelessly disorganized that the people would almost welcome a foreign ruler—at any rate at first." [118] There was really nothing Britain could do to save the situation.

116. S. Gwynn, ed., *The Letters and Friendships of Sir Cecil Spring Rice* (London, 1929), 1, 283.
117. To Villiers, August 23, 1899; ibid., pp. 285–86.
118. Same to same, January 19, 1900; ibid., p. 313.

When the predominance of one power over the other is so marked as that of Russia over England here; it is best to acknowledge it. This does not suit the papers or perhaps Foreign Office, but it is safer to stick to facts. Order is kept in this town [Tehran] by a Russian colonel and his Russian drilled troops, by the guns which the Czar gave and by the advice which the Russians are giving. Finances have been for a time set in order by a Russian loan. Corn is brought into the starving city by a Russian road. We have done nothing and given nothing and we cannot expect to get anything. Will Lord Salisbury insist on English officers being employed in the Persian Army? Will Parliament lend Persia two million, or vote another million for a road from the sea to the north? No, because it won't pay.[119]

The debate on Persian policy continued for the next several years. However, in the spring and summer of 1900 it was overshadowed by immediate dangers that threatened Britain's position in Asia. Rumors of Russian troop movements were confirmed by British Military Intelligence whose director, Sir John Ardagh, stated that, "The anticipation that Russia would profit by our embarrassments in South Africa is already fully justified." He informed the Cabinet that from sixty to one hundred and fifty thousand troops were to be concentrated on the Afghan border.

This displacement of troops is capable of no other interpretation than that of a menace designedly made at the moment when we are least capable of resenting it. . . . It is an act of insolence on the part of the powerful faction of military adventurers who have so large an influence over the policy of Russia, and is proportioned to the opportunity and the temptation afforded by our military position, to remedy which should now engross our whole attention.[120]

Sir Charles Scott, British ambassador in St. Petersburg, believed that the rumors of troop movements should not be treated lightly. The "military party" was extremely powerful, and "since

119. To Ferguson, May 28, 1900; ibid., pp. 319–20.
120. Memorandum by Sir John Ardagh, Director of Military Intelligence, Secret, Intelligence Division, February 5, 1900; F. O. 65/1614.

the Crimean war it has never been so violently hostile to England" as at that moment. Nothing would be more popular "in that part at least of the Russian army which is situated in Trans-Caspia and the Caucasus than a decision of the Emperor to take advantage of our present entanglements to make some advance southwards either into Afghan or Persian territory." The ambassador reported rumors that munitions factories in Kolomna and Mytishchi had received large orders from the Ministry of War for delivery the next spring, and that British merchants noticed unusually large troop traffic across the Caspian Sea.[121]

The visit of the Russian gunboat *Giliak* to the Persian Gulf stirred up further excitement in India and London. Curzon asked for instructions that could be issued to the navy "in the event of the Russians landing men and either hoisting their flag or endeavouring an occupation." The Viceroy suggested that in such a case the naval officer in command of the area should protest to the Russians and, if the protests were disregarded, proceed to occupy the islands of Hormoz, Qeshm, or any others the navy considered suitable for a base. Salisbury requested the Admiralty to issue such instructions to the Senior Naval Officer in the Persian Gulf. The navy was to keep the instructions absolutely secret and not to act unless the Russians took steps "clearly indicating the intention to effect an occupation or to hoist the Russian flag on Persian territory." [122] No Russian troops landed in the Persian Gulf; none crossed the Persian or the Afghan frontier. Russia looked to the Far East for new territorial acquisitions. She chose to fight Britain in Persia by other than military means.

The money the Shah had borrowed from Russia in 1900 lasted but a few months. Early in 1901 the Persian government was once again on the verge of bankruptcy. In March, Amin os-Soltān approached the Imperial Bank of Persia for an advance of £200,000. Sir Arthur Hardinge, Durand's successor as British minister at Tehran, urged his government to make it possible for the bank

121. Scott to Salisbury, No. 42, Very confidential, St. Petersburg, February 7, 1900; F. O. 65/1598.
122. T. H. Sanderson to the Admiralty, Very confidential, F. O., February 14, 1900; F. O. 60/733.

to lend the requisite sum by depositing to its credit in London £200,000 and authorizing an advance of the same amount to Persia.[123] The British government did not find it possible to subsidize the proposed advance. However, unlike its response in 1899, it did promise to recognize as binding any engagements the Persian government might make to guarantee the loan.[124]

From the outset the negotiations between Amin os-Soltān and Sir Arthur Hardinge took a familiar form. The Imperial Bank worried about its charter, which prohibited the lending of an amount larger than one third of its total capital. The Foreign Office complained of its inability to guarantee the loan. The minister in Tehran urged that money be found. Amin os-Soltān repeated that he must have funds. And the Russians bided their time.

The Grand Vizier knew that another large loan from Russia would be unpopular and would push his country further into the ever-tightening embrace of its northern neighbor. He would have liked to balance things out by borrowing from the Imperial Bank which, as a Persian institution, could lend to the Persian government without violating the restrictive provisions of the Russian loan agreement of 1900. He asked Sir Arthur whether it would be possible for the bank to lend money at 8 instead of 12 percent interest. Hardinge replied that it was in Persia's interest to support the bank by giving it business. Should the bank fail, Russia would have a financial monopoly, and Persia would be at her mercy.[125]

Unknown to Hardinge, Amin os-Soltān had begun in May new loan negotiations with Russia. However, he encountered serious difficulties because of Russia's resentment of a concession recently granted an Englishman in the South. That another concession had been bought from the Shah by foreigners was not in itself a matter to worry the Russian government. Hardly a year

123. A. Hardinge to Lansdowne, Telegram, No. 36, July 13, 1901; Memorandum on the Financial Assistance to Persia, Confidential; F. O. 60/645.

124. Francis Bertie [at the Foreign Office] to the Imperial Bank of Persia, August 3, 1901; Memorandum on the Financial Assistance to Persia; ibid.

125. A. Hardinge to Lansdowne, No. 138, Confidential, Gulahek, September 16, 1901; ibid.

passed without some privilege or other being surrendered for cash.[126] Yet the manner in which this particular concession had been granted and its very nature were bound to arouse the ire of the Russian government and most of all of the Minister of Finance, Witte.

In 1892 Jacques de Morgan, French archaeologist, published a paper in *Les Annales des Mines* claiming that oil deposits existed in southwestern Persia. Edouard Cotte, once Baron de Reuter's agent in Tehran, brought Morgan's findings to the attention of General Ketābchi Khān, Persia's Commissioner General at the Paris Exposition of 1900. The latter approached Sir Henry Drummond Wolff, who introduced him to William Knox D'Arcy, an Englishman who had made a fortune in Australian gold.[127] D'Arcy sent Ketābchi Khān, Cotte, and Alfred M. Marriott, onetime French diplomat, now D'Arcy's agent, to Tehran to negotiate an oil concession. The trio was equipped with a letter of introduction to the British minister written by Sir Henry Drummond Wolff. The methods used by Marriott, Cotte, and Ketābchi Khān were the same as those of all concession hunters in Tehran: bribery and political pressure. When asking Sir Arthur Hardinge to use his influence in furthering D'Arcy's application, Marriott frankly told him that a number of shares in the future oil company would be offered to the Persian Prime Minister.[128] Hardinge understood the potential significance of the venture but was quite sceptical about its chances of success.

---

126. As a matter of fact, that same spring the Discount and Loan Bank negotiated to build a road from Tabriz to Qazvin, a commercially important undertaking with clear military implications. The contract was signed in July 1901. The Russian bank would build the highway and hold rights to coal and oil within an area of 10 farsakhs (60 kilometers) stretching all along the road. The bank would set the tolls. Profits above 15 percent of capital invested would be equally divided yearly between the bank and the Persian government. Iran, Archive of the Ministry of Foreign Affairs, File 44/Folder 4, Registry 10, 1326.

127. There exists no detailed history of the Anglo-Persian Oil Company. B. Shwadran gives a brief account of its early years in his book, *The Middle East Oil and the Great Powers* (New York, 1955), pp. 15–40. S. H. Longrigg's *Oil in the Middle East* (London, 1954) conceals more than it reveals. N. S. Fatemi, in *Oil Diplomacy* (New York, 1957), is quite partisan, as are most of the writers on the subject be they English or Persian.

128. A. Hardinge, *A Diplomatist in the East* (London, 1928), p. 278.

If the hopes of the concessionaires are realized, and petroleum is discovered, as their agents believe will be the case, in sufficient quantities to compete with Bakou, the Concession may be fraught with important economic and, indeed, political, results. But the soil of Persia, whether it contains oil, or not, has been strewn of late years with the wrecks of so many hopeful schemes of commercial and political regeneration that it would be rash to attempt to predict the future of this latest venture.[129]

Soon after the opening of negotiations between D'Arcy's representatives and the Persian government, Hardinge "took an opportunity, as an important British enterprise was at stake, of intimating to the Atabeg-i-Azam [a new and higher title recently bestowed upon Amin os-Soltān by Mozaffar ed-Din Shah] his conviction that the investment of a large amount of British capital in Persia would be greatly to the advantage of that country." Amin os-Soltān replied that he had been all along in favor of the scheme and promised to do "his best to promote both this and all other British commercial undertakings." [130]

So great was Amin os-Soltān's personal interest in the concession that he kept the entire transaction secret, "as it was felt that if the Russian Legation got news of the project, it would attempt to crush it, and would almost certainly succeed in doing so." [131]

In his memoirs, Hardinge tells an amusing story of how Amin os-Soltān, wishing to insure himself against the wrath of his friend, the Russian minister Argyropoulo, suggested that a letter be drawn up by Hardinge embodying the main features of the proposed concession. This was submitted to the Russian legation at a time when its Oriental secretary, Stritter, was away on a brief vacation. Since no one else at the legation could read the Persian *shekasteh* script, no objections were made by the Russian minister for several days, giving the Persian government enough time to sign the contract.[132] In fact it was Amin os-Soltān himself who

129. Sir A. Hardinge to Lord Lansdowne, No. 16, Commercial, Confidential, Gulahek, May 30, 1901; F. O. 60/660 and F. O. 60/731.
130. Id.
131. Id.
132. A. Hardinge, pp. 278–79.

broke the news to an unhappy Argyropoulo. Since the Russian minister was convinced of Amin os-Soltān's Russophilia, he tried to explain the Grand Vizier's action to St. Petersburg in the most favorable light. Amin os-Soltān, he wrote,

> was undoubtedly guided by the desire to lessen English dissatisfaction with him so as to stop their participation in intrigues directed against him. . . . by pleasing the English he was probably counting on eliminating the opposition, be it even indirect, of A. Hardinge to the commercial agreement with Russia and compelling him to forgive the severity of customs regulations introduced in Southern Persia.[133]

The Russian Foreign Ministry reacted angrily and crudely. Argyropoulo was instructed to make Amin os-Soltān understand that "as long as he is in power, the repetition of anything like that, will not be forgiven by the Imperial Government."[134] A few months later E. K. Grube, the manager of the Russian Bank and Witte's agent in Tehran, telegraphed that D'Arcy had paid 50,000 tumāns in bribes to get the concession. That, in Grube's view, explained "why the Sadr [Amin os-Soltān] not only gave in to British pressure so easily and did not seek Russian aid but concealed from them the fact of negotiations with the representatives of the English concessionaire."[135]

The contract "between the Government of His Imperial Majesty the Shah of Persia, of the one part, and William Knox d'Arcy, of independent means, residing in London at 42 Grosvenor Square (hereinafter called 'the Concessionaire'), of the other part," granted the latter "a special and exclusive privilege to search for, obtain, exploit, develop, render suitable for trade, carry away and sell natural gas, petroleum, asphalt and ozokerite, throughout the whole extent of the Persian Empire for a term of sixty years as from the date of these presents."[136]

---

133. Cited in B. V. Anan'ich, "Rossiia i kontsessiia d'Arsi," *Istoricheskie zapiski*, 66 (1960), 281.

134. Ibid., p. 281.

135. Id.

136. The text in the original French, Enclosure in A. Hardinge to Lansdowne, No. 16, Commercial, Confidential, Gulahek, May 30, 1901; F. O. 60/660. The

Loans, Concessions, and Power

The concessionaire would have an exclusive right of laying pipelines (Article 2), their course to be determined by the concessionaire and his engineers (Article 5). Article 6 was of crucial importance. In the original French it read:

> Nonobstant ce qui est contenu cidessus, le privilège accordé par les présentes ne s'étendra pas aux Provinces d'Azerbaidjan, Ghilan, Mazandaran, Astrabad, et Khorassan, mais à la condition explicite que le Gouvernement Impérial Persan n'accordera à aucune autre personne le droit de construire un "pipe-line" aux fleuves du sud ou à la côte méridionale de la Perse.[137]

Article 9 authorized the concessionaire to form one or more companies to exploit the concession. Article 10 specified that within a month of the formation of the first of such companies, the latter would pay the Persian government £20,000 in cash and £20,000 in paid-up shares of the first company. "It shall also pay the said Government annually a sum equal to 16 per cent of the annual net profits of any company or companies that may be formed in accordance with the said article."

The workmen employed by the company would be Persian, but the technical staff could be foreign (Article 12). The concession would become void unless the first company authorized under Article 9 were established within two years of the date of the original agreement (Article 16). Conflicts and disputes between the contracting parties would be submitted to two arbitrators, one chosen by the company, another by the Persian government, and an umpire chosen by the two arbitrators. "The decision of the arbitrators or, in the event of the latter disagreeing, that of the umpire, shall be final."

Such was the contract that turned out to be one of the more

English version has been published in Hurewitz, *Diplomacy in the Near and Middle East*, 1, 249–51.

137. "Notwithstanding what is above set forth, the privilege granted by these presents shall not extend to the provinces of Azerbaidjan, Ghilan, Mazendaran, Astrabad, and Khorassan, but on the express condition that the Persian Imperial Government shall not grant to any other person the right of constructing a pipe-line to the southern rivers or to the South Coast of Persia."

significant documents of the twentieth century. Its subsequent fate, the vast industrial complex to which it gave rise, the passionate hatred it evoked, the conflicts it precipitated, could not have been guessed by its signers, who, in a city remote from the centers of world power, in almost total secrecy, acted out a drama of the implications of which they were only half aware.

Russia's oil interests, with whom the manager of the Discount and Loans Bank in Tehran, E. K. Grube, had close personal ties, were apprehensive lest they lose a previously noncompetitive, and therefore very profitable, market. Russian oil products had begun to appear in Persia in the 1870s. In a few years the Russians had conquered the entire market because of the ease and cheapness with which their products could be delivered from Baku. High excise taxes on oil derivatives led Russian producers to export crude oil, which was turned into high-grade kerosene by a number of small refineries in Persia. Under the pressure of international competition the Russian government, after 1896, began to refund the taxes on kerosene exported to Persia, thus making possible considerable price reductions. Though by 1900 Russia had achieved a near monopoly of the Persian kerosene market, the amount of oil she sold there was not large. In 1901 Russia exported a total of 95,079, 017 puds (approximately 1,557,489 tons of oil products, of which only 34,991 tons went to Persia).[138]

Russia sold oil products beyond Persia as well. The journal of the oil industry, *Neftianoe delo*, claimed that in 1901 90 percent of kerosene used in India was of Russian origin.[139] Moreover, India was the main transit point for Russian oil shipments to the Far East. Even southern Persia was supplied with kerosene from Bombay. This distribution pattern explains the interest which Russian oil men showed in building a pipeline across Persia to the Gulf. The first pipeline project had appeared almost simultaneously with the birth of the Russian oil industry. In 1884 S. E. Palashkovskii, the engineer who promoted railway and other projects in the Caucasus and Persia, proposed to build a pipeline from the Caspian Sea to the Persian Gulf, claiming that it would

138. *Obzor vneshnei torgovli Rossii za 1901 god* (St. Petersburg, 1903), Table IV, pp. 76–78, as cited in B. V. Anan'ich, "Rossiia i kontsessiia d'Arsi," p. 279.
139. *Neftianoe delo*, No. 8, 1902, p. 58, as cited in Anan'ich, p. 279.

bring 10,000,000 rubles in profit in its very first year of operation and eventually 100,000,000 rubles a year. Palashkovskii was so enthusiastic about the Persian Gulf that he was even willing to forget about Constantinople.

> Is it not simpler [he asked], leaving Constantinople to the jealous surveillance of our European friends, to turn where the goal is both nearer and more easily attainable? In Turkey we have to deal with all of Europe, but in Persia, where we can easily reach the ocean at the Gulf of Oman, we would have to deal with England alone.[140]

In February 1884, a special ministerial conference (Russia at the time had no cabinet in the familiar sense of the term, and ministers seldom met as a group) discussed the project and resolved to leave it "without consequences." The consensus was that the Russian government could not very well assume responsibility for an undertaking on foreign territory, "without confidence in the perpetual sympathy of the Persian government toward it."[141]

The news of the D'Arcy concession produced an immediate and vigorous reaction in St. Petersburg. The threat of British competition appeared at a time when Russia's oil industry was going through a crisis. In January 1901 the price of crude oil began to fall catastrophically at Baku. The average for 1900 had been 15.7 copecks per pud (a pud equaled 40 pounds or 16.3 kg.), for 1901 it was 8.11. The drop would continue with the 1902 average falling to 6.72, while at the bottom of the decline, in January 1902, crude oil went for 4.6 copecks a pud. According to B. V. Anan'ich's excellent account, one of the causes of the price decline was the inability of Russian oil producers to compete on world markets because of poor and expensive transportation facilities. The oil had to be carried from Baku to Batum by rail and thence by ship through the Suez Canal to India or the Far East.

The new pipeline project submitted to the Tsar in August 1901 stated that the cost of shipping a pud of oil from Baku to India,

140. Cited in Anan'ich, p. 279.
141. Cited in ibid., pp. 279–80.

even with a Baku-Batum pipe, would come to 17 copecks, whereas if oil were pumped across Persia the cost would not exceed 6 copecks. A pipeline to the Gulf would give Russia a "brilliant position" and free her of the fear of American competition. The political aspects of the issue were not neglected either:

> The laying and working of the kerosene pipeline would in any case create in the Persian Gulf real Russian commercial interests which no power would have the right to ignore . . . , and therefore would result in the growth of our influence in Persia and on the shore of the Indian Ocean.[142]

Nicholas II declared the pipeline proposal "A question of great importance which requires serious thought." The thinking was done by Witte, who asked Lamsdorff for an opinion as to whether there were any political obstacles to obtaining for the Loan and Discount Bank a concession for a pipeline from the Caspian to the Persian Gulf. Witte was so impatient that he instructed his agent in Tehran, Grube, to act before Lamsdorff had had time to alert Argyropoulo.

The idea of gaining a foothold on the Persian Gulf appealed to Witte. He had long hoped to break England's monopoly there. Only a few months before the pipeline issue had come up, he had appointed a committee on Persian Gulf trade. The committee included the director of the merchant marine department of the Ministry of Finance, Konkevich; the representative of the Ministry of War, Major General Demianovich; the representative of the Moscow Exchange Committee, a leading Moscow merchant, Aleksandr Naidenov; the representatives of the St. Petersburg and Odessa exchange committees; and others. It recommended that regular steamship communications be established between Odessa, Bushehr, and Basra with a subsidy of 3 rubles per mile, since the line would otherwise lose money.[143]

The committee also recommended that a consulate and a bank be opened at Bushehr, and that they be guarded by Russian soldiers with a naval vessel permanently stationed in the Persian

---

142. Cited in ibid., p. 283.
143. Many Russian shipping lines were regularly subsidized.

Gulf.¹⁴⁴ These recommendations had been acted upon. Now another step must be taken by Witte firmly to establish Russia in the Gulf.

Witte's haste, his reliance on his own agents, and insufficient coordination with the Ministry of Foreign Affairs created some antagonism between Grube and Argyropoulo. Sir Arthur Hardinge wrote:

> M. Grube is inclined to talk rather too frankly, and I think that his consciousness of the important political position which he occupies here, as the de facto equal of the Russian Minister and holder of Persia's purse strings, may have led him to exaggerate the greatness of his influence, but the views expressed by him are I venture to think worth noting in so far as they indicate, which within certain limits they probably do, the inner mind of M. de Witte.¹⁴⁵

The assumption of equality of status by Grube must have been extremely offensive to Argyropoulo, a taciturn diplomat of the old school.¹⁴⁶ Friction developed between the two as soon as Grube arrived in Tehran early in 1901. However, the minister quickly realized that his own superior, Count Lamsdorff, was dominated by Witte and that resisting Grube would be dangerous. He therefore became cooperative to the point of supplying the bank manager with information even before reporting it to the Ministry of Foreign Affairs.¹⁴⁷

Argyropoulo had originally opposed the pipeline project on the grounds that it would have serious political consequences, that

144. Memorandum by Consul-General John Michell, January 3, 1901, Enclosure No. 1 in Scott to Lansdowne, No. 5, Commercial, Confidential, St. Petersburg, January 7, 1901; F. O. 65/1628.

145. A. Hardinge to Lansdowne, No. 32, Very confidential, Tehran, March 14, 1902; F. O. 60/660.

146. K. M. Argyropoulo was a professional diplomat schooled in the traditions of the Asiatic Department of the Ministry of Foreign Affairs. "The diplomatists of the Asiatic Department . . . were distinguished as a class by excessive reticence and were therefore reluctant to allude to any local political topics; and Mr. Argyropoulo was no exception to this depressing rule." A. Hardinge, A *Diplomatist in the East*, pp. 274–75.

147. A. Hardinge to Lansdowne, No. 32, Tehran, March 14, 1902; F. O. 60/660.

the line would be expensive, and that it could not be protected "from attempts of any voluntary or hired malefactor who, on a dark night and in a deserted spot, should put under it a small dynamite or power charge." Witte did not appreciate Argyropoulo's caution. In a letter to Lamsdorff he expressed his regret that "a concession of similar sort had been granted to the English without our minister's knowledge." Pressing forward his attack, Witte wrote:

> Apparently the latter [the English], while endeavoring to obtain their recently acquired concession for the development of Persia's oil wealth, did not hold opinions such as have been expressed by Privy Councilor Argyropoulo and were not afraid of the political consequences of laying a pipeline across Persia, for otherwise they would not have persisted in obtaining this concession and would not have gained it.[148]

Argyropoulo was not prepared to fight the Minister of Finance. Whatever his private feelings may have been, he would henceforth give Grube his complete cooperation.

The campaign for a pipeline concession was linked to the loan issue. In September 1901, when Amin os-Soltān's need for funds, both to pay government officials and satisfy the Shah who wanted to go to Europe, became acute, Grube expressed willingness to provide 10,000,000 rubles. Russia's conditions were: the conclusion of a new commercial treaty, the elimination of British influence from the Tehran mint, and the granting to the Loan and Discount Bank of a pipeline concession.[149] All three were hard to meet because of inevitable British opposition, yet Amin os-Soltān felt that he had no other choice but to comply. Having played false to the Russians in the matter of D'Arcy's oil concession, he had to give them something in return to keep their goodwill. If the price was high, it was the nation, not Amin os-Soltān, who would pay.

On learning of Russo-Persian loan negotiations, Sir Arthur Hardinge addressed a note to the Grand Vizier stating:

148. Cited in Anan'ich, pp. 283–84.
149. Cf. Anan'ich, p. 284.

the rapid decision to conclude a loan with Russia, after you had repeatedly assured me that one was not comtemplated at present, and the intimation which I received from you on Thursday that the matter had been practically settled before His Majesty's Government had had time to suggest any alternative course, would produce a regrettable impression in London, especially as the renewal of conditions of the former loan might exclude for another two years the exclusive financial dependence [sic] of Persia upon Russia, and thus prolong the disturbance of the equilibrium and equality of influence between the two powers of which we had right to complain.[150]

Hardinge bent every effort to prevent further strengthening of Russian control over Persian finances. On October 5 he asked Argyropoulo about the loan negotiations and was told that none were in progress and that the Russian minister had not even written about it to St. Petersburg. In an attempt to draw him out, Hardinge suggested that Persia's attitude on the tariff question might determine whether or not Russia gave her a loan. Argyropoulo denied this, claiming that the two questions were separate and that tariffs had nothing to do with loans.[151]

The first overt act, showing Persian acceptance of Russia's three demands, occurred on October 10 when a Belgian financial adviser to the Persian government, Engels, officially informed the Master of the Mint, Maclean, a British subject, that he, Engels, had been appointed administrator of the mint.[152] Engels asked Maclean to call on him on the thirteenth and "hand over various papers connected with that institution." Sir Arthur Hardinge, suspecting political intrigue, advised Maclean to act cautiously because an attempt might be made to provoke or force him into resigning his post. The advice proved superfluous. During their brief interview, Engels simply handed Maclean the letter of dismissal from the Grand Vizier. "Mr. Engels at the same time informed Mr. Maclean that it had been decided in consequence

---

150. Sir A. Hardinge to the Grand Vizier, September 22, 1901; F. O. 60/645.
151. A. Hardinge to Lansdowne, No. 151, Gulahek, October 5, 1901; ibid.
152. Belgian advisers habitually collaborated with the Russian legation.

of Russian representations to grant the Russian Bank the exclusive right of minting silver for the Persian Government." [153]

Hardinge was infuriated by Maclean's account of the treatment he had received. On the same day he called on the Grand Vizier, spoke very strongly to him, stating that he "considered this summary dismissal of an English official, on no other ground than that of his nationality, as a slap in the face to His Majesty's Government" and to himself as the representative of England, and that he "especially resented the precipitous and unceremonious way in which it had been effected," without giving him time for friendly remonstrance.

> I pointed out that though the Shah had a perfect legal right to dismiss his own servants at his discretion, the political position of England and Russia in relation to Persia rendered the treatment by the Persian Government of their respective officials in its service to some extent a political question, regarded as it was by the Persian people as a criterion of the Government's views and tendencies in the domain of foreign policy, and that the least I had the right to expect was that if a change of thinking had to be made, it should be carried out in a tactful and considerate manner. The Shah would not dream, though he had the abstract right to do so, of dismissing a Russian Cossack officer from the Persian army in such fashion.[154]

Amin os-Soltān could have had no illusions as to Hardinge's knowledge of the facts in the Maclean case, yet he maintained that Russia had nothing to do with the Englishman's dismissal. The government had acted because of merchants' complaints of the unsatisfactory state of coinage. The Russian legation and bank had also complained of the number of cracked coins in circulation. Amin os-Soltān showed Hardinge a letter from the merchants, but Sir Arthur thought it had been "paid for with Russian money." [155]

On the same day Hardinge asked Argyropoulo whether the

153. A. Hardinge to Lansdowne, No. 155, Tehran, October 15, 1901; ibid.
154. Id.
155. Id.

Russian bank would be given a monopoly on minting. Argyropoulo replied that he knew of no such project and did not believe Grube contemplated it. Hardinge now felt that Engels "had committed an indiscretion" and had "unwittingly betrayed an arrangement which M. de Witte may have authorized M. Grube to make with the Persian Government" but which had not been formally concluded. The Belgian financial administrator had not been as secretive as the Russian diplomats, but even without his statement to Maclean the British had enough facts to perceive the pattern. So did everyone else in Tehran. The dismissal of the English Master of the Mint was interpreted as a moral victory for Russia, "indicating that the Grand Vizier's financial necessities had compelled him to capitulate to Russia." [156] Sir Arthur had learned his first lesson.

> From that moment . . . [he says in his memoirs] I began to realize that where the interests of Russia were concerned I could not rely on the Grand Vizier, that the Shah, who was merely an elderly child, was himself a broken reed, and that the Persian monarchy itself was an old, long-mismanaged estate, ready to be knocked down at once to whatever Foreign Power bid highest, or threatened most loudly its degenerate and defenceless rulers.[157]

British diplomacy in Persia was still failing. The Grand Vizier was not telling Hardinge the whole truth and paid relatively little attention to English representations and protests. Argyropoulo feigned ignorance. Belgian financial advisers recently hired by the Persian government, seemed to sense the decline of British power in Tehran and entered into friendly, even close, relations with the Russians. Lord Lansdowne, Salisbury's successor at the Foreign Office, decided to deal directly with St. Petersburg and instructed Charles Hardinge, who had previously served in Tehran, to propose to the Russian Foreign Minister, Count Lamsdorff, that the two powers issue a joint loan to Persia.

To Charles Hardinge's initial inquiry about Russo-Persian loan negotiations, Lamsdorff had replied by denying that any such

156. Id.
157. A. Hardinge, A *Diplomatist in the East*, p. 280.

negotiations were conducted. When confronted with overwhelming evidence, he promised to ask Witte whether there was any truth to the reports. The comedy went on for weeks. On November 2 Lamsdorff told Charles Hardinge that,

> M. Witte had replied that the Persian Government, in one of those periodical phases of desperate impoverishment, had applied in terms of despair for a loan, and that he had complied with their request by the Russian Bank entering into negotiations with the Persian Government, and had even granted them quite a small sum in advance.
>
> Count Lamsdorff said that he had reproached M. Witte with having kept him in the dark respecting these negotiations, and for having been the indirect cause of his denial to me of the existence of any such negotiations for which he now expressed to me his regret.[158]

He further said that he had mentioned to Witte the British proposal of a joint loan to Persia, but that "in view of the present state of negotiations it could be of no practical utility to discuss it." Lamsdorff refused to reveal the amount of the proposed loan or its terms, while admitting that it had been concluded. The next day he reversed himself and claimed that the talks were still continuing.[159]

In his November 3 meeting with Lamsdorff, Charles Hardinge used much plainer language than before. When Lamsdorff made some pious statements about the independence of Persia, and pointed to "the fact that the Persian Government could of its own free will apply to Russia for a loan" as a proof of such independence, Hardinge asked

> whether it could not be fairly said that the independence of Persia was compromised when a foreign power availed itself of a moment of financial necessity to wring concessions from the Persian Government which were not only injurious to the interests of Persia but to those of other foreign governments. I mentioned the case of the recent tariff negotiations, and

158. Charles Hardinge to Lansdowne, No. 314, St. Petersburg, November 3, 1901; F. O. 60/645.

159. Id.

said that there appeared to be no doubt that M. Witte's agents in Persia had threatened the Persian Government with withholding any further financial assistance for them unless concessions were made in favour of Russian commercial enterprises by imposing heavy duties on articles of foreign importation such as Indian tea etc., a proceeding which was contrary to the interests of Persia and to those of other Powers.[160]

Lamsdorff denied the facts and maintained that there was no connection between Persian tariff revisions and loan negotiations. Charles Hardinge found himself in the same position vis-à-vis Lamsdorff as Sir Arthur Hardinge was in vis-à-vis Argyropoulo.

Having been rebuffed at St. Petersburg, the English returned to the attack in Tehran. Sir Arthur Hardinge gathered that the Persian government needed £1,200,000 or even £1,500,000 to cover the following expenses:

Budgetary deficit for 1901	£300,000
Debt to the Imperial Bank of Persia	£216,000
Debt to the Russian bank on account of advances received in August and September	£150,000
Cost of the forthcoming trip of the Shah to Europe	£300,000
Construction of the Qazvin-Tabriz-Jolfā road	£250,000

He also learned that the loan negotiations with Russia had not been concluded, partly because of the Shah's resistance to a Russian demand for a concession for the Qazvin-Tabriz-Jolfā road.

The Russians had on several occasions asked the Persians to grant them that concession. To avoid it, the Shah had promised some years earlier that Persia would herself build the road within five years and that if she did not, Russia could have the concession. Now the time was almost up, and the Russians were demanding that the Shah live up to his promise. Hardinge urged

160. Id.

Amin os-Soltān to grant the concession rather than borrow more money from Russia to build the road in the remaining time. However, the Shah for once fought hard against giving foreigners more privileges. Hardinge was surprised.

> I cannot well account for H. M.'s obstinacy on this matter. It may be, of course, that he feels that to give the Russians the right to build the road through Azerbaijan would be a more visible and therefore a more dangerous Concession than the alienation on paper of some new source of revenue which his subjects would not know of. It may be that he shares the belief, which I have heard expressed in other quarters that the road if built by the Russians will be so constructed as to be easily convertible into a light military railway.[161]

The British proposal of a joint Anglo-Russian loan greatly alarmed the Shah and the Grand Vizer. The latter confessed to Sir Arthur "that the day that he most dreaded for Persia was that on which the Russian and the British Governments came to an agreement." Moreover, the Shah and Amin os-Soltān evidently feared that the Russians would resent their having discussed the loan with the English. If the Shah was afraid of anything more than of Russia's wrath, it was of being denied the loan and left without money. "The English refuse me all assistance themselves and try to interfere with my obtaining it from others!" was his constant complaint during those tense days. Mozaffar ed-Din was entirely absorbed in his plans for a tour of Europe and nagged at Amin os-Soltān for money without which it could not be undertaken.

> "When I go," said His Highness, "to the palace I hear His Majesty laughing and talking with his courtiers, but as soon

---

161. A. Hardinge to Lansdowne, No. 173, Very confidential, Tehran, November 3, 1901; ibid. (If the Shah's opposition was real and not a mere bargaining device, and if it was he rather than Amin os-Soltān who foresaw the conversion of the Jolfā-Tabriz road into a railway, he must be given credit for possessing a higher degree of intelligence than his contemporaries were willing to allow him. In 1914 the Russians did convert the Jolfā-Tabriz highway, which had been suitably built, into a railway.)

as I come in there are long faces; the Shah assumes a mournful air, says that so much more albumen has been found that morning in his water, that it is a crime to prevent him from going to Contrexeville, and that he wants to know the last news about the loan." [162]

Though Hardinge had been repeatedly disillusioned in Amin os-Soltān, he fully appreciated the Grand Vizier's predicament. The only way to make it possible for him to break away from Russia was to provide him with enough money to satisfy the whims of the Shah and to increase his own already enormous wealth. Sir Arthur's dispatches to Lansdowne were very emphatic on this point. Like Charles Hardinge before him, Sir Arthur was trying to overcome the apathy and the balanced budget mentality that reigned in London. His strongest support came from the Viceroy of India.

Curzon learned of the Russian loan negotiations late in the game. Unlike London, he was prepared to do everything in his power to prevent Persia from sinking ever more deeply into Russian debt. In spite of its strained financial circumstances, the Government of India would find the money. On October 1, 1901, Curzon telegraphed the India Office: "We are not only willing to provide 500,000l, and can do so without inconvenience, but we think that the present opportunity one of the greatest political importance, which should not be lost." [163] On November 8 he requested the India Office that all Foreign Office dispatches to the minister in Tehran be repeated to him so as to keep him fully informed. Sir William Lee Warner, Undersecretary of State, who was in perpetual disagreement with the Viceroy, felt that the cost of sending a copy of every dispatch to India by telegram would be too high and that security would be endangered. "I think that when the loan is accepted, if ever, it will be time enough to tell the Viceroy all particulars." This time, however, Lord George Hamilton overruled his budget-conscious subordinate. At the bottom of the sheet on which W. L. W. defended His Majesty's

---

162. Id.
163. From Viceroy, October 2, 1901; L.I., 89, 1901, No. 1407.

exchequer he wrote, "I think the Viceroy should have the telegrams but through us." [164]

The Viceroy's offer was eventually transmitted to Hardinge in Tehran, and, on November 7, he communicated it to Amin os-Soltān. The first question the Grand Vizier asked was whether a British loan would not violate the Russian loan contract of 1900 in which Persia had promised not to borrow from other sources at least until 1910. Hardinge replied that he understood the 1900 agreement to mean that foreign loans "in the sense of the sale of Persian securities to the general public on the open market" were prohibited, but not transactions such as Britain was now proposing, namely a direct governmental loan to Persia. Amin os-Soltān was nervous.[165] It was well and good for the British minister to spin sophistries, he must have thought, but how could he confront Argyropoulo with such a specious argument? He promised to consult the Shah and bring His Majesty's answer the same afternoon.

Mozaffar ed-Din's reply, provided undoubtedly by the Grand Vizier himself, stated that the British government was aware that the 1900 loan contract prohibited Persia from borrowing abroad except in Russia.

> He [the Shah] must have an assurance that the acceptance of the proposed advance was not contrary to that engagement. If the Persian Government could receive such an assurance direct from Russia, or if His Majesty's Government could obtain it for them, they would be only too glad to discuss with us an arrangement which was, he admitted, in the highest degree advantageous to them. But without some guarantee of the kind the risk of a serious misunderstanding with Russia was too great.[166]

The Persians were saying in effect, if you want us to borrow from you rather than from the Russians, you should protect us from their wrath. Hardinge agreed.

164. I. O. Minute Paper, Secret Department, Register No. 1316, Subject: Persia, November 11, 1901, L.I., 78, 1901.

165. A. Hardinge to Lansdowne, No. 175, Confidential, Tehran, November 13, 1901; F. O. 60/645.

166. Id.

There followed a long conversation in which Amin os-Soltān reminded the British minister that it was England's refusal of assistance that drove him to seek Russia's aid in 1899. The equal balance of influence between the two great powers was thus destroyed.

> His greatest wish was to restore that balance in the interests of Persia, but he could not do so at the risk of a quarrel with Russia, in which Persia would be placed in the wrong, as breaking her engagements. Russia was their neighbour along an immense line of frontier from Armenia to Afghanistan, and there were a thousand ways in which, if they really offended her, she could injure them.[167]

Since the British ambassador at St. Petersburg got nowhere with his proposals of a joint Anglo-Russian loan, the English finally made Persia a unilateral offer. Sir Arthur wrote Amin os-Soltān on November 20 that he was authorized to inform His Highness of the British government's readiness to advance Persia a sum "not exceeding half a million pounds out of the revenues of India, repayable in ten years, or earlier by agreement, and secured on the customs of Fars and the coast of the Persian Gulf." Hardinge further stated that these customs, "being excluded from the operations of the Russian loan of 1900 could be assigned for this purpose without conflicting with Persia's contract with the Russian Bank or diminishing the latter's security." In regard to Persia's desire that Britain obtain Russia's agreement to the proposed loan, Hardinge wrote that while the British government was always glad to discuss with Russia terms of a joint advance to Persia, it "does not regard it as within its province to request the consent of the Russian Govt. in respect of an agreement to which it is not itself a party." In conclusion Hardinge said that he would have no objection to his memorandum being shown to the Russian government, if the Persian government "deems it necessary to obtain the consent of the latter to the acceptance of the offer of a British loan." [168]

Hardinge knew that Argyropoulo would turn down any request

---

167. Id.
168. A. Hardinge to the Grand Vizier, Tehran, November 20, 1901; ibid.

from Amin os-Soltān to help obtain the consent of the Russian government to a British loan. To force the Russian minister's hand, Hardinge worked out an ingenious scheme. The Shah should send for Argyropoulo and Hardinge and, "after calling upon me [Hardinge] to formulate it [the offer] so as to preclude all possibility of misunderstanding, should invite M. Argyropoulo to obtain the necessary consent of the Russian Government." Hardinge himself realized that his plan was a bit too clever for Mozaffar ed-Din Shah, who was unlikely to accept the role assigned to him by the British minister. Monsieur Joseph Naus, a Belgian financial expert in the service of the Persian government, agreed, when told of the scheme, that the old Shah would have gone along, but the present one was too shy and nervous.[169] The Russian legation was immediately informed of Hardinge's plan by Naus himself, who claimed that the British minister had tried to make him persuade the Shah to call in the two ministers and ask them to request their governments to issue a joint loan to Persia. According to Naus' version as transmitted to St. Petersburg, Hardinge told him that he "wished to obtain the Shah's initiative in order to achieve common action of England and Russia in Persia." [170] That Naus' version of Hardinge's plan, or rather Naus' version in Russian transmission, differed from Hardinge's is not surprising. What is surprising is that the British minister confided in the Belgian, who had already acquired the reputation of a friend of Russia.

The developments of the next few days closely approximated Hardinge's anticipation. Amin os-Soltān showed the British note to Argyropoulo, who refused to transmit it to St. Petersburg. The manager of the Russian bank, E. K. Grube, transmitted the text by telegram to Witte, who replied that the advance offered by Britain "was a loan by a foreign government and that he would not authorize the Persian Government to accept it." However, Witte promised to conclude the negotiations which had been dragging on for months and issue Persia a loan on the same

169. A. Hardinge to Lansdowne, No. 184, Tehran, November 29, 1901; ibid.
170. Central State Historical Archive in Leningrad, as cited in Anan'ich, "Rossiia i kontsessiia d'Arsi," p. 285.

conditions as those of 1900.[171] Grube reported that the Grand Vizier urged the Shah to reject the offer of the British government because its control over southern customs would create complications with Russia, which was exactly what Hardinge wanted in order to force Russia to agree to divide Persia into spheres of influence, bringing about the destruction of the Shah's authority.[172]

While awaiting Persia's decision, Sir Arthur raised several other issues with Amin os-Soltān: one concerned a new tariff, the other Seistān. For the past several months Persia had been negotiating with Russia a revision of tariffs. When asked for specific information on the proposed new convention, Amin os-Soltān was evasive, saying only that the new tariffs "would prove highly satisfactory" to Britain.[173]

The second issue was that of Seistān. The British had heard rumors that the Shah would pledge the revenues of that strategically important province as a guarantee for a new Russian loan. Sir Arthur requested of the Persian government a formal statement signed by the Shah to the effect that Seistān's revenues would never be "alienated to a foreign power." Why did Lansdowne want such a guarantee, Amin os-Soltān asked on November 28. Hardinge explained

> that the peculiar position in which the loan contracts had placed Persia toward Russia . . . made it natural that we should demand special securities for our own interests, in case these should be in danger of being mortgaged or sacrificed as the price of fresh Russian financial assistance. It would be moreover a protection to Persia to place them beyond such risk, by being able to invoke previous engagements with ourselves. As regards independence, the declaration I had asked for in no way encroached upon it. The Persian Government had accepted the loan contract which did really

171. A. Hardinge to Lansdowne, No. 184, Tehran, November 29, 1901; F. O. 60/645. A. Hardinge, No. 80 (in cypher), 1901; L.I., 89, 1901, No. 1407 (2674).

172. Anan'ich, p. 285.

173. A. Hardinge to Lansdowne, No. 184, Tehran, November 29, 1901; F. O 60/645.

limit Persian sovereign rights and practically placed her in a position not unlike that of Afghanistan or the late Transvaal Republic, which could not make foreign treaties, any more than she could make foreign loans, without the consent of a third power.[174]

Whether he realized it or not, Hardinge's taunting words, which visibly wounded the feelings of the Grand Vizier, testified to his own frustration. Like Mortimer Durand in 1899, and Ronald Thomson twenty years earlier, he was venting his spleen on the Persians because they were subservient to Russia. But what had he or his predecessors done to back the Persians in moments of crisis? They had long walked the tightrope between the two powers. However, in 1901, much more than in 1879 or even in 1899, putting one's trust in British aid or protection would have been foolish. Amin os-Soltān, though selfish and venal, was doing his best to prolong the life of his country, begging and buying for her at least a few years of apparent independence. Iran was still alive, at least in name, and if it had to be kept alive at the expense of British interests, so much worse for British interests.

Weeks passed without a Persian reply to the British loan offer. Hardinge must have sensed that it would be turned down in the end. He urged Lansdowne to negotiate with Russia directly since "We can discuss the matter with Russia as equals, but Persia cannot." [175] He had learned another lesson:

> I am so convinced that the financial question dominates others, with a corrupt and spendthrift Government like this, that I regard the recovery of our right to lend money to Persia as an absolute condition of our doing anything, or even maintaining our position here, and therefore as an advantage worth purchasing by pretty heavy concessions and risks. Once that is regained, everything else follows: as it is, we are ploughing the sands. Reasoning, arguments, the interests of their country in the future are nothing to the Persian Ministers; they understand only two things—force and money. With the latter we can do anything with them; but it must

174. Id.
175. Lord Newton, *Lord Lansdowne* (London, 1929), p. 235.

be given, not bargained about. Had we been willing so to arrange our offer that it could have been accepted by them without conflicting with their Russian engagements, we should have won the trick; but, as you say, the India Office and Treasury would not see the thing from the point of view of "Nothing venture, nothing have," and we must be content with having at least made a proposal, which has shown them that they can still turn to us in an emergency.[176]

At last, on January 7, 1902, Amin os-Soltān told Hardinge that Witte would not permit Persia to borrow from England and that he demanded, as a condition for issuing a Russian loan, the right to build a pipeline across Persia. Hardinge at once pointed out that this would conflict with Article 6 of the D'Arcy concession, which specified that "the Persian Imperial Government shall not grant to any other person the right of constructing a pipeline to the southern rivers or to the South Coast of Persia." Amin os-Soltān said that Witte had consulted his lawyers and had been assured that Article 6 did not prohibit the construction of a pipeline to the Gulf "for the conveyance in transit of petroleum originating outside Persia." Hardinge noted that "The Grand Vizier spoke with extreme bitterness of the treatment of the Persian Government by M. de Witte. He was weary he said of the difficulties, obstacles and fresh demands which that Minister was continually putting forward." [177] The official letter, declining the British loan offer, was delivered to the legation on January 8. It was dated December 5, 1901, and stated that the Shah expressed his gratitude for the kind offer of assistance,

> but owing to the loan Contract of 1900 with the Russian Bank according to which the Persian Govt. is precluded from raising a foreign loan for 10 years without the consent of Russia, which consent the Russian Govt. on being approached declined to give, it is not possible for the Persian Govt. to accept it, and there is no doubt that the British Govt. will not admit any difficulty prejudicial to the friendly intercourse

176. Id.
177. A. Hardinge to Lansdowne, No. 3, January 7, 1902; F. O. 60/660.

between the two countries, Persia and Russia, to arise on this account.[178]

Amin os-Soltān refused to give any information on the proposed tariff revision. However, he softened the blow by including in a separate note a paragraph concerning Hardinge's demand for a guarantee that the internal revenue of Seistān would not be "pledged to any other Government or its subjects." The Shah, Amin os-Soltān, wrote, "was much astonished at this request, since the Persian Government had never had and has not any such intention, and is of opinion that any formal documentary guarantee to this effect is unnecessary and inconsistent with the dignity of an independent sovereign."[179] Thus Persia in fact acceded to England's demand on Seistān revenue, while ostensibly rejecting it and avoiding giving needless offence to Russia.

There was little Sir Arthur Hardinge could do to improve Britain's position in Tehran. He had Lansdowne's support, but the Foreign Secretary confessed that his own attempts to find money for Persia had failed. "The Treasury met us with an absolute *non-possumus*," he wrote, and "the India Office was suspicious and could not be induced to move at more than half speed."[180] In January 1902 Hardinge made another attempt to stir his government into action.

> I am bound to inform His Majesty's Government [he wrote in a long dispatch] that the position of affairs here is in the highest degree unsatisfactory, and even dangerous to British interests; that the decomposition of Persia is proceeding with great rapidity; and that unless the country, including the northern shores of the Persian Gulf and south-western land frontier of our India Empire, by which the Russians can turn the flank of Afghanistan, is to become in all but name a Rus-

178. Atabeg-i-Azam [the title granted to Amin os-Soltān by Mozaffar ed-Din Shah] to Sir A. Hardinge, December 5, 1901 [Delivered on January 8, 1902], Enclosure in A. Hardinge to Lansdowne, No. 7, January 8, 1902; ibid.

179. The Atabeg-i-Azam to Sir A. Hardinge, Translation, December 5, 1901, Enclosure in A. Hardinge to Lansdowne, No. 9, Confidential, Tehran, January 13, 1902; ibid.

180. Newton, *Lord Lansdowne*, p. 233.

sian dependency, we must be prepared not merely to risk money in the form of advances on inadequate security, but perhaps also expend it on a fairly large scale for exclusively political, as distinct from financial returns.[181]

Hardinge compared Russia's power over the Persian government to that of the Parliament in Britain:

> Like our Parliament in the seventeenth century, M. de Witte, when he grants Supply, requires of the Shah, as a preliminary condition, "redress of grievances," in other words, the surrender to Russia of some fresh political advantage. The leverage thus acquired by him is being used without scruple or mercy in the present instance for the purpose of extorting from Persia a preposterous Concession for pipe-lines to the Persian Gulf, which will probably never be carried into actual effect, but will, nevertheless, afford an excuse for covering Southern Persia with surveyors, engineers, and protecting detachments of Cossacks, and preparing a veiled military occupation.[182]

Hardinge had not lost hope. The Shah's proposed European visit might give Britain an opportunity to save her position in Tehran. The Shah might be "emancipated from the overshadowing influence of Russia," the financial circles in the City "might help to extricate her [Persia] from her financial embarrassment," and Hardinge himself might gain an opportunity to establish a better personal relationship with the Shah during his stay in England. Hardinge was very much disturbed by the hesitation of the government to receive the Shah right after Edward VII's coronation. A postponement of the trip in the summer of 1903 would offend the touchy ruler. Moreover, "Russian influence might have grown in the interval so dangerously strong that a situation susceptible of being repaired to-day might prove much harder to repair a year hence." [183]

---

181. A. Hardinge to Lansdowne, No. 11, Confidential, Tehran, January 29, 1902; F. O. 60/660.
182. Id.
183. Id.

British prestige in Tehran was low. It was generally felt that a second Russian loan would transform Persia into a Russian dependency similar to Bukhara. Many Persians "could not understand the apparent indifference of England to her own interests," and her assumption of the role of a silent spectator of Russia's advance. Mokhtār os-Saltaneh, former chief of police, told Mr. Grahame, the vice consul, that the time had come for energetic action. "You should put heart into the Shah, for he has none. Throw a stone. Wake him up; he is asleep. Now is the time. . . . Make direct representations to him that a fresh loan from Russia means binding Persia hand and foot—the entire sacrifice of his own independence." [184]

At St. Petersburg the British ambassador, Sir Charles Scott, continued his wearisome representations on the loan issue. He expressed to Lamsdorff his surprise that Russia would not permit Persia to borrow from Britain, and asked on what grounds she did so. Lamsdorff promised to speak to Witte. Scott reported that he had pointed out

> frankly to the Russian Government that according to the reports that had reached them [the British] of the use which was being made of Persia's embarrassed condition, and of the clause attached to the Loan Contract with the Persian Government, of which I was able to give him instances by the information transmitted in Sir A. Hardinge's telegrams . . . it was calculated to particularly [sic] reduce Persia to a condition of complete dependence on, and subserviency to, Russia, which was scarcely compatible with the assurances repeatedly exchanged between our two Governments and with Count Lamsdorff's expressed desire to respect the perfect freedom of action in that State.[185]

Lamsdorff listened patiently, made a few quiet objections, and let the matter drop.

By the middle of January 1902 all but one question in regard to the Russian loan had been settled, the remaining issue being that

184. Enclosure in A. Hardinge to Lansdowne, No. 17, Confidential, Tehran, February 4, 1902; ibid.
185. Scott to Lansdowne, No. 59, St. Petersburg, February 20, 1902; ibid.

of the pipeline. Political and economic motives combined to make Witte insist on getting the concession. A pipeline across Persia would gain for Russia a foothold on the Gulf almost as effectively as if she had built a railway. Pumping stations, repair depots, and other installations along the pipeline would have to be guarded, offering an excuse for stationing Russian troops from one end of the country to the other. The Baku oil industry would also benefit. In recent years it had suffered greatly at the hands of its most ruthless competitor, Standard Oil, which was driving Russian oil products out of European and Asiatic markets.[186] In a memorandum addressed to the Minister of Agriculture and State Properties, the Baku oil producers bitterly complained of their plight: the position of the oil processing industry in Baku had reached the point at the end of 1901 where many refineries were compelled to decrease and even suspend production, while quite a few of the refineries worked at a definite loss, leading to destruction and ruin.[187] A pipeline to the Persian Gulf would lower the costs of transportation to the point where Russian oil products would be competitive once more.

In Tehran the negotiations were conducted by Grube and Argyropoulo, though the latter played a subordinate role. On February 4, 1902, Grube telegraphed St. Petersburg that Amin os-Soltān had agreed to the concession. A week later the Shah signified his assent with the proviso that the Russian government assume responsibility for the violation of the D'Arcy concession.[188] Amin os-Soltān was fully aware that the British would see in the pipeline concession an infringement of D'Arcy's rights.

Several weeks earlier D'Arcy had obtained an opinion from Mr. Crackenthorp, King's Counsel, that "the construction by Russia of the suggested pipe-line from Baku to the Persian Gulf would, unless consented to by Mr. D'Arcy, be an unlawful interference

---

186. For documents on the position of Russia's oil industry in international competition, see Akademiia Nauk S.S.S.R., *Monopolisticheskii kapital v neftianoi promyshlennosti Rossii, 1883–1914* (Moscow, 1961), pp. 155–296.

187. Memorandum of the XVIth Congress of Baku Oil Producers to the Ministry of Agriculture and State Properties, July 18 [31], 1902; ibid., p. 263, document No. 103.

188. Anan'ich, "Rossiia i kontsessiia d'Arsi," p. 286.

with the exclusive right conferred on him by the Concession."[189] Sir Arthur Hardinge so informed Amin os-Soltān. In a conversation with the Persian Prime Minister he pointed out that his chief objection to the Russian demand was political:

> As a business scheme it [the pipeline] is absurd, and cannot pay; probably the line will never be laid down. But it will afford the concessionaires an excuse for sending a host of engineers and surveyors (accompanied by small Cossack detachments for their protection) on the coast of the Persian Gulf, and if they get into trouble with the natives there, for establishing a disguised military occupation.[190]

Hardinge further explained that the D'Arcy concession gave Persia a good excuse for refusing the Russian demands on the ground of legal complications. The British government and the Parliament were "alive to the importance of affairs in Persia," and it would be a pity to alienate them before the Shah's forthcoming trip to England.[191]

Amin os-Soltān confided to Hardinge that he was still urging St. Petersburg to abandon the demand for the pipeline. He felt that Count Lamsdorff shared the view that Persia should be granted the loan without insisting on this concession, but the Russian Foreign Minister "was not strong enough to prevail against M. de Witte, who, on these matters, was apparently all powerful with the Emperor." The Grand Vizier suggested that the British ambassador at St. Petersburg

> might find means of representing to His Imperial Majesty the expediency of not making its acceptance a *sine qua non* of the loan. He had told the Russian Government that if it was so treated the negotiations would have to be abandoned, but the Shah and Court insisted on having the money for

---

189. Enclosure in Hardinge to Lansdowne, No. 14, Confidential, Tehran, February 1, 1902; F. O. 60/660.

190. Memorandum for guidance of Abbas Kuli Khan (Assistant Oriental Secretary) in conversation with the Grand Vizier, dated January 26, 1902, Enclosure No. 1 in A. Hardinge to Lansdowne, No. 14, Confidential, Tehran, February 1, 1902; ibid.

191. Id.

Loans, Concessions, and Power 381

their European tour, and he might, therefore, however unwillingly, be forced to yield.[192]

Though ostensibly Amin os-Soltān had already yielded, he was still trying to block the concession by using the English as a shield. Hardinge seized the opportunity, promised to forward the Persian request to Lord Lansdowne, and offered to raise the question with Argyropoulo. Amin os-Soltān, not wanting the Russian minister to know that he was working against Russia, declined the latter offer.[193]

Having received instructions from Lansdowne, Sir Charles Scott, British ambassador to Russia, called on Lamsdorff to tell him that Article 6 of D'Arcy's concession bound the Persian government not to grant to any other party the right to construct pipelines to the southern rivers or the Persian Gulf. Lamsdorff, as usual, promised to take up the question with Witte and noted in passing that doubts were entertained as to the interpretation of Article 6. Scott retorted that the British government had no doubts and was not aware that the Persians did. There the conversation ended. Once again Lamsdorff evaded the issue. Scott reported to the Foreign Office that the Persian minister at St. Petersburg had made no progress either. Witte was personally conducting the negotiations, while Lamsdorff kept repeating that he "did not like to interfere with M. de Witte." [194]

Argyropoulo confirmed "that M. de Witte absolutely refused to afford Persia any financial assistance unless the pipe-line asked for to the Persian Gulf were conceded, and that Count Lamsdorff was powerless to alter this decision." When Persia needed money two years ago, he said, "England and France had both refused to help her," but "Russia had generously come to her rescue." Since then Persia had given a telegraph line in Baluchestān and an oil monopoly to England. Now Russia made a "very innocent and moderate" request, yet the Persian government would not grant it. The pipeline itself might not be built for years, if at all, "but M. de Witte attached importance to the promise that the con-

192. Id.
193. Id.
194. Scott to Lansdowne, No. 53, St. Petersburg, February 15, 1902; ibid.

cession should be given, if only as a proof of the goodwill of the Persian Government." Amin os-Soltān expressed fear of British displeasure and "insistently asked, in the name of the Shah and on his instruction, to ease the terms of the loan and postpone for a time the decision on the pipe-line." [195]

Witte, who had, in fact if not in name, taken over the functions of Minister of Foreign Affairs, paid little attention to Sir Charles' representations of February 13. He simply advised Lamsdorff to inform the British ambassador that the concession

> was sought by a private institution, the Discount and Loan Bank of Persia, and therefore the Russian Government is not in a position to give any exact explanations as to its content; but, as far as the Ministry of Finance knows, this concession, concerning exclusively the export and transit of Russian oil, cannot violate the rights of d'Arcy who, according to the sense of his agreement with the Persian Government, acquired a monopoly only in regard to native oil.[196]

A memorandum to that effect was transmitted to Sir Charles Scott.[197]

On February 17 Witte made the final decision to go ahead. It was calculated that a pipeline with a yearly capacity of 60,000,000 puds (nearly 1,000,000 metric tons) could be built in four years. The cost to Bushehr would be 80,000,000 rubles (about £8,000,000 or $40,000,000), to the Indian Ocean 110,000,000 rubles. The project would pay for itself in twenty years. Great savings would be effected on transportation. Oil pumped across Persia would sell in the Far East at 14.5 to 20 kopecks cheaper than the same oil carried through the Suez Canal, even if the pipeline functioned at only half its capacity. Thus Russia would gain a great advantage over its American competition.[198]

---

195. Amin os-Soltān reported this conversation to Hardinge. A. Hardinge to Lansdowne, No. 27, Confidential, Tehran, February 16, 1902; ibid.

196. Argyropoulo to Lamsdorff, February 3/16, 1902, as cited in Anan'ich, "Rossiia i kontsessiia d'Arsi," p. 286.

197. Witte to Lamsdorff, ibid., pp. 286–87.

198. Enclosure in Scott to Lansdowne, No. 63, February 20, 1902; F. O. 60/660.

The text of the agreement was ready in St. Petersburg by late February. It specified that the concession would remain secret and no work would be done during its first two years. In two years the concessioner, the Loan and Discount Bank of Persia, would notify the Persian government whether it would go through with the project. From the date of such notification the bank would have three years in which to begin construction and fifteen years in which to complete it. The text was general and vague. It did not even specify at what point on the southern shore of Persia the pipeline would terminate. Witte approved it on March 1 and forwarded it to Grube to be transmitted to the Grand Vizier.[199]

Grube had done his best to obtain the concession for Witte. He had used every means of persuasion to win Persian statesmen to his cause. On February 25 he urgently telegraphed St. Petersburg that "the English concessionaire of the southern pipe-line . . . [one word undeciphered] paid up to 50,000 tumāns." Grube requested Witte's permission "to promise similar reward" if the requested concession were granted. Witte replied: "You can promise 50 thousand tumāns." [200]

On February 26, unknown to Grube, Amin os-Soltān received word from the Persian minister in St. Petersburg that Russia would issue the loan without her demands for a pipeline having been met. In his article "Russia and the D'Arcy Concession," B. V. Anan'ich, who had access to Russian archives, notes the difficulty of establishing how and where the Persian minister picked up such information. "It is unlikely that he could have received it from the Ministry of Finance. Most probably it came from the Ministry of Foreign Affairs." Anan'ich feels that Lamsdorff had given up the notion of a pipeline across Persia, and points to Lamsdorff's letter to Witte of February 15/28, 1902, in which the Minister of Finance was warned that in view of British intervention one must keep in mind "the probability of our consenting to ease some of the conditions of the loan and even of exchanging in the future the above mentioned concession for some other conditions." [201]

199. Anan'ich, p. 287.
200. Cited ibid., pp. 287–88.
201. Ibid., p. 288.

Russo-Persian pipeline negotiations continued into early March, when Grube and Argyropoulo learned that D'Arcy had offered the Persian government a private loan. The original proposal of £100,000 had been made through Hardinge on January 31.[202] By the end of February D'Arcy was willing to give £300,000, and the Grand Vizier used the offer to make Witte abandon his concession demands. The pressure on the Finance Minister must have been great. He not only had to deal with Sir Charles Scott and the Persians, but also to withstand Lamsdorff, who forgot his usual docility and insisted that the loan be issued to Persia without her granting the pipeline concession in return. News of D'Arcy's proposal decided the issue. "M. de Witte, fearing that the Persian Government might borrow from English sources, and thus escape from his grasp, withdrew the demand for the pipe-line to the Persian Gulf." [203]

Since the sum offered by D'Arcy was less than a third that offered by Russia, and since borrowing from an English concern would have been politically dangerous, considering Witte's mood, Amin os-Soltān accepted a Russian loan of 10,000,000 rubles at 5 percent interest, repayable over seventy-five years. If Persia failed to meet her regular payments, Russia would be entitled to take over the administration of customs, except those of Fārs and the Persian Gulf.[204]

More than sixty years after the diplomatic battles of 1899–1902, it is hard to decide who was the victor. The loan of January 1900 was Witte's greatest achievement, giving him a tight control of Persian finances and, to a large extent, of the government. The D'Arcy concession, though privately initiated, afforded the British an opportunity to fight back. In the face of indifference or even opposition from the India Office, Sir Arthur, supported by the Viceroy of India, prevented Witte from gaining a foothold on the Persian Gulf. A Soviet historian wrote that the renunciation of

---

202. A. Hardinge to Lansdowne, No. 14, Confidential, Tehran, February 1, 1902; F. O. 60/660.

203. A. Hardinge to Sir Edward Grey, Separate and Confidential, London, December 23, 1905; F. O. 371/102.

204. Persian text of the 1902 loan agreement. Iran, Archive of the Ministry of Foreign Affairs, File 44/Folder 1.

the pipeline concession by Russia and the affirmation of the English concession "was one of the first serious defeats of Witte's economic policy in Persia on the eve of the Russo-Japanese war; and only a few years were needed to enable the Russian government fully to appreciate the significance of this defeat." [205]

While the victor may be hard to identify, there is no doubt about the loser. When Mozaffar ed-Din Shah left his country for Europe in the spring of 1902, Persia was in a worse condition than she had known under any of his Qājār predecessors.

205. Anan'ich, "Rossiia i kontsessiia d'Arsi," p. 289.

6

Seistān and the Persian Gulf:

Gates to India

The weakness of Britain's international position became manifest during the Boer War. Splendid isolation had been based on overwhelming industrial and economic superiority which had lasted till 1890, the year the United States outproduced Britain in steel. By 1900 both the United States and Germany had forged ahead of England. Though London was still the financial center of the world, industrial power passed into other hands.

To maintain her political position and protect the Empire, Britain needed allies. She had repeatedly tried to establish close relations with Germany, but the Kaiser, dreaming of sea power, refused the offers of friendship. Moreover, he encouraged Russia to act against Great Britain to the extent of telling the Russian ambassador, Osten-Sacken, during the Boer War, that he would protect Russia from attack in Europe if the Tsar chose to march on India.[1] Relations with France were strained, and not only because of the encounter in Africa: France was Russia's ally and financier. When Britain at last found a friend, it was in the Far East.

The Anglo-Japanese alliance signed on January 30, 1902, was a result of common fear of Russian expansion in Asia. Though ostensibly confined to the Far East, it had far-reaching consequences for the Middle East as well. It freed Japan for a war with Russia, thus diverting the latter from the Middle East and enabling England to pursue a more active policy at less risk.[2]

1. Osten-Sacken's report cited in F. A. Rothstein (Rotshtein), *Mezhdunarodnye otnosheniia v kontse XIX veka*, pp. 31–34.

2. For a Soviet Russian view of the alliance, see A. Galperin, *Anglo-iaponskii soiuz. 1902–1921* (Moscow, 1947).

Sir Arthur Hardinge appreciated better than any of his predecessors the strength of Russian influence in Tehran and the relative inefficacy of English measures to stay its growth. Cossack uniforms were everywhere, and the city had "a very 'Russian-Asiatic' aspect." The Russians, he complained, took the line "of being 'at home' in Persia and of just tolerating the other European representatives as Western strangers, alien from Asia, who have no real business or *raison d'être*." [3]

Many Russians were convinced that Persia would not remain an independent nation much longer. They argued that the country was tired and that the entire population of Persia looked to Russia for change.[4]

Undoubtedly many Russians had persuaded themselves that they were loved by the Persians, but Persian sources show a rather different attitude. In the summer of 1901 there circulated in Tehran a leaflet which accused Amin os-Soltān of betraying his country. "His every effort has been to make Persia a portion of Russia, and to make a Russian official Lord and master of the Persians." The leaflet charged that the Grand Vizier had armed the Armenians, squandered 20,000,000 gold coins from the treasury on wine, prostitutes, and boys, "bestowed large sums on Dervishes besotted with opium, bribed the clergy with government money and the blood of the country to win them over to his side," and handed the country over to the Russians.[5] Through the summer of 1901 Hardinge reported many instances of printed attacks on the Grand Vizier and even on the Shah himself. "All alike reproached the government with having sold out to Russia and threatened both the Shah and his Prime-Minister with death unless they speedily amend their ways." [6] Another leaflet proclaimed:

> The two-headed eagle of Russia has laid its eggs in the Gulistan Palace of the Ruler of the East. These have brought

3. Newton, *Lord Lansdowne*, pp. 232–33. Hardinge would have appreciated a popular but untranslatable Russian saying: *Kuritsa ne ptitsa, Persia ne zagranitsa.*
4. Lomnitskii, *Persiia i persy*, p. 77.
5. Leaflet entitled "Geyrat," Enclosure in A. Hardinge to Lansdowne, No. 124, Confidential, Gulahek, August 18, 1901; F. O. 60/661.
6. A. Hardinge to Lansdowne, No. 124; ibid.

forth fledglings which are cherished by the Atabeg [Amin on-Soltān]. In a year's time, when these fledglings have found their wings, they will swallow up the whole of Persia from east to west. The Atabeg has cut off the hands of England from protecting Persia. The English nation is a thousand farsakhs distant, and the thread of English policy has been broken and tangled.[7]

The campaign against the Grand Vizier was violent, and many began to expect his dismissal by the Shah. Hardinge felt that he would last another few months, and that the moment was not ripe for his downfall and for the formation of an anti-Russian ministry. Such a government would have a poor chance of success. If it were to fall from inherent weaknesses, "its failure would be considered ours and the tide of Russian reaction would flow more strongly and quickly than before."[8] To forestall Amin os-Soltān's premature downfall, Hardinge offered him to let the Shah know that the British had nothing against the Grand Vizier, and that Hardinge himself "found him very friendly and desirous of promoting friendly feelings between our two countries."[9]

During the winter of 1901–02 popular discontent focused on rumors about the new Russian loan then under negotiation. The mullas were beginning to stir. An unnamed seyyed told Hardinge that the clergy should obtain a condemnation of the proposed loan from the mojtaheds of Karbalā and Najaf; "and, if this did not deter the government, should start a movement like that against the [Tobacco] Régie."[10] In February a bitter, threatening letter, attributed to the clergy and addressed to the Shah, circulated in Tehran:

Your Imperial Majesty,
  All the Persian nation and the whole of Islam throughout the world congratulate your Imperial Majesty from the bottom of their hearts on your glorious reign!

7. Enclosure in ibid.
8. Same to same, No. 130, Confidential, Gulahek, August 22, 1901; ibid.
9. Id.
10. A. Hardinge to Lansdowne, No. 186, Confidential, Tehran, December 9, 1901; F. O. 60/645.

Seistān and the Persian Gulf

From the day when you ascended the throne of the ancient and puissant Kings of Persia till now five years have passed. You have expended 150 korours [75,000,000 tumāns] in cash, and, moreover, you have contracted debts to the amount of 70 korours, and now, by a further loan of 22 korours of tomans from Russia, you are about to sell the Government and the faith of Persia to Christians by your own whim and caprice. A hundred thousand congratulations on your Imperial glory and justice. Truly you have merited the title of "Glory of the Sovereigns of Iran." . . . Alas! a thousand times alas! You have brought down the time-honoured name of Persia to dust, cast the ruins of the Kingdom of Persia beneath the foot of the Emperor of Russia, and darkened the day of Islam and of Persia. . . .

By God Almighty and the Holy Ones of Islam, we all, loyal and true subjects of your Majesty, have sworn an oath that, so far as in us lies, this dishonour shall not be thus quickly brought upon the throne. We warn you before hand that in these few days you have still time. Hasten to abandon this second loan, and cast off this son of a Georgian [Amin os-Soltān] from the Government of the Kingdom and the nation. . . . but if you continue, at the instigation of your son of a Georgian, to fall into this and that fancy, we swear by the Creator that your throne and power will go to the winds in such fashion that no trace of yourself or your children shall be left upon the earth.[11]

The government was acutely conscious of the danger of clerical opposition. It tried to bribe important mullas. Seyyed Ali Akbar, a leading ecclesiastic, had an audience with the Shah and emerged with a valuable ring and a large sum of money.[12] Amin os-Soltān remembered the Tobacco Régie. So did the British. A decade ago the clergy, supported by Russian officials, had broken up an English concession. Could it not, with English encouragement, break up a Russian loan?

11. Seditious letter sent to H. M. the Shah, Translation, Enclosure in A. Hardinge to Lansdowne, No. 19, Tehran, February 4, 1902; F. O. 60/660.
12. A. Hardinge to Lansdowne, No. 23, Secret, Tehran, February 14, 1902; ibid.

On February 5, the British vice-consul, Mr. Grahame, had an interview with one of the great mojtaheds, Seyyed Abdollāh Behbehāni, long a friend of the English. The Seyyed complained that his condolences on the death of Queen Victoria and congratulations on the accession of Edward VII had been ignored. To create rapport, Grahame presented to Seyyed Abdollāh "a very small souvenir and unworthy token" of esteem, a silver clock. "The Seyyed took the clock out of its case, wound it up, played with it, and appeared pleased, although he referred to the gold watch [a gift of the late Queen] as having been valued for him by a friend from Stamboul at 200 l." Clearly the silver clock was not as rich a gift.[13]

When Grahame mentioned the Russian loan, Seyyed Abdollāh expressed his disapproval and the determination of the mojtaheds to prevent it. The only trouble was that some clerics were timorous, others venal. "He required money to bring them over, and he wished to feel assured that their actions on this matter would be appreciated by England, in whose interests, as much as in those of Persia, he was acting in this matter." Grahame was in no position to make promises, but said he would transmit the message to his superiors. The Seyyed indicated that opposition was being organized, "'but there are too many lukewarm fellows who must be bought and we must feel that we have some support at our back in case of need.' 'Moral support?' 'Yes moral support. Secret of course!'"

The visit lasted an hour and a half. When Grahame rose to leave, Seyyed Abdollāh said he hoped they would meet again soon. His parting words were: "'I have been casting about to see from whom I could raise a loan of, say, 2,000 tomans. That ought to be enough to assure the others, to stop their mouths.'"[14]

Hardinge reported the interview to Lansdowne, who had the dispatch printed for circulation to various government departments, omitting an important passage:

> Your Lordship will observe that the Seyid, after deploring the venality of his reverent brethren, suggested in a soliloquy,

---

13. Memorandum by Mr. Grahame, Tehran, February 5, 1902; Enclosure in ibid.
14. Id.

or "aside," that the sum of 400 pounds, if placed in his own hands might enable him to bring them into line. I told Mr. Grahame that it was out of the question for me to give so large an amount out of secret service funds, with no security as to its proper employment, but that he might take an early opportunity of leaving 50 pounds (in Russian rouble notes) with the Seyid, hinting delicately that more might be forthcoming should any practical result, in the form of a clerical protest against the loan, appear.[15]

Amin os-Soltān knew of the rising clerical opposition, negotiated with the mullas, and made efforts to bribe them over to his side. The mojtahed Seyyed Ali Akbar was invited to the palace to interpret a dream of the Shah's, though some said it had been made up to test the mulla's sentiments.

"In my dream," he [the Shah] told the Seyyid, "I saw you appear before me clad in the Ihram . . . [a linen cloth worn by pilgrims in Mecca] and bearing on your back a heavy bag. I was angry and rebuked you for entering my presence in such scanty attire, when suddenly the sack fell from your shoulders and from its mouth flowed gold and silver. Immediately there was a dazzling light and I saw in the heavens a moon of extraordinary brightness. I awoke greatly agitated and now call on you to explain this vision."

The Seyyed replied:

Your Majesty saw me in the primitive Moslem garb throw a sack at your feet whence flowed gold and silver, this means that my ancestor the Prophet bids you to make no fresh loans from unbelievers, but to trust for the restoration of your finances to your subjects and fellow servants of the faith. And the brilliant moon which Your Majesty beheld is His Highness the Atabeg-i-Azam [Amin os-Soltān], who draws his light from yourself as his sun.

The Shah was angered at the mention of the loan and accused the clergy of neglecting religion in favor of politics. The Seyyed

15. A. Hardinge to Lansdowne, No. 23, Tehran, February 14, 1902; ibid. Typewritten and signed in Hardinge's hand.

denied this, but added that pious Moslems were disturbed at the idea of a fresh Russian loan.[16] Seyyed Abdollāh's statement to Grahame was not idle talk. The clergy had taken the offensive.

The British vice-consul and the mojtahed met again on February 23. The mulla reported that Amin os-Soltān had tried to ascertain his views on the loan but that he had refused to express an opinion. He proceeded to talk of the need for collective action on the part of the clergy. Emissaries must be sent to Mashhad, Rasht, Najaf, Esfahān, and Shirāz, where a number of mullas were prepared to act. "In fact throughout the country the ulema [divines] are like a train of gunpowder, awaiting a spark to produce an explosion." Funds were needed for traveling expenses.

Grahame replied that the minister had foreseen the needs and sent 250 tumāns, which he turned over to Seyyed Abdollāh on the understanding "that any action taken must be consistent with loyalty to the Shah and the Govt. (Shah-parasti ve Doulat-parasti)." The Seyyed accepted both money and hypocrisy. "Of course," he said. "What other means are open to us?" He then spoke of the necessity of warming the hearts of certain clerics in Tehran.

> I pointed out [Grahame reported to Hardinge] that the Minister before spending any large sums would have to see a sign or token from such people, that however much confidence might be felt personally by the Minister in Seyyid Abdullah it might be necessary to furnish our Govt. with some proof that collective and not individual action was being taken.
>
> The Seyyid said that of course receipts were not to be thought of. It must be carefully concealed that there were any foreigners interested in the movement, otherwise certain people might say—"you are only taking us from one set of Kuffar to hand us over to another."
>
> Before leaving I repeated that the sum of 250 tomans

16. A. Hardinge to Lansdowne, No. 32, Tehran, February 27, 1902; ibid. One is tempted to give an alternative interpretation of the Shah's dream. Mozaffar ed-Din was hinting that the clergy should open its heavy bags and let some of the gold and silver flow to him. Of course, the Seyyed would be careful not to suggest such an interpretation.

handed to the Seyyid was intended to cover working expenses such as travelling charges and gratuities and that further sums which might be given by the Minister would depend on what satisfactory symptoms might show themselves.[17]

Whether Vice-Consul Grahame knew it or not, he was watching the first steps of the Persian revolution. The country was indeed a train of gunpowder, but only the clergy could produce the spark to set off the explosion. Hardinge's action in providing Seyyed Abdollāh Behbehāni with a few hundred pounds did not cause the upheaval. Without his connivance, however, the clergy might have hesitated. Had Hardinge assumed an adamantly pro-Shah position in full harmony with his Russian colleague, the clergy almost certainly would have drawn back, and the course of events would not have been the same.

Hardinge's encouragement of anti-Russian, and therefore anti-Shah, agitation extended to the provinces. The consul general in Esfahān, Mr. Preece, was instructed to exercise great care in dealing with the clerical movement. The governor, Mas'ud Mirzā Zell es-Soltān, was a friend and, though a brother of the Shah, was prepared to act against him. He had even asked Preece for money for that purpose, but the legation hesitated to pay. "The sum asked by Zil is absurdly large," Hardinge wrote, "but if you want 400 tomans to stimulate local mollahs you can have them. Only nothing must pass in writing which would indicate this, and your dealings with them must be direct not through Zil who had better not know of any presents we may give to clergy."[18] Consul General Preece found that though the clergy were willing to work against the Russian loan, not even their leader, Āqā Najafi, would do a thing for fear of the governor, the ruthless and cruel Zell es-Soltān. "Unless Zil es Sultan tells them to preach and work," Preece telegraphed the legation, "you may be certain that nothing will be done here [even if I spent 20,000 tomans

---

17. Memorandum by Mr. Grahame, February 23, 1902, Enclosure in A. Hardinge to Lansdowne, No. 32, Secret, Tehran, February 27, 1902; ibid.

18. A. Hardinge to Preece, No. 4, Tehran, March 16, 1902, Enclosure in A. Hardinge to Lansdowne, No. 55, Secret, Tehran, April 1, 1902; ibid. The above passage was bracketed at the Foreign Office. In the margin was the notation: "Omit."

among Mollahs I should not succeed in getting Mollahs to move, it rests entirely in Zil's hands.]"[19]

At the end of April, Hardinge himself visited Esfahān where he conducted personal discussions with several powerful clerics. Sheykh ol-Arāqeyn, a wealthy mulla and a relative of the celebrated Āqā Najafi, told him that the authority of Zell es-Soltān was so great that the clergy would hesitate to participate in any political movement without his approval. Zell es-Soltān, the mulla said, was sympathetic but did not want the trouble to start in Esfahān, "as he might be suspected of having encouraged it." However, Āqā Najafi and others were prepared to appeal to the Sultan of Turkey and ask him to convey to the Shah the strong objections of the Persian clergy and people to any further concessions being made to Russia. Hardinge advised against such an appeal, in which he saw the influence of Pan-Islamic ideas of Seyyed Jamāl ed-Din Afghāni.[20]

Eventually Zell es-Soltān permitted the clergy to act and even joined the movement in the hope of supplanting his incapable brother on the Persian throne. There can be little doubt that in the absence of British encouragement he would not have done so.

As the clerical movement gathered momentum, the Tehran divines appealed for support to the mojtaheds of the holy cities of Iraq: Najaf and Karbalā. The appeal, which was circulated in Tehran, was strongly anti-Russian. The Persian government, it said, was yielding to the infidels. "If once we fall into the grasp of Russia our wives and children are no longer our own. The most sacred ties are under the control of the foreigners. All power is taken from the Ulema [divines]. How is Islam humbled!"[21]

The leaders of the movement maintained constant contact with the British. They felt the need for an informal agreement whereby the English would guarantee their safety. Hāji Mirzā

19. Preece to Hardinge, March 17, 1902; Enclosure in A. Hardinge to Lansdowne, No. 55, Secret, Tehran, April 1, 1902; ibid. Brackets added to the original document at the Foreign Office. In the margin the notation: "Omit."

20. A. Hardinge to Lansdowne, No. 77, Confidential, Tehran, May 5, 1902; ibid.

21. A. Hardinge to Lansdowne, No. 55, Secret, Tehran, April 1, 1902; ibid.

Seyyed Abu Tāleb Zanjāni, one of the most influential and, in Hardinge's view, one of the most enlightened, of the Tehran mojtaheds, met with the British minister and Vice-Consul Grahame to ask them what protection the clergy could expect if it were persecuted for opposing the loan. Hardinge gave an equivocal answer:

> I thought it best to state frankly that with the exception of bast (sanctuary) we were not in a position to guarantee protection to Persian subjects against the consequences of acts by them displeasing to their Government. No doubt if, as a consequence of a protest by them against concessions to Russia of a nature to endanger the national independence, the authors of the protest were to be arrested and exiled, I could and would make a strong remonstrance to the Persian Government, but it is not probable that such a step would be taken.[22]

It was more likely, Hardinge went on, that the Grand Vizier would use other pretexts and opportunities to remove them, in which case the legation would be powerless to intervene. It was impossible for the minister "to give any undertaking as to what the British Government might or might not do, in the event of the Shah's calling in Russian aid to put down possible risings against an anti-national policy." He had his own ideas on the subject, and personally thought that if the Russians invaded Persia on the pretext of reestablishing order, Britain might possibly, by cooperating with Russia on the same lines in regions nearer her borders, "neutralise the more dangerous consequences of such intervention," but he "should not be justified in expressing such an opinion to a Persian Minister much less to a private person without distinct authority" from Lord Lansdowne. He repeated that he could not countenance "anything in the form of violence or uprisings against lawful authority." With this proviso, Hardinge was prepared to cooperate with the clerical movement. He even offered small sums of money "to induce others to join the national party in constitutional and loyal protest, as distinct from anything like a revolutionary movement." Since Hardinge

22. Id.

knew that the Russian loan had already been concluded, he felt that no action of the clergy would affect it. Riots would only help the enemies of Persian independence.[23]

Step by step a secret alliance between the British legation and the clerical leadership was forged in Tehran, Esfahān, and elsewhere. Hardinge did not doubt the value received for small payments which the legation made from time to time. In the case of the second Russian loan, the clergy's protest had come too late.

> But with a timid and superstitious Prince like the present Shah the warning against further concessions to Russia may not prove ineffective, and it is therefore I think very desirable with this end in view that we should maintain the relations which I have endeavoured to establish with them, and thus to some extent control their action and keep it if possible within safe and reasonable bounds.

Hardinge conceded that there were "very few leaders among them whose religious zeal is proof against bribes," but an open commitment now would make it harder for the clergy to change their position in the future without risking a loss of prestige.[24]

Hardinge's words about nonviolent and constitutional methods of opposition were nothing but cant. His agents reported that on the eve of the Shah's departure for Europe, tension was rising. Everywhere there was talk of demonstrations and riots. A French merchant was told by a member of the Russian legation to shut up his shop when the Shah left, "as there would be riots 'and another China in Tehran.'" In the presence of Amin os-Soltān's own secretary, a mulla declaimed "against the sale of the country" to Russia "and declared that the Shah on his return from Europe would not be permitted to reenter his dominions unless he signed a pledge to make no further Russian loans and grant no more concessions to Russia." He recalled how Nāser ed-Din Shah had been forced to dismiss his Grand Vizier twenty-nine years before. The people would be equally firm with his successor. "The Government no doubt relied on the Cossack Brigade," the mulla continued, "but the men composing it were in the main Persians and

23. Id.
24. Id.

Moslems and the clergy had but to remind them of their duty to their faith to make them turn and kill their Russian officers." [25]

In his attempts to save Britain's position in Persia, Hardinge was prepared to use every available means of influencing the ruling circles and, most of all, the Shah himself. He believed that Mozaffar ed-Din should visit England. "The sight of London, of our resources, etc., and a cordial reception by the King and British Government would, I am sure, have an excellent effect," he wrote Lord Lansdowne.[26] Sir Arthur also wanted the Shah to be awarded the Order of the Garter as his father had been before him. Lansdowne agreed, and Hardinge intimated to Mozaffar ed-Din that he would receive the honor.

Through some oversight, Edward VII had not been informed of the plan until shortly before the Shah's arrival. The King was very much upset by this lapse. He may even have felt that the government was attempting to abrogate one of the few remaining royal prerogatives, the granting of decorations and titles. Ignoring the precedents set in the cases of Nāser ed-Din Shah in 1873 and the Sultans Abdul Majid in 1856 and Abdul Aziz in 1867, he declared that it was undesirable to confer the Garter on non-Christians.[27]

Hardinge and Lansdowne urged the King to confer the decoration. Sir Nicholas O'Connor, British ambassador in Constantinople, protested that if this were done the Sultan, Abdul Hamid, bloody tyrant and murderer of Armenians, would also covet the honor. Disappointment might even drive him into an alliance with Germany or Russia. Hardinge argued that "although Mozaffar ed-Din Shah could not be regarded as a great Sovereign, he was not, like his father, stained by the horrible persecution of the Babis; and that his short reign had, generally speaking, been if not brilliant, at least unstained by any atrocious acts of cruelty." [28]

The Shah arrived in London on August 18. Two days later he visited the King on his yacht at Portsmouth. Lansdowne, still trying to resolve the issue, produced a memorandum stating that the

25. A. Hardinge to Lansdowne, No. 62, Tehran, April 9, 1902; ibid.
26. Cited in Newton, Lord Lansdowne, p. 234.
27. Lee, King Edward VII, 2, 155.
28. A. Hardinge, A Diplomatist in the East, p. 289.

statutes of the Order of the Garter would be amended to admit non-Christians and that the Shah would be one of the first to be so honored. Knowing full well that his own father and two sultans of Turkey had been admitted to the order in the past, Mozaffar ed-Din took the whole thing to be a way of refusing him membership, and King Edward was furious at his Foreign Secretary who, he felt, was forcing his hand. The King offered the Shah a "jewelled portrait," which he promptly refused and left the country a very unhappy man.[29]

The Bishop of Rochester; Lord A. Knollys; Lord Lansdowne; Sir Arthur Hardinge; the Prime Minister, Mr. A. J. Balfour; and the King himself hotly debated various trivia in the statutes of the order and spent a great deal of energy and time on the problem of whether a Moslem prince was worthy of being admitted to the sacred community of the Knights of the Garter. However, when the King refused to give in, letting the Shah leave garterless, the incident assumed major proportions. Sir Arthur Hardinge, who had promised the Shah the Garter as an inducement for him to visit England, threatened to resign. A Cabinet crisis was in the making. "The consequences of repudiating an assurance to the Persian Government were too dangerous, however, to allow the King's objections to prevail." Balfour concealed from the Cabinet the letter full of complaints against Lansdowne which His Majesty had written him; and in reply sent the King "a strongly worded memo" which pointed out "that Lord Lansdowne had acted under a misapprehension, and commented upon the disastrous results which would follow if the promise were repudiated."[30] In November the King surrendered " 'from patriotic motives and a high sense of duty though with the greatest reluctance,' " as he put it.[31]

On February 2, 1903, a special mission headed by Lord Downe arrived in Tehran to invest the Shah with the Order of the Garter. Several prominent Persians, including Amin os-Soltān, were also decorated amid general enthusiasm.[32] It was a brilliant

29. Lee, 2, 155–56; Newton, pp. 236–37.
30. Newton, pp. 237–38.
31. Lee, 2, 156.
32. A. Hardinge to Lansdowne, No. 31, Tehran, February 9, 1903; F. O. 60/679. The entire volume is devoted to the Garter Mission.

Seistān and the Persian Gulf

occasion, but it stirred up further trouble for the King. The Emperor of Japan learned of the Downe Mission. "This naturally created . . . 'a very bad feeling' in Japan, and eventually it became necessary to send a similar Mission to Tokio." [33] In view of the treatment the Shah had received in London, it is doubtful whether the eventual bestowal of the Garter produced the desired effect on him and his ministers. One must rather conclude that the entire episode was only a bit of comic relief in an otherwise deadly serious play.

The grimness of the situation in Persia was conveyed to Lord Lansdowne in detail by Sir Arthur Hardinge when he came to London during the visit of the Shah in August 1902. Having already gone quite far in supporting the clerical movement, Hardinge wanted more precise instructions on the extent to which it should be encouraged, "if they asked our assistance or advice, to promote either a constitutional or a revolutionary agitation against the further Russification of Persia." Hardinge wanted to know whether, "If money for instance were requisite, should we give it *sub rosa*, as the Russians did at the time of the Régie, to the leaders of the Clerical party?" The question was not settled, but Sir Arthur put on record his view that he "should have funds for the careful payments to the principal men of the Church party, both in Persia and at Najaf and Karbala." Later Lansdowne commented: "We could not mix ourselves up in a cabal against the Shah, but a moderate sum might well be spent in establishing closer relations with the Church party." [34] Hardinge conceded that the difficulties he foresaw might not arise, "that the clergy, though they may talk, will not act, or that they will be bought by Russia (as has happened before), both in Persia and Arabia, and that the Persian Government will muddle along for a few months longer." But Britain must be prepared for all eventualities, and he must have definite instructions.[35]

The clergy might arise and even excommunicate the Shah, precipitating disorders such as had occurred during the Tobacco

33. Newton, pp. 239–40.
34. A. Hardinge to Lansdowne, Most Secret, Rosenau, Datchet, August 27, 1902; F. O. 60/733. Lansdowne's comment written in the margin of Hardinge's memorandum.
35. Id.

Régie. "The Shah, threatened with deposition, may be unable to put down trouble. The Russians might then come in." On hearing this Lansdowne said he thought

> that if Russian troops crossed into Persia to repress a popular movement such as that described above, His Majesty's Government would be prepared to intervene *pari passu* in the South and in Seistan, the parts nearest to our own bases, and to occupy—ostensibly on the same principle as Russia was acting upon in the North, and with the same professed object, viz., the maintenance of internal order—the various ports of the Persian Gulf, remaining there as in China, till we had, jointly with Russia, whom we should then oblige to discuss the Persian question with us, re-establish the authority, solvency, and independence of the Shah's Government, or, should this prove impossible, till we had found other means of securing British interests in those regions.[36]

The substance of Lansdowne's conversations with Hardinge was embodied in a most secret memorandum the latter wrote and the former circulated to a number of interested persons. The Prime Minister, Arthur Balfour, generally agreed with the points made by the minister in Tehran and the Secretary of State. He did not expect a clash with Russia, but if the troops of the two powers met in Persia, war might result. "Given a war between England and Russia, in which Persia was involved;—would Persia be a suitable theatre in which to utilize our small army in an offensive movement against the enemy, or ought we to content ourselves with holding seaports and organizing native resistance to the invader?" No dogmatic solutions were possible, "But the War Office should certainly be turning it over in their minds." Balfour concluded his comments with a word of caution: "It goes without saying that even the smallest *appearance* of military activity on our part, whether by way of massing ships or otherwise, should follow, not precede, any threatening language or movement on the part of Russia, but it should follow it immediately." [37]

36. Id.
37. Mr. A.J. Balfour to the Marquess of Lansdowne, Whittingehame, Prestonkirk, September 6, 1902; ibid.

Seistān and the Persian Gulf

The War Office received a copy of Hardinge's memorandum of August 27 and gave much thought to the problem of what to do in case of Russian aggression in Persia. Lieutenant Colonel W. R. Robertson, of the Military Intelligence, stated the essence of British policy in Persia as being "the maintenance of the *status quo;* and, in case of the *status quo* being disturbed, to prevent any other Power establishing its supremacy in the Persian Gulf, or in Southern Persia." Russia's aims, on the other hand, were the seas —in Persia, in the Mediterranean, and in China. In the Mediterranean Russia had to reckon with Germany as well as with Britain. In the Far East the Anglo-Japanese alliance had checked Russia's progress. Persia was the only area where Russia confronted England alone.

Russia's position with regard to northern Persia was "one of over-whelming superiority." A strong position on the flank of India, even if not used for invasion, would constitute a constant threat and "tend to make us more amenable with regard to the Black Sea and the Persian Gulf." Should Russia reach the Persian Gulf, Britain would be entirely excluded from Persia. Therefore it was necessary to decide on the line beyond which Russia would not be allowed to advance. Robertson suggested that such a line could be drawn across Persia from Seistān, via Kermān, Yazd, and Esfahān, to Kermānshāh. "Assuming that Russia would consent to such a division, our share must be either annexed outright, or formed into a protectorate, or turned into a buffer State under the best Persian Chief we could lay hands on." However, division of the country would not assure everlasting peace. Britain would have to maintain armed forces sufficient to repulse a Russian attack. At least fifty thousand and perhaps as many as a hundred thousand troops would be needed. Robertson knew that no such forces were available. "It hardly seems necessary to say more," he noted sadly, "in order to show that, unless our military system be revolutionized, we cannot carry out the policy laid down."

Moreover, there was no sign that Russia was willing to divide Persia into spheres of influence. Robertson quoted the *Birzhevye Vedomosti* of St. Petersburg to the effect that "There can be no division of spheres of influence in Persia, which, together with the waters which bathe its shores, must remain the object of Russian material and moral protection." And the *Novoe Vremia:* "Let England once understand that we do not want India, but only the Persian Gulf, and the whole question is settled." The only way to confront Russia, Robertson went on, was to hold at least Bandar Abbās and the Gulf islands. When it came to specific suggestions, Robertson had none to offer. Britain must make preparations for Persia's "dismemberment," pending which she should push her influence and "endeavour to prevent Russia from strengthening her present dominating position." [38]

Lieutenant Colonel E. A. Altham generally concurred with Robertson. "War with Russia . . . would probably entail also war with France." Such a struggle would inflict upon the British Empire "a period of humiliating disasters, from which recovery will be most difficult." He saw the dilemma facing Britain as follows:

> If we take steps to counteract a Russian advance into Persia, we risk a war in which our chances of success are very doubtful; if we do nothing and let Russia gradually absorb Persia, the evil day is but put off to a time when we shall be forced to fight Russia for India under still more unfavourable conditions.

Altham advocated military reorganization and the conclusion of alliances. Specifically he wanted an agreement with Germany on Asia Minor and Persia similar to the one with Japan on the Far East. Under such circumstances Russia would not risk war, "or, if the war ensued, it would be a war the results of which we need not fear." [39]

Lieutenant General Sir W. G. Nicholson, Director General of Military Intelligence, forwarded his subordinates' papers to Lord F. Roberts, the Commander in Chief, with a brief note stating that it seemed impossible to maintain British interests in Persia

38. Strategic Relations between England and Russia with regard to Persia, Lieutenant-Colonel W. R. Robertson, A.Q.M.G. Intelligence Division (2), October 4, 1904, War Office Memoranda on Sir A. Hardinge's Letter of August 27, 1902 and Papers annexed to it; ibid.

39. Lieutenant-Colonel E. A. Altham, A.Q.M.G., Intelligence Division (2), October 14, 1902, W. O. Memoranda . . . ; ibid.

unless an understanding was arrived at with either Germany or Russia. He preferred the German alternative since "the interests of England and Russia are so obviously antagonistic that any agreement as to spheres of influence in Persia would probably be infringed by Russia whenever it suited her purpose to do so." Nicholson felt that Seistān must be held. However, "Any idea of the military occupation of Southern Persia cannot, I think, be entertained, as the requisite troops could not be provided without dangerously weakening the garrison of India." [40]

Finally, the Secretary of War, St. John Brodrick, read the papers. Being a civilian, he saw the issue in an entirely different light. First, he refused to admit that the British army was as weak as the military claimed. Second, he felt that they had concentrated too much on Persia. "Any engagement with France and Russia would, in the very unlikely contingency of our having no ally, be conducted in a good many spheres besides Persia." Moreover, Brodrick did not believe that France would fight on Russia's side:

> It is not clear [he wrote] that it is to France's interest to establish Russia in the Persian Gulf, while it is very clear that it is not to Germany's interest that these two powers [France and Russia] should monopolize the trade of that region, and in the event of hostilities we are exceedingly unlikely to stand alone.[41]

The India Office under Lord George Hamilton was in its usual pessimistic mood. Sir William Lee Warner, Undersecretary of State, insisted that Britain must be prepared to act alone in case of war. Should any other power intervene, Russia would have northern Persia in her sole occupation, while England would be sharing the south with other European powers. Hamilton did not believe that Britain could hold all of southern Persia, and advised that this limitation of capabilities be faced "at the beginning of any new departure of policy." [42] The India Office wanted a con-

40. Lieutenant-General Sir W. G. Nicholson, D.G.M.I., October 16, 1902, W. O. Memoranda . . . ; ibid.
41. St. J[ohn] B[rodrick], November 4, 1902, W. O. Memoranda . . . ; ibid.
42. Persia, Most Secret, India Office Minutes on Sir A. Hardinge's Letter of August 27, 1902, and Papers annexed to it; ibid.

ference with the Foreign Office, the War Office, and the Admiralty to discuss the Persian problem.

The conference was held at the Foreign Office on November 19, 1902. The Admiralty was represented by Prince Louis of Battenberg, Director of Naval Intelligence, and Captain Armstrong; the Foreign Office by Sir Thomas Sanderson; the India Office by Sir W. Lee Warner and Sir A. Godley; the War Office by Lieutenant General Sir W. Nicholson and Lieutenant Colonel Altham. It was agreed that in the event of war with France and Russia, Britain would seize Bandar Abbās and occupy the Gulf islands of Qeshm, Hengām, and Hormoz. In case of disorders in Persia leading to Russian occupation and the entry of British troops into Persian territory, though not against Russia, it was decided to limit action by the following conditions:

(i) We have no troops available for the effective occupation of Persian territory, or even of any large number of Persian ports; and it is by troops and not by ships that positions on the sea coast must be held.

(ii) We should run the risk of creating a most unfortunate impression upon India if we occupied any ports or districts from which we might probably be forced to retire, either in view of an impending collision with Russia, or subsequently to an out-break of hostilities.

(iii) Whatever steps we might take should be such as to involve as little as possible the risk of further complications by the intervention of other foreign Powers in any temporary measures taken to preserve order in Persia.[43]

If need be, Britain would occupy Bandar Abbās, the islands, and Seistān, but it was held that no other occupation of territory or operations inland should be attempted. To prepare for the possible occupation of Seistān, it was decided to extend the Baluchestān railway beyond Nushki and encourage the growth of British trade.

It was [also] agreed that in reality the most effective check to Russian progress towards South Persia lay in the comple-

43. The Persian Question, Secret, Minutes of a Conference held on Wednesday, November 19, 1902; ibid.

tion of the railway from Constantinople to Bagdad, as it would bring the Turks in force on the flank of a Russian advance, and that it would be a great mistake to oppose the project, which we ought on the contrary to encourage to the best of our power, provided we can acquire our proper share in the control of the railway and its outlet on the Persian Gulf.[44]

The decisions of the conference ratified the policy of abandonment and withdrawal long urged upon the government by Hamilton and several of his subordinates at the India Office. It is significant that of those present no one shared either Lord Curzon's or Sir Arthur Hardinge's views on Persia, nor was any of them except Lee Warner and Godley particularly well informed in regard to the Middle East. The policy established on November 19 was not that of the Viceroy, the Secretary of State for Foreign Affairs, or the minister in Tehran, yet it proved prophetic of things to come. Three years later the Liberals would come back to power after ten years in the wilderness of loyal opposition. Their Foreign Secretary, Sir Edward Grey, would endorse most of the decisions of November 19.

Sir Arthur Hardinge was entirely disappointed in the outcome of consultations to which he had given rise by his memorandum of August 1902. He found the conclusions of the interdepartmental conference of November 19, 1902, "almost tantamount to an abdication" of Britain's position in Persia. His worry was increased in the summer of 1903 when the domestic situation in Persia deteriorated still further, and the Russian Minister intimated to the Grand Vizier "that if the helplessness of the Persian Government should occasion more serious troubles at Tabreez and in other parts of Azerbaijan, Russian troops may be obliged to cross the frontier." [45]

General war was one thing, but the entry of Russian troops into Persia occasioned by local events was something else again. If British intervention were confined to the Gulf ports and Seistān, the Russians would take over the rest of the country by default.

44. Id.
45. A. Hardinge to Lansdowne, No. 88, Secret, Gulahek, June 17, 1903; ibid.

Persia would become a Russian Egypt, "and English influence would be as completely dead and buried, not merely at Tehran, but throughout the length and breadth of the land, as French influence has been in the Nile Valley since the day when Colonel Marchand hauled the tricolour down at Fashoda." Hardinge would not abandon Persia but rather would enter into an alliance with Bakhtiāri, Arab, and other tribes of the southwest and hold it, together with Esfahān, "the old, historical metropolis of Persia," depriving Russia "of any excuse for advancing further south on the pretext of preserving the Shah's authority in the southern portion of his kingdom." Russia, Hardinge felt, would not consider "British participation in the pacification of Persia a *casus belli.*" [46]

Government machinery was slow. It was February 1904 when the Government of India made its contribution to a debate now two and a half years old. Many things had happened since Hardinge penned his memorandum. Russia had become heavily involved in a Far Eastern adventure that would soon explode in war with Japan. Witte, one of the prime movers of Russia's Persian policy for over a decade, was no longer Minister of Finance. But the British government was still operating along the lines arrived at by the interdepartmental conference of November 19, 1902, Hardinge's letter to Lansdowne not having had much effect.

The Government of India shared St. John Brodrick's view that in case of war Persia was unlikely to be the main theater of operations. Furthermore, Curzon did not believe that Russia intended to annex Persia. He proceeded to give an astonishingly correct analysis of Russia's modus operandi. Russia, he argued,

> greatly prefers to control the Government of the countries, which she desires to influence, through the prevailing form of government and dynasty, and to utilize them as the instruments through whom she may obtain supreme political influence and unchallenged commercial control. . . . For these purposes it is necessary that the unit with which she is dealing for the time being be so weak as to be dependent,

46. Id.

Seistān and the Persian Gulf

but not so weak as to fall absolutely to pieces. The screen of the native Government must be kept intact, so as to cover what might otherwise have the appearance of hostile designs.

If Russian troops entered Persia to suppress internal disorders and establish military occupation, British forces should follow suit.

We should enter as the supporters of the dynasty, in order to insure a return to the *status quo ante*, and to save those parts of the country lying nearest our borders or in which our interests are paramount, from the risks of disorder . . . Above all, though this may sound paradoxical, we should enter in order to accelerate, under proper conditions, evacuation by the Russians as well as ourselves.

Curzon agreed with Hardinge that, in addition to Bandar Abbās and Seistān, Britain should, in the event of a Russian move, occupy Bushehr and Mohammareh, the latter being nearest Tehran. However, the surest preventive against a Russian move into Persia was her knowledge of the consequences of her actions. "If she is fully convinced that a move upon Tabreez or Meshed will be at once followed by a British move in the South, and particularly upon the Gulf ports, she will probably think twice about a step that would risk so much for so problematic a gain." [47]

Whatever differences of opinion existed between British statesmen, soldiers, and diplomats on the proper policy to be pursued vis-à-vis Russia in Persia, and the differences were great, they all agreed at least on the proposition that Seistān and the Persian Gulf were vitally important to Britain and must be protected in case of a Russian attempt to occupy the rest of the country.

"Seistan is practically a badly tilled oasis in the midst of deserts and swamps." [48] It is a vast land, stretching along the Afghan

47. Government of India to Mr. Brodrick, Fort William, February 4, 1904, Enclosure No. 1 in I. O. to F. O., Most Secret, February 20, 1904; ibid. The letter was signed by Curzon, Kitchener, and others, but the thoughts as well as the style are Curzon's.
48. L. Fraser, *India under Curzon and After* (New York, 1911), p. 116.

and Baluch borders, isolated from the rest of the world by hundreds of miles of almost impenetrable sand and rock. Once upon a time Seistān was prosperous. Legend made it the home of Persia's great champion, Rostam, the "grave" of whose mythological father, Zāl, is shown to this day to interested travelers by the main highway between Qāen and Zāhedān.[49] With the rise of Afghan power, Seistān temporarily fell under the rule of various petty princes of Herāt, Qandahār, and Kābul, but in the second half of the nineteenth century, Persia reimposed her authority on a major part of the province. The dispute with the Afghans was settled in 1872 by an arbitration commission headed by Sir Frederic Goldsmid.

To the English, Seistān was of great strategic value. "It's possession would be an important preliminary to a comprehensive advance upon India, or an invasion of Afghanistan."[50] Russian advances in Central Asia in the 1880s had provoked much fear in India that Khorāsān, Seistān, and Afghanistan might be next to fall. However, British counteraction had been confined largely to intelligence gathering.

A network of native agents spread all over Central Asia. Some worked for the British, some for the Russians, and some for both. The Government of India was extremely sensitive to spies and infiltrators. Its own intelligence center in Mashhad constantly reported on Russian troop movements in Turkestan as well as on the movements of seemingly insignificant individuals in Khorāsān. The opening of Russian and British consulates in Khorāsān and Seistān was a part of the same game of secret politicking and spying.

Both Russians and Englishmen found Khorāsān and Seistān difficult assignments. Isolation and loneliness were hard to bear in such places as Birjand, Qāen, or Nosratābād, small dusty towns where society consisted of a couple of provincial officials, a mulla, and the consul himself. There was almost no work to do, and time had to be killed playing cards or drinking. Occasionally a consul would study Persian language and literature and escape the demoralizing routine of consular life.

49. The author visited the spot in 1943 and noted that Zāl had been thoroughly assimilated by the local population to the pantheon of Moslem saints.
50. Fraser, p. 116.

Seistān and the Persian Gulf

Under such conditions spies provided welcome relief and excitement. While British agents quietly made their way north, Russian agents, posing as merchants, cruised along the Afghan and Indian borders. The first permanent Russian agent in Seistān, a certain Rahim Khān, seems to have arrived there in 1891. He was arrested and flogged by order of the local chief, Mir Ali Akbar Khān Heshmat ol-Molk, for "unnatural offences," and his property was confiscated. The Russian legation in Tehran openly intervened in his behalf. Rahim Khān's property was restored to him, and he was allowed to live in Seistān to the humiliation of Heshmat ol-Molk. Rahim Khān engaged in propaganda, telling people that the Russians would soon come and show favor to those who helped him. The chief mulla, "a man of great influence amongst the people," was recruited by Rahim Khān, and helped him to incite the people against the government.[51]

In 1895 Lieutenant Colonel H. Picot, Britain's military attaché in Tehran, and Colonel C. E. Yate, on a visit from Mashhad, discussed "the advisability of extending our Agency system of espionage in Central Asia and the Caucasus." During the war scare of 1895, Picot pointed out in a memorandum to Sir Mortimer Durand, then British minister, the only information about Russian troop movements into Transcaspia came from Mr. Peacock, consul at Batum. Since then the consulate general at Mashhad had been established and kept watch on Central Asia as far as Samarkand but could report on Russian troops only after they had arrived in Central Asia. There was a need for intelligence from Baku, Petrovsk, Astrakhan, and Tiflis.[52]

In 1897 the Russians took a long step in extending their own intelligence in eastern and southeastern Persia. Under the pretext of preventing the plague, which had broken out in Bombay, from reaching Russia, her minister in Tehran, Evgenii Bützow, requested that the Persian government allow a number of Russian

51. Government of India to I. O., Foreign Department, No. 137, Secret, Frontier, Simla, July 24, 1894; L. I., 1894.
52. Memorandum respecting News Agencies in Central Asia and the Caucasus by Lt. Col. H. Picot, Tehran, July 1, 1895, Appendix 5, Enclosure in Memorandum by Sir M. Durand on the Situation in Persia, December 1895, Confidential (6704); F. O. 60/581.

doctors to establish quarantine posts along the Perso-Afghan border and the highways leading into Khorāsān from Seistān. No sooner had the Persian government acceded to this request than General A. N. Kuropatkin, disregarding the agreement reached by Bützow and the Persian Foreign Minister, Mohsen Khān Moshir od-Dowleh, that the doctors would be protected by a Persian military escort, began to insist upon an escort of one hundred and twenty Russian Cossacks. The Persian minister at St. Petersburg pointed out to the Minister of Foreign Affairs, Count M. N. Murav'ev, that Kuropatkin's demand contravened the agreement already reached, and that the British legation at Tehran had protested against the stationing of Russian troops on the Perso-Afghan border.[53]

Charles Hardinge, who was in charge of the legation in the absence of Sir Mortimer Durand, believed that "The object of the Russians was to penetrate as far south as Seistan in order to be able to turn the flank of the frontiers of India." In his memoirs he took credit for having thwarted the Russians and forced them to decamp by bringing some Indian troops to the frontier.[54] Lord Hardinge of Penshurst, reminiscing in his old age about the diplomatic feats of young Mr. Charles Hardinge, may be forgiven a few inaccuracies. Indeed, he had tried to take vigorous action against the Cossacks, but Salisbury, who was then hoping for a détente with Russia, advised him not to emphasize the Cossack escort. Thereafter Hardinge remained silent, especially since he had learned "that Count Muravieff had informed the Persian Minister in St. Petersburg that Her Majesty's Government had consented to the entry of Russian troops into Persia for service on the Afghan frontier." [55]

Once the Cossacks had arrived, they stayed. Gradually their officers began to assume administrative functions and issue orders to local civil and military authorities. They intervened in local affairs, usually taking the side of the population against corrupt government officials. A British secret agent testified that the Russians took up "the cause of the people against their own [the

53. C. Hardinge to Salisbury, No. 23, Tehran, March 14, 1897; F. O. 60/584.
54. C. Hardinge, *Old Diplomacy*, p. 64.
55. C. Hardinge to Salisbury, No. 23, Tehran, March 13, 1897; F. O. 60/584.

Persian] government." This made the Russians popular, though it distressed local officials.[56]

The Persian government, when pressed by the British, agreed that the object of the Cossack cordons "was not so much the exclusion of plague as the placing of every conceivable obstacle in the way of commercial intercourse between India and Khorasan."[57] But it was utterly incapable of forcing the withdrawal of the Cossacks.

The quarantine system was a continuous annoyance to the British. Its two dozen stations strung along the Afghan border were so many thorns in the side of the Government of India. Captain H. Smyth of the Cheshire Regiment reported to Consul General Trench in Mashhad that the posts were commanded by Captain Iyas (?), an officer of the Russian Imperial Guard.

> He is a very capable officer, speaking French, English, Persian very well, and some Urdu and Pushtu. He is high-handed and arbitrary, interfering freely with the Persian officials. He is well supplied with excellent Russian maps, far better than any we possess, and he does a large amount of intelligence work, being able to cross-examine men coming from every direction.[58]

The British tried to get the Russians out. In 1902 Lord Lansdowne personally spoke about it to Amin os-Soltān. The latter blamed Amin od-Dowleh, during whose brief administration the Russians had been admitted. They were interfering in Persia's internal affairs and disrupting Indian trade, but it was difficult, if not impossible, to dislodge them.[59]

In the summer of 1898 Russia appointed a consul to Seistān.

---

56. Memorandum of Information received during the month of August 1897, regarding affairs beyond the North-West Frontier of India, Enclosure in Government of India to the I. O., Foreign Department, Secret, Frontier, No. 129, Simla, September 8, 1897; L. I., 45, 1897.

57. Government of India to Hamilton, No. 110, Simla, July 3, 1902; L. I., 146, 1902, No. 967.

58. Captain H. Smyth's Report to Consul General C. Trench, Meshed, May 2, 1902, Enclosure in ibid.

59. See various papers concerning the Russian sanitary cordon in Khorāsān in F. O. 60/732.

Since there were no Russian subjects anywhere near, and no Russian trade or any other interests, the step was clearly calculated to demonstrate to the British that they had no monopoly on southeastern Persia. The British consul at Kermān, Captain Percy M. Sykes, urged the Foreign Office immediately to appoint an English consul. Soon Sykes himself was transferred to Seistān, where his principal task was to watch his Russian colleague.[60]

That same summer three Englishmen, engaged in a "topographical survey" in the vicinity of Panjdeh, crossed into Russian territory. They were discovered and conducted back across the frontier. In September a Russian surveyor and three assistants appeared on the Perso-Baluch border near Mirjāveh.[61] The great game went on.

The arrival of George Curzon in India coincided with increased Russian activity in East Persia. The new Viceroy, reversing the cautious policy of his predecessor, urged that Britain protect Seistān. He began to build a railway from Quetta to Nushki and a road thence to the Persian frontier. Postal and telegraph service was opened, and posts established for the military protection of trade.[62] But Curzon's principal goal in Seistān was the exclusion of Russia, a formidable task at a time when Britain was diplomatically isolated and militarily involved in Africa.

In the tense atmosphere of 1900 and 1901 rumors spread far and wide, and truth was often hard to distinguish from fancy. The Russian consul in Seistān, A. Miller, was known for his extreme Anglophobia. Several Russians were traveling through the land and one of them, named Zarudnyi, was reported to have distributed rifles as presents to tribesmen.[63] In April 1901 the Government of India was alarmed at the persistent rumors picked up by the Major Chevenix Trench, consul general at Mashhad, that Persia intended either to let Russia "farm" Seistān's revenues or sell the province outright.

60. See various documents in L. I., 106, 1898, Register No. 870, September 1898.
61. Ibid., No. 1023, November 4, 1898.
62. L. Fraser, *India under Curzon and After*, p. 121.
63. From the Viceroy [Telegram], No. 273, February 20, 1901, Foreign, Secret; L. I., 130. 1901.

Seistān and the Persian Gulf

We think [Curzon cabled London] that in no circumstances, direct or indirect, ought Seistan to pass under Russian control. An intimation to the Persian Government of the interest that we take in Seistan, and of our inability to acquiesce in its extinction, might forestall any such move, if contemplated.[64]

Similar intelligence was received later concerning Khorāsān, where Shojā' od-Dowleh, Governor of Quchān, was known as a Russian puppet who kept his money in Russian banks. It was reported that all along Khorāsān's northern border Persian officials were in Russia's pay, Russian-Armenian money lenders were buying up agricultural land, letters and telegrams were opened and their contents communicated to the Russian agent in Quchān. The agent himself was said to be "the governor's chief adviser" and the districts of Daregaz and Quchān "already regarded by the Russians as part of Russian dominions." From Tehran orders had reportedly been sent to the governor to sell the Crown lands to Persian subjects, "and Russian subjects had been adopting the plan, so usual in Persia, of buying land in the name of some Persian subject." [65] The India Office reacted with great calm. Britain had Persia's promise that the customs of the south would not be turned over to foreign control. An undersecretary of state (probably W. Lee Warner, the signature is illegible) thought that Seistān was included in "Southern Persia," and, if not, there was no objection to asking Persia to include it. As for the rumor itself, Chevenix Trench had "proved somewhat bombastic and inaccurate," and it was improbable that Russia was about to move as alleged.[66]

The India Office called Lord Lansdowne's attention to Curzon's telegram of April 28, and the Foreign Secretary instructed Sir Arthur Hardinge to verify the rumors. "We cannot, of

64. Viceroy to India Office, Telegram in cypher, Simla, April 28, 1901; L. I., 132. 1901.
65. Memorandum of information received during the month of December 1901, regarding affairs on and beyond the North-West Frontier of India; L. I., 141, 1902, No. 199.
66. India Office, Minute Paper, Register No. 513; ibid.

course," he added, "tolerate any tampering with Seistan by Russia." [67] Hardinge quickly discovered that in the spring of 1901 the Persian government, desperately looking for cash, decided to sell a portion of Seistān's Crown lands, which made up most of the province. The British minister believed it possible that the Russians had considered a plan to buy these lands. The hereditary governor of Seistān, Heshmat ol-Molk, a friend of the British, suggested that, as a way of preventing the Russians from acquiring the Crown lands, the English help him buy them. Hardinge favored the scheme but warned that it must be concealed from the Persian government.[68]

Heshmat ol-Molk's proposal did not meet with approval among Indian officials. Colonel C. E. Yate, governor-general's agent in Baluchestān, wrote that if Britain were "to purchase the country in Hashmat-ul-Mulk's name, we should have no hold upon him after the purchase was completed, but to purchase it in our own name would be quite a different matter." [69]

Yate did not believe that the Persian government would sell the land but hoped the Government of India could get it on a ninety-nine years' lease. Curzon was willing to grab Seistān under any arrangement. Hearing that a couple of Mashhad merchants had bid for Crown lands, the Viceroy telegraphed Sir Arthur Hardinge: "Whatever course is proposed, whether purchase or lease of Seistan lands, or farm of Seistan revenues, our desire would be to outbid all others." [70] Next day Hardinge replied that it was impossible either to buy Seistān lands outright or to secure them through Heshmat ol-Molk.[71] Curzon confessed that he too doubted the advisability of working through Heshmat ol-Molk; but he already had a new plan. Let Hardinge, taking advantage of the Shah's pecuniary difficulties, offer Persia a loan on the security of Seistān revenue. As for Hardinge's suggestion that he obtain

67. Lansdowne to A. Hardinge, No. 12, May 6, 1901; *L. I.*, 134, 1901, No. 769.
68. A. Hardinge to the Foreign Secretary of the Government of India, Telegram, May 7, 1901; same to same, Telegram, May 9, 1901; ibid.
69. Col. C. E. Yate to the Secretary of the Government of India, Foreign Department, No. 81, Confidential, Quetta, May 20, 1901; ibid.
70. Curzon to A. Hardinge, Telegram No. 2384F, Simla, May 28, 1901; ibid.
71. A. Hardinge to Curzon, Telegram, May 29, 1901; ibid.

from the Persian government a promise not to alienate lands without giving notice to the British, it had only negative value, since such a promise "would imply that alienation to Russia is possible—a contingency which we would not accept." [72] Thus the British, who started out by reacting to a mere rumor of Russia's alleged plan for buying land in Seistān, found themselves seriously considering precisely such a course of action.

The whole scheme was abandoned as rapidly as it had originated. The only loser was the unfortunate Heshmat ol-Molk who had earned himself the distrust of his own government and the hatred of Russian agents in Seistān and Khorāsān. While Hardinge and Curzon exchanged telegrams, the Persian government, encouraged if not instigated by the Russians, demanded from Heshmat arrears of revenue. The British consul at Mashhad urged Hardinge to authorize the vice-consul at Seistān to make Heshmat ol-Molk a "present of £2000 to relieve present pressure." He feared that "otherwise Heshmat may be led to accept pecuniary help from Russia and become her dependent instead of ours." [73]

The first signs of trouble for Heshmat ol-Molk had appeared earlier that year. In his official diary for the period ending April 11, Captain R. A. E. Benn, vice-consul in Seistān, had reported the local rumor that Heshmat ol-Molk had been "severely censured" for allowing British officers to obtain so much influence. Moreover the Russian consul, A. Miller, succeeded in intimidating him to such a degree that he had "somewhat modified the friendliness of his conduct" toward the English.[74]

H. S. Barnes, India's Foreign Secretary, wrote Hardinge that the Government of India attached the highest importance "to the assertion of the paramount interest of Great Britain in Seistan." It held

> that in no circumstances should Seistan be permitted to pass, like the northern provinces of Persia, under the control or

72. Curzon to A. Hardinge, Telegram, No. 1319F, Simla, May 31, 1901, ibid.

73. A. Hardinge to Secretary of the Government of India, Foreign Department, Telegram, No. 12, May 22, 1901; ibid.

74. From H. S. Barnes to A. Hardinge, No. 1291F, Simla, May 29, 1901, L. I... 134, 1901, No. 723.

even the preponderating influence of Russia, and that British prestige and influence in that quarter should be constantly and actively maintained.

Barnes freely admitted that though commercial considerations were important, "the object of the Government of India in opening the route to Quetta and pushing trade had been mainly political." (In the original document someone other than its writer underlined the word "political" and put a cross next to it.)

> In these circumstances [Barnes went on] the downfall of the present Governor of Seistan would be a serious blow to the plans which the Government of India have in view, since the substitution of a less friendly and accommodating Governor could hardly fail to affect the trade injuriously, and in this way to weaken our claim to regard Seistan as manifestly and exclusively within our sphere of influence.[75]

The letter contained an interesting admission. It had become the fashion in the nineteenth century to justify aggressive action, interference in the internal affairs of nations, and even war, by the supposed interests of commerce. Industry and trade had been raised to the status of gods in the new bourgeois mythology, and the presence of commercial interests was believed to bestow the right to intervene in their defense. Once this ethic became established, all sorts of noneconomic interests were justified or defended in the guise of commerce and trade. Britain's position in Seistān was a case in point. The profits a few Indian merchants derived from trading in Seistān would not have sufficed to maintain British consulates and secret agencies in eastern Persia, let alone pay for highways and railways over hundreds of miles of desert in Baluchestān, the military outposts, the telegraph lines, and the salaries of hundreds of Englishmen involved in the effort. Only in a secret letter would a high Indian official admit to the minister in Tehran the obvious truth that "the object of the Government of India in opening the route to Quetta and pushing trade had been mainly political." Thus the British, whose various

75. Id.

representatives in Tehran loved to lecture the Persians on the autonomy, if not the primacy, of business, were acting, at least in Seistān, exactly the way the Russians did in every province of northern Persia, making an artificially created commerce serve as a screen for, and a justification of, political penetration and intervention.

Curzon was determined to save Heshmat ol-Molk, whose "friendly attitude toward the British Government, particularly in the matter of encouraging trade with Quetta," had been "misrepresented by A. Miller, the Russian Consul," and who was, "in consequence, likely to incur the displeasure of the Persian Government." The Viceroy asked Hardinge to use his influence in behalf of Heshmat ol-Molk, who had been ordered by his government to go to Tehran, though it was "more than doubtful whether he will obey the summons." [76] Consul General Trench, himself an official agent of the Viceroy, also urged prompt action.

Sir Arthur was prepared to talk to Amin os-Soltān about Heshmat ol-Molk. On June 22 he cabled Lansdowne:

> The Persians always reproach us with not supporting our friends, and say that this is why we have lost so many. I fear that, if we let him [Heshmat ol-Molk] fall, we shall lose our influence in Seistan to Russia. A hint that, if trouble arose there in consequence of his recall, an Indian military detachment might . . . be sent over the border for protection of Indian traders would, in the last resort, probably prove effective.[77]

On the twenty-third the Foreign Office replied that in talking to the Grand Vizier, Hardinge should dwell "on importance of our commercial interests in Seistan, which we cannot afford to neglect." The Foreign Office deprecated any action on the part of the Persian government that would cause disturbances in Seistān and thereby compel the British "to take measures for the protection of those interests." However, London was not as firmly de-

76. Government of India to Lord Hamilton, No. 91, Secret, Simla, June 6, 1901; ibid.
77. A. Hardinge to F. O., Telegram, No. 30, June 22, 1901; ibid.

voted to Heshmat ol-Molk as was Simla, and did not wish to insist "in so many words on retention of Heshmat who may after all prove a broken reed." [78]

There was no agreement between Whitehall and Simla on how far Hardinge should go in pressing the Persian government on various matters concerning Seistān. Curzon had entered into direct communications with Hardinge and had tried, with some success, to conduct England's foreign policy from India. Since Hardinge's own views were on the whole closer to Curzon's than to Lord George Hamilton's, the Viceroy preferred not to go through the India Office where his recommendations were likely to be disregarded entirely or, at best, modified beyond recognition. Neither the Foreign Office nor the India Office approved of Curzon's methods. Hamilton undertook to point out to him that the instructions Hardinge had from the Foreign Office in regard to Seistān did not go as far as the Government of India wanted and asked for in the Viceroy's dispatches to the Minister at Tehran.

> I take this opportunity [Hamilton went on] to point out that inconvenience must inevitably arise from direct correspondence with Tehran on a matter of Imperial policy, in respect of which the British Minister is receiving his instructions from the Foreign Office, while Your Excellency is in communication with myself upon it. In these circumstances it seems to me manifestly preferable that any suggestions which the Government of India may consider it desirable to make in similar circumstances should be made to this Office.[79]

The courtesy of the traditional ending, "I have the honour to be, My Lord, Your Lordship's most obedient humble Servant," could not palliate the pain which the sensitive, proud, and ambitious Viceroy must have felt at having been administered this blunt reprimand.

Heshmat ol-Molk was saved by the British, but their position was still precarious. The angry, muffled struggle between the

78. F. O. to A. Hardinge, Telegram, No. 22, June 23, 1901; ibid.
79. Hamilton to Curzon, No. 10, Secret, July 5, 1901; ibid.

representatives of the two great powers involved Baluch tribesmen, whom the British wanted to protect from Russian influence and whom the Russians supplied with guns; Cossacks, who used quarantine procedures to disrupt Indian trade; Belgian customs officials, who were supposed to be neutral but served Russia; and the plain people of small, poverty-ridden Persian towns, who suddenly became an object of solicitude on the part of foreigners.[80]

Though appeal to the masses had not yet become a major aspect of Anglo-Russian rivalry, psychological warfare was practiced on a small scale at Nosratābād, where Consul Trench, before having been transferred to Mashhad, used to hold weekly tent-pegging practices for the horsemen of his Indian escort as a means of impressing the people.

As Major Trench has already reported, this weekly "gymkhana" is generally attended not only by the local inhabitants, but by villagers from outside Nasratabad. Tea, *kalian* [water pipes], are always served, and keen interest is displayed in the proceedings. The Russian Vice-Consul and his party are always invited and invariably attend. To-day Mr. Miller excused himself on the plea of ill health, and before long it was evident that he had prepared a counter attraction in the shape of a native band with a performing monkey, etc. A crowd of boys and children from the Fort took up its position a few yards behind my darbar tent, which does duty for a "grand stand" on these occasions, and began the most distracting programme. Men, who were recognized as Russian servants, were also sent round among our spectators to draw attention to the rival show; but I am glad to say without result. Not a man even left his place and the band retired to the city. I trust I may be pardoned for recording so trivial an occurrence in an official diary; but the incident affords a good example of the childish schemes Mr. Miller resorts to to belittle my appointment here and damage our popularity.[81]

80. See the various documents in L. I., *140, 1901*, Nos. 1475* and 1481.
81. April 6th, Diary No. 6 of Captain R. A. E. Benn, His Britannic Majesty's Vice Consul for Seistan and Kain for period ending 11th April, 1901; L. I., *133, 1901*, No. 645.

One would give much to see the Russian counterpart of this unique document; one would give even more for a film, recording for posterity this particular encounter of the two empires.

The episode with the monkey may seem amusing in retrospect, but it was taken seriously by the participants. Personal relations between Miller and Benn deteriorated, reaching the breaking point early in 1902. In tones befitting important matters of state, Captain Benn reported to his superior in Mashhad that at a dinner party in January Miller had drunk too much, become boisterous, and related "indelicate incidents which had occurred to him in Kirman." In May Miller arrived drunk at Benn's party in honor of the King's birthday. "After dinner in the drawing-room, M. Miller very rudely insisted on interrupting the conversation, and finally fell asleep in his chair." Benn interpreted Miller's behavior as an insult to His Majesty's Government and requested that it be brought to the notice of the minister in Tehran so that "such measures as may be deemed necessary by His Excellency may be taken to prevent the repetition of it." In the meantime, Benn would neither invite Miller nor accept his hospitality.[82] Reading these sad reports one can imagine the tensions within the European community consisting of half a dozen people thrown upon its own entirely inadequate spiritual resources in a small, hot, isolated town on the edge of a great desert, full of boredom and gossip, seething with intrigue, rancor, and hate. Perhaps in its own grotesque way the European community at Nosratābād symbolized the vast world of imperialist politics of which it was a reflection.

The excessive sensitivity of Captain Benn must have resulted partly from the prominent role Consul Miller was then playing in the Mirjāveh dispute, also known as the Dozdāb question.

Late in 1901 a small detachment of Anglo-Indian troops under Captain Webb Ware established an outpost at Mirjāveh, a village on the right bank of the Talab River in what was generally acknowledged as Persian territory. The initiative came from British officials on the Northwest Frontier who believed that

82. R. A. E. Benn to Lt. Col. J. F. Whyte, Consul-General in Khorasan and Seistan; No. 105, Confidential, Seistan, June 4, 1902; L. I., 146, 1902, No. 1038.

Mirjāveh, as a source of supplies for the Seistān trade route, was of the utmost importance to the British, whereas Dozdāb (now Zāhedān) would be of greatest importance to Russia should she plan to build a railway through eastern Persia to the Persian Gulf. For the British, wrote Colonel C. E. Yate, governor-general's agent in Baluchestān, the possession of Dozdāb "would be a spoke in the wheel of the projected Russian Railway." [83]

Immediately after the British arrived at Mirjāveh, Persia lodged a vigorous protest with Sir Arthur Hardinge, who suspected that the Russians may have given Amin os-Soltān the courage to demand the prompt withdrawal of British outposts from Persian territory. The Government of India ordered Webb Ware to retire to the left bank of the Talab, enabling Hardinge to inform the Persians that the captain, who had occupied some Persian territory "under a misapprehension," had been instructed to withdraw.[84]

The Government of India was anxious to negotiate with Persia on "rectification" of the border in such a way as to obtain both Mirjāveh and Dozdāb. Hardinge advised against it. The Shah was very suspicious of British designs on Baluchestān, and the Grand Vizier would probably consult the Russian legation, which would almost certainly advise him to insist on retaining Dozdāb, and promise him the support of the Russian government. "As the tract in question is, in the words of your dispatch under reply, 'not worthy to be subject of sustained controversy,' I think it would be simpler to accept and mark out by cairns or pillars the line indicated on the map." [85]

The Persian government adopted a firm, yet conciliatory line. It stated that the right bank of the Talab was as Persian as Qom or Kāshān and that it expected the British government to recognize the undoubted rights of Persia, "and instruct its officials not to interfere in the frontier which would be contrary to the

---

83. Col. C. E. Yate to the Secretary to the Government of India in the Foreign Department, No. 233, Confidential, Camp Ziarat, June 27, 1902; L. I., 149, 1902, No. 1526A.

84. A. Hardinge to Moshir od-Dowleh, April 6, 1902; L. I., 145, 1902, No. 854

85. A. Hardinge to Barnes, No. 14, Tehran, April 11, 1902; ibid.

friendly relations of the two Powers." At the same time Persia did not reject Hardinge's suggestions for a boundary-marking commission.[86]

Russia entered the Mirjāveh-Dozdāb question at the start. Her ambassador to Britain made inquiries in regard to the dispute, indicating his government's interest and concern. Fishing for information, Hardinge mentioned this to the Belgian Director of Persian Custom, M. Joseph Naus, who worked closely with the manager of the Russian bank, Grube, and knew much. Hardinge expressed his regret that the Persians had involved the Russians in the Mirjāveh issue. Naus said that the Persian government had not appealed to Russia, but that the Russian legation had itself approached and pressed them on the subject.

> He added in the strictest confidence, that the Russians had informed them that if they allowed us to occupy Mirjawar [sic] or to rectify to our advantage the frontier as shown on the map attached to the Holdich Protocol, the Russian Government would insist on a corresponding rectification of the boundary and the cession of territory in Northern Khorasan.[87]

The Russian archives being closed, Naus' claims cannot be verified. It is possible that Persia would not have raised the Mirjāveh issue had not the Russians threatened to demand compensation in Khorāsān. It is equally possible, and more probable, that in the face of the unceremonious behavior of Captain Webb Ware, Amin os-Soltān requested Russian support, which was promptly granted. Naus may have been instructed by the Persians or the Russians to give his version to the British in order to protect the Persian government from retaliation and to impress upon Hardinge Russia's determination not to allow Britain to annex Mirjāveh and Dozdāb. If the latter surmise is correct, Naus achieved his purpose.

86. Mushir-ed-Dowleh to A. Hardinge, May 14, 1902, Enclosure in C. L. des Graz, Chargé d'Affaires at Tehran, to the Secretary to the Government of India in the Foreign Department, No. 20, Gulahek, May 26, 1902; L. I., 149, 1902, No. 1526A.

87. A. Hardinge to Lansdowne, No. 65, Confidential, Tehran, April 10, 1902; L. I., 150, 1902, No. 1713A.

Seistān and the Persian Gulf 423

In May the Russian press chimed in. *Novoe Vremia* ran an article attacking Hardinge and the methods of British diplomacy in general:

We have already called attention to the endeavours of England to lay hands on Persian Baluchistan, and, if possible, on Seistan also, in view of the considerable political and strategic importance of these provinces. With this object we find them constantly full of British Agents, sowing discontent among the tribes, and suborning them and the authorities. . . .

Undoubtedly, all the representatives of the Persian Administration along the borders of British Baluchistan have been bought with British gold. Many of them have long been in British pay, as have also some of the Baluch Chiefs.

If the question of the occupation by sepoys of points in Persian territory is left to the examination of British Agents only, in communication with the local Governor, or even with Persian Plenipotentiaries, sent from Tehran, it may easily be shown that the English acted correctly, and only occupied what belonged to them by right.

The next paragraph had an ominous ring:

It is therefore necessary that, to the point where the territorial rights of Persia have been infringed upon, we should send Russian Plenipotentiaries to carry out, in conjunction with the Persian authorities, a precise examination of the whole question in dispute. . . . We cannot continue to leave South-Eastern Persia to the mercy of England—the question affects our most vital interests. We have long tried to avoid a "Seistan question," but circumstances demand it, we must bring it forward.[88]

The warning to Britain was unmistakable. The article in *Novoe Vremia*, the inquiries made by the Russian ambassador in London, and the ostensibly sincere confidences of Monsieur Naus were all

88. Extract from "Novoe Vremya" of the 7th May 1902 (Translation), Enclosure No. 1 in Scott to Lansdowne, No. 162, St. Petersburg, May 7, 1902; L. I., 149, 1902, No. 1526A.

part of the same campaign designed to bring Russia into the Mirjāveh-Dozdāb question. Another warning was given to the British by Consul Miller. Accompanied by a sizable and well-armed escort, he traveled along the Perso-Baluch frontier in open defiance of the English, challenging their pretentions to a special position in Seistān. The British response was half-hearted. The Foreign Office called the attention of the Russian ambassador, "in the most moderate language," to Miller's demonstration

> under conditions which were likely to disturb the minds of the population on both sides of that frontier, and we had intimated that, if M. Miller's action should unfortunately have this result, it might be necessary for us to strengthen our forces on the British side of the frontier, which we did not at all desire to do.

The Russian ambassador was also told that even if the British had encroached on Persian territory at Mirjāveh, it was a dispute between England and Persia, and that it was "somewhat singular" that "Baron Von Graevenitz [the ambassador] had come to this office in order to protest against it, before we had heard anything on the subject from Tehran." [89]

England's bluster did not frighten Russia in the least. An increase in Indian troops in Baluchestān was of no consequence and did not have to be taken seriously. Having diagnosed British threats as a bluff, Russia objected in rather strong terms against British complaints about Miller. The correctness of her diagnosis was borne out by Lansdowne's instructions to Sir Charles Scott, British ambassador in St. Petersburg, not to refer any more to troops in his discussions with the Russian government.[90]

Scott continued to complain about Miller, saying that the British government thought it "eminently undesirable that an impression should be allowed to prevail that the Russian Vice-Consul's movements are directed in a spirit of antagonism to the tranquility of the adjoining British territory." On May 28 Scott repeated his complaints against Miller to Count Lamsdorff. "His

89. Lansdowne to Scott, No. 141A, May 10, 1901; ibid.
90. Same to same, No. 145, May 21, 1902; ibid.

Excellency listened in silence, and evinced no desire either to invite discussion or to take note of my remarks." [91]

Vice-Consul Benn, Miller's enemy, accused him and his brother, Dr. Miller, of fomenting trouble all along the frontier. British officials across the border in Baluchestān were angrily demanding that action be taken against him. At the India Office Sir W. Lee Warner commented that Benn had said nothing new about Miller. "It is M. Miller's duty to stir up trouble." He was doing the British all the mischief he could. The English protest had been received with surprise. "We returned to the charge and met with silence . . . I venture to think that we had better leave it alone." [92]

Months passed before Lord Lansdowne obtained full documentation on the Mirjāveh-Dozdāb case. Having read all the papers and correspondence, Lansdowne saw how flimsy Britain's position was. The officers on the Northwest Frontier had acted on their own and embarrassed the government. Sir Thomas H. Sanderson, Undersecretary of State at the Foreign Office, wrote to the India Office that Lansdowne could very well understand the dissatisfaction of the officers with the frontier established by a joint commission in 1896. However, it must be respected until modified by mutual agreement.

> The map attached to Colonel Holdich's report of 5th April 1895 . . . shows what was the line intended by the Commissioners, and the argument advanced by Captain Webb Ware for giving their decision a different interpretation appears to Lord Lansdowne to be scarcely worthy of serious discussion. His Lordship cannot but think that Captain Webb Ware's action in establishing a military post on the other side of the line marked on the map without any reference to the Government of India for instructions was altogether indefensible. His action has not unnaturally given rise to much irritation and suspicion on the part of the Persian Government, and Lord Lansdowne, after reading these pa-

---

91. Scott to Lansdowne, Telegram, No. 47, St. Petersburg, May 28, 1902; ibid.
92. Note on the question of protesting to Russia against M. Miller's behavior, 28 VII 1902, Signed W.L.W.; L.I., 146, 1902, No. 1038.

pers, is not surprised at the observations which have been addressed to him in recent conversations both by the Shah and the Persian Grand Vizier [both were visiting England in August 1902] as to the necessity for strict control over British officers stationed in the neighbourhood of the frontier.[93]

Hamilton forwarded a copy of Sanderson's letter to the Viceroy, with a note of his own requesting His Excellency to issue such instructions as he might consider necessary to insure the boundary laid down by the Joint Commission in 1896 being scrupulously respected by officers on the frontier until it was modified by mutual agreement between the governments concerned.[94]

Only Consul Miller emerged with an enhanced reputation from the events of 1902. If his superiors ever learned of his allegedly ungentlemanly behavior at Captain Benn's dinner party, they must have secretly savored the Englishman's embarrassment and discomposure. Moreover, it is possible that Miller was a gentleman and, as such, never insulted anyone unintentionally. His boorish behavior may have been a part of a well-calculated campaign to rattle the English. Miller's reward was the Order of St. Anne and a promotion to the post of consul at Kermān.[95]

British retreat in the Mirjāveh-Dozdāb dispute stabilized the situation in southeastern Persia but did not diminish the rivalry between the great powers. The British subsidized tribal chiefs, the Russians controlled the Belgian customs' administration, whose Director in Seistān, Molitor, confessed that his actions, which the British interpreted as hostile, had been, as Benn reported,

> the result of specific orders received from his superiors in Tehran; that these orders were the result of Russian intrigue generated by M. Miller in Seistan; that the customs work here is being subjected to an interference by the Russian Vice-

---

93. F. O. to I. O. August 26, 1902; ibid.
94. Hamilton to Curzon, No. 39, September 5, 1902; ibid.
95. Memorandum of information received during the month of July 1902, regarding affairs on and beyond the North-West Frontier of India; L. I., 147, 1902, No. 1155.

Seistān and the Persian Gulf

Consul, which, if allowed to continue will develop into surveillance, which must eventually prove hostile to the prospects of the Department [Customs] and to the growth of British trade; and finally he would convince us that the unscrupulous nature of M. Miller's intrigues in Seistan is a factor in the general situation which demands the serious attention of his own Department, and in the interests of the embryo trade route, he ventured to add, of His Majesty's Government also! [96]

Molitor's expression of dissatisfaction with Miller may have been genuine: the Russian consul was not a particularly pleasant or attractive individual. However, it may have been a ruse designed to avert British anger and make it easier for the Belgians to function in an area where English influence was overwhelmingly strong. Whatever Molitor may have felt, he acted in close concert with the Russians, while one of his assistants, Cesari, was even suspected of being in Miller's pay.[97]

The Persian Gulf, no less than Seistān, was an area in which the British were eager to maintain a monopoly of influence and power. No one has ever expressed the imperialist position more clearly or eloquently than George Curzon.

> A Russian port in the Persian Gulf, that dear dream of so many a patriot from the Neva or the Volga, would, even in times of peace, import an element of unrest into the life of the Gulf that would shake the delicate equilibrium so laboriously established, would wreck a commerce that is valued at many millions sterling, and would let loose again the passions of jarring nationalities only too ready to fly at each others' throats. Let Great Britain and Russia fight their battles or compose their differences elsewhere, but let them not turn into a scene of sanguinary conflict the peaceful field of a hard-won trade. I should regard the concession of a port upon the Persian Gulf to Russia by any power as a

---

96. Benn to Trench, No. 3, Confidential, Seistan, August 2, 1902; L. I., *145*, 1902, No. 826.

97. Diary No. 14 of Major R. A. E. Benn for the period 16th to 31st October 1902; L. I., *150*, 1902, No. 1650A.

deliberate insult to Great Britain, as a wanton rupture of the *status quo*, and as an intentional provocation to war; and I should impeach the British minister, who was guilty of acquiescing in such a surrender, as a traitor to his country.[98]

Man and nature seemed to have conspired to turn the Persian Gulf into one of the most desolate and horror-filled areas in the world. Unbearable heat, sand storms, insects, and disease had their human counterpoint in slavery, piracy, corruption, and general lawlessness that had few parallels anywhere. From the narratives of occasional travelers and the reports of British officials, one receives the impression of general decay, disorder, and violence.[99]

The most important local ruler on the Persian shore of the Gulf, Moezz os-Saltaneh, chief of the Ka'b Arabs and hereditary governor of Mohammareh, opposed the extension of British commerce because it brought Persian officials in its wake and threatened to diminish his medieval autonomy.[100] In the spring of 1897 he was murdered by his own brother, Khaz'al, who thereupon assumed the dignity of the Sheykh of Mohammareh. The British, fearful of disturbances that might endanger their interests or threaten English lives, sent a gunboat to the Kārun River, for which they received the Shah's thanks.[101]

The Persian government, showing full understanding of the realities of the situation, telegraphed the fratricide, whose accession it did not dispute, that his chief duty was, and his very existence depended upon, "the good services you render to British

---

98. Curzon, *Persia and the Persian Question*, 2, 465.

99. Cf. the excellent report by Percy Sykes, consul at Kermān, who visited the Gulf in late 1896: Report by Consul Sykes on the Karun Question, Enclosure in Durand to Salisbury, No. 5, January 19, 1897; F. O. 65/1547.

100. Id.

101. C. Hardinge to Salisbury, No. 80, Gulahek, June 20, 1897; F. O. 65/1548.
Charles Hardinge, then chargé d'affaires in Tehran, in his memoirs written years later, commented briefly that when the Sheykh of Mohammareh was murdered,
No general disturbance followed as, at the request of the Shah, I sent a British ship to maintain order. Twenty years later, when Viceroy of India, I met the Sheikh at Mohammerah and could hardly realize that such a courtly old gentleman could have been the direct instigator of the murder of his brother. [*Old Diplomacy*, p. 65.]

Seistān and the Persian Gulf

trade." If Khaz'al wished to gain the favor of the Persian government, he would "act in such a way for the maintenance of the peace and for the security of British traders that they, and especially Messrs. Lynch . . . may telegraph to the British Charge d'Affairs an expression of their satisfaction with you." [102]

Khaz'al, who had little respect and less liking for the Persian government, accepted this particular piece of advice. It stood him in good stead. Several years later, when the Persian government had disintegrated further and the whole Empire seemed about to fall apart, an Englishman thus described the Sheykh's position:

> He is wealthy and has already shown himself able to mobilize 25,000 cavalry and infantry in some operations against turbulent tribes. He renders nominal fealty to the Shah, possesses a Persian title, married a Persian princess, flies the Persian flag, and tries to keep on good terms with Tehran; but he levies his own taxes, maintains his own troops, and in practice is more than semi-independent . . . He is a warm friend of the British and looks to them for advice and support.[103]

When, at Russia's urging, Persia established a modern customs administration directed by a group of Belgian experts, Khaz'al felt threatened. In January 1901 Monsieur Simais, a customs official, came to Mohammareh from Tehran to negotiate with the Sheykh the establishment of government control of customs in the area under his jurisdiction. Sheykh Khaz'al had been paying Tehran 60,000 tumāns a year for the privilege of farming the customs. Now the government offered him 30,000 a year to give up the privilege, and promised another 12,000 to 15,000 as pension.[104] When Khaz'al showed no intention of obeying Tehran, the British saw the difficulty of the situation:

---

102. Nezām os-Saltaneh to Sheykh Khaz'al, Enclosure in C. Hardinge to Salisbury, No. 80, June 20, 1897; F. O. 65/1548.

103. Fraser, *India under Curzon and After*, p. 105.

104. Lt. Col. C. A. Kemball, Officiating Political Resident in the Persian Gulf, to the Secretary of the Government of India, Foreign Department, No. 50, Confidential, March 9, 1901; L. I., 132, 1901, No. 508.

> We cannot but admit that the desire of the Persian Government to establish their Customs in the place is reasonable and their right to do so unquestionable, but on account of our trade interests and of the possibility of serious trouble and dislocation of trade being occasioned by the introduction of the new regime, we are undoubtedly within our rights in claiming an interest in the matter and in ascertaining from the Persian Government what their proposals are.[105]

Sheykh Khaz'al stood firm. He had served the British long and faithfully. Now it was their turn to support him. He enumerated the favors he had rendered the English: he took off the Shatt ol-Arab boats which his brother had run in competition with the British firm of Lynch Brothers; he patrolled the Shatt and made it safe from pirates; but he must look out for himself and his family. As the British Vice-Consul reported from Mohammareh,

> Circumstances have changed: Russians and French frequently come here. It is well known that Russia is omnipotent in Tehran, and can do what it likes with the Persian Government; if he [Khaz'al] persists in encouraging British trade, the Russians will use their influence in opposing him and encouraging the Persians in establishing customs and other measures for undermining his power.

Ten years before, the Persians had sent a Kārgozār (agent of the Foreign Ministry) to Mohammareh, followed by a passport agent; then they established a quarantine station.

> Next the customs will come. Then the Persians might begin selling his lands . . . Is he to sit still and let all this happen? He has promised to support our [British] trade and to take our advice, but, if we do nothing for him, he will have to ask to be released from this promise. What do we advise him to do?[106]

The British vice-consul at Mohammareh, who had to listen to

---

105. C. A. Kemball, Consul General for Fars and Khuzistan, to A. Hardinge, No. 55, April 25, 1901; L. I., 133, 1901, No. 446.
106. Kemball to Hardinge, No. 92, Confidential, Bushire, July 2, 1901; L. I., 136, No. 989.

Seistān and the Persian Gulf

Khaz'al's complaints, said that Britain would "never allow this country to pass into the hands of a foreign Power." With irrefutable logic Khaz'al replied that this might be so, but if the English allowed the Persians to destroy him, the future would "have no interest for him or his family." He wished, of course, to be loyal to the Persian government, but if they attacked him, what would the English do? Interpreting the Sheykh's position for Hardinge, Lieutenant Colonel C. A. Kemball, Officiating Political Resident in the Persian Gulf and Acting Consul General for Fārs and Khuzestān, wrote that Khaz'al had kept the customs out of Mohammareh until now by bribing the right people; but such a state of affairs could not last much longer, and he was hinting that if the British did not help he might have "to place himself in the hands of others," although he would prefer to stay with the British.

Kemball was aware that it had been the professed policy of Britain not to assist the Sheykh in resisting legitimate demands of the Persian government. At the same time he thought that "recent events may have caused His Majesty's Government to reconsider its policy in regard to Persia, more particularly with reference to British interests in the south, and the preservation of a friendly Power at Mohammerah might certainly be of importance to us." [107]

Kemball, like many other Anglo-Indian officials, would have gladly taken up the cause of any local lord, whether Heshmat ol-Molk in Seistān or Khaz'al at Mohammareh, against the central government. Sir Arthur Hardinge, himself a proponent of strong action, would not go that far. He instructed Kemball to tell Khaz'al that he hoped to visit the Sheykh at Mohammareh. The Sheykh should "come to fair arrangement" with the Persian government in regard to customs. "There is no question of taking away or undermining your political authority over your tribesmen. Be patient," Hardinge advised Khaz'al. The British minister was uncertain whether the Arab ruler would listen to advice. He bluntly asked Kemball: "If Sheikh were to resist Persians forcibly, how many men could he put in the field?" [108]

107. Id.
108. Hardinge to Kemball, Telegram, No. 46, Tehran, July 28, 1901; L. I., 137, 1901, No. 1154.

While trying to prevent Khaz'al from resisting the government by force, Hardinge looked for a method of satisfying him and keeping his allegiance. He proposed to the British government that it guarantee to Khaz'al the payments the Persian government promised to make to him in compensation of his loss of the privilege of farming the customs.[109]

Khaz'al accepted the government's demands for a new customs regime, but hesitated about admitting Belgian administrators. To the British vice-consul at Mohammareh it seemed that the Sheykh was "doubtful if he had acted right in giving way to a certain extent in the matter of Customs." He claimed that the khans of Dashtestān and the Bakhtiāri chiefs had promised him support if he resisted by force the establishment of Persian customs.[110] Hardinge again urged that it was "wiser to come to a compromise than to create disturbances the ultimate consequences of which it is not easy to calculate." [111]

Hardinge's proposal that Khaz'al be given support was strongly seconded by George Curzon, Viceroy of India, who felt that the Kārun River was of the utmost importance and that "A main cause of our weakness in Persia is our failure to support those chiefs and officials who are disposed to side with us." [112] Lansdowne shared Curzon's and Hardinge's views but was afraid of making a positive commitment. He thought that Hardinge should go no further "than to say that so long as Sheikh acts in accordance with our advice and remains a faithful subject of the Shah, he will have our good offices and support." [113] This was exactly the kind of wording which infuriated those who dealt with British diplomats: ambiguous, self-contradictory, and binding upon one party only, with the other given complete freedom to judge whether the bargain had been kept.

The Persian government knew of the close relationship existing

109. Hardinge to Kemball, Telegram, No. 52, Tehran, August 15, 1901; ibid.
110. The Resident, Bushire, to the Minister, Tehran, No. 20, March 28, 1902; L. I., 144, 1902, No. 671.
111. Minister, Tehran, to Resident, Bushire, No. 23, March 29, 1902; ibid.
112. Telegram from Viceroy, November 26, 1902; L. I., 150, 1902, No. 1562A.
113. F. O. Draft of telegram to Viceroy, n.d. Never sent, drafted about the end of November 1902; ibid.

Seistān and the Persian Gulf

between Sheykh Khaz'al and the British. It could not avoid discussing the issue of customs at Mohammareh with the British minister. During his meeting with Amin os-Soltān on December 1, 1902, Sir Arthur Hardinge was brutally frank. He thus reported the conversation:

> I had no wish to call in question the Shah's sovereignty over the Chief or the people of Mohammerah, which His Majesty's Government had always recognized. Our experience in Seistan had, however, been a lesson in the effects on our interests which the presence of a Russian Consul, and of Belgian Customs officials, who were not always judicious, could produce . . . On the Karun, as in Seistan, the Russians had no *bona fide* commercial interests, and their recent appointment of a Consul could have only political objects. We were determined not to have, if we could help it, another Seistan in Mohammerah, and to let Sheikh Khazal, therefore understand that if Russian Agents attempted to intimidate him, or insinuate that they could bring pressure to bear on him owing to the influence which they exercised at Tehran, we on our side were ready to support him. It was because threats of this kind had been made by Prince Dabija, Russian Consul at Isfahan, when he visited Mohammerah, that I had felt obliged to intimate to the Sheikh that our naval forces in the Gulf were more powerful than those of Russia, and that they might be employed in certain eventualities for the purpose of maintaining the status quo in which he and we were equally interested.[114]

Hardinge's statement, stripped of diplomatic verbiage, meant that Mohammareh and the lower Kārun had been virtually removed from Persian sovereignty and placed under British protection. Amin os-Soltān told Hardinge that the Shah would be distressed if he reported this to His Majesty. The Grand Vizier could not resist assigning the blame for the growth of Russian influence to the British themselves. It was the "unsympathetic policy" pursued in Tehran during Hardinge's predecessor's time "and the

114. A. Hardinge to Lansdowne, No. 167, Confidential, Tehran, December 5, 1902; F. O. 60/660.

British Government's refusal to help Persia financially, notwithstanding the urgent representations made by Sir M. Durand himself," that had driven the Persian government into the position of which the English now complained.[115]

Later in the year Sheykh Khaz'al again asked whether the British would protect him against attempts by foreign powers (he was not afraid of the Shah) to overthrow him. Hardinge replied that if Mohammareh were attacked, "we should, I believe, interfere, provided you had acted in accordance with our advice, and our fleet, which is the strongest of any in the Gulf, would be employed to prevent any forcible measures against you."[116]

The first Russian incursions into the Persian Gulf area had occurred in the summer of 1899. On June 4 three Russians, the consul in Esfahān and two Cossacks, arrived in Bushehr from Shirāz. The British political resident, uncrowned king of the Gulf, telegraphed Hardinge that the purpose of their mission was to inspect the island of Hormoz "as to suitability for a coaling station."[117] The Russian consul at Esfahān, Prince Dabizha, scion of a Moldavian family that had settled in Russia in 1812, belonged to the same school of active imperialists as Miller. In Hardinge's opinion Dabizha and his Cossacks, as well as other Russian travelers reported in the vicinity of Bandar Abbās, were the spearhead of a dangerous enemy force. He telegraphed the political resident at Bushehr: "You should watch his movement and the movements of other Russians in the Gulf ports. You may be quite certain that Russia and France are working in unison."[118]

Hardinge's reference to France was prompted by the fact that Dabizha was the guest in Bushehr of the French vice-counsul, but the British had been worrying about French activity in the Persian Gulf for at least the past five years. In 1894 France had

115. Id.
116. A. Hardinge to the Sheikh of Mohammerah, December 7, 1902, Enclosure in A. Hardinge to Lansdowne, No. 167, Confidential, Tehran, 1902; ibid.
117. Political Resident in the Persian Gulf to A. Hardinge, Telegram No. 79, Bushire, June 5, 1899; L. I., 114, 1899, No. 692.
118. A. Hardinge to the Resident in the Persian Gulf, Telegram, No. 61, June 7, 1899, ibid.

opened a consulate at Masqat (Muscat). Her consul, Ottavi, was fluent in Arabic and an able diplomat (to the British "intriguer"). He turned the ruler of Oman, Sheykh Seyyed Faysal, against the British and obtained from him the right to establish a French coaling station there. When the British made inquiries in Paris, the Minister of Foreign Affairs, Theophile Delcassé, claimed that he knew nothing about it.

In 1899 the Government of India instructed the political resident in the Persian Gulf, Colonel M. J. Meade, to insist with the Sultan that the concession for the coaling station be revoked. Meade went to Masqat accompanied by Admiral Douglas in H.M.S. *Enterprise*, flagship of the East Indies Squadron. The Sultan refused to listen to Meade's demands, and Admiral Douglas let him know that "if he did not come off to the flagship at a given time and accede in full to British demands, he would bombard his palace, which stands at the water's edge. The Sultan came off. That was the end of the French coaling station." [119]

Throughout his stay in the south, Prince Dabizha was surrounded by British spies who observed his every movement and overheard many of his conversations. It was reported that he asked a merchant, Āqā Mohammad Shafi', whom the British had prosecuted for fraud and who had spent time in jail on their insistence, to build a house on the outskirts of Bushehr for a Russian consul who would soon arrive there.

In Mohammareh, Dabizha was treated most unceremoniously. He was placed in quarantine on the pretext that Bushehr, whence he had come by ship, had been declared a plague zone. Dabizha protested vehemently, "saying that there was no plague in Bushire, and demanded to be shown an authority from the Shah or the Sadr Azam." Knowing that he had been quarantined on orders of an English doctor, Dabizha gave the incident a political interpretation.

After remaining a few days, he threatened to leave the quarantine station by force and proceed up the Karun. As it was not considered advisable to use force to keep him in quaran-

---

119. Fraser, *India under Curzon and After*, p. 88. Cf. Ronaldshay, *The Life of Lord Curzon*, 2, 45–46.

tine, the Chief of Mohammerah, Sheikh Khazal, arranged to give him a steam launch to convey him to Ahwaz, on the understanding that he did not communicate with the shore until the remaining period of quarantine.[120]

If the English were high-handed in causing Dabizha's virtual imprisonment and expulsion, the Russian consul was inquisitive, and arrogant. In a conversation with one of Sheykh Khaz'al's men he remarked that the Sheykh "was a servant of the English, that the British Consul was the real Governor, and in support of his statement he added that H.B.M.'s Consul General at Bushire had offered to give him a letter of introduction to Sheikh Khazal, but that he had refused to take it." That no such offer had been made by the British consul in Bushehr bothered Dabizha not in the least as long as the story served to enhance his stature.

When Dabizha met Khaz'al, he told the Sheykh that Russia intended to have a port in the Gulf but that England was raising obstacles. British quarantine stations on Hormoz and Qeshm islands had been established "with the intention of fortifying them," but Russia would not consent to such arrangements. The people of the northern provinces were happy "and the 'Mujtaheds' had made overtures to Russia to take the Northern Provinces of Persia under her protection." [121]

British apprehensions were further aroused by the demands in the Russian press for the acquisition of a port on the Persian Gulf, preferably Bandar Abbās. Few threats had a stronger effect on the English, especially on those whose careers had involved them closely with India. For such Englishmen the Persian Gulf was *mare nostrum*, and any foreign intrusion a violation of rights bought by centuries of exertion and blood.

> For nearly three hundred years [one of them wrote] our flag has flown upon its waters . . . It was flying in the Gulf of Oman before the *Mayflower* sailed from Plymouth. We have

120. Memorandum on a visit of Prince Dabija, Russian Consul at Ispahan, to Bushire and Khuzistan, Enclosure in Lt. Col. M. J. Meade, Political Resident in the Persian Gulf, to the Secretary of the Government of India, Foreign Department, No. 107, Bushire, July 10, 1899; L. I., 115, 1899, No. 791.

121. Id.

Seistān and the Persian Gulf

sacrificed and fought and traded and ruled throughout the narrow seas of the Middle East until every rival has gone down before us. By innumerable sacrifices of blood and treasure, by the unflinching valour of our seamen, by the lonely and forgotten graves upon those burning shores, by the very merit and restraint of our control, we have earned thrice over the right to keep our paramountcy inviolate.[122]

In the midst of the Boer War, when Britain's forces were committed elsewhere, Russian ships appeared in the Persian Gulf. One of them, the gunboat *Giliak*, quietly entered the harbor at Bandar Abbās on February 14, 1900. The British Admiralty had already been instructed to observe the Russians. Should they hoist their flag on the shore, or contemplate establishing a base, land a force, or attempt to control a port, the British Senior Naval Officer would protest. If his protest were disregarded, he would "hoist the British flag on Hormuz or Henjam or Kishm." [123]

The *Giliak*'s captain asked for coal, three hundred tons having been ordered by the Russian authorities from Bombay. The coal was delivered, but *Giliak* could not take that much aboard. The Captain therefore began negotiations with the local governor to leave part of the coal in Bandar Abbās, thus making of it a Russian coaling station.[124] The *Giliak* sailed away, leaving behind twenty-five tons of coal. "This looks like thin edge of the wedge, and is in remarkable contradiction of Muravieff's assurances," Curzon telegraphed. At the India Office an unsigned and uninitialed minute was attached to the Viceroy's telegram, saying in part: "I think that we ought to stop this," and below, "All we want to do is to show that we have and mean to assert interests in Bunder Abbas if the Persians are selling off." [125]

The local governor had refused the Russians permission to store coal. Whether he had "developed healthy suspicions," as an English writer states, or was frightened by the sudden and un-

122. Fraser, p. 82.
123. Secretary of State for India [Hamilton] to the Viceroy [Curzon], February 14, 1900; L. I., 120, 1900, No. 355.
124. The Viceroy [Curzon] to the Secretary of State for India [Hamilton], Secret, February 17, 1900; L. I., 119, No. 244.
125. From Viceroy, March 3, 1900, in Cypher, Foreign, Secret; ibid., No. 298.

expected arrival of H.M.S. *Pomona*, which "took absorbing interest in the proceedings," he decided that it was safer to refuse distant Russia than Britain, which was observing him through *Pomona*'s gunsights.[126]

The *Giliak* called at several other Gulf ports and steamed away, leaving the British in expectation of the coming of other ships to establish a base at Bandar Abbās. A voluminous correspondence was carried on between the Foreign Office, the India Office, the Admiralty, the Government of India, the British minister in Tehran, and the political resident in the Persian Gulf. Investigations were conducted into the political situation of the various coastal sheykhs with whom deals could be made over the head of the Persian government. Sites of possible naval bases were surveyed on several islands, and new telegraph lines were planned.[127] That no major steps to implement the plans were taken may be explained partly by official inertia, partly by a lull that fell on the Gulf after the brief storm caused by Dabizha and the *Giliak*.

Prince Dabizha returned to the Gulf in March 1901 in connection with the expected arrival in Bushehr of the Russian merchant ship *Kornilov*.[128] He began to negotiate the purchase of a house for a Russian consulate.[129] Once again telegraph wires between London, Tehran, the Persian Gulf, and India came alive with messages, instructions, and warnings. Once again the Russian press beat the drums, evoking a clear and, for the English, ominous echo in Paris. The *Journal des Débats* wrote that the English were strengthening their position by building new coaling stations, interfering with the local rulers, intriguing in the Najd, Kuwayt, and Yaman, and consolidating their sovereignty in Baluchestān. The Russians too were active. They established consulates in Basra and Bushehr and inaugurated steamship communications between Odessa and Gulf ports. The *Journal des Débats* deplored the fact that the French did not take part in this activity. *Novoe Vremia* welcomed France to the Gulf. "It is not

126. Fraser, pp. 91–92.
127. Cf. various documents in F. O. 60/733.
128. Lt. Col. Kemball to A. Hardinge, No. 31, Confidential, Bushire, March 8, 1901; L. I., 122, 1901, No. 542.
129. Same to same, No. 51, Confidential, Bushire, March 9, 1901; ibid.

easy for us to carry on the struggle against the English, who hitherto have been all powerful in these regions, and we gladly welcome our good friend and ally, who by working with us will obtain exactly identical advantages." [130]

Indeed Russian activity in the Gulf increased sharply in the spring and summer of 1901. Commerce, shipping, and consulates were the means of establishing the Russian presence there. The British consul general in St. Petersburg, Michell, reported that on orders of Grand Duke Aleksandr Mikhailovich, Syromiatnikov, a staff writer on the *Novoe Vremia* who signed his articles with the name "Sigma," had been sent to the Persian Gulf in the summer of 1900 to study the trade of the Gulf ports. Upon his return, he submitted a report to Witte, stating that there was a potential market for Russian sugar. The only sugar currently sold in the Gulf was French, of inferior quality. There was also a market for kerosene, cotton and wool goods, grain spirits, and so forth. Such trade, however, would necessitate the establishment of a steamship line which would have to be subsidized by the government in order to compete with the British. Russian banks and consulates should also be opened. Finally, Syromiatnikov recommended that a Russian man-of-war be stationed in the Gulf at all times and coaling stations established at Bushehr and Basra.[131]

The voyage of the old merchant ship *Kornilov*, which excited the admiration of the Parisian press, raised hopes at St. Petersburg, and frightened the English, was uneventful and unprofitable. In October the *Kornilov* called at Bandar Abbās and landed 5,000 cases of kerosene. At Langeh she landed three bales of cotton goods, at Bushehr 12,000 cases of kerosene and 100 cases of glassware. She then touched at Basra, returned to Langeh, and finally left, carrying 4,600 bags of tobacco for Beirut, 60 cases of gum tragacanth for Odessa and London, 17 bales of cotton for Odessa, and 2 cases of opium for Alexandria.[132] This was just

---

130. C. Hardinge to Lansdowne, No. 277, St. Petersburg, September 27, 1901; F. O. 65/1622.

131. Memorandum by Consul-General Michell, St. Petersburg, January 3, 1901, Enclosure No. 1 in C. Scott to Lansdowne, No. 5, Commercial, Confidential, St. Petersburg, January 7, 1901; F. O. 65/1628.

132. Memorandum by Vice-Consul Sequeira, December 18, 1901, Enclosure in

about the sum total of Russian trade in the Gulf for the year 1901.

The opening of Russian consulates in the Gulf ports was an easier matter. The consul at Basra, Adamov, received detailed instructions from the ambassador at Constantinople, that old master of Middle Eastern diplomacy, former Director of the Asiatic Department of the Ministry of Foreign Affairs and, before that, Minister at Tehran, the strong Anglophobe, I. A. Zinov'ev. In a survey of English malefactions "Zinov'ev stressed that Russia could not remain indifferent toward English intrigues in this region and that therefore it was necessary to struggle in every way against English political and economic dominance in the Persian Gulf zone." [133] Or, to adopt W. Lee Warner's pronouncement on Consul Miller: It was Monsieur Adamov's duty to stir up trouble.

In August 1901 Curzon heard talk of Russia's appointing a consul to Masqat. The British political agent there wanted to know how to advise the Sultan, since one had to consider that a French consul was already in Masqat. Curzon felt that the relationship of France and Russia to Masqat was not analogous. The former had had relations with the Sultanate for many years and signed a treaty concerning it with Britain in 1862. Russia had neither old ties nor new interests, her total trade with Masqat for 1900–01 being valued at $10,000.[134] In the end no Russian consul was appointed to Masqat. The English hold there was far too strong.

The sight of Russian ships and consulates in the Persian Gulf made Curzon resume his old battle with Whitehall. On November 7, 1901, he sent to London a dispatch in which he referred to his memoranda of September 21, 1899, and September 6, 1900. "Subsequent events," he wrote in the name of the Government of India, "have more than confirmed the forecasts that were contained in our earlier letter, and have lent additional weight to our

---

Kemball to A. Hardinge, No. 173, Bushire, December 22, 1901; L. I., 141, 1902, No. 214.

133. Foreign Policy Archive cited by G. L. Bondarevskii, *Bagdadskaia doroga i proniknovenie germanskogo imperializma na Blizhnii Vostok* (Tashkent, 1955), p. 194.

134. Curzon to Hamilton, No. 142, Simla, August 8, 1901; L. I., 126, 1901, No. 1005.

Seistān and the Persian Gulf

appeal for a clear and emphatic enunciation of British policy in regard to that country." Curzon enumerated the advantages Russia had recently gained. The events of the past two years strengthened his conviction that "the question of Persia and the Persian Gulf is on the verge of becoming the most critical issue in Central Asian politics."

Turning to the Gulf specifically, the Viceroy wrote:

> We take it to have been a commonplace of British statesmanship throughout the past century that in Southern Persia and the Persian Gulf British influence should remain supreme; and that while at no time could the commercial competition of other Powers be reasonably resented, or legitimately opposed, yet, the creation of rival political interests in that quarter could not be permitted, without seriously compromising the interests of India and therefore of Great Britain. We know of no Indian Administration and of no responsible British statesmen, who have not subscribed to these views.

In a frontal attack on Lord George Hamilton and a number of high officials at the India Office, Curzon stated:

> More recently we have observed indications of a willingness in some quarters to recede from this attitude, and to argue that the political predominance which has been acquired by Great Britain in the region in question, at so great an expenditure of energy and treasure, may with impunity be challenged by others, and can safely be shared with them.

The Government of India, Curzon reiterated, had no objections to the granting of commercial access to the Persian Gulf, by railways or other means, to Russia, but felt strongly that

> the acquisition of political interests or rights by the Russian Government in those quarters would be fraught with positive danger to the security of the Indian Empire; and we hope that any such idea or proposal may continue in the future, as it had done in the past, to meet with the strenuous opposition of His Majesty's government.[135]

[135]. The Government of India to Lord Hamilton, No. 183, Secret, Simla, November 7, 1901; L. I., 139, 1901, No. 1376.

Curzon's memorandum was circulated in the India Office and the Cabinet with a long note by Hamilton, who accused the Viceroy of never descending from the level of generalities and failing to propose practical measures that could be enacted in Persia. Indulging in some generalizing of his own, Hamilton argued that "Our pretentions and policy in that country are based upon an order of things that is passing away, whilst the Russian advance has behind it modern forces and agencies that are becoming more and more potent." He repeated his contention that the development of a network of railways had altered the balance of power in the Middle East in Russia's favor.

> The forces in the north behind Russia, military, diplomatic, and financial, are on the wax, ours on the wane. So conscious is Russian diplomacy that time is on their side, that they play a wary and cautious game, giving us no opportunity even if we wished it, of overtaking their progress by threat of war.

The very independence of Persia, Hamilton went on, had become a Russian instrument for gaining concessions and monopolies.

> It is self-evident that so long as we adhere to our old policy and methods of recognizing and supporting an independence that does not exist, our position will become worse and worse, and we shall neither maintain Persia's liberty of action nor protect our special but limited interests.[136]

Hamilton disagreed with Curzon's suggestion that Britain issue a warning to Persia not to grant Russia any concessions or privileges that might endanger British interests in southern Persia, yet he, even less than Curzon, whom he reproached for it, had no concrete proposals to offer. Pushed to its logical conclusions, his position would require a total abandonment of Persia and the Persian Gulf. Hamilton represented a defeatist element, or a pessimistic streak that was not uncommon in English statesmen. However, his views were shared more by the opposition than by his own colleagues in the Cabinet. Lord Lansdowne felt closer to Curzon and did not admit that England was as weak as Hamilton

136. Minute by G[eorge] H[amilton], December 27, 1901; Persia, I. O., No. 1376/07; ibid.

Seistān and the Persian Gulf

claimed. Moreover, like Curzon, he found it difficult to believe in the "natural" or "inevitable" advance of Russia. When in March 1899, Sir A. Godley, who was Undersecretary of State at the India Office and who shared many of Hamilton's and W. Lee Warner's views, used the terms in a letter to Curzon, the Viceroy replied that such remarks only excited horror in his mind.

> You reason from what you regard as the inevitable; and it is a familiar argument in modern politics. . . . I will no more admit that an irresistible destiny is going to plant Russia in the Persian Gulf than in Kabul or Constantinople. South of a certain line in Asia her future is much more what we choose to make it than what she can make it herself.[137]

Lansdowne would have approved this language. When it was time to speak, his own voice was more moderate than the Viceroy's, but it reflected Curzon's rather than Hamilton's thinking.

Rising in the House of Lords on May 5, 1903, Lord Lansdowne declared that Britain's policy was to promote and protect British trade in the Persian Gulf. Britain's efforts, he said, were not directed toward the exclusion of the legitimate trade of other nations; however, "we should regard the establishment of a naval base or of a fortified port in the Persian Gulf by any other power as a very grave menace to British interests, and we should certainly resist it with all the means at our disposal." [138]

Curzon was elated. On May 14 he wrote to his principal opponent and immediate superior, George Hamilton:

> You may judge how satisfied I was when . . . I read the statement of a British Foreign Minister in Parliament, that Great Britain would in no circumstances tolerate the creation of a naval base by any foreign Power in the Persian Gulf. This is what I contended for in a language which has since become famous in my book eleven years ago; it is what I have argued and pleaded for in scores of letters to you during the last four years. . . . and therefore if at the end of all these discussions I find that the view that I have so re-

---

137. Curzon to Godley (private), dated April 12, 1899; cited in Ronaldshay, *The Life of Lord Curzon,* 2, 99.

138. Parliamentary Debates (Lords), 4th series, 121, 1348.

peatedly pressed has at length prevailed in the highest quarters, I cannot help feeling some personal sense of congratulations.[139]

The Russian ambassador in London "unused to such directness of speech by British statesmen on delicate subjects" spoke to Lansdowne the day after the latter's famous declaration and denied any desire on the part of Russia to establish a naval base in the Persian Gulf. However, he refused to be drawn into a discussion of the possibility of an understanding between Britain and Russia on Persian matters and expressed doubt that "the time had come for any such general discussion, or for consideration of any Agreement under which the respective spheres of influence of the two countries would be formally recognized." [140]

George Curzon was not a man quietly to enjoy his hour of triumph. Lansdowne's declaration in the House of Lords, "our Monroe Doctrine in the Middle East," [141] must be dramatized so as to make it absolutely convincing for friend and foe alike. He decided to make a tour of the Persian Gulf, visit its various ports, and display the might of the British navy. Sir Arthur Hardinge, who wondered how to present the proposed voyage to the Persians, was instructed by the Foreign Office that "It would be a mistake to regard Viceroy's tour as a threat to any one; it is the natural outcome of the friendly interest which we take in Persian affairs, and our existing relations with the Sultan of Muscat and the chiefs of the West side of the Persian Gulf." [142]

Sir Arthur had already informed the Persian Foreign Minister, Mirzā Nasrollāh Khān Moshir od-Dowleh, of the proposed visit. He hoped that the Viceroy would be suitably received in Persian ports, and that the Persian government would see in the visit "a fresh proof of the determination of the British Government to maintain its rights and interests which are in harmony with those of His Majesty the Shah." [143]

139. Curzon to Hamilton (private), dated May 14, 1903; cited in Ronaldshay, 2, 311–12.

140. Ronaldshay, 2, 312.

141. Fraser, *India under Curzon and After*, p. 83.

142. F. O. to A. Hardinge, cypher, No. 92, October 2, 1903; F. O. 60/730.

143. A. Hardinge to Mushir od-Dowleh, Tehran, September 26, 1903, Enclosure in A. Hardinge to Lansdowne, No. 152, September 27, 1903; ibid.

Seistān and the Persian Gulf

The Shah and his ministers did not see Curzon's tour in such a light. To them it was a disturbing and embarrassing affair. The Russians would undoubtedly make compensatory counterdemonstrations, heavy expenses would be incurred in entertaining the distinguished visitor and his staff, commitments might have to be made or turned down, antagonizing one or the other great power in the process. Mozaffar ed-Din and Amin os-Soltān would have preferred to be left alone.

Curzon toured the Gulf in November and December 1903 in grand style. The fleet, consisting of the steamship *Hardinge*, four cruisers, and several smaller boats, sailed from port to port, dazzling the Arab sheykhs and assuring them of Britain's superior might. On the Persian side of the Gulf things did not work out so well.

Sir Arthur Hardinge, who accompanied the Viceroy on most of the trip, had made arrangements that Curzon would be received by the Persian government at Bandar Abbās and Bushehr. Alā od-Dowleh, Governor of Fārs, begged that Bandar Abbās not be included. He gave no reasons, but the distance of that town from Shirāz, the hardships of travel, and the enormous expense of moving the governor, a large ceremonial staff and military guard, were sufficient to explain his reluctance to go. Curzon agreed to be met at the landing in Bushehr but refused to accept an official residence from the Persian government. A long hassle developed about whether Alā od-Dowleh should call on Curzon first in the Viceroy's residence, or the Viceroy on the governor in his. Another difficulty arose over the gun salute. Curzon would have a thirty-one gun salute. Alā od-Dowleh asked for equal treatment, but the British admiral, who would do the firing, refused to give him more than nineteen.

On December 2 the glittering armada entered the harbor at Bushehr. Curzon was planning to land, proceed to the British residency, and there receive a visit from Alā od-Dowleh. The latter refused, saying that he would visit Curzon if the Viceroy stayed at a place provided by the Persian government, thus giving him the privileges of a guest. Otherwise Curzon should call on the governor first. From Tehran, Alā od-Dowleh received orders to stand pat. Negotiations lasted all day while the British naval squadron lay at anchor and Curzon fumed at the Persians for the insult inflicted upon a representative of His Britannic Majesty. The next day the Viceroy of India sailed away without having been welcomed to Bushehr.[144] His Persian visit had been a total fiasco. English writers who have claimed that this so-called "triumphal tour" increased Britain's prestige were either uninformed or indulging in wishful thinking.

The meeting between Curzon and Sir Arthur Hardinge gave them an opportunity to discuss British policy and to discover that they agreed on its general lines but not on some important specifics and not on the means of achieving mutually desired end. Curzon's great failing was arrogance. Himself sensitive to every slight, quick to feel insults, always on guard against any attempt to lower or humiliate him, he was largely indifferent to the feelings of others. Of his affection for Persia, a country he knew better than almost any European then alive, there could be little doubt; yet he blamed Hardinge "for being too courteous and diplomatic with the Persians, and treating mendacious Asiatics as if they were European statesmen." Curzon felt that the Persians should be treated "with the frank, and, if need be, brutal directness" that he found successful with the rulers of Afghanistan and Nepal. Hardinge saw the flaw in Curzon's logic:

> He forgets that India overshadows them in a manner to which the position here affords no parallel, and that he has not to deal with the active competition on the spot of intriguing Russian diplomatists, not to speak of Frenchmen and Germans, all meddling in the vortex of Persian politics.[145]

There was another flaw in Curzon's logic, which Hardinge did not see: "brutal directness," which usually meant brutal manners, made the Persians hate the English almost as heartily as they hated the Russians, those other masters of "brutal directness." How the Persians felt did not matter to either power in 1903, but would matter a great deal some fifteen years later. Persia, which

---

144. Memorandum on the Bushire Incident by Lord Curzon [countersigned by Sir A. Hardinge], December 3, 1903, off Bushire, Enclosure in A. Hardinge to Lansdowne, No. [illegible], December 4, 1903; ibid.

145. A. Hardinge to Lansdowne (private), February 1904, as cited in Newton, *Lord Lansdowne*, p. 243.

Curzon knew so well and to whose welfare he was not indifferent, would see in him only an enemy; and when his dream of a Persia, safe under British protection, would be about to come true, she would rise and shatter it forever, inflicting upon him a humiliating and painful defeat.

7

War, Revolution, and the Reconciliation of the Antagonists

The Shah's trip to Europe in the summer of 1902 had cost Persia an enormous sum of money. The 10,000,000 rubles borrowed from Russia in April were spent before the end of the year. When Amin os-Soltān went to the Russian bank for another loan, the manager, E. K. Grube, "used very plain language," telling him "that he had orders from M. de Witte to grant no further loan without a guarantee that the money would be employed for definite public purposes, and not squandered amongst the courtiers and h.H.'s own worthless dependents."[1] The Belgian Director of Customs, J. Naus, on the contrary, claimed that Witte was "not indisposed" to extend additional aid to Persia, though he agreed with Hardinge's view that the Russians would probably demand a reorganization of the "maliat" (taxes).[2]

Hardinge was sceptical about the success of reforms and felt that another loan was inevitable. Should Amin os-Soltān get another Russian loan, he would have to pay heavily for it in political concessions to Russia, "such, for instance, as placing of Russian controllers over the 'maliat,' or the granting of the pipelines to the Persian Gulf," unless Britain again come forward with a counteroffer, "either by means of an advance through the Imperial Bank or from Mr. D'Arcy, and thus beat down the Russian terms by obliging M. de Witte to lower them, or to see Persia borrow elsewhere."[3]

This time the British government backed its minister, making

1. A. Hardinge to Lansdowne, No. 183, Confidential, Tehran, December 30, 1902; F. O. 60/660.
2. Id.
3. Id.

it possible for him to offer Persia a loan through the Imperial Bank. The sum was small, but it staved off a total collapse of the Persian government. The agreement, signed by Amin os-Soltān and Joseph Naus for Persia and Joseph Rabino for the Imperial Bank on April 4, 1903, provided for a loan of £300,000 at 5 percent, repayable over twenty years from the income of Caspian fisheries. If such income proved insufficient, postal revenues, as well as the customs receipts of Fārs and the Persian Gulf ports, would be used.[4]

Anticipating future financial battles, Sir Arthur proposed that the British government buy the controlling interest in the Imperial Bank of Persia, an institution without which England would be in no position to compete with Russia. Lord Lansdowne wrote back that a number of objections to Hardinge's proposal had been raised. It was said, first, that the Bank was "concerned in transactions which, from an English point of view, would be regarded as usurious and somewhat shady." Second, "If such transactions were discontinued shareholders' profit would be largely diminished, and they would have a grievance." Third, the prices of shares would go up if it were known that the British government was buying. Fourth, the prospects of the bank's failing were remote while the possibility of its falling into other than English hands was excluded, "Since the majority of directors must be English under the Charter."[5]

Patiently and in great detail, Sir Arthur tried again to explain the reasons for his proposal that the British government buy a controlling interest in the Imperial Bank of Persia. Though the bank had showed profit every year since its foundation, except 1894–95, one or two unfavorable annual balances could lead to its liquidation by the owners. Moreover, there was nothing that would prevent foreigners from gaining control over this private institution.

> I believe that last year it was intimated to Monsieur de Witte
> . . . that he could influence the policy of the Bank by buying

---

4. Iran, Archive of the Ministry of Foreign Affairs, File 44/Folder 1, year 1326 A. H.

5. Lansdowne to A. Hardinge, Telegram, No. 31, Secret, March 28, 1903; F. O. 60/668.

some [shares], upon which Monsieur Grube declared that the Russian Banque d'Escompte was strong enough to destroy its rival without incurring this unnecessary outlay. Monsieur Grube has indeed stated to a diplomatic colleague of mine that the blows which he is dealing will achieve this end in another four or five years at most, and the persistent reports which he spreads of the insecure position of the Imperial Bank have not been without effect on the timid, credulous, and suspicious Persian merchants, several of whom have observed to me that our English Bank is after all a mere private, and they hear somewhat shaky, concern, whilst the Banque d'Escompte is as firm as the Russian Government.[6]

Since loans meant political power, Hardinge went on, Russia was in a better position than England. The former could be compared in its powers in Persia to the House of Commons, the latter to the House of Lords, "and accordingly in any determined struggle between the two, it is Russia which is almost sure to win." The balance of power would not be righted until Russia's control of "supply" was broken. Her power of the purse dominated Persian politics and confronted Britain at every turn.

It would be of less importance if the Shah and his advisers were enlightened and public spirited enough to economise, to develop the resources of their country, and by paying off . . . the Russian debt to regain their freedom of borrowing in the open market. But they are . . . extravagant, fatalistic, and careless of the future beyond belief. Even the Atabeg-i-Azam [Amin os-Soltān], the only statesman among them, is a kind of political Micawber, buoyed up, like that hero, after brief periods of acute depression, by cheery hopes, begotten of a singularly sanguine and genial temperament, that at the last moment "something will turn up" to save Persia from the ruin she is courting.

The only way by which, so it appears to me, we can mitigate the grave dangers of this situation is to take a lesson from Monsieur de Witte and place the Imperial Bank in a

6. A. Hardinge to Lansdowne, No. 38, Secret, March 29, 1903; F. O. 60/665.

position as nearly analogous as possible to that of the Banque d'Escompte de Perse.⁷

The struggle of the banks went on year after year, with the English usually on the defensive. In the summer of 1902 the Russian bank was about to open a branch in Mashhad with a manager and staff of twelve assistants. Plans were being made for another branch office in Seistān. Curzon saw "what opportunities for Russian interference would be created, and how largely Russian interests in Seistān would increase, by the establishment of a Russian banking business." The Government of India did not know whether the Imperial Bank of Persia would find it profitable to open a branch in Seistān, but, Curzon wrote, "the measure would be of great advantage to our interests, and we would suggest that . . . the Bank should be approached on the subject." ⁸

Though the Imperial Bank of Persia had an official monopoly on the issuance of bank notes, the Russian bank, in October 1903, began to circulate what it called "bons de caisse." Being payable to the bearer and backed by an institution whose credit was of the highest order, these notes were as good as money, and an infringement on the rights of emission held by the Imperial Bank. The Imperial Bank's manager, Joseph Rabino, complained to Hardinge, who protested to the Foreign Minister, Nasrollāh Khān Moshir od-Dowleh. On October 11 a meeting was held to discuss the problem. Hardinge, Moshir od-Dowleh, Naus, Rabino, and others, agreed on nothing.⁹ The issue would remain alive for years.

At times the financial rivalry of the two banks exploded in open warfare. On Wednesday, March 14, 1906, the manager of the Russian bank, E. K. Grube, invited a number of *sarrāfs* (petty money changers who performed most of the day-to-day banking functions in the bazar) to a meeting at the bank. They were persuaded to stage a run on the Imperial Bank of Persia. If enough notes were presented, Grube thought, the Imperial Bank

7. Id.
8. Curzon to Hamilton, No. 104, Simla, June 26, 1902; L.I., 146, 1902, No. 937.
9. A. Hardinge to Lansdowne, No. 164, Tehran, October 11, 1903, and enclosures 1, 2, and 3; F. O. 60/666.

would run out of coin and would have to stop payments until additional supplies could be brought in. The closing of the bank's doors, even if temporary, would be a blow that could ruin its standing forever.

On Monday, March 19, the run began. A crowd of people presented notes to the sum of 540,000 qerāns (54,000 tumāns). In the midst of the hubbub there arrived a messenger from the Russian bank with notes for another 800,000 qerāns. Counting coin is a slow job. So anxious was the Russian bank messenger to exhaust the Imperial Bank's supply of silver, that he proposed to take the money without counting it.[10] By the end of the day the bank had paid out 1,340,000 qerāns. On Tuesday it paid 500,000 more, on Wednesday 378,000. Thursday was Now-Ruz (New Year's Day), and Friday, as usual, no business was transacted. On Saturday, March 24, a further 329,000 worth of notes were cashed in. The total withdrawn in four days reached 2,547,000 qerāns, of which 1,647,000 had been claimed by "the public" and 900,000 by the officials of the Russian bank. The resources of the Imperial Bank proved adequate, and the run failed.[11]

The British chargé d'affaires in St. Petersburg complained against the Russian-engineered run on the Imperial Bank in a private letter to Lamsdorff. The latter denied everything. The British chargé d'affaires in Tehran, Grant Duff, Lamsdorff wrote, had privately mentioned to Grube Rabino's allegations. Grube had replied that had such complaints been made officially, they would have provoked an equally official action by the Russian bank through the Russian legation against Mr. Rabino on the grounds of calumny.[12]

Sir Arthur's advice of March 1903 that the British government should acquire control of the Imperial Bank and treat it as a

---

10. Tradition has it that the employees of the Imperial Bank on that particular day took a long time counting money so as not to pay out too much before closing time, thus giving the bank's agents an opportunity to collect more silver for the next day.

11. Joseph Rabino, manager of the Imperial Bank of Persia, to E. Grant Duff [Chargé d'Affaires], Tehran, March 26, 1906, Enclosure No. 3 in E. Grant Duff to Sir Edward Grey, No. 74, Confidential, Tehran, March 27, 1906; F. O. 371/108.

12. Lamsdorff to Spring Rice, April 10/23, 1906, Enclosure No. 1, Spring Rice to Grey, No. 281, Confidential, St. Petersburg, April 24, 1906; ibid.

political rather than a commercial venture had not been accepted. In spite of periods of severe difficulty, the bank somehow survived as a private institution in competition with the Russian Ministry of Finance.

Through the spring and summer of 1903, Persia's internal situation continued to deteriorate. The Court was utterly demoralized, corrupt, and rife with intrigue. Rumor had it that the Shah's favorite wife, sister of Abdol Hoseyn Mirzā Farmānfarmā, was plotting her husband's overthrow. It was said that Amin os-Soltān had lost his influence because he had opposed the Shah's wish to go on a pilgrimage to Mashhad. Some attributed the decline of the Grand Vizier's influence to the fact that

> when the Shah recently ordered a pension of £ 3000.- a year, besides a large lump sum down, to be paid to his favourite astrologer, because His Majesty had dreamt that he had saved him from drowning, the Atabeg [Amin os-Soltān], who was struggling at the time with the usual loan difficulties, lost his temper and said that he had raised large sums to pay for the Shah's tours and toys, but must protest against paying for his dreams.[13]

By the end of April the various factions at Court eagerly anticipated Amin os-Soltān's fall. The Russian minister, Petr Mikhailovich Vlasov, who had succeeded Argyropoulo in 1902, and Monsieur Naus, his close collaborator, expected Soltān Majid Mirzā Eyn od-Dowleh, an extreme reactionary, to take power. The British would have preferred the more patriotic Amin od-Dowleh, who made overtures to the English, even offering to overthrow his long-time rival. In a letter to Hardinge, Amin od-Dowleh expressed the sentiments of a number of Persians who grieved over the catastrophic decline of their nation and feared its probable extinction. He wrote:

> I deplore the fall of my country into the clutches of Russia and cannot understand how it is that you are silent. Are you not aware of the actual facts, or, being aware of them

13. A. Hardinge to Lansdowne, No. 64, Confidential, Tehran, April 27, 1903; F. O. 60/665.

is the British Government content to see Persia turned into a Russian dependency like Bokhara? I am neither a partisan of England nor am I a servant of Russia, but I am proud to be a patriot.[14]

Hardinge replied that he could not work against the Prime Minister but that England stood ready to help Persia whenever she asked for help.[15]

In the capital there was at least peace and a semblance of order, but in the provinces anarchy spread from town to town. The regular machinery of government broke down in Āzarbāyjān, where the governor, Mohammad Ali Mirzā, heir to the throne, resorted to criminal elements to help him keep his hold on the province. The notorious brigand, Rahim Khān, a tribal chieftain from Qaradāgh who had been condemned to death a year earlier but whose life had been spared by the prince-governor, was appointed commander of the prince's horsemen.[16] The Russian consul general at Tabriz, Ivan Fedorovich Pokhitonov, wielded great influence over the Valiahd (Crown Prince). An extreme nationalist and imperialist, crude and violent in his methods, Pokhitonov had "the reputation of detesting everything English." When the British acting consul, H. F. Stevens, tried to establish friendly relations with Pokhitonov, he was not only given no encouragement, Stevens reported, but was publicly slighted.[17]

When antiforeign riots broke out in Tabriz, Acting Consul Stevens suspected Turkish agents of instigating them. Unlike Stevens, who was not privy to all the secrets of the Tehran legation, Hardinge knew that the movement was headed by Persian clergy. He had been almost a charter member of that movement himself. What alarmed him was Pokhitonov's loud declaration that Russian troops, which had massed along the Persian border, would be used in Persian territory to protect Russian engineers working on the Jolfā-Tabriz-Qazvin road.[18]

14. Id.
15. Id.
16. Acting Consul H. F. Stevens to A. Hardinge, No. 7, Secret and Confidential, Tabriz, June 25, 1903; F. O. 60/666.
17. Id.
18. A. Hardinge to Lansdowne, No. 101, Secret and Confidential, Gulahek, July 6, 1903; ibid.

He communicated with Lansdowne and was authorized to tell Amin os-Soltān that any entry of Russian troops into Persia for the purpose of suppressing revolutionary disturbances would oblige the British "to take identical measures in the south and east." There can be no doubt that this information was communicated to the Russian legation at once.[19]

Lacking the necessary documents it is impossible to say whether the Russian government intended large-scale armed intervention in Persia in the summer of 1903. War clouds were rapidly gathering in the Far East, diverting to some extent the attention of Russia's rulers from other areas of potential imperial expansion. However, small-scale incursions into Persian territory did take place. As far back as December 15, 1894, the Tsar had approved a set of regulations permitting Russian border guards to cross into Persia in pursuit of bandits and to operate in Persian territory until such bandits were destroyed. The regulations were reaffirmed and amended on August 7, 1903. Furthermore, Russian troops were authorized, when operating in Persian territory, to punish those who were "guilty of sheltering fugitive criminals." In his "Instruction" to the newly appointed minister at Tehran, Aleksei Nikolaevich Speyer, Lamsdorff explained that such measures resulted from the inability of the Persian government to keep order on the frontier.[20]

In December a punitive expedition was sent to Persia over the protests of her government. In March 1904, a month after the outbreak of the Russo-Japanese War, the Russians suspended the regulations allowing her troops to enter Persia, but soon restored them "because of continued banditry" along the frontier.[21]

Antiforeign agitation in Tabriz and elsewhere easily transformed itself into outbursts against minorities. In Tabriz and other towns of Āzarbāyjān, Christians were threatened. In Hamadān the Jews lived in constant fear of their lives. Throughout the country Baha'is became the target of hostility instigated

19. Sir A. Hardinge to Sir Edward Grey, Separate and Confidential, London, December 23, 1905; F. O. 371/102.
20. Lamsdorff's "Instruction," "Tsarskaia Rossiia i Persiia v epokhu russko iaponskoi voiny," *Krasnyi Arkhiv*, 4(53) (1932), 23. (*Krasnyi Arkhiv* shall henceforth be cited as K. A.)
21. Id.

and directed by the more fanatical of the clergy. The bloodiest incidents of the summer occurred in and around Yazd, where the governor, Mahmud Mirzā Jalāl od-Dowleh, son of Zell es-Solṭān, inspired by the prominent Esfahān divine, Āqā Najafi, unleashed a mob of several thousand against the Baha'is. In a few days of horror over one hundred men, women, and children were tortured and put to death, houses looted and burned, fruit trees uprooted, and field crops trampled out.[22]

Amin os-Solṭān admitted that the Yazd massacres "had been traced to Agha Najafi, who had attempted to provoke similar massacres in many other towns of Persia, and had sent emissaries for this purpose to Sultanabad, Kazvin and Tehran." The Persian government was taking military measures to preserve order, he claimed. To reassure all Western representatives that Christians were not in danger, the Grand Vizier told Sir Arthur Hardinge of a telegram that had been received by the Shah from the four chief mojtaheds of Karbalā and Najaf, "disavowing the anti-Christian and anti-European agitation at Tabriz, but approving the execution of Babi [Baha'i] heretics at Isfahan and Yezd and expressing a hope that the Persian Government would encourage their repition [repetition] in other cities."[23] Amin os-Solṭān said that he was satisfied with the stand taken by the clerical leaders, "since attacks upon Christian schools and officials might have greater results than a mere outcry against Babism,"[24] which was a way of saying that whereas attacks on Christians might lead to European protests and interference, the massacre of a few hundred Baha'is would not and therefore would have no importance in the eyes of the Persian government.

The dismissal of Amin os-Solṭān by the Shah in September was greeted with joy. The old Vizier had wielded enormous power for a quarter of a century. He had grown rich, fat, and cynical. For

22. For a detailed account see M. T. Mālmiri, *Tārikhe shohadāye Yazd* (Cairo, 1342 A.H.).

23. A. Hardinge to Lansdowne, No. 102, Secret and Confidential, Gulahek, July 9, 1903; F. O. 60/666. (A letter of E. Eldred, British consular agent in Yazd, attached to the above dispatch, reported that the governor had a Babi (Baha'i) blown from a cannon and another's throat cut "to appease the crowd." The governor refused to take any measures to stop the murders.)

24. Id.

War, Revolution, and Reconciliation

Mozaffar ed-Din he felt only contempt, for his country a love too weak for sacrifice. Unprincipled, shrewd, charming, and selfish, he was feared, envied, and hated by many of his compatriots who saw in him the embodiment of every vice of the old regime.

His successor, Soltān Majid Mirzā Eyn od-Dowleh, was a grandson of Fath Ali Shah and Mozaffar ed-Din's son-in-law. Born about 1847, he had occupied a succession of provincial governorships, becoming Minister of the Royal Domain and Governor of Tehrān in 1901. Like most of his contemporaries in government, he amassed a large fortune by speculation and extortion, and gained a reputation for narrow-mindedness, ignorance, xenophobia, and cruelty that shocked even the hardened commander of the Persian Cossack Brigade, Colonel Kosogovskii, who characterized the prince as "a man of low morality, and, evidently, cruel: during his two months stay in Māzandarān [in 1896] among his original punishments was that one of the guilty men was shod, like a horse, with horseshoes, nails having been driven into his bare heels, into the flesh." [25] His only apparent qualification for high office was the influence he wielded over the Shah.

In normal times Russia would have been satisfied with the appointment of Eyn od-Dowleh and with the increasingly chaotic conditions in Persia. However, times were not normal. On February 9, 1904, Japan struck, and Russia found herself embroiled with an unexpectedly powerful enemy. Her limited financial, industrial, and military resources were strained. It was no longer possible to pour millions of rubles into Persia or to risk a clash with England while the Japanese invested Port Arthur and pushed into Manchuria. It was Russia's turn to reevaluate her Persian policy.

On June 20 a Special Conference was called at the Ministry of Foreign Affairs under the chairmanship of Count Lamsdorff to determine the proper economic and financial policy in Persia under conditions imposed by the war in the Far East. Among the participants were: the Minister of Finance, V. N. Kokovtsov; the Ambassador at Constantinople, I. A. Zinov'ev; the Senior Counselor of the Ministry of Foreign Affairs, K. M. Argyropoulo; the

---

25. Kosogovskii, *Iz tegeranskogo dnevnika*, p. 79.

Director of the First Department of the Ministry of Foreign Affairs, N. Hartwig; the Chairman of the Board of the Discount and Loan Bank of Persia, P. Bark.

Lamsdorff and Kokovtsov brought to the attention of the conference that the first Russian loan to Persia (22,500,000 rubles) had been made in 1900, the second (10,000,000) in 1902, and that since then the Persian government had been constantly asking for more loans or delays in payments of the accumulated debts. Because of political considerations, most of her requests had been satisfied, and Persia now owed Russia 3,000,000 rubles in short-term credit. Since the Persians had proved their inability to fulfill their financial obligations, and since "the existing system of management of state economy in Persia can in no wise serve as a guarantee of a more correct attitude toward affairs on the part of the government of the Shah," it was necessary to adopt a policy in case of new requests of the Persian government for financial aid.

Persia, whose richest and most populous provinces were located along the Russian border, had been naturally exposed to the influence of a state that was culturally superior to her. In recent years special efforts had been made to widen this largely commercial influence. Russia did not stop with loans to the Shah but actively participated in the economic life of the nation.

The most outstanding Russian enterprise in Persia was the Discount and Loan Bank, on which the Russian Treasury had spent 11,300,000 rubles in addition to credits of 10,000,000 rubles extended to it by the State Bank. The ever-widening activity of the bank demonstrated the strength and purposefulness of this enterprise. Its political importance was determined by its ability considerably to hamper the activities of the British Imperial Bank of Persia. Other Russian enterprises included road building, transportation and insurance, and the commercial shipping line to the Persian Gulf, the latter costing the government 200,000 rubles a year in subsidy.[26]

The conference agreed with Kokovtsov that all questions of financial policy in Persia must be approached with great caution. To spend money there, while many of Russia's most important

26. Special Conference on economic policy in Persia, June 7/20, 1904; "Anglo-russkoe sopernichestvo v Persii v 1890–1906 g.g.," K. A., 1(56) (1933), 49–50.

domestic needs remained unsatisfied, was permissible only if such spending brought real advantages. One must distinguish between investment in banks, roads, and transportation and loans to the government. In the first instance sacrifice was justified by the resultant growth of Russian commerce, in the second Russia reaped only popular dissatisfaction, which endangered her prestige. Kokovtsov stated that the Russian Treasury must not give direct assistance to the Shah except in extraordinary circumstances where some specific advantage was sought from the Persian government. Investment in productive enterprises should be allowed,

> but even that should be limited as far as possible to Northern Persia, no further than the line passing through Esfahān; to the south of that line competition with other powers, especially England, appears to us extraordinarily difficult and capable of unfavorable influence upon our relations with those powers.[27]

The conference took note of the fact that Persia was in disarray and that no amount of purely financial help would rescue her. The Persian government had worked out a reform project but, "It is not open to doubt . . . that without outside help Persia will be unable to . . . realize the reforms." They would affect mostly the governing class and the clergy, who would oppose them. The intervention of Russia in favor of reforms, which would probably fail, would only decrease Russia's "charm" (*obaianie*). They could succeed if England and Russia simultaneously pressed for them, but then considerable internal upheavals would occur. "At the present time, however," the conference concluded, "any significant complications in the countries neighboring on Russia must be recognized as extremely undesirable."[28]

Since the conference discussed economic issues at a time of great financial stringency brought about by the war, the tone of the discussions and the decisions reached were cautious and conservative. The overall policy of the Russian government was much

27. Ibid., p. 51.
28. Ibid., p. 52.

more comprehensively stated in the instructions written by Lamsdorff in October 1904 for the guidance of the new Russian minister at Tehran, A. N. Speyer.

Lamsdorff acknowledged that the war in the Far East was not going well and that rumors, exaggerating Russian reverses, circulated in Tehran.[29] He continued:

> the Ministry of Foreign Affairs in its instructions to the Legation in Tehran, as well as in its relations with other departments in connection with Persia, has undeviatingly maintained the basic principle that Russia cannot and must not go back and give up active work wherever her real interests are concerned, especially when the established aims have already been partly achieved. As a result, the Persian government was soon convinced of the absence of any change in the relations of Russia toward Persia even in financial questions, since it was able last spring to take advantage of our financial assistance in its pressing budgetary needs.[30]

The steadiness and perseverance with which the Russians pursued their goals in Persia were truly impressive. About a year before the outbreak of war, the able and knowledgeable correspondent of *The Times*, Valentine Chirol, wrote of the "persevering hands of Russian statesmen, whose breadth of grasp and continuity of purpose are liable to no disturbance from the fluctuations of public sentiment or the precariousness of parliamentary majorities." [31] Not even war could deflect the Russian Government from its Persian goals

> to preserve the integrity and the inviolability of the possessions of the Shah; without seeking territorial accretions for

29. Three days after Japan attacked Russia, the Shah asked Hardinge to provide him with accurate news of the war. Hardinge promised to keep him informed. "News of the Japanese success," he wrote, "produced an immense impression here, and appears to have given much satisfaction to the Persian Court." A. Hardinge to Lansdowne, No. 19, Telegraphic, February 12, 1904; F. O. 60/684. If the reputedly Russophile court rejoiced in Japanese victories, one can imagine the jubilation in the openly anti-Russian circles.

30. "Instruction," "Tsarskaia Rossiia i Persiia v epokhu russko-iaponskoi voiny," K. A., 4(53) (1932), 13–14.

31. V. Chirol, *The Middle Eastern Question or Some Political Problems of Indian Defence* (London, 1903), pp. 17–18.

ourselves, without allowing the hegemony of a third power, gradually to subject Persia to our dominant influence . . . In other words, our task is to make Persia politically an obedient and useful, i.e. sufficiently powerful, instrument in our hands, and, economically, to preserve for ourselves the large Persian market for a free application of Russian labor and capital. The close interrelationship and interaction of political and economic results which have already been achieved by us, will create that firm basis upon which we must develop our fruitful activity in Persia.[32]

The struggle between Russia and Britain went on. The two agreements, those of 1834 and 1888, affirming the territorial integrity of the Shah's domain could not be interpreted extensively, as far as St. Petersburg was concerned. Any attempt to see in them "some condominium of Russia and England in Persia," or a definition of spheres of influence was, "self-evidently, a basic violation of the above stated main task" of Russia and therefore inadmissible.

Sir Henry Drummond Wolff had been the main proponent of Anglo-Russian understanding. However, "All attempts of this statesman to induce Russia to enter into a definite agreement with England in regard to Persian affairs have not achieved, and could not have achieved, success due to the reasons expressed above and which lie at the basis of the old Russian policy." [33]

England's chase after concessions, through which she hoped to ensure her domination over most of Persia, had not been successful either. The British had looked to railways to establish their influence, but railway construction was postponed, first to 1900 then to 1910. The Tobacco Régie was a complete failure; Kārun navigation did not return expected profits. Even a viable institution such as the Imperial Bank had not been able to withstand serious Russian competition. It was able to maintain its position vis-à-vis the Discount and Loan Bank only because it enjoyed extraordinary privileges such as the right to issue bank notes. On the contrary, Russia, because of certain economic and financial

32. "Instruction," K. A., 4(53) (1932), 14.
33. Ibid., p. 16.

measures, had been able not only to strengthen her position in northern Persia but even to gain a firm foothold in the Persian Gulf.[34]

Far from desiring a détente, Lamsdorff was apprehensive lest Russian defeats in the Far East prompt Britain to press Russia into an agreement in Persia.

> It should not be overlooked that merely to enter into negotiations with Great Britain could do us very serious harm by undermining confidence toward Russia, which we have undoubtedly been able to create in the Persians.

Wherever Russian and English interests collided, Russia must consistently and firmly follow her aims, proving to the Persians and the British that her determination to defend her rights had not weakened.

> Finally, for the extreme eventuality of aggressive measures on the part of the English in Seistān, where in recent years their work has assumed an especially active character, we are taking military precautions in Central Asia in order to be ready for every eventuality.[35]

Lamsdorff proceeded to deal with specific aspects of policy. Russia feared that on the death of the sick Mozaffar ed-Din, Zell es-Soltān, his half-brother, would try to ascend the throne. The Russian legation and the commander of the Persian Cossack Brigade, now Colonel Chernozubov, had taken appropriate measures to prevent this. Since Mohammad Ali Mirzā was the lawful heir, it was hoped that Britain could be induced not to support other claimants. For Russia the Valiahd (Crown Prince) was the most suitable candidate

> because in Tabriz he not only proved his constant attention to Russia's very important interests in Āzarbāyjān, but demonstrated visible inclination toward everything Russian, having even learned, with the help of his teacher, Mr. Shapshal, the Russian language to a sufficient extent. In conse-

---

34. Ibid., p. 17.
35. Ibid., p. 18.

quence of this, and taking into account the future, the Imperial government on its part has tried to establish the best relations with the heir to the Persian throne, and last spring cooperated in the liquidation and consolidation on more favourable terms in the Discount and Loan Bank of all of the Valiahd's debts, simultaneously guaranteeing him, through a secret agreement, the immediate issuance of a loan in case of extraordinary events and the need quickly to leave Tabriz.[36]

The British, Lamsdorff continued, were anxious to shake loose the ties between the capital and the provinces, but the Russians used the Shah to foil their intrigues and supported the government in Tehran. As long as a Persian Prime Minister was not openly anti-Russian, he would receive Russia's backing.

Lamsdorff noted that Tehran rumors predicted the fall of Eyn od-Dowleh and the return to power of Amin os-Soltān. In November 1902 the latter had expressed to the Russian minister, Vlasov, his deep conviction of the inevitability of an alliance between Persia and Russia.

> In such an alliance, correctly established, one could not fail to see that last step which would entirely and finally ensure us the achievement of our basic aims and therefore this thought received in principle the august approval of the Sovereign Emporer; however, the practical realization of the alliance appeared premature mainly because we did not dispose in the vicinity of Persian frontiers of sufficiently impressive forces, which would guarantee the distant southern regions of Persia from any encroachment, and therefore would free from risk our allied obligations.[37]

The Russian government knew that its position in Persia rested essentially "upon the forces with which we are capable of defending that position." The continuing construction of the Orenburg-Tashkent railway and other measures, such as the concentration of troops in Central Asia, made it ever more firm.

36. Ibid., pp. 19–20.
37. Ibid., pp. 20–21.

Lamsdorff was aware that Amin os-Soltān's proposal of alliance was motivated by his desire to maintain his own power, yet it was consonant with the "slowly ripening demands of life" and rested on firm, real foundations. The moment for its conclusion had not yet arrived, but Lamsdorff suggested to Speyer that he base his activity in Tehran on the idea of a closer union between the two countries, without touching upon the forms which the alliance might assume. "You will find fertile ground for preparatory work in this direction both in the numerous negative aspects of Persia's internal life, and in her lack of security from external dangers," Lamsdorff preached.[38]

Speyer was to seek the appointment of Russian officers as instructors in the Persian army. However, the appearance of a general army reorganization must be avoided. Persian finances were incapable of supporting real military reform which, moreover,

> would not correspond to our own interests, since on the question of any basic reforms—if, contrary to expectations, Persia found the money and the government capable of making them—our aim does not consist in accepting the unknown . . . and assuming an active role in the cares for the complete revitalization of that country.[39]

Any intervention in Persian internal affairs would inevitably arouse against Russia the hatred of the population, and harm Russian interests through complications of an international character.

Even minor advantages and minor dangers should not be overlooked. Speyer was to seek the appointment of a Russian doctor to the Court, "which circumstance would bring us undoubted political advantage." The minister must also concern himself with anti-Russian propaganda conducted by Armenian agitators who found a protagonist in the British consul, Churchill. However, Speyer must avoid antagonizing the Armenians, because many of them were "a useful conductor of our economic influence."

38. Ibid., p. 21.
39. Ibid., pp. 22-23.

Wealthy Armenians had a material interest in Russian trade and were unlikely to approve of anti-Russian propaganda.[40]

Russia's economic policy, which had been determined by an interministerial conference in June 1904, was summed up by Lamsdorff in six points:

1. To reject as far as possible all Persian requests for economic aid.

2. To make loans only in most extraordinary circumstances, out of political and economic considerations and with sufficient guarantees.

3. Not to seek unprofitable concessions.

4. To develop and improve the already existent Russian enterprises such as the bank, the roads, transport agencies, etc.

5. To oppose railway construction.

6. To participate in the development of the telegraph network as an enterprise supplementary to road building.[41]

In spite of diminished credits for the year 1904, sizable sums had been appropriated for the principal construction projects. The Jolfā-Tabriz and Qazvin-Hamadān highways were assigned 3,500,000 rubles, while 400,000 were granted for the equipment of the harbor at Anzali.[42]

In discussing eastern Persia, Lamsdorff stressed the importance of Seistān, where the British and the Russians came into closest contact. The former had bribed Showkat ol-Molk and Heshmat ol-Molk, rulers respectively of Qāenāt and Seistān. The same system of bribery and threats was practiced by the English throughout Baluchestān as well. They built roads to the Persian frontier and telegraph lines in Persian territory. They made a display of force by sending Major MacMahon with an escort of 1,000 men to delimit a section of the border.[43]

Speyer's goals were mutually contradictory: he was instructed to improve relations with Heshmat ol-Molk, and strengthen the authority of the Shah. Some steps had already been taken, Lams-

40. Ibid., pp. 24–25.
41. Ibid., p. 34.
42. Ibid., pp. 34–35.
43. Ibid., p. 25.

dorff wrote. On Russian initiative postal service and a telegraph line under secret Russian control had been established between Mashhad and Nosratābād. The customhouse in Seistān hampered the Indian merchants. A permanent representative of the Discount and Loan Bank had settled in Nosratābād. The guard at the Russian vice-consulate had been increased to match that at the British. An army officer was attached to the Seistān vice-consulate and another stationed at Torbate Heydari.[44]

Finally, in connection with Seistān, Speyer was instructed to press the Persian government for the establishment of plague-control stations, and to have his consular agents travel through the countryside, developing contacts with local khans. The agents would supply Speyer with information, and he would be in a position to advise the Persian government and guide its activity in accordance with Russia's views.[45]

Southern Persia, Lamsdorff believed, presented a wide sphere for Russian activity. British pretentions to exclusive domination in that area had been proved baseless. However, Russia's recent Far Eastern reverses had a particularly unfavorable effect in South Persia because the region was full of open and secret British agents who had extensive connections and spread Arabic and Indo-Persian newspapers with most tendentious stories about Russia. Still, Russia's position was basically firm. The central government, which feared for the integrity of its rule in the Gulf, for its authority and dignity; local rulers such as Sheykh Khaz'al of Mohammareh or officials such as the Kārgozār of Langeh, who had suffered more than once from clashes with England and had become her enemies; and, finally, the masses of the population, all had welcomed the Russians as a counterweight to the English.[46]

The time had arrived to open a branch of the Discount and Loan Bank in Bushehr, permanently to station a Russian naval vessel in the Gulf (one was being built expressly for that purpose), and to appoint a Russian doctor to the customs at Bandar Abbās. The latter port was of special importance. Situated at the

44. Ibid., pp. 26–27.
45. Ibid., pp. 27–28.
46. Ibid., p. 28.

entrance into the Persian Gulf, it was visited by all Russian ships and served the provinces of Larestān, Kermān, and Bam, as well as certain districts of Baluchestān, Seistān, and Yazd. The Russian government was determined to establish a consulate at Bandar Abbās. Commerce and shipping alone would justify this step, "but political considerations further move us to accept this measure as necessary," Lamsdorff wrote. Moreover, Bandar Abbās was a good intelligence outpost, close to the island of Qeshm where the British had a naval station.[47] To establish an agency there was worth spending money even while an unsuccessful war was being waged with Japan.

Undoubtedly with Curzon's recent tour of the Gulf in mind, Lamsdorff advised Speyer to think of a trip south. The visit, of course, would have to be made in suitable style. It would have great moral and political effect:

> in the sense of a visible affirmation of the equality of rights of Russia and England and a demonstration of the importance we attach to our own interests in those regions, such a measure would have the best consequences for our consular representatives, agents among the native inhabitants, and all persons who in any way come into contact with the Russian element, in the sense of unifying and strengthening their activity, raising their personal prestige, and creating a more palpable consciousness of the work in which they, albeit in different ways and degrees, participate.[48]

As for western Persia, its significance lay in its proximity to the holy cities of Mesopotamia. The British, who fully appreciated the influence the leading mojtaheds of Najaf and Karbalā exerted on Persia's internal affairs, stopped at nothing, not even at fraud, to use it to their own advantage. Though the British system of bribery, Lamsdorff thought, was least effective in the fanatical milieu of the Shiite clergy, the English had influenced the mojtaheds against Amin os-Soltān and even tried to have them provoke ferment among the Shiites of Transcaucasia. Speyer was

47. Ibid., pp. 29–30.
48. Ibid., p. 30.

given overall responsibility for guiding the activity of Russian agents who watched for British intrigues.[49] The principal city of western Persia, Kermānshāh, could not be neglected not only because of its proximity to Najaf and Karbalā but also because of the person of its governor, Abdol Hoseyn Mirzā Farmānfarmā, and the role that city would play in the future, when the Baghdad railway was constructed, in the spread of German commercial and political influence.

> In accordance with above-mentioned circumstances we have rejected for ourselves, in spite of attempts of Farmānfarmā to ingratiate himself, any participation in his concession for the construction of the road Khāneqin-Kermānshāh-Hamadān, the very construction of which we have attempted to prevent in Tehran, since such a road would only facilitate the admission of Germany into the internal Persian market.[50]

Lamsdorff's style was atrocious, but the clarity of aims belied the confusion of language. Not even military defeat in the Far East would make Russia give up her traditional goals in Persia. It would take a revolution and the German threat to force her to abandon the dream of absorbing the entire country rather than only its northern half. Even then the renunciation would be incomplete, and secret hopes would not die.

In the light of Lamsdorff's instructions to Speyer, Curzon's and Hardinge's pleas for a stronger British policy in Persia become more understandable. One also comes to appreciate the insights of a journalist whose analysis of Russia's aims and methods was unusually penetrating.

> As surely as Russia's ascendency is to-day impregnably established in the North of Persia, so will it gradually, and with the increased momentum of acquired speed, be established throughout Persia down to the Gulf and to the confines of India, if it is given time to extend the sphere of its operations through all different agencies which it controls, either directly or through the nominal rulers of the country.[51]

49. Ibid., p. 31.
50. Ibid., p. 31.
51. Chirol, *The Middle Eastern Question*, pp. 303–04.

Why does not Russia annex Persia? "Russia prefers a feeble and bankrupt Oriental neighbour to an annexed dependency. She has learned the secret of ruling an Eastern State through its nominal owners, if only they are weak, corrupt, and in her pay." [52]

On April 8, 1904, after prolonged negotiations, Britain and France signed an agreement settling their differences over Morocco, Egypt, and Siam. Though Germany was not even mentioned, Berlin did not miss the significance of the agreement, which laid the foundation of an alliance of great consequence to the fate of Europe and of the world. With the sensitivity peculiar to the frightened and the persecuted, Persian statesmen saw in the agreement a prelude to a wider entente that would include Russia. Early in May, Alā ol-Molk, former ambassador at Constantinople, came to ask Hardinge whether the rumors of an impending Anglo-Russian agreement were true. Sir Arthur said that such an agreement would be good for all concerned. Alā ol-Molk argued the opposite.

> His remarks [Hardinge wrote] were of no special interest and I should not have mentioned them or alluded to the subject had I not thought it worth while again to note the extreme anxiety displayed by the ruling classes in this country at the merest rumour, however slight, that the Russians and ourselves may make up our differences in Asia.[53]

Persia's fears were premature. If there was some inclination on the British side, an inclination which increased as Japanese victories made Russia look less formidable and dangerous, to reach an agreement with her, no corresponding desire was discernible on the Russian side. In a summary of events in Persia during 1905, the British legation in Tehran listed Russian activities:

1. Russia made demands that a lighthouse be built in the Persian Gulf and buoys placed in ports. She would survey the coast and do the work. (The Shah turned it down and did the work himself.)

---

52. Ibid., p. 298.
53. A. Hardinge to Lansdowne, No. 81, Confidential, Tehran, May 10, 1904; F. O. 60/682.

2. Opened consulates at Langeh and Bandar Abbās.

3. Had Prince Amatouni, of the Ministry of Commerce, travel through the south promoting Russian trade.

4. Russian citizens were buying up land around Mashhad and Anzali.

5. Russian agents stirred up the population against the Seistān border commission.

6. Interfered in the case of an American missionary, Labaree, who had been murdered in Urumiyyeh.

7. Promoted schemes for automobile traffic along her roads in the north.

8. Made an attempt to get absolute control of the Mashhad-Seistān telegraph.[54]

9. Through financial pressure attempted to gain complete control of the Persian army.

10. To secure the favor of Mohammad Ali Mirzā, the heir apparent, advanced him £100,000 with no strings attached.

11. Intrigued against the Indian Commercial Mission.

12. Spread rumors.[55]

The list shows how energetically and systematically Lamsdorff's instructions were being carried out. The opening of the consulate in Bandar Abbās had been accomplished with amazing speed. The consulate at Langeh and Amatouni's travels were part of the same expansion of commitments in the Gulf area. Stirring up the population in Seistān, promoting automobile transport, pressing for the control of the army, lending money to the Valiahd, all these were tasks given to Speyer in the summer of 1904. His success would have been impressive under any circumstances. That he was able to achieve it while his country was losing a war was truly remarkable.

Russia's attempts to weaken or embarrass Britain were not confined to Persia. Even South Africa was considered a proper arena for striking a blow at England, thus diverting her attention

---

54. Russia already had control, but the British apparently did not know it yet. See supra, p. 466.

55. Report on the Events in Persia in 1905, Enclosure No. 1 in E. Grant Duff to Sir Edward Grey, No. 53, Confidential, Tehran, February 27, 1906; F. O. 371/106.

from the Middle East and Far East. A Boer general, Joubert-Piennaar, proposed to the Russian minister in Lisbon, Koiander, "to organize in South Africa an uprising of the Blacks," who were allegedly ready for it, because of the influx of the Chinese into South Africa. Canadian and Australian riffraff who had been brought in "to exterminate us," were also ready to rise up against their own government.[56]

Lamsdorff told the Tsar that the project could be useful. Nicholas hated the English, often using expressions "in which no distinction was made between the Jews and the English or the English and the Jews."[57] He was delighted at the prospect of giving them trouble. The question was discussed with the Minister of Finance, Kokovtsov, who would have to provide the £80,000 for which Joubert had asked. The Russian ambassador in Paris, Nelidov, advised Lamsdorff against involvement in Joubert's scheme. What did Russia know about him? How could he be trusted with £80,000? What if the British discovered Russia's participation? What would be the advantage to Russia of an uprising in South Africa? Japan did not need British help, and a diversion of this sort would serve no useful purpose.[58]

Lamsdorff's caution and good sense, which must have temporarily deserted him under the stress of the Japanese war, eventually triumphed, making him drop the plan and its author. However, this minor episode shows how far Russia would go in her search for means to strike at Britain. If the Russian government seriously contemplated giving £80,000 to an unknown adventurer who made dubious promises of an uprising in South Africa, it would certainly not hesitate to spend ten or twenty times as much in Persia, where it already controlled most of the ministers and the heir apparent, if not the Shah himself.

In February 1905 the Persian government, needing money for a reorganization of the army, which had virtually ceased to exist, approached Russia for another loan. In spite of the poor state of

56. Koiander to Lamsdorff, Lisbon, February 10/23, 1905; "Nikolai II, 'Imperator Kafrov,'" K. A., 2–3 (69–70) (1935), 242, 243–47.
57. Witte, Vospominaniia (Moscow, 1923), 2, 372.
58. Nelidov to Lamsdorff, Secret, Paris, March 17/30, 1905; K. A., 2–3 (69–70), 250–52.

her own finances, Russia offered £350,000 on condition that instead of hiring Austrian officers, as the Shah intended, the Persian army be placed under Russian control. "The scheme practically amounted to the extension to the whole Persian army of an organization similar to that of the present Cossack Brigade." [59] When the Shah hesitated, the Russian Bank applied pressure, demanding payment of arrears on old debts. In their distress the Persians turned to the British. The Imperial Bank "dallied with the proposal for some time, but finally informed the Persian Government that they were warned by their legal adviser that, by the terms of their charter, they were not legally entitled to make further advances to the Persian Government." [60] In May the British government offered £200,000 if Persia would grant England control over irrigation works on the Kārun. The Shah refused.[61] In June the Persian minister in London, Alā os-Saltaneh, told Lord Lansdowne that Russia was making new efforts to bring the Shah under her influence. The point of it all was that the Shah needed £150,000 or £200,000.[62] Once again no money was forthcoming from the British, and the Persians went, hat in hand, to the Russians.

Russia was in turmoil. In February 1905 Kuropatkin, the Commander in Chief in the Far East, was defeated at Mukden. In June Admiral Z. P. Rozhestvenskii's fleet, which had traveled half way around the world from the Baltic to the China Sea, was destroyed in the Straits of Tsushima. Every defeat reverberated throughout the vast, sullen land of Russia. Strikes, demonstrations, riots, and armed uprisings broke out in the two capitals and through most of the provinces. By midsummer it was evident that a revolution was in progress. Yet even then the Russian government refused to neglect Persia.

On August 25, 1905, Lamsdorff told a special ministerial conference that the Shah was on his way to Russia. The Prime

59. Report on the Events in Persia in 1905, Grant Duff, No. 53, Tehran, February 27, 1906; F. O. 371/106.
60. Id.
61. Id.
62. Lansdowne to A. Hardinge, Draft, No. 100, Secret, June 20, 1905; F. O. 60/697.

Minister, Eyn od-Dowleh, had informed the Russians that the Shah had reached a final decision "to renounce the policy of vacillation between English and Russian influences and irrevocably to turn to the side of Russia." There was no doubt that upon arrival the Shah would ask for money. Kokovtsov, the Minister of Finance, expected the request to be for £1,000,000.[63]

Russia had already invested 69,526,918 rubles in Persia. She had made the following distributions:

highways and Anzali harbor	10,632,000
3. The Tabriz highway	2,535,000
4. The Persian Insurance and	
1. The Discount and Loan Bank	21,350,000
2. The Anzali-Tehran and Hamadān Transport Society	200,180
5. Persian Gulf shipping	1,180,000
6. Long-term loans	29,114,738
7. Short-term loans of 1903, 1904, 1905	2,975,000
8. Loans and credit to the Persian heir apparent	1,540,000

Should she now give the Shah another 10,000,000 rubles?

The loan would be purely political. A country with a budgetary deficit of 3,000,000 rubles a year would not be able to repay it. Should the loan be made, it must be hedged with guarantees that Persia would not come back for more, or turn to Britain. The conference agreed that a pledge on the part of Persia henceforth not to borrow from England (the Imperial Bank) would constitute a real guarantee. "Such an obligation should, it would seem, also correspond to the intentions of the Shah as declared to the Imperial government, if he has sincerely decided in the future to avoid dependence upon England." [64]

The conference agreed that under existing circumstances Russia should not attempt an extensive reorganization of the Persian

---

63. Special Conference of August 12/25, 1905; "Anglo-russkoe sopernichestvo v Persii," K. A., 1(56) (1933), 55–56.

64. Ibid., pp. 56–57.

army, an expensive undertaking fraught with dangerous complications. The Persians had recently placed orders for arms in France and tried to get the requisite sum of 5,000,000 francs from the Paris-Netherlands Bank. Russia intervened, and on her advice the bank declined the request. Russia would not cooperate in the financing of such purchases abroad, but the War Minister suggested that she "could provide Persia with weapons, preferably old models, from her own stores." [65]

The conference decided that:

1. Persia would be given a loan of up to 10,000,000 rubles.

2. She would undertake not to borrow from England (the Imperial Bank).

3. The Discount and Loan Bank should be given the exclusive right of supplying the Tehran mint with silver.

4. The Persian government would undertake not to grant concessions in provinces bordering on Russia without her consent.

5. The Persian government would undertake not to enter any negotiations in regard to railway construction before the expiration of the current moratorium, and would not reach any further decisions on that score without reaching an agreement with Russia.

6. Russia must assume a negative attitude toward any purchases of arms by Persia. Really necessary arms could be provided by Russia from her old stores.

7. Russia should strengthen somewhat the Persian army with Russian cadres, without increasing the total number of its foreign instructors.[66]

British statesmen could not believe their eyes. A beaten country, its army demoralized, its cities seething with the violence of strikes and pogroms, its countryside aflame with peasant revolt, could not possibly pursue a forward policy abroad and subsidize a foreign government. Yet the Persian minister at St. Petersburg, Moshir ol-Molk, told the British chargé d'affaires, Cecil Spring Rice, that a new loan was being negotiated.

65. Id.
66. Ibid., p. 59, Notation by Nicholas II: "Agreed. Peterhoff, August 18 [31], 1905."

It would appear to be a somewhat remarkable step for Russia to take, in her present financial condition [wrote Spring Rice], to offer a pecuniary advance to Persia; but the idea cannot be dismissed as incredible with regard to a Government which, on the eve of the conclusion of peace with Japan, appointed a Committee to consider the question of forest regulations in the Liaotung Peninsula.[67]

When Spring Rice wrote his dispatch to Grey in January 1906, his diagnosis was already out of date. In October 1905 a general strike broke the resistance of the Tsar. Witte, who had signed the peace treaty with Japan on September 5, was put at the head of the government. He prevailed on the Emperor to publish a manifesto granting the nation a number of democratic freedoms and modifying the regime to the extent of instituting an elective assembly, the Duma. The revolution seemed to have triumphed. The old-line statesmen of the Empire were bankrupt. Deeply shaken, they lost for a moment their self-assured and combative spirit, and accepted the sad need of changing the course of Russia's foreign policy.

Great changes had occurred in Britain also. The Conservatives who, under Salisbury and Balfour had ruled the Empire for over ten years, lost their mandate and were succeeded by the Liberals. Sir Henry Campbell-Bannerman, the new Prime Minister, and Sir Edward Grey, his Foreign Secretary, approached old problems in a spirit quite different from Salisbury's or Lansdowne's.

Persia was stirred, too. In December 1905 Tehran merchants, inspired by leading mullas, Seyyed Abdollāh Behbehāni, Seyyed Mohammad Tabātabāi, and Āqā Seyyed Jamāl ed-Din, demanded the dismissal of the hated Grand Vizier, Eyn od-Dowleh. The Government reacted by arresting or exiling some of the leaders and breaking up street mobs. Through the winter and spring of 1906 the situation continued to deteriorate. In July the ecclesiastical leaders staged an exodus from the capital and took refuge in the holy city of Qom. Between July 19 and 23 more than 5,000 persons took *bast* (sanctuary) in the British legation.

67. Spring Rice to Grey, No. 12, St. Petersburg, January 12, 1906; F. O. 371/103.

In another week their numbers swelled to between 12,000 and 14,000. On July 30 the Shah dismissed Eyn od-Dowleh, but the crowd in the British legation made a new demand—a Constitution. Mozaffar ed-Din Shah had neither the power nor the inclination to suppress the movement. On August 5 he capitulated.[68]

Both in St. Petersburg and Tehran the political situation was highly unstable. Sir Edward Grey felt that the instability and uncertainty could be utilized to effect a rapprochement with Russia. The idea was not new. Even at the height of Russophobia under Disraeli, a substantial segment of English opinion favored an understanding with Russia. Liberal statesmen had consistently leaned in that direction and found support among a portion of conservatives.

On more than one occasion between 1889 and 1900 the British government, directly and through private channels, hinted at a rapprochement. Sir Henry Drummond Wolff, whose inept efforts to introduce Persia to the "benefits" of European capitalism had exacerbated the rivalry between England and Russia, had been an ardent champion of Anglo-Russian cooperation. Rebuffed by Dolgorukov and Giers in 1889, he remained an optimist. When relations between the two countries reached their nadir in 1900, he wrote a confidential letter to Baron Staal, Russian ambassador in London, proposing an agreement. The best place for the two powers to start resolving their differences, he wrote, was Persia. Russia wanted an exit on the Persian Gulf and Wolff felt that "this object is legitimate and laudable provided it is pursued peacefully." The three governments concerned would sign a convention on the basis of a neutralization of Persia; the construction of a network of railways, among them the line from Anzali to Mohammareh; the collection of transit dues to service a loan

---

68. There is a growing literature on the Persian revolution. Of older works, E. G. Browne's *The Persian Revolution of 1905–1909* is the best in spite of serious shortcomings. *Tārikhe enqelābe mashrutiyate Irān* by Mehdi Malekzādeh is a seven-volume compendium containing much useful information. Ahmad Kasravi's *Tārikhe mashruteye Irān* must also be mentioned. M. S. Ivanov's *Iranskaia revoliutsiia 1905–1911 godov*, though published in 1957, is a good example of Soviet history writing of "the period of the cult of personality," or, more plainly, of the Stalin era. Dr. Nikki Keddie of the University of California at Los Angeles is currently engaged in a detailed study of the revolution.

guaranteed by the three powers; and so forth.[69] Staal showed no interest.

Upon the death of Queen Victoria, the British government had made new attempts to improve relations with Russia. While planning an alliance with Japan, Britain calculated its probable effects on Anglo-Russian relations and hoped that it would make Russia more amenable to an understanding in regard to the Middle East. In fact, Manchuria was not a principal area of Anglo-Russian conflict. The British government was much more concerned about Russia's relations with Afghanistan and her southward movement in Persia. Lansdowne discussed Persia with the Russian ambassador in October 1901, suggesting that the division of the country into spheres of influence might provide a solution to the Persian problem.

> His Excellency [the ambassador] observed that the Russian Government had never been in favour of the virtual partition of Persia into British and Russian spheres of interest. They believed that Great Britain had interests in Northern Persia just as Russia had interests in the southern portion of that country, through which she hoped some day to obtain an outlet for her trade.[70]

For Russia the price of an agreement with Britain would have been the renunciation of newly established relations with Afghanistan and, what was much more important, the renunciation of southern Persia. "The Russian government wanted neither to break with Afghanistan, nor to give to the English a part of Persia. The tsarist government found English proposals unacceptable." [71]

The Anglo-French entente of 1904 made it more desirable than ever that Britain and Russia compose their differences. King Edward VII was anxious to move in this direction, but the outbreak of war in the Far East prevented any immediate improve-

---

69. Sir H. Drummond Wolff to M. de Staal, Confidential, London, January 20, 1900; Enclosure in Appendix IV, Memorandum on Persian Railways, I. O., June 20, 1911; F. O. 371/1886.

70. Lansdowne to Hardinge, No. 287, Draft, October 29, 1901; F. O. 65/1618.

71. V. M. Khvostov, "Zavershenie borby za razdel mira," Potemkin, ed., *Istoriia diplomatii*, 2, 158.

ment of Anglo-Russian relations. However, in April 1904 in Copenhagen, where he had gone to celebrate King Christian's birthday, Edward VII talked to Aleksandr Izvolskii, who represented the absent Tsar. After lunch the two discussed affairs for three quarters of an hour, and the King "found a new coadjutor" in Izvolskii's person. Edward promised that his new ambassador to Russia, Charles Hardinge, would apply himself to the task of establishing cordial relations between the two countries.[72]

Sir Charles Hardinge arrived in St. Petersburg in May. Russia was at war with Japan, and Britain was widely blamed for having made it possible for the Japanese to fight. British aggression in Tibet, where Colonel F. Younghusband had occupied Lhassa, increased the anti-British sentiment in the government and at Court. The Dane Mission to Afghanistan, sent by the Government of India in October 1904, gave rise to additional suspicions and bad blood. However, it was the Dogger Bank incident that marked the low point of Anglo-Russian relations, bringing the two nations nearer to war than they had been at any time since 1885. On the night of October 21–22 the Russian Baltic Squadron was steaming across the North Sea on its way to the Far East. Admiral Zinovii Petrovich Rozhestvenskii was in command of an ill-disciplined, insufficiently trained crew. Rumors of Japanese torpedo boats and destroyers lurking off the coasts of Sweden, Norway, Denmark, Germany, and Britain did not seem ridiculous to the admiral and his officers. When they met a fleet of some fifty British fishing boats in the dark of the night, panic seized the armada. Ships began to fire in every direction, sinking one and hitting several others, and inflicting considerable damage on one another. The "battle of Dogger Bank" which lasted for about twelve minutes, could have triggered a war with England.[73]

However, wars seldom, if ever, start accidentally. Russia could not afford to fight England and Japan simultaneously. England had no desire to fight anyone at all. There was a great public out-

72. Lee, *King Edward VII*, 2, 284–85.

73. Rozhestvenskii's name is persistently misspelled by Western writers who insist on adding a *d* to it, no doubt by analogy with *rozhdestvo* (Christmas). A vivid description of the panic is given in the novel *Tsushima* by N. Novikov-Priboi, who was a sailor on the battleship *Orel* at the "battle of the Dogger Bank."

cry, threats were uttered freely, but in the end the incident was referred to arbitration and quietly settled. Through it all Sir Charles Hardinge continued to pursue a cautious and friendly course.

When he was chargé d'affaires in Tehran, during a prolonged absence of Sir Mortimer Durand in 1897–98, Charles Hardinge had tried but failed to induce the British government to provide the Shah with money to prevent him from accepting a Russian loan. He thus had had firsthand experience of Anglo-Russian rivalry in Persia. It is probable that the experience disheartened him and made him feel that Britain's old influence at Tehran could not be regained, that it was to Britain's advantage to arrive at an understanding with Russia, thus saving at least Seistān and most of the Persian Gulf coast from absorption by Russia.

Before leaving St. Petersburg in January 1906 to assume his new post as permanent undersecretary at the Foreign Office, Hardinge did all he could to impress on the Russians Britain's goodwill and his own sympathy. A defeated and humiliated Russia, paralyzed by revolution, did not seem frightening or dangerous any longer. Hardinge told Lamsdorff that English public opinion had changed in favor of Russia. "I had been particularly impressed [he said] at hearing prayers offered up in a small country church a few weeks ago for the restoration of peace and tranquility in Russia and I regarded such an incident as an indication of the feeling of all classes." [74]

He mentioned that Grey expected Russia not to try to modify the status quo in Persia. Lamsdorff agreed that "there was no fear at present of any policy of adventure being adopted in Persia or elsewhere." Hardinge observed

> that it was not so much the action of officials or of the Ministry for Foreign Affairs which was to be feared as that of persons such as M. Grube, who, though belonging to the Ministry of Finance, acted in Persia quite independently of the Russian Legation.
>
> Count Lamsdorff assured me that with the present Min-

74. C. Hardinge to Grey, No. 32, St. Petersburg, January 6, 1906; F. O. 371/121.

ister of Finance [Vladimir Nikolaevich Kokovtsov] I need feel no alarm on that score, and that it was not likely that anything would now be done in Persia without his being previously consulted.[75]

Several months earlier, when Witte was returning to Russia from Portsmouth, New Hampshire, where he had signed the peace treaty with Japan, he had met the first secretary of the Russian embassy in London, S. A. Poklewski-Koziell, "a person very close to King Edward VII." Poklewski told Witte that he had come to invite him in the name of the King, and with the knowledge of the Russian ambassador, Count Benckendorff, to visit England. Since the purpose of such a visit would have been to discuss a possible Anglo-Russian agreement, Witte declined the invitation.[76] He would have preferred talks with France and Germany, leading to a continental coalition, though he was willing to maintain correct relations with Britain:

> however, should I be in power [he wrote] I would not consent to the conclusion with Britain of conventions the content of which was reported to me by Poklewski. I would not consent because I feel that Russia, in spite of the incautious war with Japan, has still remained such a great country that she must have her hands free and not bind herself with treaties.[77]

During his brief service as Prime Minister, Witte refused to move closer to Britain, though he strongly disapproved of the Bjorko treaty imposed by the overbearing Kaiser Willie on the befuddled Tsar Nikkie.

The Tsar's Bjorko gaffe was totally rejected by his own ministers, and he was compelled to repudiate it, thus removing a momentary obstacle to the improvement of relations with Britain. In December 1905 a Liberal government was formed in England. It proceeded to work with vigor and determination for the achievement of an agreement with Russia.

In the first part of 1906 several important changes in diplo-

75. Id.
76. Witte, *Vospominaniia*, 2, 371–72.
77. Ibid., p. 372.

matic personnel took place. A. N. Speyer, an Anglophobe of long standing, was recalled from his post in Tehran. The Persian minister at St. Petersburg, Moshir ol-Molk, said that Speyer was persona grata neither at St. Petersburg nor at Tehran, where his conduct was regarded as "violent and tactless." [78] It was said in the Persian capital that the main reason for removing Speyer was his poor management of the Russian legation, "which has for the last year been the scene of most unedifying and most public quarrels." The minister and his first secretary, Somov, had clashed when the former invited the legation staff to a picnic immediately after the destruction of the Russian navy by Admiral Togo. Somov had refused to attend, and, Speyer believed, had planted a story critical of the minister in the Russian press.[79] Speyer was replaced by N. G. Hartwig, who had been Director of the Asiatic Department of the Foreign Ministry. Before leaving for Tehran, he called on the British chargé d'affaires, Cecil Spring Rice. His attitude seemed friendly, and he talked of cooperation "in the good work of improving the relations" between the two countries.[80]

Spring Rice himself left St. Petersburg for Tehran in June. He had previously served in Persia for a number of years and had learned the language, a rather unusual accomplishment for a European diplomat. He was sceptical about an Anglo-Russian understanding and was not in sympathy with the policies of Sir Edward Grey. Lord Kitchener, Commander in Chief in India, who, like most Anglo-Indian civil and military officials, was opposed to a rapprochement with Russia, said in a letter to Spring Rice: "We out here are indeed glad that you are in Persia, and we feel the utmost confidence while you are there, that all that can be done, will be done, to protect Indian and Imperial interests, and to follow the line of policy in accord with British traditions." [81]

78. Spring Rice to Grey, No. 12, St. Petersburg, January 2, 1906; F. O. 371/103.
79. E. Grant Duff to Grey, No. 66, Tehran, March 2, 1906, Confidential; F. O. 371/107.
80. Same to same, No. 187, St. Petersburg, March 14, 1906; F. O. 371/124.
81. Kitchener to Spring Rice (private), Simla, June 17, 1907; Gwynn, *Letters*, 2, 101.

In May the colorless, competent, timid Lamsdorff resigned under a barrage of abuse from certain groups at Court and a section of the press. The new Foreign Minister, Aleksandr Petrovich Izvolskii, had made a brilliant career by happening to be in the right place at the right time to please the right persons. Careful of dress and appearance, ingratiating of manner, he produced an excellent impression on those who knew him not too well. An English diplomat wrote:

> He is not without vanity and ambition; nervous, somewhat timorous of responsibility, and most susceptible to criticism. He is quick and intelligent, and though unused to hard work, he loyally endeavours to master the subjects with which he has to deal. . . . His amiable social qualities render him very popular at the Court and in society, but I should doubt if his opinions carry much weight with them. His means are slender, and both he and his charming wife would, for many reasons prefer a comfortable well-paid Embassy to the drudgery and responsibility of a Cabinet Minister, with a comparatively inadequate salary. . . . He is loyal and sincerely anxious for an understanding with Great Britain." [82]

Two weeks after Izvolskii had assumed the post of Foreign Minister, Sir Arthur Nicolson, the new British ambassador, arrived in St. Petersburg. Like Sir Charles Hardinge who had preceded him at the St. Petersburg embassy, Nicolson had briefly served in Persia and had neither liked nor understood the country. Over the years he had come to feel that Germany, not Russia, constituted the greatest threat to Britain. In this he was at one with Hardinge, now permanent undersecretary at the Foreign Office, and Sir Edward Grey. Together the three men had considerable freedom in shaping Britain's foreign policies in the crucial years before the First World War. All three were single-minded in their determination first to gain, then to retain, the Russian alliance. With Nicolson the desire for Russian friendship became an *idée fixe*, an obsession to which he would sacrifice not

---

82. Sir A. Nicolson to Grey, No. 4, St. Petersburg, January 2, 1907; F. O. 371/318.

only abstractions such as truth, fairness, or honor, but at times even the concrete interests of his country. It would seem that he was afflicted with the need to believe in the righteousness of one's allies and the evil of one's enemies.

Shortly after his arrival, Nicolson opened negotiations that would last over a year. The intricacy of the problem, the enormous quantity of details that had to be mastered, discussed, and agreed upon, the unexpected complications that arose from time to time, made the negotiating of the Anglo-Russian agreement a classic example of the art of diplomacy. As diplomatic technicians Nicolson, Izvolskii, and the rest proved that they possessed skills of a high order. Though Persia was the most important question at issue between the two powers, their rapprochement was a result of the pressure of forces that lay entirely outside Persia. She was only an obstacle, an unfortunate impediment that had to be removed somehow. The same was true of Afghanistan and Tibet, the two other areas of Anglo-Russian conflict in Asia.[83]

For Russia an agreement with Britain on Persia meant a radical departure from an old and firmly established tradition. Izvolskii, who was primarily interested in the Balkans and the Straits, hoped that by sacrificing potential domination over all of Persia, Russia would gain control of Constantinople. Sir Edward Grey had dropped meaningful hints that England "might no longer object" to the reopening of the Near Eastern question.[84] However, anti-English sentiments in the Russian governing circles were strong and tenacious.

The Tsar himself was essentially pro-German, as was the Empress Aleksandra Fedorovna. Grand dukes Mikhail Nikolae-

---

83. Since the Anglo-Russian agreement of 1907 was a major link in the chain of events leading to World War I, it has received a great deal of attention from historians. A vast number of documents has been published. Gooch and Temperley devoted most of Vol. 4 of their *British Documents on the Origin of the War* to the agreement. R. P. Churchill's *The Anglo-Russian Convention of 1907* is a detailed factual study. Most works on the diplomatic history of the prewar period or on the origins of the war give a résumé of the convention and of the negotiations that led to it. I do not propose to tell the familiar story again, but shall give only an outline sufficient for the purposes of this study.

84. Grey to Nicolson, Private, November 6, 1906; E. Grey, *Twenty-five Years: 1892–1916* (London, 1925), 1, 162–63.

vich and Nikolai Mikhailovich; the Minister of the Court, Baron V. B. Fredericks; his assistant, Prince N. S. Dolgorukov; the Court's Marshal, Count P. K. Benckendorff, inclined toward Germany. Among ministers and members of the State Council, A. V. Krivoshein, P. Kh. Schwanebach, I. L. Goremykin, and P. N. Durnovo had German sympathies. At the Foreign Ministry the "German party" included K. A. Gubastov, Assistant Minister of Foreign Affairs in 1906–07; Baron M. A. Taube, Counselor of the Ministry; Iu. P. Bakhmetev, Ambassador to Japan; R. R. Rosen, Ambassador to the United States; Count N. D. Osten-Sacken, Ambassador to Germany; Prince L. P. Urusov, Ambassador to Austria; and others.[85]

The diplomatic service was an especially traditionalist branch of government. Most of the important posts were occupied by old men with personal contacts at Court. (Grand Duchess Maria Pàvlovna was known for her ability to secure desirable appointments.) The personnel of the diplomatic service was heavily German. In 1907, of the 315 Russian diplomats stationed abroad, 138 were Baltic German nobles. A vast majority of the diplomats were extremely conservative. Most of the ambassadors were between seventy-five and eighty years old, with fifty years of service behind them, relics of another epoch, representing the mentality and the outlook of the Russia of Nicholas I.[86]

The military, too, were generally opposed to an English orientation. The traditions of Turkestan were strong, and the memories of the Crimean War had not disappeared completely. Sir Arthur Nicolson, who did his best to cultivate the government and Court circles and in the process had become an apologist for almost everyone and everything Russian, was afraid of the influence of the military. He defended the Tsar against imputations of weakness and despotism ("I do not imagine that any impartial man of whatever shade of politics could deny to His Majesty the possession of qualities which are admirable and exemplary"), but admitted that "The military party is a powerful one, and its sentiments cannot be ignored. I anticipate that it is in that quarter

85. I. V. Bestuzhev, *Borba v Rossii po voprosam vneshnei politiki* (Moscow, 1961), p. 46.
86. Ibid., p. 63.

that serious obstacles to a good understanding with Great Britain will be found." [87]

Izvolskii was also uneasy about the Russian military:

> l'Etat Major Général [he complained] semble n'avoir rien appris et rien oublié et parle du Seistan, du Golfe Persique, de l'Océan Indien etc. exactment comme on parlait avant la guerre avec le Japon—de la Mandchourie, de la Corée, de l'Océan Pacifique. . . . La lutte entre tout ce monde et moi sera chaude et malheureusement je suis très mal secondé par mon propre personnel dont les uns me sont ouvertement, les autres sourdement hostiles.[88]

The Foreign Minister's apprehensions were well founded. The General Staff had discussed the possibility of an understanding with Britain in an extremely negative spirit. The military declared their opposition to an agreement with a nation that had always acted as "the energetic, pitiless, and harmful" enemy of Russia. The Tsar's one-word comment, penned in his own hand, was: "Correct." [89]

The issue was discussed at great length in the various ministries. I. A. Zinov'ev, ambassador at Constantinople, submitted a memorandum in which he gave it half-hearted conditional approval. He enumerated the measures that had been taken in years past to increase Russian influence in Persia: the formation of the Cossack Brigade, the organization of the Russian bank, the establishment of plague quarantine in Khorāsān (which, he added, should be extended to Seistān "due to the ambitious views of England"), the opening of consulates in Bushehr and Bandar Abbās. Russia had rejected every British proposal for the division of Persia into spheres of influence. Such a division would hurt Russia's prestige; but, on the other hand, she could not compete with Britain in the south because her industry was not strong

---

87. Nicolson to Grey, No. 4, St. Petersburg, January 2, 1907; F. O. 371/318.

88. Izvolskii to Benckendorff, Strictly personal, St. Petersburg, September 14/27, 1906; A. Iswolsky, *Au service de la Russie* (Paris, 1937), 1, 378.

89. Document from the Central Main Military-Historical Archive (*fond* 200c, *opis* 1, *delo* 155, *listy* 95–124) as cited in A. V. Ignat'ev, *Russko-angliiskie otnosheniia nakanune pervoi mirovoi voiny* (Moscow, 1962), p. 59.

enough. An agreement with Britain was desirable. Would it not be possible, Zinov'ev asked, to obtain British support for Russia's interests in the Straits by making certain concessions on Afghanistan? Clearly the old diplomat did not want an agreement. He was proposing to give up nothing substantial in exchange for Constantinople.[90]

At a special ministerial conference held on September 20, 1906, Izvolskii argued in favor of the proposed agreement.

> It must not be forgotten [he said] that a choice must be made between an agreement capable of firmly securing at least a part of our interests and rivalry under circumstances in which we lack the assurance that questions which concern us would not de decided without us and to the detriment of all our advantages [sic; *"v ushcherb vsem nashim polzam"*].[91]

The Minister of Finance, Kokovtsov, gave Izvolskii strong support. Russia, he said, must admit that her importance in Persia had decreased. It was correspondingly necessary to change one's views in regard to Eastern policy, a policy whose basic flaw was that the forces at Russia's disposal had not been commensurate with the aims she had set herself. The policy of reaching the Persian Gulf had been erroneous. Britain dominated the Gulf, and Russia's strength was insufficient to challenge her.[92]

In view of the current situation in Persia, Kokovtsov went on, "the establishment of an exclusive Russian influence would threaten to lead to military suppression of the entire country." Therefore Russia should not get deeper into Persia. However, Russian interests in the northern provinces were too great to be abandoned. They must be defended against British as well as German penetration. A line drawn from Qasre Shirin through Hamadān, Tehran, and Mashhad to Ashkhabad would indicate the limits of the natural Russian sphere. This line

---

90. Zinov'ev's secret memorandum of August 25, 1906, on the question of agreement between Russia and England; "K istorii anglo-russkogo soglasheniia 1907 goda," K. A., 2–3(69–70) (1935), 5–18.

91. "Anglo-russkoe sopernichestvo v Persii v 1890–1906 g.g.," K. A., 1(56) (1933), 60.

92. Ibid., p. 61.

on the one hand closes the entrance to Persia to the Baghdad road and protects the approaches to the Transcaspian railway; and on the other, taking in the capital of the country, draws a natural limit to the sphere in which we have already obtained concessions and, in general, have firmly planted our feet. We must limit ourselves to this line and make a firm decision not to go further.[93]

Kokovtsov wanted Russia to stop giving Persia money. It was time to get back some of the 72,204,754 rubles Russia had already invested there. The government of the Shah owed Russia 28,972,124 rubles in long-term and 3,223,810 in short-term debts. The Crown Prince had been advanced 1,627,500 rubles. Against her total debt of 32,823,434 rubles to Russia, Persia owed Britain no more than 2,000,000 rubles. In Kokovtsov's opinion the financial sacrifices of the two great powers were not proportionate to their respective influence. Indeed, one must spend money, but one "must [also] possess moral strength, otherwise one cannot gain firm influence in an exotic land." [94]

The Chairman of the Board of Directors of the Discount and Loan Bank of Persia, formerly its Tehran manager, E. K. Grube, explained that monies lent to the Shah had been spent on his whims or to enrich his favorites. "The universal system of tax farming is ruining the country, and Persia needs not new loans but new men who could put the country in order . . ." Grube, who had found it easy to make a Russian tool of Monsieur Joseph Naus and his Belgians, felt that they were best qualified for this task.[95]

The War Minister, Lieutenant General A. F. Roediger, agreed with Izvolskii and Kokovtsov and spoke in favor of an understanding with England. Lieutenant General F. F. Palitsyn, Chief of the General Staff, whom Sir Arthur Nicolson regarded "as one of the chief obstacles to the agreement," [96] said that Russian military interests in Persia had nothing to do with Persia as such, since

93. Ibid., p. 62.
94. Ibid., p. 61.
95. Ibid., p. 63.
96. Nicolson to Grey, No. 4, St. Petersburg, January 2, 1907; F. O. 371/318.

that country posed no threat to Russia. It was England that Russia was concerned with, and it was English insistence on controlling Seistān that would constitute the subject matter of forthcoming negotiations. Acting Chairman of the Council of State Defense, Lieutenant General A. P. Protopopov, added that Russia's *drang nach* Persian Gulf could not be explained by economic considerations alone. Russia needed intermediary naval stations in that part of the world, and the navy was interested in Chāhbahār, a port at the entrance of the Persian Gulf. Thus the position of the military was ambiguous. On this occasion they did not openly state their opposition to an agreement but rather put forward terms that would make it impossible.[97]

Izvolskii argued his case again on February 14, 1907, at a conference which included V. N. Kokovtsov; the Russian Ambassador in London, Count A. K. Benckendorff; the Minister of the Navy, I. M. Dikov; the Minister of Commerce and Industry, D. A. Filosofov; generals Palitsyn, Polivanov, and Ermolov; K. M. Argyropoulo; and others. Up until recently, Izvolskii began, the idea of an understanding with England found no support in Russian public opinion, and in the governing circles there existed the conviction that

> Persia must fall entirely under Russian influence and that we must strive for a free exit on the Persian Gulf, with a railway line running across all of Persia and the creation of a fortified point on the said Gulf. However, the events of the last years have made clear the unfeasibility of this plan and have posed the question of the necessity of removing the grounds of conflict with England, the most suitable means for which is the delimitation of spheres of influence.[98]

Izvolskii also pointed out the close connection between the proposed agreement and Germany's project of the Baghdad railway. The Russians had been quick to see the threat that the Baghdad railway would pose to their dominant position in Persia. As early as 1900, V. A. Sakhanskii, an engineer concerned with railway

97. K. A., 1(56) (1933), 63.
98. Journal of the conference of February 1/14, 1907, "K istorii anglo-russkogo soglasheniia," K. A., 2–3(69–70) (1935), 19.

projects in Persia, called for the construction of a road from Russia to Central Persia before Germany, "a competitor more dangerous than Britain," built a line across Turkish territory.[99]

The Soviet historian, A. Popov, has claimed that "the concrete question which laid the basis for the review in principle of the entire line of Russian foreign policy was the question of railways, particularly the question of railway construction in Persia, immediately related to the question of the Baghdad R.R." In Popov's opinion, the reappraisal began with a memorandum submitted in 1903 by the Russian ambassador in Peking, P. M. Lessar, who had served in Central Asia and in London, and was well acquainted with Middle Eastern problems. Lessar was afraid of the effects of a German-built Baghdad railway and advocated the construction, in agreement with Britain, of a line running from Transcaspia to India across eastern Persia. Argyropoulo and Zinov'ev had opposed his scheme, while the Russian minister at Tehran, Vlasov, and the consul in Bombay, Klemm, favored it. Witte went even further, advocating a railway from Central Asia to India across Afghanistan. Ill feeling between Russia and Britain prevented the realization of this plan, Popov wrote.[100] Though Popov exaggerates the importance of the Baghdad project in bringing about the Anglo-Russian understanding, it is true that fear of German penetration of the Middle East was felt sharply in St. Petersburg, at least in the circles whose principal spokesman was Izvolskii.[101]

At the conference of February 14, 1907, Izvolskii invited his colleagues' comments and views on the Persian question and the Baghdad railway. The response was unenlightening. The assembled statesmen, soldiers, and diplomats seemed uncertain. Many either expressed no opinions or failed to have them recorded. Kokovtsov spoke at some length. He believed that the construction of the Baghdad railway was inevitable and that it remained for Russia to seek compensations from Germany. The Minister of

99. V. A. Sakhanskii in Lieutenant P. A. Rittich's confidential report, *Otchet o poezdke v Persiiu i persidskii Beludzhistan v 1900 godu* (St. Petersburg, 1901), p. 35.

100. A. Popov, "Stranitsa . . . ," pp. 150–52.

101. For a discussion of German policy in Persia from 1890 to 1905, cf. Bradford G. Martin, *German-Persian Diplomatic Relations, 1873–1912*, Chap. 2, pp. 50–91.

Trade and Commerce agreed with the Minister of Finance, and added that while the Baghdad railway was bad enough, a branch line to Persia would be worse. In negotiating with Britain and Germany, Russia should make sure that no such branch lines would be built, and that the "sterilizing" agreement prohibiting railway construction in Persia would be extended for another ten years (to 1920).

The demarcation line between the Russian and British spheres of influence was also brought up for discussion. Kokovtsov proposed that it run from Qasre Shirin through Hamadān, Tehran, and Mashhad, to Gowdān on the Russian border. General Palitsyn, Chief of the General Staff, wanted it to run much further south, from Qasre Shirin to Esfahān, including Kermānshāh in the Russian zone, to Yazd and thence to the Afghan border. All of Khorāsān would fall into the Russian zone, and Russia would ensure for herself "the existing strategically very important roads to Afghanistan which run through northeastern Persia." [102]

Izvolskii accepted Palitsyn's suggestion in regard to the demarcation line and incorporated it in a counterdraft which he handed to Nicolson on February 20. On March 10 the British replied that they would not agree to Russia's zone touching the Afghan frontier.[103]

With the arrival of spring the negotiations gathered speed. An obstacle arose in June when the British suggested that in the preamble to the proposed convention mention be made "of the special interests which Great Britain had in the maintenance of the status quo in the Persian Gulf." Izvolskii objected strongly, arguing that the Anglo-Russian convention should not touch the interests of other powers, since he had given Germany assurances to that effect. "M. Izvolsky did not deny, and this was stated in writing, that Great Britain had special interests in the Persian Gulf, but he declined to insert any allusion to the above in the

102. K. A., 2–3(69–70) (1935), pp. 21–25.
103. For a summary of negotiations, cf. General Report on Russia for the Year 1907, Enclosure in Nicolson to Grey, No. 57, St. Petersburg, January 29, 1908; F. O. 371/514.

War, Revolution, and Reconciliation

Convention itself." [104] Nicolson, believing that insistence on this point might endanger the ultimate success of the negotiations, "willingly gave up the quest." [105] Izvolskii on his part agreed that the convention should be supplemented by a note from Grey reaffirming England's special position in the Gulf and Russia's assent to it.[106]

While negotiations went on in St. Petersburg, revolution had broken out in Tehran, complicating the issues and threatening to demolish the intricate structure of compromise painstakingly reared by Nicolson and Izvolskii. It was natural for the nationalists to seek sanctuary in the garden of the British legation in August 1906. The chargé d'affaires, E. Grant Duff, could not very well have refused the traditional right of *bast* to a throng one of whose leaders was Seyyed Abdollāh Behbehāni, an old friend of the English. For several years the British had encouraged the clergy to oppose Russian loans and concessions. The distinction between "constitutional" and other means of opposition may have been clear to the Oxonian and Cantabrigian English diplomats in Tehran; it was utterly meaningless for Persians, who, as subjects of a despot, knew that opposition was the equivalent of sedition and loyal opposition a contradiction in terms. The encouragement they had received from Sir Arthur Hardinge was understood by the clergy as a promise of support, and no qualifying clauses made any impression. When the revolutionaries sought protection behind the tall brick walls of the legation garden, Grant Duff could not shut its gates to them.

The Russian legation was aware of the friendly relations between the mullas and the English. The Soviet historian, M. S. Ivanov, refers to a document in the Central State Historical Archive of Leningrad which shows that in August 1906 Grant Duff handed Seyyed Abdollāh Behbehāni a letter thanking him and Seyyed Mohammad Tabātabāi "for their closeness to the British Legation." The letter is alleged to state that each of the

104. Id.
105. R. P. Churchill, *The Anglo-Russian Convention of 1907* (Cedar Rapids, 1939), p. 166.
106. General Report on Russia for the Year 1907, F. O. 371/514.

two mojtaheds was granted a pension of 1,500 tumāns per month by the British.[107] That the English in Tehran sympathized with the nationalist movement was, of course, an open secret.

The new Russian minister, N. G. Hartwig, formerly Director of the First (Asiatic) Department of the Ministry of Foreign Affairs, had only recently arrived from St. Petersburg, where he had posed as a friend and supporter of Izvolskii. Once in Tehran, he began to conduct himself exactly like a Dolgorukov, a Zinov'ev, or a Speyer. He felt he should uphold the Shah. "He also knew that Persia was not yet ready for a constitution, and that the Shah and only the Shah, was the foundation stone of order in his country." [108]

The sight of over ten thousand Persians taking *bast* in the British legation was proof enough for Hartwig that the British government had launched an attack on Russian positions in Persia. He firmly believed that Britain sought to create complications in pursuit of an aggressive plan. The Russian ambassador in London, Count Benckendorff, denied that England had any such intention. The policies of the new Cabinet were clear. The reductions in the army and the navy, the granting of a constitution to Transvaal, the various ministerial speeches, were indications of a policy of peace and appeasement.[109] Sir Edward Grey, Benckendorff wrote, knew nothing about Persia. "Pourtant si, évidemment, il est constitutionnaliste en Russie, il n'en est pas de même pour la Perse, il trouve cela folie." [110]

Benckendorff pleaded for cooperation between the Russian and British legations in Tehran. The Foreign Office had admitted to him that the granting of *bast* to the nationalists in the legation's garden had been a mistake. Hartwig and the new British minister,

---

107. M. S. Ivanov, *Iranskaia revoliutsiia 1905–1911 godov*, p. 202. It should be noted that M. S. Ivanov is generally extremely tendentious.

108. E. Schelking, *Recollections of a Russian Diplomat* (New York, 1918), p. 240.

109. Benckendorff to Izvolskii, West Cowes, July 25/August 7, 1906; Iswolsky, *Au service de la Russie*, 1, 339–40.

110. Ibid., p. 341.

Spring Rice, should frankly discuss the situation.[111] However, Benckendorff had no confidence in Hartwig and did not consider his conduct "sound." He accused the minister in Tehran of turning the possible into the probable and the probable into the certain. Hartwig was uncritical and failed to check the information that reached him. He wanted Benckendorff to ask the Foreign Office whether the Tehran rumors that King Edward had sent "incendiary telegrams" to the Persian revolutionaries were true. To ask Benckendorff to do such a thing, "c'est vouloir me mettre dans la situation qu'on se moque de moi et ce qui est pire, de notre crédulité!" Why did not Hartwig do the simple thing and ask Grant Duff? "Savez-vous qu'on répand le bruit de télégrammes du Roi; savez-vous qu'on prétend que c'est vous et l'Angleterre que êtes à la tête de l'agitation; savez-vous qu'on vous accuse d'avoir invité et paye les réfugiés? Je vous en préviens." [112]

Britain, Benckendorff argued, though sympathetic to constitutionalism in Russia, did not consider Persia ripe for the same thing. The English believed that Persia should have reforms "imposed by common Anglo-Russian action." Russia on her part should not be hostile to all reform; she already had enough of a reputation for that: "Intervenir en tout, à coup de conseils constants, comme l'indiquent les rapports de Hartwig, n'est-ce pas exactement pratiquer la politique d'ingérence égoïste que nous reprochons de tout temps à l'Angleterre, la taxant sans hésitation d'intrigues constantes?" [113]

The British knew that Hartwig was an old hand at provocation and intrigue. Grey, no less than Izvolskii, "was afraid of Hartwig spiking Isvolsky's guns before the latter got under way." [114] Actually Hartwig was much more opposed to the Persian revolutionary movement than to an agreement with the British, unless the agreement were to promote revolution. When Spring Rice arrived in Tehran at the end of the summer, he found Hartwig at

111. Benckendorff to Izvolskii, London, July 26/August 8, 1906; ibid., p. 343.
112. Same to same, London, July 27/August 9, 1906, ibid., pp. 345–46.
113. Ibid., p. 348.
114. Grey to Spring Rice, November 30, 1906; Gwynn, Letters, 2, 83

least outwardly friendly. He, the French minister, and Spring Rice desired the entente. The Persians hated it, and so did many English officials. As Spring Rice wrote his journalist friend Chirol, "all the staff here, and especially all the Indian Consuls, are dead set against reconciliation which is contrary to all their traditions and also takes away their occupation. So you see that the task even of getting on with the Russians here without friction is a very hard one." [115]

A few months in Tehran produced a marked change in Spring Rice's sentiments. He had been met with open arms by Persian nationalists, who hoped he would "continue the support which they believed they had already received." Spring Rice told them that the British government sympathized with their cause but would not promise any assistance.

> I quoted the Koran to prove that if liberty was not won by the people for themselves it was not worth having. But I can't say I gave satisfaction. The general belief is that we have given Persia up as a bad job and that we have sold her to the Russians as a part of a general scheme of buying and selling, which we call peace negotiations.[116]

A month later he wrote to Chirol: "I can't tell you how refreshing it is to hear the Persians talking about their new liberties and the things they are ready to do for their country." [117]

Spring Rice's admiration for the national movement led him to join the ranks of the opposition to Grey's policy of partitioning Persia. His dispatches, full of eloquent arguments against buying an ephemeral agreement at the price of cutting Persia in pieces, only annoyed Sir Edward, whose mind had been made up even before he had become Foreign Secretary and whose stubbornness was utterly unshakable.[118] In his private correspondence, Spring Rice revealed some of the bitterness he had begun to feel toward

---

115. Spring Rice to Chirol, November 6, 1906; ibid., p. 85.
116. Same to same, December 5, 1906; ibid., p. 86.
117. Same to same, January 3, 1907; ibid., p. 88.
118. Cf. various documents in *British Documents on the Origin of the War*, Vol. 4, and Churchill, *The Anglo-Russian Convention of 1907*, pp. 164–65

the ruthless politician with the deceptively mild exterior who was conducting Britain's foreign affairs.

> Politics here are highly amusing [he wrote]. The Russians are engaged in spoiling their own Duma at home and teaching the Shah how to spoil his Mejlis here. The dear Liberals at home are trying to get social recognition from the Russian Emperor, and to obtain this are encouraging him in his policy of extinguishing the liberties of Persia. Some day I shall have the great amusement of showing the whole game up. I shall be dead then; but won't my ghost have a good time! [119]

Russia was a "predatory bureaucracy" and no agreement with her could be relied upon, wrote Spring Rice, using language almost identical with that of a then obscure Russian émigré in Switzerland, V. I. Lenin.[120] Moreover the forthcoming Anglo-Russian agreement would do little to protect British interests. The agreement meant little unless backed by force; and if backed by force, it was needless. All it would do would yield to Russia without a struggle what Britain used to yield after a struggle. "You can't keep an elephant out of a potato plot by tying a parchment to his trunk. The defence of India must be men, not paper." Spring Rice was willing to be as Machiavellian as any. Persia was "a damned hole hardly worth an outside sheet of the Times," he wrote a friend. "If he [Grey] can get *real* agreement with Russia, it is well worth sacrificing Persia—though," and here his Machiavellianism sagged, "I doubt whether a great country can afford to be mean even in the smallest things." [121]

On January 1, 1907, Mozaffar ed-Din Shah signed the Constitution. He died a week later and was succeeded by Mohammad Ali Shah, who promised to uphold the new constitutional order. Almost immediately friction developed between the autocratic Shah and the Majles (Parliament). Every reform proposed by the latter was opposed by the former. Most of the reforms were also

---

119. Spring Rice to Helen Ferguson, April 23, 1907; Gwynn, *Letters*, 2, 98.
120. Spring Rice to Chirol, May 24, 1907; ibid., p. 100.
121. Spring Rice to Ferguson, June 21, 1907; ibid., p. 102.

opposed by Hartwig because of their anti-Russian and libertarian tendency.

The Cossack Brigade was attacked in the Majles by the Mojtahed Āqā Seyyed Mohammad Tabātabāi, who protested against its Russian-style uniforms, epaulets, and decorations, and against its practice of showing military honors to the Russian minister in Tehran but not to the Persian Minister of War.[122] Seyyed Mohammad might have gone further and questioned the effectiveness of the Brigade, which had greatly deteriorated in the past few years under Colonel Chernozubov. Its Persian officers, discontented and restive, tried to limit the power of the commander in such matters as pay and promotions. A committee elected by them investigated the Brigade's finances and were said to have discovered that Colonel Chernozubov had been stealing their pay. Russian officers confirmed the allegation. Chernozubov left for Russia, and on September 15 a new commander, Colonel Vladimir Platonovich Liakhov, arrived in Tehran.[123] Under him discipline was tightened, efficiency improved, and the Brigade was able to play its inglorious role in the suppression of the revolution.

The attack on the hated Director of Customs, Joseph Naus, was another proof of the anti-Russian tendency of the Majles. The Belgians in the customs' administration had been working hand in hand with Russia ever since their arrival on the Persian scene in Amin od-Dowleh's administration.[124] British officials throughout Persia, Anglo-Indian officials, English and Indian merchants, ceaselessly complained to Sir Arthur Hardinge about them, but Hardinge deemed it wiser not to conduct a frontal

---

122. G. P. Churchill of the British legation in Tehran wrote that Seyyed Abdollāh Behbehāni joined the national movement out of personal motives. "Seyyed Mohammad, another prime mover among the Mojtaheds in opposition to the Government, had other and less sordid motives, a real desire for reform being one of his objects." Memorandum by Mr. G. P. Churchill, April 14, 1906, Tehran; Enclosure in Grant Duff to Grey, No. 101, Confidential, Tehran, April 22, 1906; P. O. 371/109.

123. Lt. Colonel J. A. Douglas to Grant Duff, No. 53, Gulahek, September 20, 1906; Enclosure No. 1 in Grant Duff to Grey, No. 246, Confidential, Tehran, September 26, 1906; F. O. 371/105.

124. Cf. Lamsdorff's instructions to Speyer, K. A., 4(53) (1932), 33.

attack on Naus.[125] The Russians in Tehran, especially the voluble E. K. Grube, made no secret of their power over the Belgians. As he said to the United States minister, "he had them all under his thumb, including M. Naus." [126]

Though the new Shah dismissed Naus, he would not continue indefinitely to obey the will of his subjects sitting in the Majles. He was determined to rule as his ancestors had before him, autocratically and arbitrarily. As a first step toward the restoration of royal authority, he recalled from Europe the old Amin os-Soltān who had been living abroad in retirement that looked very much like exile. In early May 1907 he returned to the post of Prime Minister. The more extreme elements among the nationalists interpreted his reappearance on the political scene as the first blow against their cause. Amin os-Soltān was cordially hated by most nationalists. He was identified in the popular mind with the endless series of concessions that Mozaffar ed-Din Shah, and his father before him, had granted to Europeans. He was identified, above all, with the Russian loans of 1900 and 1902. It was against him and his policies that the clergy had originally agitated; and, much earlier, it was he who had been the target of the bitterest invectives in Malkam Khān's *Qānun*. As the summer wore on, it became apparent that a confrontation between the Shah and the Majles was inevitable. The atmosphere was charged with tension and heavy with forboding of strife and bloodshed.

Rumors of an Anglo-Russian entente added to the fears and anxieties of the Persians. They had suspected as early as November 1905 that a rapprochement might be in the offing. Since Persia saw in the rivalry of the two great powers her only guarantee of survival, she trembled at every sign of improved relations between them. The Persian minister in London, Mohammad Ali Khān Alā os-Saltaneh, asked Lord Lansdowne whether there was any truth to the rumors that Russia and Britain were about to arrive at an understanding in regard to their interests in Persia. "I told Ala es-Sultaneh that the report was without foundation,"

125. A. Hardinge, *A Diplomatist in the East*, p. 85.
126. A. Hardinge to Lansdowne, No. 32, Very confidential, Tehran, March 14, 1902.

Lansdowne telegraphed Grant Duff. However, he did tell the Persian minister that with the end of the Japanese war "many quarters" manifested a desire "to bring back a better understanding between the two countries." If these ideas ever took shape, "the Persian Government might rest assured that we had no intention of in any way encroaching upon the integrity and independence of Persia." [127] From then until September 1907 Persia was kept in the dark as to the intentions of the two powers in regard to her.

The Anglo-Russian convention on Persia, Afghanistan, and Tibet was signed in St. Petersburg on August 31, but the Foreign Office feared to the very last moment that Russia might back out and wreck their dreams. On August 25 Sir Charles Hardinge warned that though the Russians were apparently ready to sign, "we must take care that they do not back out during the interval." [128]

Russia had no intention of backing out. Witte, the opponent of agreement with Britain, had had a short tenure as Prime Minister. His successor, Goremykin, lasted a little over a year and was in turn succeeded by Petr Arkad'evich Stolypin, a man primarily concerned with domestic affairs and willing to leave foreign policy to Izvolskii. On August 24, only a week before the signing of the convention, Stolypin presided over a Special Conference at which the Foreign Minister reiterated the reasons for the understanding. The goal of Russian foreign policy, he said, was to shield Russia from the threat of a war with Japan and her ally, England. Great upheavals could be expected in Europe, in Austria or the Balkans for instance.

> If Russia should be tied up by the ambiguous situation in the Far East and unable to raise her voice at such a moment of solution of European problems, she would immediately descend to the level of a second-rate power. We must put our interests in Asia in their proper place otherwise we would

---

127. Lansdowne to Grant Duff, No. 159, Draft, November 15, 1905; F. O. 60/697.
128. C[harles] H[ardinge] to Mallet, F. O., August 25 [1907], Russia No. 28647; F. O. 371/325.

ourselves become an Asiatic state, which would be the greatest calamity for Russia.[129]

Izvolskii was seconded by a member of his own ministry, Stolypin's son-in-law, Sergei Dmitrievich Sazonov, who stressed the domestic necessity of insuring external tranquility.

> Our internal situation does not allow us to pursue an aggressive foreign policy. The absence of alarm from the point of view of international relations is extremely important for us since it would give us an opportunity with perfect calm to dedicate all our strength to the ordering of affairs within the country. Under these conditions the conclusion of an agreement on Eastern affairs must be recognized as most consonant with our interests.[130]

At this late date there was no longer any overt opposition to the convention. It remained for Izvolskii and Nicolson to affix their signatures to the document. On August 31 Sir Arthur triumphantly telegraphed: "Convention with the supplementary documents was signed today by the Minister for Foreign Affairs and myself." [131]

The Anglo-Russian Convention of 1907 is too well known to require detailed exposition. The preamble made the traditional bow to the "integrity and independence of Persia," while the text cut up the country into three unequal spheres. The northern, and largest, was reserved for Russia, Britain promising "not to seek for herself, and not to support in favour of British subjects, or in favour of the subjects of third Powers, any concession of a political or commercial nature." The line defining the Russian sphere ran from Qasre Shirin through Esfahān and Yazd to the point on the Persian frontier where the Afghan and Russian borders intersected. Britain promised also "not to oppose directly or indirectly, demands for similar Concessions in this region which are sup-

---

129. Journal of the Special Conference of August 11/24, 1907 concerning the conclusion of an agreement with England on the Afghan question; K. A., 2-3(69-70) (1935), 36.
130. Id.
131. Nicolson to Grey, No. 178, Telegram; F. O. 371/325.

ported by the Russian Government." Russia on her part undertook identical obligations in regard to the zone beyond the line running from the Afghan border through Birjand and Kermān and ending at Bandar Abbās. The remaining articles on Persia dealt with loan issues and were, relatively speaking, of minor significance.[132]

The British minister in Tehran was mortified. He had received no official notification about the signing of the agreement and had been denying its existence when the Persian government already had a copy of the text.

> They have thrown a stone into the windows here and left me to face the policeman. Neither Nicolson nor the F. O. informed me that the agreement was signed till three days after it had been published here. This was, I suppose, a sign that the Persian public opinion was not to be considered.[133]

Unwilling to hide his feelings or to conceal from his superiors the true state of affairs in Tehran, Spring Rice wrote Sir Edward Grey that it was impossible to ignore the disorganization of the Persian government, the feud between the Shah and the people, the conviction that Russia was secretly on the side of the Shah who was determined to organize disorders so as to provoke foreign intervention, and the belief that the two great powers knew the Shah's plan and had made arrangements to profit by it. "We are worse off than the Russians because we are not feared as they are, and because we are regarded as having betrayed the Persian people." British and Russian assurances were not believed since it was well known that "those who are supposed to be in the confidence of Russia and are known to frequent the Russian Legation are the open enemies of the new order of things." The English were seen as the accomplices of Russia and of Persian reactionaries. Mincing no words, Spring Rice went on:

---

132. The text of the convention has been published many times. The part on Persia appears in Hurewitz, *Diplomacy in the Near and Middle East*, 1, 266–67. The Russian text, with minor deletions, was published in Iu. V. Kliuchnikov and A. Sabanin, *Mezhdunarodnaia politika noveishego vremeni v dogovorakh, notakh i deklaratsiiakh* (Moscow, 1925), Part I, No. 326, pp. 333–36.

133. Spring Rice to Chirol, September 1907; Gwynn, *Letters*, 2, 103.

I am, of course, quite incapable of judging the political situation in England. But it would seem that there is at least a prima facie case for those who are ready to criticise you for all you do either in cooperation with an autocratic power or in opposition to the liberties of smaller nations. . . . And I need not remind you of what you said yourself, namely that the value of the agreement will depend on the manner in which it is carried out. It is possible that Russia will use the agreement as she used the agreement with Japan about Corea, in order to carry on her old designs under a new cover. It will be more serious from the point of view of public opinion if the old policy is still carried on under the new Convention. For the breach by treachery of a formal agreement is a far more serious matter than the open prosecution of a policy of undisguised hostility.[134]

Persian reaction was one of desperate anger. Its bitterness was directed much more at Britain than at Russia. The latter had been known for a long time as a brutal enemy. In Russia the Tsar was torturing, exiling, shooting, and hanging thousands of domestic revolutionaries. That was to be expected. What was unexpected, incomprehensible, and painful was Britain's participation in the rape of Persia. The deep indignation of the Persians was in part a result of the moralizing tone British diplomacy had always assumed in Tehran. The two Thomsons, Sir Mortimer Durand, Sir Arthur Hardinge, and the various chargés d'affaires never tired of lecturing the Persians on probity and honor, never missed a chance to point to England as a paragon of virtue. England was the home of constitutionalism and democracy. Her Parliament was the mother of parliaments. It is easy to understand why Persian nationalists expected British support and were shocked by the Anglo-Russian convention.

The influential nationalist newspaper *Habl ol-Matin* published a series of articles on the agreement, attempting to explain the motives behind it and in the process condemning it.[135]

134. Spring Rice to Grey, September 13, 1907; ibid., pp. 103–05.
135. The four articles are reprinted in E. G. Browne, *The Persian Revolution*, pp. 175–90.

On September 30 it printed a long article showing that the agreement was of enormous advantage to Russia and that in the future Britain would suffer defeat. Persia, betrayed by England, would join Russia. "In this matter the British Government has proved herself to be the enemy of civilization and humanity. In other words, England has now acquired the title of 'enemy of civilisation and justice' which for ages was only applicable to Russia." [136]

It was in September 1907 that the modern Persian image of England crystallized. Grey and Nicolson had been dishonest. R. P. Churchill, on the whole a sympathetic chronicler of the negotiations of 1906–07, states that "Even in diplomacy Nicolson had used most deceitful language," when he assured the Persian minister at St. Petersburg " 'that the arrangement was eminently favourable to Persia, and how baseless were the reports that Russia and Great Britain had contemplated a partition of Persia.' " [137] Such instances of deceit could easily be multiplied. However, it was not any single act of dishonesty that mortified the Persians. What shocked and oppressed them was the atmosphere of uncertainty and hypocrisy that Sir Edward Grey managed to create, and the sudden realization that Britain was not the moral force they had believed her to be. Justifiably or not, most Persians would, from then on, be prepared to believe only the worst of England. Perfidy, greed, the blackest crimes against humanity, would be attributed to her. The image of a cynical people totally indifferent to the sufferings of the rest of mankind, buying and selling entire nations, trading in opium, purposely starving millions of its colonial subjects, and secretly controlling the destinies of the world, would survive the departure of British power from the Middle East, Indian independence, and the decline of Britain to the rank of a secondary power.

In Britain opinion was sharply divided. Sir Henry Drummond Wolff claimed credit for the agreement, which to some extent followed the lines he had advocated eighteen years earlier. He boasted that both Nicolson and Izvolskii were his old colleagues,

136. Translation of an article in the Habl ul-Matin, No. 11, dated Calcutta, September 30, 1907; Russia, No. 39793; F. O. 371/325.
137. Churchill, *The Anglo-Russian Convention of 1907*, p. 315.

perhaps implying that he had in some measure influenced their views.[138]

Sir Edward Grey spent years defending the agreement of which he and Nicolson were the principal English authors. "The cardinal British object . . . was to secure ourselves forever, as far as a treaty would secure us, from further Russian advances in the direction of the Indian frontier." [139] Grey firmly believed that he had achieved this purpose. Like Lord George Hamilton, Curzon's one-time antagonist at the India Office, Sir Edward had no faith in Britain's ability to defend herself against Russia in Asia. Russia was too strong, Russia's advance was inevitable, Russia could not be stopped. Yet he believed that a scrap of paper would prevent the inevitable. Grey never bothered to resolve the contradiction. He would only play variations on the same theme: "We are freed from an anxiety that had often preoccupied British Governments; a frequent source of friction and a possible cause of war was removed; the prospect of peace was made more secure." [140]

Grey believed, moreover, that the agreement of 1907 was onesidedly in Britain's favor. "What we gained by it was real—what Russia gained was apparent." Such a view made sense only to those who shared Grey's premises, the same premises from which Hamilton had argued against Curzon seven years before, namely that Russia's hold on northern Persia was permanent and could under no circumstances be shaken; that the British hold on south Persia was tenuous and could not be maintained by force. The strange thing was that Grey held on to this view through Russia's defeat in war and through her revolution of 1905–06. When Russian power failed at Port Arthur, Mukden, and Tsushima, when the government of the Tsar was repudiated in the streets of St. Petersburg and Moscow, in the factories of Ivanovo-Voznesensk, and on the decks of the *Potemkin*, Grey continued to seek Russia's friendship. Unlike the leader of his own party, Campbell-Bannerman, he never expressed sympathy for the revolution, but wrote, "I am impatient to see Russia reestablished as a factor in European politics. Whether we shall get an arrangement

138. H. D. Wolff, *Rambling Recollections*, 2, 378.
139. Grey, *Twenty-five Years*, 1, 159–60.
140. Id.

with her about Asiatic questions remains to be seen; I will try when she desires it and is ready." [141]

Grey's views were fully shared by Nicolson, Charles Hardinge, Sanderson, and a number of other Foreign Office professionals. Sir George Buchanan, writing after the First World War, felt that the agreement had paved the way for Anglo-Russian collaboration in European questions.

> It proved, indeed, in the end more successful in promoting an understanding, that was outside the purview of the written agreement, than in reconciling their conflicting interests in Persia, which up to the very eve of the Great War occasioned constant friction.[142]

Here, indeed, was the answer to the question of Grey's motives. He was not a world statesman. His horizon was limited to Europe. European problems occupied his mind, often to the exclusion of all else. He saw the Convention of 1907 from a purely European and largely anti-German point of view.

Opposition to the agreement came from many sources. There was, for instance, Professor Edward G. Browne, a lover of Persia and her culture, friend of a number of leading nationalists and vociferous defender of the popular cause. There was Mr. H. F. B. Lynch, of Lynch Brothers, the firm that ran the steamers on the Kārun and traded in Mohammareh, Bushehr, and throughout the south. There were the imperialists and the Government of India. Last but not least, there were numerous groups and associations, including labor organizations, which execrated the alliance with a despot who had just dispersed Russia's first parliament, the Duma, and instituted a regime of counterrevolutionary repression. Dozens of petitions and letters of protest were sent to Sir Edward Grey. They came from all over the country; from the South Place Ethical Society, the Cowdenheath Branch of the Social-Democratic Federation, the Society of Friends of Russian Freedom (forwarding a resolution adopted at a meeting in Trafalgar Square), the Wales District Council of the Social Demo-

---

141. Grey to Spring Rice, February 19, 1906; Gwynn, *Letters*, 2, p. 65.
142. George Buchanan, *My Mission to Russia*, 1, 91.

War, Revolution, and Reconciliation

cratic Federation, the Oxford Branch of the Independent Labour Party, the Fabian Society at Edinburgh University, and many more. Grey did not comment, but Sir Charles Hardinge wrote in the margin of the letter from the Streatham Women's Liberal Association "It looks as though this was inspired by a Jewess Secretary." [143]

Eight years later the radicals were still denouncing the Anglo-Russian agreement. In 1915, in one of its Labour and War Pamphlets, the Independent Labour Party declared:

> From the standpoint of British interests the Convention was an obvious and, we must suppose, a deliberate surrender. Russia was a beaten Power, with an empty Treasury, a demoralized army, and a people seething in revolt, while her footing in Persia had been lost by the victory of the Persian democracy. We proceeded to place the greater part of the country under her influence, presumably because we wished to buy her goodwill in our European rivalry with Germany.[144]

The imperialists found their strongest voice in Lord Curzon. In his view the convention was deplorable:

> It gives up all that we have been fighting for for years, and gives it up with a wholesome abandon that is truly cynical in its recklessness. Ah, me, it makes one despair of public life. The efforts of a century sacrificed and nothing or next to nothing in return.[145]

Curzon led the attack on the agreement in the House of Lords, while Earl Percy spoke against it in the Commons. The debate sounded like an attenuated echo of the old exchanges between Lord Curzon, the Viceroy, and Lord Hamilton, the Secretary of State for India. The same arguments, in a form suitable for the public, were brought forward; but it seems that no one, except the debaters themselves, paid much attention. The issue had been settled long in advance, the Liberals had a solid majority, and

143. No. 37605; F. O. 371/324.
144. Independent Labour Party, "Persia, Finland, and Our Russian Alliance," Labour and War Pamphlets, No. 12 (London, 1915).
145. Cited in Ronaldshay, *The Life of Lord Curzon*, 2, 38.

Curzon's eloquence could do nothing to change that basic and decisive fact.[146]

As an epitaph to the debate in England one might quote the opinion of Harold Nicolson, Sir Arthur's son and admiring biographer:

> Even as an Asiatic agreement the Anglo-Russian Convention was a feeble and artificial growth. It was popular neither in England nor in Russia. It was cordially disliked by the Government of India as well as by all the Russian and British officials on the spot. It proved unworkable and damaging in Persia, and it was never recognized by the Amir of Afghanistan.[147] It was in essence an attempt to reconcile two fundamentally divergent attitudes, to reconcile the Slav tendency toward disintegration with the Anglo-Saxon tendency toward preservation—to combine the British policy of creating a chain of self-supporting and independent States on the borders of India with the Russian policy of "spontaneous infiltration." It was a regrettable alliance between the sanddune and the sea.[148]

Russian public opinion was by and large hostile to the agreement. The Duma, which had no power over the conduct of foreign affairs, heard a brief statement by Izvolskii and some favorable remarks by P. N. Miliukov.[149] The press was either sceptical or unfavorable. *Rech*, the organ of Miliukov's own Constitutional Democratic party, approved the convention but felt that Britain had received greater advantages than Russia. Speaking for Moscow capitalists who were directly involved in Persia, *Golos Moskvy* disapproved and deplored the diminution of Russia's prestige in the eyes of the Asiatics.[150]

146. R. P. Churchill, in *The Anglo-Russian Convention of 1907* is too critical of the opposition and too favourable to the government spokesmen in this debate. Even a close reading of *Parliamentary Debates* (4th series, 183 and 184) fails to convince that Fitzmaurice, Sanderson, Reay, or the Earl of Crew got the better of the opposition.

147. Nor was it recognized by the Persian government.

148. H. Nicolson, *Portrait of a Diplomatist*, p. 191.

149. Cf. Churchill, *The Anglo-Russian Convention of 1907*, pp. 332–33.

150. P. N. Efremov, *Vneshniaia politika Rossii* (1907–1914 gg.) (Moscow, 1961), pp. 65–66.

Few Russians defended the convention. Prince G. N. Trubetskoi felt that Russia had gained from the recognition of her preponderant interests over a large territory that was a natural market and a field for the application of Russian enterprise. Neither Britain nor Russia, but *tertium gaudens* (Trubetskoi borrowed Lansdowne's expression) could derive an advantage from the competition, rivalry, and enmity of the two powers. "Our renunciation of an active policy in the south of Persia was not accompanied by real material losses." [151]

Some expressed the view that Russia could dominate all of Persia commercially, agreement or no agreement.

> Two or three railway lines within the limits of the Russian sphere of influence from our borders into the depth of Persia would play a decisive part in the cause of the strengthening of commercial position all over Persia; it is an old truth that commercial success is the most mighty and solid conductor of political influence.[152]

The anonymous writer, reversing Sir Edward Grey's reasoning, argued that Britain had not gained a comparable advantage. Her sphere was important strategically but barren commercially.[153]

Old-line Russian imperialists were as much distressed by the agreement as their English counterparts. I. A. Zinov'ev, who had spent most of twenty-seven years (1856–83) in Persia, and eight more (1883–91) as Director of the Asiatic Department of the Ministry of Foreign Affairs, felt that

> Only those international agreements are reliable and fruitful which in an equal measure ensure the dignity and the rightful interests of both contracting parties, but not those which subordinate the interests of one party to the benevolent judgment of the other. The agreement of February 1907 [signed in August] between Sir Edward Grey and A. P. Izvolskii belongs undeniably to the second category. Such an agree-

151. G. N. Trubetskoi, "Rossiia, kak velikaia derzhava," V. P. Riabushinskii, ed. *Velikaia Rossiia* (Moscow, 1910), 1, 76.
152. P. A. T., "Zheleznodorozhnyi vopros v Persii i Velikii Indiiskii put," *Velikaia Rossiia*, 2, 253–54.
153. Id.

ment would hardly satisfy even a secondary power. A first-rate power like Russia can reconcile itself to it even less.[154]

However, because of his official position as ambassador at Constantinople, Zinov'ev had to remain silent, at least in public, until his retirement in 1912, when he poured out his scorn of Izvolskii's policies in a 174-page book called *Russia, England and Persia*.

S. Iu. Witte, who had done a great deal to bring Persia under Russian domination, saw his efforts dissipated and his positions abandoned.

> One could say that Persia [he wrote in retirement], especially all its northern part, the most populated and most productive, had long been under our dominant influence. With the conquest of the southern parts of the Caucasus, which had once been provinces of Persia and Turkey, the entire northern part of Persia was, as if naturally, destined in the future if not to become a part of the great Russian Empire, then, in any event, to become a country under our complete protectorate.
>
> For such a result we have sacrificed our Russian blood.

Witte was convinced that the destiny of Persia should have been left to history and that Russia should not have tied her own hands. She should have patronized Persia and "just as the other provinces of the south of Caucasus united with Russia, the northern part of Persia must in the near future gradually become provinces of the Russian State."

The convention gave both Britain and Russia influence over the central government, Witte wrote, but since the government resided in Tehran, Britain acquired a means of exercising influence in the north.

> What have we got in the end? We can't annex Persia politically because that would contradict the agreement with England. We can't have any economic advantage at all because obviously we cannot compete with the Germans in the north of Persia under the condition that Persia should give

---

154. Zinov'ev, *Rossiia, Angliia i Persiia* (St. Petersburg, 1912).

War, Revolution, and Reconciliation

the Germans the same economic conditions as she gives us. As a result it is clear that we have signed a convention under which we shall lose Persia in the future.[155]

The similarity of Witte's and Zinov'ev's views is not surprising. Witte knew and respected Zinov'ev and referred to him as "a very honorable outstanding diplomat who has excellent knowledge of the affairs of the Middle East." [156] In a certain sense Witte and Zinov'ev shared the view of Grey and Nicolson. They too believed that Britain could not stop by force the southward march of Russia and that therefore an agreement securing southern Persia to Britain was entirely to the latter's advantage. Therefore for Russia the agreement was a great and unnecessary sacrifice. Paradoxically, those Russians whose analysis of the relative strength of the two great powers in Persia coincided with that of Grey, and who agreed with him that what Britain had renounced was only apparent, whereas what Russia had given up was real, would never have signed the convention.

155. Witte, *Vospominaniia*, 2, 407–08.
156. Ibid., p. 423.

8

The Uneasy Alliance

The Russian government believed that the Persian clauses of the Convention of 1907 contained an implicit British promise not to interfere with any Russian activity in the Russian sphere and that the words of the preamble about the independence and territorial integrity of Persia were no more than a ritualistic tribute to a popular idea. Sir Edward Grey tacitly encouraged such an interpretation. Years later he wrote:

> I had never expected that the Agreement would diminish Russian activity in the north of Persia. It was impossible that the hands of the clock, which had already marked so much time in the lapse of Persian independence, should be put back, but I hoped that the clock might be stopped. And so in a way it was, for the Russians kept their interference strictly to the north. Russian Foreign ministers, freed from the apprehension of British rivalry at Tehran, were ready to be easy and to go slow, but Russian agents were apt to regard themselves as having a free hand in the Russian sphere, and in that sphere things were frequently done that were not consistent with the "integrity and independence." [1]

Thus Grey had hoped to stop the clock, and in a way it did stop, but frequently it did not. Such was Grey's logic.

The Persian revolution followed its stormy course. On the day the Anglo-Russian convention was signed, Amin os-Soltān was shot dead by a Tabriz fanatic, Abbās Āqā, member of a terrorist political club (*anjoman*). The life of the Shah himself was openly threatened in the press.

---
1. Grey, *Twenty-five Years*, 1, 167.

The tyrant falleth aye by self-wrought ill:
The Rook is lost: the Pawn advances still:
Bishop and Knight we to the task will bring:
The Premier's slain—'tis check-mate to the King.[2]

The Shah and his supporters had no intention of coming to terms with the Majles. They were encouraged in their anticonstitutionalist attitude by the Russian minister, N. G. Hartwig. Reared in the atmosphere of the Asiatic Department of the Ministry of Foreign Affairs and firmly committed to its imperialist traditions, Hartwig

> was one of those who considered at the time of the signature of the Convention, that his country was being deprived of the ripe fruit which was ready to fall into her lap, and he seems to have thought that the only way in which the results of Russian diplomacy of past years were to be secured was in the retention, at all costs, on the throne of Mohammed Ali Shah, who, as Valiahd at Tabriz, had shown himself thoroughly amenable.[3]

The Russian minister would have used force to suppress the revolution; but for the moment Izvolskii was anxious not to disturb the British, whose support he needed in the Balkans. The Persian revolution was discussed at a Special Conference in November 1907. Izvolskii spoke against measures "equivalent to the establishment of a protectorate" over Persia and called for a solution "on the basis of the agreement with England." This was unpalatable to the military, who argued that joint action with Britain was especially undesirable, since "having established herself on the shores of the Persian Gulf with our help, she will kill the last of our influence in Persia and will forever bar our move-

---

2. E. G. Browne, *The Persian Revolution*, p. 152. Browne writes: "All the pieces in the game of Chess are here mentioned; the King (*Shah*), the Queen (called *Farzin* or *Wazir*, 'The Prime Minister'), the Rook or Castle (*Rukh*), the Pawn (*Piyada*), the Bishop (called *Pil* 'the elephant'), and the Knight (*Asp*, 'the horse')."

3. Sir G. Barclay to Sir E. Grey, No. 18A, Confidential, Tehran, February 10, 1910; F. O. 371/956.

ment to the Persian Gulf."[4] The military refused to entertain the idea of joint Anglo-Russian "pacification" of Persia, while Izvolskii, supported by Stolypin and Kokvtsov, did not want to engage in unilateral military action at the risk of breaking the agreement with England.[5] It was decided to refrain from open intervention.

Secret intervention was not barred, and Hartwig was busy, urging the Shah to get rid of the Parliament, the Constitution, the free press, and all the democratic trappings that both he and the Shah ardently hated.[6] For several weeks past the Cabinet had

4. Minutes of a Special Conference chaired by Izvolskii as cited in Bestuzhev, *Borba v Rossii po voprosam vneshnei politiki*, p. 149.

5. In his *Borba v Rossii po voprosam vneshnei politiki*, I. V. Bestuzhev claims that one of the two most important motives for the conclusion of the Anglo-Russian agreement of 1907 was the "need for a joint struggle against the revolutionary movement in Persia" (p. 148). This would indicate that Britain was at least as guilty as Russia of suppressing the Persian revolution. However, a page later, having either forgotten his thesis or failed to see the inconsistency, Bestuzhev writes: "It was becoming evident that intervention in Persia could be undertaken [by Russia] only at the price of breaking the agreement which had just been concluded with England" (pp. 148-49).

The source of Bestuzhev's view is Lenin's article "Inflammable Material in World Politics," published in *Proletarii* in Geneva on August 5, 1908. Lenin wrote:

Shamefully defeated by the Japanese, the armies of the Russian tsar are taking their revenge by zealously serving the counter-revolution. The exploits of the Cossacks in mass shootings, punitive expeditions, manhandling and pillage in Russia are followed by their exploits in suppressing the revolution in Persia. That Nicholas Romanov, heading the Black Hundred landlords and capitalists, scared by strikes and civil war, should be venting his fury on the Persian revolutionaries, is understandable. It is not the first time that Russia's Christian [in the original "Christ-loving," *Christophilous*] soldiers are cast in the role of international hangmen. That Britain is pharisaically washing her hands of the affair, and maintaining a demonstrably friendly neutrality towards the Persian reactionaries, is a somewhat different matter. The British Liberal bourgeoisie, angered by the growth of the labour movement at home and frightened by the mounting revolutionary struggle in India, are more and more frequently, frankly and sharply demonstrating what *brutes* the highly "civilized" European "politicians," men who have passed through the high school [in the original "higher school"] of constitutionalism, can turn into when it comes to a rise in the mass struggle against capital and the capitalist colonial system, i.e. a system of enslavement, plunder, and violence. [*Collected Works* (English translation. 4th ed., Moscow, 1963), 15, 182.]

6. David Fraser, an English correspondent unsympathetic to the Persians and their constitutional movement, wrote:

It was notorious in Tehran that while Monsieur de Hartwig . . . acted osten-

been headed by the mildly liberal Abol Qāsem Khān Nāser ol-Molk, an Oxonian who numbered among his friends Sir Edward Grey (who had been his classmate), Lord Curzon (with whom he used to debate at Balliol), Spring Rice, and many other leading figures in English political and diplomatic circles. On December 14 Nāser ol-Molk resigned. Next morning he was in jail with a heavy chain on his neck. Only his personal friendships with prominent Englishmen saved him from the vengeance of the Shah. The British legation intervened, and Nāser ol-Molk was allowed to leave for Europe. Meanwhile the streets had filled with a mob demonstrating against the Majles, which was accused of being an assembly of Babis and infidels. The Cossack Brigade was called out, but not to put down the demonstration. The Shah used it to intimidate the Majles and its supporters.

If at this psychological moment the troops had moved to occupy the mosque [Sepahsālār's mosque next to the Parliament building] and the temporarily closed Parliament building, complete victory would have been on the side of the Shah. Instead he called the Ministers, who had already resigned, for negotiations; it became clear to everyone that the Shah, unsure of his power, was seeking a compromise.... The temper changed radically: the supporters of the Constitutional regime, together with revolutionaries, seeing the balance of material power tipping in their favor, raised their heads, while the Shah and his entourage began to lose their spirit.[7]

---

sibly with the British *chargé d'affaires* in the matter of joint representations to the Shah relating to the restoration of the Constitution, he habitually spoilt the effect of the joint action in subsequent private interviews with the Shah or his advisers. . . . M. de Hartwig in fact belonged to the old school which only knew the traditional forward policy. He represented the reactionary and military party in Russia which looks with scant favour upon the Anglo-Russian agreement and all that it implies. [*Persia and Turkey in Revolt* (London, 1910), p. 9. Hartwig was reflecting the attitude of the Tsar himself. Cf. note 39, infra.]

7. Hartwig's dispatch of December 7/20, 1907; Russia, Ministry of Foreign Affairs, *Sbornik diplomaticheskikh dokumentov kasaiushchikhsia sobytii v Persii s kontsa 1906 g. po iiul 1909 g.* (St. Petersburg, 1911–13), 1, 57–58. Hereafter cited as *S.D.D.*

That Hartwig's sympathy was all with the Shah can be seen even from the expurgated version of those of his dispatches which the Russian government found fit to publish. He was disappointed that the Shah had not dealt the final blow to the Majles when he had the opportunity. An unnamed correspondent wrote to E. G. Browne from Tehran:

> The blow came as a surprise to the Assembly ... Heaven only knows what stopped the Shah from following up his first *coup*, and dealing the decisive blow. Perhaps it was only a part of the irresolute policy of this wretched man. Perhaps, and this seems the true reason, he could not count on his troops. ... On the morrow the *Majlis* and the *anjumans* recovered from their inaction.[8]

The Shah's forces melted away, leaving him no other choice but negotiation with the Majles. On orders from St. Petersburg and London, the Russian and British legations stepped in. On December 20 their dragomans were received by the Shah. They advised him to come to terms with the Majles. He thanked them, promised to achieve pacification, but said that he deemed it necessary to remove from the Majles certain members who participated in the activities of the political clubs (*anjomans*). However, he had lost the opportune moment. The Majles was receiving reenforcements, and its power grew as that of the Shah declined.[9]

On December 22 Hartwig and Charles Marling, British chargé d'affaires, made additional representations to the Shah, advising him to abide by the constitution which he had sworn to uphold.[10] His Majesty promised to follow their suggestions, without specifying whether he was referring to the joint advice given publicly or to the advice he received from Hartwig behind closed doors. Though he lost a battle against the nationalists, Mohammad Ali had good reason to feel he could win the war. On the very day that Hartwig and Marling urged him to cooperate with the Majles, the Russian minister received a telegram from Izvol-

---

8. Browne, *The Persian Revolution*, p. 165.
9. Two telegrams from Hartwig, December 7/20, 1907; S.D.D., 1, 49–50.
10. Hartwig to Izvolskii, December 9/22, 1907; ibid., pp. 52–53.

skii authorizing him to inform the Shah that while "respecting the inviolability and integrity of Persia, the Imperial Government will contribute by all available means to the personal safety of Mohammad Ali and his family." [11]

Hartwig's restraint in public was a result of the position assumed by his government under the mild urging of Sir Edward Grey, who preached nonintervention. Grey wrote to Count Benckendorff that Persia should be left alone to work out her own form of government. He was anxious to cooperate with Russia toward noninterference, which Persians would appreciate. "They will then look to us both with confidence instead of attempting to intrigue with others against us." [12] Relations between the Shah and the Majles did not improve, but a certain détente was achieved. Hartwig told Marling that he had been acting the peacemaker, discussing matters with the leaders of the nationalists and also urging the Shah to demonstrate his goodwill.[13]

From St. Petersburg Sir Arthur Nicolson spread optimism. In his annual report to Sir Edward Grey (for 1907) he pointed out that Russia had abandoned her offensive policy and wished "to concentrate her energies in consolidating her position in the northern portion of Persia . . . The anxiety lest Russia should aspire to obtain a footing in the Gulf has apparently been shown to be groundless." [14] Nicolson reluctantly admitted the existence of some difficulties with Russia, but to him these served only to emphasize Izvolskii's good faith and that of the military who had joined him in refusing to allow a movement of Russian troops toward Persian frontiers.[15]

Nicolson had referred to the Russian local officials in Persia as a source of trouble. The most troublesome of them all was undoubtedly Ivan Fedorovich Pokhitonov, consul general at Tabriz.

11. Izvolskii to Hartwig, Telegram, December 9/22, 1907; ibid., p. 54.
12. Grey to Benckendorff, Fallodon, Christon Bank, Northumberland, December 28, 1907; Iswolsky, *Au service de la Russie*, 2, 109.
13. Hartwig to Izvolskii, telegrams of January 1/14 and 9/22, 1908; S.D.D., 1, 79–81.
14. General Report on Russia for the year 1907, Enclosure in Nicolson to Grey, No. 57, St. Petersburg, January 29, 1908; F. O. 371/514.
15. Id.

Day after day he sent messages to Hartwig and directly to St. Petersburg—for he had the privilege of bypassing the minister whenever he wished—describing the alleged depredations of the revolutionaries and the resulting anarchy. In January 1908 he complained that party strife had compelled the closing of the Tabriz bazar for twelve days. Pokhitonov was afraid that Russian toll collectors of the Tabriz-Jolfā highway would leave their job. "Russia," he telegraphed St. Petersburg, "as the party which has the greatest interest in general and specifically in the highway, is suffering considerable losses." Pokhitonov called for Cossacks to guard the highway. "All foreigners openly express their surprise at our seeming indifference to our interests." [16]

The eager consul did not get the Cossacks, but Izvolskii instructed Hartwig to draw Persia's attention to the disorders in Āzarbāyjān. The message to the Persian government contained an open threat:

> Be good enough . . . to call the most serious attention of the Shah's Ministers to the fact that their continued inactivity in this question might lead to consequences equally undesirable for Russia as well as Persia and might force us to take all measures which might seem necessary for the protection of our subjects and interests.[17]

Disappointed in Izvolskii's reaction, Pokhitonov made another request. Could he have permission to recruit the mayor of Marand, a small town in Āzarbāyjān, to guard the highway? The mayor had a number of horsemen who were his "relatives" and were for hire.[18] Izvolskii agreed that such a method of raising troops would be cheaper and, he might have added, less troublesome vis-à-vis Britain. He asked Hartwig's opinion.[19] The latter, seeing eye to eye with Pokhitonov, replied that he had no objections.[20] The consul was now ready to recruit a private army on Persian soil.

16. Pokhitonov to Izvolskii, Tabriz, January 16/29, 1908; S.D.D., 1, 81–82.
17. Izvolskii to Hartwig, Telegram, St. Petersburg, January 17/30, 1908; ibid., pp. 88–89.
18. Hartwig, Telegram, January 31/February 13, 1908; ibid., p. 90.
19. Izvolskii, Telegram, February 1/14, 1908, ibid., p. 90.
20. Hartwig to Izvolskii, Telegram, February 3/16, 1908; ibid., p. 91.

The Uneasy Alliance

In the highest governmental and court spheres there was talk of restoring Russia's position in Asia. The Viceroy of the Caucasus, Count I. I. Vorontsov-Dashkov, wrote to the Tsar: "Our influence on the East close to the Caucasus—on Persia and Asia Minor—has been shaken; but we will regain it, and with great interest, when Russia gets stronger." [21]

From July 1908 to March 1910 the government held more than ten special conferences on the Persian question. The Viceroy of the Caucasus advocated intervention. Kokovtsov, who had earlier sided with Izvolskii, grew more belligerent and interventionist as time passed. Izvolskii continued to argue that

> such measures as the dispatch of our troops to Persia, toward which English public opinion and, following it, the London Cabinet, tend to react with a certain sensitivity, ought to be undertaken with special caution in order not to disrupt the good understanding existing between the two powers.[22]

It seems that the Tsar tended toward aggressive unilateral action, whereas Stolypin favored cooperation with the British.[23]

The agreement with England prevented large-scale intervention against the constitutional authorities in Tehran but did not prevent local military action along the Russo-Persian border. When on April 13, 1908, a Russian officer, Dvoeglazov, accompanied by some soldiers, crossed into Persian territory and was killed by Shāhsavan tribesmen, the Russians blew up the incident to major proportions. Hartwig lodged a protest with the Persian Foreign Minister, claiming that the Shāhsavans had crossed into Russia and killed Dvoeglezov on Russian soil.[24] On May 16 Izvolskii informed Hartwig that three tribal chiefs in the Āstārā area, where the shooting had occurred, had received Russian demands to pay compensations and a warning that "in case banditry is not stopped, our detachments will burn the

---

21. I. I. Vorontsov-Dashkov to Nicholas II, Tiflis, February 24/March 9, 1908; K. A., 1 (26) (1928), 110, No. 6.

22. Document from Central State Historical Archive of Leningrad, *fond* 1276, *opis* 3, *delo* 700, *list* 243, as cited in Bestuzhev, *Borba v Rossii*, p. 313.

23. Bestuzhev, *Borba v Rossii*, p. 313.

24. Marling to Grey, No. 95, Tehran, April 23, 1908; F. O. 371/516.

villages of all who participate in looting or hide the bandits and will punish the guilty without pity." [25]

From Batum the British consul, Stevens, reported that Russian troops had entered Persia under orders to burn villages along the line of the expedition.

> Accordingly, so far as report goes, several villages within a radius of 12 versts [7.9548 miles] from the frontier which were visited by the troops were razed to the ground, and the expedition having thus far attained its object, General Snarsky and his detachment are withdrawing to Russian territory.[26]

Before Snarskii's troops withdrew to Russia, the general issued an ultimatum to the governor of Āzarbāyjān. He announced that he had been sent by the Viceroy to exact retribution. "The insolent seizure of Russian land has been punished. The constructed village—annihilated." The governor was given six days to pay certain sums decided upon by the Russian frontier court, to promise to pay to the families of Dvoeglazov and the others compensation in the sum to be designated by the Russian government, to pay for damages resulting from the occupation of Russian territory near the post Dymanskii, and to pay the expenses of Snarskii's own punitive expedition. "In case of a late answer or a negative answer to even one point, I shall consider myself entitled to cross the frontier and seek satisfaction on all the enumerated issues with force of arms." [27]

The Persian government bowed to the ultimatum. The Minister of Foreign Affairs complained to Hartwig that Persia could not raise the required sums at once and asked whether they could be added to her long-term debt.[28] The case was closed but resentment against Russia among Persian constitutionalists increased further. Hartwig freely admitted to Charles Marling that the Russian version of Dvoeglazov's death had been incorrect, "and

---

25. Izvolskii to Hartwig, St. Petersburg, May 3/16, 1908; S.D.D., 1, 153.

26. Consul Stevens to Grey, No. 5, Batum, May 13, 1908; F. O. 371/516.

27. Text of Snarskii's ultimatum, transmitted by Kokhanovskii, Tiflis, May 25, 1908; S.D.D., 1, 177–79.

28. Hartwig to Izvolskii, Tehran, May 10/23, 1908; ibid., pp. 163–64

that the incident really took place on the Persian side of the frontier, which the unfortunate officer crossed with some of his men in pursuit of a runaway horse." [29] Marling wrote:

> It appears from all the Persian official accounts of the incident that the Russian soldiers committed most serious excesses to avenge the death of the Russian officer at Belaswar, who, moreover, was admittedly in the wrong in crossing the frontier. This is confirmed by the meager independent testimony I have received. That Russia should demand compensation for injuries which are insignificant as compared with the murders and damage committed on Persians by her own troops has consequently aroused great indignation here.[30]

A Salisbury or a Lansdowne would have given the Persian government at least verbal support in a case such as that of Dvoeglazov. Grey chose to ignore it completely. When Sir Charles Hardinge met Izvolskii at Reval in June he did not even mention the incident until Izvolskii said that he was preoccupied with the state of affairs along the Perso-Russian frontier, and that "it might be necessary to exact some compensation from the tribes" for the murders they had committed. That Sir Charles was aware of all the facts in the Dvoeglazov case is evident from the appearance of his initials in the margins of all the dispatches from Batum, Tehran, and St. Petersburg dealing with it. Yet he endorsed Russian behavior:

> I replied that it was not a matter in which we wished to interfere, that since the conclusion of our Convention we had confidence in Russia's intentions toward Persia but that we earnestly hoped that a satisfactory and amicable solution of the difficulty could be found.[31]

The Reval meeting between King Edward VII and Tsar Nicholas II was another step toward a closer Anglo-Russian

29. Marling to Grey, No. 115, Gulahek, May 20, 1908; F. O. 371/516.
30. Marling to Grey, No. 128, Tehran, May 30, 1908; ibid.
31. Memorandum by Sir Charles Hardinge, Secret, 20885/08, H. M. Yacht *Victoria and Albert*, June 12, 1908; F. O. 371/517.

entente. The visit of the King to Russia evoked strong protests from a large segment of British society. Radical and Labour members of Parliament "regarded the visit as unjustified . . . and there was a growing popular impatience . . . with the Tsar's autocratic methods of government and corresponding sympathy with the revolutionary movement." [32] In an article published in the *Labour Leader* toward the end of May, Ramsay MacDonald described the Tsar as a " 'common murderer' and objected to the King, as the head of a state which prided itself on its constitutional freedom, 'hob-nobbing with a blood-stained creature' like the Tsar." [33] A debate was held in the House of Commons with Labour members, Keir Hardie and James O'Grady, and the Liberal, Arthur Ponsonby, speaking against the visit, and Grey defending it. When the vote was taken, it showed 225 for and 59 against the visit.[34] The Foreign Office received a large number of letters from individuals and from labor groups objecting to the proposed trip.[35]

Secure in its majority in the House of Commons, the government could disregard popular sentiment. The King and Queen made their voyage and were welcomed by the Tsar aboard his yacht, *Shtandart*. Edward was accompanied by Charles Hardinge and Nicolson, Nicholas, by Stolypin and Izvolskii. The latter held several long conversations with Hardinge, who pointed out that Britain deeply distrusted Germany because of her naval armaments.

> In seven or eight years' time [Hardinge said] a critical situation might arise, in which Russia, if strong in Europe, might be the arbiter of peace and have more influence in securing the peace of the world than at any Hague Conference. For this reason it was absolutely necessary that England and Russia should maintain toward each other the same cordial and friendly relations as now existed between England and France.[36]

32. Lee, *King Edward VII*, 2, 587.
33. Id.
34. Ibid., pp. 587–89.
35. Many of the letters are in F. O. 371/517.
36. Memorandum by Sir Charles Hardinge, Secret, H. M. Yacht *Victoria and Albert*, June 12, 1908; ibid.

The Uneasy Alliance 521

If the Reval meeting produced no concrete results, it certainly helped to confirm the impression in the minds of Russian statesmen that Britain placed great value on her new-found friendship with Russia. Izvolskii had plans for the revision of the status of the Straits and various other Balkan matters for which he would need British support, or at least abstention from opposition. He was therefore gratified by the attitude of the King. Ten days after the two monarchs had parted, a third put their cooperation to a severe test.

Mohammad Ali Shah never achieved a satisfactory relationship with the Majles. To his Qājār mind all constitutionalists were traitors. A large number of his subjects agreed, not because they loved him but because they too were convinced that resistance to the Shah, Shadow of God, Kiblah of the Universe, could never be legitimate. Hartwig adroitly exploited the Shah's despotic sentiments. "Between the abortive coup d'état and the destruction of the Medjliss in June," the British legation reported, "his advice and efforts were directed, not to trying to effect any reconciliation between the sovereign and the assembly, but merely towards strengthening the material forces upon which His Majesty's throne depended." [37]

Hartwig's closest associate in making plans for the overthrow of constitutional government was Colonel Vladimir Platonovich Liakhov, commander of the Cossack Brigade. Six feet four inches tall, "with a small bullet-shaped head and a trimmed yellow beard," he looked youthful at thirty-nine. "He wore a beautiful dark uniform and walked with graceful, light movements that gave him an air of great distinction . . . He had blue, deep-set, gentle eyes, and a strong chin." [38] He had also an iron will and was completely devoted to autocracy.

Liakhov and Hartwig advised the Shah "to abolish the Constitution, disperse the Majlis, and, by means of a whole series of manoeuvres, so as to escape the insistence of the European Powers, to return to the former absolute form of government." [39]

37. Barclay to Grey, No. 18A, Confidential, Tehran, February 10, 1910; F. O 371/956.
38. J. M. Hone and P. L. Dickinson, *Persia in Revolution* (London, 1910), p 117.
39. Report No. 59, Secret, "To the General Staff of the Military District of

The Shah was willing to accept Russian advice, which corresponded so perfectly with his own views and inclinations. On June 3 Mohammad Ali left Tehran and camped at Bāghe Shāh, a large garden on the outskirts of the city. From there he made his demand that the press and popular orators stop attacking him. The Majles countered with the request for the dismissal of Amir Bahādor Jang, the Shah's close friend; Shapshal, his Russian tutor; and four other extreme reactionaries.[40] Since neither side would give in or compromise, force seemed the only way out of the impasse.

Encouraged by his Russian advisers, the Shah demanded that the Majles expel and exile eight deputies whom he found especially obnoxious, including the popular orators Malek ol-

---

the Caucasus. To the Quartermaster General." As cited in E. G. Browne, *The Persian Revolution*, p. 221. Four of Liakhov's reports, which are reproduced in the original Russian on pp. 432–36 of Browne's book, were obtained and sent to the English Orientalist by a Bulgarian, Panov (Panoff), who was in Persia as correspondent for the Russian newspaper *Rech*. The Russian government repudiated the reports as forgeries. However, before the revolution even Marxist writers accepted their authenticity without question. Only in the 1950s did Soviet historians return to the Tsarist position and accuse Browne of spreading forgeries. The Soviet government has not published any documents on the coup d'état of June 1908. A careful study of the reports reproduced by Browne shows their great accuracy in describing events that neither Panov nor Browne witnessed. Practically every statement made by Liakhov in Report No. 60 (p. 434) can be confirmed from independent sources. Report No. 62 and evidence for its possible authenticity are dealt with below. If positive proof were available that Liakhov's reports were forgeries, one would still have to conclude that the forger was a person very close to either Liakhov or Hartwig to have been able to compose papers which reflected their sentiments and actions with such accuracy.

That Nicholas II himself advised the Shah to act against the Constitution is admitted by M. S. Ivanov, who quotes the Tsar's own words: "'The Shah can save the throne only by an immediate dispersal of the Majles and other such revolutionary gatherings. This is my only answer.'" (M. S. Ivanov, *Ocherk istorii Irana*, p. 223.)

40. Of Shapshal, very little is known. E. G. Browne writes on the authority of an unnamed Englishman long resident in Russia:

Shapshal is a Karaite Jew. His relatives are proprietors of a well known tobacconist firm. I know no details of his early life, except that he was a pupil at a private grammar-school in St. Petersburg (Gurevich's), and that he completed a course at the Oriental Faculty of the St. Petersburg University. It is very possible that he was intended for the Consular Service, since most of the students of the Oriental faculty work with a view to entering either the Consular or the Diplomatic Service. [Browne, *The Persian Revolution*, pp. 419–20.]

Motakallemin and Seyyed Jamāl ed-Din Esfahāni. During the next several days, while fruitless negotiations continued, the Shah marshaled his forces and prepared for a trial of strength.

On or about June 22 he appointed Colonel Liakhov military governor of Tehran. Martial law was proclaimed, and the Cossack Brigade began to concentrate in the city. On June 23 the Brigade, commanded by Liakhov, Perebinosov, Blaznov, and Ushakov, surrounded the Majles.[41] Sharp fighting broke out. Liakhov, a firm believer in the therapeutic value of bloodshed, ordered artillery to be brought up. Shells were fired into the Bahārestān (Majles building) and the adjoining mosque of Sepahsālār. Several hundred persons were killed before nationalist defenses collapsed. Through the rest of the day the Shah's troops, especially those under Amir Bahādor Jang, looted private houses and arrested scores of nationalists. The next morning Malek ol-Motakallemin, the orator, and Mirzā Jāhāngir Khān, the editor of a nationalist newspaper, were strangled. Seyyed Jamāl ed-Din fled the city, but he too was caught and put to death.[42]

At the very moment of Hartwig's triumph, when he was ready at last to extirpate the revolution root and branch, the minister was informed that a number of constitutionalists had found refuge in the British legation. Hartwig would not allow the old tradition of *bast* (sanctuary) to interfere with his plans. To prevent hundreds of men running to the English for protection, he ordered Liakhov to surround the British legation with Cossacks. This was an unprecedentedly bold step. The English gasped at the Cossack Colonel's arrogance but could not help admiring the man's determination.

> The only Russian for whose behaviour I have the slightest admiration [an English resident of Tehran wrote]—rather the sort of admiration one would accord to Judge Jeffreys of Claverhouse—is Liakhov. He has just gone straight ahead

41. The names are given in Pavlovich's preface to V. Tria, *Kavkazskie sotsialdemokraty v persidskoi revoliutsii* (Paris, 1910), p. 5.

42. These events were reported with barely suppressed glee by Hartwig to Izvolskii, Zargandeh, June 18/31, 1908; S.D.D., 1, 224–26. See also Annual Report on Persia for the year 1908, Enclosure in Barclay to Grey, No. 18A, Confidential, Tehran, February 10, 1910; F. O. 371/956.

without caring what anyone cared, thought, or said. He makes no secret of it; he has played for the greater glory of Russia and what is to him, and to many others of his kidney, the natural corollary—the humbling of England. He carried out the coup d'état; he determined that his work should not be spoilt by a Bast at the British Legation; he deliberately insulted the Legation by posting his many Cossacks round it, perfectly indifferent of the consequences, quite heedless of any paper agreements or humbug of that sort; he let go, even if he did not send, all his Cossacks round the town to say that if there was a Bast *chez nous* he would bombard the Legation; he did his damnedest to make us eat dirt, to destroy our name among the people, in the evidently justifiable conviction that his Government would take no notice of his extraordinary action.[43]

The English were aware that Liakhov had not acted on his own. The posting of Cossacks around the legation park to prevent Persians from entering was a serious matter. It was Hartwig who had ordered the step when he saw that thirty or forty nationalists had found refuge at the British legation and others might follow, preventing him from finishing the job of killing the revolution. "M. de Hartwig's disappointment at the obstacles which now arose in the way of the thorough execution of his scheme to reestablish the Shah as an absolute monarch, then vented itself on His Majesty's Legation." [44]

Hartwig openly accused the British chargé d'affaires, Charles Marling, of supporting the nationalists against the Crown. His language was immoderate and offensive. "For several days the tension was so great as not only seriously to endanger the relations between the two Legations, but even to jeopardize the success of the Anglo-Russian accord." [45] In London the Foreign Office complained of Hartwig's actions. It rejected his allegations of Marling's intervention on the side of the nationalists as absurd:

---

43. One of the British Legation Staff to Spring Rice, Tehran, July 16, 1908; Gwynn, *Letters*, 2, 106–07.
44. Barclay to Grey, No. 18A, February 10, 1910; F. O. 7/956.
45. Id.

"the last thing we want is a lot of refugees in the Legation but it is impossible always to refuse." It was pointed out that "A complication of this kind would be most unfortunate at this moment and would have a very disastrous effect on our Entente."[46]

Among themselves the Russians admitted Hartwig's role in the coup d'état of June 23 and his responsibility for posting Cossacks around the British legation. In Benckendorff's opinion the cause of the trouble lay in the difference of interpretation Hartwig and Marling gave to the term "nonintervention." "Mais j'avoue," he wrote Izvolskii, "que l'interprétation de Marling me semble s'être maintenue beaucoup plus près de celle qui a été stipulée entre vous et Grey, que celle qui ressort et de télégrammes de Hartwig et des paroles que Marling lui attribue."[47] Marling had precipitated the crisis by doing nothing; Hartwig had achieved the same result by doing too much. He had organized and encouraged the Shah's supporters, and had treated Marling as if he were an inferior or even a subordinate. Hartwig's behavior had been so brazen that even the French ambassador in London, Cambon, found it necessary to discuss it with Benckendorff.[48]

British pressure was unusually strong. Engrossed in Balkan matters, Izvolskii did not want to see the collapse of the Anglo-Russian agreement. Hartwig was ordered to lift the guard from the British legation, but his usefulness in Tehran had been gravely impaired. He was persona non grata to the British. King Edward himself bluntly told Benckendorff that new ministers were needed in Tehran. Since Spring Rice had already left Persia, this could be interpreted only as a request for the recall of Hartwig. Benckendorff agreed that "No matter what he [Hartwig] did, his judgement would be mistrusted as would be his understanding of cooperation and non-intervention."[49]

Both Izvolskii and Benckendorff felt that S. A. Poklewski-Koziell, counselor of the embassy in London, would make a good minister in Tehran. Benckendorff characterized him as intelligent,

---

46. Mallet to Benckendorff, London, June 25, 1908; Iswolsky, *Au service de la Russie*, 2, 170–71.

47. Benckendorff to Izvolskii, London, June 19/July 2, 1908; ibid., p. 174.

48. Same to same, London, June 23/July 6, 1908; ibid., p. 178.

49. Id.

energetic, and deeply versed in political affairs. Moreover, in English eyes he was above suspicion of double dealing.[50]

Stanislaw Alfonsovich Poklewski-Koziell, a rich Polish nobleman, was a good friend of Izvolskii under whom he had served in the Russian legation in Tokyo before the Japanese war. Witte attributed to "evil tongues" the rumor that Poklewski helped Izvolskii financially. During the several years he spent in London, Poklewski made himself popular in English society. Like Benckendorff and Izvolskii, he displayed moderately liberal tendencies and advocated Anglo-Russian friendship; in fact he was a principal go-between in the early exploratory stages of the negotiations that led to the conclusion of the convention of August 31, 1907.[51]

Izvolskii "showed the greatest anxiety to maintain the cooperation between the two powers in Persia, and the Emperor himself subsequently conveyed to Sir A. Nicholson [sic] a message reiterating his desire that the Anglo-Russian accord should be observed." [52] However, getting rid of Hartwig was more difficult than making Nicholas "reiterate his desire" for Anglo-Russian friendship. Madame Hartwig, "a lady of great force of character," was close to the "grand ducal circles in St. Petersburg." [53] Hartwig had powerful friends, which explains his independence of Izvolskii and his disregard of the latter's instructions.

Nothing demonstrated Hartwig's exceptional strength better than the incident of the Cossacks of the British legation and his subsequent defiance of the policy of his own superior, Izvolskii. Though it was "generally admitted" in Tehran that the officers of the Cossack Brigade had been under Hartwig's orders and that "the real responsibility for the surrounding of the legation by Cossack patrols rested with no less a person that Hartwig," [54] it was Liakhov who had to answer for the action. In a report to his military superiors in the Caucasus he stated that he had been called to the Russian legation by the minister on June 18 and told

50. Id.
51. Witte, *Vospominaniia*, 2, 372.
52. Barclay to Grey, No. 18A, February 10, 1910; F. O. 371/956.
53. Id.
54. Id.

that the English had guessed that a coup was being prepared and that they "intended to give sanctuary to malcontents, so as thereby to weaken the effects of our action." Measures were to be taken to prevent *bast* in all foreign legations, but Hartwig advised Liakhov "that more special measures should be taken against the British Legation than against the rest." [55]

Hartwig continued in his post for several more months, playing a double game of cooperating with the English in public while urging the Shah in private to extend the counterrevolution. The minister was concerned about the role played by Caucasian revolutionaries in Persian political affairs. After the dispersal of the Majles on June 23, 1908, the nationalists of Tabriz refused to recognize Mohammad Ali as the legitimate ruler. The authority of the royal governor collapsed, the nationalists political societies (*anjomans*) took over and prepared to defend the city against the Shah's army. The nationalists also appealed to the Social Democrats in the Caucasus for help against despotism. The Oblast Committee of the Social Democratic party decided to recruit a number of experienced revolutionaries and former soldiers skilled in fighting and send them to Persia armed with guns and bombs. Soon dozens of Georgian Social Democrats were in Tabriz. The Dashnaktsutiun (Armenian Revolutionary Federation) did not immediately join the nationalists. It had to take into account the possible reaction against Armenian populations in other Persian towns. As the struggle in Tabriz intensified, the Dashnaks tended to give up their neutrality. At last in October 1908 they joined in the defense of Tabriz and contributed greatly to its success.[56]

---

55. Liakhov's Report No. 62 of June 12 (25), 1908; Browne, *The Persian Revolution*, p. 224.

56. Tria, *Kavkazskie sotsial-demokraty*, pp. 9–10. The participation of Russians and Caucasians in the Persian revolution has been given great prominence by Soviet writers. M. S. Ivanov creates the impression that Bolsheviks were one of the major forces in the struggle against the despotism of the Shah. See his *Ocheck istorii Irana* and *Iranskaia revoliutsiia 1905–1911 godov*. See also E. Bor-Ramenskii, "K voprosu o roli bolshevikov zakavkaz'ia v iranskoi revoliutsii 1905–1911 godov," *Istorik marksist*, No. 11 (1940). Ivar Spector in his book, *The First Russian Revolution, Its Impact on Asia* (Englewood Cliffs, 1962), has relied on Russian sources, mostly secondary. It should be pointed out, however, that while Caucasian revolutionaries undoubtedly played a major role, the Bolsheviks did not. They remained until after 1921 a minority, overwhelmed by

Hartwig regularly reported the doings of the Caucasians to St. Petersburg.[57]

Though Tehran was firmly held for the Shah by Liakhov and his Cossacks, large areas of the country were falling into the hands of the nationalists. Mohammad Ali was unable to impose his authority on Tabriz. Rasht, the principal city of Gilān, was taken over by the nationalists under the leadership of the Dashnak Yefrem Khān Davidiants. In central and southwestern Persia, Bakhtiāri and other tribesmen were restless and ready to explode.

The British felt strongly that the only way to preserve order was to make the Shah keep the fundamental laws and convoke the Majles. Sir Arthur Nicolson urged the Russians not to waste time and invited them to make a joint communication to the Shah.[58] The Assistant Minister of Foreign Affairs, N. V. Charykov, replied that he was asking Hartwig to do so jointly with Marling.[59]

The willingness of the Russian Ministry of Foreign Affairs to cooperate in restraining Mohammad Ali Shah, and, by implication, Hartwig, was caused by the need to have British support in an intricate Balkan game. Early in 1908 Austria's Foreign Minister, Count Alois von Aehrenthal, proclaimed his country's intention to build a railway from Bosnia through the Sanjak of Novibazar and on to Salonika. Izvolskii urged his government to pursue a more aggressive policy in the Balkans. He wanted to obtain for Russian warships the right of passage through the Straits. Relations with Japan had improved, and peace was assured in the Far East. The situation in the Near East, however, demanded vigorous action. Russia must not neglect her interests there; otherwise " 'she risked losing the fruits of centuries of

---

the Georgian Mensheviks, Armenian Dashnaks, and Azerbaijani Musavatists. On the relative strength of the various parties in Transcaucasia before and during the Russian revolution, see F. Kazemzadeh, *The Struggle for Transcaucasia, 1917–1921* (Oxford, 1951). Moreover, in Russia itself the distinction between Bolshevik and Menshevik was, until after 1917, not as clear as Soviet historians made it appear during the Stalin era.

57. Various telegrams from Hartwig in *S.D.D.*, 1.
58. Nicolson to Charykov, August 21/September 3, 1908; *S.D.D.*, 1, 249–50.
59. Charykov to Nicolson, August 21/September 3, 1908; ibid., p. 250.

effort, losing the role of a Great Power, and assuming the rank of a second rate State whose voice is inaudible.' " [60]

The Chief of the General Staff, Palitsyn, was the only one to support Izvolskii. The Assistant Minister of War, General Polivanov, and the Naval Minister, Dikov, said that Russia's armed forces were not ready to fight a war. The Finance Minister, Kokovtsov, vehemently objected to taking risks, and Stolypin expressed the same view. The Prime Minister felt that it was not time to pursue an adventurous foreign policy. " 'A few years from now, when we will have achieved complete tranquillity at home, Russia will start again to speak in her old language.' " [61] A week later the Council of State Defense emphatically repudiated any policy which might involve Russia in a war in the Balkans.[62] To achieve his ambitious project, Izvolskii had to rely on diplomacy alone. British goodwill and support were indispensable. Izvolskii would gladly sacrifice Mohammad Ali Shah to unrestricted Russian navigation of the Turkish Straits.

In September 1908, when Nicolson proposed that Britain and Russia jointly advise the Shah to maintain the Constitution and reconvoke the Majles, Izvolskii was on his way to Austria and negotiations with Aehrenthal. In July a revolution had erupted in Turkey. Both Austria and Russia were ready to take advantage of the fall of Abdul Hamid, but Izvolskii wished to avoid for the time being any further complications in Persia.

The Izvolskii-Aehrenthal meeting at Buchlau resulted in a verbal agreement between them that Austria would annex Bosnia and Herzegovina, after informing Russia of her intention to do so. In return Austria would assume a friendly "benevolent" position should Russia deem it necessary to take steps to gain free passage for Russian warships through the Dardanelles. Izvolskii then proceeded to Germany, Italy, and France. At a railway station near Paris he learned from a newspaper that Austria was planning to annex Bosnia and Herzegovina. On October 6 the annexation was

60. *Vestnik N.K.I.D.*, No. 1, 1919, p. 20 as cited in Efremov, *Vneshniaia politika Rossii*, p. 79; cf. also V. M. Khvostov, "Borba Antanty i avstro-germanskogo bloka," in Potemkin, ed., *Istoriia diplomatii*, 2, 187–88.
61. *Vestnik N.K.I.D.*, No. 1, 1919, p. 22, as cited in Efremov, p. 80.
62. Ibid., p. 81.

proclaimed in Vienna, but Aleksandr Petrovich Izvolskii had not been notified.

In London he was badly disappointed by Grey's refusal to support Russian plans for the revision of the status of the Straits. Indeed, Sir Edward would have found it difficult to explain to the English public why Britain should support Russia against Turkey at the very moment when her bloody Sultan had been overthrown and a revolutionary government installed.

In the next several months Austria, Serbia, Russia, and Germany took Europe to the brink of war. On March 22, 1909, the German ambassador in St. Petersburg, Count F. L. Pourtales, demanded that Russia recognize the Austrian annexation of Bosnia-Herzegovina. It was clear to Izvolskii that Russia must either accept the fait accompli or fight a war against Austria and Germany in defense of Serbia. Russia complied with the German ultimatum.

Through the tense months from October 1908 to April 1909, Russia either left Persia more or less to herself or cooperated with the British in maintaining an uneasy balance between the Shah and the nationalists. In November Hartwig finally left Tehran, though his wife remained and continued to exercise a great deal of influence on the Court. The Russian chargé d'affaires, Sablin, learned that the Shah would publish a manifesto expressing his "intention not to restore the Majles which contradicted religion and the views of the people." The two legations at once called His Majesty's attention to the promises he had earlier given to Britain and Russia.[63] Later that day the manifesto was published. It was addressed to the mojtaheds of Tehran who were told that the Shah would defend Islam and protect the law of the Prophet.

> Now that you have proved that the institution of the Majles is contrary to Islam and have declared the Majles *harām* (forbidden), and the Mojtaheds in the provinces have adopted a similar decision, We give up Our previous intention and there will be no more talk of such a Majles.[64]

63. Sablin's telegram, Tehran, November 9/22, 1908, *S.D.D.*, 2, 5.
64. Dastkhatt [manifesto] of November 22, 1908, Enclosure in Sablin's dispatch, Tehran, November 14/27, 1908; ibid., p. 28.

The Uneasy Alliance

The dragomans of the two legations called on His Majesty, who met them with complaints about the dangers of the reconvocation of the Majles. He claimed that the clergy opposed it and the Persian people were not ready for it. The dragomans suggested that a stricter electoral law could prevent the election of ignorant deputies. The Shah pretended to be interested and promised to appoint a consultative council to work out a new electoral law. "According to my conviction", Sablin telegraphed, "shared by the British Minister also, there is no basis for taking any energetic measures of pressure upon the Shah at this time." [65]

Looking back at the events of 1908, Sir Arthur Nicolson summed up Russia's policy as one of return to European affairs.

> If the results of the war with Japan had been other than what they were, it is possible that Russia would have lost much of her interest in the questions which agitate South-Eastern Europe and would have sought to create for herself a vast Asiatic Empire. The Japanese war effectively dissolved these dreams.[66]

Defeat and revolution forced Russia to reorganize her system of government, her army, her navy, and her general administration. She saw the need of liquidating as rapidly as possible all outstanding questions with Japan and of coming "to an arrangement with Great Britain, the great neighbour of Russia in Asia." When all this had been accomplished, the Russian government

> could endeavour to re-establish Russia in her position in Europe, and to return, perhaps subdued and chastened, to their former field of political interests and activity which they had abandoned in the pursuit of the mirage of Asiatic predominance.[67]

Turning to Persia, Nicolson pointed out that Russia was very much alarmed at the connection between the leader of Tabriz nationalists, Sattār Khān, and the Young Turks, and feared the

---

65. Sablin's telegram, Tehran, November 15/28, 1908; ibid., pp. 12–13.
66. Annual Report on Russia for the year 1908, Enclosure in Nicolson to Grey, No. 92, St. Petersburg, February 8, 1909; F. O. 371/727.
67. Id.

establishment in Āzarbāyjān of an independent socialist republic. "This nervousness on the part of the Russian Government proved that their anxiety was sincere." Having satisfied himself that nervousness was a proof of the sincerity of anxiety, whatever that meant, Nicolson praised Russia for her "patience and forebearance in not adopting active measures of intervention." [68] The Russian government had acted loyally in the spirit of the understanding with Britain.

> It is inevitable that on certain points their views may not have been in exact harmony with those of His Majesty's Government, but I think that they have shown always a desire to meet the wishes of Great Britain, and when the traditions, habits, and methods of Russian bureaucracy and diplomacy are taken into consideration, it is in my mind remarkable and satisfactory that the co-operation of Russia has been so cordial and of so liberal a character. The Anglo-Russian Convention, in so far as Persia is concerned, has led to more beneficial results than the most sanguine could have been anticipated [sic].[69]

Thus the ambassador dismissed as insignificant and unimportant the bombardment of the Majles by Liakhov's Cossacks, the posting of guards around the British legation, the arrests and executions of nationalists, and all the other measures either proposed or encouraged by the Russian minister in Tehran.

Hartwig's departure somewhat eased the tension between the British and Russian legations. The new British minister, Sir George Barclay, was well disposed toward the agreement of 1907. The Russian chargé d'affaires, Sablin, was not strong enough to pursue an independent policy and followed Izvolskii's line. The unusually friendly relations between the two legations permitted them to reach an agreement on the situation in Tabriz in the spring of 1909.

The principal city of Persian Āzarbāyjān had risen against the Shah on the day it learned of the Tehran coup d'état and the

68. Id.
69. Id.

dispersal of the Majles. Mohammad Ali was determined to crush all resistance. He concentrated around Tabriz large forces under the command of the ruthless and reactionary Eyn od-Dowleh and the unprincipled Sepahdār, a wealthy landowner from Gilān. The investment of the city was completed on February 3. For the next three months Tabriz was cut off from the rest of the country and received no supplies.

The leaders of the nationalist-revolutionary forces, Sattār Khān and Bāqer Khān, had fewer than two thousand men at their command, while the Shah's troops numbered perhaps six thousand, consisting of some four hundred well-disciplined Cossacks and a few detachments of other regular troops.

> But the main force consisted, not of soldiers, but of savage tribesmen . . . bloodthirsty brigands who, by terrorizing villages and wayfarers from time immemorial, have gained a a reputation for fierceness, which should not be mistaken for a reputation for bravery. . . . They were out for loot with the minimum of risk. To starve Tabriz and then to pillage it was the dazzling prospect which kept them in their camps.[70]

Calling upon the nomads to subdue a city, inviting the tribes to murder and loot townspeople, were actions every Tehrāni, Esfahāni, or Shirāzi could understand. The Shah had betrayed his trust; he now appeared in the eyes of millions of his subjects as a promoter of anarchy, a traitor to the sacred duty of ruler and protector of his people.

Tabriz was starving. Sattār Khān tried to break through the ring of the Shah's troops and the hordes of tribesmen, but his forces were inadequate. Only a handful of nationalists and the Caucasian revolutionaries were willing to fight to the death.[71] The Russian acting consul general, A. Miller, appealed to his government for Russian troops to "protect" the foreign colony and open the road to Tabriz so that food might be brought in.

70. Arthur Moore, *The Orient Express* (London, 1914), p. 4.
71. In late April Sattār Khān's forces were joined by Arthur Moore, a British newspaperman, and Howard C. Baskerville, an American schoolteacher (B.A. Princeton, 1907). Baskerville was killed in battle on April 21. Cf. Browne, *The Persian Revolution*, pp. 440–41.

The foreigners were not in any danger of violence, but the famine was a real threat to everyone. Barclay and Sablin decided to ask the Shah for a six-day truce during which the population could be supplied with food.[72]

Izvolskii instructed Sablin to tell the Shah in "a categorical form" that the actions of his troops endangered the peaceful population and foreign consulates in Tabriz. The Shah's "most serious attention" was to be called to the immediate need to order Eyn od-Dowleh to permit the entry into the city of food supplies.

> At the same time warn the Shah that if the commander of the Shah's troops does not immediately fulfil this demand, we would be forced at once to take decisive measures for the opening by armed force of a road for the transportation of food and for the defense of foreign subjects and institutions in Tabriz, while all the responsibility for the consequences would fall on His Majesty.[73]

Russia gave the Shah twenty-four hours to make up his mind, but the emphatic tone of Sablin's demarche compelled Mohammad Ali to give his consent that same day. He telegraphed Eyn od-Dowleh an order granting the truce and permitting a specified amount of food to be brought into Tabriz.[74] Before learning of the Shah's compliance, the Russian government instructed the Viceroy of the Caucasus to send "by forced march a detachment of sufficient strength for the protection of Russian and foreign institutions and subjects." [75] Before the troops had crossed the border, St. Petersburg received notice that its demands had been met. The Viceroy was told to keep the expeditionary force in readiness in case of need.[76]

72. Sablin to Izvolskii, Telegram, Tehran, April 7/20, 1909, S.D.D., 2, 132.
73. Izvolskii to Sablin, Telegram, St. Petersburg, April 7/20, 1909; ibid., p. 133.
74. Sablin to Izvolskii, Telegram, Tehran, April 7/20, 1909, ibid., p. 135.
75. Izvolskii to the Acting Consul General at Tabriz, Telegram, St. Petersburg, April 7/20, 1909; ibid., p. 135.
76. To H. M.'s Viceroy in the Caucasus, Telegram, St. Petersburg, April 8/21, 1909; ibid., p. 138.

In his camp outside Tabriz the proud, stiff-necked Soltān Majid Mirzā Eyn od-Dowleh, Governor of Āzarbāyjān, claimed that he had received no orders to lift the siege. Fighting continued in spite of joint representations made by the Russian and British consuls, A. Miller and A. C. Wratislaw. The former then requested that Russian troops be dispatched immediately to open the Jolfā-Tabriz road.[77] The troops were ordered to march on April 22,[78] and Izvolskii sent to his envoys in London, Berlin, Paris, Washington, Rome, Madrid, and elsewhere, a circular telegram explaining the motives of Russian armed intervention.[79]

Tabriz was in agony. People ate grass. Many died of starvation, "and in every street lay fearsome figures, all but naked, scarcely recognizable as human beings."[80] Another few days and the nationalists would have to surrender to Eyn od-Dowleh and open the gates to the wild tribesmen of the bandit Rahim Khān. The Shah begged Russia to stop her troops. Izvolskii said they would not be stopped now that they were on their way. However, he promised to keep them from entering Tabriz if by the time they reached its outskirts the Shah, faithful to his promise, established the truce and lifted the blockade.[81]

On the twenty-ninth of April one hundred and twenty Cossacks, sixty-five riflemen, and twenty-four machine gunners with two machine guns reached the Āji-Chāy bridge at Tabriz. Since the Shah had not lifted the blockade, Acting Consul Miller ordered the detachment to enter the city.[82] Wagons loaded with food rolled in behind Russian troops. The English correspondent, Arthur Moore, who had participated in the defense of Tabriz, acknowledged that the city had been saved by the coming of the Russians.

77. Miller's telegram of April 9/22, 1909; ibid., p. 141.
78. Telegram to the Viceroy in the Caucasus, St. Petersburg, April 9/22, 1909; ibid., p. 141.
79. Circular Telegram of the Minister of Foreign Affairs to Russia's Representatives in London, Berlin . . . , St. Petersburg, April 10/23, 1909; ibid., p. 144.
80. Moore, *The Orient Express*, p. 20.
81. Izvolskii to Miller, Telegram, April 14/27, 1909; *S.D.D.*, 2, 152.
82. Telegram from Miller, Tabriz, April 16/29, 1909; ibid., p. 153.

Their entry into the town was the direct cause of the opening of the roads, the dispersal of the disappointed armies of the Shah, the promulgation of the Constitution and the appointment of a Constitutionalist Ministry. It saved Tabriz from a surrender which could not otherwise have been delayed for three days longer, and thereby it averted the complete collapse of the Constitutional movement.[83]

Moore exaggerated the importance of the arrival of the Russians. Tabriz was relieved on April 29. About a week earlier nationalist detachments from Rasht had occupied Qazvin and continued on to Tehran. The anti-Shah Bakhtiāri tribesmen under Samsām os-Saltaneh and Sardār As'ad approached from the south. These were the forces that eventually overthrew Mohammad Ali, while the presence of Russian troops in Tabriz neutralized that city, taking its nationalists out of the revolutionary struggle. It is true, however, that the arrival of Russian troops saved Tabriz and its nationalist defenders. Though Russian troops behaved badly and rapidly antagonized the population, which had welcomed them with open arms, the Tabrizis were fortunate not to have been conquered by Rahim Khān's cutthroats.

Russia's intervention appeared paradoxical, since it was to the advantage of the nationalists and hurt Mohammad Ali. Published Russian documents do not fully explain her course of action. It would seem that the dispatch of troops was motivated by fear for the fate of the consulate staff and other Russian subjects in Tabriz. On April 17 the Tabriz *anjoman* (political society or council), which was the de facto revolutionary government of the city, met with consuls Miller and Wratislaw, who were told that the supply of grain

> was all but exhausted; the great majority of the population of over two hundred thousand souls was starving; and they feared that it would not be possible to hold them in check much longer. They might break out at any moment into

83. Moore, pp. 20–21.

rioting and pillaging the richer houses, in which they hoped to find food.[84]

On the eighteenth and nineteenth hungry crowds roamed the streets, and there was talk of attacking foreigners. "The Russian subjects, conscious of their unpopularity, were in a state of panic, and crowded into their Consulate and the houses round it." The consulate was guarded by thirty Cossacks with two machine guns and could have withstood a mob attack, but Miller may have recalled the fate of Griboedov and decided not to take the risk. Once the two consuls stepped in, Russian troops broke the blockade in a few days.[85]

The arrival of Russian troops in Tabriz put an end to the fighting there. Royalist bands, bitterly disappointed that they would not have the pleasure of sacking and looting the city, dispersed. Elsewhere in the country revolutionary activity rose ever higher.

Mohammad Ali Shah had failed to consolidate his position after the coup d'état. His greatest single problem was financial. Already in 1906 the Persian government had opened negotiations for another foreign loan, but the revolution intervened. The Majles consistently refused to borrow abroad. In October 1908 the British chargé d'affaires reported from Tehran: "The Treasury is empty. . . . the taxes are being paid with the greatest irregularity." [86] By February 1908 the Majles realized the necessity of borrowing, but Russia preferred to advance money to the Shah rather than to the government now that the distinction between state funds and the Shah's privy purse was real. On October 7, 1907, the counselor of the Russian embassy in London, Poklewski-Koziell, suggested to Sir Charles Hardinge that Britain and Russia give the Shah a personal loan,[87] but Britain "refused to be party to any loan not made publicly and not

84. A. C. Wratislaw, *A Consul in the East* (Edinburgh, 1924), p. 253.
85. Ibid., pp. 254–55.
86. Marling, No. 230, October 10, 1907, as cited in Memorandum respecting Question of Joint Anglo-Russian Advance to the Persian Government (August 1907 to February 1910); F. O. 371/947.
87. Poklewski to C. Hardinge, October 7, 1907; ibid.

recognized by the Persian Government." [88] Hardinge believed that a loan granted directly to the Shah without the Majles' endorsement "might easily lead to his deposition or assassination." [89]

In April 1908 the newly appointed French financial advisor, Monsieur Bizot, testified that Persia had reached the end of her resources.[90] "Such was the position when the *coup d'état* of the 23-d June converted a penniless constitutional Government into a bankrupt despotism." [91] Two weeks after the coup the Shah was asking for a loan. The British replied that

> "so long as the Constitution is suspended" they could not lend money to Persia on the double ground that, in the event of the revival of the Constitution, the Assembly might repudiate such a loan, and that under the personal government of the Shah no confidence could be felt that the money lent would be employed for the good of the country.[92]

The Russians pressed the British to give the Shah money, but from Tehran Marling recommended that "far from giving assistance to the Shah, his position should be made as difficult as possible—that every source of revenue should be cut off, and that His Majesty's Government should press for the overdue interest on the 1903-4 loan." [93] The Russians warned that the Shah would fall if not helped. "Mr. Marling was rather of opinion that his deposition would 'not be a bad solution' of the problem." [94] In St. Petersburg Hartwig exploited Nicolson's exaggerated fear of Germany, telling him that, if driven to despair, the Shah would borrow in Germany, allowing her to enter the Persian situation.[95]

The British government informed Marling that it was willing to advance money to the Shah jointly with Russia, but on certain conditions: "The loan shall not be employed for the suppression

88. C. Hardinge to Poklewski, October 15, 1907; ibid.
89. C. Hardinge to A. Nicolson, No. 397, November 19, 1907; ibid.
90. Marling, No. 103, April 30, 1908; ibid.
91. Id.
92. Telegram to Marling, No. 166, July 8, 1908; ibid.
93. Marling, No. 253, September 10, 1908; ibid.
94. Marling, November 18, 1908; ibid.
95. Nicolson, No. 604, December 22, 1908; ibid.

The Uneasy Alliance 539

of the Constitution, but advanced in such a manner as will allow of its being used as a lever for supporting it." [96] Nicolson was told that one of the conditions of the loan would be the restoration of the Constitution.[97] The Russians did not like the British conditions. Hartwig and Izvolskii, as well as the new Persian minister at St. Petersburg, Eshāq Khān, and the Shah's special envoy, Alā ol-Molk, urged Nicolson that funds be advanced immediately on the promise of steps being taken later toward the restoration of the Constitution.[98]

Fruitless negotiations continued through the winter and spring of 1909. Though he received no cash, Mohammad Ali was given much advice. On April 8 Izvolskii and Nicolson reached an agreement that the Russian and British governments would jointly advise the Shah, (1) to remove immediately his ultrareactionary Prime Minister, Moshir os-Saltaneh, and his equally reactionary friend, Amir Bahādor Jang; (2) to restore the Constitution; (3) to appoint a cabinet composed of worthy persons selected from a list of candidates privately supplied by the two legations ("obviously, should the Shah's choice fall upon persons who do not inspire the necessary confidence," Izvolskii wrote to Nicolson, "Persia will not be granted an advance of any kind"); (4) to grant an amnesty to his opponents; (5) to fix a date for the election and the convocation of the Majles. As soon as the Shah accepted all five conditions, Russia might give him a loan of 2,500,000 francs. Britain would advance the same amount upon the approval of the new Majles.[99]

The terms agreed upon by the two powers were presented to the Shah, who was reminded that he had repeatedly broken his promises and listened to bad advice. He could have been reconciled with his people and bettered his country. Instead disorder reigned throughout the land. Now the two powers declared that if

96. To Mr. Marling, Telegram, No. 244, September 5, 1908; ibid.
97. To Nicolson, Telegram, No. 672, December 23, 1908; ibid.
98. Telegrams from Nicolson, Nos. 604, 605, 613 of December 1908; ibid.
99. Memorandum transmitted to the Embassy of Great Britain in St. Petersburg, March 26/April 8, 1909; S.D.D., 2, 115–17. Cf. A. Nicolson, No. 232, April 8, 1909, cited in Memorandum respecting Question of Joint Anglo-Russian Advance . . . ; F. O. 371/947.

His Majesty did not accept in all its details the program recommended by them, they would refrain from giving further advice, and His Majesty would "not be in a position to count upon any support from them or their agents." [100] The Shah had no choice but to obey. Russian troops had crossed the border in Āzarbāyjān. Nationalist bands were marching toward the capital from the north, while Bakhtiāri tribesmen approached from the south. He only pleaded that in case of serious disorders "during which he personally, his family, and the Qājār throne could suffer," the two powers guarantee his safety. Barclay and Sablin replied "that the very best written guarantee to the Shah will be the Memorandum which we transmitted . . . on April 9." [101]

For several days Mohammad Ali Shah evaded the issue. He dismissed from the government Moshir os-Saltaneh and appointed his own uncle, Kāmrān Mirzā Nāyeb os-Saltaneh, in his place. But he also dismissed Russia's favorite, Sa'd od-Dowleh, and refused to appoint the English protégé, Nāser ol-Molk. The two legations, working in unusually close accord, protested against the appointment of Nāyeb os-Saltaneh.[102] From St. Petersburg the Acting Minister of Foreign Affairs, N. V. Charykov, insisted on the reinstatement of Sa'd od-Dowleh and the appointment of Nāser ol-Molk.[103]

On May 4 the Shah capitulated. On the fifth he published a rescript fixing the date of elections to the Majles.[104] On the tenth another decree completely restored the Constitution. "Anglo-Russian representations took effect," Sablin telegraphed. "The Cabinet suggested by the Legations with Nasr [sic] ol-Molk at its head and Sa'd od-Dowleh as Minister of Foreign Affairs is making a serious impression." [105] The new Minister of Foreign

---

100. Enclosure in Sablin, Tehran, April 11/24, 1909; S.D.D., 2, 160–65.
101. Sablin, Telegram, Tehran, April 11/24, 1909; ibid., p. 146.
102. Sablin, Telegram, April 18/May 1, 1909; ibid., pp. 154–55.
103. Acting Minister of Foreign Affairs to the Chargé d'Affaires in Tehran, Telegram, St. Petersburg, April 20/May 3, 1909; ibid., p. 156.
104. Sablin, Tehran, April 22/May 5, 1909; ibid., p. 158.
105. Sablin, Telegram, Tehran, April 27/May 10, 1909; ibid., p. 164. Foreigners, including scholars, often fail to perceive the distinction between Nasr, Nāser, and Nasir.

Affairs addressed a letter to the two legations reminding them that on December 22, 1908, they had given the Shah verbal guarantees. "Since there is no document about this and since His Majesty does not remember the content of those guarantees," Sa'd od-Dowleh wrote, "I have the honor most humbly to request of you to communicate to me their written text signed by you." [106]

The British were not anxious to make written commitments, but a letter to Sa'd od-Dowleh was drafted and signed by Barclay and Sablin. The guarantee was given with certain qualifications.

> To the extent to which Your Majesty shall sincerely perform the duties of a constitutional Monarch, You will have the support and the good will of England and Russia, and both States shall, in case of need and of your request in this connection, give protection to your Person. However, both representatives are convinced that the best guarantee against the danger which Your Majesty anticipates, would be the restoration of the constitutional regime and sincere cooperation in its regular functioning.[107]

Written guarantees were not enough. At the end of May, Russia advanced Mohammad Ali Shah 2,500,000 francs at 6 percent.[108] But money was not enough either. The Rasht nationalists led by Yefrem Khān, a Turkish Armenian with considerable revolutionary experience, captured Qazvin. The figurehead leader of the Rasht contingent, Mohammad Vali Khān Sepahdār, was no constitutionalist. Until the spring of 1909 he had been a faithful servant of Mohammad Ali. He had even participated in the unsuccessful siege of Tabriz; but a personal quarrel with the insufferable Eyn od-Dowleh drove him home to his vast estates in Gilān. There he was intimidated by the nationalists into joining their cause. In Qazvin the Russian consul, Ovseenko, tried but failed to persuade Sepahdār to abandon the march on

---

106. Sa'd od-Dowleh's letter of May 10, 1909, Enclosure in Sabin, Tehran, May 2/15, 1909; ibid., p. 179.

107. Barclay and Sablin to Sa'd od-Dowleh, May 10, 1909; Enclosure in Sablin, Tehran, May 2/15, 1909; ibid., pp. 179–80.

108. Sablin, Telegrams Nos. 1 and 2, Tehran, May 17/30, 1909; ibid., pp. 202–03.

Tehran.[109] Indeed, Sepahdār could not have stopped the advance of the columns whose nominal commander he was. The Caucasian revolutionaries, whether Social-Democrats or Dashnaks, would have shot him without hesitation had he attempted to play false. On June 29 the mojahedin ("holy warriors"—the name given to members of revolutionary fighting units) began to advance on Yenge-Emām on the Qazvin-Tehran road. Simultaneously armed bodies of Bakhtiāri cavalry were making their way toward the capital from the south.

Messrs. Churchill and Romanovskii, representing the two legations, warned both the fadāiyān ("those who sacrifice themselves"—another name given to the revolutionary fighting men) and the Bakhtiāri leaders that "The only means of avoiding foreign intervention" was the immediate restoration of order. Armed demonstrations were unjustifiable mutinies, which served only to complicate an already critical situation.

> Neither Russia nor England threaten the independence of Persia by the advice they give, being guided only by a feeling of friendship for their neighbour. The Shah has really restored the Constitution and confirmed extremely liberal electoral laws. The Government, which could under no circumstances be reproached with nursing reactionary schemes, is approaching reform on the firm basis of law. Those to whom Persia is dear must patiently and quietly wait for the convocation of the Majles.[110]

The Shah was desperate. Barclay and Sablin had repeatedly assured him that the restoration of the Constitution would end sedition and heal the country.

> "I did everything you told me [Mohammad Ali complained]. You see the results. The country is in complete anarchy, and I am openly threatened. Now I call upon your friendship."

---

109. Survey of events in Tehran from June 12/25 to June 19/July 2, 1909, Enclosure in Sablin, Zargandeh, June 19/July 2, 1909; ibid., pp. 242–43.

110. Sablin, Telegram, Tehran, July 4, 1909; ibid., p. 232. Churchill and Romanovskii talked to Sardār As'ad, the Bakhtiāri leader, in this sense on July 5. Sardār As'ad made only a few remarks and, when saying good-bye, added "do svidaniia v Tegerane" ("until we meet in Tehran").

The Uneasy Alliance 543

We [Barclay and Sablin] replied to His Majesty thus: "For ten months we kept persuading Your Majesty to give the Constitution back to the country. For eight months you did not heed our advice. Meanwhile your adversaries . . . grew stronger and armed themselves. Both Legations have done everything possible to prevent the crisis.[111]

Their audience with the Shah depressed both Barclay and Sablin.[112] The latter must have felt especially uncomfortable since his legation had been primarily responsible for exacerbating the relations between the Shah and the Majles. Sablin certainly knew what sort of advice Hartwig had been giving before his departure. At this late date the best Izvolskii could do for Russia's trusted friend, Mohammad Ali, was to instruct Benckendorff to raise with Sir Edward Grey the question of giving the Shah sanctuary in one of the legations.[113]

Russia was not opposed to intervention. Tabriz was already held by her troops. A special ministerial conference decided on July 3 that the entrance of the fadāiyān and the Bakhtiāris in Tehran might endanger Russian residents and institutions. The Russian government felt a moral responsibility to protect them.

> With this in view the Conference has resolved to send at once a detachment composed of one Cossack regiment, one infantry battalion, and one battery, from Baku to Anzali. This detachment shall be moved no further than Qazvin, ensuring communications between that point and the Caspian Sea. Further movements of units of this detachment shall depend upon the course of events and shall take place only upon the demand of the Imperial Legation in Tehran.[114]

Within a few days Russian troops began to arrive in Qazvin.[115] The Gilān nationalists and the Bakhtiāris joined forces near

111. Sablin, Telegram, Tehran June 19/July 2, 1909; ibid., p. 224.
112. Id.
113. Izvolskii to Benckendorff, Telegram, St. Petersburg, June 20/July 3, 1909; ibid., p. 228.
114. Same to same, St. Petersburg, June 20/July 3, 1909; ibid., pp. 227–28.
115. Izvolskii to Sablin, Telegram, June 23/July 8, 1909; ibid., p. 234.

Tehran. After some indecisive fighting, they outmaneuvered royalist troops and entered the capital on Tuesday, July 13. The Shah sought refuge at the summer residence of the Russian legation a few miles north of the city. The episode was described in a dispatch of the Russian chargé d'affaires, Sablin:

> The Shah's suite arrived in Zargandeh at 8 o'clock in the morning. The Shah with his children arrived a half hour later. I am not eloquent enough to describe the solemn sadness of the moment when the Shah, pale and thin, entered the Legation garden on horseback. I and the members of the Legation greeted His Majesty, the Cossacks of the convoy presented arms. The Shah said to the guard in Russian "Zdorovo." With visible excitement the Shah shook my hand and entered the Minister's house.[116]

The Cossack squadron guarding the Shah was soon joined by the Sepoys from the British legation. Russian and British flags were raised. During the night, while "A cossack and a sepoy guarded His Majesty's rest," his treasures were transported from Tehran to Zargandeh to the safety of the Russian legation. With the jewels and the money came the Shah's servants, retainers, and some five hundred faithful troops.[117]

On the sixteenth Mohammad Ali was formally deposed and his twelve-year-old son, Ahmad Mirzā, proclaimed Shah. On the eighteenth the fat little boy left the sanctuary of the Russian legation and drove to Tehran escorted by Cossacks and Sepoys, to take the oath to uphold the Constitution.[118]

Now that they were victorious, the Constitutionalists began to

---

116. Sablin, Telegram, Tehran, July 3/16; ibid., p. 255.
117. Id.
118. Survey of events in Tehran from 3/16 to the 10/23 of July, 1909, Enclosure in Sablin, Zargandeh, July 11/24, 1909; S.D.D., 3, 2. The Soviet writer, Il'inskii, stressed Mohammad Ali's closeness to the Russians. "The slavish admirer of Russian tsarism, Mohammad Ali was a faithful servant of the Russian government." He was heavily subsidized by Russia. "However, Mohammad Ali stopped at nothing to obtain money: during his governorship over Iranian Āzarbāyjān he secretly directed bands of highwaymen who shared with him their loot." (Rostovskii et al., *Novaia istoriia kolonialnykh i zavisimykh stran*, 1, Chap. 24, 541).

settle old scores. Large-scale arrests of Mohammad Ali's supporters, among them the reactionary mojtaheds Sheykh Fazlollāh, Ali Akbar Borujerdi, and Ākhund Āmoli, were carried out on July 30. Several of the former Shah's military aides and the chief of police, Sardār Afkham, were also jailed. The next day, before a jubilant crowd that included his own son, Sheykh Fazlollāh was hanged. The former artillery commander who had participated in the bombardment of the Majles, Ājudān Bāshi Esmāil Khān, was hanged on August 1.[119] The Russian chargé d'affaires, Sablin, asked the new Persian government not to indulge in vengeance, but the Persians paid no attention. Sablin complained to the Acting Minister of Foreign Affairs, S. D. Sazonov, who instructed the Russian ambassador in London to tell Grey that since the Persians had no desire to accept the advice of the two powers "we shall probably have to resort to threats in order to prevent manifestations of political vengeance." [120]

Far more important to the Russian legation than the lives of a few reactionaries was the fate of the Cossack Brigade and its officers. On the very day of Mohammad Ali's overthrow, the legation's dragoman, Baranovskii, met with Sepahdār, Sardār As'ad, and Yefrem Khān, leaders of the provisional government, and demanded that the Brigade be left under its Russian colonel. Furthermore, Baranovskii insisted that all Cossack officers and enlisted men who had defended the Shah be granted complete amnesty. He obtained a written promise that

> provisionally the Persian Cossack Brigade will remain as before under the command of the Colonel [Liakhov] on condition of his complete subordination to the responsible Minister of War who will be appointed today, and that he execute all orders which would be given to him by this Minister.[121]

---

119. Survey of events in Tehran from July 17/30 to July 24/August 6, 1909, Enclosure in Sablin's dispatch, Zargandeh, July 25/August 7, 1909, S.D.D., 3, 26.

120. Sablin to the Acting Minister of Foreign Affairs [Sazonov], Tehran, August 12/25, 1909. Sazonov to the Ambassador in London [Benckendorff], St. Petersburg, August 12/25, 1909; ibid., pp. 56–57.

121. The Engagement of Sepahdār and Sardar As'ad in regard to His Majesty the Shah's Cossack Brigade, Tehran, 27th of Jamādi os-Sāni 1327 (July 16, 1909), Report of the First Dragoman of the Legation, Baranovskii, to the Imperial

The survival of the Cossack Brigade having been assured, the Russian legation undertook the task of securing the position of its agents at Court. The Constitutionalists were anxious to remove the boy-shah from the exclusive influence of his Russian tutor, Captain Smirnov, and his physician, Sadovskii. The former was refused admission to the Shah. "There is no doubt," Sablin telegraphed home, "that the government spheres do not wish to see Staff Captain Smirnov in the Palace any longer. However, I supposed that we should insist that Mr. Smirnov be kept as the tutor of the Shah." [122] When the English doctor, Lindley, was officially appointed first physician to Ahmad Shah, both Sablin and Barclay tried to restrain the Persian government from flouting Russia's wishes. Sablin repeatedly pointed out how patient Russia had been. He had had so many pretexts to call Russian troops to Tehran, but had not done so "out of respect for the national movement" and in the hope "that the new people would understand and appreciate Russia's policy." Sablin was disappointed: "They . . . have not understood, have not appreciated it." Useless governors had been appointed to provinces contiguous with Russia; Smirnov and Sadovskii had not been confirmed in their positions; the Russian bank had received no cooperation in suing its Persian debtors; the right of *bast* had not been respected. Sablin asked his government to instruct him as to what strong means he could use to influence the Persians so that "they would, once and for all, understand that our nonintervention is not synonymous with connivance." [123]

The new Russian minister, Stanislaw Poklewski-Koziell, arrived in Tehran on September 21. Liberal in his inclinations and friendly to the British, Poklewski intended to pursue a conciliatory policy. The Smirnov-Sadovskii case was one of the first he had to deal with, and he brought to it a reasonableness and tolerance seldom displayed by his predecessors. He would be satisfied if Captain Smirnov relinquished his position as exclusive

---

Chargé d'Affaires in Persia, Enclosures in Sablin's dispatch, Zargandeh, July 11/24, 1909; ibid., pp. 4–5, 7.

122. Sablin's telegram, Tehran, August 17/30, 1909; ibid., p. 76.
123. Sablin's telegram, Tehran, August 18/31, 1909; ibid., pp. 77–78.

The Uneasy Alliance

tutor to the Shah and remained as instructor of military science.[124] Izvolskii had other views. He saw in Persia's attempt to remove Captain Smirnov and Dr. Sadovskii an unfriendly act. Poklewski was to make this clear to the Persians and to demand the restoration of the status quo.[125] Poklewski immediately changed his tone, and the Persians gave in at once, stating that they "would never dare to take such a hostile step as the firing of Messrs. Smirnov and Sadovskii." [126] However, Smirnov's monopoly was broken. He remained at Court as one of several tutors of the young Shah. Izvolskii changed his mind and accepted the solution. He claimed to understand "that with the change of the entire political regime in Persia one cannot expect the education of the Shah to be entrusted to a foreign officer." [127]

Another issue between Persia and the Russian and British legations concerned the status and finances of the former Shah. Mohammad Ali and his friends were hated by a great number of people. Even the Tsar's diplomats conceded that the reactionaries who had found refuge in the Russian legation compound at Zargandeh were "the representatives of the camarilla which had brought the country to utter ruin and which had for centuries oppressed all of Persia." [128] Clearly Mohammad Ali and his entourage would have to leave Persia and find refuge in Russia. Therefore it was in the interests of the Russian government to obtain for the former Shah a financial settlement that would take care of his expenses and would prevent his becoming a burden on the Russian treasury.

The negotiations were conducted in behalf of Mohammad Ali

---

124. Poklewski-Koziell's telegram, Tehran, September 17/30, 1909; ibid., p. 137.

125. Telegram of the Minister of Foreign Affairs [Izvolskii] to the Minister in Tehran [Poklewski-Koziell], St. Petersburg, September 18/October 1, 1909; ibid., p. 138.

126. Poklewski's telegram, Tehran, September 20/October 3, 1909; ibid., p. 144.

127. Telegram of the Minister of Foreign Affairs [to Poklewski], Yalta, September 24/October 7, 1909; ibid., p. 150.

128. The *bast* of Mohammad Ali Mirzā in the Imperial Legation in Tehran from July 3/16 to August 27/September 9, 1909, Enclosure in Sablin's dispatch, Zargandeh, September 5/18, 1909; ibid., p. 119.

by Sablin. Under his pressure a protocol was signed on September 7, specifying among other things that Mohammad Ali would return to the State any Crown treasures he may have taken with him (or, to put it bluntly, stolen). The Persian government would assume the Shah's debts (1,413,434.00 tumāns to the Russian bank alone). The government would take over the Shah's estates but would pay him and his family 100,000 tumāns per annum, starting from the day he left the country. Britain, which associated herself with the agreement, and Russia promised to make representations to the former Shah to abstain from political activity abroad. Moreover, the Russian government promised

> to take all effective measures not to allow such agitation on his part. If His Majesty Mohammad Ali Mirzā should leave Russia, and if it should be proved to the satisfaction of both Legations that he conducted political agitation against Persia from a country other than Russia, the Persian Government would have the right to stop the payment of his pension.[129]

The protocol stated that Mohammad Ali would leave Persia forty-eight hours after its signing. At four o'clock in the afternoon on September 9 the former Shah, accompanied in behalf of the Russian legation by Vice-Consul Nekrasov and in behalf of the British legation by Vice-Consul Cowan (the Russian document gives his name as *Kovan*) departed from Tehran.[130] The Persian government proceeded to count the Crown jewels and other treasures the Russian legation turned over to it on the Shah's departure and discovered that many items were missing. A special committee showed that the Shah had given some Crown jewels to his uncle, Kāmrān Mirzā Nāyeb os-Saltaneh, to sell to European dealers. Kāmrān Mirzā had stolen them. Other valuables had been disposed of by the Shah through his favorite, Mojallal os-Saltaneh. The Government wanted to sue Kāmrān Mirzā for 1,000,000 tumāns, but the chances of recovery were small. The first dragoman of the Russian legation felt that "the missing

129. Article 11 of the Protocol of September 7, 1909, Enclosure in Sablin's dispatch, Zargandeh, September 5/18, 1909; ibid., pp. 123–26.
130. Sablin's telegram, Tehran, August 27/September 9, 1909; ibid., pp. 92–93.

The Uneasy Alliance

treasures must apparently be considered forever lost to the Shah's treasury."[131]

The financial plight of the new Persian government was such that it could hardly pay its day-to-day expenses. The additional burdens of supporting the former Shah and paying the nationalist forces now in Tehran exhausted its already meager reserves. When Mohammad Ali had applied for a joint Anglo-Russian loan in the spring of 1909, Russia, wishing to strengthen his position, had approved the draft agreement, but the Shah fell before the advance had been made.[132] Almost immediately upon assuming power, the new government asked the Imperial Bank of Persia for £100,000. The English were agreeable but did not want to antagonize the Russians, who had every reason to feel that the Persian government harbored anti-Russian sentiments.[133] In September the Persians applied to the two powers for an advance of 400,000 tumāns. Again Britain was willing, but Russia made demands for economic concessions with strong political implications. Persia would have to permit her to introduce motor vehicles on the Tehran-Rasht road, to grant a concession for mining copper in the Qarajadāgh, and to permit Russian subjects to organize shipping on Lake Urumiyyeh. The Persians let the negotiations die.[134]

On December 13 the Persian government once again asked Britain and Russia for money to help restore order in the country.[135] Eventually a large loan would be needed, but for the moment £500,000 would suffice. On December 26 Nicolson wrote Izvolskii that Britain was not disposed to make a large loan, but that "the most urgent question was to provide the Persian government with sufficient funds to enable them to introduce

131. *Bast* of Mohammad Ali . . . , Enclosure in Sablin's dispatch, Zargandeh, September 5/18, 1909; ibid., pp. 114–15.

132. Sir G. Barclay, No. 431, Telegram, June 1, 1909, cited in Memorandum respecting Question of Joint Anglo-Russian Advance to the Persian Government (August 1907 to February 1910); F. O. 371/947.

133. Memorandum respecting Question of Joint Anglo-Russian Advance . . . ; ibid.

134. Id.

135. Barclay to Grey, No. 221, Confidential, Tehran, December 27, 1909; F. O. 371/950.

some order into the administration and to re-establish their authority." [136] Izvolskii replied that an advance of £400,000 which Nicolson had suggested would accomplish nothing. The money would be spent paying off the bureaucrats and the military. Russia would rather tie the advance to a larger loan to be jointly issued by the two powers on certain conditions.[137] In a telegram to Benckendorff, Izvolskii explained that he opposed giving Persia a small advance because desirable conditions could not be attached to it.[138]

Sir Edward Grey had asked Izvolskii to instruct Poklewski-Koziell to work out mutually agreeable conditions with Barclay. Izvolskii informed his minister that Russia wanted a control commission to be set up in Tehran. It would include the directors of the British and Russian banks and would (1) control the expenditure of government funds, (2) supervise the budget, and (3) cooperate with the Persian Ministry of Finance in a revision of tax laws.[139] In addition previous Russian demands must be satisfied and the advance must be made part of a larger loan.

After a month of negotiations Barclay and Poklewski presented their joint proposals to the Persian government. These embodied the original Russian position without any serious modifications. Barclay had retreated before Poklewski on every point.

The Persian government was told that its request for an advance would be granted on following conditions:

1. The Persian government would prepare a program of expenditures for the approval of the two legations. Disbursements would be made under the control of a commission made up of the government's financial adviser and the chief administrator of customs (or their deputies), two members of the Majles, and two Persian officers, the Minister of Foreign Affairs presiding.

---

136. Nicolson to Izvolskii, St. Petersburg, December 13/26, 1909, Enclosure 1 in Nicolson to Grey, No. 676, Confidential, St. Petersburg, December 27, 1909; F. O. 371/947.

137. Aide-Memoir communicated to Sir A. Nicolson by M. Izvolsky, Enclosure No. 1 in Nicolson to Grey, No. 11, Confidential, St. Petersburg, January 6, 1910; ibid.

138. Minister of Foreign Affairs to the Ambassador in London, St. Petersburg, January 9/22, 1909; S.D.D., 4, 10–11.

139. Minister of Foreign Affairs to the Minister in Tehran, Telegram, January 3/16, 1910; ibid., p. 6.

2. The Persian government must hire seven French financial experts. No money would be paid to Persia until her government officially requested the French for such experts.

3. Persia must establish a military force sufficient to provide security of commercial communication. The government would invite foreign instructors but only with the prior approval of Britain and Russia.

4. Persia undertakes not to give any concession for the building of railways in Persia without first offering an option to the Imperial Russian Government and the Royal British Government. This right of option shall not apply in cases of concessions being granted to Persian subjects for the construction and exploitation of railway lines exclusively with Persian capital if it is proved to and accepted by the Russian and British Governments that such capitals are really of native origin.

5. The Society of the Jolfā-Tabriz Road shall get a concession for the navigation of lake Urumiyyeh.

6. The advance would constitute the first payment of a larger loan, if Russia and Britain should agree to grant one. Otherwise the advance would be repayable in ten annual installments. The interest would be 7 percent per annum and the customs revenues would serve as guarantee of repayment.[140]

The Persian government could not accept such onerous conditions. Poklewski reported that the proposed terms

> made a crushing impression on the Persian Government. The terms indicated by the powers seem to a majority of ministers quite heavy. The Government has not dared to submit the joint note to the deliberations of the Majles but rather carefully hides from the public the demands of Russia and England.

The press commented that until then no Prime Minister had ever dared "to foist upon Persia such heavy and humiliating condi-

---

140. Translation of a joint note communicated to the Acting Minister of Foreign Affairs of the Shah, Saqat ol-Molk, by the Imperial and the British Ministers on February 3/16, 1910, Enclosure in Poklewski-Koziell's dispatch, Tehran, February 6/19, 1910; 4, ibid., pp. 50–52.

tions, which would deprive Persia of her independence." The newspaper *Irāne Now*, one of whose editors was the Caucasian revolutionary, the future leader of the Musavat Party and of the independent republic of Azerbaijan (1918–20), Mohammad Amin Rasulzādeh, protested against the loan and advised the sale of Crown jewels to raise funds. Another newspaper, the *Majles* (No. 77), said that Russian troops remained in Persia in order to force the government to accept the terms proposed by the powers.[141]

Persia made several attempts to secure money from private sources, bypassing the British and Russian governments. In December 1909 Barclay learned of the arrival in Tehran of a Mr. Joseph Woolf and a Mr. Osborn. "They gave out that they had come for sport but had had the misfortune to lose their rifles in Russia . . . it was some days before my suspicions were aroused," the minister telegraphed London.[142] Soon he discovered that Woolf was discussing financial matters and had suggested a loan secured by Persian shares of the Anglo-Persian Oil Company.[143]

While the Persian government tried to keep things secret, Woolf contacted the London firm of Samuel & Co., which had sufficiently large sums at its disposal to finance the loan. Samuel and his partner, Walter Levy, who had interests in many Asiatic countries, wanted to obtain the support of the British government. In February they informed the Foreign Office of their plans and were promised that this information would not be repeated to the Russians.[144] The diplomats betrayed the money lenders. No sooner had Grey learned of the scheme than he instructed Nicolson to reveal it to Izvolskii and to suggest that both governments stop Persia from securing the loan.[145] In Tehran Barclay had already warned the Persians against dealing with Woolf and his associates.

141. Survey of events in Tehran from February 5/18 to 12/25, 1910; Enclosure in Poklewski's dispatch, Tehran, February 12/25, 1910; ibid., pp. 60–62.

142. Barclay to Grey, No. 36, Very Confidential, Tehran, March 15, 1910; F. O. 371/954.

143. Memorandum by Mr. Churchill, Enclosure in ibid.

144. Mr. J. Woolf to Sir C. Hardinge, International Oriental Syndicate, Ltd., London, April 8, 1910; ibid

145. Grey to Nicolson, No. 118, Telegram, March 18, 1910; ibid.

The Uneasy Alliance

His Majesty's Government [he wrote] cannot agree to the hypothecation by the Persian Government of any sources of its public revenue to any advance except that now under negotiation between the British and the Russian Governments on the one side and the Persian Government on the other.[146]

The Persians protested that negotiations with the two powers "cannot do away with the full power of the Government over its uncharged resources," [147] and the two powers agreed to recognize Persia's right to borrow from third parties provided the customs revenues pledged to Russian or British loans were not pledged to new loans, and provided that Persia entered into an agreement for the regularization of payments to Britain and Russia on her old debts.[148]

Messrs. Samuel and Co. were duly notified by the Foreign Office that Britain and Russia had instructed their ministers in Tehran to oppose private loans.[149] Woolf was furious. The Foreign Office had not only broken its promise and informed the Russians, it had directly opposed the entrepreneurs in Tehran. In a letter to Sir Charles Hardinge, Woolf declared that two separate financial groups were prepared "to carry through with my syndicate the reorganization of Persian finances." Defying the Foreign Office, he added: "Whatever the view of the Foreign Office on this matter as a result of the Anglo-Russian Convention may be, I am compelled to point out that the consolidation of the Persian debt will be undertaken at once." [150]

146. Barclay to the Persian Government, March 15, 1910, Enclosure No. 1 in Barclay to Grey, No. 43, Tehran, March 24, 1910; ibid. Poklewski issued an almost identical warning on the same date. He repeated Barclay's arguments, adding that under the agreements of 1900 and 1902 the Persian government had no right to borrow abroad without the prior consent of the Russian government. Cf. Translation of the Note of the Russian Minister in Tehran to the Acting Minister [Director] of Foreign Affairs of March 2/15, 1910 (3 Rabi ol-Avval 1328), Enclosure in Poklewski's dispatch, Tehran, March 5/18, 1910; S.D.D., 4, 97–98.

147. Persian Government to Sir G. Barclay, Enclosure 2 in Barclay to Grey, No. 43, F. O. 371/954.

148. Joint Note Communicated to the Persian Government, Tehran, March 25/April 7, 1910, Enclosure No. 1 in Barclay to Grey, No. 50, Tehran, April 8, 1910; ibid.

149. Louis Mallet to Messrs. Samuel and Co., F.O., March 12, 1910; ibid.

150. See note 144 on p. 552.

Russian diplomats were quick to take advantage of the opening made by Grey. Count Benckendorff proposed that the two powers press the Persian government to promise not to grant any concessions to foreigners without the approval of Russia and Britain. The projected note to Persia would contain a threat: "If the Persian Government do not act in conformity with this desire of the two Powers, the latter will not fail to take such measures as they might find it necessary to defend their interests." [151] Grey hesitated. How would one justify such an action to other powers and to the Parliament? He felt that it was enough to impose limitations on Persia's freedom in regard to her means of communications, telegraphs and ports. The last sentence of the proposed note sounded like an ultimatum to him and should be softened, he felt.[152]

Nicolson presented Grey's view to Izvolskii, who produced a modified version of the original draft. The softened redaction read:

> before granting any concessions for means of communication telegraphs and ports [no punctuation marks in the original] to a foreign subject, the Persian Government will enter into an exchange of views with them [Britain and Russia] in order that measures may be devised whereby the political or strategic interests of the two Powers may be duly safeguarded. Any act in contravention of this principle would be regarded as contrary to the traditional friendship so happily existing between Britain and Persia.[153]

The note was delivered to the Persians by Poklewski and Marling. The Foreign Minister, Hoseyn Qoli Khān Navvāb, replied that Persia would never agree to any concession not consonant with her friendship with the two powers. Yet, he added, "The Persian Government is obliged to protect its independence

---

151. Cited in Grey to Nicolson, No. 233, Telegram, May 15, 1910; F. O. 371/954.

152. Id.

153. Aide-memoire: Proposed Amended version for communication to the Persian Government, Enclosure No. 1 in Nicolson to Grey, No. 233, St. Petersburg, May 17, 1910; ibid.

The Uneasy Alliance

and the undoubted rights of freedom possessed by this country." [154] Even this mild assertion of independence was not allowed to pass unchallenged. Both legations returned the note to the Foreign Minister on the next day.[155] Before the summer was over Woolf and his associates withdrew from the field.

Other capitalists appeared on the scene even before Woolf's scheme had fallen through. In May the London firm of Seligman Brothers wrote to the Foreign Office that their group was prepared to negotiate with Persia for a loan. C. D. Seligman wanted the Foreign Office to allow him to mention in the prospectus that the loan was approved by the Government.[156] Louis Mallet replied for the Foreign Office that if the terms of Seligman's contract were satisfactory to His Majesty's Government, Sir Edward Grey would "consider favourably" the request for the mention of government approval. "He [Grey] could not, however, give his approval to any contract which was not agreeable to the Russian Government" Mallet concluded.[157]

Grey would not approve of anything or anyone objectionable to Russia. He made it clear to Count Benckendorff that Britain was not encouraging the loan and that Seligman was working independently of the Foreign Office.[158] The Russian government confessed that it would be "disturbed" by a large loan from British sources.[159]

On October 10, 1910, the Persian government formally applied to Seligman Brothers for a loan of £1,200,000. This would be enough to pay off old debts and free Persia from the tight noose of Russian and British financial control. C. D. Seligman notified

154. Hussein Kuli Khan to Sir G. Barclay (Translation), September 3, 1910 (28 Shaaban 1328), Enclosure No. 1 in Barclay to Grey, No. 169, Gulahek, September 6, 1910; ibid.

155. Joint Note communicated to Hussein Kuli Khan [refusing to accept his note of the previous day], September 4, 1910, Enclosure No. 2 in Barclay to Grey, No. 169; ibid.

156. Messrs. Seligman Brothers to the F. O., London, May 13, 1910; F. O. 371/958.

157. F. O. to Messrs. Seligman Brothers, May 21, 1910; ibid.

158. Sir Edward Grey to Mr. O'Beirne [chargé d'affaires at St. Petersburg], No. 184, Confidential, July 5, 1910; ibid.

159. O'Beirne to Grey, No. 275, Telegram, St. Petersburg, October 9, 1910; ibid.

the Imperial Bank of Persia's intention to pay off her debt with money borrowed from him. His letter was left unanswered. On October 21 he wrote again, informing the Foreign Office that the loan would be floated in England only. He received no reply until the twenty-fourth when a Mr. Maxwell at the Foreign Office wrote him that the Imperial Bank of Persia was interested in furnishing Persia a loan and that Sir Edward Grey would not be able to support Seligman Brothers until the results of the bank's negotiations with Persia were known. Maxwell also admitted that the Foreign Office would prefer the Imperial Bank of Persia as a lender to the government of the Shah. Like Reuter, Talbot, Woolf, Samuel, and many others, Seligman tasted the bitterness of international politics in Persia.

> In the future [he wrote to the Foreign Office] should the Persian Government ever require a fresh loan, no responsible firm would negotiate, knowing that at the eleventh hour the Foreign Office is liable to be used in support of a competing house, in spite of the fact that a formal application has been made by the Persian Government and the fact noted by the Foreign Office; in other words, it means that the Imperial Persian Bank can dictate what terms they like to the Persian Government.[160]

Originally the Imperial Bank of Persia had no intention of lending Persia any more money. When on September 14, 1910, almost a month before making a formal application to Seligman Brothers, the Persian government requested £100,000 on the security of Crown jewels, the Imperial Bank "regretfully" declined the business "in view of the large sums outstanding with the Persian Government."[161] As late as October 6 its board of directors refused to issue even a small loan.[162] Then on October 7, after one of the directors had talked with Seligman, the bank de-

---

160. Messrs. Seligman Brothers to the F. O., London, October 25, 1910; ibid.

161. Telegram of the Imperial Bank of Persia in Tehran to the Imperial Bank of Persia headquarters [in London], September 14, 1910; Telegram of the Bank's board in London to the Bank in Tehran, same date, Enclosures in Imperial Bank of Persia to the F. O., London, October 24, 1910; F. O. 371/965.

162. Imperial Bank, London, to A. O. Wood, Tehran, October 6, 1910; ibid.

The Uneasy Alliance

cided that its interests were threatened.[163] The manager in Tehran, A. O. Wood, was asked to find out what terms Seligman had proposed to the Persians.[164] He cabled the terms, adding that "Persian Government much prefer Imperial Bank of Persia arrange business instead of Seligman Brothers." [165] The next day he was instructed to assure the Persian government that the bank could "issue a loan on as favourable terms as anyone." Further, the directors let Wood know that it was "all-important in the interests of the Imperial Bank of Persia to prevent the business going into other hands." [166]

The Persian government must have been anxious to explore the possibility of getting money from the Imperial Bank. After all, Seligman, through no fault of his own, could not be relied upon. Woolf and his associates had been frozen out by the Foreign Office, and there was nothing to prevent it from getting rid of Seligman as well. A high government official, Vakil or-Roāyā, hinted to Wood that the Persian government would prefer to borrow from the Imperial Bank rather than from Seligman. He claimed that he had been authorized by the government to ask for a loan of £1,200,000. On October 25 A. O. Wood learned that the Persians had not broken negotiations with Seligman. He wrote to the Finance Minister and, having received no answer, requested a meeting with him and the Minister of Foreign Affairs. The two admitted that they had asked Vakil or-Roāyā to approach Wood "with a view of obtaining a quotation." Wood replied that if Persia wanted the money, she would have to apply in writing.[167]

Seligman's representative in Tehran, W. A. Moore, learned of Vakil or-Roāyā's conversations with Wood. The ministers assured him, however, that Vakil or-Roāyā had acted on his own and that they were still dealing with Seligman.[168] On the

163. Same to same, October 7, 1910; ibid.
164. Same to same, October 18, 1910; ibid.
165. A. O. Wood, Tehran, to the Bank, London, October 18, 1910; ibid.
166. Imperial Bank, London, to A. O. Wood, Tehran, October 19, 1910; ibid.
167. Barclay to Grey, No. 198, Tehran, October 31, 1910; F. O. 371/958.
168. Mr. Moore to Sir G. Barclay, Tehran, October 28, 1910; Enclosure No. 3 in Barclay to Grey, No. 198; ibid.

thirtieth Moore discovered that the Foreign Office had backed the Imperial Bank of Persia against Seligman. He wrote to Sir George Barclay, the British minister in Tehran: "I wish it clearly understood that I do definitely bring a charge of bad faith against the Foreign Office . . . The whole facts will be put before Parliament the moment it meets." [169]

Actually the British legation had not even begun to exercise pressure in favor of the Imperial Bank of Persia, though Grey had instructed Barclay to do so and to prevent Seligman from placing his loan. Sir George felt that his intervention "at this juncture would tend rather to prejudice than to further negotiations." He would act "only if it appears to me that the Persian Government wish to deal with Seligman Bros. rather than with the Bank." He saw no evidence of such a desire, but felt that, on the contrary, the Persians were anxious to come to terms with the Imperial Bank.[170]

The Imperial Bank of Persia had deep roots in Persian economic and political life. Even without Foreign Office support it probably could have won against Seligman. Moreover, the members of the bank's board in London belonged to the establishment. Sir T. Jackson, Chairman, and Sir T. Gordon, member of the board, dealt easily with high government officials who trusted them to act in the interests of the Empire. Seligman, on the contrary, was an outsider. Jackson and Gordon delicately pointed out to Sir Edward Grey that the Seligmans' "chief house was in New York." [171] Grey came to look upon Seligman Brothers as a foreign firm which should be opposed in favor of British companies.[172] Though no one said a word about it, the fact that Seligman and his associates, as well as Woolf, Samuel, and Levy, were Jews and had international connections, probably militated against them. Sir George Buchanan, British ambassador in St. Petersburg, pointed out to Grey that Russia's financial agent in

169. Same to same, October 31, 1910; ibid.
170. Barclay to Grey, No. 415, Telegram, Tehran, October 22, 1910; F. O. 371/965.
171. Grey to Barclay, No. 43, April 11, 1911; F. O. 371/118.
172. Grey to Sir George Buchanan, No. 120, Telegram, April 13, 1911; ibid.

Washington, Vilenkin (Wilenkin), was married to a Miss Seligman.[173]

Though a subtle anti-Semitism may have played its part, the main reason for Grey's support of the Imperial Bank was the political reliability of an institution that could be, and had been at times, an instrument of British policy. Before permitting the bank to go ahead with the loan, the Foreign Office approached the Russians. K. M. Argyropoulo, senior counselor at the Ministry of Foreign Affairs, said he knew all about the proposed loan and had no objections "provided, of course, that the conversion of the Russian Bank debt is first concluded." [174]

Grey was anxious to obtain Russian consent to the Imperial Bank loan as quickly as possible and without waiting for the conversion of old Persian debts to the Russian bank. "Unless this is done," he telegraphed the chargé d'affaires at St. Petersburg, Mr. Hugh O'Beirne, "either some other house will step in or the bank will conclude the business in spite of our dissent." [175] The Russians refused to be rushed. K. M. Argyropoulo knew the game well, having served for five years (1897–1902) as minister in Tehran.

In trying to make the Russians give their immediate assent to an Imperial Bank loan, the British chargé d'affaires at St. Petersburg made the mistake of saying that the bank could issue the loan without the consent of the British government. The new Minister of Foreign Affairs, Sazonov, reacted strongly to what he must have perceived as an implied threat.

> His Excellency observed [O'Beirne reported] that if the loan were concluded the impression created here would be very bad, and, further, that to withdraw Russian troops from Kazvin would then be quite impossible. The Russian Government would have to keep the force in north Persia for years, a mea-

---

173. Buchanan to Grey, No. 103, April 13, 1911; ibid
174. O'Beirne to Grey, No. 297, Telegram, St. Petersburg, November 4, 1910; F. O. 371/965.
175. Grey to O'Beirne, No. 667, Telegram, November 4, 1910; ibid.

sure which would be unpleasant for the Russian Government, and, he supposed, equally so to us.[176]

Grey wanted Sazonov to understand the general lines of British policy in Persia. England supported Russia in everything involving the latter's vested interests. However, British trade in the south was suffering "and the Russian Government would be placing us in an invidious position were they to expect us to use all our influence to prevent the Persian Government from obtaining the means to restore order, which is essential to our commercial interests." Britain had consistently supported the Russian minister in Tehran and expected "equal consideration at the hands of the Russian Government."

> As to troops, it might be remarked that, when their presence is no longer necessary, or is unnecessary, in the places where they are, their indefinite stay in full strength would be inconsistent with the maintenance of any native government at all in Persia, especially when combined with refusal or prevention of all financial help to Persian Government.[177]

Grey did not specify the instances of Russian obstruction, but they were numerous. In addition to her refusal to give Persia a loan jointly with Britain, Russia opposed all other measures that could improve Persia's financial position. In May 1910, when the British legation in Tehran had asked the Russian legation whether it would agree to a joint loan, the Government of India providing £200,000 and Russia £200,000, the Russian government had stated that it would not "unless the payments of capital and interest on this sum are duly guaranteed by reliable sources of income of the Persian Government." [178] This meant that Persia would have had to accept the same terms she had already rejected. Three months later, when the British had proposed to have the Anglo-Persian Oil Company lend the Persian Government £500,000, a Sazonov had told O'Beirne "That the said deal

176. O'Beirne to Grey, No. 315, Telegram, St. Petersburg, November 15, 1910; ibid.
177. Grey to O'Beirne, No. 692, Telegram, November 18, 1910; ibid.
178. Memorandum transmitted by the Ministry of Foreign Affairs to the Chargé d'Affaires of Great Britain, St. Petersburg, June 3/16, 1910; S.D.D., 4, 206–07.

was inconvenient for us, as it would probably have repercussions upon the question, very important for us, of the consolidation of small debts which the Shah's Government owes us." [179]

Now, in the fall of 1910, Anglo-Russian relations were visibly deteriorating. Russia was seeking a better understanding with Germany. Izvolskii, known as a Francophile and Anglophile, had been removed from the Ministry of Foreign Affairs and sent to Paris. In November Nicholas II and his new Minister of Foreign Affairs, Sergei Dmitrievich Sazonov, went to Potsdam to negotiate an agreement with Germany in regard to the Baghdad railway and Persia. The British were not at all sure how far the Tsar would go and what secret understanding he and Wilhelm might conclude.

In Tehran, Poklewski and Barclay did not deal with problems of grand political strategy. Yet their relations reflected the increasing tension between the two powers. The Imperial Bank's proposed loan and Sazonov's open threat of indefinite military occupation of northern Persia made it necessary for the British to take a stand, a thing Grey hated to do. When Barclay told Poklewski that the Imperial Bank was ready to go through with the loan, the Russian minister was "considerably annoyed." The priority of the conversion of Persia's debts to Russia had not been waived by his government, he said, "and spoke of sending in an ultimatum to the Persian Government in the event of signature of Imperial Bank loan contract threatening seizure of customs if conversion was not completed without delay." [180]

At the Foreign Office there was no agreement on how to deal with the loan question. Russia's position was clear. She did not want anyone to lend Persia money unless Russian terms were first met. Money in the Persian treasury would reduce the dependence of the Persian government on Russia and make it less docile. Sir Edward Grey could not make up his mind. While some of his subordinates felt that it was too late to retract the promise of the loan, others wanted to wait and see. Arthur Nicolson, as usual,

179. Acting Minister of Foreign Affairs [Sazonov] to the Minister in Tehran, Telegram, St. Petersburg, August 3/16, 1910; S.D.D., 5, 59.
180. Barclay to Grey, No. 492, Telegram, Tehran, November 28, 1910; F. O. 371/965.

championed the Russian cause with obstinate singlemindedness. Grey agreed that it was too late to go back on the loan. "On the other hand," he wrote "we cannot object to the Russians putting pressure on the Persians about the Conversion, if the Persians are obstinate after getting their loan." [181]

In the end the Russians won. The Imperial Bank did not sign its loan contract with Persia until the Russians achieved what they wanted, namely a favorable consolidation of the various debts Persia owed them. A treaty to that effect was signed on January 10, 1911, in Tehran. The consolidated debt was to be paid off over the next fifteen years. Interest was set at 7 percent, and the receipts of all customs, except those of Fārs and the Persian Gulf ports, were pledged as security.[182]

The Imperial Bank was at last free to issue the loan. On May 8, 1911, the contract was signed by A. O. Wood and Esmāil Khān Momtāz od-Dowleh. The bank agreed to give Persia £1,250,000 at 5 percent. Customs receipts served as security.[183] Commenting on the terms, Poklewski stated that they were unfavorable to the bank, considering Persia's poor credit. He explained the willingness of the bank to make the loan in terms of its fear of Seligman's firm. The Imperial Bank had accepted not only the burden and expense of floating the loan but even undertook to pay "the old claim of the London Exchange on the Persian Government in connection with the swindle perpetrated by one of Persia's Ministers in London in connection with a proposed issue of Persian lottery tickets on that Exchange." [184]

For the Persian government, money was essential for the restoration of order and the resumption of normal activities. However, neither end could be achieved as long as Russian troops re-

---

181. Minutes by RCL, LM, and EG, Persia No. 43277, November 28, 1910, Imperial Bank proposed loan; ibid.

182. Text of the Treaty in Poklewski's dispatch, Tehran, January 6/19, 1911; S.D.D., 6, 5–8.

183. Imperial Bank of Persia to the Foreign Office, London, June 1, 1911; F. O. 371/1184.

184. Minister in Tehran to the Acting Minister of Foreign Affairs, Neratov; June 15/28, 1911; *Mezhdunarodnye otnosheniia v epokhu imperializma*, 2nd series, 1900–13 (Leningrad, 1939), 18 (Part 1, document No. 138), 149–51. Hereafter cited as M. O. The reference was to Malkam Khān, cf. supra, Chapter 4.

mained on Persian territory, at Tabriz, Rasht, and Qazvin. The British, too, would have liked the Russians to evacuate Persia. During the Tsar's visit to King Edward VII at Cowes in August, 1909, Izvolskii and Benckendorff had discussed Persian problems with Asquith, Grey, and Nicolson. Grey urged the Russians to withdraw their troops: "The longer they stayed the greater was the risk of an anti-Russian agitation in Persia, and, if such an agitation did spring, it would be more difficult than ever to withdraw the troops." [185] Izvolskii professed his desire to recall the troops but wanted guarantees that commercial roads would remain open, and "that affairs in Tehran would not become worse than ever." Izvolskii stressed the role of Caucasian revolutionaries in "recent disturbances" and pointed out "that the new chief of police in Tehran was a Russian revolutionary who had committed terrorist outrages in Russia, and had fled from the Russian police." [186]

From Tehran, Poklewski added his voice to that of Sir Edward. The new Persian government had established correct relations with Russia. The issue of the young Shah's doctor and tutor had been solved; the officers of the Cossack Brigade were well treated; the Cabinet took into account not only the rights but even the wishes of the Russian legation; and there was no threat to the foreigners. England, once the hope of the nationalists, had disappointed them by cooperating loyally with Russia in the affair of Mohammad Ali's *bast* and by refusing to lend money without Russian approval. The continued presence of Russian troops would only feed discontent. The Majles, which was about to reconvene, would discuss the topic to the exclusion of everything else.

> From within the walls of the Majles agitation would spill over to the street, spread through the country, assume a strong anti-Russian character; and we would then not only be unable to recall our troops from Persia and maintain with Persia normal friendly relations, but would be compelled to take

185. Sir Edward Grey, Memorandum, Secret, August 16, 1909, 30520, August 13, 1909; F. O. 371/732.
186. Id. The reference was to Yefrem Khān, who was an Armenian from Turkey, not from Russia as Izvolskii implied.

measures which could take us too far in the business of active intervention in Persian affairs.[187]

Poklewski's analysis was confirmed at once by the behavior of the press. *Irane Now* and *Sharq* were especially vociferously anti-Russian. The publishers of all Tehran papers had been told to change their tone. The ministers and deputies of the Majles were discussing the introduction of censorship. In the meantime the publisher of *Sharq*, Seyyed Ziā ed-Din, was removed from his post, it having been discovered that he was only nineteen years old whereas the law required a publisher to be at least thirty.[188]

Izvolskii was willing to recall the troops at least from Qazvin and even telegraphed Poklewski that this would be done, leaving only fifty Cossacks as the consulate's convoy. Though the total number of Russian soldiers would not decrease, the rest of the Qazvin force being assigned to the consulates at Rasht and Anzali, Izvolskii wanted the step advertised in Persia as an expression of Russian friendship.[189] But Izvolskii himself was under pressure from the right-wing circles and their press.

> In Tehran it is our duty to start speaking Russian once again [thundered *Moskovskie Vedomosti* on September 6 (19?), 1909]. And if England should want to prevent it, the Ministry ought immediately to break the agreement which ties hand

---

187. Poklewski-Koziell's telegram of October 11/24, 1909; S.D.D., 3, 181–82.

188. Survey of events in Tehran from October 23/November 5 to October 30/November 12, 1909, Enclosures in Poklewski's dispatch, Tehran, October 31/November 13, 1909; ibid., p. 221.

Sir George Barclay had written in his annual report that *Sharq* was actually run by an Armenian who was a reactionary and a provocateur. It was he
> who had stated to the Russian Minister that, in his view, there is no hope whatever of Persia saving herself, and had urged that the Russian troops at Kazvin should be brought on to Tehran. He appears to be working for the latter end by endeavouring to inflame public opinion against Russia. The daily attacks against Russia which appear in this paper must therefore be considered in this light. [Annual report on Persia for the year 1909, Enclosure in Barclay to Grey, No. 19, Confidential, Tehran, February 10, 1910; F.O. 371/956.]

One wonders whether the owner of *Sharq* was paid by some Russians without Poklewski's knowledge.

189. Minister of Foreign Affairs to the Minister in Tehran, Telegram, St. Petersburg, October 17/30, 1909; S.D.D., 3, 191–92.

and foot the freedom of our national policy and which should not have been concluded at all.[190]

At a St. Petersburg salon a Russian diplomat told a lady

> that at this time our Minister of Foreign Affairs is not Izvolskii but George [sic] Grey, that we do everything to please England: we have overthrown the Shah in Persia, we are supporting the party of "progress and union," we are helping to overthrow the King of Greece.[191]

Russian troops lingered on in the north, and the Majles, which had convened on November 15, made their prolonged stay its chief subject of debate. Why did not the Russian army go home, the deputies asked. Adib ot-Tojjār declared:

> their presence and their unexpected actions are little by little destroying all hopes of the Persian people. In Ardebil for instance, a gang of Shāhsavan brigands rides out to plunder. Immediately the Government sends a detachment to restore order and punish the outlaws. No sooner had the detachment approached Ardebil and the moment of the thieves' ruin arrived, a Russian detachment appears and misunderstandings arise. Rahim Khān, the famous bandit who won fame through brigandage and violence, has always done this. No sooner had a government . . . army appeared in Qarajadāgh and the moment of his complete defeat arrived, than a Russian detachment appeared in Ahar. Why these appearances? [192]

Seyyed Hasan Taqizādeh, deputy from Āzarbāyjān, said that the presence of Russian troops caused disorder in the state. Ten Cossacks in a Persian town were enough to halt the administrative machine. The Russians occupied various cities in the north under false pretexts, but the Cabinet had not done all it should.

> He [the Minister of Foreign Affairs] says that he has taken steps. At the usual Wednesday receptions in the Ministry of

190. Cited in Bestuzhev, *Borba v Rossii* . . . , pp. 311–12.

191. Bogdanovich, *Tri poslednikh samoderzhtsa*, entry for October 30/November 12, 1909, p. 469. The diplomat in question was Schelking.

192. Majles session of February 5, 1910 [Russian text], Enclosure in Poklewski's dispatch, Tehran, January 30/February 11, 1910; *S.D.D.*, 4, 31–44.

Foreign Affairs, when all the ministers call on him, he, perhaps, asked the Russian Minister during a conversation over a cup of tea: "When will your troops leave Persia?" and heard in reply, "Enshāollāh!" [God willing].[193]

Though the tone of the debates in the Majles had been moderate and no insults had been flung at Russia, her government found in them a pretext for postponing evacuation. With feigned sorrow Izvolskii wrote Poklewski-Koziell that Russia had been prepared to discuss the slow withdrawal of her troops.

> The more saddening is the rude interference of the extreme nationalists in this question in the Majles, since under any kind of threat we would be deprived of opportunity to carry out our intentions.
> Kindly bring this to the attention of the Shah's Government and induce them to take all measures . . . toward the cessation of the harmful agitation begun by the nationalists.[194]

Poklewski spoke to the Assistant Minister of Foreign Affairs, Saqat ol-Molk, about the "tactless and aimless gesture of the Majles." [195] Sepahdār, the Prime Minister and a revolutionary *malgré lui*, told the dragoman of the Russian legation, Baranovskii, that in his opinion Persia could exist only in friendship with Russia. He and a majority of ministers would resign rather than follow any other policy toward her. Sepahdār wanted to know whether Russia would withdraw her troops if the Persian government were friendly. Poklewski sent word that he wanted to see Persian deeds. As long as the Persian government had not acceded to Russian demands on four or five issues, he would not conduct even private conversations on the subject of the evacuation of troops.[196]

Upon learning of the Majles' decision to seek the withdrawal of

193. Id.
194. Minister of Foreign Affairs to the Minister in Tehran [copy to London], Telegram January 25/February 7, 1910; ibid., p. 28.
195. Poklewski used the strong and insulting term *vykhodka: "o bestaktnoi i bestselnoi vykhodke Medzhlisa."*
196. Poklewski's telegram, Tehran, January 26/February 8, 1910; *S.D.D.*, 4, 29–30.

The Uneasy Alliance

Russian troops and to protest if they remained, Grey instructed Barclay to declare to the Persian government that while "sympathizing with its desire for the evacuation, the London Cabinet has complete confidence in the promises of the Imperial Government [Russia] and does not believe that the proposed protest would achieve its aim." [197] Barclay had no choice but to carry out policies decided upon in London. However, he did not conceal from Grey his misgivings. "The Persian Government are, I feel," he telegraphed, "being driven to desperation by the line that Russia is pursuing, and I believe there is a danger of the Cabinet tendering its resignation, a step which might again bring about chaotic conditions." [198]

Sir Charles Hardinge was also disturbed. Something might be said to Count Benckendorff. "It cannot be to the real interests of Russia that chaos and hostility toward Russia should reign in Persia," he wrote.[199] In fact he did speak to Benckendorff about the need for adopting a generally conciliatory attitude, pointing out specifically the presence of Russian troops and the desperate financial situation as possible causes of a downfall of the Tehran Cabinet.[200]

From St. Petersburg Sir Arthur Nicolson rushed to Russia's defense.

> It cannot be denied [he wrote upon reading Barclay's dispatch of February 11] that the retention of the Russian troops in Persia has continued for a longer period than would seem to be justified by the circumstances, but the proceedings in the Medjliss occurred at the very moment when M. Izvolsky was on the point of proposing their withdrawal. I would submit that we should be careful to avoid giving the impression here that we have any inclination to disapprove of Russia's attitude, or that we are falling in with the views of the Persian Government.

197. Ibid., p. 28.
198. Barclay to Grey, No. 62, Telegram, Very Confidential, Tehran, February 11, 1910; F. O. 371/952.
199. Attitude of Russian Government towards Persia, Minutes, Persia, No. 4956, February 11, 1910; ibid.
200. Grey to Barclay, No. 28, Telegram, February 12, 1910; ibid.

The Russian government had always been patient with Britain. It said not a word when British troops were landed at Bushehr, or when the British seized a depot of arms.

> If we were now led to take any action, or make use of any language, whereby the Persians might be induced to believe that there was a divergence of views between the two Governments, the good and cordial feeling which has up to now characterized the execution of our convention would thereby be impaired.[201]

Three separate conversations on the subject of the evacuation of northern Persia showed Nicolson that Izvolskii's reasons for keeping the troops in Persia were not convincing. He admitted as much in two telegrams to Grey,[202] but persisted in his view that Russia was right and that no objections should be raised to her actions in Persia. Later in the year, as relations between Britain and Russia deteriorated, Russian behavior in Persia grew more and more arbitrary and insolent.

> Complaint after complaint poured in upon Downing Street. Nicolson was at pains to defend Russian misdeeds. It is still recounted in the Foreign Office that he minuted a bulky memorandum on Russian violations of the Convention [of 1907] with the words: "I have not read this document. But if, as I assume, it contains criticisms of Russian procedure in Persia, it is largely based on prejudice and false assumptions." [203]

Persia's chargé d'affaires at St. Petersburg, Ali Qoli Khān Moshāver ol-Mamālek, addressed a note to Izvolskii asking for the evacuation of Russian forces in view of the fact that the Persian government had secured order, thereby eliminating the causes that had originally brought in the troops. Ali Qoli Khān was given to understand that the raising of the issue appeared to

---

201. Nicolson to Grey, No. 55, Telegram, St. Petersburg, February 13, 1910; ibid.
202. Same to same, No. 95, St. Petersburg, February 19, 1910, and No. 100, St. Petersburg, February 21, 1910; ibid.
203. H. Nicolson, *Portrait of a Diplomatist*, p. 258.

Russia quite unfortunate "since our troops would under no circumstances be evacuated from Persia under any pressure." Poklewski was instructed to tell the Persians that Izvolskii would not even give a written reply to Ali Qoli Khān's note.[204]

Russia's adamant position on the issue of troop withdrawal and its unreserved defense by Nicolson decided Grey to abandon his brief attempt to support Persia. On February 12 he had agreed with Charles Hardinge that "something" should be said to Benckendorff. On the fifteenth he showed Benckendorff the text of a telegram he had just sent to Barclay, instructing him

> to remind the Persian Government of the respect to which the Russian and the English Governments are entitled, and to state that in the opinion of the Government of Great Britain the Russian Government cannot take any measures in regard to the troops issue under any pressure, and that the Majles should correct its last gesture through some kind of pacificatory demonstration.[205]

Dreary negotiations over the issue of the troops continued for more than a year. At no time did the Russian government admit that it had in fact imposed a permanent occupation on northern Persia. There were always incidents that provided excuses for keeping the detachments in Qazvin, Rasht, Tabriz, and elsewhere. Late in February 1910 there occurred in Gilān a dispute between Lianozov, the Russian entrepreneur who controlled the fishing rights, and local authorities about the limits of his fisheries and his right to sublet to Russian subjects. The Persians organized a boycott of Lianozov's enterprise. Poklewski saw in this an attempt to force Lianozov to give up his concession, and asked St. Petersburg to dispatch one hundred Cossacks from Baku to Anzali to augment the force of fourteen Cossacks already on the

---

204. Minister of Foreign Affairs to the Minister in Tehran, Telegram, St. Petersburg, January 31/February 12, 1910; S.D.D., 4, 44–45. (Twenty years later Moshāver ol-Mamālek served as Persian ambassador in Moscow. Though I was only seven years old when I saw him last, I have preserved a vivid memory of his strikingly handsome and majestic appearance. F.K.)

205. Count Benckendorff's telegram, London, February 2/14, 1910; S.D.D., 4, 48–49.

spot.²⁰⁶ The Persian government immediately gave in and promised to "punish the guilty." ²⁰⁷

In Tabriz Russian officials picked up every rumor of trouble to justify continued military occupation. Early in March 1910 the Turkish acting consul told the Russian consul general that the nationalist leader, Sattār Khān, was abnormal and capable of wild acts. Disorders could occur in Tabriz. No less a personage than the Chairman of the Council of Ministers, P. A. Stolypin, showed interest in the gossip and forwarded the information to the Viceroy of the Caucasus, Count I. I. Vorontsov-Dashkov, who would be called upon to suppress an anti-Russian movement in Āzarbāyjān should one break out.²⁰⁸

Waiting for Sattār Khān to go mad and furnish a pretext for further intervention did not suit the Russian government. The nationalist leadership must be removed. "Insolent sallies of the fadāiyān, Sattār and Bāqer, and agitation against our detachment in Tabriz continue to grow without meeting the necessary retort," Izvolskii telegraphed. Poklewski was to demand that the Persian government disarm and expel the fadāiyān and their leaders. "If this demand is not fulfilled," Izvolskii threatened, "we shall be forced to take the necessary measures on our own." The Viceroy of the Caucasus was sending to Jolfā two infantry battalions with two guns and a Cossack hundred, "and if the Persian Government does not immediately take the measures indicated above, they will be moved to Tabriz." ²⁰⁹ Poklewski obeyed his orders but could not conceal his doubts. Miller, in charge of the consulate at Tabriz, was an old Anglophobe who believed in the maximum use of force and belonged to the same school as Zinov'ev and Hartwig. Poklewski had difficulty sharing his apprehension of a Persian attack upon the Russian detachment at Tabriz.²¹⁰

206. Poklewski's telegram, Tehran, February 15/28, 1910; ibid., pp. 64–65.
207. Same, Tehran, February 19/March 4, 1910; ibid., p. 67.
208. Chairman of the Council of Ministers to the Viceroy of the Caucasus, St. Petersburg, Telegram, February 23/March 8, 1910; ibid., p. 78.
209. Minister of Foreign Affairs to the Minister in Tehran, St. Petersburg, February 25/March 10, 1910, ibid., pp. 78–79.
210. Poklewski's telegram, Tehran, February 27/March 12, 1910; ibid., p. 81.

The Uneasy Alliance

Again the Persian Government had no choice but to comply. Sattār and Bāqer were invited to come to Tehran. For the two revolutionary adventurers this meant the loss of power and position. Their refusal to go was gleefully communicated to Izvolskii by Miller, who probably secretly hoped they would stay, causing more Russian troops to enter Tabriz.[211] Only a few hours later Poklewski was instructed by Izvolskii to warn the Persian Prime Minister, Sepahdār, that Russia expected "decisive action from him, otherwise the detachment in Jolfā will cross the border."[212] The government did all it could, and the two nationalist leaders promised to leave Tabriz, whereupon Stolypin asked the Viceroy of the Caucasus to halt his troops.[213]

The failure of the Persian government to obtain the withdrawal of Russian forces contributed to a Cabinet crisis in mid-April. The Russian legation feared the formation of a more radical ministry and advised St. Petersburg to threaten Persia with repressive measures. Russia could tell the Persians that she would refuse to maintain relations with any Cabinet which did not have her confidence; increase the strength of the Russian army of occupation; demand an immediate payment of old debts; and even occupy Tehran. "Though the last measure," Poklewski wrote, "is, of course, very undesirable, because extreme, it seems to me that such a threat would of itself suffice."[214]

Following closely Grey's policies, the British legation in Tehran attempted to induce the Persians to assume a more conciliatory attitude toward Russia. On June 27, 1910, the chargé d'affaires, Charles M. Marling, told the Bakhtiāri leader and cabinet member, Sardār As'ad, that he "could not understand the extraordinary folly" of Persian nationalists.

> Could they not realise that as Persia must have relations with Russia, it was well that these relations should be good and friendly, and were they so insensate as to imagine that they

211. Miller's telegram, Tabriz, March 4/17, 1910; ibid.
212. Minister of Foreign Affairs to the Minister in Tehran, St. Petersburg, March 4/17, 1910; ibid.
213. Chairman of the Council of Ministers to H.I.M.'s Viceroy of the Caucasus, St. Petersburg, March 6/19, 1910; ibid., p. 105.
214. Poklewski's telegram, Tehran, April 6/19, 1910; ibid., p. 146.

could struggle against a Power whose armed forces alone were equal to one-third of the entire population of Persia?

Marling advised As'ad to restrain the Majles Russophobes such as Taqizādeh, Hoseyn Qoli Khān Navvāb (former Minister of Foreign Affairs), and Hakim ol-Molk, who formed the majority of the foreign affairs committee.

Sardār As'ad tried to present to Marling the Persian point of view, or as the Englishman put it,

> to ventilate some of the grievances of Persia against Russia, but I cut short his tale of woe saying he was doing exactly what I had tried to warn him against, namely expatiating on Persia's wrongs instead of going to discuss them with the Russian Minister, who would always meet him in a most conciliatory spirit.[215]

Sardār As'ad dutifully went to Poklewski who repeated to him old demands which Persia must satisfy before the Russian government agreed to withdraw its troops. These included an extension of the Qarajadāgh mining concession, the right to import free of duty sixty automobiles to work on the Rasht-Tehran road, and the return of the Cossack Brigade to its original privileged status.[216]

The domestic situation in Persia was greatly influenced by foreign affairs, reflecting their every change. Russian intransigence in the troops issue produced a conflict in the nationalist camp. The radicals demanded defiance of Russia, while the more conservative pleaded for caution and accommodation. The clergy, who until then had been supporting the revolution, began to have doubts. In Najaf, a holy city in Iraq, the mojtaheds denounced Seyyed Hasan Taqizādeh, a Majles deputy from Āzarbāyjān, of whose radical nationalism they disapproved. On July 15 Seyyed Abdollāh Behbehāni, a cautious and opportunistic cleric, was assassinated in his own home. Some said that the murder had been committed "on the instigation of Taqizādeh and his party who were seeking revenge for the deceased's refusal to intercede

215. Marling to Grey, No. 117, Gulahek, July 4, 1910; F. O. 371/962.
216. Id.

The Uneasy Alliance 573

for Taqizādeh before Najaf mojtaheds." Others were convinced that the Russians had killed Seyyed Abdollāh to provoke disorders which would serve as a pretext for the occupation of Tehran.[217] *Sharq* reprinted an article from a Constantinople newspaper, *Shams*, about the relations of the Russian consul in Baghdad with the mojtaheds, whose negative attitude toward the anti-Russian policy of the radicals it attributed to the influence of the consul.[218]

Sepahdār's cabinet finally resigned and was succeeded by a more radical, or anti-Russian one, headed by Mostowfi ol-Mamālek, with Hoseyn Qoli Khān Navvāb as Minister of Foreign Affairs and Ahmad Khān Qavām os-Saltaneh as Minister of War. To balance "the radicals" and keep the support of the conservatives, Abdol Hoseyn Mirzā Farmānfarmā was made Minister of the Interior. Charles Marling commented in a dispatch to Grey that "to be reduced to enlisting the services of such a notorious exponent of government by tyranny and extortion as Farman-Farma is in itself a confession of failure." [219] Marling noted that Mirzā Hoseyn Qoli Khān Navvāb was "violently anti-Russian." Poklewski also noted that the members of the new Cabinet had "at all times supported anti-Russian agitation in the country and tirelessly got in the way of the previous ministry in its attempts to establish normal relations with us." [220]

Mr. Charles M. Marling undertook to enlighten Mirzā Hoseyn Khān on the subject of Russian friendship. His report of the conversation he had with the new Persian Foreign Minister is an incredible document, which deserves to be quoted at some length.

> I think [Marling wrote] that I succeeded in mitigating, at least for the moment, the Nawab's mistrust of Russian mo-

---

217. Poklewski's telegram, Tehran, July 3/16, 1910; and Survey of events in Tehran from July 2/15 to July 9/22, 1910, Enclosure in Poklewski's dispatch of July 10/23, 1910; S.D.D., 5, 3, 10–11.

218. Survey of events in Tehran from August 1/14 to August 7/20, 1910, Enclosure in Poklewski's dispatch, Zargandeh, August 7/20, 1910; ibid., p. 67.

219. Marling to Grey, No. 138, Confidential, Gulahek, July 29, 1910; F. O. 371/950.

220. Poklewski's telegram, Tehran, July 21/August 3, 1910; S.D.D., 5, 30.

tives. His Excellency is, I am sure, ready to admit M. Poklewski's personal goodwill, but he is less than half convinced of the sincerity of the Russian Government's professions of friendliness, while as for the Russian officials in Persia, he regards the great majority of them as "agent provocateurs," whose sole business is to provide excuses for the retention of the Russian troops.

Marling insisted that in every case he had investigated he found that the Russian officials gave essentially correct accounts of events.

> I fear, however [he went on], that the Minister's confidence in his official information—so remarkable in an official who cannot but have had a large experience in his countrymen's inventive talents—was not in the least shaken, and in this case I fear that discussion of incidents between him and M. Poklewski cannot fail to be difficult.[221]

Through the rest of the summer the Persian government pleaded with Russia to withdraw her troops. The answer was always the same: Russia awaited "real proofs of the willingness of the Shah's Government to establish firm, sincere relations with Russia, which would be possible only if it met our wishes." [222] The Russian position grew harsher every day, and St. Petersburg began to talk about "the necessity of entering the path of reprisals." [223]

Sir George Barclay on his return from a trip home tried to restrain the Russian legation, but Russia was now determined to bring down the Cabinet. Poklewski wanted the Majles dissolved. A new Majles might be more reasonable, he felt. Barclay was doubtful. "Unless it were packed at our instigation—which is, of course, out of the question—I see no ground for this hope." [224]

221. Marling to Grey, No. 144 [last paragraph Confidential], Gulahek, August 4, 1910; F. O. 371/963.
222. Acting Minister of Foreign Affairs [Sazonov] to the Minister in Tehran, Telegram August 20/September 2, 1910; S.D.D., 5, 79–80.
223. Same to same, St. Petersburg, September 6/19, 1910; ibid., p. 104.
224. Barclay to Grey, No. 383, Confidential, Tehran, September 26, 1910; F. O. 371/964.

In a conversation he had with his British colleague, Poklewski "spoke with bitterness" of England's "desire to come to the assistance of the Persian Government with financial aid, which, he said, would go to the support of a Cabinet which was hostile to Russian interests." [225]

Barclay's appeals for moderation and conciliation made no impression on Poklewski, who grew more and more agitated and blunter in expression as the conversation went on.

> M. Poklewski spoke with some asperity [Barclay wrote] of the support I was lending a Cabinet which was hostile to Russia by not discouraging the offer of loans to it.
>
> He spoke of this legation as a nest of nationalists, and observed that the attitude of certain persons in England—he had just read a foolish letter from Professor Browne to the "Manchester Guardian" and a leading article upon it in that paper—was calculated to give the Persian Government the impression that the cooperation of the two Powers in Persia was apparent rather than real. Russia could not stand much longer the total disregard with which the present Cabinet treated her interests.[226]

Had the fall of the Persian Cabinet been likely to relieve the tension between the powers in Persia, Barclay would have been

---

225. Barclay to Grey, No. 385, Telegram, Gulahek, September 26, 1910; ibid. At the Foreign Office Mr. H. Norman commented:

M. Poklewski is becoming daily more irate and unreasonable.

The money is wanted to restore order and unless this is done no progress can be made. It is not wanted to support the Cabinet though indirectly it would have that effect.

It looks as though M. Poklewski and his Govt. did not really wish to see Persia orderly and prosperous but wanted her to remain weak and disturbed so that she may be more completely dominated by Russia. This is a reversion to the attitude to which it was hoped that the Anglo-Russian Agreement had put an end and is entirely opposed to the letter and the spirit of that instrument. [Persia, No. 34960, September 26, 1910, Oil Company Loan Negotiations, Minutes.]

226. Barclay to Grey, No. 184, Very Confidential, Gulahek, October 3, 1910; ibid. Professor Edward G. Browne of Cambridge University, a distinguished Orientalist and author of books on Persian literature, the Babi religion, and his own travels in Persia, was a passionate defender of the Persian revolution, about which he wrote extensively.

happy to see it fall. However, he was made uncomfortable by Poklewski's hints that the idea of intervention was gaining ground in Russia. "I must point out," he telegraphed to Grey, "that Russia could at any moment create a situation which would, in the eyes of the world, be sufficient ground for intervention, by permitting intrigues among her influential protégés in this country." The particular protégé whom Barclay had in mind was Mohammad Vali Khān Nasr os-Saltaneh, Sepahdār, leader in spite of himself of the Gilān revolutionaries in 1909, cautious Prime Minister, and secret collaborator with the Russians.[227]

London did not want to hear evil, see evil, or speak evil. "The suggestion that Russia, through Sipahdar, is stirring up trouble in Persia in order to justify intervention is most unpleasant," wrote Mr. Norman, an undersecretary at the Foreign Office. "In the present state of Anglo-Russian relations I find it hard to believe that it can be the case."[228] Sir Edward Grey was ready to believe in but not to admit Russia's bad faith. Unilateral Russian action in Persia might lead to the collapse of the 1907 agreement and must therefore be prevented at all cost.

> It is absolutely essential [he instructed Barclay], on European and not merely on local grounds, that the solidarity of action of the two Powers in Persia should be maintained, and care should be taken not to allow any divergence of views with your Russian colleague, to assume undue proportions. If joint action of the two Powers should lead to resignation of Cabinet it would be unfortunate, but consideration should not be allowed to impair the harmony now existing between the two legations.[229]

Simultaneously in St. Petersburg Mr. O'Beirne, the chargé d'affaires, communicated to the Acting Minister of Foreign Affairs, Sazonov, the contents of Grey's instruction to Barclay (Telegram No. 283 of September 28). O'Beirne pointed out that

227. Barclay to Grey, No. 384, Very Confidential, Telegram, Gulahek, September 26, 1910; F. O. 371/964.
228. Persia, No. 3495, September 26, 1910; Russo-Persian Relations, Minutes; ibid.
229. Grey to Barclay, No. 283, Telegram, September 28, 1910; ibid.

Grey "Had gone a long way to meet the views held by M. Poklewsky," to the extent of being willing to exercise pressure on the Persian government to make it accept all Russian demands. Grey was prepared to do so, O'Beirne told Sazonov, "at the risk of bringing about the fall of the present Persian Cabinet." [230]

Russia's growing intransigence in Persia reflected the general deterioration of Anglo-Russian and the corresponding improvement of Russo-German relations. Within the ruling circles at St. Petersburg, powerful forces worked for the reversal of Izvolskii's policies of alliance with France and friendship with England, compelling the minister to resign in the autumn of 1910. The reactionary press baited France and Britain and praised Germany. "It is time to recoil at last from he nightmare created through an excessive closeness to the universal corrupter, France, and the ancient enemy of Russia, England," wrote *Russkaia Zemlia* on October 24, 1910.[231]

To strengthen the position of the Anglophile elements at the Tsar's Court and in the government, and to prevent the Germanophiles from destroying the Agreement of 1907, Grey was willing to force the Persians into granting all Russian demands. On the occasion of a visit to London of the Regent-Elect of Persia, Abol Qāsem Khān Nāser ol-Molk, a political moderate with an Oxford education, Sir Arthur Nicolson "took the opportunity of impressing on . . . him the folly of the Persian Government in adopting an antagonistic attitude to Russia." [232] Grey himself urged his old friend and schoolmate not to oppose Russian interests in the north. Cynically and perversely, Grey reiterated his faith in Russia's good intentions. "I assured him," he wrote, "that Persia could safely adopt a policy of conciliation towards Russia, as Russia had no incentive to pursue a forward policy in Persia, since all suspicions of us have been removed by the Anglo-Russian Agreement." [233] Two weeks later at a special ministerial conference the new Minister of Foreign Affairs, Sergei Dmitrievich

230. O'Beirne to Grey, No. 397, St. Petersburg, September 29, 1910; ibid.
231. Cited in Bestuzhev, *Borba v Rossii* . . . , p. 331.
232. Grey to Barclay, No. 174, October 15, 1910; F. O. 371/964. The conversation took place on October 8.
233. Same to same, No. 296, Telegram, October 12, 1910; ibid.

Sazonov, stated that "the manifestly unfriendly tone which has been adopted toward us by the Government of the Shah . . . , as well as the complete ignoring of our demands compel us to take certain punitive measures in regard to Persia." [234] The measures themselves were being discussed with Poklewski-Koziell. Quickly and without debate the conference decided, "in conformity with circumstances, to take such repressive measures as he [Sazonov] may find most convenient at any given moment." [235]

Russian determination further to increase intervention in Persia was strengthened, perhaps unwittingly, by British complaints against brigandage in the south and threats to use force for the protection of commerce. The old system of law enforcement had broken down completely, and the roads were left unguarded. In July in Barclay's absence Charles Marling, the chargé d'affaires, proposed to Grey that an ultimatum be issued to Persia stating that if order were not restored by September, Britain would act on her own.[236] Barclay, who was on leave in London, wanted the Persians either to restore order by September or create under British-Indian officers a special force similar to the Cossack Brigade.[237] His advice was accepted, and the decision communicated to Sazonov, who replied that Russia had no objections as long as the proposed force stayed out of the Russian zone.[238]

The Persian government was unable to restore order throughout its vast and underpopulated country. Revolution had upset and disorganized the old system and freed the tribes of their fear of Tehran. To control them and to police thousands of miles of roads would have required large sums of money which the government did not have. Though the British were aware that Persia lacked the means to organize a special force in the south, they

234. Journal of a special conference on Persia, October 15/28, 1910; K. A., 3 (58) (1933), p. 57.

235. Id.

236. Marling to Grey, No. 114, Gulahek, July 2, 1910; F. O. 371/958.

237. Persia, No. 25923, July 18, 1910; Present Situation in Persia, Minutes; ibid.

238. Aide-memoire communicated to Mr. O'Beirne by Mr. Sazonov [on August 22, 1910], O'Beirne to Grey, No. 355, St. Petersburg, August 24, 1910; F. O. 371/958. Cf. O'Beirne's Memorandum to Sazonov, August 12, 1910; S.D.D., 5, 42–45.

persisted in demanding it. When in October bandits threatened the town of Langeh, on the Gulf shore, and the Persian government could do nothing against them, the British landed one hundred and sixty sailors and four guns.[239]

British pressure made it more difficult for the Persian government to resist Russia's demands and withstand her hostility. The appointment of Ivan Fedorvich Pokhitonov to the post of consul general in Tehran must have struck fear into the hearts of Persian nationalists, for Pokhitonov, who had served for many years in various Russian consulates in northern Persia, was known as a fanatical monarchist, imperialist, and ardent supporter of the deposed Shah. Upon his arrival in Tehran, Pokhitonov set up "an establishment apart from the legation," and equipped himself with "his own staff, Cossack escort, and gholmas [servants]." [240]

Hoseyn Qoli Khān Navvāb, the Minister of Foreign Affairs, could no longer continue in office. He resigned at the end of December. Sir George Barclay attributed Hoseyn Qoli Khān's departure from the Cabinet to "his despair of maintaining the independence of Persia in the face of what he calls the arbitrary acts of Russia, and to his anxiety lest the scheme of policing the southern trade routes should be insisted on by His Majesty's Government." Barclay did not conceal from London that his own letter of December 24 to Hoseyn Qoli Khān, demanding an answer to the British request for the formation of a force to restore order in the south, had pushed the Foreign Minister into resigning.[241]

Mr. H. Norman, an undersecretary at the Foreign Office, understood that Hoseyn Qoli Khān's departure was a regrettable loss. No better man was likely to be found for the job, though it was clear "that agreement between him and M. Poklewski was impossible." Norman also realized that little could be done to solve the dilemma: "The worst is that any Persian Minister of

239. Poklewski's telegram, Tehran, October 18/31, 1910; *ibid.*, p. 164.
240. Monthly summary of events by Mr. G. P. Churchill, Enclosure 1 in Barclay to Grey, No. 244, Confidential, Tehran, December 27, 1910; F. O. 371/1184.
241. Barclay to Grey, No. 512, Telegram, Confidential, Tehran, December 28, 1910; F. O. 371/967.

F. A. who shows a more complaisant spirit towards Russia runs a very good chance of being driven from office by public opinion, so that something very like a deadlock is to be feared." Arthur Nicolson's comment was brief and typical: "I hardly think Hussein Khan is a great loss to us." [242]

Hoseyn Qoli Khān's despair of maintaining his country in independence was well justified. But before they gave up the unequal struggle, the Persian government and the Majles made a last valiant attempt to raise the nation to its feet.

242. Persia, No. 46829, December 29, 1910; Resignation of the Persian M. F. A., Minutes; ibid.

9

"The Strangling of Persia"

In August 1910 Poklewski and Barclay learned that the Majles intended to invite a number of foreign advisers to reform Persia's financial administration and civil service. St. Petersburg and London did not like the prospect of Frenchmen running Persia's ministry of finance, Italians training a gendarmerie, and Austrians the army. Assistant Minister of Foreign Affairs, A. A. Neratov, and British chargé d'affaires, Hugh O'Beirne, agreed that the Persian government should be prevented from hiring subjects of any but minor powers.[1] In reply to the Italian ambassador's question whether Britain and Russia had objections to Italians' serving the Persian government, Grey wrote that the engagement of Italian subjects "would place the two Powers in a most difficult position."[2]

After a long debate on the relative merits of the Belgians, the Italians, and the Swiss, the Majles decided to invite Americans. As citizens of a great power they would not be intimidated by Russia or Britain; yet, as Americans, they would not pose a threat to anyone since, to quote the Russian minister in Tehran, "the United States are not a great European power and have no political interests here."[3] Neratov, now Acting Minister of Foreign Affairs, also felt that the invitation of American advisers did not threaten Russian interests. However, he felt that the Persian

1. O'Beirne to Grey, No. 349, St. Petersburg, August 20, 1910; F. O. 371/963. Parts of this chapter have appeared in my article "Russia vs. Morgan Shuster," *Ventures*, 4 (1964), 41-48
2. Grey to the Marquis Imperiali, August 19, 1910; F. O. 371/963.
3. Poklewski's telegram of August 28/September 10, 1910; S.D.D., 5, 87-88.

government's decision to disregard Russian and British advice, and engage citizens of a great power, constituted a dangerous precedent.[4]

The British assumed a favorable attitude toward the Persian project of inviting American advisers, even defending it in St. Petersburg. Reluctantly Neratov acquiesced, though he hated giving way to Persia, and "to avoid the appearance of so doing" instructed Poklewski "to inform the Persian Government in a peremptory form that the Russian Government 'authorized' them to employ Americans as proposed."[5] Simultaneously the Russian ambassador in Washington, Roman Rosen, in an aide-memoire to the United States Department of State, expressed Russia's concern and the hope that America would refuse the Persian invitation to send advisers to Tehran.[6]

On December 25, 1910, Ali Qoli Khān Nabil od-Dowleh, Persian chargé d'affaires in Washington, was instructed to request the United States Secretary of State to put him in communication "with impartial American financial people" for the purpose of employing experts for the Persian Treasury.[7] The Secretary of State, Philander C. Knox, promised to take the matter under kindly consideration.[8] The Russian embassy in Washington reported to St. Petersburg that Knox had consulted the British and, finding that they did not object to the employment of American technical experts by the Persian Ministry of Finance, recommended five. "The American Government," the report said, "is not taking part in the negotiations which are being conducted

4. Acting Minister of Foreign Affairs to the Minister in Tehran, St. Petersburg, August 26/September 8, 1910; ibid., p. 87.

5. O'Beirne to Grey, No. 379, St. Petersburg, September 14, 1910; F. O. 371/963.

6. A. Yeselson, *United States–Persian Diplomatic Relations*, pp. 108–09.

7. The Minister of Foreign Affairs to the Persian Minister in Washington, Telegram, Tehran, December 25, 1910, Inclosure in the Persian Chargé d'Affaires to the Secretary of State, No. 21, Washington, December 28, 1910; File No. 3891.51/37, *Papers Relating to the Foreign Relations of the United States*, 1911 (Washington, 1918), p. 679.

8. The Secretary of State to the Persian Chargé d'Affaires, No. 34, Washington, January 5, 1911; ibid.

concerning the conditions under which the Americans will enter Persian service." [9]

On January 26 the officials of the Foreign Office read in their morning papers a brief dispatch from New York stating that the *New York Times* of January 25 carried a telegram from Washington to the effect that Secretary of State Knox had conferred with the Secretary of the Treasury, Franklin MacVeagh, who submitted to him names of five financial experts for transmittal to the Persian minister. A sheet of Foreign Office paper was clipped to the little piece of newsprint and sent on its appointed round. "Have we heard of this?" scribbled L[ouis] M[allet]. "Not till this morning, except from the papers," replied A[rthur] N[icolson]. "I have told Count Benckendorff of this," added E[dward] G[rey]. On the same day Mr. James Bryce, British ambassador in Washington, confirmed the accuracy of the New York dispatch.[10]

Russia complained mildly. Benckendorff informed Grey of a letter from the Minister of Foreign Affairs, Sazonov, who was said to have raised "serious objections." [11] Sir Arthur Nicolson noted that Sazonov had previously agreed to the employment of Americans by Persia and had so informed Tehran. "I do not see how we could change this attitude now, even if there were time to stop the appointments." [12] Grey instructed Sir George Buchanan, the British ambassador in St. Petersburg, to tell Sazonov that it was now too late to reopen the question.[13] Even the Russian minister in Tehran, Poklewski, felt that matters had "advanced too far to upset the engagement of American advisers, and that a bad effect would be produced by doing so in view of our [Russian and British] previous statements." [14]

9. Prince Kudashev's telegram, Washington, January 13/26, 1911; S.D.D., 4, 12.

10. Persia, Confidential, No. 3116, Minutes, Clipping of Reuter's New York Dispatch. Mr. Bryce to Sir Edward Grey, No. 10, Washington, January 26, 1911; F. O. 371/1185.

11. Benckendorff to Grey, London, January 29, 1911; ibid.

12. Persia, No. 3823, Minute by A. Nicolson, January 30, 1911; ibid.

13. Grey to Buchanan, No. 32, Telegram, February 4, 1911; ibid.

14. Barclay to Grey, No. 36, Telegram, Tehran, February 3, 1911; ibid.

The principal adviser suggested by the State Department on the recommendation of the Secretary of the Treasury was W. Morgan Shuster, of whom the British ambassador in Washington, wrote:

> He is described as a man of considerable force of character and unquestioned integrity. He seems to be also rather unbending in temper and rigid in methods. He enforced the customs regulations in the Phillippine Islands with a stringency which occasionally became vexatious, and certainly rendered him unpopular. He is said to have also taken up the cudgels for the natives with a vigour which caused some little embarrassment to the administration, and which would appear to have led to his return home.[15]

Energetic, idealistic, and honest to a fault, Morgan Shuster swept into the summer heat of Tehran like a thunderstorm. No sooner had he been appointed Treasurer General and received authority from the Majles to reorganize the nation's finances than he found himself in a head-on collision with all the vested interests that profited from the confusion and corruption of the old administration. The Russian legation noted with certain satisfaction that the Americans were being accused of planning to stop paying pensions and various other grants to individuals, thus creating much dissatisfaction. Appealing to "the fanaticism of a benighted population," Shuster's enemies loudly accused the Americans of being Babis.[16]

When, in accordance with law, Shuster requested the Belgian head of Persian customs, Mornard, to deposit custom receipts in the treasurer's account, Mornard refused. Thereupon the Imperial Bank of Persia, whose manager was "warmly in favour of the new arrangement," would no longer honor Mornard's checks. The Russian legation took Mornard's side, offering him "moral support and accusing Shuster of seeking popularity with the nationalists."[17] The Russian minister himself sought to intimidate

15. Bryce to Grey, No. 45, Confidential, Washington, February 16, 1911; ibid.
16. Survey of events in Tehran from June 8/21 to June 14/27, 1911, Enclosure in Poklewski's dispatch, Tehran, June 15/28, 1911; S.D.D., 4, 178–79.
17. Survey of events in Tehran from June 15/28 to June 21/July 4, 1911, Enclosure in Poklewski's dispatch, Tehran, June 29/July 5, 1911; ibid., pp. 189–90.

Shuster by talking about him "in the most bellicose and unmeasured terms" in front of the British minister and the manager of the Imperial Bank. Indeed, Poklewski's language had been so abusive that he found it necessary later to apologize to Sir George.[18] The British legation took no part in the dispute, and Sir Edward Grey approved of Sir George Barclay's neutrality, "merely judging from the merits of the case." Moreover, Grey believed that Shuster should be allowed to establish financial order from which both Russia and Britain would gain.[19]

To Russia, Britain's benevolent neutrality in the Shuster-Mornard case was a veiled form of support for the former. In a telegram to Benckendorff, Neratov complained that American advisers had taken over the conduct of all affairs in Persia, which was "undoubtedly dangerous." Grey "leans to the side of Shuster, who is supported by Barclay, in spite of what he told Poklewski." [20]

Following Poklewski's lead, the German minister, Count Quadt zu Wykradt und Isny, addressed a note to the Persian government upholding Mornard and containing a "somewhat discourteous reference to Mr. Shuster." [21] The French and the Italians also rallied to Mornard's defense, but Shuster had gained the complete confidence of the Majles and was assured of its enthusiastic backing. Mornard retreated and grudgingly accepted a truce.

The Mornard case had not yet been settled when Shuster found himself in another and much more serious conflict with Russia. To make possible the collection of taxes in a country verging on anarchy, the Majles had authorized Shuster to organize a Treasury gendarmerie.[22] He immediately offered the command

18. Extract from a letter from Mr. Wood, June 24, 1911; F. O. 371/1192. Minute by Mr. Norman in Persia, No. 29939, July 31, 1911; ibid.

19. Barclay to Grey, No. 232, Telegram, Gulahek, July 5, 1911, and Grey to Buchanan, No. 319, Telegram, July 6, 1911; F. O. 371/1192.

20. Acting Minister of Foreign Affairs to the Ambassador in London, Benckendorff, Telegram No. 855, June 26/July 9, 1911; M. O., 2nd series, 18 (Part 1, No. 184), 201–02. The same document was published with omissions in S.D.D., 6, 199–200.

21. Barclay to Grey, No. 371, Telegraphic, Gulahek, August 2, 1911; F. O. 371/1192.

22. Barclay to Grey, No. 234, Telegraphic, Tehran, July 7, 1911; ibid.

of the new force to the British military attaché, Major Charles Stokes, who had the reputation of knowing Persia and her language better than any other foreigner in Tehran.

That the Foreign Office was ambivalent in regard to the Stokes appointment is evident from intradepartmental memoranda. "From the Russian point of view the choice of Major Stokes is most unfortunate as he is fanatically anti-Russian," commented Undersecretary Norman. "On the other hand," he added, "the appointment will be a good one from the general point of view." Unless the Government of India objected (Stokes' commission was in the Indian army), and it should have no reason to do so, Britain should acquiesce in the appointment, for "to throw obstacles in its way would look like opposing the efforts of the Majles, who have approved of it, to reform Persia." Louis Mallet wrote that the Russian government would suspect Shuster of anti-Russian designs. "It would be very unfortunate if Mr. Shuster . . . [one word illegible] this hostility of the Russian Govt who can thwart him and make his task impossible, if they wish to do so." Sir Edward Grey added that

> If Major Stokes is appointed, he should be cautioned to suppress all anti-Russian feeling & Sir G. Barclay might tell Mr. Shuster . . . [a word illegible, perhaps "delicately"] what the situation is and point out how essential it is that no employe in Shuster's administration should show anything but complete impartiality between nations.[23]

On July 10, 1911, Neratov told Buchanan that while he had no objections to the gendarmerie as such, he would prefer its command being given to an officer representing a minor power. "If it were possible, on the other hand, to split up the command, he thought that the posts might be filled by Russian and British officers respectively." [24] Grey was willing to accept Neratov's solution [25] and instructed Barclay to suggest to Shuster that he appoint a Swede instead of an Englishman.

23. Persia, No. 26457, July 7, 1911, Treasurer-General, Minutes; ibid.
24. Buchanan to Grey, No. 148, Telegraphic, St. Petersburg, July 11, 1911; ibid.
25. Grey to Buchanan, No. 199, Telegraphic, July 13, 1911; ibid.

Shuster refused to be guided by Barclay's advice and told the British minister that he needed Stokes, who was the only man capable of accomplishing the difficult task of forming a gendarmerie. Barclay reported that the Persian government would not accept the two-command solution "unless under compulsion," in which case Shuster would resign.[26]

The longer the Foreign Office studied the Stokes case, the less it liked it. A director of the Anglo-Persian Oil Company, Charles Greenway, called on Norman and said he hoped the British Government would "forbid" the appointment of Major Stokes as contrary to British interests,

> because Major Stokes was entirely identified with the most extreme nationalists in Persia and attended the meetings of their *anjumans*. He was nearly as anti-British as he was anti-Russian and lost no chance of denouncing the iniquity of British policy in Persia especially as regards the difficulties which have been put in the way of loans. In his new position he will have every opportunity of damaging the position of Great Britain in Persia and of spreading his opinions among Persians.[27]

Norman, who had been aware of Stokes' views, admitted that he had no idea that the military attaché had gone so far as to join a Persian revolutionary society. To a Foreign Office private telegram inquiring about Stokes' opinions and actions, Sir George Barclay replied that the major had often expressed to him "in private strong condemnation of the policy of H. M. Government." Barclay had never heard of Stokes' attending *anjomans*, but "He has always been in close touch with extreme nationalists, and is in the general opinion closely identified with that party."[28] Russia could not permit an English officer to command a Persian force in the north. "It seems to me," Poklewski telegraphed home, "that we could agree to the appointment of Mr. Stokes

26. Barclay to Grey, No. 252, Tehran, July 14, 1911; ibid.

27. Persia, No. 27787, July 17, 1911, Treasury Gendarmerie, Minute by Norman; ibid.

28. Decypher telegram from Sir G. Barclay, Tehran, July 18, 1911, Private and Confidential, File No. 28250; ibid.

only if a Russian officer is given the same position in our sphere of influence, or if the organization of Persian military forces is entrusted to our instructors." [29] Benckendorff had several conversations with Nicolson, who was very unhappy over the Stokes affair. He did not know how Britain could stop Stokes from entering Persian service if he chose to resign his commission.[30] Neratov pressed the issue. "We consider it impossible in principle to remain indifferent to the invitation of Stokes to the post of chief of financial gendarmerie which would function in our sphere of influence." [31]

The Russian press opened a campaign against the Stokes appointment. On August 3 *Novoe Vremia* warned that the appointment could adversely affect the 1907 Anglo-Russian agreement. When the London *Times* stated that the British government had no legal means of preventing Stokes from resigning from British service, *Novoe Vremia* retorted that the only possible conclusion was that the Agreement of 1907 was "*a merci* of any adventurer and, therefore, remained a scrap of paper without real significance." [32] Sir George Buchanan reported from St. Petersburg that public opinion had been aroused and official circles disturbed. Neratov insisted that Grey issue "a declaration of the readiness of His Majesty's Government to support any demand for compensation that the Russian Government might eventually put forward in order that Russian public opinion might receive some moral satisfaction." [33]

Grey tried to compromise. On August 8 Barclay warned the Persian government that it could insist on employing Stokes only if his activities did not spread to the Russian sphere of influence. Otherwise Britain would recognize Russia's right to defend her interests in the north. But Russia grew ever more intransigent.

29. Poklewski's telegram, Tehran, June 25/July 8, 1911; S.D.D., 6, 198.

30. Benckendorff's telegram, London, July 4/17, 1911, ibid., pp. 6–7.

31. Acting Minister of Foreign Affairs to the Ambassador in London, Telegram, St. Petersburg, July 11/24, 1911; S.D.D., 1, 25–26.

32. *Novoe Vremia* No. 12699 of August 3 and No. 12704 of August 2, 1911, as cited in M. O., 2nd series, 18, (Part 1), 312, note 1.

33. Buchanan to Grey, No. 228, St. Petersburg, August 9, 1911; F. O. 371/1192.

Even the appointment of a Russian officer to an equivalent post in the gendarmerie would not do. "That would return us to the policy of rivalry," wrote Neratov.³⁴

Count Benckendorff feared that the Stokes incident might seriously harm Anglo-Russian relations. In a conversation with Grey on August 15 he emphasized that the Russian government did not blame Britain. However, the Russian public was convinced that the Stokes appointment was a violation of the "parallélisme de notre situation réciproque en Perse." Grey said that he would not be the cause of deterioration of friendly relations between the two powers over such an issue as the Stokes case; but he did not know what to do except postpone the acceptance of Stoke's resignation from the Indian army. Benckendorff was convinced of Grey's good faith.³⁵ In a long letter to Neratov he expressed his certainty that England had no secret designs on northern Persia. Grey had already repudiated Stokes but did not want to oppose Shuster, wishing to avoid the inevitable reproach that the powers always put obstacles to any serious reforms in Persia. Benckendorff concluded with a warning that Germany would take advantage of a rift between Britain and Russia.³⁶

"Little Neratov," as his colleagues called him,³⁷ finally succeeded in provoking the phlegmatic Sir Edward Grey. Replying to the threats reported by Buchanan on August 15, Sir Edward repeated that Stokes had acted independently of the British government. Neratov must realize this.

> He has not, as far as I am aware, made any objections at Tehran, and it seems to me time that he should make some communication there . . . in support of my warning. . . . At present the Persian Government must look on me as more Russian than the Russians. . . . The Acting Minister of Foreign Affairs should explain to the public that the sole reason why the appointment has not been made has been

34. Neratov to Benckendorff, Telegram, No. 1079, August 2/15, 1911; M. O., 2nd series, 18 (Part 1, No. 320), 323–24.
35. Benckendorff to Neratov, Letter, August 2/15, 1911; ibid. (No. 322), pp. 325–26.
36. Same to same, Letter, August 2/15, 1911; ibid. (No. 323), pp. 327–30.
37. Eugene de Schelking, *Recollections of a Russian Diplomat*, p. 230.

our action, and do in the present case what I have done in this country in keeping public opinion patient over the continued presence of Russian troops in Northern Persia and the actions of Colonel Liakhov in past years.

I have had to defend these matters several times, and if I had been as exacting over them as Russia is now the good understanding between Great Britain and Russia would have come to an end long ago.[38]

Grey's fortitude vis-à-vis Russia was exceedingly limited. On August 16 he blustered, on August 17 he gave in and told Benckendorff that Stokes would not be allowed to resign from the Indian army, thus preventing him from accepting the appointment as commander of Shuster's gendarmerie. Grey said that he could be attacked in Parliament for occupying himself more with Russian interests in the north than British interests in the south. His performance, as reported by Benckendorff, was undignified. He had surrendered unconditionally and now pleaded for Russian initiative in Tehran to protect himself against embarrassment in the Parliament.[39]

On the nineteenth Poklewski transmitted to the Persian government a formal note, protesting Stokes' nomination as commander of the gendarmerie and reserving the right to take the necessary measures to safeguard Russia's interests in northern Persia. On the same day Barclay made a similar brief statement, adding only "that His Majesty's Government cannot accept Major Stokes' resignation in view of the well-founded Russian objections to his appointment." [40]

The very next day Shuster paid a visit to Poklewski and put before him a new proposal—to hire Stokes but not keep him in Tehran for more than six months, at the expiration of which the major would be sent to Shiraz. Shuster explained his plans for reform, intimating that he had, if not the support, at least the sympathy of the British. Should Russia continue to frustrate his

38. Grey to Buchanan, No. 441, August 16, 1911; F. O. 371/1192.

39. Benckendorff to Neratov, Telegram No. 189, August 4/17, 1911; M.O., 2nd series, 18, (Part 1, No. 331), 343-44.

40. Barclay to Grey, No. 162, Gulahek, September 4, 1911, Enclosures 4 and 5; F. O. 371/1192.

"The Strangling of Persia"

every effort, he would have to resign and leave the country. "I must confess that the conversation with him impressed me," Poklewski wrote home.[41] He was even willing to contemplate a compromise such as Shuster was proposing, though he told Barclay that he did not think the Russian government would change its policy.[42] The Russian ambassador in London, Count Benckendorff, suggested the acceptance of the compromise to spare Grey political difficulties.[43]

The conversations between the Treasurer General and the Russian minister continued. "Would it be possible," Poklewski asked, "to arrange that, after six months, one of the Swedish officers should be put in command of the whole Gendarmerie and that Major Stokes should then work nominally under him and outside the so-called Russian zone . . . ?"[44] Shuster found it difficult to formulate an agreement with Stokes to the satisfaction of both the Russians and the Majles. However, increased personal contact with Poklewski was making it easier to find an acceptable middle ground. Shuster pleaded that the Russian government, as a gesture of generosity, agree to a contract of nine months which Stokes would spend in Tehran. In the margin of Poklewski's telegram reporting Shuster's request, the Tsar wrote, "No yielding. Peterhoff, August 26 [September 8], 1911."[45] Though negotiations continued a while longer, the issue was permanently closed.

Russia's policies in Iran in 1910 and 1911 were closely related to European and even African affairs. Her opposition to Shuster and Stokes was the result not only of Persian developments but of the general international situation in which Russia found herself after the Bosnian crisis. Germany in particular exercised a powerful influence on the course of events in Tehran.

41. Poklewski to Neratov, Telegram No. 702, August 8/21, 1911; M. O., 2nd series, 18 (Part 1, No. 351), pp. 361–62.

42. Barclay to Grey, No. 348, Telegraphic, Gulahek, August 21, 1911; F. O. 371/1192.

43. Benckendorff to Neratov, No. 192, August 9/22; 1911; M. O., 2nd series, 18 (Part 1), 365, note 3.

44. Poklewski to Shuster, Tehran, September 2, 1911; W. M. Shuster, *The Strangling of Persia* (New York, 1912), pp. 391–92.

45. Poklewski to Neratov, No. 739, August 25/September 7, 1911; M. O., 2nd series, 18 (Part 1, No. 411), 415.

German involvement in Persia in the nineteenth century and the early years of the twentieth had been small. Russia and Britain were too well entrenched to be seriously challenged. However, the construction of the Baghdad railway aroused grave fears in both Russia and England. The former was especially sensitive to the possibility of a German-owned branch line connecting Baghdad and the Shiite holy cities of Karbalā and Najaf with Khāneqin, on the Perso-Turkish border. When Ivan Alekseevich Zinov'ev, now ambassador in Constantinople, first learned of the plans for such a line in March 1902, he told the Persian ambassador that a railway from Persia to the holy cities of Iraq would greatly increase the flow of Persian pilgrims, which would constitute an additional drain on Persian finances. Persia should demand of Turkey, under the threat of closing the borders to the pilgrims, that she postpone the construction of the line.[46] Russia was equally alarmed at the prospect of the extension into Persia of the British railway from Quetta to Nushki. Lamsdorff wrote that the realization of such projects was "in contradiction to Russia's tasks." [47]

Defeat in the Japanese war momentarily weakened Russia's determination to prevent all railway construction in Persia. On August 25, 1905, a Special Conference presided over by Lamsdorff agreed that it was inexpedient to press Persia to extend the "sterilizing" agreements of 1890 and 1900 beyond 1910.[48]

It was the German threat in Europe that made Britain and Russia compose their differences over Iran. Shortly before the conclusion of the Anglo-Russian Convention of 1907, Germany, trying to forestall the formation of a hostile combination directed against her, informed the Russian government that she was willing not to seek concessions for railways, highways, or telegraphs in northern Persia if Russia allowed her commercial freedom and

46. G. L. Bondarevskii, *Bagdadskaia doroga i proniknovenie germanskogo imperializma na Blizhnii Vostok*, pp. 244–45. Bondarevskii refers to the Foreign Policy Archive of the Ministry of Foreign Affairs of the U.S.S.R., Dossier No. 3625, pp. 329/31.

47. Project of a secret instruction to Vlasov [Minister in Tehran], September 10/23, 1902, as cited in Popov, "Stranitsa . . . ," p. 148.

48. The Journal of the Conference in "Anglo-russkoe sopernichestvo v Persii v 1890–1906 g.g."; K. A., 1 (56) (1933), 57–58.

built a line from Tehran to Khāneqin to connect with the Baghdad railway.⁴⁹

The Russian government was particularly unhappy over the prospect of a German railway penetrating Persia from the west and opening the door to an influx of German goods into an area that was commercially an exclusive Russian preserve.⁵⁰ The military raised the strongest objections, stating their firm belief in the "impossibility of reconciling the Baghdad Railway with Russia's strategic interests." ⁵¹

Between 1907 and 1910 Russia, whose relations with Germany were cool, could not fail to be alarmed at the evidences of the continued growth of German influence in the Middle East. After the Bosnian fiasco, pro-German circles in St. Petersburg made a determined effort to improve relations between the two countries. In 1910 they succeeded in forcing Izvolskii's resignation from the post of Minister of Foreign Affairs and initiating negotiations with Berlin.

On October 10, 1910, Hugh O'Beirne telegraphed Grey that the Russian and German emperors would meet at Potsdam and that Persian problems would be discussed.⁵² A week later O'Beirne was informed by the new Minister of Foreign Affairs, Sazonov, that the Russians had already been negotiating with the Germans and had "bound themselves to agree to the junction of the Baghdad-Khanikin branch with a railway to be eventually built by Russia from the frontier to Tehran." ⁵³

The Persian question was discussed in detail at a ministerial conference presided over by Sazonov on October 28. The Foreign

---

49. Erusalimskii, "K istorii potsdamskogo soglasheniia 1911 g."; *K. A.*, 3 (58) (1933), 47. Some of the material on the railway question appears in my article "Russian Imperialism and Persian Railways," *Russian Thought and Politics*, Harvard Slavic Studies, 4 (The Hague, 1957), 355–73.

50. Protocol of deliberations of the Council of Ministers of October 15/28, 1910; B. de Siebert, *Entente Diplomacy and the World, Matrix of the History of Europe, 1909–1914* (New York, 1921), p. 477. Hereafter cited as *E. D.*

51. Id.

52. O'Beirne to Grey, No. 276, Telegraphic, St. Petersburg, October 10, 1910; *British Documents on the Origin of the War, 1898–1914*, 10 (Part 1), 549. Hereafter cited as *B. D.*

53. Same to same, October 17; ibid. (No. 599), pp. 550–51.

Minister reviewed for his colleagues the course of Russo-German negotiations. Russia had proposed to conclude an agreement with Germany on the following principles: (1) Russia would not oppose the construction of the Baghdad railway; (2) the Baghdad railway would not be linked with future Persian lines without prior agreement with Russia; (3) Germany would declare that she had no political interests in Persia, would accept the existence of special Russian strategic and commercial interests in the northern zone of Persia, and would not seek concessions in that zone. On the basis of these proposals Sazonov hoped to arrive at an understanding which would lead to improved relations, for "At present one could say that the hostile influence of Germany is felt, in one form or another, everywhere, assuming at times forms extremely unpleasant for us." [54]

The news of pourparlers with Germany concerning Persia evoked a storm of indignation in the Russian business community, which knew it could not compete with Germany without the help of such political measures as preferential tariffs, discriminatory freight rates, or even outright export subsidies. A group of Moscow industrialists led by P. P. Riabushinskii, one of Russia's wealthiest men, met with several sympathetic Duma deputies to question a representative of the Foreign Ministry on the government's position in regard to German penetration of Persia. He stressed the volume and importance of Russo-Persian trade and noted that 80 percent of Russian exports to Iran consisted of cotton goods in which Moscow businessmen, as owners of textile mills, were especially interested. The achievements of Russian commerce in Persia were due to customs and tariff agreements which were extremely disadvantageous to Persia and favorable to Russia. But even with all the one-sided agreements, Russian trade would not prosper without constant government subsidies. The extension of a German railway into Persia would upset old arrangements, make it impossible to continue business as usual, and lead to disastrous consequences for Russian commerce. Riabushinskii wanted Persia to have no railways, considering any and all of them a potential threat to the interests of Russian business. A

54. Journal of a special conference on Persian affairs, October 15/28, 1910; "K istorii potsdamskogo soglasheniia 1911 g."; K. A., 3 (58) (1933), 53.

Soviet writer commented that "The Russian bourgeoisie demanded that tsarism conduct in Persia the usual politically reactionary line of keeping Persia roadless, and stubbornly insisted that feudal-military protection secure its interests in Persia."[55]

Sazonov himself felt that it would have been better if no railways were built in Persia. He hoped that Russia, while promising Germany to construct the Tehran-Khāneqin line, would be able to evade this obligation. Moreover, he believed that the German railway would not reach Baghdad for another ten to fifteen years.

> The Khāneqin line will not be started before that time elapses [Sazonov said]. Thus we will have much time to take measures firmly to consolidate our Persian markets and, should we be successful in treading this path, we need not fear the Khāneqin line at all. In the meantime the Germans are apparently attaching great significance to our agreement to link the network [nonexistent] of Persian railways with the Baghdad line. This agreement, which under certain circumstances could easily turn out to have been fictitious, will achieve for us a very essential result, namely a general improvement of our relations with Germany.[56]

It is abundantly clear that, given freedom of choice, the Russian government would have preferred to keep Persia without railways. However, fearing a further deterioration of her relations with Germany, Russia felt compelled to placate her powerful western neighbor by promising to connect Tehran with the projected Baghdad line. It would have been possible to allow the Germans themselves to build this line, but that would have lead to the establishment of important permanent German interests in the Russian sphere. Russia was understandably reluctant to spend money to facilitate German commercial competition, nor was she willing to turn the construction over to some international concern, for that would have only hastened the disaster. The policy that seemed the most satisfactory was to dodge, procrastinate,

---

55. Erusalimskii, "K istorii potsdamskogo soglasheniia 1911 g."; *ibid.*, p. 50.
56. Journal of a special ministerial conference; *ibid.*, p. 54. Cf. S. D. Sazonov, *Vospominaniia* (Paris, 1927), pp. 34–35.

and hope that something would come up to change the international situation in Russia's favor.

The British failed to understand Sazonov's game. The ostensible willingness of the Russian Foreign Minister to accept German demands in regard to the Khāneqin-Tehran line struck them as foolish and harmful. Even the experienced Sir Arthur Nicolson did not appreciate Sazonov's gamble or understand his motives. It seemed to him that Sazonov had "light-heartedly surrendered to Germany all that Izvolsky was determined to withhold from her," and that he seemed "to have made this surrender without receiving anything at all in exchange for it." Baffled by it all, Nicolson wrote: "I cannot understand how he [Sazonov] can be so completely blind to the consequences of what he is doing."[57] Sir George Buchanan thought that the agreement was a diplomatic victory for Germany and attributed its conclusion to Sazonov's mistake "in allowing himself to be entrapped during his conversations with M. Kiderlen-Waechter into giving verbal assurances, of which he did not at the time realize the full significance."[58]

The emperors Wilhelm and Nicholas met at Potsdam in November 1910, but the final agreement on Persia was not signed until August 1911. It formally acknowledged Russia's "special interests" in Iran, whereas Germany was declared to have only "commercial ends" there. Germany promised not to seek railway, highway, or telegraph concessions in the Russian zone, and Russia in return pledged herself to build the Tehran-Khāneqin line within a specified period of time from the completion of the northern section of the Baghdad railway.[59] Germany also secretly promised not to construct branch lines leading from the Baghdad railway in the direction of either the Caucasus or Persia. Turkey, which was vitally interested in such lines for the prosperity of her eastern provinces, had not been consulted.[60]

57. A. Nicolson to Sir F. Cartwright (private), F. O. February 6, 1911, B. D., 10 (Part 1, No. 678), p. 650.

58. Buchanan, *My Mission to Russia*, 1, pp. 97–98.

59. Buchanan to Grey, St. Petersburg, August 23, 1911; B. D., 10 (Part 1, No. 714).

60. Neratov to Benckendorff, August 25/September 7, 1911; E. D., No. 643, p. 576.

"The government of the tsar decided to compensate itself for the concessions made to Germany by strengthening its positions in Persia at England's expense," writes a Soviet historian.[61] The connection between Russia's improved relations with Germany and her increased belligerency in Persia is quite clear. It is equally clear that Russia was able to take advantage of the Moroccan crisis to advance her interests in Persia in the knowledge that Britain would not dare to engage in simultaneous conflicts with Germany and Russia.

On April 27, 1911, Moulai Hafid, the Sultan of Morocco, appealed to France for help against rebels in the cities of Fez, Rabat, and Meknez. When French troops went to the Sultan's rescue, Germany, realizing that the country had fallen entirely into French hands, demanded compensation. On July 1 the gunboat *Panther* appeared off shore at Agadir. A Franco-German war seemed about to break out. The British reacted with unusual firmness. In a speech at the Mansion House, Lloyd George placed Britain squarely on the French side. When the German ambassador, Metternich, protested to Grey, the latter sent for the First Lord of the Admiralty and told him to have the navy in readiness, since it might be attacked at any time. Germany had to choose between war and retreat. Like Russia in the Bosnian crisis, she withdrew.

Taking advantage of the critical situation in Europe, Russia made a great effort that summer to regain the dominant position she had occupied in Tehran in the reigns of Mozaffar ed-Din Shah and Mohammad Ali Shah. The simplest and the least dangerous way of achieving this end was to restore the latter to the throne.

In his exile at Odessa the former Shah ceaselessly worked to regain the Crown. Dozens of ardent supporters came to him for instructions and returned to Persia to intrigue and plot in favor of their deposed master. Mohammad Ali's propaganda was especially effective among the Turkoman tribes of the Gorgān, where rumors of his impending return spread as early as March 1910.[62] The Persian government informed Sir George Barclay that Mohammad Ali was inciting the tribes to rebellion and that he had

61. Efremov, *Venshniaia politika Rossii* (Moscow, 1961), p. 119.
62. Telegram of Dolgopolov, Astarābād, March 17/30, 1910; S.D.D., 4, 124.

invited two chiefs on the Ja'farbāy Turkomans to Baku where they were given large sums of money for distribution in Persia.[63] Such actions, the Persian government claimed, were incompatible with the stipulations of the protocol signed by England, Russia, and Persia.[64] The Russian government, of course, denied everything, but promised nevertheless to warn the former Shah against any such actions.[65]

St. Petersburg was well aware of Mohammad Ali's plans and activities. Being totally dependent on his hosts, the former Shah did not even try to conceal from them his desire to return to Persia. He had on several occasions approached the Russian government through his closest collaborators, including the former Prime Minister, Sa'd od-Dowleh, in regard to his restoration.

At the Russian Foreign Ministry the Persian revolution was seen as an English plot to undermine the authority of the shahs, who had over the years become obedient tools of Russia. Therefore Mohammad Ali's dreams of restoration found a sympathetic, though somewhat equivocal, response. He was devoted to Russia and "under the skilled guidance of the Imperial Russian Legation" could become a "useful" ruler. However, the Foreign Ministry realized that the partisans of the Shah were disunited and disorganized. There was no certainty that Mohammad Ali and the tribes loyal to him could take Tehran without the open support or large financial aid from Russia. Yet, anarchy and disorder in Persia could produce an independent movement in favor of Mohammad Ali. His partisans might gain strength and be joined by the young Ahmad Shah. Then the appearance of Mohammad Ali on Persian soil would be timely, and Russia "should not create any obstacles to it." [66]

63. Poklewski's telegram of September 25/October 8, 1910, Tehran; *S.D.D.*, 5, 129–30.

64. Hussein Kuli Khan [Hoseyn Qoli Khān] to Sir G. Barclay (Translation), October 2, 1910, Enclosure in Barclay to Grey, No. 185, Gulahek, October 5, 1910; F. O. 371/996. A Foreign Office official wrote in the margin "This is not our concern and probably is not true."

65. Captain Khabaev's telegram, Odessa, October 6/19, 1910; *S.D.D.*, 5, 113. Acting Minister of Foreign Affairs to the Minister in Tehran, St. Petersburg, October 6/19, 1910; ibid., p. 145.

66. Neratov to Poklewski, St. Petersburg, July, 1911, M. O., 2nd series, 18 (Part 1, No. 133), 143–46.

"The Strangling of Persia"

In reply to Mohammad Ali's questions about Russia's position vis-à-vis his restoration, the Foreign Ministry replied that in principle Russia had nothing against it, but doubted its possibility. He should not count on Russian aid. If he wanted to go back to Persia he would have to do so at his own risk.

> However, if the movement in his favor assumed serious proportions, if the people really demanded his return and his own son and successor, having joined his partisans, abdicated in his favor, then, of course, we would be the first to hail him and would, on our part, give him all the cooperation which depended on us.[67]

The former Shah knew that the Russian government would welcome his return to Persia. In mid-October he expressed the desire to travel incognito to western Europe, ostensibly for medical treatment. The Tsar gave his permission, and Mohammad Ali left Odessa for Vienna on October 31.[68]

The Persian government, having accumulated a vast amount of evidence of Mohammad Ali's intrigues, stopped paying his pension. The Russian and British ministers protested, claiming that the allegations made against the former Shah had not been proved. Hoseyn Qoli Khān Navvāb, Minister of Foreign Affairs, refused to comply with the demand of the two powers to resume payments, whereupon Poklewski and Barclay sent legation servants to deliver to him another note.

> They were to go to the Ministry of Foreign Affairs and wait till the money was paid. If it was not paid, they were to follow Minister for Foreign Affairs to his house or elsewhere. This is a custom followed by creditors in Persia for recovery of debts.[69]

For three days the legations' servants dogged the steps of the minister until, humiliated and disgusted, he paid.

---

67. Id.
68. Acting Minister of Foreign Affairs to Captain Khabaev, assigned to the person of H. M. the Shah, Telegram, St. Petersburg, October 16/29, 1910; ibid., p. 159. Captain Khabaev's telegram, Odessa, October 18/31, 1910; ibid., p. 164.
69. Barclay to Grey, No. 447, Telegraphic, Tehran, November 3, 1910; F. O. 371/966.

When the Persian minister in London complained about the indignity inflicted upon Hoseyn Qoli Khān, Nicolson replied that the complaint's "tone was injudicious," though he admitted to his colleagues that the incident had been unfortunate. Grey agreed.[70] He instructed Barclay "not to cooperate in steps of that nature," and so to inform his Russian colleague in Tehran.[71]

In Vienna Mohammad Ali met one of his younger brothers, Abol Fath Mirzā Sālār od-Dowleh, and his devoted supporter, Arshad od-Dowleh. Plans were made for the former to invade Persia from Turkish territory, while the latter would raise the Turkomans around Astarābād. N. G. Hartwig, former Russian minister in Tehran now serving at Belgrade, came to Vienna to discuss the former Shah's project. In an army camp near Varāmin on the eve of his execution by government troops, which had defeated and captured him on September 5, 1911, Arshad od-Dowleh recalled the discussion.

> The Russian Minister came to see us, and we asked for help. He told us that Russia could not help us. Russia and England had an agreement in regard to Persia, from which neither would depart. They had resolved not to interfere in any way internally. "But, on the other hand," he said, "the field is clear. If we can do nothing for you, we equally will do nothing against you. It is for you to decide what are your chances of success. If you think you can reach the throne of Persia, then go. Only remember, we cannot help you, and if you fail we have no responsibility."

They asked Hartwig for money. He said Russia could not provide any but suggested they raise money on the receipt for some jewels the former Shah had deposited at the Russian Bank in Tehran.[72]

70. Translation of a telegram received October 31, 1910 (Communicated by Mirzā Mehdi Khān), November 2; Nicolson's minute, Persia No. 39970, November 3, 1910, Ex-Shah's pension; Grey's Minute, Persia, No. 40066, November 4, 1910; ibid.

71. Grey to Barclay, No. 187, November 8, 1910; ibid.

72. Arshad od-Dowleh's confession was recorded on the spot by Arthur Moore, a correspondent of the London *Times* who knew Persian. (Moore, *Orient Express*, pp. 33–34.) Cf. Ambassador in London Benckendorff to the Acting Minister of Foreign Affairs, Neratov, Telegram No. 273, October 29/November 11, 1911;

Since the Soviet government has not published the relevant documents, it is impossible to determine exactly when and under what conditions Mohammad Ali was allowed to begin his counter-revolutionary campaign. However, by December 5 he was receiving diplomatic support from Sazonov, who informed the British chargé d'affaires, Hugh O'Beirne, that an emissary had come to Russia with the proposal to restore the former Shah. Sazonov claimed that he had discouraged the unidentified emissary, but did not see the scheme as altogether impracticable. O'Beirne reported to the Foreign Office:

> When I remarked that it would be madness on the part of the ex-Shah to have anything to do with it, and that the only result would be the loss of his pension, Monsieur Sazonov replied that he was not so sure that there might not be something in the idea, or words to that effect, adding that things in Persia were going very badly.[73]

Having received this information, Grey sent word to Sazonov that "the return of the late Shah might have most embarrassing consequences." [74]

While the Russian government pretended to know nothing about it, the former Shah's agents were active in the Caucasus and in Transcaspia. The bandit leader Rahim Khān, who had retreated to Russia after Mohammad Ali's overthrow, was preparing to return to Persia at the head of a rebel force. When the Persian government asked Russia to stop him from crossing the border, Sazonov telegraphed the Viceroy of the Caucasus, Count Illarion Ivanovich Vorontsov-Dashkov, that Russia could not

---

M. O., 2nd series, 18 (Part 2, No. 860), 354. Cf. also Shuster, *The Strangling of Persia*, p. 107.

After Shuster published Moore's record of Arshad od-Dowleh's confession in a letter to the London *Times* (October 21, 1911), the Russian government issued an official communique denying the alleged meeting in Vienna between Mohammad Ali and the Russian ambassador, M. M. Giers. Technically the Russians were correct. Shuster learned later in Vienna that Mohammad Ali had negotiated not with Giers but with his old friend Hartwig. (Shuster, p. 107.)

73. O'Beirne to Grey, No. 475, Secret, St. Petersburg, December 6, 1910; F. O. 371/967.

74. Grey to Buchanan, Draft of a telegram, No. 317, Secret, December 20, 1910; ibid.

prevent Rahim Khān, who was not a captive, from returning to his own country. The Viceroy was also asked to warn Rahim Khān that if he went to Persia and engaged in antigovernment activities, he would not be readmitted to Russia since it was impossible to allow him to use Russian territory as a base of operations.[75]

Early in July, in front of a large number of people at a dinner party, the Russian minister, Poklewski-Koziell, predicted that the Persian government would cease to exist within a few weeks.[76] Lacking documentary evidence, it is impossible to tell whether he had received secret information from St. Petersburg, or was only engaging in prophecy like the rest of Tehran. The city was full of rumors.

On July 12, having learned that Sardār Arshad (Arshad od-Dowleh), Leys os-Soltān, and Mansur ol-Molk, three prominent supporters of Mohammad Ali, had been seen in Baku, the Persian government through its chargé d'affaires in St. Petersburg, Ali Qoli Khān Moshāver ol-Mamālek, requested their detention. The Russian government agreed to inform the authorities in the Caucasus, but told Ali Qoli Khān that "the arrest of the persons named by him was inadmissible under law; as long as they have done nothing prejudicial they can only be placed under surveil-

---

75. Poklewski-Koziell, Telegram, Tehran, November 22/December 5, 1910; Consul A. Miller, Telegram, November 22/December 5, 1910; Minister of Foreign Affairs to H.I.M.'s Viceroy in the Caucasus, St. Petersburg, November 22/December 5, 1910; S.D.D., 5, 218–19. Until then the infamous bandit chief, Rahim Khān Chelebiāni of Qaradāgh, had been freely permitted to use Russian territory as a sanctuary where he could hide from government troops. Occasionally he looted Russian property in Persia, and the Persian government would receive Russian demands that it pay for the damage. Sir George Barclay wrote to Sir Edward Grey: "It is more than unusually difficult for Persian Government to give satisfaction for depredations of rebel chief, in view of the fact that his plunder is stored in Russia. M. Poklewski has on more than one occasion brought this to the attention of his Government, and suggested the confiscation of Rahim Khān's ill-gotten property." (Barclay to Grey, No. 95, Telegraphic, Tehran, March 10, 1910; F. O. 371/952.) Needless to say, Poklewski's suggestions were ignored, the Russian government having decided in January 1910 that Rahim Khān could not "be considered a common bandit" but "rather an insurgent." (Minister of Foreign Affairs to the Minister in Tehran, Telegram, December 29, 1910/January 11, 1910; S.D.D., 3, 310.)

76. Shuster, *The Strangling of Persia*, p. 108.

lance."[77] In a telegram to the diplomatic officer assigned to the Viceroy of the Caucasus, the Ministry of Foreign Affairs defined Russia's position thus:

> Strictly observing the principle of non-interference in internal affairs and, in particular, in the struggle of parties in Persia, and being by no means hostile in principle to the return of Mohammad Ali, we must abstain from any opposition to his partisans in their endeavor for his restoration. At the same time it is very important for us that no proof of Mohammad Ali's direct intrigues should fall into the hands of the Persian Government since it would then have a basis for depriving him of his pension and we would have to take care of him.[78]

The authorities in the Caucasus willingly entered the spirit of the game. Colonel Pastriulin, chief of the secret police in Baku, telegraphed the Viceroy's office in Tiflis that he had no information concerning the presence in Baku of Sardār Arshad and the others.[79]

Persia's Regent, Abol Qāsem Khān Nāser ol-Molk, privately inquired at the British legation whether the English would oppose the return of the former Shah or remain neutral. The British informed Poklewski, who asked them to tell the Regent that Russia was giving Mohammad Ali neither moral nor material support. Having thus admitted by implication that the former Shah was making attempts at restoration, Poklewski indicated to Barclay that in his opinion barring the Shah from passing through Russia on his way to Persia would constitute a departure from neutrality and "active assistance to the present Persian government."[80]

77. Telegram to the Diplomatic Official assigned to H.I.M's Viceroy in the Caucasus, St. Petersburg, June 30/July 13, 1911; S.D.D., 6, 207.

78. Telegram to the Diplomatic Officer assigned to the Viceroy in the Caucasus, No. 877, July 1/14, 1911; M. O., 2nd series, 18 (Part 2), 146, note 1.

79. Telegram of Kokhanovskii [Viceroy's office], Tiflis, July 2/15, 1911; S.D.D., 7, 3.

80. Minister in Tehran, to the Acting Minister of Foreign Affairs, Neratov, Telegram, No. 556, July 4/17, 1911; M. O., 2nd series, 18 (Part 1, No. 211), 223–24.

The Russian ambassador in London feared that his government was going too far. Mohammad Ali had proved that he was not a strong man. Should he be restored, he would have to resort to Russian financial assistance and would stay on the throne only through Russian protection. English public opinion would never rally to the Shah, and Russia would lose Britain's support and cooperation. Benckendorff advised Neratov to declare that Russia recognized the young Shah and that allowing Mohammad Ali to use Russia as a base of operations in a Persian civil war was incompatible with the obligations she had assumed. "If there is to be a civil war, we should not have contributed to it." [81] Benckendorff did not know that the former Shah had already arrived in Persia.

Accompanied by a few faithful companions, Mohammad Ali, carrying a Persian passport in the name of Khalil, made his way from Vienna to Petrovsk, a small Caspian port north of Baku. There he and his party boarded a Russian chartered steamer *Christopher*, to which were transferred boxes labeled "Mineral Water," containing two machine guns and a good supply of ammunition purchased by Arshad od-Dowleh in Austria and transported across Russia without the slightest interference from the police.[82] On July 17 the former Shah landed at the Turkoman village of Gomoshtappe, near Astarābād. A small group of supporters welcomed him at the shore. Later they were joined by some Turkomans. A brief meeting was held and it was decided to march on Astarābād without delay. The Shah's younger brother, Malek Mansur Mirzā Shoā' os-Saltaneh, who was in command of the expedition, sent messages to various Turkoman tribes to come to the aid of the returned King.

The next day the authorities at Astarābād received Mohammad Ali's letter demanding submission and stating that he would grant an amnesty to those who had fought against him in the past, preserve the Constitution, maintain security, and punish inciters of disorder. The town officials, leading merchants, clergy, and the local *anjoman* (revolutionary society) decided to submit.

81. Ambassador in London to the Acting Minister of Foreign Affairs, Neratov, Telegram, No. 152, July 5/18, 1911; ibid., pp. 227–28.

82. Arshad od-Dowleh's confession, Moore, *Orient Express*, p. 34.

A number of frightened Constitutionalists took *bast* in the Russian consulate.

"To the thunder of cannon and joyous shouts of the crowd the Shah entered Astarābād today at the beginning of the tenth hour," the Russian consul, Ivanov, telegraphed on July 22.[83] The consulate became the nerve center of the town and Ivanov its "master." While maintaining the fiction of noninterference in Persian affairs to the extent of abstaining from visiting Mohammad Ali, he aided and encouraged him in every way. The former Shah "found no words to express his gratitude for all the attention which I [Ivanov] gave him." [84]

The Persian government found itself in a most difficult situation. Even before the telegraph had brought the news of Mohammad Ali's landing at Gomoshtappe, anarchy had been widespread. Kordestān had been invaded, in accordance with the plans of the former Shah and his friends, by Abol Fath Mirzā Sālār od-Dowleh. Āzarbāyjān, Gilān, Khorāsān, Fārs—the fairest provinces of the Empire—seethed with discontent. Governors often refused to obey Tehran. Bandits made all highways, except those patrolled by the Russians, unsafe. A Cabinet crisis of late June was a symptom of deep sickness which held the country in its morbid grip. There was virtually no force that could oppose the bands of the former Shah. The Cossack Brigade was useless since its commander, Prince Vadbolskii, took his orders from the Russian minister who had been empowered by St. Petersburg to decide in every instance whether the Brigade's Russian officers would or would not obey the Persian government.[85] Diplomacy seemed to be the only instrument left to the Persians.

83. Ivanov's telegram, Astarābād, July 9/22, 1911, S.D.D., 1, 21.

84. Report of the Collegiate Counselor Ivanov, Astarābād, July 20/August 2, 1911; ibid., pp. 59–73.

85. Acting Minister of Foreign Affairs to the Minister in Tehran, Poklewski, St. Petersburg, July 6/19, 1911; ibid., p. 14. In October Poklewski wrote "The Brigade is now almost independent of the Persian government, which not only exercises no control over its finances and operation but also lacks the ability to dispatch any part of it without the consent of the Colonel, and often of the Legation or of St. Petersburg." (Minister in Tehran to the Acting Minister of Foreign Affairs, Neratov, Telegram No. 941, October 1/14, 1911; M. O., 2nd series, 18 [Part 2, No. 631], 168.)

In a note transmitted to Poklewski on July 19, the Persian government reminded him that it had repeatedly brought to his attention Mohammad Ali's intrigues. Contrary to the expectations of the Government of the Shah, the note said, His Excellency had not deemed it necessary to help apprehend Arshad od-Dowleh, Mansur ol-Molk, and Leys os-Soltān, thus permitting them to go to Petrovsk, negotiate with the Turkomans, and enter Persian territory.

> Considering the good neighbourly and friendly relations of the two countries, the Government of the Shah does not know to what to ascribe the prejudice and the indifferent attitude expressed to it under these circumstances by the Government of His Majesty the Emperor. It is hard for the Government of the Shah to believe that for a year the Russian Government could not take measures toward the cessation of the agitation organized by Mohammad Ali Mirzā and his agents.

The Persian government, the note continued, in accordance with the Protocol of September 7, 1909, would no longer pay Mohammad Ali's pension and divested itself of all responsibility for the damages that might result from the landing of Mohammad Ali "who arrived on the Persian shore from Russia in a Russian ship." [86]

The Russian government did not reply to the Persian note for nine days. In the interim it discussed the issue of Mohammad Ali's return with the British and took measures to assure the success of the former Shah, or at least further to weaken the Persian government. On July 19 Neratov instructed Benckendorff to propose to Grey that the two powers abstain from any action that might aid either party in the Persian struggle.[87] Benckendorff spoke to Nicolson, who expressed surprise at the appearance of the former Shah in Persia and added that he must have

86. Note addressed by the Imperial Minister of Foreign Affairs to Russia's Minister in Tehran, July 19, 1911, No. 11678, Enclosure in Poklewski's dispatch of July 13/26, 1911; S.D.D., 7, 29–32.

87. Acting Minister of Foreign Affairs to the Ambassador in London, St. Petersburg, July 6/19, 1911, ibid., p. 15.

traveled through Russia under an assumed name. Nicolson had prepared a dispatch to Buchanan, which he now showed to the Russian ambassador, proposing that the two powers issue a statement denying recognition to Mohammad Ali, supporting the Persian government, and agreeing that it need no longer pay his pension. When Benckendorff suggested that the former Shah might achieve a quick victory, Nicolson replied that it was impossible. There would be a long and bloody civil war, the responsibility for which would fall on the former Shah. Benckendorff telegraphed home that it was necessary to dissociate Russia from any responsibility for the latter's actions. This could be achieved only by going along with the British and issuing a declaration hostile to Mohammad Ali. "Une déclaration différente de celle de l'Angleterre soulignerait une différence principelle, favoriserait lutte intestine en Perse et rendrait, je crains, impossible sincère coopération ultérieure anglaise." [88]

Neratov did not accept Benckendorff's advice but asked him to tell Nicolson "that the appearance of Mohammad Ali in Persia was as much of a surprise for us as for the London Cabinet." The Shah had received no subsidies from Russia, and his travel incognito over Russian territory could hardly have been prevented. Now that he was in Persia Russia could only remain strictly neutral.[89] Neratov had talked with Sir George Buchanan about the proposed joint declaration and accepted the point about the former Shah's pension. However, he was not prepared to take any action against Mohammad Ali or to make prior declarations of nonrecognition. "Having entered Persian territory, Mohammad Ali has burnt his boats and only one thing is left for him: to go forward, either to win or to perish. Therefore I remain of the opinion that in this affair it is best to remain neutral." [90]

Though negotiations between St. Petersburg and London continued for another ten days before an agreement was reached on

88. Ambassador in London to the Acting Minister of Foreign Affairs, Neratov, Telegram No. 154, July 6/19, 1911; M. O., 2nd series, 18 (Part 1, No. 219), 237.

89. Acting Minister of Foreign Affairs to the Ambassador in London, St. Petersburg, July 7/20, 1911; S.D.D., 7, 17.

90. Same to same, Telegram No. 926, July 7/20, 1911; M. O., 2nd series, 18 (Part 1, No. 228), 246–47.

what to tell the Persians, Neratov suggested that Poklewski reply to the Persian note of July 19 that the Russian government had not ignored Persian representations concerning intrigues in favor of Mohammad Ali. Russia had repeatedly warned him against actions inimical to the existing regime.

> However, since the Persian Government never buttressed its statements with any proof and since Mohammad Ali Shah claimed to be innocent of any agitation, there was good reason to suppose that the latter was conducted without His Majesty's knowledge and only in His name by other persons.

The Russian government was not responsible for the Shah's transit through Russian territory since he traveled incognito. Significantly enough, the note kept referring to Mohammad Ali as the Shah and His Majesty.

Having exhausted his defensive resources, Neratov went over to the attack. The Imperial government could not but note that during the two years since the exile of Mohammad Ali Shah, the Persian government had done almost nothing for the pacification of the country. "Constant cabinet crises, petty party struggles, and the mostly fruitless activity of the Majles" characterized this period and undoubtedly prepared the ground for the return of the former Shah.

> In view of these considerations the Imperial Government does not deem it possible to divest the Persian Government of responsibility for damages which might be suffered by Russian subjects from the appearance of Mohammad Ali Shah and will continue to consider it responsible for any loss which might be inflicted upon Russian governmental and private interests by Persian internal disorders.[91]

Though Poklewski and Barclay officially announced that their

91. Acting Minister of Foreign Affairs to the Minister in Tehran, Poklewski, Telegram, St. Petersburg, July 15/28, 1911; ibid. (No. 256), pp. 268–69. The Soviet historian Il'inskii writes: "The Tsarist government decided that the time had now come to restore Mohammad Ali. Having supplied the former Shah with a false passport, money and a guard of detectives and policemen in mufti, the Russian authorities sent this gang from Petrovsk to Iran on the steamer 'Christopher.' " (Rostovskii et al., *Novaia istoriia kolonialnykh i zavisimykh stran*, 1, Chap. 24, 550.)

"*The Strangling of Persia*" 609

governments would not interfere in the struggle between the Persian government and Mohammad Ali, Russian military and consular authorities paid no attention to such declarations. On the contrary they interfered directly and effectively. A certain Rashid ol-Molk, Russia's friend and former Governor of Ardebil, had been sent to fight Shāhsavan tribesmen who had always supported Mohammad Ali. In spite of the superiority of his force, Rashid ol-Molk was defeated and fled in disgrace back to Tabriz. There he was accused of high treason. The local *anjoman* wanted to hang him in order to intimidate the former Shah's sympathizers. The Russian consul, A. Miller, who felt that Rashid ol-Molk's execution would produce an impression disadvantageous to Russia, asked Poklewski for instructions.[92] Poklewski replied immediately that Russia could neither allow his execution nor the infliction "of any punishment without a prior impartial trial."[93]

On July 27 Miller demanded that Rashid ol-Molk be released at once. The acting governor informed him that the prisoner was held on orders from the government in Tehran, whereupon Miller "sent 300 Russian soldiers, fully armed, to the Governor's palace, beat off the Persian guards, insulted the Acting Governor, liberated Rashidu'l-Mulk and took him away."[94] He made his way to the armed camp of the reactionary Governor of Marāgheh, Samad Khān Shojā' od-Dowleh, who was preparing to conquer Tabriz in the name of the former Shah.

Shojā od-Dowleh had gathered a considerable force between Tabriz and Sarāb.[95] In Tabriz some one thousand nationalists were ready for defense, when once again Miller interfered, informing both Samad Khān and the Tabrizis that Russia would not tolerate any fighting capable of damaging Russian property or endangering foreign lives in the city.[96] Thus the defenders would

92. State Counselor Miller [Consul], Telegram, Tabriz, July 13/26, 1911; *S.D.D.*, 7, 28.
93. Poklewski's telegram, Tehran, July 13/26, 1911; ibid.
94. Shuster, *The Strangling of Persia*, pp. 122–23.
95. Miller claimed that Samad Khān Shojā' od-Dowleh had three thousand horsemen, but this is undoubtedly an exaggeration. (Report of the State Counselor Miller, Tabriz, August 17/30, 1911; *S.D.D.*, 7, 113–15.)
96. Same, telegram, Tabriz, August 27/September 10, 1911; ibid., pp. 122–23.

have to meet Samad Khān's force in the open country, where his cavalry would have a clear advantage, whereas in the narrow streets of Tabriz the nationalists would have had the edge.

The Russians knew that hundreds of Armenian, Georgian, and Azerbaijani revolutionaries who had fled the Caucasus would join the fight against Mohammad Ali as they had done in 1908–09. Poklewski even expected a fresh influx of Russian subjects from Transcaucasia. He requested his government to increase the surveillance over the border both east and west of the Caspian.[97] He also asked the Persian government to turn over to Russian consuls for repatriation all suspicious persons, and he threatened "that in case of non-compliance of the Persian Government with such demands our Consuls would arrest such undesirable Russian subjects independently." He authorized Russian consuls in Tabriz, Ardebil, Qazvin, Rasht, and Mashhad so to act.[98]

Persia's new Foreign Minister, Mirzā Hasan Khān Vosuq od-Dowleh, tried to mollify the Russian government in the hope of preventing its agents in the north from giving open support to Mohammad Ali. He suggested to Poklewski that leading members of the Cabinet and Majles had come to the conclusion that the policy of hostility to Russia was ruinous. They would like to know "on what conditions would Russia assume a benevolent attitude toward the present Government." Poklewski replied that the question could have been answered much more easily before civil strife had begun, but that essentially Russia wanted Persia to pursue a friendly policy in harmony with the spirit of the 1907 Anglo-Russian agreement. Vosuq od-Dowleh then requested an answer to a last question:

> If the Imperial Government became certain that the Government of the Shah would henceforth follow a friendly policy toward Russia, consonant in everything with the letter and the spirit of the Anglo-Russian Agreement, could the Imperial Government provide all its agents in Persia with such instructions that our [Russian] present neutrality could

97. Poklewski's telegram, Tehran, July 10/23, 1911; ibid., p. 22.
98. Ibid., p. 23.

not be interpreted in a sense hostile to the Government of the Shah and favorable to Mohammad Ali Shah? [99]

As Mohammad Ali's bands advanced on Tehran, the coalition of disparate groups, parties, and interests that had ruled the country for the past two years showed signs of breaking up. The Bakhtiāri khans, who had been instrumental in overthrowing the Shah, were no longer certain that he would not return to the capital in triumph. Russia's obvious support of his cause made them fear for their future. One of their leaders, Samsām os-Saltaneh, the Prime Minister, approached Poklewski privately and told him that both he and his brother, Sardār As'ad, sought an understanding with Russia. They, as well as the other khans, were dissatisfied with the Majles and would demand that it increase the powers of the Crown and the government. If the Majles refused, they would withdraw from politics, opening the way for the restoration of Mohammad Ali. The British minister, Samsām os-Saltaneh said, had been kept fully informed of their views.[100]

The Bakhtiāri khans could desert the Constitutionalist cause, obtain Mohammad Ali's pardon, and withdraw to the safety of their mountains. The majority of nationalists, however, had no hope of surviving the former Shah's triumph and were determined to fight. Military affairs were entrusted to the chief of Tehran police, the Armenian revolutionary Yefrem Khān. Much of the work of organizing and supplying combat units, which marched eastward to meet the advancing cavalry led by Sardār Arshad (Arshad od-Dowleh), fell to Morgan Shuster. By virtue of his position as Treasurer General, his loyalty to the regime that employed him, and his personal identification with the revolutionary cause, he became a central figure in organizing resistance and a symbol of defiance and hope. His leading role in thwarting

---

99. Minister in Tehran to the Acting Minister of Foreign Affairs, Neratov, Telegram No. 664, July 27/August 9, 1911; M. O., 2nd series, 18 (Part 1, No. 309), 312–13. In the margin someone, most probably Neratov, wrote: "In my opinion the Government in Persia is now an empty sound. Soon we will be definitely convinced of this." The same document, with omissions, appeared in S.D.D., 7, 81–82.

100. Same to same, Telegram No. 683, August 4/17, 1911, Secret; M. O., 2nd series, 18 (Part 1, No. 388), 350–51.

Mohammad Ali's attempt at restoration has been acknowledged by friend and foe alike.[101]

On September 5, 1911, near Varāmin, Sardār Arshad was defeated and captured by government troops. The next morning he was executed by a firing squad and with him died Mohammad Ali's hopes of entering Tehran.[102] A desultory struggle continued for many weeks, but it was clear that only direct Russian intervention could reverse the course of events in Persia.

In spite of the sympathy the former Shah evoked at the Russian Court and in the government, the latter was not prepared to use armed force to put him back on the throne. British opposition to Mohammad Ali's person was unequivocal. Not only old Benckendorff but also Izvolskii argued against "nonintervention," a term used by Russian diplomats to describe their policy of aiding the former Shah. Izvolskii admitted that a victory of the government would ruin Russia's position in Tehran. But the restoration of Mohammad Ali would only get the powers back to their old difficulties. "It seems to me," he wrote, "that it would be more advantageous to accept the English proposal to support the present regime, but on such conditions and with such guarantees as would make us and England masters of the situation." [103]

The Russian government had no intention of withdrawing support from Mohammad Ali or aiding the Persian government

101. Minister in Tehran to the Acting Minister of Foreign Affairs, Neratov, No. 739, August 25/September 7, 1911; ibid. (No. 411), p. 415. In a recent violently anti-American propaganda pamphlet, *Nachalo ekspansii S. Sh. A. v Irane* (*The Beginning of U. S. Expansion in Iran*) (Moscow, 1963), pp. 30–31, Z. Z. Abdullaev represents Shuster as an agent of American imperialism, and a rather sinister figure. Yet even he says that though "the principal role in repulsing the counterrevolutionaries was played by the progressive forces of the Iranian people, one cannot deny that the actions of Shuster and his assistants also contributed to the ruin of the counterrevolutionary plans of the ex-Shah."

102. Unlike most of Mohammad Ali's friends and supporters, Arshad od-Dowleh was both faithful and brave. The *Times* correspondent, Moore, witnessed the execution. "When he heard the command 'Ready' he shouted 'Zindabad Vatan' (Long live my country). Fire! The volley rang out and he fell, but rose again to his knees with no sign of injury, and cried twice 'Zindabad Mohammed Ali Shah.' The second section fired, and all was over. I could not watch again, but I heard his gallant cry." (Moore, *Orient Express*, p. 36.)

103. Ambassador in Paris to the Acting Minister of Foreign Affairs Neratov; M. O., 2nd series, 18 (Part 1, No. 332), 345.

in restoring order. St. Petersburg reacted negatively to every attempt made in Tehran to reestablish a modicum of security in the country. Early in October the Persian government proposed to hire a number of Swedish officers to train the army. Neratov admitted that Russia had no legal right to protest, though he felt that the Persian plan was harmful for Russia. In the margin of Neratov's dispatch Nicholas II wrote: "Since it is harmful to Russia, it is therefore impermissible. We are the masters in the North of Persia." [104]

St. Petersburg had concluded that the most harmful thing for Russia, and therefore the most inadmissible, was the continued presence in Tehran of the Treasurer General Morgan Shuster. A final conflict between him and the Russians was inevitable, its outcome predetermined. St. Petersburg could never forgive him the role he had played in thwarting Mohammad Ali's attempted restoration, and searched for a pretext for his removal. Shuster's own inexperience and zeal provided Russia with an opportunity for decisive intervention.

Malek Mansur Mirzā Shoā' os-Saltaneh, one of Mohammad Ali's younger brothers and a leader of counterrevolutionary forces, had been outlawed by the Majles. On October 4, 1911, the Council of Ministers instructed Shuster to seize his property. To avoid possible complications with foreign legations, the Minister of Foreign Affairs, Vosuq od-Dowleh, informed both Barclay and Poklewski that the properties of several persons who had participated in the rebellion would be confiscated. Poklewski drew Vosuq od-Dowleh's attention to the fact that the prince was a Turkish subject (he had assumed Turkish citizenship to protect himself against possible prosecution by Persian authorities), and that if the Persian government took over his properties it would become responsible for the debts of the owner to the Russian bank. On October 9 Shuster formally took possession of Shoā os-Saltaneh's house and garden in the city, as well as a suburban estate at Dowlatābād, thus unknowingly precipitating an international incident of major proportions.

104. Acting Minister of Foreign Affairs to the Minister in Tehran, Poklewski, Telegram No. 1407, September 23/October 6, 1911; ibid. (Part 2, No. 537), p. 84. The Tsar's marginal notation dated Livadia, September 28/October 11, 1911.

The Treasurer General's action was immediately reported to the Russian consul general, Ivan Fedorovich Pokhitonov, who had arrived in Tehran less than a year before. Pokhitonov had had a long career in Persia and belonged to the extreme nationalist group that deplored the Anglo-Russian understanding of 1907 and yearned for a return to the glorious days of unrestrained rivalry. During the chaotic years of the Persian revolution, Pokhitonov had been Consul General in Tabriz where his doings were virtually uncontrolled. Now in his new post he acted as if he were still his own master. George Churchill, the old and experienced English official, had noted in a report to his minister that "He [Pokhitonov] is setting up an establishment apart from the legation and will have his own staff, Cossack escort, and gholams." [105] Pokhitonov rarely consulted his superior, Poklewski. Their relations had long been unpleasant and strained.

Having been informed of Shuster's move, Pokhitonov acted on his own initiative and authority. "In view of the fact that this house, as well as the Prince's estates, serve as collateral for his debt to our Bank, and that its seizure without the knowledge of the Consulate General was contrary to the treaty, I sent Petrov and Hildebrand with four cossacks with instructions to remove the violators of our rights, which was accomplished by those I sent without a clash." [106]

Shuster at once sent a telegram to Poklewski at Zargandeh, informing him of the incident and explaining the circumstances under which the government order for the confiscation of Shoā' os-Saltaneh's property had been carried out.

> I feel sure [Shuster stated in conclusion] that Your Excellency will recognize that this action of your officers is wholly unwarranted and unlawful and I therefore request you in this friendly manner to give immediate orders to your Consulate to have their force withdrawn and to inform me of their withdrawal.[107]

105. Barclay to Grey, No. 244, Confidential, Tehran, December 27, 1910, Enclosure No. 1; F. O. 371/1184.
106. Pokhitonov's telegram, September 28/October 11, 1911; S.D.D., 7, 171–72.
107. Shuster, *The Strangling of Persia*, pp. 139–41.

"The Strangling of Persia" 615

Within an hour Poklewski replied that if all rights of Russian subjects were safeguarded, the legation would not oppose the Persian government's measures against Shoā' os-Saltaneh's properties but would hold it responsible for any claims Russian subjects might have against the prince.[108] Later that afternoon Poklewski telephoned Pokhitonov and asked him why he had intervened between Shoā' os-Saltaneh and the Persian government. "A heated argument took place over the wire, at the conclusion of which the Russian Minister demanded to know what justification Pokhitanof [sic] had for his action. The latter replied that he had his reasons." The conversation was overheard by a Persian employee of the telephone exchange who knew Russian and who reported everything to Shuster that same evening.[109]

Having received Poklewski's telegram, Shuster notified him that he would make a second attempt to take over Shoā' os-Saltaneh's property. On October 10 the Treasurer General's two assistants, F. S. Cairnes and J. N. Merrill, called on Pokhitonov, read to him the government order of confiscation, and requested the withdrawal of Cossacks. Pokhitonov, who was angered by Cairnes' demeanor, replied that the prince's property was mortgaged to the Russian bank and that no measures should be taken against it until the issue was clarified between the Persian government and the Russian legation. He flatly refused to withdraw the troops from Shoā' os-Saltaneh's house and garden.[110] Thereupon Cairnes informed him that he would take possession of the property by force. This was done immediately and without injury to anyone.

In the afternoon Pokhitonov's subordinates, vice-consuls Petrov and Hildebrand, accompanied by a Persian officer of the Cossack Brigade, made an unsuccessful attempt to intimidate Shuster's gendarmes and enter the garden. There exist several mutually contradictory versions as to what took place at the gate. Pokhitonov sent his version to Neratov in St. Petersburg without notifying Poklewski. It claimed that the Persian gendarmes had

108. Ibid., p. 142.
109. Ibid., p. 151.
110. Ibid., pp. 145–47. Pokhitonov's version in his telegram of September 28/ October 11, 1911; S.D.D., 7, 173–74.

aimed their rifles at the uniformed officials of the Russian consulate and publicly insulted them.[111] Poklewski's version was communicated to St. Petersburg in three separate telegrams on October 12 and 13. It pointed out that Shoā' os-Saltaneh was a Turkish subject and not under Russian protection. The prince was not in debt to the Russian bank, though he had given it a false document mortgaging some of his estates. This had been done in 1908 for the purpose of protecting his property, but the fictitious character of the transaction was known to everyone in Tehran.[112]

Persian officials had informed the legation of their intention to confiscate Shoā' os-Saltaneh's properties. Pokhitonov's intervention was unauthorized, and he was given "categorical orders" not to meddle. Next day Shuster's gendarmes took over Shoā' os-Saltaneh's house and removed five Persian Cossacks who had been stationed there by Pokhitonov. The latter did not dare to act openly this time, but requested the commander of the Cossack Brigade, Prince Vadbolskii, to send a detachment to restore Cossack occupation of the house. Vadbolskii refused.

> I find that the action of the Consul General constitutes not only a rude and inexplicable insult to the Persian Government, but also a grave offense against the Legation. . . . in case of a new act of insubordination or of any scandal, I would be compelled, for the restoration of service discipline, to take, independently and on my personal responsibility, necessary measures against individual officers or even the entire staff of the Consulate General.[113]

The Persian government, Poklewski went on, sent him a note complaining against the consulate general and asking that Pokhitonov and Petrov be recalled. Poklewski replied orally that the inability of the Persians to protect Russia's flag and her subjects against insults from government forces "places Persia so

---

111. Pokhitonov's telegram of September 28/October 11, 1911; ibid.

112. Minister in Tehran to the Acting Minister of Foreign Affairs, Neratov, Telegram No. 924, September 29/October 12, 1911; M. O., 2nd series, 18 (Part 2, No. 603), 146–47.

113. Same to same, Telegram No. 924, September 30/October 13, 1911, Personal and Very Secret, No. 2; ibid. (No. 616), pp. 154–55.

to speak outside the law." He therefore refused to accept the protest but promised to investigate the case, report it to St. Petersburg, and act "according to my conscience." [114]

Neratov reacted sharply. He knew that the document purporting to show Shoā' os-Saltaneh's indebtedness to the bank was fictitious, but he felt that Pokhitonov had to protect Russian interests "without entering the question of the fictitious nature of the Bank document, since it is entirely clear that we would never admit that this document is fictitious." All the blame in the incident belonged to the Persians, whose insolence in demanding the recall of Pokhitonov and Petrov was "unexampled" and necessitated "the sharpest repulse." Poklewski was instructed to demand that the Persian government remove its gendarmes from Shoā' os-Saltaneh's house and put it under the protection of the Russian officered Cossack Brigade and that, irrespective of the results of the investigation, the Persians apologize for threatening the officers of the consulate general. Finally, Poklewski was to return the note in which Persia had requested the recall of Pokhitonov and Petrov and declare "that if the Persians should once again permit themselves anything of the sort, you would cease communicating with the Cabinet." The draft of Neratov's telegram was shown to Nicholas II at Livadia and bears his notation: "Good." [115]

Poklewski did not obey his instructions. He telegraphed Neratov that Shuster was in the right, and that the matter should not be pushed any further. Russia would only be accused of trying to create an incident because of the failure of Mohammad Ali to regain the throne. The future would provide many "good pretexts" which would "allow us to break the obstacles we meet on our path under the present regime." The regime itself might be indirectly modified.[116]

Further reflection on the events of the last several days only

114. Same to same, Telegram No. 924, September 30/October 13, 1911, No. 3; ibid. (No. 617), pp. 155–56.

115. Acting Minister of Foreign Affairs to the Minister in Tehran, Poklewski, Telegram No. 1498, October 2/15, 1911; ibid. (No. 6363), 170–71. A garbled version of this document appears in S.D.D., 7, 182.

116. Minister in Tehran to the Acting Minister of Foreign Affairs, Neratov, Telegram No. 957/b, October 5/18, 1911; M. O., 2nd series, 18 (Part 2, 661), 182–83.

increased Poklewski's anger against the insubordinate Pokhitonov and against Neratov who gave the consul tacit approval by endorsing his actions. Pokhitonov had taken it upon himself to decide Russian policy in Persia, completely disregarding the minister. Moreover, his actions had been so blatantly unjust, so crude and arrogant, that Poklewski could no longer stomach them. How could he, a wealthy Polish aristocrat, friend of Izvolskii and of the late King Edward VII, bow to such indignities? He sent another telegram to Neratov, his third that day, stating that he did not share the views of the Ministry of Foreign Affairs (read Neratov) on the Shoā' incident and did not feel it possible to carry out his instructions. He would rather resign his post and return to St. Petersburg.[117]

From London Count Benckendorff conveyed to Neratov British fears that, as a result of Russian pressure, an ultranationalist government might come to power in Tehran and that the Regent might resign. Nicolson had complained that anarchy in Persia hurt British interests in the south and that Grey was vulnerable in Parliament.[118] Benckendorff called for a policy of compromise between the two powers and Persia, but Neratov, backed by the Tsar, disregarded his advice. He paid no more attention to O'Beirne, British chargé d'affaires in St. Petersburg, to whom he intimated on October 19 that though Russia had not yet decided to take "extreme measures," the possibility of sending troops to Persia, if the situation did not improve, was not excluded.[119]

In a telegram to Poklewski dispatched on October 22, Neratov reiterated his support of Pokhitonov, in whose actions he saw "only an entirely correct understanding and execution by him of his duties." [120] Neratov felt that there had been no disagreement in principle between the minister and the consul, though Poklewski had assumed a milder tone. The Persians must be taught a

117. Same to same, Telegram No. 957v, October 5/18, 1911; ibid., p. 183 note 1.
118. Ambassador in London to the Acting Minister of Foreign Affairs, Neratov Letter, October 7/20, 1911; ibid. (No. 674), pp. 193–95.
119. British Chargé d'Affaires in St. Petersburg to the Acting Minister of Foreign Affairs, Neratov, Letter, October 7/20, 1911, Urgent; ibid. (No. 671), p. 192.
120. Acting Minister of Foreign Affairs to the Minister in Tehran, Poklewski, Telegram No. 1567, October 9/22, 1911; ibid. (No. 691), p. 206.

lesson, and Poklewski would be provided with Russian troops to enforce all his demands. As for Persian opinion, "one should not forget that the Persians bow only to force and explain every concession by the weakness of the opposite side." (The Tsar noted in the margin, "Very good.") [121]

In a fourth telegram of the same date Neratov instructed Poklewski to inform the Persian Foreign Minister of Russia's views, return the Persian note asking for the recall of Pokhitonov and Petrov, and demand the immediate withdrawal of Shuster's gendarmes as well as apologies to the Russian consulate for the insults inflicted on its officials.[122] Finally, in a personal telegram, he stated that the presentation of Russian demands could no longer be postponed. As for Poklewski's request to leave Tehran, he could not accept it without the Tsar's permission, which could not be obtained quickly.[123]

Poklewski found himself in a most unenviable situation. Not only Pokhitonov in Tehran but also Miller in Tabriz, Dabizha in Mashhad, Nekrasov in Rasht, and others, began to go over his head directly to Neratov. The consuls advocated a hard line and in unison called for Russian armed intervention. A full month before the Shoā' incident, Consul Nekrasov had appealed for a gunboat and a squadron of Cossacks with machine guns.[124] Poklewski objected, pointing out to Neratov that Nekrasov refused to pay attention either to the situation in Persia or to the aims pursued by the Russian government there. Were the measures proposed by him adopted, Russia would have to occupy and assume direct rule over Gilān. "The possibility of such an issue is, of course, not excluded for the future, but as of now there is no sufficient basis for it."[125] Neratov delayed his answer until October 25. When he finally wrote to Poklewski, the latter saw

121. Same to Same, Telegram No. 1572, October 9/22, 1911, No. 3; ibid. (No. 693), pp. 207–08.
122. Same to same, Telegram No. 1568, October 9/22, 1911, No. 4; ibid. (No. 694), pp. 208–09.
123. Same to same, Telegram No. 1569, October 9/22, Personal; ibid. (No. 695), p. 209.
124. Nekrasov's telegram No. 135, August 29/October 11, 1911; ibid., p. 233.
125. Poklewski to Neratov, Telegram No. 777, September 2/15, 1911; ibid.

that the Ministry of Foreign Affairs had sided with Nekrasov. Neratov had accepted the latter's evaluation of the situation, indirectly accused Poklewski of passivity, and declared that if the Persians failed to meet every Russian demand, the Russians would take such measures as they considered necessary for the protection of their interests. In such a case the Cossacks stationed in Rasht, who would have been reinforced by another squadron, would be ordered to act.[126]

Pokhitonov's insubordination and the aggressive behavior of the other consuls, who acted in complete disregard of the minister in Tehran, laid the foundation for the legend promoted and exploited by Edward Grey, Arthur Nicolson, George Buchanan, and other proponents of Anglo-Russian friendship at any price. The legend proclaimed that the Russian government tried loyally to live up to the letter and spirit of the Anglo-Russian Agreement of 1907 but was often frustrated by its own agents in Persia, agents who represented the unregenerated remnant of the old Asiatic Department school.

As with all legends, this one contained an element of truth. An overwhelming majority of Russian agents in Persia, whether consular, financial, or military, were anti-British, anti-Constitutionalist, and imperialist. However, they did not subvert the polices of St. Petersburg. On the contrary, they were much more sensitive to the real feelings of the top policy makers, and of the Tsar himself, than the unfortunate Poklewski-Koziell.[127]

Pressed by Neratov for stronger action, and aware of the weakness of his own standing with St. Petersburg, Poklewski once more stated his views on the Shoā' case. He repudiated Pokhitonov's version of the incident, relegating "to the realm of fantasy" the complaint about the gendarmes aiming their rifles at the officials of the consulate.[128] Poklewski stressed that Po-

---

126. Neratov to Poklewski, Letter No. 760, October 12/25, 1911, Secret, Urgent; ibid. (No. 721), pp. 233–35.

127. On October 24 Neratov submitted to the Tsar a report on the Shoā' case (based on the Pokhitonov version of the incident) together with copies of his own correspondence with Poklewski. In the margin of Neratov's report the Tsar wrote: "I entirely approve your instructions. Livadia, October 16/29, 1911." (Report of the Acting Minister of Foreign Affairs to Nicholas II; ibid. [No. 706], pp. 219–20.)

128. Minister in Tehran to the Acting Minister of Foreign Affairs, Neratov, Telegram No. 993, October 14/27, 1911, No. 1; ibid. (No. 745), pp. 258–59.

khitonov knew his views on the question of Shoā' os-Saltaneh's properties, knew that the entire affair concerned the legation exclusively, yet interfered in it.

for the maintenance of service discipline and for the prevention in the future of dangerous play with military force on the part of the Russian Consulate, I find it absolutely necessary (1) that Pokhitonov be ordered to follow the instructions issued to him by the Legation on the 27th of September [October 10] last . . . (2) that the Consulate General be ordered from now on to present to the Legation copies of all its telegraphic and other reports to the Ministry of Foreign Affairs.

Poklewski explained Pokhitonov's motives thus:

After Mohammad Ali's failures, Pokhitonov, who is strongly inclined toward him, arrived at the conviction that the Imperial Government should give up the policy of nonintervention and give active aid to the ex-Shah and his local supporters. Seeing that in this question the Legation, without special directives of the Ministry, does not transgress the limits of legal defense exclusively of the interests of Russian subjects and persons who are really under our protection, the Consul General took advantage of the Shoā' affair for independent action, hoping to carry with him the Legation and the Imperial Government. Having been ordered to stop intervening in this affair, he did nothing to prevent the possibility of an incident with Persian cossacks, but on the contrary, either himself or his dragomans, tried to create a big misunderstanding between the Cossack Brigade and the Persian Government. When they failed in this, the Consulate General wanted to blow up the incident between the dragomans and the gendarmes and thus to achieve our active intervention in the Shoā' case. Having failed in this also, the Consulate General sent to the Ministry, over the head of the Legation, a report evidently complaining about the Minister and in the unconcealed hope of achieving his replacement.[129]

129. Minister in Tehran to the Acting Minister of Foreign Affairs, Neratov, Telegram, No. 993, October 14/27, 1911, Personal, No. 2; ibid. (No. 746), pp. 259–60.

Neratov's reply was a curt reprimand. He expressed his regret that, in spite of twice-repeated instructions, Poklewski had failed to act. As for Poklewski's latest telegram, "I see neither in it nor in the letter anything that could change my point of view on the affair." [130] Poklewski had no further choice. On November 2 he returned the Persian note to the Foreign Minister, Vosuq od-Dowleh, and presented Neratov's demands.

Vosuq od-Dowleh confessed to Poklewski that the Cabinet disapproved of Shuster's methods and would like "to bridle him." However, Russia should not hurry the Persian Cabinet since pressure would only increase Shuster's popularity "among unbalanced Persian politicians." Poklewski stated that he had formal instructions and needed a quick reply.[131]

The Majles was fully committed to Shuster. Vosuq od-Dowleh himself, as well as his brother, Ahmad Khān Qavām os-Saltaneh, had been originally friendly to him. However, the Treasurer General had investigated "the gross frauds and malversations" that had occurred in the tax system in Āzarbāyjān. Private sources informed him that the tax collector had made a fortune and that he sneered at the government and the Treasurer General. "That he thought himself safe in so doing," Shuster wrote, "was perhaps due to his being the father of the two ministers just referred to: Wuthuqu'd-Dawla and Ghavamu's-Saltana. That they should become suddenly hostile to me . . . is perhaps explainable by the same relationship." [132]

Vosuq od-Dowleh's hostility to Shuster may have been caused by personal considerations, but many Persian politicians were beginning to feel that the Treasurer General had gone too far. Shuster himself did not fully appreciate the seriousness of the situation he had unwittingly created. He probably did not even know that Russia had raised with Britain the question of his removal from Persia. Benckendorff suggested to Nicolson that a stop must be put to Shuster's activities. Nicolson agreed, and

---

130. Acting Minister of Foreign Affairs to the Minister in Tehran, Poklewski, Telegram No. 1641, October 18/31, 1911; ibid. (No. 764), pp. 276–77.

131. Minister in Tehran to the Acting Minister of Foreign Affairs, Neratov, Telegram No. 1015, October 20/November 2, 1911; ibid. (No. 784), pp. 290–91.

132. Shuster, *The Strangling of Persia*, p. 210.

"The Strangling of Persia"

added that Shuster had taken the wrong road the moment he arrived in Persia. However, Sir Arthur did not want to force him out, preferring to see him resign. This would avoid polemics in the press, in Parliament, and especially in America.[133] While the stage was being thus set for an attack on the Treasurer General, and with the Shoā' incident still unresolved, Shuster added oil to the fire by appointing an Englishman, Lecoffre, to the post of financial inspector at Tabriz in the heart of the Russian zone of Persia.

The Lecoffre appointment demonstrated Shuster's lack of sensitivity to the realities of power politics. He had learned nothing from the Stokes case, and provoked a new crisis at the most inappropriate time imaginable. Lecoffre had lived in Persia for several years, working first for the Imperial Bank and later for the Ministry of Finance. He had attracted the attention of the Russian legation as a Russophobe and a "participant in the national revolutionary movement."[134] Poklewski immediately suggested to Neratov that Russia should protest against the Lecoffre appointment.[135] Neratov agreed and expressed the hope that Sir George Barclay would support the protest. The Tsar was impatient. "Such protests," he commented in the margin of Neratov's draft, "can only elicit smiles."[136]

On November 6 the Persian government gave a negative reply to Russian demands for the withdrawal of gendarmes from the Shoā' country estate, house and garden. It pointed out that the Russian legation had received prior notification that the rights of Russian subjects would be protected. The consul general had been asked in accordance with law to abstain from interference.

---

133. Ambassador in London to the Acting Minister of Foreign Affairs, Neratov, Letter, Very Confidential, October 12/25, 1911; M. O., 2nd series, 18 (Part 2, No. 722), 235–36.

134. Sablin's review of events, No. 38, July 11/24, 1909, as cited in Minister in Tehran to the Acting Minister of Foreign Affairs, Neratov, Telegram No. 1023, October 21/November 3, 1911; ibid. (No. 793), pp. 296–97.

135. Id.

136. Neratov to Poklewski, Telegram, St. Petersburg, October 22/November 4, 1911; S.D.D., 7, 209 (incomplete version). The Tsar's marginal comment dated Livadia, October 29/November 11, 1911; M. O., 2nd series, 18 (Part 2), 297, note 1.

In view of the innocence of the Persian officials, it would be harmful and undignified for the Persian government to accept Poklewski's demands.[137]

On the same day Sir Arthur Nicolson instructed Sir George Barclay to express to Shuster strong disapproval of any appointment of an Englishman in northern Persia and to tell him "that the English Government considers any appointment of such a nature as could evoke doubts in Russia about the good faith of the English Government to be contrary to the spirit of its agreement with Russia." [138] Barclay called on Shuster and read him the text of Grey's telegram.

> I replied to Sir George Barclay [Shuster reports in his book] that I always had been and was still most anxious to observe all the legitimate interests of Russia and the other powers in Persia, but that I could not, as he well knew, in this case, any more than in the Stokes case, recognize the existence in Persia of foreign "spheres of influence," a thing which the Persian Government had officially forbidden me to do on more than one occasion.[139]

Neither the Persian government nor its Treasurer General were prepared to surrender to Russia. Neratov eagerly pressed forward, ordering Poklewski to repeat the demands in writing and to let the Persians know that in case of a negative reply Russia would take any measures she considered necessary for the protection of her interest. A Russian force would be sent to Qazvin where it would await Poklewski's call to march to Tehran and remove Shuster's gendarmes from Shoā' os-Saltaneh's property. Neratov also informed Poklewski that the above instructions had been approved by the Tsar and their execution must be reported to St. Petersburg by telegram.[140]

Suddenly the Russian press opened a violent attack on Shuster.

137. Minister in Tehran to the Acting Minister of Foreign Affairs, Neratov, Telegram No. 1015, October 24/November 6, 1911; ibid. (No. 815), p. 316.

138. Ambassador in London to the Acting Minister of Foreign Affairs, Neratov, Letter, October 25/November 7, 1911; ibid. (No. 823), pp. 320–21.

139. Shuster, *The Strangling of Persia*, pp. 160–61.

140. Acting Minister of Foreign Affairs to the Minister in Tehran, Poklewski, Telegram No. 1734, October 26/November 8, 1911; M. O., 2nd series, 18 (Part 2, No. 835), 330.

"The Strangling of Persia"

The United States ambassador in St. Petersburg reported that the newspapers were "accusing him of being a Jew and having been unnecessarily offensive to both the British and the Russians."[141] Obviously the decision to break Persian resistance, by force if necessary, had been made and was being implemented. Poklewski was completely discredited at St. Petersburg, and no one listened to the pleas of old Benckendorff not to permit Pokhitonov to decide Russian policy and ruin the Anglo-Russian understanding.[142] Pokhitonov's policy was that of the Tsar and Neratov. Both were prepared to risk British displeasure for the sake of gaining firm control of "their" sphere of Persia.

The Russian ultimatum was handed to Vosuq od-Dowleh by a secretary of the Russian legation on November 11. It contained familiar terms: the substitution of Persian Cossacks for Shuster's gendarmes and an apology to the officers of the Russian consulate.[143] The Persian government was given forty-eight hours to reply, but the very next day Neratov began making preparations for the use of force. He asked the Chairman of the Council of Ministers, Vladimir Nikolaevich Kokovtsov, to instruct the Viceroy of the Caucasus to have a detachment ready for transportation to Qazvin.[144] Simultaneously the Information Bureau of the Russian government published an official version of the Shoā' incident based on Pokhitonov's dispatches. "Having considered the said affair," the release stated, "the Russian Government recognized the actions of the Consul General and the officials subordinate to him as correct and consonant with circumstances."[145]

The Persian Prime Minister, Samsām os-Saltaneh, frightened

---

141. Cited in Yeselson, *United States-Persian Diplomatic Relations*, p. 117.

142. Ambassador in London to the Acting Minister of Foreign Affairs, Neratov, Letter, Personal, October 26/November 8, 1911; M. O., 2nd series, 18 (Part 2, No. 836), 331–33.

143. Minister in Tehran to the Acting Minister of Foreign Affairs, Neratov, Telegram [unnumbered], October 29/November 11, 1911; ibid. (No. 866), pp. 359–60.

144. Acting Minister of Foreign Affairs to the Chairman of the Council of Ministers, Kokovtsov, Letter No. 803, Secret, Urgent, October 30/November 12, 1911; ibid. (No. 868), p. 364.

145. Government bulletin, St. Petersburg, October 30/November 12, 1911 S.D.D., 7, 224–27.

by open Russian military activity, ordered Shuster to withdraw the gendarmes from Shoā' os-Saltaneh's properties. The Treasurer General refused, arguing that the confiscation order having been signed by the entire Cabinet, its revocation must be signed by the entire Cabinet as well.[146] There was no agreement among the ministers on the course the government should follow, nor did the Majles have much confidence in a Cabinet headed by a Bakhtiāri chieftain. In an attempt to gain time, Samsām os-Saltaneh and Vosuq od-Dowleh resigned, and the rest of the Cabinet followed. There was now no one who could reply to the Russian ultimatum.[147]

Neratov, who learned of the fall of the Persian Cabinet from a telegram sent by the Tehran correspondent of the London *Times*, urged Poklewski to announce immediately the termination of his relations with the Persian government, "whereupon we shall give orders for the dispatch of a detachment to Qazvin."[148] He chose to interpret the resignation of the Prime Minister and the Minister of Foreign Affairs as a refusal to submit to Russian demands.[149] On November 16 Kokovtsov instructed the Viceroy of the Caucasus to send four thousand men to Persia. Of these, two thousand would march on Tehran and two thousand stay in reserve at Qazvin.[150] Simultaneously Neratov sent a note to Grey enumerating Russia's grievances against Persia and informing the British government of the dispatch of troops to Qazvin and, if need be, to Tehran.[151]

The news of a major invasion of Persia pained Sir Edward Grey. He told Benckendorff that Russia should have been satis-

146. Shuster, pp. 161–62. Minister in Tehran to the Acting Minister of Foreign Affairs, Neratov, Telegram No. 1091, November 1/14, 1911; M. O., 2nd series, 19 (Part 1, No. 9), 10–11.

147. Poklewski to Neratov; ibid.

148. Acting Minister of Foreign Affairs to the Minister in Tehran, Poklewski, Telegram No. 1773, Urgent, November 1/14, 1911; ibid. (No. 1), p. 1.

149. Same to same, Telegram No. 1782, November 2/15, 1911; ibid. (No. 10), p. 11.

150. Kokovtsov to the Viceroy, Telegram [unnumbered], November 3/16, 1911; ibid., p. 14, note 5.

151. Acting Minister of Foreign Affairs to the Ambassador in London, Benckendorff, Telegram No. 1798, November 3/16; ibid. (No. 16), pp. 15–16.

fied with a seizure of customs and reserved more energetic measures for the support of further demands "such as the recall of Shuster, for instance." The British government would not object to that, but Grey was anxious to protect Russian moves from adverse criticism of an alarmed public.[152] On November 18 Sir George Buchanan, who had just returned to St. Petersburg from a prolonged leave, told Neratov that Grey understood Russia's demands and felt they were consonant with Russia's position in Persia. However, the dispatch of troops was undesirable because of the adverse effect it could have on Anglo-Russian relations, which Grey cherished. There was not a problem in the world on which England and Russia did not see eye to eye except Persia. "English public opinion," Buchanan said, "is extremely sensitive of the latter question, and the English Government cannot disregard this." The current Russian invasion of Persia, taking place while Britain's new King, George V, was visiting India, might produce manifestations of sympathy among his Moslem subjects. Buchanan expressed the hope that Russia would give the Persians time to change their minds before sending troops to Tehran. He pointed to the existence of British sympathies for the Regent, Abol Qāsem Khān Nāser ol-Molk, and added that the restoration of Mohammad Ali would not be favorably received, especially if it appeared to be the result of Russian military intervention.

Neratov replied that Russia valued her relations with Britain, that she had carefully considered the measures which had been taken in Persia, and that further developments depended on the situation which would obtain after Russian troops reached Qazvin. The Anglo-Russian agreement remained in full force, and Russia would avoid everything capable of creating difficulties for the British government. However, the longer Russia's troops stayed in Persia, the longer would grow the list of her demands. Russia might then insist on the dismissal of Shuster "even though we understand that measures which are ordinary in Persia, cannot be applied to him as a foreigner." Neratov also mentioned Pokhitonov, saying that the consul general knew Persia and her

152. Ambassador in London to the Acting Minister of Foreign Affairs, Neratov, Telegram No. 279, November 4/17, 1911; ibid. (No. 30), p. 29.

customs. If his subordinates had been too zealous, they would be reprimanded, but that was a purely domestic Russian issue. As for Mohammad Ali, Neratov said that Russian actions were in no way connected with his fate.[153] Buchanan reported that Kokovtsov had repeated this assurance to him the next day and made a formal promise that Russia would not annex any Persian provinces or violate her territorial integrity.[154]

The Russians were prepared to make promises concerning Persia as long as the British left them free to do what they pleased. Kokovtsov assured Buchanan that "Russian troops would be recalled as soon as her two demands were satisfied, i.e. formal apologies of the Persian M[inistry of] F[oreign] A[ffairs] to the Russian Minister in Tehran and the substitution of Persian Cossacks for the gendarmes at Shoā' os-Saltaneh's estate."[155] However, on the same day Neratov telegraphed Poklewski that Russia would not be satisfied with a Persian acceptance of the two demands. The Acting Minister of Foreign Affairs was actually afraid that Persia might accede to them before the arrival in Anzali of the Salianskii Regiment, which had left Baku the day before, thus compelling the troops to return home.

> Should the Persian Minister of Foreign Affairs request that you receive him so that he could comply with our demands, kindly use some well-sounding pretext such as the necessity of asking for additional instructions to postpone meeting him until the arrival in Anzali of the Salianskii Regiment. . . . This is necessary in view of my statement to Buchanan that if the acceptance of our previous demands did not occur before the arrival of our troops in Persia, we would put forward new demands, including, probably, the firing of Shuster.[156]

153. Acting Minister of Foreign Affairs to the Ambassador in London, Benckendorff, Telegram No. 1810, November 5/18, 1911; ibid. (No. 31), pp. 30–32.

154. Buchanan to Grey, Telegram No. 288, November 19, 1911, deciphered at the Russian Ministry of Foreign Affairs; ibid., p. 32, note 3.

155. Acting Minister of Foreign Affairs to the Minister in Tehran, Poklewski, Telegram No. 1833, November 7/20, 1911; ibid. (No. 42), pp. 40–41.

156. Same to same, Telegram No. 1840, Urgent, November 8/21, 1911; ibid. (No. 47), p. 43.

Shuster had become Russia's bête noire. Neratov wanted him removed from Tehran and inquired how this could be done "without any direct action against Shuster personally" since he was a citizen of the United States, whose intervention in Persian affairs should be avoided.[157] If Neratov had misgivings about the position of the United States, they were dispelled by the American ambassador in St. Petersburg, Guild, who told him that the United States government was "not at all interested in the fate of Shuster . . ." whose course of action it did not approve. Should the Russian government demand Shuster's removal from Persian service, the United States would refrain from any interference.[158]

Poklewski, perhaps trying to restore his standing in the eyes of the Foreign Ministry at St. Petersburg, urged his government to take advantage of the invasion of Persia to ensure future "normal" relations with that country. One of Shuster's basic goals was the rupture of the Anglo-Russian agreement, which his actions had already endangered.[159] How to get rid of Shuster? One could hardly count on his voluntary resignation or on the consent of the Majles, which hoped that foreign powers would prevent Russian troops from entering Tehran.

> However, the movement of our troops on Qazvin and especially on Tehran will encourage all the opponents of the present discredited regime and the enemies of Shuster, and the removal of the latter will be achieved by means of a coup d'état in one of three ways: first—by the Bakhtiāris in their

---

157. Same to same, Telegram No. 1805, November 4/17, 1911; ibid. (No. 26), pp. 26–27.

158. Same to same, Telegram No. 1830, November 7/20, 1911; ibid., p. 26, note 6. A month later in a conversation with Guild, the Russian Minister of Foreign Affairs, Sazonov, stressed that "Mr. Shuster's selection was particularly disagreeable to Russia, not only on account of his action, but because he is a Jew. I ventured to say," Guild reported, "that in this at least I thought he was mistaken, but he insisted upon it with great emphasis." (The American Ambassador to Russia to the Secretary of State, No. 129, St. Petersburg, December 15, 1911; *Papers Relating to the Foreign Relations of the United States*, 1911, p. 685.)

159. From London Benckendorff telegraphed that according to "established" local opinion, "the main thought of the Majles and Shuster is the rupture of the Anglo-Russian agreement." Telegram No. 289, No. 3, November 12/25, 1911; M. O., 2nd series, 19 (Part 1), 49, note 1.

own interests . . . , second—in case of complete withdrawal of the Bakhtiāris from affairs [of state], by the partisans of Mohammad Ali Shah with the purpose of restoring him to the throne, and third—by ourselves at the occupation of Tehran, in which case we would probably have to retain the present Shah and Regent.[160]

Urged by Sir George Barclay, who transmitted to them Kokovtsov's promise to Buchanan that Russian troops would not invade Persia if she fulfilled the two original demands, the Persians formed a cabinet that included members who until then had been objectionable to the Majles. Poklewski reported that in all probability Russian terms would be accepted immediately.[161] Neratov replied that Buchanan had misrepresented Kokovtsov's position. The Chairman of the Council of Ministers had not stated positively that Russia would be satisfied with Persian acceptance of the original demands after the entry of Russian troops in Persia.[162] On that very day, November 22, 1911, the first contingent of the Russian expeditionary force landed at Anzali.

Sir George Buchanan brought to Neratov's attention the fact that the new Persian Cabinet had already accepted the original Russian demands. Would Russia be satisfied and halt her troops or recall them if they had already landed in Persia? Neratov answered that it was too late. The troops had reached Anzali the day before, the situation had changed, and Russia could no longer be satisfied with the acceptance of her original ultimatum by Persia. Would Russia at least refrain from advancing beyond Rasht, Buchanan asked.

> I did not conceal from Buchanan [Neratov wrote] that the resistance which we could meet on this issue [the dismissal of Shuster] on the part of the Persians might compel us to

---

160. Minister in Tehran to the Acting Minister of Foreign Affairs, Neratov, Telegram [unnumbered], November 8/21, 1911; ibid. (No. 55), pp. 48–50.

161. Same to same, Telegram No. 1124, November 8/21, 1911; ibid. (No. 56), p. 50.

162. Acting Minister of Foreign Affairs to the Minister in Tehran, Poklewski, Telegram No. 1851, November 9/22, 1911; ibid. (No. 59), p. 55.

"The Strangling of Persia" 631

decisive action. Buchanan replied that with all the confidence the London Cabinet had in us, it was doubtful that the latter could sympathize with the realization of our goals by nonpeaceful means because secret intentions would be immediately seen in our violent actions.[163]

Russia's wrath was further increased by the publication in Tehran of a Persian translation of a letter Shuster had written to *The Times* denouncing Russian policies. Neratov brought this "offence" to the attention of the Russian Cabinet, which decided to use force against the recalcitrant foreigner.[164] He also instructed Poklewski to resume relations with the Persian Cabinet now that it had accepted the original Russian demands in the Shoā' case, but to warn it that since the publication of Shuster's letter and the arrival of Russian troops at Anzali, Russia could no longer be satisfied with that. Persia must dismiss Shuster and Lecoffre. She must undertake not to invite foreign advisers without the prior consent of Britain and Russia, and the advisers must be subjects of minor powers. Finally, "the Persian Government must, without procrastination, undertake to solve through negotiations all the accumulated affairs and questions." For Poklewski's eyes Neratov added:

> If the present Persian Government deem these demands unacceptable or declare them impossible of fulfillment because of opposition on the part of radicals, we would have to move a detachment to Tehran, propose to the Regent to dismiss the ministers and form a new cabinet, which would first of all dissolve the present illegally sitting Majles and order new, strictly legal, elections with the simultaneous formation of the Senate, and then would fire Shuster and fulfil the rest of our demands.... Should the Majles refuse to dissolve at the bidding of the Government, we would have to compel it by force in a way that appeared best according to local circumstances. In case of the Regent's resignation

---

163. Same to same, Telegram No. 1856, Urgent, November 10/23, 1911; ibid. (No. 70), pp. 65–66.

164. Same to same, Telegram No. 1861, November 10/23, 1911; ibid., p. 66, note 3.

we would have to appoint one in agreement with the English or carry out the above-mentioned measures on our own.[165]

In London and in St. Petersburg, through Benckendorff and Buchanan, Grey pleaded for moderation. Already under pressure in Parliament because of his decision to defend Russia's actions in Persia, he could not go further and condone a Russian occupation of that country. Benckendorff advised his government to help Grey by giving assurances that the Russian expeditionary force would be quickly withdrawn. It could always be sent back to Persia.[166] Buchanan told Neratov that Grey had instructed him to point out that the Persians had accepted the two Russian demands, and that therefore Grey considered it necessary "that Russian troops should not land, or, if they had already landed, should be recalled as soon as possible." [167] Still, Neratov would not be moved. Buchanan attributed his position to "public opinion," a tired concept that helped British diplomats explain to their own satisfaction the hard policies of the Russian government. "In Russia," Buchanan recorded his memoirs, "the despatch of troops to Kaswin and the contemplated occupation of Tehran were regarded as measures which it was incumbent on her to take for the vindication of her outraged honour." [168]

The British ambassador was under the impression that Neratov's position in the Persian issue was harder than that of his chief, the Chairman of the Council of Ministers, Kokovtsov.[169] However, Neratov was prepared, in deference to English sentiments, to halt the Russian troops at Rasht at least for a while; Kokovtsov felt that in the question of troop movements deeper into Persia, Russia should think not in terms of the attitude of the British government but in terms of the preservation of her own dignity and the satisfaction of the just demands of her public opinion. A withdrawal could take place only if the Persians

165. Same to same, Telegram No. 1859, Urgent, November 10/23, 1911; ibid. (No. 71), pp. 66–67.
166. Ambassador in London to the Acting Minister of Foreign Affairs, Neratov, Telegram, November 10/23, 1911; ibid. (No. 70), pp. 68–69.
167. Ibid., p. 66, note 2.
168. Buchanan, *My Mission to Russia*, 1, 101.
169. Cf. ibid., pp. 99–100.

acceded not solely to the original demands made in the Russian ultimatum but also to any others Neratov might find it expedient to make at any given moment. "In particular, I entirely share your Excellency's opinion of the necessity of presenting to the Persian Government in one form or another of a demand for the dismissal of Morgan-Shuster." [170]

Russian troops had begun their march from Anzali to Rasht when Sir George Barclay succeeded in bringing together Vosuq od-Dowleh, Foreign Minister in the reconstituted Cabinet, and Poklewski. The Persian minister made his apologies for the "insults" inflicted on the officials of the Russian consulate general and informed Poklewski that Shuster's gendarmes had already been withdrawn from the Shoā' property. It was 3 P.M. on November 24. Poklewski replied that the step now taken by the Persian government made possible the resumption of relations between him and the Cabinet. However, he added, Russian troops had already landed in Persia. This was an expensive and inconvenient measure. Moreover Shuster had spread in Tehran his letter full of lies and insults. "In view of all this," he concluded, "I do not think that the Imperial Government could be satisfied now with the fulfillment of our first two demands." [171]

The Persians had not expected such a turn of affairs. They had been assured by Barclay that the acceptance of the two Russian demands in the Shoā' incident would spare their country a Russian occupation. "It was only too plain that Russia proposed to keep pouring her cossacks into Northern Persia, whatever the British or the Persian Government might do or say." [172] In Tehran "almost everybody" attributed the Shoā' incident and its consequences to Russia's desire to restore Mohammad Ali. Poklewski pointed out to Neratov that "indeed, the entry of our troops in Tehran could, given certain preparation, lead to such a result." The supporters of the former Shah had already ap-

---

170. Chairman of the Council of Ministers to the Acting Minister of Foreign Affairs, Neratov, Letter No. 774, Urgent, Secret, November 10/23, 1911; *M. O.*, 2nd series, 19 (Part 1, No. 85), 80–81.

171. Minister in Tehran to the Acting Minister of Foreign Affairs, Neratov, Telegram No. 1141, Urgent, November 11/24, 1911; ibid., No. 90, p. 85.

172. Shuster, p. 166.

proached the Russian legation. However, Poklewski felt that without Russia's "active and direct support" Mohammad Ali's cause could not win.[173]

Clutching at straws, the Persian government turned to the United States. Vosuq od-Dowleh knew that the next Russian demand would be for the dismissal of Shuster; "and in this matter the affairs of Persia and Russia will reach the point of extreme difficulty," he cabled Ali Qoli Khān Nabil od-Dowleh in Washington, "in such a manner that we might either consent to Mr. Shuster's removal or to the actual, immediate destruction of the country." Vosuq od-Dowleh wanted to know what, in the opinion of the United States government, Persia should do in such circumstances.[174] The American reply was short, cold, and, to the Persians, heartbreaking:

> In view of the circumstances under which the Persian Government selected and engaged Mr. Shuster, an American citizen, to fill an important post as an official of Persia, the Government of the United States recognizes that the difficulties indicated present for the decision of the Government of Persia political questions in regard to which the Secretary of State does not find it appropriate to offer any suggestions.[175]

If the State Department was cold, the Congress was frivolous:

> the Majles appealed to the House of Representatives. But this ideological plea to the generosity of a sister democracy was not even answered. In fact, it was the cause of some jocularity in Congress. After a clerk read the message in French (its original form) to the accompaniment of laughter, a translation was read, and the document was referred to the Committee on Foreign Affairs.[176]

173. Acting Minister of Foreign Affairs, Neratov, Telegram No. 1146k Personal, Very Secret, November 12/25, 1911; M. O., 2nd series, 19 (Part 1, No. 101), 96.
174. Minister of Foreign Affairs to the Persian Legation in Washington, November 25, 1911, Enclosure in the Persian Chargé d'Affaires to the Secretary of State, No. 64, Washington, November 25, 1911; *Papers Relating to the Foreign Relations of the United States*, 1911, p. 683.
175. Aide Mémoire, The Department of State to the Persian Legation in Washington, November 27, 1911; ibid., pp. 683–84.
176. Yeselson, *United States–Persian Diplomatic Relations*, p. 119.

Sir Edward Grey continued to play his game of publicly defending Russian actions in Persia while complaining against them in private. On November 28 he told the Parliament that the Agreement of 1907 had not been violated. Next day he appealed to the Russian government not to violate the agreement by occupying Tehran, which "would in fact reduce this independence of Persia to simple fiction." [177] Neratov thanked Grey for his speech to the House of Commons and totally disregarded his requests for moderation.[178]

At noon on November 29 the dragoman of the Russian legation handed to the Persian Minister of Foreign Affairs a new ultimatum. Persia was given forty-eight hours to dismiss Shuster and Lecoffre, undertake not to hire foreign advisers without the "prior consent" of the Russian and British legations, and agree to idemnify Russia for the expenses of her current military expedition in Persia.[179]

Sir Edward Grey told the Persian minister in London that "the Persian Government must submit to Russian demands without delay." [180] Identical advice was proffered to the Persians in Tehran by Sir George Barclay.[181]

Time was rapidly running out. On December 1 the Cabinet urged the Majles to accept the ultimatum. The deputies sat in deep silence. The tension was almost unbearable when the voting began.

> And when the roll call was ended every man, priest or layman, youth or octogenarian, had cast his own die of fate, had staked the safety of himself and family, and had hurled back into the teeth of the great Bear from the North the unanimous answer of a desperate and downtrodden people who

177. Ambassador in London to the Acting Minister of Foreign Affairs, Neratov, Letter, November 16/29, 1911; M. O., 2nd series, 19 (Part 1, No. 114), 103-05.
178. Acting Minister of Foreign Affairs to the Ambassador in London, Benckendorff, Telegram No. 1903, November 16/29, 1911; ibid. (No. 112), p. 102.
179. Copy of the Note of the Imperial Russian Minister in Tehran to the Shah's Minister of Foreign Affairs of November 16 [29], 1911, No. 158; S.D.D., 7, 266.
180. Telegram of Count Benckendorff, London, November 18/December 1, 1911; ibid., p. 270.
181. Minister in Tehran to the Acting Minister of Foreign Affairs, Neratov, Telegram No. 1188, November 19/December 2, 1911; M. O., 2nd series, 19 (Part 1, No. 142), 125.

preferred the future of unknown terror to the voluntary sacrifice of their national dignity and of their recently earned right to work out their own salvation.[182]

The streets of the city filled with people. Shouts of "death or freedom" were heard on all sides. Russia was loudly cursed. Poklewski's good friend, Alā od-Dowleh, well known for his Russophile proclivity, was shot dead in front of his house. Powerless and frightened, the Cabinet tendered its resignation.[183] Its last act was the dispatch of a melancholy note rejecting the Russian ultimatum and proclaiming Persia's readiness to begin negotiations for the modification of Russia's demands.[184] Neratov at once instructed Poklewski to order the Russian troops at Rasht to march on Qazvin.[185]

Caught between rising domestic opposition and the intransigence of the Russians, Grey spared no effort to salvage the Agreement of 1907. He urged Benckendorff "that Russian troops should not go to Tehran except in the very last resort." Nor should any more demands be put forward by Russia without consulting Britain.

> I was afraid [Grey wrote] that Government of Russia did not realize how suddenly Persian question, if it was mismanaged, might raise the whole question of foreign politics. If further demands were to be put forward with regard which [sic] we might be obliged to say that they were not justified or inconsistent with the entente, the Persian question would disappear and the much more serious question of foreign politics, both for us and Russia, would take its place.[186]

182. Shuster, p. 182.

183. Minister in Tehran to the Acting Minister of Foreign Affairs, Neratov, Telegrams No. 1175 and 1180, November 18/December 1, 1911; *M. O.*, 2nd series, 19 (Part 1), 119.

184. Translation of the Note of the Shah's Minister of Foreign Affairs of 9th Zi-hajjeh 1329 [December 1, 1911], No. 14545, Poklewski's telegram No. 1193, November 20/December 3, 1911; ibid. (No. 146), pp. 128–29.

185. Acting Minister of Foreign Affairs to the Minister in Tehran, Poklewski, Telegram No. 1916, November 18/December 1, 1911; ibid. (No. 126), p. 115.

186. Grey to Buchanan, copy handed to Benckendorff, Ambassador in London to the Acting Minister of Foreign Affairs, Neratov, Telegram No. 307, November 19/December 2, 1911; ibid. (No. 140), p. 122.

Neratov pretended not to understand the cause of Grey's apprehension. He was willing to order Russian troops not to advance beyond Qazvin but noted that circumstances might compel them to enter Tehran. New demands might also be made in case of Persian armed resistance. These, however, would be confined to the Russian sphere and would relate to such questions as railway construction in northern Persia, the organization of a Russian controlled armed force in Tabriz, and so forth. Of course, he added, "no demands of general political character" would be made without prior agreement with the British.[187]

Sensing the insecurity of Grey's position at home, Benckendorff warned Neratov that the British Foreign Secretary might resign, bringing about the formation of a new Cabinet and a new political orientation. Would Russia risk a return to the old rivalry for the sake of secondary issues? All Grey wanted was an assurance that Russia would remain faithful to the preamble of the 1907 convention. For him this was not a question of prestige only, but a practical necessity if he were to maintain himself in power.[188] Grey had the support of a majority in the country and of the press, but within the Liberal party opposition was growing. The Liberals advocated better relations with Germany. Should Grey fall, a rapprochement with Germany would follow. "It is evident that for those who desire the breach of this [Anglo-Russian] entente the Shuster affair is a powerful lever." [189]

A. P. Izvolskii added his voice to that of Benckendorff in support of the Anglo-Russian entente which had demonstrated its efficacy the previous summer:

> there can be no doubt that Germany, who had thought of establishing herself at Morocco, retreated only before the perspective of a clash with France, England, and with us. I understand all the difficulty of harmonizing our present actions in Persia with English wishes. Nevertheless I implore

187. Acting Minister of Foreign Affairs to the Ambassador in London, Benckendorff, Telegram No. 1951, November 21/December 4, 1911; ibid. (No. 148), p. 130.

188. Ambassador in London to the Acting Minister of Foreign Affairs, Neratov, Telegram No. 311, November 21/December 4, 1911; ibid. (No. 150), p. 131.

189. Same to same, Letter, same date; ibid. (No. 151), p. 134.

you not to lose sight of the incalculable consequences of a break with England over Persian affairs.[190]

Having turned down the Russian ultimatum of November 29, the Persian Cabinet tried to resign, but the Regent refused to accept the resignation, and Samsām os-Saltaneh, Vosuq od-Dowleh, and their colleagues had to carry on the best they could. Russian actions had evoked an outburst of national sentiment. Meetings and demonstrations were held in Tehran as well as the principal provincial towns. The Democratic faction of the Majles called for armed resistance. Pleas for support were sent to the parliaments of all nations, including the Congress of the United States. However, Poklewski, who carefully observed the situation, felt that the decision rested largely with the Najaf clergy and the Bakhtiāri khan, Sardār As'ad.[191]

The Bakhtiāri leaders had grievances against Shuster and the Majles. Samsām os-Saltaneh, Prime Minister and brother of Sardār As'ad, would have accepted all Russian demands long before had it not been for the Treasurer General and his radical supporters. Two of the Bakhtiāri khans told Poklewski in November that they were debating whether to stage a coup d'état, getting rid of Shuster and the Majles, or to withdraw from the capital, leaving the country prey to Mohammad Ali. They assured Poklewski that a government formed by the Bakhtiāris after a coup d'état would be prepared to act in agreement with Russia and England, fire Shuster, disband the Majles, and make one of their own khans regent. They had discussed the entire scheme with Barclay, who refused to give advice.[192]

Before meeting the Bakhtiāri khans, Poklewski had discussed the matter with his English colleague. The two ministers agreed to assure the tribes that they would be justly treated by any central authority if they returned to their home land. For the time being they would not be encouraged to stage a coup d'état.

The khans were politically sensitive. Though for half a century

190. Ambassador in Paris to the Acting Minister of Foreign Affairs, Neratov, Letter, November 24/December 7, 1911; ibid. (No. 170), p. 158.

191. Minister in Tehran to the Acting Minister of Foreign Affairs, Neratov, Telegram No. 1206, November 23/December 6, 1911; ibid. (No. 166), p. 155.

192. Same to same, Telegram No. 1125, Urgent, November 8/21, 1911; ibid. (No. 57), pp. 50–51.

"The Strangling of Persia"

they had been on friendly terms with the English, though many owned shares of the Anglo-Persian Oil Company or received outright subventions from the British government, the Bakhtiāris came to feel that their future depended largely on their ability to establish good relations with Russia. To buy her favor they offered Poklewski to withdraw their old opposition to Mohammad Ali. They told him that the torrents of blood recently spilled prevented them from taking an active part in the restoration of the former Shah. However, they would not oppose it if they were allowed to leave Tehran with guarantees of safety. After the passage of a year or so, they would be prepared to participate in the affairs of state once more as faithful servants of the Shah.[193]

Grey refused to encourage any action by the Bakhtiāris, and Neratov, who did not wish to antagonize him on this score also, instructed Poklewski to deal with the khans in close agreement with Barclay, though he was to make sure "not to repulse the Bakhtiāris and not to impel them to give up energetic actions against Shuster and the Majles desirable from our point of view." [194]

On December 5, after Persia had rejected the Russian ultimatum, several Bakhtiāri khans called on Poklewski and told him that they would try to press the Majles to accept Russian demands. "In case of failure," Poklewski telegraphed, "they will try to close down the Majles, and, should this fail too, they will withdraw from affairs entirely and will try to leave Tehran before the arrival of our troops." [195] Though the Russians were willing to use the Bakhtiāris against Shuster and the Majles, they did not trust the khans, whose economic and political interests tied them closely to the British. Moreover, the Russians feared that Sardār As'ad might attempt to usurp the throne, a contingency "most undesirable" in the eyes of Russia, whose government was firmly committed to the Qājārs.[196]

193. Id.
194. Neratov to Poklewski, Telegram No. 1879, November 13/26, 1911; ibid., p. 51, note 1.
195. Minister in Tehran to the Acting Minister of Foreign Affairs, Neratov, Telegram No. 1199, November 22/December 5, 1911; ibid. (No. 160), p. 150.
196. Acting Minister of Foreign Affairs to the Ambassador in Paris, Izvolskii, for Sazonov, Telegram No. 1958, November 22/December 5, 1911; ibid. (No. 154), p. 141.

The Russians were determined "to appoint a government which would fire Shuster, dissolve the Majles, and restore order." [197] Both the Persians and the British feared that this meant the return to power of Mohammad Ali. Sir George Buchanan went so far as to tell Neratov that Grey would rather risk the fall of the Cabinet than recognize the former Shah. Moreover, Russian recognition of Mohammad Ali's restoration would, in the eyes of the English public and Parliament, lead to the destruction of Anglo-Russian agreement. Grey wanted the Russian government to let him announce in the Commons that neither government would, under any circumstances, recognize the former Shah. Neratov was willing to promise only that Russia would refrain from recognizing him as long as her expeditionary forces remained in Persian territory. "We cannot," Neratov stated, "now undertake not to recognize him, when he independently returns to the throne and is recognized by the people, which would perhaps realize that this was the only way to restore order in the country." [198]

Taking advantage of Sazonov's presence in Paris, the British government through its ambassador, Sir Francis Bertie, communicated to him a memorandum expressing Grey's views on the Persian question. Grey admitted that "the outcome of the present situation must be to secure the establishment of a Government in Persia that will conform to the principles of the Anglo-Russian agreement and pay proper regard to the special interests of Great Britain and Russia respectively." However,

> 2. It would not be consistent with the dignity of England to recognize a restoration of the Ex-Shah after the manner in which he disregarded the warnings given to him by both the Russian and the British Governments not to return to Persia. . . . Sir E. Grey therefore trusts that the Russian Government will not add to the embarrassments of the situation by permitting the restoration of the Ex-Shah to be the outcome of the present crisis.

197. Id.
198. Same to same, for Sazonov, Telegram No. 1959, November 22/December 5, 1911; ibid. (No. 155), p. 141.

"The Strangling of Persia"

Sir Edward wanted Poklewski and Barclay to agree on a financial adviser to Persia, the two powers providing her with a loan as a measure for the prevention of chaos. However, financial assistance would have no effect if Russia insisted upon exacting from Persia an indemnity for the current military expedition. "Sir E. Grey hopes," the memorandum continued, "that when the present crisis is past the Russian Government will find means of avoiding the difficulty which would be caused by an insistence on the payment of an indemnity." Finally,

> 6. Sir E. Grey understands that as soon as the Russian demands have been complied with and order in Northern Persia has been restored, the military measures and occupation of Persian territory which are now in progress and are stated to be provisional and not permanent will cease.[199]

In spite of mounting British pressure, St. Petersburg stood firm. Buchanan continued to protest against the possible Russian occupation of Tehran and the restoration of Mohammad Ali. He emphasized again and again that the occupation of the capital would "be regarded in England as a blow struck at the independence of Persia, and consequently at our understanding with Russia." Neratov "remained obdurate on this point, and at the same time refused to sanction a statement being made in the House of Commons to the effect that the two Governments had agreed under no circumstances to recognize the ex-Shah." [200] He restated his position in a memorandum which declared that Russian military operations had nothing to do with the affairs of the former Shah. Should he take advantage of the presence of Russian troops to achieve his ends, the Russian government would not recognize him without previous agreement with Britain. Russian troops concentrated at Qazvin would not march on Tehran before December 21 unless an emergency compelled the Russian minister in Tehran to call them before that date. Russia

---

199. Memorandum transmitted by the British Ambassador in Paris to the Russian Minister of Foreign Affairs, November 25/December 8, 1911; ibid. (No. 176), pp. 163–64; also Telegram No. 186 in S.D.D., 7, 296.
200. Buchanan, *My Mission to Russia*, 1, 100.

wished to withdraw the Qazvin detachment as soon as possible and would do so when the Persians accept her demands. The Russian government hoped, Neratov concluded, that no new incidents such as "violence against the person of a Russian agent, an attack on Russian institutions or our troops, acts of provocation toward Russia, troubles in general, etc." would occur.[201] The caveat was so broad as to make the promise of withdrawal meaningless. The exchange of memoranda and personal negotiations in St. Petersburg, London, and Paris had failed to restrain Russia.

Incidents were, of course, unavoidable. They were also easily provocable by men such as Pokhitonov, Miller, or Prince Dabizha. The latter telegraphed Neratov from Mashhad that the situation there was "extremely serious." The authorities were paralyzed. Caucasian émigrés, local revolutionaries, and the clergy were agitating against the foreigners and arming the people to resist the Russian ultimatum concerning Shuster. The population was excited, and Russian troops were needed to prevent complications. The seventy Cossacks with two machine guns already stationed at Mashhad were not enough. Dabizha wanted two more Cossack squadrons and an infantry battalion as well as an infantry battalion with four machine guns for Quchān.[202]

The Persian government was rapidly losing all hope of outside support. Foreign parliaments ignored the appeals of the Majles. European cabinets were too deeply absorbed in their own problems and not at all interested in the fate of Persia. The domestic coalition of nationalists, clergy, and Bakhtiāri chiefs, which had governed the country since the overthrow of Mohammad Ali, was coming apart at the seams. Vosuq od-Dowleh did everything possible to modify the Russian ultimatum. He assured Poklewski that the Cabinet was willing to fire Shuster and pay an indemnity. However, he begged for a change in the phrasing of the second

201. Memorandum of November 27/December 10, 1911, Enclosure in Acting Minister of Foreign Affairs to the Chairman of the Council of Ministers, Kokovtsov, Letter No. 885, Secret, November 28/December 11, 1911; M. O., 2nd series, 19 (Part 1, No. 189), 175–76.

202. Consul General in Mashhad to the Acting Minister of Foreign Affairs, Neratov, Telegram No. 146, November 24/December 7, 1911; ibid. (No. 175), pp. 162–63.

article of the Russian ultimatum. The article in question required Russian and British prior "consent" to the appointment of foreign advisers by the Persian government. Both Vosuq od-Dowleh in Tehran and Moshāver ol-Mamālek in St. Petersburg tried to substitute for it the word "agreement."[203] Neratov felt that Russia should not be lenient. If Persia accepted all three points of the ultimatum, and if no further incidents occurred, Russian troops would withdraw from Qazvin. The general improvement of Russo-Persian relations, according to Neratov, depended entirely upon Persia. However, the Majles, as then constituted, would never allow the government to reestablish order. Therefore, if the Cabinet were able to do so, Russia could only recommend that it dissolve the Majles immediately and set a date for new elections.[204] On December 12 Poklewski informed Vosuq od-Dowleh that the ultimatum was not subject to negotiation.[205]

The Persian government procrastinated and tried to induce the Russians to negotiate on the demand concerning foreign advisers. Vosuq od-Dowleh offered to promise that "in questions pertaining to the invitation of foreign functionaries and officers the Persian Government will be ready for a prior exchange of opinions with the Russian and British legations in Tehran."[206] On December 13 Sazonov returned to Russia and next day resumed the direction of the Foreign Ministry. His position on Persia was essentially the same as Neratov's but without Neratov's rigidity. He telegraphed Poklewski that Russia would accept Vosuq od-Dowleh's phrasing of Article 2 of the ultimatum with a small change, the pertinent part reading, "The Persian Government, wishing to reach agreement on questions relating to the above named functionaries." Thus Sazonov in fact was making no

203. Various telegrams exchanged between Neratov and Poklewski, ibid. (Nos. 104, 183); also S.D.D., 7, 295.

204. Acting Minister of Foreign Affairs to the Minister in Tehran, Poklewski, Telegram No. 2000, November 26/December 9, 1911; M. O., 2nd series, 19 (Part 1, No. 185), 172–73.

205. Minister in Tehran to the Acting Minister of Foreign Affairs, Neratov, November 29/December 12, 1911; ibid., p. 181, note 1.

206. Persian proposals cited in Minister in Tehran to the Acting Minister of Foreign Affairs, Neratov, Telegram No. 1242, November 29/December 12, 1911; ibid., note 2.

concession at all, though seemingly assuring a more reasonable attitude than Neratov's.[207]

Since the Persians still had not accepted the ultimatum, Poklewski made preparations for the occupation of Tehran. He asked for instructions concerning his relationship to the future Russian military commander of the city, inquired into the course of action to be pursued in case the Persian government remained in the capital and in case it left Tehran, asked what to do with Shuster and how to treat Yefrem Khān, the Dashnak chief of Tehran's police.[208]

Russian forces were spreading steadily over the north. They appeared at Khoy and moved toward Urumiyyeh to the consternation of the Turks, whose troops also began to encroach on Persian territory.[209] The Viceroy of the Caucasus, Count I. I. Vorontsov-Dashkov, believed that Turkey would fight for the Persian districts she had occupied. Turkish preparations for war could not be ignored, and Russia must immediately begin similar preparations, he advised.[210]

Late at night on December 20 the Majles found itself surrounded by armed Bakhtiāris and Yefrem Khān's police. Under the muzzles of their pistols, the deputies accepted Russia's ultimatum.[211] Poklewski was notified the next day. On the twenty-fourth the Majles was disbanded and Shuster dismissed. Within a few days he left Persia. "His aims were admirable and just," Sir Edward Grey commented years later, "but he had not realized that Russian interference in the north of Persia could only be ousted by force. . . . He attempted what was good, but what could only be done by force; and there was no force available for the purpose." [212] Sir George Barclay, who had faithfully carried

207. Minister of Foreign Affairs to the Minister in Tehran, Poklewski, Telegrams Nos. 2043 and 2044, December 1/14, 1911; ibid. (No. 200), p. 186.

208. Minister in Tehran to the Minister of Foreign Affairs, Telegram No. 1268, December 5/18, 1911; ibid. (No. 222), pp. 207–08.

209. Consul General in Erzerum, Stritter, to Sazonov, December 9/22, 1911; ibid., p. 209, note 1.

210. Viceroy of the Caucasus to the Minister of Foreign Affairs, Telegram No. 7666, December 5/18, 1911; ibid. (No. 224), pp. 208–09.

211. Survey of events in Tehran from December 8/21 to December 14/27, 1911 (Poklewski's dispatch of December 15/28, 1911), S.D.D., 7, 370–71.

212. Grey, Twenty-five Years, 1, 169.

out Grey's policy of undermining Shuster, admitted that "It is enough to make the angels weep to see all Shuster's machinery fall into incapable hands. . . . I *really* liked that man." [213]

With the dispersal of the Majles and Shuster's departure, Persia virtually ceased to exist as a state. A small group of men, some patriotic others traitorous, tried to control events the magnitude of which dwarfed them and revealed their impotence. In northern Persia Russian troop commanders and consuls ignored the local authorities and assumed the functions of government. The consuls were especially vociferous and aggressive in promoting Russian imperialist interests and relying on force. Pokhitonov had done so in Tehran and Miller in Tabriz. In Rasht, Astarābād, or Mashhad, they were always the hardest, most belligerent of Russian officials.

Consul Nekrasov in Rasht complained directly to Sazonov that the Persians boycotted Russian goods and even made attacks upon Russian forces. The Minister of Foreign Affairs suggested the arrest and court-martialing of Russian subjects who took part in such attacks, the disarmament of Persian revolutionary units "and other disorderly elements," and the arrest and exile to Russia of the leaders of the nationalist movement.[214] Nekrasov acted even before receiving instructions. On December 21 the Cossacks sacked a printing plant suspected of printing anti-Russian leaflets. The Cossacks claimed that someone, perhaps a Persian gendarme, had fired a shot. No one had been injured, but Russian fire killed or wounded thirty Persians.[215]

Nekrasov arrested a number of Persians, including members of *anjomans* and clergy, and planned to ship them to Baku. "While admitting that this measure is not foreseen by the existing juridical norms, I deem it my duty," he wrote, "to call the attention of the Imperial Legation to the fact that existing circumstances utterly preclude the application of such norms intended for normal international relations." [216] He predicted a catas-

213. Cited in Nicolson, *Portrait of a Diplomatist*, p. 259.

214. Minister of Foreign Affairs to the Consul in Rasht, Nekrasov, Telegram No. 2117, December 10/23, 1911; M. O., 2nd series, 19 (Part 1, No. 245), 235–36.

215. Consul in Rasht to the Minister of Foreign Affairs, Sazonov, Telegram No. 330, December 13/26, 1911; ibid. (No. 267), pp. 248–49.

216. Id.

trophe unless more Russian troops were sent to Rasht, and accused the British and Turkish consuls of inciting and protecting Persian authorities against Russia.[217] "In general," Nekrasov claimed, "one must regard the attack of December 8 [21] as an ambuscade prearranged by Persian government troops which were aided by fanatical Persian and Turkish Armenians and, morally, by the Turkish and British consuls." [218]

Poklewski was afraid that Nekrasov's doings would provoke a mass uprising in Gilān. "Moreover, his fantasy is apparently limitless, and he finds it possible to ignore the norms of both [local] law and international law." [219] Having been taught a lesson by Pokhitonov, Poklewski was not as peremptory with Nekrasov.

> However [he telegraphed the consul], further arrests of Persian subjects on the basis of suspicion alone, searches in the houses of the Moslems, and especially any measures against the clergy seem to me utterly undesirable and capable only of inflaming public passions. Neither should you arrest Turkish subjects, nor deport Persian subjects to Baku unless you receive specific permission from St. Petersburg.

Poklewski expressed his "deep conviction" that tranquilization could be achieved only through common action between Nekrasov and the Kārgozār (representative of the Persian Ministry of Foreign Affairs).

> The Cabinet is doing everything possible in this direction, and the new governor, who should soon arrive in Rasht with an escort of two hundred Persian Cossacks, is equipped with corresponding instructions. You, on the contrary, evade meeting the Kārgozār, who has been ordered to cooperate in every possible way in the restoration of the normal state of affairs in Gilān.[220]

217. Same to same, Telegram No. 343, December 14/27, 1911; ibid. (No. 343), pp. 253–54.

218. Same to same, Telegram No. 360, December 17/30, 1911; ibid., p. 254; note 1.

219. Minister in Tehran to the Minister of Foreign Affairs, Sazonov, Telegram No. 1306, December 15/28, 1911; ibid. (No. 278), p. 258.

220. Poklewski to Nekrasov, Enclosure in Minister in Tehran to the Minister of

"The Strangling of Persia"

Perceiving the contradiction between Sazonov's suggestions and Poklewski's instructions, Nekrasov complained that the latter were imprecise. What should he do about those already arrested and deported to Baku, among whom only three had actually participated in an attack on Russian troops? What about those whose role in the attack had not been clearly established? What about a man who had been "active in the crowd which attacked our troops and had the temerity to traduce the August name [Nicholas II] and received a bayonet wound but of whom it is not known whether he was armed or not?"[221] Obviously Nekrasov was hoping that St. Petersburg would overrule Poklewski once again and institute a reign of terror in Rasht. In his clash with his superior, he had every reason to feel confident. How could Poklewski's instructions of December 29 be reconciled with Sazonov's, who had telegraphed on the same day that

> Punitive measures against those guilty of attacks on our troops must be carried out with all necessary severity and speed by agreement between the commanders of our detachments and the consuls. Among punitive measures the commanders of the detachments, in agreement with the consuls, should be permitted . . . to make monetary exactions from the population which supports actions hostile to us.[222]

In Tabriz, Consul Miller, who had served in the same capacity in Seistān, was even more belligerent than Nekrasov. He belonged to the extreme imperialist wing of the consular service, was a friend of Pokhitonov and an old enemy of the British. Like most of his colleagues he felt nothing but dislike and disdain for the Persians. Miller's experience in Tabriz, the most staunchly revolutionary city in Iran, had been unhappy until he managed to have Russian troops enter it in 1908. However, they had not

---

Foreign Affairs, Sazonov, No. 1305, December 16/29, 1911; ibid. (No. 283), p. 261.

221. Consul in Rasht to the Minister of Foreign Affairs, Sazonov, Telegram No. 372, December 19, 1911/January 1, 1912; ibid. (No. 294), pp. 271–72.

222. Minister of Foreign Affairs to the Minister in Tehran, Poklewski, Telegram No. 2156, December 16/29, 1911, copies to Miller and Nekrasov; ibid. (No. 279), p. 258.

completed their task: Mohammad Ali had not been restored, a tame Persian had not been appointed governor of Āzarbāyjān, the administration of the province had not been taken over by himself, and Caucasian revolutionaries had not been returned to Russian jails. A minor incident with Russian troops created an opportunity for the achievement of most of Miller's goals.

About ten o'clock in the evening on December 20, ten Russian soldiers were repairing a telegraph line in Tabriz. A few had climbed the roof of a private building next to the local police headquarters. Persian gendarmes drove them away. The Russians returned with reenforcements and entered into a loud quarrel with the gendarmes. There are several versions as to who provoked whom, but all agree that in the ensuing fight one Russian was slightly injured and two Persians fell dead to the ground. Next day shooting broke out in several parts of the city. Shortly after 9:30 P.M. six Russian mountain guns stationed in the Bāghe Shomāl began to shell the citadel. Armed revolutionary bands, joined by the populace, attacked the Russian consulate, but were thrown back. Consul Miller reported to St. Petersburg that the Persians tortured captive Russian soldiers.[223] The Persian governor and foreign eye-witnesses on their part accused the Russians of committing brutalities on a large scale. An English traveler wrote:

> In some cases houses were entered and men, women, and children were shot indiscriminately. There were a great many women and children killed, but most of this happened during the shelling by the Russians of certain houses from which Persians had been firing. The Russian soldiers systematically looted and destroyed every house from which they had been fired upon.[224]

The Viceroy of the Caucasus, Count I. I. Vorontsov-Dashkov, proposed an immediate march on Tehran. He urged the most

---

223. Report of the State Counselor Miller, Tabriz, December 27, 1911/January 9, 1912; S.D.D., 7, 410-25.

224. G. D. Turner in the Manchester *Guardian*, September 3, 1912, as cited in E. G. Browne, *The Reign of Terror in Tabriz* (London, 1912), pp. 9-10. Also cf. Shuster, *The Strangling of Persia*, pp. 219-20.

"The Strangling of Persia"

energetic measures against strikes, boycotts, looting, and disorder. Nationalist fighters, the *fadāiyān*, should be arrested, and, in case of resistance, exterminated. It was Russian procrastination in moving on to Tehran, he said, that gave courage to the Persians to attack Russian Troops.[225] Vorontsov-Dashkov called for vengeance:

> the insolent attack on our detachment in Tabriz and the tortures inflicted on the wounded demand the most severe retribution, in view of which I would propose to General Voropanov, upon his arrival with the detachment, to blow up the citadel and to set up courts-martial which would try all the instigators of the attack upon our detachment, those guilty of torturing our wounded and also all our subjects hiding in Persia who have joined in the armed attack upon our detachment. The sentences to be executed immediately.

And in another telegram on the same day:

> I hotly insist upon the measures of repression which must be applied in Tabriz and Rasht in retribution for the spilled Russian blood. All the guilty must be court-martialed and in Persia, on the spot where the crimes were committed; and they should under no circumstances be sent to Russia to be confined in the prisons of the Caucasian Military District where all the prisons are full to overflowing and where the trial of these heavily accused criminals would be infinitely prolonged and the verdict might be relatively mild.[226]

The Russian Council of Ministers met on December 26 to discuss the Tabriz situation and decide on the policy to be pursued there. It was reported that from the twentieth to the twenty-fifth one Russian officer and thirty-nine enlisted men had been killed, five officers and forty-two enlisted men had been wounded. Reenforcements had been sent, including four infantry regiments,

225. The Viceroy of the Caucasus to the Minister of Foreign Affairs, Sazonov, Telegram No. 7637, December 10/23, 1911; M. O., 2nd series, 19 (Part 1, No. 257), 236–37.
226. Two telegrams from the Viceroy of the Caucasus to the Minister of Foreign Affairs, December 11/24, 1911; ibid., p. 239; see also note 4 on that page.

five Cossack squadrons, three batteries of three guns each, a mortar platoon, and half a company of sappers. Another force of four thousand men had been sent from the Caucasus to Anzali, Rasht, and Qazvin. The gunboats *Kars* and *Ardahan* had been dispatched to Anzali. The Chairman of the Council of Ministers had instructed the Viceroy of the Caucasus to institute courts-martial to try the instigators of attacks on Russians, those who tortured Russians, and Russian revolutionaries who took part in anti-Russian activities in Persia.[227] The Council of Ministers confirmed previous actions of the Ministry of Foreign Affairs, issued additional instructions, and stated that Russian troops should be withdrawn from Persia upon the restoration of order, but in the meantime authorized punitive measures against the Persians.

The Viceroy of the Caucasus was not satisfied with the Cabinet's stand, which he considered too mild. In a telegram to the Tsar he described the struggle in Tabriz and the heroism of Russian soldiers, and called for vengeance. "Any procrastination and the show of excessive humanity in this case would be interpreted as a manifestation of weakness on our part and our dependence on powerful outside influences." The hint was clear: the Persians must not be allowed to think that Britain had the power to moderate Russian behavior.[228] The Tsar replied:

> I am indignant at the insolent attack of the Persians on our troops in Tabriz. Entirely approve of the order you gave to General Voropanov to act harshly and quickly. Convey to the units which have suffered losses my cordial thanks. Nicholas.[229]

Encouraged by the Tsar himself, Consul Miller proceeded to execute prisoners. On December 31, corresponding to the Ashurā (the tenth of Moharram), a holy memorial day in the Shiite

227. Special journal of the Council of Ministers, December 12/26, 1911; ibid. (No. 264), pp. 242–47.

228. The Viceroy to the Tsar, December 16/29, 1911; ibid., p. 263.

229. Court Minister [Baron Fredericks] to the Minister of Foreign Affairs, Sazonov, Telegram No. 3225, Livadia, December 16/29, 1911; ibid. (No. 286), pp. 263–64.

calendar, the Russians hanged the chief mojtahed of Āzarbāyjān, Saqat ol-Eslām. Several others, both clergy and lay, shared his fate on the same day. Hangings continued for more than a week, Hāji Ali Davāfurush, a leading nationalist, being put to death on January 6, 1912. Miller felt that the executions were beneficial:

> Among the population this punishment has produced the very best impression for us and considerably alleviated the anger of our military personnel evoked by the sight of the soldiers and Cossacks bestially tortured to death by the *fadāiyān*. Altogether fifteen have been executed. Of those arrested and court-martialed twenty-six have been released and pardoned on my request.[230]

While the Russians were pounding the center of Tabriz with their cannon and court-martialing their enemies, the notorious reactionary Samad Khān Shojā' od-Dowleh, hovered on the outskirts with his tribesmen. A devoted follower of Mohammad Ali since the latter's years as governor of Āzarbāyjān, he was waiting to be admitted by his Russian friends into Tabriz where he hoped to be recognized as governor and formally to proclaim the restoration of his royal master. Buchanan, who knew of this plan, asked Sazonov not to permit Shojā' to carry it out. It seems that the British government had made of Mohammad Ali a symbol of their own humiliating failure in Persia. Russia could not be effectively opposed and would inevitably achieve her aims, but one could turn the fat and vicious former Shah into a scapegoat and achieve a certain satisfaction from preventing his restoration. Opposition to the person of the former Shah absorbed most of their energies and became the principal task of the British in Persia.[231] Sazonov paid little attention to Grey's wishes. Russia, he claimed, could not oppose Shojā' od-Dowleh's entry into the city, to which he had been invited by the population, without committing an act of intervention in Persia's internal affairs.

---

230. Miller's telegram, Tabriz, December 24, 1911/January 6, 1912; S.D.D., 7, 206–07.

231. Benckendorff to Sazonov, Telegram No. 336, December 19, 1911/January 1, 1912; M. O., 2nd series, 19 (Part 1), 273, note 3.

However, Sazonov was willing not to extend to him formal recognition, which would not prevent Miller from dealing with Shojā' as the de facto governor. "Miller could suggest to Shojā' to refrain from a solemn proclamation of Mohammad Ali [as Shah]." [232]

Consul Miller had not waited for either Sazonov or Poklewski to instruct him about Shojā', who entered the city on January 1 and proceeded to massacre his enemies and loot the population, while promising to act in everything in accordance with the directives of the Russian government.[233] The indiscriminate killings, tortures, and vandalism of Shojā' od-Dowleh's followers far surpassed the brutality of Russian troops.

Sir George Barclay was shocked by the reign of terror in Tabriz. In his opinion the execution of Saqat ol-Eslām had been a "catastrophe of such major importance that it is impossible to foresee all its consequences." [234] Sir Louis Mallet showed Barclay's telegram to Benckendorff, who begged Sazonov to publish justificatory documents showing that Russia had resorted to reprisals because of attacks on her soldiers. Across Benckendorff's dispatch Nicholas II wrote "The nervousness of the English is beginning to bore me." Sazonov replied to Benckendorff that Russian public opinion was indignant over the "bestialities" committed by the Persians on Russian soldiers. Harsh punishment was inevitable, and could fall upon the members of the clergy such as Saqat ol-Eslām. "However, precedents of execution of such persons can be found both in Persia and in Turkey." [235]

Ali Qoli Khān Moshāver ol-Mamālek, Persian minister in St. Petersburg, tried to protest against the Tabriz massacre. He asked Sazonov for the withdrawal of Russian troops, the removal of

232. Minister of Foreign Affairs to the Minister in Tehran, Poklewski, Telegram No. 2194, December 20, 1911/January 2, 1912; ibid. (No. 296), p. 273.

233. Miller's telegram No. 796, December 22, 1911/January 4, 1912; ibid., p. 273, note 4. Also Miller's telegram of December 19, 1911/January 1, 1912; S.D.D., 7, 395.

234. Ambassador in London to the Minister of Foreign Affairs, Sazonov, Telegram No. 341, December 21, 1911/January 3, 1912; M. O., 2nd series, 19 (Part 1, No. 301), 276.

235. Sazonov to Benckendorff, Telegram No. 2206, December 22, 1911/January 4, 1912; ibid., p. 276, note 3.

Shojā' od-Dowleh, and the punishment of those guilty of hanging Saqat ol-Eslām on a holy day. Otherwise the Persian Cabinet would resign and declare that it had been compelled to do so by Russian actions. Sazonov rudely replied that the Persian protest was out of place and warned Ali Qoli Khān of the serious consequences that would follow the resignation of the Persian Cabinet. He also instructed Poklewski to make it clear to the Regent and the ministers that they "would bring upon the country only immeasurably greater calamities." Should they listen to reason, Poklewski could indicate to them that Russian troops would not remain in Persia "beyond the time necessary for the establishment of a normal state of affairs." [236]

The Persian government stopped protesting but continued its feeble efforts to reestablish at least the outward forms of its authority in Tabriz. The Bakhtiāri khans who had forced Mohammad Vali Khān Sepahdār out of the Cabinet, proposed him for the governorship of Āzarbāyjān, hoping to weaken through him the power of Shojā' od-Dowleh who had plans for the conquest of the capital and the restoration of Mohammad Ali. Sazonov had instructed Consul Miller to let Shojā' od-Dowleh know that his expedition against Tehran would be utterly aimless and "would not meet with our [Russian] approval" because of the promises made to Britain not to recognize Mohammad Ali's restoration so long as there were Russian troops in the vicinity of Tehran.[237] Shojā' od-Dowleh obeyed his masters, but the Persian government nevertheless preferred to have the weak Sepahdār rather than the violent tribesman at the head of the phantom government in Āzarbāyjān.

Sazonov was willing to let Sepahdār come to Tabriz but wanted Shojā' od-Dowleh to be assured that "his goodwill toward us has earned him our sympathy and he can count on our support in the future." [238] Poklewski told Vosuq od-Dowleh, the

236. Minister of Foreign Affairs to the Minister in Tehran, Poklewski, Telegram No. 2216, December 23, 1911/January 5, 1912; ibid. (No. 320), pp. 295–96.
237. Minister of Foreign Affairs to the Consul General in Tabriz, A. Miller, Telegram No. 66, January 11/24, 1912; M. O., 2nd series, 19 (Part 2, No. 384), 39.
238. Minister of Foreign Affairs to the Minister in Tehran, Poklewski, Telegram No. 218, February 2/15, 1912; ibid. (No. 471), p. 132.

Foreign Minister, that Russia would agree to Sepahdār's appointment if Persia formed a Cossack brigade in Tabriz and granted an amnesty to Shojā' od-Dowleh's supporters. The Cabinet accepted both conditions.[239]

Shojā' od-Dowleh had no intention of giving up the post granted him by the Russians. He accused the Tehran authorities of fomenting disorder and threatened to "resign." [240] Poklewski felt that Shojā' had misunderstood Sepahdār's intentions and failed to realize that "they both serve not only the Persian but the Imperial [Russian] Government as well." [241] Sazonov was not certain of Sepahdār's loyalty, and was afraid that the abandonment of Shojā' od-Dowleh by Russia would be interpreted as a sign of her weakness.[242] His apprehensions were fed by Russian consuls who were firmly committed to Shojā' od-Dowleh and resented the prospect of Sepahdār's participation in the government of Āzarbāyjān. Consul Beliaev in Ardebil and Acting Consul General Preobrazhenskii in Tabriz tried their best to block Sepahdār's appointment and to sabotage the policies of their chief in Tehran.[243]

Poklewski must have relived his bitter experience with Pokhitonov in the Shoā' incident when he read copies of Preobrazhenskii's telegrams to Sazonov. In hot anger at his agents in Āzarbāyjān, he accused Shojā' od-Dowleh of arrogant lying and Preobrazhenskii of excessive credulity.

> In general it is time [he telegraphed Sasonov] that the Consulate General begin to display a more critical attitude toward the statements of Shojā' and stop transmitting his nonsensical opinions about the person of Sepahdār who is much better

---

239. Minister in Tehran to the Acting Minister of Foreign Affairs, Neratov, Dispatch No. 33, July 5/18, 1912; ibid. (Part 1, No. 329), pp. 335–37.

240. Ibid. (Part 2), p. 409, note 3.

241. Minister in Tehran to the Minister of Foreign Affairs, Sazonov, Telegram No. 522, June 17/30, 1912; ibid., 20 (Part 1, No. 247), p. 239.

242. Minister of Foreign Affairs to the Minister in Tehran, Poklewski, Telegram No. 1229, June 19/July 2, 1912; ibid. (No. 253), p. 246.

243. Acting Consul General in Tabriz to the Minister of Foreign Affairs, Sazonov, Telegram No. 350, June 22/July 5, 1912; ibid. (No. 271), p. 264.

known to the Legation than to the Consulate General and to Shojā'.²⁴⁴

This time Poklewski's old antagonist, Neratov, came to his aid. In a letter to the Assistant to the Viceroy of the Caucasus, Nikolai Pavlovich Shatilov, he wrote that Sepahdār was still judged as the former leader of revolutionary bands which had marched from Gilān to Tehran to help overthrow Mohammad Ali Shah. However, it was forgotten that he had been forced to assume that role and that he had not only never been a revolutionary but not even a convinced Constitutionalist. On the contrary, Neratov continued, there were ample reasons to think "that he had been one of the secret partisans of the former Shah during the latter's recent unsuccessful attempt to regain his lost throne."²⁴⁵ The problem was finally settled when Shojā' od-Dowleh accepted the post of assistant governor, retaining the substance of power, under Sepahdār—the perennial figurehead.

The real issue in the case of Shojā' od-Dowleh was the restoration of Mohammad Ali. After the defeat of his forces, the former Shah had retreated to the Gorgān plain, where he sought additional Russian help and made arrangements for the protection of his person. The Governor General of Turkestan, A. V. Samsonov, was instructed by Neratov to take the Shah to the Caucasus and thence to Odessa. In case of extreme need he could be transported to Astrakhan or Petrovsk in a naval ship, though a private vessel would be preferable. Without obtaining the opinion of the Foreign Minister, Neratov added, he could not say who would pay the expenses, but he had no doubt that the Russian government would take care of them.²⁴⁶ Mohammad Ali was not evacuated in October 1911. He and his entourage lingered on, hoping for Russian intervention on their behalf. "Here everything is held together by the hope of Russian aid," wrote Consul Ivanov from

244. Ibid., note 3.
245. Acting Minister of Foreign Affairs to the Assistant to the Viceroy of the Caucasus, Shatilov, Letter No. 926, Secret, August 7/20, 1912; ibid. (Part 2, No. 515), 54–55.
246. Acting Minister of Foreign Affairs to the Governor General of Turkestan, Samsonov, Telegram No. 1559, October 8/21, 1911; ibid., 18 (Part 2, No. 682), 201.

Astarābād. "The Turkomans are always ready to desert the Shah and could even make an attempt on his life. The Shah in turn cannot continue without the Turkomans who are his best support." [247]

Russian officials, military and diplomatic, did everything possible to keep up Mohammad Ali's spirit and hope. Ivanov himself turned over to him 267 rifles and much ammunition. On October 29 the former Shah was entertained at dinner aboard the Russian naval vessel *Astarābād*. When he went ashore, he was given a Russian military escort to guard his person. Poklewski felt that should such acts of Russian officials become known, Russia would be badly compromised. The Tsar disagreed. Having read Poklewski's report, he wrote in the margin, "There is nothing special in this." [248]

Poklewski was not kept fully informed of the activities of his own consuls, but he suspected that they had secret instructions from St. Petersburg to work for the restoration of Mohammad Ali. Miller in Tabriz was smart enough to give to his installation of Shojā' od-Dowleh the appearance of Persian action. Neither Nekrasov at Rasht nor Beliaev at Ardebil had gone too far. However, the Astarābād consulate under Ivanov devoted itself openly and entirely to Mohammad Ali's cause.

> In general both Ivanov and the consular agent in Bandare Gaz render open services to the ex-Shah and visibly cooperate in the strengthening of his authority in the Astarābād province. This is reported from Persian sources, by the English agent at Astarābād, and by Belgian customs officials.

Moreover, Poklewski wrote to Sazonov, a Russian adventurer, Amirajibi, was recruiting Ingush and other Caucasian mountaineers for Mohammad Ali's forces. Several hundred had already arrived in Persia. None of this, Poklewski felt, was compatible with the dignity and prestige of Russia,

> and it is in our interests to terminate this abnormal situation either by placing the ex-Shah on the throne, or by asking him

247. Telegram from Ivanov, Astarābād, December 4/17, 1911; S.D.D., 7, 330.
248. M. O., 2nd series, 19 (Part 1), 318, note 3.

"The Strangling of Persia"

to leave Persia. If the Imperial Government chose the second decision, it would be necessary thereafter to take serious measures to uproot the official laxity that has recently developed in our consular practice here, which reflects harmfully upon the dignity of the Imperial legation and makes unification of the activities of all our agents in Persia impossible for it.[249]

Russia's decisions on the fate of Mohammad Ali were ultimately based on considerations of political grand strategy. Late in 1911 Benckendorff began to see signs of British desire to improve relations with Germany. He warned Sazonov in December that Persia was not the only problem between Russia and Britain, but that there was a considerable body of opinion in England that viewed relations with Germany as unnecessarily tense. The Russian Ministry of Foreign Affairs intercepted and deciphered Grey's telegram to Buchanan, informing the latter of Lord Haldane's mission to Berlin for a "frank exchange of views with the German Government." France had made an agreement with Germany over Morocco; Russia had settled some of her problems at Potsdam. Therefore, Grey went on, "it is very desirable that we should also settle now our questions, or our relations with Germany might become worse."[250] However, even without such telegrams Sazonov had begun to feel that the time for aggressive action in Persia had passed. Russia had taken full advantage of the Moroccan crisis to consolidate her position in northern Persia. Britain had remained virtually silent while Russia succeeded in getting rid of Shuster, occupying Persia's northern provinces, destroying the revolutionary movement in Tabriz, and killing her enemies. Now the European situation was improving and Britain was turning her attention to Persia once more.

Benckendorff feared that a full-fledged discussion of the Persian question between St. Petersburg and London might lead to the collapse of Grey's entire foreign policy. Sir Edward's position was

249. Minister in Tehran to the Minister of Foreign Affairs, Sazonov, Telegram No. 1373, December 31, 1911/January 13, 1912; ibid. (No. 344), pp. 318–19.

250. Secretary of State for Foreign Affairs, Grey, to the English Ambassador in St. Petersburg, Buchanan, Telegram No. 96, January 25/February 7, 1912; ibid. (Part 2, No. 429), p. 85.

not particularly strong, and no foreign secretary could remain in power long if attacked by members of his own party and the opposition.[251] An informal coalition of dissident Liberals, Conservatives, and Labourites used Russian activities in northern Persia to discredit Grey's policies and push for better relations with Germany. Many Englishmen were particularly unhappy over the situation in southern Persia where Britain could either pursue a policy of strength, leading to military occupation, or of nonintervention. The Conservatives preferred the first alternative, the Liberals the second. Grey hoped to solve the south Persian problem by strengthening the central government to the point where it could restore and keep order on its own. Such was Benckendorff's analysis.[252]

Sazonov began to move toward moderation. He told Buchanan that understanding with Britain was the alpha and omega of his policy.

> In order to maintain it and to meet the wishes of His Majesty's Government [Buchanan wrote to Grey], he had, in defiance of Russian public opinion, stopped the advance of the Russian troops on Tehran, facilitated an amicable arrangement with the Persian Government, consented to the joint advance of £200,000, sacrificed the ex-Shah, and, in fact, done everything which we had asked him to do. . . .
>
> Not only had he been attacked in the Press, but he had been reproached in other quarters with sacrificing Russia's interests at our dictation. He had had to overcome considerable opposition in the Council of Ministers, and after the attacks made on the Russian troops at Tabriz last December he had received three letters telling him that he was not fit to direct Russian foreign policy and threatening his life.[253]

On January 29 Buchanan received a formal note on the normalization of the situation in Persia. It proposed that the Persian

251. Ambassador in London to the Minister of Foreign Affairs, Sazonov, Letter, January 15/28, 1912; ibid., No. 397, pp. 50–52.

252. Ambassador in London to the Minister of Foreign Affairs, Letter, January 3/16, 1912; ibid. (No. 350), pp. 3–5.

253. Buchanan to Grey, Private letter, n. d., cited in Buchanan, *My Mission to Russia*, 1, 111.

government enter into direct negotiations with Mohammad Ali with a view to putting an end to their struggle. The Russian government could empower its consul at Astarābād to mediate between the two sides. The former Shah did not consider his cause hopeless but might withdraw if offered a pension. Furthermore, Russia felt that Persia needed money and an improved military force.

The existing Persian forces were useless or worse. The fadāiyān (mojāhedin) consisted of "local dregs and those newly come, predominantly Caucasian anarchists, criminals, and such like refuse." They should be disbanded and the foreigners exiled. Persian armed forces should be no larger than was absolutely necessary, and Russia and Britain should have some say as to where they would be deployed.

Other specific demands which Russia put forth included the preservation of the Qājār dynasty, the granting to Russia of additional concessions in her zone, the settlement of all claims of the Russian Discount and Loan Bank, the solution of the problem of land ownership (Persian law forbade foreigners to own land), and so forth.[254] What the Russian government was asking for was the acceptance by Britain of the Russian interpretation of the Persian clauses of the Agreement of 1907. Northern Persia was to be handed over to Russia, and neither Britain nor the Persian government in Tehran was to interfere with it.

Britain was prepared to accept Russia's proposals, but wanted assurances that Mohammad Ali would be removed from Persian soil and never recognized as Shah. A written statement by him to the Russians that he would not try to return to Persia in the future would, the British thought, provide some security against his reappearance on the Persian scene. Sazonov was prepared to sacrifice Mohammad Ali, but not forever to destroy his usefulness. He refused to ask the former Shah for a promise never to return. "Equally we do not consider it possible to undertake an obligation never and under no circumstances to recognize the Shah in case of his return to the throne," he wrote to Bencken-

254. Note of the Minister of Foreign Affairs to the English Ambassador in St. Petersburg, Buchanan, January 16/29, 1912; M. O., 2nd series, 19 (Part 2, No. 398), 54–56.

dorff, but crossed out the sentences and added a promise and a threat. Russia would make a new attempt to establish firm friendly relations with the Persian government. However, "should the latter prove unworthy of our confidence this time as well, we would have to discuss the . . . situation with the London Cabinet." [255]

On September 6 Poklewski offered to mediate between the former Shah and Tehran. The offer was accepted, and Consul Ivanov was instructed "to offer Mohammad Ali Shah in behalf of the Persian Government a pension of 50,000 tumāns a year and a full amnesty to his supporters on condition that he voluntarily and immediately leave Persia." Poklewski advised Ivanov to tell the former Shah that Russia considered these conditions very favorable. If he refused to accept them, he was to be told bluntly that Russia had decided to end the disturbances in Persia by supporting the government, thus increasing the latter's chances of winning the struggle against him.[256]

Ivanov, obeying his instructions, conveyed to a stunned Mohammad Ali the wishes of the Russian government. The former Shah wrote out a statement which he gave to the Consul. It read in part:

> I had begun this affair [the counterrevolutionary attempt of 1911] supposing that the sympathies of Russia were with me and wanted to act here in accordance with the wishes of the Russian Government. Unfortunately I did not succeed in my intentions and efforts. In any case I shall undertake nothing contrary to the will of His Imperial Majesty, and if such is the wish of the Russian Government I am ready to stop and leave. But when my victory is near, when Khorāsān, Āzarbāyjān and the entire Caspian seashore are for me, and perhaps all of Persia, it is unfair to compel me to give up my rights in favor of people who style themselves the government

---

255. Minister of Foreign Affairs to the Ambassador in London, Benckendorff, Telegram No. 78; January 13/26, 1912; ibid. (No. 392), pp. 43–44.

256. Minister in Tehran to the Minister of Foreign Affairs, Sazonov [copy to the Consul in Astarābād], Telegram No. 75, January 25/February 7, 1912; ibid. (No. 430), pp. 85–86.

and whose offer to me I do not consider befitting my dignity.[257]

Mohammad Ali made a last attempt to salvage his shattered cause. In a letter given to Consul Ivanov for transmission to the Russian government, the former Shah promised in writing that he would act in all affairs of state in accordance with the wishes of the Tsar, even in the British zone. The Russian minister in Tehran, Mohammad Ali added, "must under no circumstances know [about it]; for the time being it would be of no advantage either to the Russian Government or to me [if Poklewski knew]." Verbally the Shah explained to Ivanov

> that he had long ago arrived at the conviction of the necessity for Persia of a Russian protectorate and was therefore willing to give the Russian Government a written obligation concerning his acceptance for Persia of a Russian protectorate in any form.[258]

Mohammad Ali's stratagem was too simpleminded and transparent to be taken seriously at St. Petersburg. He had nothing more to offer the Russian government, and it withdrew support. It was Ivanov's painful task to explain to the former Shah that "upon mature reflection" the Russian government had come to the conclusion "that under the present circumstances the restoration of His Majesty to the throne was impossible."[259] The Russians were careful not to shut the door to the possibility of future cooperation. It was "under present circumstances" that restoration was impossible. When the Persian government begged the two powers to issue a statement that Mohammad Ali would never be recognized, Sazonov refused to assume an obligation "which under certain conditions might turn out to be unfulfillable."[260] However, this was only a safety measure intended for

257. Consul in Astarābād to the Minister in Tehran, Poklewski, Telegram No. 9, January 27/February 9, 1912; ibid., p. 86, note 1.

258. Consul in Astarābād to the Minister of Foreign Affairs, Sazonov, Telegram [number lacking], January 31/February 13, 1912; ibid. (No. 465), p. 127.

259. Minister of Foreign Affairs to the Minister in Tehran, Poklewski, Telegram No. 210, February 1/14, 1912; ibid. (No. 467), p. 128.

260. Minister of Foreign Affairs to the Minister in Tehran, Poklewski, Telegram No. 169, January 27/February 9, 1912; ibid. (No. 441), p. 98.

the distant possibility that the Persian situation underwent a radical change some time in the future. At the moment the former Shah had nothing more to do than bargain for money.

Abandoning every vestige of imperial dignity, Mohammad Ali quibbled over his pension. He even wanted the Persian government to pay off his Turkoman and Caucasian mercenaries.[261] Poklewski, who wanted to save the Anglo-Russian agreement and the appearance of Persian independence on which it was predicated, worked out a compromise between the former Shah and the government. On February 29, 1912, the manager of the Bandare Gaz branch of the Russian Discount and Loan Bank, sent home a brief telegram: "The Shah's affairs are being settled. He is leaving Persia today." [262]

The Russian ultimatum of November 29, the dismissal of Shuster, and the Tabriz massacre had brought Khorāsān to the verge of explosion. Prince Dabizha, Russian consul general in Mashhad, was as much of an imperialist as Pokhitonov, Miller, and Nekrasov. Like them, he was a proponent of the use of armed force and a strong partisan of Mohammad Ali. Anticipating an anti-Russian outbreak, he wrote to the Governor General of Turkestan, Aleksandr Vasilievich Samsonov, that the Persians were preparing for holy war.[263] Samsonov obtained Sazonov's consent for the dispatch of troops to Khorāsān, but met with opposition on the part of Poklewski, who felt that such action was untimely, "the more so since the appearance of our armed forces in these fanatical places could serve precisely to increase anti-Russian agitation." [264]

The relative quiet was broken more than a month later not by the nationalists and revolutionaries but by the partisans of Mohammad Ali and Russian agents. Vosuq od-Dowleh complained to Barclay that Russian officials were recruiting Turkomans for Mohammad Ali's force, and agitating in his favor. On Grey's instructions, Buchanan brought this to the notice of the Russian

261. Ibid., p. 175, note 4.
262. Ibid., p. 180, note 2.
263. Governor-General of Turkestan to the Minister of Foreign Affairs, Sazonov, Telegram No. 788, December 14/27, 1911; ibid. (Part 1, No. 274), p. 254.
264. Poklewski to Sazonov, ibid., p. 254, note 2.

government.²⁶⁵ He also complained to Sazonov about Prince Dabizha, whose attitude, he wrote, had "not been a strictly impartial one." Agents of the consulate general in Mashhad had been accused of agitating in favor of the former Shah and leading Mashhad mobs in defiance of the police.

> The accumulation of evidence [Buchanan went on] showing that the ex-Shah is being encouraged by Russian agents —acting, as His Majesty's Government are well aware, in disregard of the orders of the Imperial Government—causes grave anxiety to His Majesty's Government, and compels them to ask the Imperial Government to send further urgent instructions to their Representatives in Persia on this subject. His Majesty's Government trust that the Russian Representatives will be at once instructed to refrain from giving assistance, either direct or indirect, to the ex-Shah or to his supporters. His Majesty's Government further trust that some serious notice will be taken of the action of Prince Dabija at Meshed.²⁶⁶

Consul Dabizha claimed that he had done his best to prevent "ferment" at Mashhad. He had even expelled from the consulate a certain Sardār Yusef upon becoming aware of the latter's connection with agitation. As for Russians' leading mobs and being otherwise active in behalf of the former Shah, Dabizha wrote: "I do not deny the participation of Russian subjects in the ferment, but I have given them timely orders to abstain from such participation; but I cannot, nor do I have the right, to prohibit them from visiting mosques." In the margin of Dabizha's telegram there is a curious notation which reads, "In accordance with the wish of Mr. Minister [Sazonov] this telegram is *not* being sent to the Tsar. S. P.b. January 29 [February 11], 1912." ²⁶⁷ Perhaps

265. Memorandum of the English Embassy to the Russian Minister of Foreign Affairs, January 22/February 4, 1912; ibid. (Part 2), p. 81, note 5. Also Memorandum of the English Embassy of January 24/February 6, 1912, Urgent; ibid. (No. 424), pp. 81–82.

266. Memorandum of the English Embassy at St. Petersburg to the Minister of Foreign Affairs, January 24/February 6, 1912, Urgent; ibid.

267. Dabizha's telegram No. 5, January 25/February 7, 1912; ibid., p. 83, note 2.

Sazonov felt that Nicholas might take a favorable view of the activities of the consul who, after all, was only continuing to do that which, until a few days ago, had been encouraged by the highest authorities in St. Petersburg. Sazonov and the Cabinet had decided not to cause any further deterioration in Anglo-Russian relations and had abandoned Mohammad Ali. Dabizha must accept the decision.

The Mashhad situation was growing tenser. On February 19 a notorious bandit and partisan of the former Shah, Mohammad of Nishāpur, arrived in the city with a band of twenty followers and took *bast* at the shrine of the eighth Imam, Rezā, for the Shiites the holiest spot in Persia. The bandit Mohammad and Sardār Yusef Khān now jointly demonstrated in favor of Mohammad Ali. They were encouraged by Shoā' os-Saltaneh, who sent a telegram to the clergy announcing the early arrival of the former Shah in Mashhad.[268] Dabizha had been too deeply committed to Mohammad Ali to reverse himself as rapidly as Poklewski and Sazonov demanded. He continued to provide secret support to the reactionaries who had taken *bast* at the holy shrine. The British consul, and future historian of Persia, Major Percy M. Sykes, reported that Dabizha had transmitted to the clergy Shoā' os-Saltaneh's telegram, and that he refused to cooperate with Sykes. St. Petersburg politely inquired whether this was so, while Poklewski, who knew the truth, bluntly ordered Dabizha "to put an end to the agitation which is now taking place in Mashhad." [269]

News of Dabizha's support of Mohammad Ali was picked up by foreign correspondents in Tehran and St. Petersburg. The Prime Minister, V. N. Kokovtsov, asked Sazonov, "in view of the extreme undesirability of the spread of such information," to repeat to the Russian consuls, Dabizha in particular, that their actions must strictly conform to their instructions and the government's attitude toward the former Shah.[270]

268. Consul General in Mashhad to the Minister of Foreign Affairs, Sazonov, Telegram No. 17, February 9/22, 1912; ibid. (No. 517), p. 172.

269. V. Klemm to Dabizha, Telegram No. 279 [St. Petersburg], February 11/24, 1912. Poklewski to Dabizha, No. 130, February 13/26, 1912; ibid., p. 178, note 1.

270. Chairman of the Council of Ministers to the Minister of Foreign Affairs, Letter, Confidential, February 10/23, 1912; ibid. (No. 524), p. 178.

"The Strangling of Persia" 665

Only three days before he left Persian soil for the last time, Mohammad Ali sent a telegram to Dabizha, asking him to inform the mojtaheds, the merchants, and the entire population of Khorāsān that they had been right to turn to the Tsar without whose help there could be no order in Persia. "God willing," the telegram continued, "I will soon be in Mashhad, bow before the grave of the holy Imam and, together with you, march on Tehran." Dabizha did not dare to transmit the telegram without permission from St. Petersburg. He asked for instructions and reported that the Shah's supporters were growing in number, that they now held the compound which included the shrine of the Imam, but that they had changed their attitude toward Russia, which had become another enemy in their eyes.[271] Sazonov replied that he must not transmit the former Shah's telegram but must, together with Sykes, take all measures to stop the activities in favor of Mohammad Ali.[272] Poklewski went even farther, instructing Dabizha to let Mohammad Ali's partisans know that the Russian detachment in Mashhad was there to maintain order and that any acts of violence would be put down by military force. "In case of extreme need this threat may have to be carried out." However, Poklewski believed that agitation in favor of the Shah could have developed only in the hope of support from the Russian consulate and Russian troops. Therefore, as soon as the parties concerned were convinced that Dabizha followed his instructions, the danger of disorders would diminish.[273]

The former Shah left Persia as he had arrived, aboard a Russian ship. His fanatical followers in Mashhad refused to accept the inevitable. To the great embarrassment of the Russian government they sat in the sanctuary of the shrine, untouchable and protected by ancient tradition. It was said that someone had fired a shot at a Russian soldier. Consul Dabizha was nervous. Negotiations with the Governor of Khorāsān, consultations with the insurgents in the shrine, unsatisfactory encounters with Major

271. Consul General in Mashhad to the Minister of Foreign Affairs, Telegram No. 18, February 13/26, 1912; ibid. (No. 541), p. 191.
272. Sazonov to Poklewski, Telegram No. 310, February 16/29, 1912; ibid., note 4.
273. Minister in Tehran to the Minister of Foreign Affairs, Telegram No. 134, February 16/29, 1912; ibid. (No. 564), pp. 215-16.

Sykes, and the abandonment, to some betrayal, of Mohammad Ali by Russia, must have embittered the consul general. Like Miller, Nekrasov, and Pokhitonov, he preferred to rely on Russian troops.

> I deem it necessary [he telegraphed on March 4] immediately to take authority into our own hands and to put the city under martial law; I see no other means for the establishment of order and therefore request instructions in that sense. Otherwise I cannot answer for any consequences.[274]

The partisans of the Shah turned the great mosque and its companion buildings into a fortress from which they emerged to harass the population, shoot at the police, and loot houses and shops in the center of the city. The governor admitted that he could not restore order. On March 24 Dabizha asked General Red'ko to take over.[275] Next morning the streets were patrolled by Russian soldiers, order was restored, and the Persian governor, Rokn od-Dowleh, resigned. Only the shrine remained in the hands of the reactionary fanatics.[276]

From his sanctuary in the shrine, Sardār Yusef Khān, Russia's erstwhile friend and protégé, threatened and blustered. He even telephoned the Russian consulate and told Dabizha "that the hour was near when he would emerge from the sanctuary with his men and hang and slash all Russians and other Europeans." Dabizha tried to negotiate with the mojtaheds, but their demands, such as the abolition of the constitutional regime, could not be met. The number of people in the *bast* increased in the last days of March when some two hundred armed men joined Sardār Yusef Khān. The *bast* also attracted hundreds of frightened townspeople who sought safety in the "shadow" of the martyred Imam.

About 3 P.M. on March 30, Dabizha had the shrine surrounded by Russian troops. General Red'ko made a last attempt to

---

274. Dabizha to Poklewski, Telegram No. 21, February 20/March 4, 1912; ibid., p. 235, note 2.

275. Consul General in Mashhad to the Minister of Foreign Affairs, Sazonov, Telegram No. 512, March 11/24, 1912; ibid. (Telegram No. 679), pp. 317–18.

276. Same to same, March 25, 1912; ibid., p. 318, note 1.

"The Strangling of Persia"

persuade Sardār Yusef Khān and his crowd to leave. Secure in the belief that no one would ever dream of invading the holy precincts, they defied the Russians. It was artillery's turn to speak. Deliberately and methodically General Red'ko's cannon shelled the sanctuary.[277]

Clouds of brown dust rose from shattered old brick walls. Their heavy boots crunching delicate splinters of blue, green, and gold tiles, Russian soldiers rushed through the breach into the courtyards and on toward the grave of the Imam. Though there was almost no resistance, the soldiery, unrestrained by the officers, intoxicated with the sound of the cannonade and the urge to destroy, shot at and bayoneted everyone in sight. According to Dabizha's report, "Among the Persians thirty-nine were killed." [278] The Persians claimed that several hundred, including women and children, lost their lives.

Persia stared in stunned disbelief at the great desecration perpetrated by the Russians. "O wind," cried the poet Malek osh-Shoarā Bahār, "carry the smell of blood from Tus [Khorāsān] to Yathrib [Medina], tell the Prophet of the blood-stained grave of his son!" Expressing the anger and grief of millions, the poet called on Moslems to come and see the devastation wrought by Russian guns.[279] But the spirit of the people had already been broken. There was no uprising; there was only a feeble protest

---

277. Consul General in Mashhad to the Minister of Foreign Affairs, Telegram No. 572, March 18/31, 1912; ibid. (No. 717), pp. 361–62.

278. Same to same, Telegram No. 592, March 21/April 3, 1912; ibid. (No. 725), p. 371.

279. See how this pure sanctuary was turned into a slaughterhouse . . .
Come for a moment and hear of the violence of the enemy . . .
See once again how these arrogant defenders of civilization perpetrated that which a savage would not believe.
Eight hundred men and women, local inhabitants and pilgrims, lost their lives under the attack of Russian infidel troops.

If the sanctuary of Rezā was the gathering place of rogues, why have they [the Russians] demolished the dome?
Why did these bandits, thieves, and villains loot the palace and the shrine of Rezā?
The fire of the cannon of profanation hit not the dome but the hearts of Ali and the Prophet.
—Malek osh-Shoarā Bahār, "Tupe Rus" [The Russian Cannon]

from the government and the usual expression of apprehension on the part of Sir Edward Grey who talked to Benckendorff of the importance of Mashhad in the eyes of many Moslems who were British subjects and went there on pilgrimages.[280]

Grey's remonstrances had become so routine that they bored the Tsar and impressed hardly anyone except Benckendorff. He was one of the very few Russian diplomats who felt that his country was going too far, and that too much strain was being placed on Anglo-Russian friendship. In this he was wrong because Grey's elasticity vis-à-vis Russia had no limits. As long as no Persian territory was formally annexed nor the Persian government openly abolished, Russia could do anything in her zone. Long years of residence in England, and perhaps age too, had dimmed Benckendorff's political sight. He even accepted to some extent the theory, so carefully cultivated by Russian diplomats for foreign consumption, that Russian consuls were pushing the Ministry of Foreign Affairs into situations and positions "which are not those foreseen by ministerial policy." [281]

Similar thoughts were expressed by Sir George Buchanan who believed, or out of sheer necessity pretended to believe, that "while the two Governments were doing their best to act loyally together, the Russian consuls in Persia acted in a contrary spirit." Buchanan told Sazonov that

> When, as had more than once been the case, he had told me that disorders had broken out at Meshed or at Tabriz that had necessitated the intervention of Russian troops, I had never felt quite sure whether those disorders had not been wilfully provoked by one or the other of the consuls in order to provide an excuse for intervention.
>
> Sazonov declined to admit this. He declared that Muller [Miller], his consul at Tabriz, who is now on leave, was an excellent man, and contended that the version given by Dabija of the Meshed incident was correct.[282]

280. Ambassador in London to the Minister of Foreign Affairs, Sazonov, Telegram No. 94, March 21/April 3, 1912; M. O., 2nd series, 19 (Part 2, No. 724), 370.

281. Same to same, Letter, April 3/16, 1912; ibid. (No. 767), pp. 410–11.

282. Buchanan to Grey, Private letter, n.d., as cited in Buchanan, *My Mission to Russia*, 1, 112.

Seeing that it was safer to question the conduct of individuals than to protest against Russian actions in general, the Persians complained against Russian consuls who had virtually taken over the government of the northern provinces. However, the Persian minister in London was administered a stinging rebuke by Sir Arthur Nicolson, whose Russophilia had not been shaken by the events of the last year. He expressed his surprise that the minister should take such a step.

> Moreover, he finds that in Persia they should be grateful to Russia; that it would be enough for Russia to stretch her arm and Persia would cease to exist; that Russia had proved many times her respect for the independence and integrity of Persia; that she had not interfered in the revolution which substituted the present Shah for the ex-Shah Mohammad Ali; that it was thanks to Russian as well as English action that the recent attempt of Mohammad Ali had ended in failure.

Thus on and on Nicolson lectured the Persian envoy, pouring forth a stream of sentences each of which was a lie and an insult. The British government, he concluded, did not occupy itself with the role of Russian consuls in the north any more than the Russian government occupied itself with that of the British in the south, "and it was therefore out of the question that one of the two powers communicate with the other on this subject." To add to the discomfiture of the Persian minister, Nicolson violated his confidence and repeated the conversation to Benckendorff.[283]

The Mashhad massacre was the last major crisis before the outbreak of the World War. Minor crises succeeded one another with such regularity as to become an expected feature of Persian existence.

Abol Fath Mirzā Sālāh od-Dowleh raised a rebellion in western Persia. He made Kermānshāh his base of operations and threatened to march on Tehran. The government sent Yefrem Khān with fifteen hundred men to meet the prince. The old Dashnak, who had played such a prominent part in the Persian revolution, fell in battle. A week later, as if in response to Sālār

---

283. Ambassador in London to the Minister of Foreign Affairs, Sazonov, Letter, April 28/May 11, 1912; M. O., 2nd series, 19 (Part 2, No. 886), 526–27.

od-Dowleh's successes, the Russian Cabinet decided "to maintain the strictest neutrality" between the government and the rebels, and ordered the evacuation of a part of the Qazvin detachment, thus opening for Sālār od-Dowleh the way to Tehran.[284] The situation did not become truly serious only because on May 29, 1912, government forces commanded by Farmānfarmā defeated Sālār od-Dowleh and drove him out of Kermānshāh.[285]

The suppression of Sālār's rebellion led to a breakup of the Cabinet which included disparate elements united only by their fear of Mohammad Ali and his brothers. Poklewski marveled at its survival through such upheavals as the attempt of the former Shah to regain his throne, the Shuster incident, Russian ultimatums, the Tabriz and Rasht events, the dissolution of the Majles, monetary difficulties, the forced recognition by Persia of the 1907 Anglo-Russian agreement, and, finally, the Mashhad incident. The Cabinet, Poklewski felt, had found an honorable way out of a tragic situation and courageously removed various obstacles to cooperation with Russia. He had high hopes that, having learned its lessons well, the Cabinet would make it easy for Russia to secure all her interests in Persia. However, the desire of some Persian politicians to get rid of the Bakhtiāri khans had led to a clash between the Premier, Samsām os-Saltaneh, and the Minister of the Interior, Qavām os-Saltaneh, who tendered his resignation. The Regent refused to accept it, hoping to postpone the crisis until he himself could leave the country. Neither Britain nor Russia could allow such irresponsible behavior and demanded that Nāser ol-Molk, the Regent, stay in Tehran.[286]

Poklewski was right to worry about Nāser ol-Molk's regency and the Cabinet of Samsām os-Saltaneh. Russia no longer needed to oppose them. They had been tamed, proving it by recognizing the Anglo-Russian Agreement and promising to con-

---

284. Poklewski to Sazonov, Telegram No. 424, May 6/19, 1912; ibid., 20 (Part 1), 22, note 3. Minister of Foreign Affairs to the Minister in Tehran, Poklewski, Telegram No. 988, May 14/27, 1912; ibid. (No. 87), p. 81. Poklewski to Sazonov, Telegram No. 430, May 7/20, 1912; ibid., p. 89, note 4.

285. Ibid., p. 90, note 4.

286. Minister in Tehran to the Minister of Foreign Affairs, Sazonov, Letter, Confidential, May 16/29, 1912; ibid. (No. 102), pp. 89–91.

form to its principles.²⁸⁷ The resignation of the Premier or the flight of the Regent would reopen the whole question of authority in Tehran.

The idea of restoring Mohammad Ali had not been entirely abandoned. The Tsar had always sympathized with him, and continued to recognize his titles.²⁸⁸ In the Ministry of Foreign Affairs, as well as among the military, Mohammad Ali had many friends and admirers. In Persia itself he had supporters whose number grew with each new difficulty experienced by the government. Already in July 1912 Buchanan told Neratov that rumors of Mohammad Ali's intention to return to Persia had reached London.²⁸⁹ Benckendorff reported that Sir Edward Grey's attitude toward Mohammad Ali seemed to have changed since Sir Walter Townley had taken over Sir George Barclay's post in Tehran. Though Grey still felt that restoration of Mohammad Ali would be pointless, he admitted that anything could happen in the Orient. However, for such a thing to occur, a powerful movement must come into being. Another clandestine passage through Russia would be fatal for the former Shah, for Persia, and consequently for Anglo-Russian friendship. Benckendorff commented that a return of Mohammad Ali through Russian territory would make the British feel they had been deceived by Russia, and the government would not be able to make the country swallow such a pill. One should not forget that in English eyes their government's policy in Persia had been nothing but a string of concessions to Russia, he warned.²⁹⁰

If Grey wanted a mass movement in favor of the former Shah, the Russians were happy to create one. Suddenly signs of activity

287. Same to same, Telegram No. 124 (2), February 9/22, 1912; ibid., 19 (Part 2, No. 516), 172.

288. During Mohammad Ali's first exile in Russia the Tsar himself ordered that his title of Shah be recognized and that he be addressed as His Majesty. Cf. Circular Letter of the Senior Counselor of the Ministry of Foreign Affairs [K. M. Argyropoulo], St. Petersburg, November 26/December 9, 1909; S.D.D., 3, 269.

289. Acting Minister of Foreign Affairs to the Minister in Tehran, Poklewski, Telegram No. 1325, July 4/17, 1912; M. O., 2nd series, 20 (Part 1, No. 315), 321–22.

290. Ambassador in London to the Minister of Foreign Affairs, Sazonov, Letter, July 15/28, 1912; ibid. (No. 377), pp. 380–81.

in favor of Mohammad Ali began to appear everywhere. In September 1912 the former Shah's private secretary, Heshmat od-Dowleh, informed the Russian authorities in Tiflis that Sepahdār and Shojā' od-Dowleh had agreed to invite Mohammad Ali back to Persia, and that he might appear in the Caucasus.[291]

The Viceroy asked for instructions and was told that indeed a serious movement in favor of the former Shah had developed in Persia, and that there was reason to believe that Sepahdār was one of its main inspirers. Mohammad Ali had done nothing about it, being determined "to return to the throne only with the consent of Russia and England." And finally: "In principle we do not at all consider Mohammad Ali our prisoner and have no intention of raising obstacles to his return to Persia should the Persians themselves wish it." [292]

Mohammad Ali's supporters in Iran and Russia needed a minimum of encouragement to plunge into new activities in his behalf. The acting consul general in Tabriz, Preobrazhenskii, reported that the population of Tabriz was preparing telegrams to the Cabinet in Tehran, King George V, and Tsar Nicholas II, requesting the return "to his ancestral throne" of Mohammad Ali, "who alone can bring tranquility to a country torn by civil strife." [293] Preobrazhenskii was instructed that "he should not evade receiving the petition of the population concerning the return of Mohammad Ali." [294] On September 26 Neratov cabled Sazonov, who was visiting the King of England at Balmoral, that the Tsar had received a telegram signed by influential persons, clerical and lay, requesting restoration. Four days later a similar plea arrived from the population of Zanjān.[295]

291. Lisovskii to Neratov, Telegram No. 635, Tiflis, September 8/21, 1912; ibid. (Part 2), p. 295, note 3.

292. Acting Minister of Foreign Affairs to the Viceroy of the Caucasus, Vorontsov-Dashkov, Telegram No. 1950, September 15/28, 1912; ibid. (No. 798), pp. 295–96.

293. Acting Consul General in Tabriz to the Acting Minister of Foreign Affairs, Neratov, Telegram No. 490, September 10/23, 1912; ibid. (No. 745), pp. 249–50.

294. Neratov to Poklewski, Telegram No. 1901, September 11/24, 1912; ibid., p. 250, note 2.

295. Neratov to Sazonov, Telegrams No. 1920 of September 13/26 and No. 1977 of September 17/30, 1912; ibid.

"The Strangling of Persia" 673

The agitation in favor of Mohammad Ali's restoration coincided so perfectly with the crisis brought about by the reluctance of Nāser ol-Molk, who was in Europe, to return to Persia and resume the duties of Regent that in the absence of documentation one is tempted to see a connection between these events. Abol Qasem Khān Nāser ol-Molk never sought the regency. Timorous and weak-willed, he was pushed by his British friends to assume a position for which he had no capacity. In the summer of 1912 he left for Europe and refused to return, being convinced that if he did he would be assassinated by one or another political faction. Sazonov raised the question of finding a new Regent with Grey in London, suggesting that Sa'd od-Dowleh be appointed to that post.[296] Poklewski, whose views had been solicited by Sazonov, felt that Sa'd od-Dowleh was a capable and energetic person but had a reputation for greed and shameless bribe-taking. He was suspected of being Germanophile and of having had a hand in the murder of Amin os-Soltān.

> In my own opinion, considering the present situation in Persia and the now general disillusionment with the results of the revolution of 1909, the return of Mohammad Ali Shah to the throne would be easier and more popular among wide circles of the population, than making Sa'd od-Dowleh Regent.[297]

On his trip to England Sazonov held several discussions with British statesmen on the Persian question. He was received by King George V at Balmoral on September 18. The audience lasted more than an hour. The King stressed the sincerity of his feelings toward Russia and his desire for cooperation with her. Grey pursued the same line. To Sazonov's question whether in case of war with Germany Russia could count on Britain to draw the German navy away from her Baltic shores, he replied that

---

296. Sazonov to Poklewski, unnumbered telegram, London, September 14/27, 1912; ibid., p. 311, note 3.
297. Minister in Tehran to the Acting Minister of Foreign Affairs, Neratov, Telegram No. 762, September 16/29, 1912; ibid. (No. 820), pp. 311–12. Cf. Browne, *The Persian Revolution*, pp. 154–55 for the alleged involvement of Sa'd od-Dowleh in the murder of Amin os-Soltān Atābake A'zam.

"England would make every attempt to deal the most severe blow to German naval might." The King himself said: "We shall sink every single german [sic] merchant ship we shall get hold of." [298] It was within this framework of European politics and the German threat that Persian problems were considered.

Grey agreed with Sazonov that Persia needed a strong central authority but made it clear that Mohammad Ali was unacceptable to the British. Disregarding Poklewski's advice, Sazonov proposed that the British not insist upon the return of Nāser ol-Molk to Tehran and that Sa'd od-Dowleh be appointed Regent. The conversation was inconclusive but clearly showed that the Persian crisis had passed; that in spite of a milder tone assumed by Grey, Britain would not accept the restoration of Mohammad Ali; that in his Persian policy, as in all his other policies, Grey was dominated by fear and hatred of Germany and would do nothing to alienate Russia; and that Russia could expect further concessions and retreats.[299]

The two years immediately preceding the First World War brought about no major changes in the Persian situation. The government was still drowned in a sea of problems but had no means of solving any of them. It was perpetually bankrupt. Poklewski estimated in June 1912 that Persia owed foreign countries about 12,500,000 tumāns.[300] The two powers conducted long and intricate negotiations between themselves and with Persia's new Treasurer General, Shuster's old antagonist and successor, the Belgian Mornard. Russia was willing to provide the docile Tehran government with funds, but always at a price.

The Russian government, after long discussions between various ministries, approached Tehran with a demand for a railway concession from Jolfā to Tabriz, reviving the old and forgotten Falkenhagen scheme.[301] The Persians agreed to negotiate but

---

298. Report of the Minister of Foreign Affairs to Nicholas II, October 2/15, 1912; M. O., 2nd series, 20 (Part 2, No. 1034), p. 458.

299. Ibid., pp. 459–60.

300. Poklewski's letter of June 14/27, 1912 (no number or addressee given); ibid. (Part 1), p. 295, note 2. (A tumān was then roughly equivalent to an American dollar.)

301. Neratov's correspondence with Kokovtsov; ibid., pp. 239–95, and 410–12.

gently expressed "the hope that the Imperial Government will take into consideration the situation of the Government of this country relative to the fundamental laws of the state." [302] Poklewski bluntly told the Cabinet that such statements were "vague" and "out of place." [303] From then on to all further Persian pleas for money Russia made the same reply—a demand for a railway concession.[304]

Finally on February 6, 1913, the Persian Cabinet signed an agreement with an engineer, M. Podgurskii, and the Russian Discount and Loan Bank for a concession to build and operate for seventy-five years a railway from Jolfā to Tabriz with a branch to Urumiyyeh. The bank was also given the right to exploit coal and oil deposits if such were to be found in a zone of sixty miles on either side of the railway line. The company that would operate the railway and mining would be exempt from Persian taxes and would pay the Persian government half of its net profit from the operation of the road and 5 percent of the net profit from the extraction of coal and oil.[305] All the shares of the Jolfā-Tabriz railway company were held by Russia and the board of directors consisted of Russians only, most of them functionaries of the Ministry of Finance. It included also an aristocratic name, Prince Aleksei Golitsyn.

> Thus we have before us [commented an early Soviet expert on imperialism, M. Pavlovich] a type of Russian government railway built on the territory of a foreign state. But does contemporary Persia, at least in her northern provinces, constitute foreign territory for the Russian government? [306]

Indeed, most Russians no longer thought of Persia as an independent state and expressed this view in a jingle which proclaimed

302. Persian note to Poklewski, No. 6936 of August 16, 1912, in Minister in Tehran to the Acting Minister of Foreign Affairs, Neratov, Telegram No. 647, August 4/17, 1912; ibid. (Part 2, No. 492), 35–36.

303. Poklewski to Neratov; ibid.

304. Memorandum of the Ministry of Foreign Affairs to the English Ambassador in St. Petersburg, Buchanan, September 15/18, 1912; ibid. (No. 697), p. 218.

305. M. Povlovich, *Imperializm i borba za velikie zheleznodorozhnye puti budushchego*, 1 (Part 2), 58–59.

306. Ibid., 62.

that Persia was not a foreign country just as a hen was not really a bird.³⁰⁷

The disappearance of Persian independence and, in the north, of any Persian government authority, was so clear, the actions of Russian consuls so brazen, that the British found themselves, albeit reluctantly, making representations to Sazonov and even to the Tsar. In June 1914 Buchanan warned Nicholas II that the trend of affairs in Persia "might prove fatal to the Anglo-Russian understanding." He pointed out that

> Unforeseen events had led to the occupation of certain districts in North Persia by Russian troops, and, little by little, the whole machinery of administration had been placed in the hands of the Russian consuls. The Governor-General of Azerbaijan was a mere puppet who received and carried out the orders of the Russian consul-general, and the same might be said of the Governors of Resht, Kazwin, and Julfa. They were one and all agents of the Russian Government and acted in entire independence of the central government at Tehran. Vast tracts of land in North Persia were being acquired by illegal methods, large numbers of Persians were being converted into Russian-protected subjects, and the taxes were being collected by the Russian consuls to the exclusion of the agents of the Persian financial administration. The above system was being extended to Ispahan and even to the neutral zone. We had not the slightest desire to dispute Russia's predominant interest and position in the north, but we did take exception to the methods by which that predominance was being asserted and the attempts which were being made to extend it to the neutral zone.³⁰⁸

The Tsar claimed that the entire situation had been forced upon him by circumstances and against his will. He was willing to withdraw his troops from Persia, and would have the activities of his consuls investigated by a committee of the Ministry of Foreign Affairs.³⁰⁹

307. *Kuritsa ne ptitsa,*
Persiia ne zagranitsa.
308. Buchanan, *My Mission to Russia,* 1, 115–16.
309. Ibid.

"*The Strangling of Persia*" 677

Of course, no investigation ever took place. The Persian government continued to be disregarded. Russian citizens continued to buy up large tracts of land in every northern province, circumventing the law which prohibited foreigners from owning real estate by bribing officials or registering the land in the name of Persian partners.[310] Even its own employees paid no attention to the wishes of the Cabinet. The Cossack Brigade refused to obey orders and would not conduct any operation of which its Russian commander, Prince Vadbolskii, did not personally approve. Vosuq od-Dowleh's nagging finally compelled Sazonov to write to the Russian chargé d'affaires in Tehran to investigate the complaints and talk to Vadbolskii, "who should, as far as possible, satisfy the just demands of the Government." Thus Vadbolskii was left free to decide in each case which government order was just and which was not.[311]

The British took slightly greater pains to follow the forms of international intercourse. However, in practice they too paid scant attention to the Persian government. They dealt with the Sheykh of Mohammareh and the Bakhtiāri and Baluch khans as if the Tehran government did not exist.[312]

When the First World War broke out, Britain made a feeble attempt to induce Russia to respect Persian neutrality. Grey argued that the difference between Germany and the Entente lay in the manner in which they treated neutral nations, whose rights and integrity should be protected. "To give up this principle would mean that we, like Germany, attach only relative significance to it." [313] Such representations had not the slightest effect, and Persia was turned into a battleground of Russians, British, and Turks.

On March 4, 1915, in a memorandum addressed to the British

---

310. Ter-Gukasov, *Ekonomicheskie interesy Rossii v Persii* (St. Petersburg, 1915), pp. 84–85. Cf. various documents in M. O., 3rd series.

311. Minister of Foreign Affairs to the Chargé d'Affaires in Tehran, Sablin, Telegram No. 34, January 4/17, 1914; M. O., 3rd series, 1 (No. 28), 36–37.

312. See Arnold Wilson, *South West Persia, A Political Officer's Diary, 1907–1914* (London, 1941), passim.

313. Ambassador in London, Count Benckendorff, to the Minister of Foreign Affairs, S. D. Sazonov, Telegram No. 664, October 31/November 13, 1914; E. A. Adamov, *Konstantinopol i prolivy* (Moscow, 1925), 1 (No. 22), 232. Cf. Buchanan, 1, 224.

and French ambassadors, Sazonov raised the issue of Russian annexation of Constantinople. Buchanan gave an affirmative reply to Russian proposals and stressed how great a departure from traditional policies was Britain's assent to the Russian occupation of Constantinople and the Straits. Britain wanted a Russian promise that upon gaining that city Russia would establish a free port and guarantee free commercial navigation. Sir Edward Grey was not able at the moment to state definitely British demands elsewhere, but one such demand would be for the revision of a part of the 1907 Convention, turning over to Britain the neutral zone of Persia.[314]

On March 14 Buchanan discussed the matter with the Tsar. Sazonov, who was present, remarked that Russia must be allowed complete freedom of action in her sphere; "not . . . that she had any desire to annex North Persia, but because she wanted an end put to representations which we were so constantly making about her actions there." Buchanan made a speech about the integrity of Persia in which he suggested that Russian and British representatives in Tehran "might work out an agreement under which Russia could obtain sufficient liberty of action in her own sphere without violating the principle of Persian independence." Turning to the Tsar, he said

> that after the war Russia and Great Britain would be the two most powerful empires in the world. With the settlement of the Persian question the last cause of friction between them would disappear and the world's peace would then be assured.[315]

On March 20 Russia accepted British proposals.[316] Letting Britain take over the neutral zone of Persia was a low price to pay for the acquisition of Constantinople.

Significant as it seemed, the agreement of 1915 was destined to

---

314. Memorandum of the British Embassy in Petrograd to the Russian Minister of Foreign Affairs, S. D. Sazonov, March 12, 1915; Adamov, 1 (No. 77), 275–77

315. Buchanan, 1, 227.

316. Minister of Foreign Affairs, S. D. Sazonov, to the Ambassador in London Count A. K. Benckendorff, Telegram No. 1265, March 7/20, 1915; Adamov, 1 (No. 83), 284.

last less than three years. Russia's defeat on the Western front weakened an already discredited monarchy. A violent and far-reaching revolution swept away not only the Tsar and his ministers but the whole structure of Russian state and society. The Soviet regime promptly repudiated unequal treaties, agreements, and concessions which Tsarist Russia had forced upon Persia. Simultaneously it sent units of the Red Army to occupy and hold Anzali and Rasht.

The collapse of Russia provided Britain with a unique opportunity to regain her position in Iran. Lord Curzon, who had been closely associated with Persian affairs in his many government capacities, was now Foreign Secretary. He was free to fashion and implement a policy that reflected his ideas and experiences gained over the previous quarter century. The Anglo-Persian treaty of 1919 was Curzon's own handiwork. It failed almost immediately. Curzon's thought belonged to another world, a world which had died in the fires of the World War.

New problems, new ideas, and new men emerged everywhere. A Persian officer of the Cossack Brigade staged a coup d'état and established the first strong government Persia had had in a century. The downfall of Imperial Russia and the unwillingness of Britain to hold Persia by force saved Persian independence, but the essential configuration of forces had not changed. Anglo-Russian rivalry was resumed as soon as Russia recovered from the chaos and devastation of the revolution and civil war. It would continue for many more years and after the Second World War would be absorbed into the larger struggle between Russia and the West.

BIBLIOGRAPHY

PRIMARY SOURCES

ARCHIVAL MATERIALS

France, Archive des Affaires Etrangères, Perse (various volumes).

Great Britain, Public Record Office, The Foreign Office Archives, series: F.O. 60, F.O. 65, F.O. 248, F.O. 251, F.O. 371.

———, Commonwealth Relations Office, India Office Records, *Letters from India*.

Iran, Ministry of Foreign Affairs Archives (various files).

Yale University Library, The Ghani Collection (containing letters of a number of nineteenth- and twentieth-century Persian statesmen).

———, Boone, Turin Bradford, *Persian Diary, 1911–1912* (typewritten copy).

PUBLISHED DOCUMENTS

Adamov, E. A., *Konstantinopol i prolivy* (Constantinople and the Straits), 2 vols. Moscow, Peoples Commissariat of Foreign Affairs, 1925.

Adamov, E. A., ed., and I. V. Koz'menko, compiler, *Sbornik dogovorov Rossii s drugimi gosudarstvami. 1856–1917*, Moscow, 1952.

Aitchison, Charles U., *A Collection of Treaties, Engagements and Sanads Relating to India and Neighbouring Countries*, 14 vols., Calcutta, Government of India, Central Publications Branch, 1933.

Buckle, George Earl, *The Letters of Queen Victoria*, 2nd series, Vols. 2 and 3, London, John Murray, 1926 and 1928.

Gooch, G. P., and H. Temperley, *British Documents on the Origin of the War, 1898–1914*, Vols. 4 and 10, London, His Majesty's Stationary Office, 1926–38.

Great Britain, *British and Foreign State Papers*, various volumes, London, His Majesty's Stationary Office.

Great Britain, Parliament, *Sessional Papers*, various volumes dealing with Persia between 1864 and 1914.

Grey, Sir Edward, *Speeches on Foreign Affairs, 1904–1914*, Paul Knaplund, ed., London, George Allen & Unwin Ltd., 1937.

Gwynn, Stephen, ed., *The Letters and Friendships of Sir Cecil Spring Rice*, 2 vols. London, Constable & Co., 1929.

Hagerman, Herbert J., *Letters of a Young Diplomat*, Santa Fe, The Royal Press, 1937.

Hertslet, Sir Edward, *Treaties, etc., Concluded Between Great Britain and Persia and Between Persia and Other Foreign Powers, Wholly or Partially in Force on the 1st April, 1891*, London, Harrison & Sons, 1891.

Hurewitz, J. C., *Diplomacy in the Near and Middle East*, Vol. 1, Princeton, D. Van Nostrand Co., 1956.

Il'iasov, A., *Prisoedinenie Turkmenii k Rossii* (The Annexation of Turkomania to Russia), A Collection of Archival Documents, Ashkhabad, Academy of Sciences of the Turkoman S.S.R., 1960.

Iswolsky, Alexandre, *Au service de la Russie*, Correspondance diplomatique, 1906–1911, 2 vols. Paris, Editions Internationales, 1937–39.

Kliuchnikov, I. V., and A. Sabanin, *Mezhdunarodnaia politika noveishego vremeni v dogovorakh, notakh i deklaratsiiakh* (International Politics of Most Recent Times in Treaties, Notes, and Declarations), 3 parts in 4 vols. Moscow, People's Commissariat of Foreign Affairs, 1925–29.

Meyendorff, Alexandre, *Correspondance diplomatique du Baron de Staal (1884–1900)*, 2 vols. Paris, Marcel Rivière, 1929.

Napier, George Campbell, *Collection of Journals and Reports Received from Capt. G. C. Napier, on Special Duty in Persia*, London, G. E. Eyer and Spottiswoode for Her Majesty's Stationary Office, 1876.

Pobedonostsev, K. P., *Pobedonostsev i ego korrespondenty* (Pobedonostsev and His Correspondents), 1, Moscow, 1923.

Rittikh, P. A., *Otchet o poezdke v Persiiu i persidskii Beludzhistan v 1900 godu* (A Report on a Trip to Persia and Persian Baluchestān in 1900), St. Petersburg, Military Scholarship Committee of the General Staff, 1901.

Russia, "Anglo-russkoe sopernichestvo v Persii v 1890–1906 g.g." (Anglo-Russian Rivalry in Persia in 1890–1906), *Krasnyi Arkhiv*, 1 (56) (1933), 33–64.

———, "Doklady b. ministra inostrannykh del S. D. Sazonova Nikolaiu Romanovu. 1910–1912 gg." (The Reports of the Former Minister of Foreign Affairs S. D. Sazonov to Nikolai Romanov. 1910–1912.), *Krasnyi Arkhiv*, 3 (1923), 5–28.

———, "K istorii anglo-russkogo soglasheniia 1907 goda" (Toward the History of the 1907 Anglo-Russian Agreement), *Krasnyi Arkhiv*, 2–3 (69–70) (1935), 3–39.

———, "K istorii potsdamskogo soglasheniia 1911 g." (Toward the History of the Potsdam Agreement of 1911), *Krasnyi Arkhiv*, 3 (58) (1933).

———, *Materialy po izucheniiu Vostoka* (Materials for the Study of the Orient) First issue, Confidential, 1909; Second issue, Secret, 1915, St. Petersburg, Ministry of Foreign Affairs.

———, *Mezhdunarodnye otnosheniia v epokhu imperializma* (International Relations in the Era of Imperialism), 2nd series, Leningrad, 1939. (Vol. 18, parts 1 and 2, and Vol. 19, parts 1 and 2, were especially relevant.)

———, *Monopolisticheskii kapital v neftianoi promyshlennosti Rossii, 1883–1914* (Monopoly Capital in Russia's Oil Industry), Moscow, Academy of Sciences of the U.S.S.R., 1961.

———, "Nikolai II, 'Imperator Kaffrov'" (Nicholas II, "Emperor of the Kaffirs"), *Krasnyi Arkhiv*, 2–3 (69–70) (Moscow, 1935), 241–56.

———, "Pis'ma I. I. Vorontsova-Dashkova Nikolaiu Romanovu" (Letters of I. I. Vorontsov-Dashkov to Nikolai Romanov), *Krasnyi Arkhiv*, 1(26) (Moscow, 1928), 97–124.

———, Ministry of Foreign Affairs, *Sbornik diplomaticheskikh dokumentov kasaiushchikhsia sobytii v Persii s kontsa 1906 g. po iiul 1909 g.* (Collection of Diplomatic Documents Relative to the Events in Persia from the End of 1906 to July 1909), 7 vols. St. Petersburg, 1911–13.

———, "Tsarskaia diplomatiia o zadachakh Rossii na Vostoke v 1900 g." (Tsarist Diplomacy on the Tasks of Russia in the East in 1900), *Krasnyi Arkhiv*, 5(18) (Moscow, 1926), 3–29.

———, "Tsarskaia Rossiia i Persiia v epokhu russko-iaponskoi voiny"

(Tsarist Russia and Persia During the Russo-Japanese War), *Krasnyi Arkhiv*, 4(53) (Moscow, 1932), 13-37.

———, Ministry of Finance, Department of Commerce and Industries, *Ekonomicheskoe polozhenie Persii* (The Economic Situation of Persia) [Report of an officer of the Department, M. L. Tomara, upon his investigations conducted during a trip to Persia in 1893-1894], St. Petersburg, 1895.

Siebert, B. de, *Entente Diplomacy and the World, Matrix of the History of Europe, 1909-1914,* New York, The Knickerbocker Press, 1921.

Solov'ev, A. G., and A. A. Sennikov, *Rossiia i Turkmeniia v XIX veke,* Ashkhabad, Turkoman Branch of the Academy of Sciences of the U.S.S.R., 1946.

United States of America, Department of State, *Papers Relating to the Foreign Relations of the United States,* 1911, Washington, Government Printing Office, 1918.

AUTOBIOGRAPHIES, DIARIES, MEMOIRS

Amin od-Dowleh, Mirzā Ali Khān, *Khāterāte siyāsiye Mirzā Ali Khān Amin od-Dowleh* (The Political Reminiscences of Mirzā Ali Khān Amin od-Dowleh), H. Farmān-Farmāiān, ed., Tehran, Persian Book Co., 1962.

Baddeley, John F., *Russia in the 'Eighties: Sport and Politics,* London, Longmans, Green & Co., 1921.

Blunt, Wilfred Scawen, *My Diaries,* London, Martin Secker, 1932.

Bogdanovich, A. V., *Tri poslednikh samoderzhtsa* (The Last Three Autocrats), Moscow, L. D. Frenkel', 1924.

Bompard, Maurice, *Mon Ambassade en Russie,* Paris, Plon, 1937.

Browne, Edward Granville, *A Year Among the Persians,* 2nd ed. London, Adam and Charles Black, 1950.

Buchanan, Sir George, *My Mission to Russia and Other Diplomatic Memories,* 2 vols. Boston, Little, Brown & Co., 1923.

Burne, Sir Owen Tudor, *Memories,* London, Edward Arnold, 1907.

Chirol, Sir Valentine, *Fifty Years in a Changing World* (London?), Jonathan Cape, 1927.

Dāneshvar-Alavi, Nurollāh, *Tārikhe mashruteye Irān va jonbeshe*

Primary Sources

vatanparastāne Esfahān va Bakhtiāri (The History of Iran's Constitution and the Movement of Esfahān and Bakhtiāri Patriots), Tehran, Dānesh, 1335.

Domantovich, Aleksei Ivanovich, "Vospominaniia o prebyvanii pervoi russkoi voennoi missii v Persii" (Reminiscences of the Stay in Persia of the First Russian Military Mission), *Russkaia starina*, February and March 1908.

Eastwick, Edward B., *Journal of a Diplomate's Three Years' Residence in Persia*, 2 vols. London, Smith, Elder & Co., 1864.

E'temād os-Saltaneh, Mirzā Hoseyn Khān, *Vaqāyeye ruzāneye darbāre Nāser ed-Din Shāh* (Daily Events at the Court of Nāser ed-Din Shah), Tehran, Elmi, n.d.

Feuvrier, Dr., *Trois ans à la cour de Perse*, Paris, F. Juven, n.d.

Gordon, Sir Thomas Edward, *Persia Revisited*, London, Edward Arnold, 1896.

Grey, Sir Edward, *Twenty-five Years: 1892–1916*, 2 vols. London, Hodder & Stoughton, 1925.

Hardinge, Sir Arthur H., *A Diplomatist in the East*, London, Jonathan Cape, 1928.

Hardinge, Charles (Lord Hardinge of Penshurst), *Old Diplomacy*, London, John Murray, 1947.

Iavorskii, Dr. I. L., *Puteshestvie russkogo posol'stva po Avganistanu i Bukharskomu khanstvu v 1878–1879 gg.* (The Trip of a Russian Embassy Through Afghanistan and the Khanate of Bukhara in 1878–1879), 2 vols. St. Petersburg, M. A. Khan, 1882.

Kosogovskii, V. A., *Iz tegeranskogo dnevnika polkovnika V. A. Kosogovskogo* (From the Tehran Diary of Colonel V. A. Kosogovskii), G. M. Petrov, ed., Moscow, Institute of Orientology, Academy of Sciences of the U.S.S.R., 1960.

———, "Ocherk istorii razvitiia persidskoi kazach'ei brigady" (A Sketch of the History of the Development of the Persian Cossack Brigade), *Novyi Vostok*, No. 4 (Moscow, 1923).

———, "Persiia v kontse XIX veka" (Persia at the End of the XIXth Century), *Novyi Vostok*, No. 3 (Moscow, 1923).

Kuropatkin, A. N., "Dnevnik A. N. Kuropatkina" (The Diary of A. N. Kuropatkin), *Krasnyi Arkhiv*, 2 (1922) (Moscow, 1922), 9–122.

Lamzdorf (Lamsdorff), Vladimir Nikolaevich, *Dnevnik, 1891–1892* (Diary), Moscow, Academia, 1934.

———, *Dnevnik V. N. Lamzdorfa (1886–1890)* (The Diary of V. N. Lamsdorff, 1886–1890), Moscow, Tsentrarkhiv, 1926.

Loftus, Lord Augustus, *The Diplomatic Reminiscences of Lord Augustus Loftus, 1862–1879*, 2nd series, 2, London, Cassell & Co., 1894.

Miliutin, D. A., *Dnevnik D. A. Miliutina* (The Diary of D. A. Miliutin), P. A. Zaionchkovskii, ed., 4 vols. Moscow, State Library of the U.S.S.R. named after Lenin, 1947–50.

Moayyer ol-Mamālek, Dust Ali, *Yāddāshthāi az zendegāniye khosusiye Nāser ed-Din Shāh* (Some Notes on the Private Life of Nāser ed-Din Shāh), Tehran, Elmi, n.d.

Moore, Arthur, *The Orient Express*, London, Constable & Co., 1914.

Mostowfi, Abdollāh, *Sharhe zendegāniye man yā tārikhe ejtemāi va edāriye Qājāriyyeh* (The Story of My Life or the Social and Administrative History of the Qājār Period), Tehran, Elmi, 1323.

Polovtsev, A. A., "Dnevnik A. A. Polovtseva" (The Diary of A. A. Polovtsev), *Krasnyi Arkhiv*, 4 (1923), (Moscow, 1923), 63–128.

Sazonov, S. D., *Vospominaniia* (Reminiscences), Paris, E. Siial'skaia, 1927.

Schelking, Eugene de, *Recollections of a Russian Diplomat*, New York, Macmillan, 1918.

Shuster, W. Morgan, *The Strangling of Persia*, New York, Century Co., 1912.

Tcharykov, N. V., *Glimpses of High Politics through War and Peace, 1855–1929*, New York, Macmillan, 1931.

Wilson, Sir Arnold, *South West Persia, A Political Officer's Diary, 1907–1914*, London, Oxford University Press, 1941.

Witte, Count Sergei Iul'evich, *Vospominaniia* (Reminiscences), 2 vols. Berlin, 1922, and Moscow, 1923.

Wolff, Sir Henry Drummond, *Rambling Recollections*, 2 vols. London, Macmillan, 1908.

Wratislaw, A. C., *A Consul in the East*, Edinburgh, W. Blackwood & Sons, 1924.

SECONDARY WORKS

ARTICLES

Anan'ich, B. V., "Rossiia i kontsessiia d'Arsi" (Russia and the d'Arcy Concession), *Istoricheskie zapiski*, 66 (1960), 278–90.

Bakulin, F. A., "Ocherk vneshnei torgovli Azerbaidzhana za 1870–1871 g.g." (A Sketch of the External Trade of Āzarbāyjān for 1870–1871), *Vostochnyi Sbornik*, Asiatic Department of the Ministry of Foreign Affairs (St. Petersburg, 1877), pp. 205–66.

———, "Ocherk russkoi torgovli v Mazanderane i Asterabade v 1871 g." (A Sketch of Russian Trade in Māzandarān and Astarābād in 1871), *Vostochnyi sbornik* (St. Petersburg, 1877), 269–327.

Bor-Ramenskii, E., "K voprosu o roli bolshevikov zakavkaz'ia v iranskoi revoliutsii 1905–1911 godov" (On the Question of the Role of Transcaucasian Bolsheviks in the Iranian Revolution of 1905–1911), *Istorik Marksist*, No. 11, 1940.

Boulger, Demetrius, "England and Persia," *Asiatic Review*, 7 (January–April 1889), 190–201.

Brockway, T. P., "Britain and the Persian Bubble," *The Journal of Modern History*, 13, No. 1 (March 1941), 36–47.

Frechtling, L. E., "The Reuter Concession in Persia," *Asiatic Review*, 34 (July 1938), 518–33.

Gindin, I. F., and L. E. Shepelov, "Bankovskie monopolii v Rossii nakanune velikoi Oktiabrskoi sotsialisticheskoi revoliutsii" (Bank Monopolies in Russia on the Eve of the Great October Socialist Revolution), *Istoricheskie zapiski*, 66 (1960), 20–95.

"Idhem-al-Fani," "His Imperial Majesty the Late Shah of Persia," *The Imperial Asiatic Quarterly Review and Colonial and Oriental Record*, 3rd series, 23, Nos. 45–46 (January–April 1907), 225–40.

Kazemzadeh, Firuz, "Russia and the Middle East," *Russian Foreign Policy: Essays in Historical Perspective*, Ivo J. Lederer, ed. (New Haven, Yale University Press, 1962), pp. 489–530.

———, "Russian Imperialism and Persian Railways," *Russian Thought and Politics*, Harvard Slavic Studies, 4 (The Hague, Mouton & Co., 1957), 355–73.

———, "The Origin and Early Development of the Persian Cossack Brigade," *The American Slavic and East European Review*, 15, No. 3 (October 1956), 351–63.

Keddie, Nikki R., "Religion and Irreligion in Early Iranian Nationalism," *Comparative Studies in Society and History*, 4, No. 3 (April 1962), 265-95.

Lambton, Ann K. S., "Persian Political Societies, 1906-1911," *St. Anthony's Papers*, No. 16, *Middle Eastern Affairs*, No. 3, pp. 41-89.

Langer, William L., "A Critique of Imperialism," *The Making of Modern Europe*, H. Ausubel, ed., Book 2 (New York, The Dryden Press, 1951), 918-32.

Lee, Dwight E., "A Turkish Mission to Afghanistan, 1877," *The Journal of Modern History*, 13, No. 3 (September 1941), 335-56.

Lynch, H. F. B., "The Anglo-Persian Commercial Treaty," *The Imperial and Asiatic Quarterly Review and Colonial and Oriental Record*, 3rd series, 16, Nos. 31-32 (July-October 1903), 225-30.

P.A.T., "Zheleznodorozhnyi vopros v Persii i Velikii Indiiskii put'" (The Railway Question in Persia and the Great Indian Road), *Velikaia Rossiia*, 2, Moscow, V. P. Riabushinskii, n.d.

Pavlovich, M. P., "Kazach'ia brigada v Persii" (The Cossack Brigade in Persia), *Novyi Vostok*, 8-9 (1925).

Persicus, "The Regeneration of Persia," *The Asiatic Quarterly Review*, 10 (July-October 1890), 1-17.

Popov, A. L., "Iz istorii zavoevaniia Srednei Azii" (From the History of the Conquest of Central Asia), *Istoricheskie zapiski*, No. 9 (1940), 198-242.

———, "Stranitsa iz istorii russkogo imperializma v Persii" (A Page from the History of Russian Imperialism in Persia), *Mezhdunarodnaia zhizn*, Nos. 4-5 (1924), 133-64.

Shteinberg (Steinberg), E. L., "Angliiskaia versiia o 'russkoi ugroze' Indii v. XIX-XX v.v." (The English Version of the "Russian Threat" to India), *Istoricheskie zapiski*, 33 (1950), 47-66.

Sumner, B. H., "Tsardom and Imperialism in the Far East and Middle East, 1880-1914," *Proceedings of the British Academy* (1941), 25-65.

Thornton, A. P., "British Policy in Persia, 1858-1890," *The English Historical Review*, 69, No. 273 (October 1954), 554-79, and 70, No. 274 (January 1955), 55-71.

Timofeev, A., "Imperialisticheskoe mirnoe zavoevanie Persii" (The

Imperialist Pacific Conquest of Persia), *Novyi Vostok*, No. 2, n.d., pp. 254–71.

Treue, Wilhelm, "Russland und die persischen Eisenbahnbautern vor dem Weltkriege," *Archiv für Eisenbahnwesen*, No. 2 (1939), 471–94.

Trubetskoi, Prince G. N., "Rossiia, kak velikaia derzhava" (Russia as a Great Power), V. P. Riabushinskii, ed., *Velikaia Rossiia*, 1 (Moscow, 1910), 21–137.

BOOKS AND PAMPHLETS

Abdullaev, Zakir Zul'fugarovich, *Nachalo ekspansii S. Sh. A. v Irane* (The Beginning of U.S. Expansion in Iran), Moscow, Institute of the Peoples of Asia, Academy of Sciences of the U.S.S.R., 1963.

Academy of Sciences of the U.S.S.R., Institute of Economics, *Politicheskaia ekonomiia* (Political Economy), Moscow, 1954.

Adamiyat, Fereydoun, *Bahrein Islands, A Legal and Diplomatic Study of the British-Iranian Controversy*, New York, F. A. Praeger, 1955.

Afschar, Mahmoud, *La politique européenne en Perse*, Berlin, "Iranschähr," 1921.

Allan, John, *The Cambridge Shorter History of India*, London, (1934?).

Atrpet, *Mamed Ali Shakh, Narodnoe dvizhenie v strane l'va i solntsa* (Mohammad Ali Shah, Popular Movement in the Land of the Lion and the Sun), Aleksandropol, "Shirak," 1909.

Banusevich, Anthony Michael, "Anglo-Russian Relations Concerning the Origin and Effects of the Persian Question, 1906–1911," unpublished M.A. thesis, Georgetown University, April 1950.

Bauer, Heinz, *Die englisch-russischen Gegensätze in Persien*, Tübingen, Karl Bölzle, 1940. (Doctoral dissertation.)

Baxter, William Edward, *England and Russia in Asia*, London, Swan Sonnenschein & Co., 1885.

Beliaev, Nikolai Ivanovich, *Russko-turetskaia voina 1877–1878 gg.* (The Russo-Turkish War of 1877–1878), Moscow, 1956.

Benjamin, Samuel Green Wheeler, *Persia and the Persians*, Boston, Ticknor & Co., 1887.

Bérard, Victor, *Révolutions de la Perse*, Paris, Armand Colin, 1910.

Bestuzhev, Igor Vasil'evich, *Borba v Rossii po voprosam vneshnei po-*

litiki, 1906–1910. (The Struggle over Foreign Policy Issues in Russia), Moscow, Academy of Sciences of the U.S.S.R., 1961.

Bondarevskii, Grigorii L'vovich, *Bagdadskaia doroga i proniknovenie germanskogo imperializma na Blizhnii Vostok* (The Bagdad Road and the Penetration of the German Imperialism into the Near East), Tashkent, 1955.

Bovykin, V. I., *Ocherki istorii vneshnei politiki Rossii* (Essays in the History of Russia's Foreign Policy), Moscow, 1960.

Browne, Edward Granville, *The Persian Revolution of 1905–1909*, Cambridge, Cambridge University Press, 1910.

———, *The Press and Poetry of Modern Persia*, Cambridge, Cambridge University Press, 1914.

———, *The Reign of Terror in Tabriz. England's Responsibility*, London, Taylor, Garnett, Evans & Co., 1912.

Bukharin, Nikolai, *Imperializm i nakoplenie kapitala* (Imperialism and the Accumulation of Capital), 3rd ed., Moscow, 1928.

Bullard, Sir Reader, *Britain and the Middle East from the Earliest Times to 1950*, London, Hutchinson's University Library, 1951.

Bushev, S. K., *A. M. Gorchakov*, Moscow, Institute of International Relations, 1961.

Cecil, Algernon, *British Foreign Secretaries, 1807–1916, Studies in Personality and Policy*, London, G. Bell & Sons, 1927.

Cecil, Lady Gwendolen, *Life of Robert, Marquis of Salisbury*, 4 vols. London, Hodder & Stoughton, 1921–32.

Chirol, Valentine, *The Middle Eastern Question or Some Political Problems of Indian Defence*, London, John Murray, 1903.

Churchill, Rogers Platt, *The Anglo-Russian Convention of 1907*, Cedar Rapids, The Torch Press, 1939.

Curzon, George Nathaniel, *Persia and the Persian Question*, 2 vols. London, Longmans, Green & Co., 1892.

———, *Russia in Central Asia in 1889 and the Anglo-Russian Question*, London, Longmans, Green & Co., 1889.

Dahlgren, Dorothy B., "Great Britain and the Partition of Persia," unpublished M.A. thesis, Stanford University, 1933.

Demorgny, G., *La question persane et la guerre*, Paris, 1916.

Drage, Geoffrey, *Russian Affairs*, London, John Murray, 1904.

Edwards, H. Sutherland, *Russian Projects Against India from the Czar Peter to General Skobeleff*, London, Remington & Co., 1885.

Efremov, P. N., *Vneshniaia politika Rossii* (1907–1914 gg.) (Russia's Foreign Policy), Moscow, Institute of International Relations, 1961.

Entner, Marvin L., *Russo-Persian Commercial Relations, 1828–1914*, Gainesville, University of Florida Press, 1965.

Fatemi, Nasrollah Saifpour, *Oil Diplomacy*, New York, Whittier Books, 1957.

Fitzmaurice, Edmond, *The Life of Granville George Leveson Gower, Second Earl Granville, K. G., 1815–1891*, 2d ed., 2 vols. London, Longmans, Green & Co., 1905.

Fraser, David, *Persia and Turkey in Revolt*, London, William Blackwood & Sons, 1910.

Fraser, Lovat, *India Under Curzon and After*, New York, Henry Holt & Co., 1911.

Fraser-Tytler, W. K., *Afghanistan*, London, Oxford University Press, 1950.

Gail, Marzieh, *Persia and the Victorians*, London, George Allen & Unwin Ltd., 1951.

Galperin, A., *Anglo-iaponskii soiuz. 1902–1921 gody* (The Anglo-Japanese Alliance. 1902–1921), Moscow, 1947.

Gleason, John Howes, *The Genesis of Russophobia in Great Britain*, Cambridge, Harvard University Press, 1950.

Greaves, Rose Louise, *Persia and the Defence of India, 1884–1892: A Study in the Foreign Policy of the Third Marquis of Salisbury*, London, University of London, The Athlone Press, 1959.

Grodekov, N. I., *Voina v Turkmenii* (The War in Turkomania), 4 vols. St. Petersburg, 1884.

Grunwald, Constantin de, *Trois siècles de diplomatie russe*, Paris, Calmann-Lévy, 1945.

Habberton, William, *Anglo-Russian Relations Concerning Afghanistan, 1837–1907*, Illinois Studies in the Social Sciences, 21, No. 4, Urbana, University of Illinois, 1937.

Hamilton, Angus, *Problems of the Middle East*, London, Eveleigh Nash, 1909.

Hannekum, Wilhelm, *Persien im Spiel der Mächte*, Berlin, Emil Eberling, 1938.

Hobson, J. A., *Imperialism*, London, George Allen & Unwin Ltd., 1938.

Hone, J. M., and P. L. Dickinson, *Persia in Revolution*, London, T. Fisher Unwin, 1910.

Independent Labour Party, *Persia, Finland, and Our Russian Alliance*, Labour and War Pamphlets, No. 12, London, 1915.

Ignat'ev, Anatolii Venediktovich, *Russko-angliiskie otnosheniia nakanune pervoi mirovoi voiny.* (1908–1914 gg.) (Russo-English Relations on the Eve of the First World War), Moscow, 1962.

Iskandarov, B. I., *Vostochnaia Bukhara i Pamir v period prisoedineniia Srednei Azii k Rossii* (Eastern Bukhara and the Pamirs in the Period of the Uniting of Central Asia to Russia), Stalinabad, 1960.

Ivanov, Mikhail Sergeevich, *Iranskaia revoliutsiia 1905–1911 godov*, (The Iranian Revolution of 1905–1911), Institute of International Relations, Moscow, 1957.

———, *Ocherk istorii Irana* (A Sketch of the History of Iran), Moscow, 1952.

Kazemzadeh, Firuz, *The Struggle for Transcaucasia, 1917–1921*, Oxford, George Ronald, 1951.

Keddie, Nikki R., *Religion and Rebellion in Iran*, London, Frank Cass & Co., 1966.

Korff, Sergei Aleksandrovich, *Russia's Foreign Relations during the Last Half Century*, New York, Macmillan, 1922.

Knorring, N. N., *General Mikhail Dmitrievich Skobelev*, Paris, 1939 (printed in Tallin).

Lang, David M., *The Last Years of the Georgian Monarchy, 1658–1832*, New York, Columbia University Press, 1957.

Langer, William L., *The Diplomacy of Imperialism*, 2 vols. New York, Alfred A. Knopf, 1935.

———, *European Alliances and Alignments, 1871–1890*, New York, Alfred A. Knopf, 1931.

Lee, Sir Sidney, *King Edward VII*, 2 vols. London, Macmillan, 1925–27.

Lenin, V. I., *Sochneniia*, 3rd ed., 19, Moscow, 1935.

———, *Collected Works*, 15, Moscow, 1963.

———, *Polnoe sobranie sochinenii* (Complete Works), 5th ed., 17, Moscow, 1961.

Liashchenko, P. I., *Istoriia narodnogo khoziaistva S.S.S.R.* (The History of the People's Economy of the U.S.S.R.), 3rd ed., 3 vols. 2, "Capitalism," Leningrad, 1952.

Litten, Wilhelm, *Persien von der 'pénétration pacifique' zum 'Protektorat' Urkunden und Tatsachen zur Geschichte der europäischen 'pénétration pacifique' in Persien 1860–1919*, Berlin, Walter de Gruyter & Co. 1920.

Lobanov-Rostovsky, A., *Russia and Asia*, Ann Arbor, George Wahr Publishing Co., 1951.

Lomnitskii, S., *Persiia i persy* (Persia and the Persians), St. Petersburg, A. S. Suvorin, 1902.

Longrigg, Stephen Hemsley, *Oil in the Middle East, Its Discovery and Development*, London, Oxford University Press, 1954.

Lutz, Hermann, *Lord Grey and the World War*, London, George Allen & Unwin Ltd., 1928.

Lystsov, V. P., *Persidskii pokhod Petra I, 1722–1723* (The Persian Campaign of Peter I), Moscow, 1951.

M. A., *Poslednee politicheskoe dvizhenie v Persii* (The Latest Political Movement in Persia), St. Petersburg, Trud, 1906.

Mahmud, Mahmud, *Tārikhe ravābete siyāsiye Irān bā Englis dar qarne nuzdahome milādi* (The History of Anglo-Iranian Diplomatic Relations in the 19th Century A.D.), 5 vols. Tehran, 1328–29.

Malekzādeh, Mehdi, *Tārikhe enqelābe mashrutiyate Irān* (The History of the Constitutional Revolution in Iran), 7 vols. Tehran, Soqrāt, n.d.

Mālmiri, Hāji Mohammad Tāher, *Tārikhe shohadāye Yazd* (The History of the Martyrs of Yazd), Cairo, Farajollāh Kordi, 1342 A.H. (lunar).

Markham, Clements R., *A General Sketch of the History of Persia*, London, Longmans, Green & Co., 1874.

Martin, Bradford G., *German-Persian Diplomatic Relations, 1873–1912*, The Hague, Mouton & Co., 1959.

McCarthy, Mary M., *Anglo-Russian Rivalry in Persia*, University of Buffalo Series, 4, No. 2 (June 1925).

Moezzi, Najaf Qoli Hesām, *Tārikhe ravābete siyāsiye Irān bā donyā* (The History of Iran's Diplomatic Relations with the World), Tehran, Elmi, 1325.

Mokhtāri, Habibollāh, *Tārikhe bidāriye Irān* (The History of Iran's Awakening), Tehran, 1326.

Monnypenny, W. F., and G. E. Buckle, *The Life of Benjamin Disraeli Earl of Beaconsfield*, 2 vols. London, John Murray, 1929.

Moon, Parker Thomas, *Imperialism and World Politics*, New York, Macmillan, 1926.

Nakhai, M., *L'evolution politique de l'Iran*, Bruxelles, J. Felix, 1938.

Nāzem ol-Eslām Kermāni, *Tārikhe bidāriye irāniyān* (The History of the Awakening of the Iranians), 2nd ed. Tehran, Sinā, n.d.

Newton, Lord, *Lord Lansdowne*, London, Macmillan, 1929.

Nicolson, Harold, *Portrait of a Diplomatist*, Boston, Houghton Mifflin, 1930.

Nolde, Boris, *La formation de l'Empire Russe*, 2 vols. Paris, Institut d'Études slaves, 1952–53.

Notovitch, Nicolas, *La Russie et l'alliance anglaise*, Paris, Plon, 1906.

Panikkar, K. M., *Asia and Western Dominance*, London, George Allen & Unwin Ltd., 1959.

Pavlovich Mikhail (Vel'tman), *Bor'ba za Aziiu i Afriku* (The Struggle for Asia and Africa), Leningrad, 1925.

———, *Imperializm i borba za velikie zheleznodorozhnye i morskie puti budushchego* (Imperialism and the Struggle for the Great Railways and Seaways of the Future), "Kommunist," 1 (1918); 2 (1919), Moscow.

———, *Ekonomicheskoe razvitie i agrarnyi vopros v Persii XX veka* (Economic Development and the Agrarian Question in Twentieth-Century Persia), Moscow, 1921.

Pierce, Richard A., *Russian Central Asia, 1867–1917*, Berkeley, University of California Press, 1960.

Pokrovskii, M. N., *Diplomatiia i voiny tsarskoi Rossii v XIX stoletii* (The Diplomacy and Wars of Tsarist Russia in the Nineteenth Century), Moscow, "Krasnaia nov,'" 1923.

Pokrovskii, S. A., *Vneshniaia torgovlia i vneshniaia torgovaia politika*

Rossii (The Foreign Trade and Foreign Trade Policy of Russia), Moscow, Mezhdunarodnaia kniga, 1947.

Poletika, N. P., *Vozniknovenie mirovoi voiny* (The Origin of the World War), Moscow, 1935.

Popowski, Josef, *The Rival Powers in Central Asia*, London, Archibald Constable, 1893.

Potemkin, V. P., ed., *Istoriia diplomatii* (The History of Diplomacy), 3 vols. Moscow, 1945.

Qozānlu, Jamil, *Jange dāh-sāle yā jange avvale Irān bā Rus* (The Ten Years' War or the First Russo-Persian War), Tehran, Markazi, 1315.

———, *Jange Irān-Rus, 1827–1828* (The Irano-Russian War, 1825–1828), Tehran, Tolu, 1316.

Ramazani, Rouhollah K., *The Foreign Policy of Iran, 1500–1941*, Charlottesville, The University Press of Virginia, 1966.

Reisner, I. M., *Pervaia russkaia revoliutsiia i probuzhdenie Azii* (The First Russian Revolution and the Awakening of Asia), Moscow, Znamia, 1955.

Reisner, I. M., and N. M. Goldberg, eds., *Ocherki po novoi istorii stran Srednego Vostoka* (Sketches in the Modern History of the Countries of the Middle East), Moscow, Moscow University Press, 1951.

Reisner, I. M., and B. K. Rubtsov, eds., *Novaia istoriia stran zarubezhnogo Vostoka* (The Modern History of the Foreign Countries of the East), 2 vols. Moscow, Moscow University Press, 1952.

Rittikh (Rittich), Petr Aleksandrovich, *Zheleznodorozhnyi put cherez Persiiu* (Railway Across Persia), St. Petersburg, Porokhovshchikov, 1900.

Romanov, P. M., *Zheleznodorozhnyi vopros v Persii i mery k razvitiiu russko-persidskoi torgovli* (The Railway Question in Persia and Measures for the Development of Russo-Persian Trade), St. Petersburg, Iu. N. Erlikh, 1891.

Ronaldshay, the Earl of, *The Life of Lord Curzon, Being an Authorized Biography of George Nathaniel Marquess Curzon of Kedleston, K.G.*, 2 vols. London, Ernest Benn, 1928.

Rostovskii, S. N., I.M. Reisner, G. S. Kara-Murza, B. K. Rubtsov, *Novaia istoriia kolonialnykh i zavisimykh stran* (The Modern History of Colonial and Dependent Nations), 1, Moscow, Institute of History, Academy of Sciences of the U.S.S.R., 1940.

Rotshtein (Rothstein), F. A., *Mezhdunarodnye otnosheniia v kontse XIX veka* (International Relations at the End of the Nineteenth Century), Moscow, Institute of History, Academy of Sciences of the U.S.S.R., 1960.

Rouire, Dr., *La rivalité anglo-russe au XIX siecle en Asie*, Paris, Armand Colin, 1908.

Russia, Ministry of Foreign Affairs, *Ocherk istorii ministerstva inostrannykh del, 1802–1902* (A Sketch of the History of the Ministry of Foreign Affairs), St. Petersburg, 1902.

Sāsāni, Khānmalek, *Daste penhāne siyāsate Englis dar Irān* (The Hidden Hand of British Policy in Iran), Tehran, Espander, n.d.

———, *Siyāsatgarāne dowreye Qājār* (The Politicians of the Qājār Period), Tehran, Tahvori, 1338.

Schumpeter, Joseph A., *Imperialism and Social Classes*, New York, August M. Kelley, Inc., 1951.

Schuyler, Eugene, *Turkistan*, 2 vols. New York, Scribner, Armstrong & Co., 1877.

Seeley, J. R., *The Expansion of England*, Boston, Little, Brown & Co., 1902.

Shteinberg (Steinberg), E. L., *Istoriia britanskoi aggressii na Srednem Vostoke* (The History of British Aggression in the Middle East), Moscow, Ministry of War of the U.S.S.R., 1951.

———, *Ocherki istorii Turkmenii* (Essays in the History of Turkomania), Moscow, 1934.

Shwadran, Benjamin, *The Middle East Oil and the Great Powers*, New York, Frederick A. Praeger, 1955.

Siassi, A. Akbar, *La Perse au contact de l'Occident*, Paris, Ernest Leroux, 1931.

Sidorov, A. L., ed., *Ocherki istorii S.S.S.R.* (Essays in the History of the U.S.S.R.), Moscow, Ministry of Education, 1954.

Skalkovskii, K., *Vneshniaia politika Rossii i polozhenie inostrannykh derzhav* (Russia's Foreign Policy and the Situation of Foreign Powers), St. Petersburg, 1901.

Sobotsinskii, L. A., *Persiia*, n.p., 1913.

Spector, Ivar, *The First Russian Revolution, Its Impact on Asia*, Englewood Cliffs, Prentice Hall, 1962.

Storey, Graham, *Reuter's Century*, London, Max Parrish, 1951.

Sumner, B. H., *Peter the Great and the Emergence of Russia*, London, English Universities Press, 1956.

Sykes, Sir Percy M., *A History of Persia*, 2 vols. London, Macmillan, 1915.

———, *The Right Honourable Sir Mortimer Durand*, London, Cassell & Co., 1926.

Tāherzādeh-Behzād, Karim, *Qiyāme Āzarbāyjān dar enqelābe mashrutiyate Irān* (The Rise of Āzarbāyjān in Iran's Constitutional Revolution), Tehran, Eqbāl, n.d.

Tarle, E. V., *Evropa v epokhu imperializma* (Europe in the Epoch of Imperialism), Moscow, 1927.

Taube, Baron M. de, *La politique russe d'avantguerre et la fin de l'Empire des tsars*, Paris, Ernest Leroux, 1928.

Taylor, A. J. P., *The Struggle for Mastery in Europe*, Oxford, Oxford University Press, 1954.

Terent'ev, M. A., *Istoriia zavoevaniia Srednei Azii* (The History of the Conquest of Central Asia), 3 vols. St. Petersburg, V. V. Komarov, 1906.

Terenzio, Pio Carlo, *La rivalité anglo-russe en Perse et en Afghanistan jusque'aux accords de 1907*, Paris, Rousseau & Cie., 1947.

Ter-Gukasov, G. I., *Ekonomicheskie interesy Rossii v Persii* (Russia's Economic Interests in Persia), St. Petersburg, Ministry of Finance, 1915. The second edition of this work appeared under the title *Politicheskie i ekonomicheskie interesy Rossii v Persii* in 1916.

Teymuri, Ebrāhim, *Asre bikhabari yā tārikhe emtiāzāt dar Irān* (The Silent Age or the History of Concessions in Persia), Tehran, Eqbāl, 1332.

———, *Qarārdāde 1890 rezhi, Tahrime tanbāku, Avvallin moqāvemate manfi dar Irān* (The Régie Agreement of 1890, the Prohibition of Tobacco, the First Passive Resistance in Iran), Tehran, Soqrāt, 1328(?).

Tikhomirov, M. N., *Prisoedinenie Merva k Rossii* (The Annexation of Merv to Russia), Moscow, Institute of Orientology, Academy of Sciences of the U.S.S.R., 1960.

Trevelyan, George Macaulay, *Grey of Fallodon*, Boston, Houghton Mifflin, 1937.

Tria, V., *Kavkazskie sotsial-demokraty v persidskoi revoliutsii* (Caucasian Social-Democrats in the Persian Revolution), with a Preface by M. Vel'tman-Pavlovich, "Sotsial-demokrat," Paris, 1910.

Trollope, Anthony, *The Way We Live Now* (any edition).

Vaks, L., *Ocherki istorii natsional'no-burzhuaznykh revoliutsii na Vostoke* (Sketches of the History of the National-Bourgeois Revolutions in the East), Moscow, Moskovskii Rabochii, 1931.

Vambery, Arminius, *Central Asia and the Anglo-Russian Frontier Question*, London, Smith, Elder & Co., 1874.

———, *The Coming Struggle for India*, London, Cassell & Co., 1885.

———, *Western Culture in Eastern Lands*, New York, E. P. Dutton & Co., 1906.

Ward, A. W., and G. P. Gooch, *The Cambridge History of British Foreign Policy*, 3 vols. Cambridge, Cambridge University Press, 1923.

Whigham, H. J., *The Persian Problem*, New York, Scribner & Sons, 1903.

Winslow, E. M., *The Pattern of Imperialism*, New York, Columbia University Press, 1948.

Yaganegi, Esfandiar Bahram, *Recent Financial and Monetary History of Persia*, Ph.D. dissertation, Columbia University, 1934.

Yeselson, Abraham, *United States–Persian Diplomatic Relations, 1883–1921*, New Brunswick, Rutgers University Press, 1956.

Zaionchkovskii, A. M., *Podgotovka Rossii k mirovoi voine v mezhdunarodnom otnoshenii* (Russia's Preparation for the World War in the International Aspect), Leningrad, Staff of the Workers' and Peasants' Red Army, 1926.

Zinov'ev, I. A., *Rossiia, Angliia i Persiia* (Russia, England, and Persia) St. Petersburg, 1912.

Zonnenshtral-Piskorskii, A. A., *Mezhdunarodnye torgovye dogovory Persii* (Persia's International Commercial Treaties), Moscow, Moscow Institute of Orientology, 1931.

Index

Abaza, Aleksandr Aggeevich, 232, 234
Abbās Mirzā Qājār, 5, 70, 100, 166
Abbot, 129
Abd ol-Hasan Khān of Quchān, 39-40
Abd or-Rahim Khān Sāed ol-Molk, Mirzā, 133
Abd or-Rahmān, Amir, 95-98
Abdul Hamid, Sultan, 397, 529
Abdullaev, Z. Z., 612 n.
Abu Tāleb Zanjāni, Hāji Mirzā Seyyed, 394-95, 399
Adams, Henry, 101
Adib ot-Tojjār, 565
Acrenthal, Count Alois von, 528, 529
Afghāni. *See* Jamāl ed-Din Asadābādi
Afghanistan, 49-51, 57, 68, 78, 81, 86, 93, 95, 98, 99, 219; Stoletov's mission to, 47-51, 53
Afkham, Sardār, 545
Āghāsi, Hāji Mirzā, 100
Ahmad Shah Qājār, 544, 546, 598
Ahvāz, 186, 279
Ākhāl: expeditions, 67-68, 74-76, 163; oasis, 28, 41, 42, 44, 53-56, 58-62, 66, 72, 78, 89
Ākhāl-Khorāsān border treaty, 207
Akhtar, 196-97
Alā od-Dowleh, 309-10, 445
Alā ol-Molk, 469, 539
Alā os-Saltaneh, General Mirzā Mohammad Ali Khān, 322, 330, 472, 497
Aleksandr Aleksandrovich, Grand Duke. *See* Alexander III
Aleksandr Mikhailovich, Grand Duke, 439

Aleksandra Fedorovna, Empress, 483
Alexander II, Tsar, 12, 25, 27, 36, 37, 46, 53, 57, 59, 73, 74, 84, 113, 145
Alexander III, Tsar, 73, 78, 84, 93, 98, 156, 171, 195, 197, 219-20, 223-24, 227-28
Ali Akbar, Seyyed, 389, 391-93
Ali Asghar Khān. *See* Amin os-Soltān
Alikhanov, Colonel, 88
Alison, Sir Charles, 15-16, 18, 19, 21, 102, 149, 150, 151
Alléon, concession, 158-60, 162
Altham, Lieutenant Colonel E. A., 402, 404
Amin od-Divān, Sheykh Mortezā, 303
Amin od-Dowleh, Hāji Mirzā Ali Khān, 247, 254, 302, 305, 307, 309, 310, 312, 313, 314, 315, 453-54, 496
Amin ol-Molk, 303
Amin os-Soltān, Mirzā Ali Asghar Khān, Atābak, 192-94, 195, 209, 210, 216, 217, 229, 236, 237, 246, 247, 251, 253, 254, 255, 256, 263-72, 281, 283-84, 285-86, 288, 291, 296-97, 299-300, 302, 303, 310, 318, 319, 322-23, 324, 329, 330-31, 352, 353-56, 362, 364, 365, 368-76, 379-84, 387-89, 417, 421, 433, 445, 448, 449, 450, 453, 455-56, 463-64, 497, 510, 673
Amir Bahādor Jang, 522, 539
Āmoli, Ākhund, 545
Anan'ich, B. V., 359, 383-85
Anglo-Asiatic Syndicate, 243-44
Anglo-French Entente, 469, 477
Anglo-Japanese alliance, 386, 477

Anglo-Persian Oil Company, 560, 587, 639. *See also* D'Arcy concession
Anglo-Russian agreement, 497, 498-500, 588, 592, 610, 620, 627, 629, 637, 640, 659, 662, 670; British reaction to, 502-06; early discussions of, 311-12, 480, 489; Persian reaction to, 501-02; Russian reaction to, 506-09; views on, 495, 512 n.
Anglo-Russian agreement of 1915, 678-79
Anis od-Dowleh, 112-13, 117, 118
Anzali, lagoon, 154, 216; Russians landing at, 630
Apukhtin, Aleksei Nikolaevich, 331
Āqā Mohammad Khān Qājār, 192
Ardagh, Sir John, 351
Arfa' od-Dowleh, General Mirzā Rezā Khān, 325
Argyropoulo, Kimon Manuilovich, 318, 328-29, 355-56, 361-64, 367, 371-72, 381, 457, 488, 489, 559
Armenians, 464, 527, 646
Armstrong, Captain, 404
Arshad od-Dowleh (Sardār Arshad), 600, 602, 604, 606, 611-12
As'ad, Sardār, 545, 571-72, 611, 638, 639
Āshtiāni, Hāji Mirzā Hasan, 309
Asquith, Herbert H., 563
Astarābād, province, 46, 61
Atābak. *See* Amin os-Soltān
Atrak, river, 19, 27, 33, 60

Babi-Baha'i movement, 188
Babis, 188, 445-46, 513, 585
Baddeley, John F., 96
Baghdad railway, 405, 488, 489, 561, 592-93, 596
Baha'is, 188, 190, 455-56
Bahārestān palace, bombardment of, 523
Bahreyn, 150
Bailey, E. C., 31
Bakhmetev, Iu. P., 484
Bakhtiāris, 528, 536, 540, 542, 611, 626, 629-30, 638-39, 642, 644, 653, 670

Bakulin, F. A., 169
Balfour, Arthur James, 349, 398
Balloy, Marie René Davy de Chavigné de, 187-88
Baluchestān, 150; railway, 404
Bandar-Abbās, 150, 404; Russian consulate at, 467, 470
Banque d'Escompte of Paris, 201, 232
Bāqer Khān, 533, 570-71
Baranovskii, 545, 566
Barclay, Sir George, 532, 534, 540, 541, 542-43, 550, 552, 558, 561, 567, 569, 574-76, 579, 581, 585, 586, 587, 590, 597, 599, 600, 602, 608, 623-24, 630, 633, 635, 639, 641, 644-45, 652, 662, 671
Bark, P., 458
Barnes, H. S., 415-16
Bast in the British legation, 475-76
Battenberg, Prince Louis of, 404
Beaconsfield, Lord. *See* Disraeli
Beger, Aleksandr Fedorovich, 18-19, 122, 124-25, 139-42, 155
Behbehāni, Seyyed Abdollāh, 309-10, 475, 491, 496 n., 572-73
Beliaev, Consul, 654
Benckendorff, Count Aleksandr Konstantinovich, 480, 488, 492, 525, 543, 554, 555, 563, 567, 569, 583, 588, 589, 590, 591, 604, 606-07, 612, 618, 622, 626, 632, 636-37, 652, 657-60, 668, 669, 671
Benckendorff, Count P. K., 484
Benjamin, Samuel G. W., 177
Benn, Captain R. A. E., 415, 419-20, 426
Berlin Congress, 51, 53, 57
Bertie, Sir Francis, 640
Bestuzhev, I. V., 512 n.
Binns, Mr., 257
Bismarck, Prince Otto von, 173
Bolsheviks, 527
Borujerdi, Ali Akbar, 545
Bostelman, Captain Anatolii, 277
Brackenbury, General Sir Henry, 219, 223
Brodrick, St. John, 349, 403
Browne, Edward G., 247 n., 248, 476 n., 504, 514, 522 n., 575

Index

Brunnow, Baron (later Count) E., 9, 14, 116
Bryce, James, 583, 584
Buchanan, Sir Andrew, 11, 12, 13, 19, 20
Buchanan, Sir George, 311, 504, 558, 583, 588, 589, 596, 620, 627, 628, 630, 632, 641, 651, 658, 662-63, 668, 671, 676, 678
Burne, O. T., 23
Bushehr, 61, 70; special importance for Russia, 466-67
Bützow, Evgenii Karlovich, 226, 232, 238, 247, 250-52, 255, 256, 264, 266-67, 268, 283-84, 303, 409-10

Cairnes, F. S., 615
Cambridge, Duke of, 27
Campbell-Bannerman, Sir Henry, 475
Cardoel, Buzie de, 242
Cargill, W. W., 242
Caspian fisheries, 207
Caspian Sea-Persian Gulf pipeline project, 201
Cavagnari, Sir Louis, 68
Charykov, N. V., 528, 540
Chernozubov, Colonel, 462, 496
Chirol, Valentine, 460, 468-69
Christians, 455
Churchill, George P., 464, 496 n., 542, 614
Churchill, Lord Randolph, 185
Churchill, Roger P., 502
Clarendon, George William Frederick, Lord, 12, 14, 15, 19
Clergy, Persian, 309-11, 388-97, 454, 467, 475, 493-94, 572, 642
Cleveland, President Grover, 177
Cloete, Colonel, 243
Collins, Henry M., 124, 127, 128, 130, 131, 139, 143, 146
Connaught, Duke of, 95
Cossack Brigade, Persian, 166-67, 264-65, 304, 351, 396-97, 496, 513, 521, 523, 544, 545-46, 572, 605, 616, 617, 621, 677, 679
Cotte, Edouard, 104-05, 108, 110-11, 126, 139, 354
Cousis and Theophilaktos, 280-81

Cowan, Vice Consul, 548
Crackenthorp, Mr., 379
Cross, Lord, 178
Currie, Philip, 271
Curzon, George N., Lord, 156, 188, 190, 208-09, 294-96, 330, 347-49, 352, 369, 412, 414-15, 417, 418, 427, 432, 437, 443-44, 451, 505, 679; as seen by *Novoe Vremia*, 320; memorandum of September 1899, 340-44; memorandum of August 1901, 440-41; memorandum of February 1904, 406-07; Persian Gulf tour, 444-47
Customs of Southern Persia, hypothecation, 307-08, 313-15

Dabizha, Prince, 433, 434-36, 619, 642, 662-68
D'Arcy, William Knox, 354, 355, 356, 384, 448
D'Arcy concession, 356-57, 379-81
Dashnaks, 527, 528, 542
Dashnaktsutiun, 527
Davāfurush, Hāji Ali, 651
Delcassé, Théophile, 339
Demianovich, Major-General, 360
Derby, Edward, Lord, 31, 33, 38, 129-33, 142, 144, 153
Derviz, 201 n.
Dickson, Dr. (later Sir) Joseph, 112, 117, 119-21
Dikov, I. M., 488
Discount and Loan Bank of Persia, 275, 325, 326, 327, 383, 450, 451, 452, 458, 466, 472, 473, 474, 659, 675
Disraeli, Benjamin, 51, 130, 288, 476
Dolgorukov, Prince D. I., 123
Dolgorukov, Prince Nikolai Sergeevich, 175, 187, 191, 194, 197, 198, 200, 202, 203, 204-07, 212-13, 214-18, 220-21, 225, 230, 232, 484
Domantovich, Colonel Aleksei Ivanovich, 166-68
Dondukov-Korsakov, Prince Aleksandr Mikhailovich, 88, 203-04; Persian policy proposals, 179-82
Douglas, Admiral, 435

Dowell, Admiral Sir William, 96
Downe mission, 398-399
Dozdāb question. *See* Mirjāveh dispute
Dufferin, Blackwood Frederick, Lord, 66-67, 98
Durand, Sir Mortimer, 288, 293, 297, 298, 300, 301, 303, 304, 305, 319, 323-24, 329-31, 410, 434; memorandum of *December* 1895, 289-96
Durnovo, P. N., 484
Dvoeglazov incident, 517-19

Eastwick, Edward B., 20-25
Ebrāhim Āqā, 192-93
Edward VII, King, 115, 185, 222-23, 397-98, 477-78, 493, 519, 525, 563, 618
Ermolov, 488
Eshāq Khān, 539
Esmāil Khān, Ājudān Bāshi, 545
Esmāil Khān Momtāz od-Dowleh, 562
Espionage in Central Asia, 408-13
E'temād os-Saltaneh, 209
Eyn od-Dowleh, Soltān Majid Mirzā, 453, 457, 463, 473, 475, 476, 534, 535

Falkenhagen, Baron von, 114, 134, 135, 139-42, 144-47, 152, 153, 674; concession terms, 136-39
Farhād Mirzā Mo'tamed od-Dowleh, 118
Farmānfarmā, Abdol Hoseyn Mirzā, 189, 302, 303-04, 306-07, 453, 573, 670
Fashoda, 320
Fath Ali Shah Qājār, 16, 70
Fazlollāh, Sheykh, 545
Filosofov, D. A., 488
Firuzeh, 267, 283-84
Franco-Russian alliance of 1894, 287
Fraser, David, 512 n.
Fredericks, Baron V. B., 484

Geok-Teppe, 59, 67, 75, 76
George V, King, 627, 672-74
German threat in Persia, 592-93, 595-96
Giers (legation secretary), 213

Giers, Nikolai Karlovich, 7, 46, 47-48, 59, 66, 67, 73, 84, 86, 87, 92-94, 95, 96, 187, 198, 202, 206, 212, 217-18, 220, 223-28, 230-34, 239
Giliak, 352, 437-38
Gladstone, William Ewart, 71, 72, 77, 85, 96, 98, 287
Glukhovskii, Major General, 54
Gobineau, Arthur, Comte de, 100
Godley, Sir A., 404-05, 443
Goldsmid, Sir Frederic, 408
Golestān, Treaty of, 5
Golitsyn, Prince Aleksei, 675
Golos Moskvy, 506
Gorchakov, Prince Aleksandr Mikhailovich, 7, 11, 13, 14, 15, 20, 25, 26, 36, 38, 51, 59, 93, 114, 125, 134, 145, 155, 156; memorandum of *December* 1864, 8-9; memorandum of *April* 1875, 33-35
Gordon, General Charles George, 320
Gordon, General Sir Thomas E., 247, 322, 558
Goremykin, Ivan Logginovich, 484, 498
Grahame, Vice Consul, 378, 390-93, 395
Grant Duff, E., 452, 491, 492, 493
Granville, George Granville Leveson-Gower, Lord, 21, 25, 27, 72, 81, 82, 86, 89, 91, 97, 112, 115-17, 128, 129, 132
Gray, Dawes Co., 152
Gray, Paul and Co., 149, 152
Greaves, Dr. R. L., 44, 186
Greene, Conyngham, 286-87
Greenway, Charles, 587
Greig, Adjutant-General Samuil Alekseevich, 73
Grey, Sir Edward, 405, 475, 476, 479, 481, 483, 492, 493, 494, 495, 502, 503-04, 509, 510, 515, 519, 525, 530, 543, 550, 552, 554, 555, 558, 560, 561-63, 567, 576-77, 581, 583, 585, 586, 587, 588-91, 593, 597, 600, 601, 602, 606, 618, 620, 626-27, 632, 635, 636-37, 639, 640-41, 644, 645, 651, 657, 658, 662, 668, 671, 673
Grigorovich (Arab Sāheb), 167, 253

Index 703

Grodekov, Colonel (later General) Nikolai Ivanovich, 57, 75, 76, 80
Grosvenor, R. W., 265, 271
Grube, E. K., 356, 357-58, 361, 372-73, 379, 383, 448, 450, 451-52, 479, 487, 497
Gubastov, K. A., 484
Guild, Ambassador, 629
Gunther, François, 273

Habl ol-Matin, 501-02
Hamilton, Lord George, 294, 344, 347-48, 369, 403, 405, 418, 426, 442-43; memorandum of April 1900, 346-47
Hardie, James Keir, 520
Hardinge, Sir Arthur H., 352-54, 362-65, 367-81, 384, 387-88, 393-400, 405-06, 414, 415, 418, 421, 431-34, 444, 445, 446, 448-51, 454-56, 460 n., 469, 491, 496
Hardinge, Charles (later Lord Hardinge of Penshurst), 293, 305, 306, 307, 308, 310-13, 314, 315, 322, 326, 365, 366-67, 410, 478, 479, 498, 504, 505, 519, 520, 537, 553, 567, 569
Hartington, Lord, 78-79, 82
Hartwig, Madame, 526
Hartwig, Nikolai Genrikhovich, 458, 481, 492-94, 496, 511-12, 513 n., 514, 515, 516, 517, 518-19, 521, 522 n., 523, 524, 527-28, 530, 539, 543, 570, 600
Hasan Ali Khān, 142
Hasan Ali Khān Navvāb, 253, 297
Heiden (Geiden), General Count Fedor Logginovich, 72, 73
Hengām, 404
Herāt, 21, 46, 53, 58, 73, 95, 97, 219; return to Persia, 22, 28, 68, 70-71
Heshmat od-Dowleh, 55
Heshmat ol-Molk, Ali Akbar Khān, 409, 414-15, 417-18, 465
Hildebrand (Gildebrand), 614, 615
Hormoz, 352, 404
Hoseyn Khān Moshir od-Dowleh (later Sepahsālār), Mirzā, 32, 33, 53, 54, 56, 60-66, 70, 78, 79, 92, 102, 103, 104, 108-09, 110, 111, 112, 113, 114, 115, 116, 117, 118, 119-26, 127-28, 131, 132, 135, 139-42, 144-46, 158-63, 167
Hoseyn Qoli Khān, Hāji, 177
Hoseyn Qoli Khān Navvāb, Mirzā, 554-55, 573-74, 579-80, 599-600
Hübbenet (Giubbenet), Adolf Iakovlevich von, 230, 231, 232, 234

Iavorskii, Dr. I. L., 48 n.
Ignat'ev, General Nikolai Pavlovich, 155, 197
Il'inskii, G. N., 275
Imperial Bank of Persia, 268, 270, 271, 313-17, 322, 448-52, 549, 556-59, 561-62, 584; concession terms, 210-12
Imperial Tobacco Corporation of Persia, 249-50, 254, 265, 267, 270, 271
India, dangers to and defense of, 13-14, 22-24, 28-31, 219
International Commercial Bank of Moscow, 273
Irāne Now, 552, 564
Iranian Loan Company, 272-73
Ivanov, Consul, 605, 655-56, 660-61
Ivanov, M. S., 239, 476 n., 491, 522 n., 527 n.
Izvolskii, Aleksandr Petrovich, 478, 482, 483, 485, 486, 488-92, 493, 498-99, 511-12, 515, 516, 519, 520-21, 525, 530, 534, 535, 539, 543, 547, 550, 552, 554, 561, 563, 564, 566, 568, 570, 571, 577, 596, 612, 618, 637

Jackson, Sir T., 558
Jahāngir Khān, Mirzā, 523
Jalāl od-Dowleh, Mahmud Mirzā, 456
Jamāl ed-Din Asadābādi (Afghāni), Seyyed, 181, 296
Jamāl ed-Din Esfahāni, Āqā Seyyed, 475, 523
Javād, Hāji Mirzā, 135
Jews, 310-11, 455
Jolfā-Tabriz railway, 134-36, 146, 674-75
Jolfā-Tabriz-Tehran road concession, 276-77

Jomini, Baron Aleksandr Genrikhovich, 66-67, 73
Joubert-Pienaar, 471

Kābul, 47-50, 57, 68
Kāmrān Mirzā Nāyeb os-Saltaneh, 181, 189, 193, 251, 254, 263-64, 297-99, 300, 540, 548
Kārun River, 91, 149, 152, 153-54, 158, 160-65, 186, 192, 195, 196, 197, 200, 201, 279
Kasravi, Ahmad, 476 n.
Kaufmann, General Konstantin Petrovich von, 7, 25, 26, 35, 36, 39, 46-51, 76, 155
Keddie, Nikki, 476 n.
Kemball, Lieutenant-Colonel C. A., 431
Kennedy, R. J., 253, 255-56, 258-60, 263
Ketābchi Khān, General, 354
Khārg, 52
Khaz'al, Sheykh, 315, 428-34, 466
Kheyrābād, 283
Khiva, 15, 20, 28; conquest and annexation of, 25-27
Khodāyār, Khan of Kokand, 35
Khojent, occupied by Russia, 12
Khomiakov, Nikolai Alekseevich, 201, 230, 232, 327-28
Khorāsān, 46, 56, 61, 76, 77, 79, 87, 97, 162, 180-81, 182, 219, 269
Khuzestān, 192
Kimberley, Joseph Woodhouse, Lord, 89, 287
Kitchener, Horatio Herbert, Lord, 481
Klemm, Vasilii Oskarovich, 489
Knollys, Lord A., 398
Knox, Philander C., 582, 583
Koiander, 471
Kokand, annexation of, 36
Kokarev, (Vasilii Aleksandrovich?), 169
Kokovtsov, Vladimir Nikolaevich, 457-59, 471, 473, 480, 488, 490, 517, 625, 626, 628, 630, 632
Komarov, General A. V., 84, 87, 95, 96
Konkevich, 360
Konshin, N. N., 169, 200, 230

Konstantin Nikolaevich, Grand Duke, 28, 156
Korff, Baron P. L., 201, 230
Kornilov, 438-39
Kosogovskii, Colonel (later General) V. A., 168, 188-90, 265, 296-99, 303, 304, 317-19, 457
Krasnovodsk. *See* Qizil-Su
Krivoshein, A. V., 484
Kryzhanovskii, General Nikolai Andreevich, 46
Kuropatkin, Colonel (later General) Aleksei Nikolaevich, 59, 76, 292, 339; memorandum of *February* 1900, 338
Kuzmin-Karavaev, Colonel, 264

Labour Leader, 520
Labour Party, Independnt, 505
Lamsdorff, Vladimir Nikolaevich, 194, 217, 235, 239, 361, 366-67, 378, 380, 381, 383, 424, 452, 471, 472, 479, 482, 592; Instruction to Speyer, 460-68
Langeh: British landing at, 579; Russian consulate at, 470
Lansdowne, Henry Charles, Lord, 376, 390, 397-400, 413-14, 424, 425, 432, 443, 449, 455, 457, 497-98
Lascelles, Sir Frank Cavendish, 261, 262, 263, 265, 267, 268-69, 281-83, 285-86
Lawrence, Sir John, 13-14, 20, 72
Lazarev, General I. D., 64, 67
Lebedev, Captain V., 331-32
Lecoffre, Mr., 623, 631, 635
Lemaire, General Alfred, 279
Lenin, Vladimir Il'ich, 171, 185, 495, 512 n.
Lessar, Pavel Mikhailovich, 81, 489
Lesseps, Ferdinand de, 155
Leuchtenberg, Duke Eugene of, 26
Levy, Walter, 552
Leys os-Soltān, 602, 606
Liakhov, Colonel Vladimir Platonovich, 496, 521, 522 n., 523-24, 526, 528, 545, 590
Lianozov, Stepan Martynovich, 207, 569; fisheries, 319

Lindley, Dr., 546
Lloyd George, David, 597
Loans, 307-08, 312, 319, 321-31, 448-51, 458, 471-75, 537-39, 541, 549-61, 674-75; Russian of 1900, 324-27; negotiations of 1901, 362-63, 365-78
Lobanov-Rostovskii, Prince Aleksei Borisovich, 81-83, 86, 93-94, 194, 288
Loftus, Lord Augustus, 25, 26, 32-33, 42, 114, 116
Lomakin, General N. P., 27-28, 32, 33, 40-41, 56, 58-59, 64, 67-68, 72
Lomnitskii, S., 272
Lumsden, General Sir Peter, 96
Lynch, H. F. B., 504
Lynch Brothers, 430
Lytton, Lord E., 42-44, 49, 56, 72, 154

MacDonald, Ramscy, 520
Mackenzie, Mr., 153
Maclean, 363, 365
Maclean, General C., 208, 218
MacMahon, Major, 465
MacVeagh, Franklin, 583
Mahdi, Muhammad Ahmad, 85, 94
Mahmud Khān, Mirzā, 205-06, 212
Majles, 495, 496, 497, 511, 513, 514, 521, 522-23, 527, 530-31, 537, 539, 540, 563, 565, 566, 572, 580, 581, 584, 585, 591, 610, 611, 613, 622, 629, 630, 631, 635, 638, 639, 640, 643, 644
Majles, 552
Makhdum Qoli Khān, 83
Malama, Colonel, 72
Malek ol-Motakallemin, 522-23
Malek osh-Shoarā Bahār, 667
Malekzādeh, Mehdi, 476 n.
Malet, Sir Edward, 173
Malkam Khān, Mirzā, Nāzem od-Dowleh, 38, 91, 98, 112, 117, 128, 142, 174, 178; his swindle, 242-47
Mallet, Sir Louis, 555, 583, 652
Mansfield, W. R., 14
Mansur ol-Molk, 602, 606
Mareines, Mark Iakovlevich, 275

Maria Fedorovna, Empress, 275
Maria Pavlovna, Grand Duchess, 484
Marling, Charles, 514-15, 518-19, 524-25, 554, 571-72, 573-74, 578
Marriott, Alfred M., 354
Marv, 22, 27, 28, 38, 42-45, 53, 54, 57, 66-67, 69, 70-72, 77, 79, 81, 82, 83, 86-88; annexed to Russia, 84-85
Marx, Karl, 185
Mashhad, consulates at, 208-09
Masqat (Muscat), 150
Maxwell, Mr., 556
Mayo, Lord, 20, 23
Meade, Colonel M. J., 435
Melnikov, Aleksandr Aleksandrovich, 88, 165, 174, 193
Merrill, J. N., 615
Mesbāh ol-Molk, 252
Michell, Consul, 439
Mikāil Khān, 243, 245
Mikhail Nikolaevich, Grand Duke, Viceroy, 28, 32, 37, 39, 58, 59, 73, 117, 166
Mikhail Nikolaevich, Grand Duke, 483-84
Miliukov, P. N., 506
Miliutin, General Dimitrii Alekseevich, 7, 28, 36, 37, 38, 46-47, 48, 49-50, 51, 59, 60, 68, 71, 72, 73, 84, 93, 113, 155; champions conquests in Central Asia, 7, 25, 41-42, 74
Miller, A., 412, 415, 417, 419-20, 424, 426-27, 533, 535-37, 570, 571, 609, 619, 642, 645, 647, 648, 650, 651, 652, 653, 666, 668
Mining Rights Corporation, 280
Mirjāveh dispute, 420-27
Moezz os-Saltaneh, 428
Mohammad Ali, Āqā Mirzā, 257
Mohammad Ali Mirzā. *See* Mohammad Ali Shah
Mohammad Ali Shah Qājār, 166, 188-89, 305, 306, 454, 462, 470, 497, 511, 512, 514, 515, 521, 522, 523, 527, 528, 530-31, 534, 536, 537-45, 547-48, 549, 597-601, 603-12, 617, 621, 627, 628, 630, 633-34, 638-39, 641, 642, 648, 651, 653, 655-57, 659-66, 669-74

Mohammad Āqā, 104
Mohammad of Nishāpur, 664
Mohammad Shafi', Āqā, 435
Mohammad Shah Qājār, 100
Mohammad Vali Khān Nasr os-Saltaneh. *See* Sepahdār
Mohrenheim, Baron Artur Pavlovich von, 86, 185
Mohsen Khān Moin ol-Molk, Mirzā, 101-04, 111, 128, 173, 302, 305, 307, 312, 409
Moin ol-Molk. *See* Mohsen Khān
Mojallal os-Saltaneh, 548
Mokhber od-Dowleh, 153, 303
Mokhtār os-Saltaneh, 378
Molitor, Monsieur, 426-27
Molk Ārā, 285
Moore, Arthur, 535-36
Moore, W. A., 557-58
Morgan, Jacques de, 354
Morier, Sir Robert, 185, 205-06, 223-28, 239, 269-70
Mornard, Monsieur, 584-85
Moroccan crisis and Persia, 597
Morozov, 200
Moshāver ol-Mamālek, Ali Qoli Khān Ansāri, 568-69, 602, 643, 652-53
Moshir od-Dowleh. *See* Hoseyn Khān; Mohsen Khān; Nasrollāh Khān; Yahyā Khān
Moshir ol-Molk, 474, 481
Moshir os-Saltaneh, 539, 540
Moskovskie Vedomosti, 332-33, 564-65
Mostowfi ol-Mamālek, 573
Mo'tamen ol-Molk. *See* Said Khān
Mozaffar ed-Din Mirza. *See* Mozaffar ed-Din Shah
Mozaffar ed-Din Shah Qājār, 163, 165, 188, 259, 290, 299-301, 302, 322-23, 328, 329, 367-68, 370, 372, 373, 377, 385, 388, 391, 445, 453, 456, 460 n., 476, 495, 497; the Garter affair, 397-99
Murav'ev, Count Mikhail Nikolaevich, 324, 326, 327, 339, 410; memorandum of *January 1900*, 334-37

Nabil od-Dowleh, Ali Qoli Khān, 582, 634

Nāder Shah Afshār, 70
Naidenov, Aleksandr, 360
Najafi, Āqā, 393-94, 456
Napier, Captain George Campbell, 43, 52, 53
Napier of Magdala, 30
Napoleon, 7, 100
Nāser ed-Din Mirzā, 306
Nāser ed-Din Shah Qājār, 16, 19, 32, 54, 60, 61, 64-65, 70-71, 79, 80, 81, 87, 88-89, 90, 92, 97, 104-05, 108-09, 111, 117-21, 123, 125, 126, 127-28, 132, 134, 139-41, 161, 163, 166, 167, 168, 173, 174, 180-81, 183-84, 187, 189, 190, 192, 193, 195, 198, 208, 209, 210, 217, 229, 233, 237-38, 241, 242, 246-47, 259-60, 267-68, 272, 283, 285, 286; assassination, 296-98; first trip to Europe, 111-16; third trip to Europe, 219-22
Nāser ol-Molk, Abol Qāsem Khān, 89, 90, 97, 268, 513, 540, 577, 603, 627, 670-71, 673
Nasrollāh Khān Moshir od-Dowleh, Mirzā, 445, 451
Naus, Joseph, 372, 422, 423, 448, 449, 453, 487, 496-97
Nāyeb os-Saltaneh. *See* Kāmrān Mirzā
Nazar Khān, Hāji, 195
Nekrasov, Vice Consul (later Consul), 548, 619-20, 645-47, 666
Nelidov, Ambassador, 471
Neratov, Anatolii Anatolievich, 581-82, 586, 588-89, 604, 606-08, 613, 618-20, 622-23, 625-33, 635, 636-37, 639, 640, 642-43, 655, 671, 672
Nesselrode, Count Karl von, 33, 115
New Oriental Bank Corporation, 243-44
New York Times, The, 583
Nicholas II, Tsar, 311-12, 329, 339, 360, 475, 480, 483, 484, 485, 512 n., 519, 522 n., 561, 563, 591, 596, 599, 613, 617, 619, 620, 625, 647, 650, 652, 664, 665, 668, 671, 672, 676, 678
Nicholson, Lieutenant-General Sir W. G., 402-03, 404
Nicolson, Sir Arthur, 173, 176, 183-

Index

84, 482-83, 484-85, 490-91, 499, 502, 504, 509, 515, 520, 528, 531-32, 539, 549, 554, 561-62, 563, 567-68, 577, 580, 583, 588, 596, 600, 606-07, 618, 619, 620, 622-24, 669
Nicolson, Harold, 176 n., 506
Nikolai Konstantinovich, Grand Duke, 26
Nikolai Mikhailovich, Grand Duke, 484
Norman, H., 576, 579-80, 586, 587
Northbrook, Lord, 29-30
Novikov-Priboi, N., 478 n.
Novoe Vremia, 204, 320-21, 423, 438-39

O'Beirne, Hugh, 559, 576-77, 581, 593, 601
Obruchev, General N. N., 73, 232
O'Connor, Sir Nicholas, 397
O'Grady, James, 520
Old Sarakhs, 87, 89, 92
Oppenheim (banking firm), 307
Ornstein, Julius, 257, 261, 262, 263, 271
Osborn, Mr., 552
Osipov, V. P., 175, 198
Osten-Sacken, Count N. D., 386, 484
Outram, Sir James, 149
Ovseenko, Consul, 541

Palashkovskii, S. E., 201, 230, 327-28
Palitsyn, Lieutenant-General F. F., 487, 488, 490
Palmerston, Lord, 33
Panjdeh, 89, 94, 95-97, 98
Panov, 522 n.
Paton, Robert M., 256, 258-59
Pavlovich, M. P., 675
Pelly, Lieutenant-Colonel Lewis, 149, 150
Percy, Earl, 505
Perovskii, General V. A., 6
Persian Insurance and Transportation Company, 275-76, 277
Persian Investment Corporation, 243-44
Peter I, Tsar, 4-5
Petrov, Vice Consul, 614, 615, 616, 617

Petrusevich, Colonel, 58
Pichon, M. le Baron, 17
Picot, Lieutenant-Colonel H., 289, 309, 409
Pobedonostsev, Konstantin Petrovich, 175
Podgurskii, Engineer, 675
Poggio (Podzhio), 195, 209
Pokhitonov, Ivan Fedorovich, 454, 515-16, 579, 614-21, 625, 627, 642, 645, 646, 647, 666
Poklewski-Koziell, Stanislaw Alfonsovich, 480, 525-26, 537, 546-47, 550, 551, 554, 561, 563, 566, 569, 570, 571, 572, 573, 574-77, 578, 581, 583, 584-85, 590-91, 599, 602, 603, 606, 608-11, 613-26, 629, 631, 633-34, 636, 638, 639, 641, 642, 643, 644, 646-47, 652-56, 660, 662, 664, 665, 670, 673
Poliakov, Boris, 229
Poliakov, Iakov, 272
Poliakov, Lazar Solomonovich, 199-200, 229, 230, 236, 237, 268, 270, 276-77, 326, 327
Poliakov, Samuil Solomonovich, 199
Poliakovs' enterprises, 199-200, 229, 275-78, 279
Ponsonby, Arthur, 520
Popov, A., 489
Potsdam, negotiations and agreement, 561, 593-94, 596
Pozharov, Colonel, 72
Preece, Consul General, 393
Preobrazhenskii, Acting Consul General, 654, 672
Protopopov, Lieutenant-General A. P., 488

Qānun, 242-47
Qarajadāq mining concession, 319, 549, 572
Qara Qal'e, 33, 54-56, 66
Qavām od-Dowheh, Mirzā Abbās Khān, 193, 207, 209, 216, 245, 284
Qavām os-Saltaneh, Ahmad Khān, 573, 622
Qazvin, Russian troops at, 641-43
Qazvin-Anzali road concession, 277-78

Qeshm, 352
Qizil-Ārvāt, 40, 43
Qizil-Su, 12, 18, 19, 20, 25, 58, 77
Quadt zu Wykradt und Isny, Count, 585

Rabino, Joseph, 210, 271, 273, 274, 316-18, 322, 449, 451, 452
Rafailovich, Lev, 229, 237
Rahim Khān (the spy), 409
Rahim Khān Chelebiāni (the bandit), 454, 535, 565, 601-02
Railways in Persia, 101-05, 109-10, 111, 114, 126, 127, 128, 129, 130, 134-40, 143, 144, 145, 155, 158-60, 173-76, 179, 184, 198-202, 214-19, 228-39, 327-29, 474, 489-90, 551, 592-96, 674-75
Rashid ol-Molk, 609
Rasulzādeh, Mohammad Amin, 552
Ratoul, Dr., 307-08
Rawlinson, Sir Henry, 17, 21-25
Razgonov, 50
Rech, 506
Red'ko, General, 666-67
Reuter, George, 209-10
Reuter, Baron Julius de, 63, 103-05, 108-11, 117, 122, 124, 126-34, 142-44, 146, 147, 152, 155, 156, 157, 173, 201-02, 209, 218, 242
Reuter concession, terms, 105-08
Rezā, Imam, shrine of, 182, 666-67
Riabushinskii, P. P., 230, 594
Ripon, Lord, 89
Roberts, General Sir Frederick, 68, 95
Robertson, Lieutenant-Colonel W. R., 401
Rochester, the Bishop of, 398
Roediger, Lieutenant-General A. F., 487
Rokn od-Dowleh, Mohammad Taqi Mirzā, 75, 80, 255
Romanovskii, General D. I., 12
Rosebery, Lord, 283, 287
Rosen, R. R., 484, 582
Ross, Lieutenant-Colonel E. C., 164-65
Rothstein (Rotshtein), Fedor Aronovich, 172

Rozhestvenskii, Admiral Zinovii Petrovich, 478
Rukavishnikov, 200
Russell, Lord John, 10, 17, 20
Russian Bank. *See* Discount and Loan Bank of Persia
Russian designs on India, 42
Russian pipeline project, 358-62, 375, 378-85
Russian quarantine on the Perso-Afghan border, 410-11
Russkaia Zemlia, 577
Russo-Afghan Treaty of 1878, 48
Russo-Chinese Bank, 275
Russo-Japanese War, 457, 478-79
Russo-Persian frontier issue, 1881–82, 80-83
Russo-Persian Treaty of *June 8, 1893*, 283-84
Russo-Turkish War of 1877, 45

Sablin, 530-31, 532, 534, 540-41, 542-43, 544, 545, 546, 548
Sa'd od-Dowleh, 540-41, 598, 673
Sadovskii, Dr., 546-47
Sāed ol-Molk. *See* Abd or-Rahim Khān
Said Khān, Mirzā, Mo'tamen ol-Molk, 16, 17, 19, 78, 80, 81, 83, 92, 118, 119, 125, 150, 153, 163
Sakhanskii, V. A., 488
Sālār od-Dowleh, Abol Fath Mirzā, 189, 600, 605, 669-70
Salisbury, Robert Cecil Lord, 31, 35, 51, 66, 98, 154, 162, 186-87, 191, 214, 223, 225, 238, 244, 263, 270, 279, 287, 288, 307, 312, 330, 348, 349, 352, 410; Marv policy, 44-45
Salor Turkomans, 87, 89
Samsām os-Saltaneh, 536, 611, 625-26, 638, 670
Samsonov, General A. V., 655, 662
Samuel and Co., 552-53
Sanderson, Sir Thomas H., 404, 425, 504
Sankt-Peterburgskie Vedomosti, 204
Saqat ol-Eslām, 651, 652-53
Saqat ol-Molk, 566
Sarakhs, 27, 81, 82, 83, 87, 90
Sattār Khān, 531, 533, 570-71

Savalan, 101, 111, 156
Sazonov, Sergei Dmitrievich, 499, 545, 559-60, 561, 576-78, 583, 593, 595-96, 601, 629 n., 640, 643, 645, 647, 651-54, 657, 658-59, 661-65, 668, 672, 673-74, 676-78
Schaskolskii, 273-74
Schneur, Colonel, 264
Schwanebach (Shvanebakh), P. Kh., 484
Scoble, Mr., 179
Scott, Sir Charles, 326-27, 351, 378, 381, 384
Scully, Dr., 297-98
Seligman, C. D., 555-58
Seligman Brothers, 555-58
Sepahdār, Mohammad Vali Khān Nasr os-Saltaneh, 280-81, 541-42, 545, 566, 571, 573, 654-55, 672
Shamil, Sheykh, 4, 6
Shams, 573
Shapshal, 522
Sharq, 564, 573
Shatilov, Nikolai Pavlovich, 655
Shcheglov, A., 300, 308, 312
Shir Ali, Amir, 46-51
Shirāzi, Hāji Mirzā Hasan, 261
Shoā' incident, 619, 620, 623, 624
Shoā' os-Saltaneh, Malek Mansur Mirzā, 329, 604, 613-18, 621, 624, 628, 664
Shojā' od-Dowleh, Ilkhāni of Quchān, 39, 413
Shojā' od-Dowleh, Samad Khān, 609-10, 651-55, 672
Showkat ol-Molk, 465
Shushtar, 70, 149
Shuster, W. Morgan, 584-87, 589-91, 611-12, 613-15, 617, 622-29, 631, 633, 634, 637, 638, 639, 640, 642, 644, 657
Shuvalov, Count Petr Andreevich, 25, 26, 27, 38, 57, 66, 156, 185
Siemens, C. W., 102
Skobelev, General Mikhail Dmitrievich, 35, 39, 73, 74-76, 78, 162, 204
Smirnov, Captain, 546-47
Smith, Colonel Murdock, 178
Snarskii, General, 518

Social Democrats, Caucasian, 527
Société Générale du Commerce et Industrie de la Perse, 242 n.
Somov, 481
Speyer (Shpeier), Aleksei Nikolaevich, 236, 237, 238, 249, 253, 281, 455, 464, 465, 466, 467, 481
Spring Rice, Sir Cecil, 349-51, 452, 474-75, 481, 493-95, 500-01, 525
Staal, Baron Georgii (Egor Egorovich), 99, 174, 185, 187, 201-02, 476-77
Stanhope, 67
Steinberg (Shteinberg), E. L., 48 n.
Stevens, Consul H. F., 454, 518
Stokes, Major Charles, 586-91
Stoletov, Major General Nikolai Grigor'evich, 47-50, 53
Stolypin, Petr Arkad'evich, 498, 512, 517, 520, 570, 571
Strousberg, Dr., 101-02
Sudan, 85
Sviatopolk-Mirskii, Prince Dmitrii Ivanovich, 58
Sykes, Sir Percy M., 293, 303-04, 412, 664, 665-66
Syromiatnikov (Sigma), 439

Tabātabāi, Seyyed Mohammad, 475, 491, 496
Tabriz, 169, 170; siege and relief of, 532-36; Russian terror at, 648-52
Talbot, Major Gerald F., 248, 249, 254
Taqi Khān Amir Nezām (later Amir Kabir), Mirzā, 123
Taqizādeh, Seyyed Hasan, 565-66, 573
Tashkent, 9-10
Tatishchev, S., 204
Taube, Baron M. A., 484
Taylor, Colonel R., 16-17
Tehran-Rasht motor transportation concession, 549
Tehran-Shāhzādeh Abd ol-Azim railway, 101, 103
Tekke Turkomans, 15-16, 40-41, 57, 58-59, 67-68, 75-77, 78, 80, 82, 87
Tenderden, Charles Stuart, Lord, 142
Terent'ev, General M. A., 26
Tergukasov, General A. A., 72
Teymuri, Ebrāhim, 241

Tholozan, Dr., 156-58, 160, 162, 268
Thomson, Sir Ronald F., 41, 52-57, 60-66, 71, 79, 80, 83, 87, 89, 90, 97, 157, 159-65, 167, 170, 172, 189
Thomson, W. Taylour, 28, 33, 44, 111, 112, 120, 122, 123, 124, 125-26, 128, 130, 131, 132-33, 140, 142, 144, 153, 154-55, 156
Thornton, Sir Edward, 85, 93, 95, 96
Times (London), *The*, 588, 631
Tobacco Régie, 248-67, 271-72; Armenian merchants and, 256-57; concession terms, 248-49; situation in Shiraz, 257; situation in Tabriz, 257-59; violence, 260-62, 263-65
Torkamanchāy, Treaty, 5, 6, 69, 169, 250, 251, 256
Tornau, Baron, 45
Townley, Sir Walter, 671
Treasury gendarmerie, Persian, 585-86, 590
Trench, Chevenix, 413
Trench, Colonel F., 94-95
Tret'iakov, S. M., 230, 327-28
Trollope, Anthony, 103
Trubetskoi, Prince G. N., 507
Turgenev, Ivan Sergeevich, 331
Turkomans, 194-95; Russian encroachments upon, 11-12, 27, 32
Tyrtov, Admiral Pavel Petrovich, memorandum of *February 1900*, 337-38

Urumiyyeh, shipping concession, 549, 551
Urusov, Prince L. P., 484

Vadbolskii, Prince, 616, 677
Vakil or-Roāyā, 557
Vannovskii, General Petr Semenovich, 84, 93, 232
Victoria, Queen, 96, 115, 185, 223, 477
Vilenkin (Wilenkin), 559
Vlangali, 232
Vlasov, Petr Mikhailovich, 207-08, 453, 463
Volynskii, Artemii, 4-5
Vorontsov-Dashkov, Count Illarion Ivanovich, 175, 517, 534, 570, 571, 601-03, 625, 644, 648-50, 672
Voropanov, General, 650
Vosuq od-Dowleh, Mirzā Hasan Khān, 610, 613, 622, 626, 633, 634, 638, 642, 643, 653, 662, 667
Vyshnegradskii, Ivan Alekseevich, 198-99, 232, 270

Wales, Prince of. *See* Edward VII
War Office, on policy in Persia, 400-03
Warner, Sir W. Lee, 344-45, 369, 403, 404-05, 413, 440
Watkins, Sir E., 102-03
Watson, Mr., 243
Webb Ware, Captain, 420, 421, 422, 425
Westmann (Vestman), Vladimir, 28, 32
Wilhelm II, Kaiser, 320, 386, 596
Windsor, 115
Winston, Mr., 174
Witte, Count Sergei Iul'evich, 273-74, 275, 318-19, 326-27, 360-62, 366-67, 372, 375, 380-84, 406, 448, 449, 450, 475, 480, 489, 498, 508-09, 526; memorandum of *February 1900*, 338-39
Wood, A. O., 557, 562
Wood, Consul, 305
Wolff, Sir Henry Drummond, 95, 184-88, 190-92, 193-94, 195, 196, 202-03, 204, 207, 209, 213-24, 226-30, 237-38, 241, 242, 243-44, 247, 248, 250, 251, 354, 502-03; champions Anglo-Russian agreement, 222-24, 238, 476-77
Woolf, Joseph, 552, 553-57
Wratislaw, Consul A. C., 535, 536

Yahyā Khān Moshir od-Dowleh, 92, 111, 174, 193, 204, 237, 251, 253, 254
Yaqub Khān, Amir, 68
Yate, Colonel C. E., 409, 421
Yefrem Khān Davidiants, 528, 541, 545, 611, 644, 669
Yomuts. *See* Turkomans

Index

Younghusband, Colonel Sir Francis, 478
Yuself Khān, Sardār, 663, 666-67

Zāl Khān, 192
Zell es-Soltān, Mas'ud Mirzā, 163-65, 178, 181, 184, 189, 193, 251, 285, 290, 300-01, 393-94, 462

Ziā ed-Din, Seyyed, 564
Zinov'ev, Ivan Alekseevich, 54-56, 60, 64, 71, 74-80, 159, 162, 167, 168, 171, 173, 194, 201, 202-04, 206, 212, 217-18, 220, 221, 223, 225, 227, 230-31, 232, 234-35, 253, 440, 457, 485-86, 489, 507-09, 570, 592
Zonnenshtral-Piskorskii, A. A., 172 n.

www.ingramcontent.com/pod-product-compliance
Lightning Source LLC
Chambersburg PA
CBHW061947300426
44117CB00010B/1252